The Culture of Secrecy in Japanese Religion

The Japanese Middle Ages were a period when secrecy dominated many forms of religious practice. This fascinating collection traces the secret characteristics and practices in Japanese religion, while analyzing the rise and decline of religious esotericism in Japan.

Esoteric Buddhism developed in almost all Buddhist countries of Asia, but it was of particular importance in Japan where its impact went far beyond the borders of Buddhism, also affecting Shinto as well as non-religious forms of discourse. During the Middle Ages, secret initiations became a favoured medium for the transmission of knowledge among Buddhist monks, Shinto priests, scholars, actors and artisans alike.

The Culture of Secrecy in Japanese Religion looks at the impact of esoteric Buddhism on Japanese culture, and includes comparative chapters on India and China. Whilst concentrating on the Japanese medieval period, this book will give readers familiar with present-day Japan many explanations for the still visible remnants of Japan's medieval culture of secrecy. This compelling look at a largely undiscovered field of research successfully demystifies the study of esotericism and Tantrism, and will be essential reading for scholars of East Asian Buddhism, Japanese religion and religious history.

Bernhard Scheid is a Research Fellow at the Institute for the Cultural and Intellectual History of Asia at the Austrian Academy of Sciences.

Mark Teeuwen is Professor of Japanese Studies at the University of Oslo, Norway.

The Culture of Secrecy in Japanese Religion

Edited by

**Bernhard Scheid
and Mark Teeuwen**

LONDON AND NEW YORK

First published 2006
by Routledge
2 Park Square, Milton Park, Abingdon, Oxon, OX14 4RN

Simultaneously published in the USA and Canada
by Routledge
711 Third Avenue, New York, NY 10017

*Routledge is an imprint of the Taylor & Francis Group,
an informa business*

First issued in paperback 2011

Typeset in Baskerville by
Integra Software Services Pvt. Ltd, Pondicherry, India

British Library Cataloguing in Publication Data
A catalogue record for this book is available from the
British Library

Library of Congress Cataloging in Publication Data
The culture of secrecy in Japanese religion / edited by Bernhard
  Scheid and Mark Teeuwen.
    p.   cm.
  Includes bibliographical references and index.
  ISBN 0–415–38713–2 (hardback : alk. paper)
  1. Secrecy—Religious aspects.   2. Secrecy—Japan.   3. Japan—
  Civilization—Buddhist influences.   4. Secrecy—Religious
  aspects—Tantric Buddhism.   5. Tantric Buddhism—Japan—
  History.   I. Scheid, Bernhard, 1960–.   II. Teeuwen, Mark.
  BL2211.S32C85 2006
  200.952—dc22

                                        2006003448

ISBN10: 0–415–38713–2 (hbk)
ISBN10: 0–415–54689–3 (pbk)

ISBN13: 978–0–415–38713–2 (hbk)
ISBN13: 978–0–415–54689–8 (pbk)

Contents

x   *Contents*

Illustrations

Figures

Tables

7.1	An abbreviated table of lineages of regents	178
7.2	The conflict over the *shōgyō* of the Hōon'in	186
7.3	Dōjun in Ise	189

Contributors

William M. Bodiford is Professor in the Department of Asian Languages and Cultures, University of California, Los Angeles.

Ronald M. Davidson is Professor in the Department of Religious Studies, Fairfield University, Connecticut.

Lucia Dolce is Senior Lecturer in Japanese Religions, School of African and Oriental Studies, University of London.

Bernard Faure is Professor, Columbia University, New York.

Nobumi Iyanaga is an independent scholar.

Albert de Jong is Lecturer, Faculty of Theology, Leiden University.

Kadoya Atsushi is Lecturer in the Department for East Asian Philosophy, Waseda University, Tokyo.

Susan Blakeley Klein is Associate Professor in the Department of East Asian Languages and Literatures, University of California, Irvine.

Martin Lehnert is Lecturer in the Department for Chinese Studies, University of Zurich.

Kate Wildman Nakai is Professor, Faculty of Liberal Arts, Sophia University, Tokyo.

Fabio Rambelli is Professor in the Department of Japanese Studies, Sapporo University.

Bernhard Scheid is Research Fellow, Austrian Academy of Sciences, Vienna.

Mark Teeuwen is Professor in the Department of Cultural Studies and Oriental Languages, University of Oslo.

Anne Walthall is Professor in the Department of History, University of California, Irvine.

Preface

In an age of secular rationalism we often tend to overlook that religions without secrecy are the exception rather than the rule. Most religions claim to have access to insights beyond conventional knowledge, and their priests perform rituals and manipulate objects too sacred to be shown openly. Nevertheless, these rites or objects must be partly disclosed in order to propagate the religion. Religious secrecy, therefore, always creates a tension between concealment and disclosure, which is often combined with an esoteric discourse on the supremacy of the hidden as opposed to the visible. Such a discourse may for instance lead to doctrines that set up different forms of "truth" for people with different levels of religious experience. On the level of practice, this may correspond to secret initiations that separate initiates from non-initiates. Sometimes – as in the case of the ominous "Tantric sex" – esoteric segmentation has created secret rites that transcend ethical prescriptions either in a symbolic way or in actual practice. In other cases, secret rituals took on a magical dimension and were used for mundane ends, as for instance in warfare. From the point of view of political power, religious secrecy is nevertheless an ambivalent phenomenon. It may be used to support politics by magical rituals, but it also contains a latent element of subversion in that it can never be fully controlled.

The Japanese Middle Ages – taken here as the period of political decentralization from the eleventh to the sixteenth century – were a time when all these forms of secrecy dominated religious practice. Geared by the legacy of Indian and Chinese Tantrism, secrecy and esotericism trove and prospered notably in the field of Buddhism, but spread also beyond the religious realm: secret initiations became a favored medium for the transmission of knowledge among monks specializing in esoteric Buddhist ritual as well as among kami priests, scholars or poets, and, by the late Middle Ages, even among actors and artisans. This "culture of secrecy" is the subject of this book.

The idea for this book resulted from my increasing awareness that my own research topic, medieval Shinto, was in fact firmly embedded in the conceptual matrix of esoteric Buddhism. To learn more about this subject, I organized two scientific events dealing with secrecy and esotericism in

Japanese religion. The present collection of essays is a result of this discussion process. The existence of a mailing list that grew out from our discussion group (*KudenML*, hosted by Iyanaga Nobumi) is only one of several indications that our quest has not yet been fulfilled and will hopefully produce more results in this yet underdeveloped field of research.

This book would not have been possible without the support of the Austrian Academy of Sciences that sponsored a conference on our topic in May 2004 and also contributed in many ways to the editing process of this book. In particular, I would like to thank Prof. Ernst Steinkellner, director of the Academy's Institute for the Cultural and Intellectual History of Asia, for his continuous encouragement and Cynthia Peck-Kubaczek from the same institute for her untiring efforts to polish the English of the non-native contributors to this book. Moreover, I am grateful to the European Association for Japanese Studies (EAJS) for providing a forum for our first discussions at the Warsaw Conference in 2003, when I acted as the convener of the Religions Section, together with Dr Birgit Staemmler from the University of Tübingen. I further have to acknowledge a number of institutions that graciously gave permission to publish the images in this book, most notably the Jingū Shichō, Ise, Mie prefecture (front cover), as well as the institutions mentioned below the respective figures. Finally, I would like to thank my wife Mine Scheid-Katayama for assisting me in the editorial work for this book.

Bernhard Scheid
Vienna, December 2005

Abbreviations

CDZ   *Chishō Daishi Zenshū*, 4 vols. DNBZ 25–28.

DNBZ   *Dai Nihon bukkyō zensho* 大日本仏教全書, 151 vols. Tokyo: Meicho Fukyūkai, 1978–83. (Repr.; original edition Tokyo: Bussho Kankōkai, 1912–22.)

DNZ   *Dai Nihon zokuzōkyō* 大日本続蔵経, 150 vols. Kyoto: Zōkyō Shoin, 1905–12. Reprinted in Hong Kong: The Hong Kong Committee on the Photographic Publication of a Continuation to the Buddhist Tripitaka, 1968–70.

KDZ   *Kōbō daishi zenshū* 弘法大師全集, 8 vols. Kōya-machi: Mikkyō Bunka Kenkyūjo, 1965–68. (Repr. Kyoto: Dōmeisha, 1978; Original edition in 6 vols. 1909–11.)

NDZ   *Nihon daizōkyō* 日本大蔵経, 51 vols. Tokyo: Nihon Daizōkyō Hensankai, 1914–22.

NKBT   *Nihon koten bungaku taikei* 日本古典文学大系, 102 vols. Tokyo: Iwanami Shoten, 1957–68.

NST   *Nihon shisō taikei* 日本思想体系, 67 vols. Tokyo: Iwanami Shoten, 1970–82.

SNKS   *Shinchō Nihon koten shūsei* 新潮日本古典集成, 85 vols. Tokyo: Shinchōsha, 1976–89.

SoZ   *Sōtōshū zensho* 曹洞宗全書, 18 vols. Tokyo: Sōtōshū Shūmuchō 曹洞宗宗務庁, 1970–73 (revised and enlarged edition).

ST   *Shintō taikei* 神道体系, 120 vols. Tokyo: Shintō Taikei Hensankai, 1977–94.

SZ   *Shingonshū zensho* 真言宗全書, 44 vols. Kōyasan: Shingonshū Zensho Kankōkai, 1933–39.

SZKT   *Shintei zōho Kokushi taikei* 新訂増補国史大系, 66 vols. Tokyo: Yoshikawa Kōbunkan, revised edition 1929–66.

T   *Taishō shinshū daizōkyō* 大正新修大蔵経, 85 vols. Takakusu Junjirō 高楠順次郎 and Watanabe Kaigyoku 渡邊海旭 (eds and comps). Tokyo: Taishō Issaikyō Kankōkai, 1924–34.

To   (= Tōhoku Catalogue). H. Ui, M. Suzuki, Y. Kanakura, and T. Tada (eds), *A Complete Catalogue of the Tibetan Buddhist*

       Canons (Bkaḥ-ḥgyur and Bstan-ḥgyur). Sendai: Tōhoku Imperial
       University, 1934.

TZ   *Taishō shinshū daizōkyō zuzō* 大正新修大蔵経図像, 12 vols. Tokyo:
       Taishō Shinshū Daizōkyō Kankōkai, 1975–78.

ZTZ   *Zoku Tendaishū zensho* 続天台宗全書, 15 vols. Tendai shūten
       hensanjo 天台宗典編纂所 (ed.). Tokyo: Shunjūsha, 1993.

1 Introduction

Japan's culture of secrecy from a comparative perspective

Mark Teeuwen

In 1648 a group of Shinto priests founded a library at the Outer Shrine of Ise. Their aims were to make important books accessible to the Outer Shrine priesthood and to spread correct knowledge among the general public through open lectures. In the same year, a list of regulations was drawn up that was to govern the running of this library, which was called Toyomiyazaki Bunko. The second item on this list addressed the thorny issue of secrecy:

> If members succeed in borrowing secret books (*hisho* 秘書) in the provinces, they must deposit [a copy of them] in the library. In cases where disclosure to others is deemed untoward, even members of our society may not see them. Such books must be sealed. When they are cleaned of insects, only a person with prior permission may open them and turn their pages.

> Those who read secret books in stealth will be expelled. Many books on the gods and on poetry are secret. This is so that we may dispel their misunderstandings, in these latter days. If they are read without restraint and regulation, it will be difficult to collect secret books. Therefore, it must be marked clearly in the catalogue of books which are secret and which are not.
>
> (*Bunko reijō* 文庫令条 ["Library regulations," 1648], p. 63)

This attempt at regulating the handling of secret texts in a "public" library exemplifies the tension between openness and secrecy – a tension that affected not only religion but also other forms of knowledge and expertise in medieval and early modern Japan. Most knowledge was private property, and therefore secret; at the same time, this secrecy was not absolute and it was often contested. This gave rise to never-ending battles over the status both of particular secrets and of secrecy in general. Are secret texts to be kept secret because they contain profound truths, or because they belong to someone who has the exclusive right to exploit them, or, as this item suggests, because the misunderstandings they contain must be dispelled?

As all these conceptions of secrecy intersected, they created a particular dynamic that had a great impact on the entire epistemological field of pre-modern Japan. Extending far beyond the domain of religion alone, it was so pervasive that we may speak of a "culture of secrecy," forming the context within which knowledge of all kinds was produced and reproduced. This book will explore this culture of secrecy. In doing so, we will focus especially on its relationship with esoteric Buddhism, since it was from this tradition that it derived most of its vocabulary and its procedures. In spite of the fact that Japan is a fascinating showcase of secrecy practices, there are few studies that address its functioning and its effects, let alone from a comparative perspective. The aim of this book is to investigate the development, the scope, and the decline of Japan's culture of secrecy, and to make the Japanese case available to the more general comparative study of secrecy.

Secrecy in religions: Strategy or contents?

Secrecy is an essential part of most, if not all, religious traditions. At the core of many religions we find teachings, rites, and objects that are wrapped in secrecy – or at least, we are confronted with procedures of secrecy, which may or may not conceal real secrets from outsiders. In many cases, such intentional concealment is explained as a defensive measure, taken to shield the secrets from various dangers. Secret matters must be protected from contact with the world's impurities, from the ignorant criticism of those who do not understand them, from the pressures of historical change, and, not least, from competitors in the religious arena. At the same time, secrecy serves to give information rarity value, which raises expectations and enhances the experience of those who, after much effort, finally gain access to the inner mysteries. When information is subjected to a regime of secrecy, it acquires a tantalising attraction that the same information would not have if it were freely available, and its power to fascinate increases correspondingly. Of course, secrecy also has its price. Self-imposed rules of secrecy can be a hindrance to propagation and recruitment. Secrecy may invite suspicion, condemnation and even violence if, for example, outsiders accuse insiders of conspiring to pursue all kinds of evil aims.

As a major structural constituent of religious life, secrecy has an impact on both the form and the content of religions. The need to keep certain matters secret forms institutional structures. At the same time, the need to maintain those institutions, which perceive themselves to be repositories of sacred mysteries, creates a space that will have to be filled, again and again, with real or imagined secrets. The structures of secrecy and the secrets that they conceal define both the self-perception of many religious groups and their interaction with society at large.

Yet secrecy is not easy to study. When dealing with contemporary groups, how can we be sure that what insiders tell us is a "genuine" secret? Moreover, is it ethical to expose what we have uncovered either through others' trust or by subterfuge? And when dealing with historical materials, what can we do with texts that appear to be encoded or that refer for explanation to a no longer extant "oral tradition"? What if we do succeed in recovering a secret, but it turns out to be a trivial detail that strikes us as completely meaningless or arbitrary?

Broadly speaking, secrecy appears to have been studied in two different ways. Perhaps the most obvious one is that seeking to discover what it is that a particular religious group is hiding. From this point of view, secrecy is the product of a set of inner secrets that form the core of the cult that has grown up around them. The cult must control access to its secrets to maintain their sanctity, and to safeguard their psychological impact on those who receive them. In other words, secrecy exists because there are secrets that need to be hidden.

A prominent example of this approach is Mircea Eliade's work on secrecy and initiation rites. Eliade (1958, esp. pp. 128–36) determines initiations to be an "existential experience that is basic in the human condition." He understands initiations as a "recapitulation of the sacred history of the world and the tribe," in which the neophytes "participate in the presence of the Gods or mythical Ancestors." At the centre of initiations Eliade detects a very real secret: a "central mystery," typically based on a myth about the violent death of a Supernatural Being that is "reactualized on the occasion of each new initiation" and that induces a spiritual transformation in the initiates. The secrets that are transmitted are transcendental, in the sense that they reveal to each new generation "the sum of the values received from Supernatural Beings." Eliade makes it very clear that he regards the secret contents of the archaic initiations that he finds in ancient sources and among primitive peoples of great value. Yet at the same time, he also expresses his contempt for the "recent and hybrid improvisations" of the "occult sects, secret societies, pseudo-initiatory groups [...] and the like" of modern man, whose "so-called initiation rites frequently betoken a deplorable spiritual poverty." Eliade posits a sharp contrast between those (old) initiations, which, in his view, contain a real connection to a central mystery, and (new) pseudo-initiations, which do not. As it happens, *real* initiations all belong to a bygone age, while observable reality displays alarming degeneration.

Kees W. Bolle, a student of Eliade, shows a similar bias towards a past that was more pure in his *Secrecy in Religion* (1987). Bolle argues that "not only in one tradition [i.e. Christianity – MT] but in each one, a particular mystery remains of central significance" (p. 12). All mystery-religions, he postulates, from gnosticism and pietism to Tantra, have their central mystery, even if their mysteries are not necessarily identical. Bolle traces the development of such religious movements from an initial inspired effort to "recover the one secret that counts" and to make it known to the world, to a less admirable stage in which "the original meaning of mystery has been transformed into mysteriousness, and the social sense of secret or the formation of coteries or sects has become the rule" (p. 14). Bolle, then, sees secrecy as an echo of God's own mystery, which in the course of history has been diluted due to the interference of secular society. This approach is crypto-theological, in the sense that Bolle regards human aspects of secrecy as secondary to its divine contents.

A radically different approach to secrecy was pioneered already a century ago by the German sociologist Georg Simmel (1906). The lasting importance of Simmel's work lies in his focus on the functions of secrecy rather than its contents. Simmel emphasised the positive meaning of secrecy as a necessary means for the functioning of social intercourse, both between individuals and between groups: secrecy, in his view, is no less than "one of the greatest achievements of mankind." At the same time, he also stresses that secrecy is a procedure that has value over and above its significance as a means. Simmel describes secrecy as a "stimulus of purely social derivation, quite independent of its accidental content" (p. 464). In his work, secrecy emerges as a social field that has its own dynamics, far beyond the practical necessity of hiding inconvenient pieces of information. Even when the secrets that this field contains are exposed (as they usually are), the domain of secrecy itself remains largely unaffected: "Human associations require a definite ratio of secrecy which merely changes its objects: letting go of one, it seizes another, and in the course of this exchange it keeps its quantum unvaried" (pp. 467–68). In Simmel's view, then, new secrets are created not simply because there are practical reasons for hiding the information that they contain, but also because there is an *a priori* need for a realm of secrecy of a certain size. In short, Simmel suggests that secrecy creates secrets, rather than the other way round.

Simmel has continued to inspire scholars who have analysed secrecy in sociological or anthropological terms. One eloquent example can be found in the work of Hugh B. Urban (1998, 2001), who has written extensively on secrecy in the Tantric Hindu tradition of the Kartābhajās in colonial Bengal. In his analysis of secrecy, Urban looks towards such theorists as Pierre Bourdieu and Michel Foucault. He argues that secrets are a form of symbolic capital and that the realm of secrecy is best understood as a "marketplace" with its own form of "economics." Secrets are traded on what may be described as a black market, a bazaar where peripheral groups create their own capital. Through secrecy, Urban argues, such groups can "transform information into something that can be owned, exchanged, accumulated – a commodity, something that can be bought and sold."[1] Therefore, he proposes that secrecy "is better understood, not in terms of its content or substance – which is ultimately unknowable, if there even is one – but rather in terms of its *forms* or *strategies*" (1998, p. 210). In more modern terminology than that of Simmel, Urban argues that the rationale for secrecy is not to be found in the specific information that is hidden, but rather in the strategy of creating value through scarcity and of managing the cultural capital that is produced in this way.

At first sight, the approaches of Eliade/Bolle and Simmel/Urban may appear to be mutually exclusive. However, it is also possible to argue that they offer two complementary perspectives, one from the inside and the other from the outside. For the insider, the secrets are indeed glimpses of a divine higher truth. For the outsider, however, it is clear that the machinery that surrounds the secrets is often out of proportion to their contents, and deserves an analysis in its own terms. Bolle echoes the rhetoric of the esotericists and, to a certain degree, takes their claims seriously; Urban keeps his distance and prefers to focus on what Bolle would call the "forecourt" of the temple. Bolle's approach can help us to savour the fascination of the secret to those who pursue it, in a way that Urban cannot. After all, not everything that is made scarce thereby acquires value. It needs to be accompanied by a convincing discourse and, more importantly, by a systematic performance that persuades the audience that the object or matter in question is not just rare, but in some way unique. It would indeed seem that a direct link to a "central mystery" is a common *topos* across cultures and religious traditions.

Is there no way, then, to approach the enchantment of the secret other than through sociological or theological means? Is it not possible to discuss the fascination of the secret in terms other than its function as symbolic capital or its roots in divine mystery? One valuable suggestion for an alternative perspective is Fabio Rambelli's (2002) analysis of the semiotics of secret buddha images (*hibutsu* 秘仏) in Japan.[2] Rambelli focuses on cult objects, especially buddha images, that are subject to a particular regime of invisibility and hiding. While acknowledging the social aspects of secrecy (especially of selective secrecy), Rambelli looks beyond these aspects towards questions of signification: How can objects convey meaning if they are invisible? How can we explain that there are cases where invisibility functions to intensify sacredness? He argues that secret buddha images have a special ontological status as liminal mediators between the visible and the invisible, the manifest and the formless. In this sense, these images are perceived as standing at that crucial spot where the unconditioned, undifferentiated world of the Dharma-realm intersects with the conditioned, differentiated world of karmic existence. As an "invisible presence," they give real, physical form to the metaphysical. While all buddha images, hidden or not, are understood to embody the unconditioned buddha body, *secret* buddha images, by remaining invisible, do better at "display[ing] the very concept of buddhahood – omnipresent but out of sight" (p. 302).

Rambelli describes the signification of buddha images in general as an example of the semiotic phenomenon of ostension, which, in Umberto Eco's definition, "occurs when a given object...is 'picked up' by someone and *shown* as the expression of the class of which it is a member" (Eco 1976, pp. 224–25). Unseen objects are objects "without characteristics," to use a Buddhist term, and are therefore more easily given collective, or even universal, metaphysical status. Secret objects (or teachings) create a void that begs to be filled with meaning. They are present and concrete, and yet they remain out of reach and abstract; for that very reason, they stand on the threshold between this world and another realm of unknown characteristics. In this sense, the secret buddhas of Japanese temples are perhaps representative of the realm of secrecy as a whole: the secret is a vacuum displayed in a conspicuous place. It may be filled with particular secrets, but even when these are exposed the vacuum remains in place, with its magic undiminished.

Cultures of secrecy and historical change

It goes without saying that even though secrecy in itself is a universal phenomenon, this does not mean that it will function in the same way at all times and in all places. Secrecy practices and even the concept of secrecy itself are subject to regional variation and historical development. A comparative study of secrecy is most valuable if it can identify clear differences between conceptions of secrecy in different periods and places.

Eloquent examples of such variation can be found in Kippenberg and Stroumsa's collection of essays on secrecy in Mediterranean and Near Eastern religions (1995). Here, the contrast between secrecy in ancient Greece and that in Egypt is particularly pronounced. Writing about the Greek mystery cults, Luther Martin (1995) argues (while referring to the work of Walter Burkert and Erwin Rohde) that here secrecy had little to do with concealed information: the mystery contents were "either trivial or public all along," so that "there was essentially no secret to let out." For the participant in Hellenistic mystery cults, "the 'doing' of secrecy...is not primarily a concealing of some knowledge, but rather embodies the ritual procedures necessary for the formation and maintenance of social boundaries" (pp. 109–10). The primary function of secrets was to define "clubs" of initiates. Those who had no interest in joining such a club were on the whole also uninterested in its secrets because the secrets in themselves were not thought to be particularly rare or valuable.

A radically different conception of secrecy is sketched by Jan Assmann (1995), whose chapter in the same volume deals with ancient Egypt. Here, secrecy was informed by a belief in the divine status and thaumaturgical power of the ancient liturgical texts. Knowledge of these texts was to be the privilege of priests and, ultimately, the priest-king. With this knowledge came the responsibility to perform the liturgy correctly, in order to "ensure the continued functioning of the world" (p. 55). In Egypt, then, in contrast to the Greek mystery cults, secrecy was concerned with very real secrets that consisted of information and objects that needed to be hidden. Moreover, these secrets were the domain of an official cult, not a private club. They constituted the professional knowledge of the official priesthood, and as such they had nothing to do with esotericism or mysticism, if these terms are understood to refer to a personal quest for a higher insight. The contrast to the Hellenic mystery cults could not be greater. Clearly, we can discern here two quite different "cultures of secrecy," which would be difficult to subsume under a single general definition of secrecy.

This difference between Egypt and Greece is an example of regional variation; such variation is further complicated by historical change. At the end of his chapter, Assmann (p. 60) points out that in Ptolemaic and Roman Egypt, the secret texts of the official cult found a new role as a part of the revelatory literature of groups of initiates. With the formation of these groups, the knowledge transmitted in the texts acquired a host of new functions (for example, to lead individuals to personal salvation, or to deliver individuals from misfortunes). In the process, the rationale for and management of secrecy underwent radical changes as well.

An example of a comprehensive history of secrecy practices in a particular religious tradition can be found in Paul Christopher Johnson's *Secrets, Gossip, and Gods: The Transformation of Brazilian Candomblé* (2002). Candomblé is an Afro-Brazilian religion with a focus on spirit possession, not unlike Voodoo in Haiti and Santeria in Cuba. It features an elaborate series of initiations, each giving the initiates access to secret knowledge of a higher level. Secrecy, then, has always played a major role in Candomblé, and Johnson offers a comprehensive analysis of "the historical layers of secrecy" in this religion (Part II, pp. 59–100). In the first phase, Yoruba uses of secrecy came to Brazil with the slave ships. Then, a new layer was added under the brutal regime of the slave masters, who looked at "black sorcerers," "hidden dances," and "altars of idols" with suspicion and disgust and repressed them with harsh measures. Even after the abolition of slavery in 1888, Candomblé was denied recognition as a legitimate religion. It was outlawed as a form of illegal medicine or sorcery, and treated as a "tumour," a cancer that had to be excised from the nation if Brazil was to become a truly modern state. This changed in the course of the 1930s, when Candomblé evolved from an Afro-Brazilian ethnic symbol into a national one. In the years when Brazilian national identity became a popular concern, the public perception of Candomblé began to change from dangerous slave magic to a hallmark of Brazilian national culture. At the same time, Candomblé moved into new social settings, and more formalised institutions and procedures were established. As an effect of

Candomblé's emergence onto the national stage, many of its secret practices and myths were pulled into the public domain.

The result, however, was not a decline of secrecy; rather, as Johnson writes, "the secrets receded to a more protected place":

> The response to the anthropological Clouzots,[3] who went sneaking into the locked rooms, was not to buy stronger locks. The response was a shift in the frame of secrecy. [...] The boundary was moved back, and the door shielding recusant secrets from the public was already elsewhere. Now, it would be found in the most elusive of places: in the closed bodies of prepared initiates and in secretism, discourses on secrets.
>
> (Johnson 2002, p. 100)

Johnson describes how even without "real" secrets, secrecy continued to be "embodied" and "performed" in Candomblé. He calls this ritual performance of secrecy "secretism," a neologism that he defines as "the active milling, polishing, and promotion of the reputation of the secrets." As secrets slipped out of the religion's control, they were replaced by ritualised secretism: "It is through secretism, the circulation of a secret's inaccessibility, the words and actions that throw that absence into relief, that a secret's power grows, quite independently of whether or not it exists" (p. 3). One characteristic of secretism in Candomblé is nostalgia for a time when there were real secrets – not unlike the nostalgia displayed by Eliade and Bolle.

These examples from Greece, Egypt, and Brazil must suffice to underline that secrecy can take on a variety of guises in different cultural and historical settings. From a socio-economic point of view, a secret, like any other commodity, can only retain its value as long as it is *perceived* to have value; and this perception can change rapidly under new historical circumstances. From a theological view, ideas can change as to what should be protected from desacralisation through concealment, and what should be revealed to all in the interests of proselytisation. From a semiotic perspective, the void of the secret may be perceived either as a passageway to another dimension or as a breach through which polluting heterodoxies invade the realm of sacred truth.

Secrecy in Japan

What is striking about secrecy in Japan is that it seems to belie Simmel's hypothesis that societies require "a definite ratio of secrecy" whose quantum remains unvaried. In Japan secrecy appears to have come in waves. Many authors have pointed out that the entire field of Japanese Buddhism came under the sway of esotericism in the late classical period (from the eleventh century onwards). In subsequent centuries, esoteric habits spilt over into adjoining and ever more peripheral fields of cultural practice. Secret initiations, for example, became a favoured medium for the transmission of knowledge not only among monks, but also among court poets, theatre actors, and even carpenters and blacksmiths. There seems to have existed a "culture of secrecy" in medieval Japan that cut across divisions of religion, sect, class, and occupation. This fact presents us with a range of questions: Where did this sudden predilection for secrecy and esotericism come from and what factors contributed to its success?

These questions become even more pressing when we see that this culture of secrecy came under attack quite abruptly in the seventeenth century, when the Tokugawa shogunate (1603–1868) established a new social order in the country. Across the intellectual field, secret teachings lost much of their prestige and authority in this new setting. Texts that in the medieval period had been transmitted within closed lineages were now made available to the public by way of the printing press. Oral transmissions were held up against newly compiled collections of canonical works, and rejected as "frauds of a later age" when they failed to satisfy strict criteria of scriptural orthodoxy and philological hermeneutics. Whereas earlier, all that was "secret" had been associated with profound truth and superior powers, the word now quite suddenly became a synonym for "fake." Again, we are left to wonder how this dramatic turn was possible.

Did these changes mark the end of Japan's culture of secrecy? In one sense, they did: the secret never regained as dominant a position within Japanese society as it had earlier held. Yet it is not difficult to see elements of continuity, or even expansion. The social setting of the secret was the transmission lineage, and never in the history of Japan were there so many lineages (*ryū* 流) as in the Tokugawa period, when large urban centres spawned new specialisations. In the martial arts alone, hundreds of lineages sprang up all over the country, each transmitting its own secret techniques and oral traditions. In places that were less exposed to the new intellectual mood (e.g. among *yamabushi* mountain ascetics), secrecy appears to have retained its medieval power to the full. Anne Walthall's essay in this book (Chapter 14) shows that even at the shogunal court, secrecy was transformed rather than discredited; it could be argued that the imperial court was even more secretive. What happened is perhaps best described not as the downfall of secrecy, but rather its relativisation, caused by the rise of a new culture of openness and historical criticism. The secret no longer dominated the field alone.[4]

In an attempt to sketch a very tentative historical outline of Japan's culture of secrecy, we may discern three periods: the classical period, before the wave of esoterisation set in; the medieval period, when secrecy in all its forms pervaded society; and the early modern period, when secrecy was offset by new demands for openness and became either marginalised or transformed. The transitions between these periods can roughly be dated to the twelfth and seventeenth centuries, respectively.

How can these shifts in the functioning of secrecy be described and explained? As a first step, we propose to approach this question from two different perspectives: discourses of secrecy and practices of secrecy.

Discourses of secrecy

The changing roles that secrecy has performed in Japanese society can be described in terms of a shift from one discourse of secrecy to another. The secret, as a category of knowledge, carried different associations in different periods. Secrecy had both positive and negative connotations, and the more positively secrecy was valued, the more widely and actively it was used. Surveying the essays gathered in this book, a picture emerges of three such competing discourses on the secret, two positive and one negative. At the risk of gross simplification, they may be roughly labelled as "typical of":

1   (exoteric) Mahāyāna
2   esoteric Buddhism
3   Confucianism.

In fact, these discourses cross the (ill-defined) boundaries of these three categories with great ease, and it is therefore perhaps more helpful and accurate to describe them by their key concepts:

1   the secret as a skill in means (*upāya*)
2   the secret as a mandala
3   the secret as a violation of the public good.

Of course, none of these conceptions of secrecy were peculiarly Japanese, and we shall see that their origins must be traced to the Asian continent. In this introduction, our aim will be to sketch how these three concepts of secrecy functioned in Japanese society in different historical periods. We propose that together these three notions of the secret formed the conceptual framework within which the Japanese discourse on secrecy took shape.

1   *The secret as a skill in means*

A typical example of what we may cautiously refer to as a Mahāyāna type of secrecy can be found in the *Upāyakauśalya-sūtra* (Skill-in-means sutra). This early Mahāyāna sutra (first century BCE?) closes with instructions on its transmission, beginning with the following injunction:

Son of the family: This teaching of skill in means is to be kept secret. Do not explain it in the presence of inferior sentient beings whose store of merit is small.

Why so? This teaching is not the stage of the auditors (*śrāvakas*) and independent buddhas (*pratyekabuddhas*)[5] – what need to mention sentient beings whose store of merit is small?

Why so? They are untrained in [this skill in] means. They have no need for it. No one but a bodhisattva is a fit vessel for this [teaching of] skill in means; no one else is to be trained in this teaching.

(Tatz 1994, p. 87)

Secrecy is here linked directly to stages of training. Those who have not reached the level of a bodhisattva will not benefit from this sutra's teaching, nor will they understand what to use it for. Therefore it must not be taught to them.

In another typical move, the sutra notes that when this teaching was first taught, those who had not reached the right stage of training were physically unable to perceive it:

Then all among the four assemblies of the world, including the gods, who were fit vessels heard this doctrine. All who were not fit vessels did not have it enter their ears.

(Tatz 1994, p. 88)

The secret, then, is that which one *must not* teach to those who are not ready to receive it, or that which *cannot* be taught to, or even heard by them.

To know what to teach to whom is the very essence of skill in means, the prime achievement of the bodhisattva. Out of compassion, the bodhisattva adapts his teachings to the needs of his hearers. He employs secrecy by hiding the true intentions behind his actions and words, so as to avoid misunderstandings. For example, the Skill-in-means sutra explains that the Buddha (before his enlightenment, when he was still a bodhisattva) chose to be born from the womb of a mother rather than manifest himself directly as a buddha because "in that case, some sentient beings would suspect that he is a god, a *gandharva*,[6] a magical creation, or some local spirit. With such suspicion, they would not listen to doctrine" (Tatz 1994, p. 53). Everything the bodhisattva does is in this way geared towards the benefits it brings to sentient beings. Secrecy is an intrinsic element of the bodhisattva's skilful strategies to lead all sentient beings to enlightenment.

The same view on secrecy is elaborated further in the Lotus sutra (*Saddharmapuṇḍarīka-sūtra*). In the second chapter of that sutra (also entitled "Skill in means"), the Buddha reveals that until then he had taught only provisional teachings to sentient beings, but had hidden the "true Dharma." The teaching that there are three vehicles (those of *śrāvakas*, *pratyekabuddhas*, and bodhisattvas) is not true; it is only through the one vehicle of full buddhahood that the sentient beings can be liberated. In the third chapter ("A parable"), this revelation is further illustrated by the tale of the burning house in which the Buddha is compared to a father who deceives his sons in order to save them. This method of teaching by skilful deception presupposes secrecy: if the deceit is revealed too soon, it will not produce the desired results.

As did the Skill-in-means sutra, the Lotus sutra warns that not all are fit to receive its teachings:

> I say [to you], Śāriputra! / Those who slander this sutra, / if I told the tale of their evils, / I could not exhaust them in a whole kalpa. / For this cause and reason / I especially say to you:

> Amongst undiscerning people, / do not preach this sutra. / If there be any who are clever, / of clear wisdom, / learned and of strong memory, / who seek after the Buddha-way, / to such people as these, / then, you may preach it.

> > (Katō *et al.*, 1975, p. 107)

In this case, the sutra must be hidden not from those who do not understand it, but from those who want to harm it. But the conditions for receiving the teaching of the Lotus are the same as in the Skill-in-means sutra: wisdom and a sincere desire for buddhahood.

There is a striking continuity in the understanding of secrecy in Mahāyāna doctrine. In China, we encounter much the same ideas that we already saw in the Skill-in-means and Lotus sutras. Misaki Ryōshū (1988, ch. 2) has analysed the notion of the secret (Chin. *mi* or *bimi* [*mimi*], Jap. *mitsu* or *himitsu* 密・秘密) in the thought of Chinese Tiantai masters and their Japanese Tendai heirs. He found that in the works of Tiantai thinkers, "secret" referred to two kinds of knowledge: knowledge that must not be divulged to those who are not ready or worthy to receive it and knowledge that cannot be divulged because it is beyond human comprehension, the domain of fully enlightened buddhas alone. As we have seen above, both of these meanings were already foreshadowed in the Skill-in-means sutra.

Michael Pye (1978, p. 160) has pointed out that in China, the concept of skilful means was developed into a very productive hermeneutical tool. It was used to explain why the Buddha taught different things at different times, and to range his teachings on a scale from more to less "expedient," or less to more "real." Tatz (p. 16) argues that this was a later development, not yet evident in the Skill-in-means sutra. Such hermeneutics came into their own with the development of Chinese sutra schools, notably the Huayan and the Tiantai schools. These schools ranked sutras according to their level of truth in a process called *panjiao* 教判 ("tenet classification"). *Panjiao* lists identified progressive levels of teaching, which become more exclusive (or more comprehensive) as they approach the ultimate truth – the truth that is known only to fully enlightened buddhas. It was in this sense that Tiantai thinkers understood the Lotus sutra's self-designation as the "storehouse of the secret" (*bimizang* 秘密蔵).

Looking back on these notions of the secret, two points are worth making. First, the main term used in Buddhist Chinese for "secret," *mi* 密, carries both the meaning of "secret" and that of "dense, concentrated, thick." In fact, in pre-Buddhist sources the second meaning was much more common than the first.[7] That "secret" conveyed the meanings both of "that which is hidden," and of "the inner essence, [truth] in its most condensed form," was therefore a simple and inescapable matter of Chinese semantics. Second, in this Buddhist realm there was a continuum from the "secret" (that which is known to some people and intentionally hidden by them from others) to the "esoteric" (that which is known to higher beings and is beyond the grasp of ordinary humans). *Mi* is an esoteric truth that has been revealed to mankind – buddha-wisdom that is beyond human understanding, and yet available in the form of sutras believed to contain the secret of buddhahood.

2   *The secret as a mandala*

The concept of revealed esoteric truth was developed further in esoteric Buddhism. As has been pointed out by many scholars, "esoteric Buddhism" (*mikkyō* 密教) is by no means an unproblematic term. To begin with, it is used in a variety of meanings. In the Japanese context, it refers first of all to one school of Buddhism, Shingon, which occasionally called itself also by the name "Mikkyō." It is also used to designate esoteric aspects of Japanese Tendai (often referred to as Taimitsu 台密, "Tendai esotericism," although the Tendai school did not use this term itself).[8] The border between esoteric and exoteric teachings was drawn differently in China and in Japan, in Tendai and in Shingon, and, as discussed in detail by Lucia Dolce in this book, it shifted quite radically over time.[9] The word *mikkyō* itself is of Chinese origin (*mijiao*), but as Robert Sharf (2002) has pointed out, *mikkyō* and *mijiao* are not the same:

> The compound *mijiao* is ubiquitous in Chinese translations of Indian scriptures, where it is used to denote the sublime and subtle teachings of the Buddha. More important, the distinction between teachings that are "explicit" (*xian* 現) and those that are "hidden" (*mi* 密) is found in the *Da zhidu lun* 大智度論, from whence it made its way into the fully articulated Tiantai tenet-classification system of the Tang. Yet in none of these sources does the term "esoteric" denote an

independent institution, sect, or even doctrine. Rather, it refers to the fact that the Buddha's sermons were understood in different ways by different people, depending on their individual capacities. The explicit or manifest teachings were those witnessed by all, irrespective of their prior spiritual accomplishments. The more advanced teachings were deemed esoteric or secret, because only advanced beings possessed the spiritual wherewithal to discern them.[10]

As we have seen above, these same meanings of "secret" can be traced back all the way to the early Mahāyāna Skill-in-means sutra.

Sharf's rejection of the notion of a Chinese *mijiao* school is confirmed from a different perspective by Ryūichi Abé.[11] Abé shows that as a rubric of Buddhism, Mikkyō was an invention of the Japanese monk Kūkai (774–835). In Chinese catalogues of Buddhist scripture, esoteric texts were "randomly scattered among Mahāyāna scriptures"; but Kūkai created "a wholly new bibliographical taxonomy" that set esoteric texts apart from exoteric, and defined them as a separate "vehicle," designated variably as the vajra vehicle (*kongōjō* 金剛乗) or the "unsurpassable vehicle" (*saijōjō* 最上乗). Such a vehicle, as Sharf agrees, had not yet been envisioned in China.

What characteristics did Kūkai's esoteric or secret category have? His central point, repeated in a number of texts, was that exoteric teachings are teachings preached by the *nirmāṇakāya-buddha* (the Buddha as he appears to ordinary sentient beings), and are adapted to the capacities of their audiences. They do not represent the absolute truth; they merely offer a relative truth, a truth that is helpful to the teachings' intended audience. In contrast, the esoteric teaching is preached by the *dharmakāya-buddha* (the Buddha in his absolute, transcendent form, the "Dharma-body") and represents the inner wisdom of the Buddha in its purest form. Kūkai maintained that the Dharma-body is not silent, but speaks to us in its own secret language, constituted by the so-called "three mysteries" (a term in which "mysteries" is yet another translation of *mitsu*). These mysteries are direct expressions of the body, speech and mind of the Dharma-body itself. They are ritually replicated in the form of mudras (hand gestures), mantras, and visualisations of mandalic forms – although in a wider sense, all sounds, sights and forms of the world are such mysteries in essence.[12]

What was different in this new discourse on the secret? Kūkai presented the esoteric as a new category of Buddhism, a new vehicle that rose above earlier *panjiao* ladders of truth, and that constituted the inner essence of them all. In addition, he gave a voice to the inner secret of the Buddha by making the Dharma-body speak. In doing so, he created the concept of non-dual, absolute speech. While the exoteric teachings consisted of words that *refer* to helpful but conditional teachings, the esoteric mysteries of the Dharma-body *are* the stuff of enlightenment, in a direct, absolute, non-dual manner.

It is this last point that makes it meaningful to speak of an "esoteric Buddhist" concept of secrecy, differentiated from the more general (exoteric) "Mahāyāna" view. In both cases, secret refers to the knowledge of a buddha; the difference is that in the esoteric view, this knowledge is said to be physically present in this world and instantly accessible to all sentient beings. It is this presence that is the esoteric secret.

Of course, the notion of this secret presence was not new in itself. In fact, Kūkai himself referred (among other scriptures) to the non-esoteric *Laṅkāvatāra-sūtra* when arguing for the notion of the Dharma-body's preaching.[13] What characterises the category of the secret in esoteric Buddhism is its concreteness. It is not so much the general *principle* of the Dharma-body's preaching that is secret, but its concrete *forms*. These forms consist first of all of the "three mysteries" mentioned above, and of their ritual use. It is these mysteries that unlock the secret realm of absolute truth, embodied in the Dharma-body. When used correctly, in the ways that have been transmitted in a direct line from the Dharma-body to our own age, they can make the enlightened realm, the "glory of the mandalas,"[14] manifest in samsara. The mysteries are as much instruments of concrete power as of truth: they can be used to unleash the powers of the divine figures that are mapped and made manifest in the mandalas.

In medieval Japan, the notion of the "glory of the mandalas" as a physical presence was ubiquitous. By "mandalising" places, objects, and even texts, they could be transformed into specimens of the non-dual power of the Dharma-body. Specific and not so specific sites were envisioned as mandalic power points, where the Dharma-body itself saves the sentient beings through objects, buildings, and landscapes that represent "True Reality." In fact, some texts do not hesitate to identify the whole of Japan as the "one-pronged vajra" of the Dharma-body. Such ideas were certainly not limited to the Shingon school alone.

As an example, let us take a brief look at a fourteenth-century text on the shrines of Ise, entitled *Reikiki* 麗気記. In a passage that the text's unknown authors attribute to the Tendai patriarch Saichō (767–822), the imperial shrines of Ise are described as the "Dharma-realm on earth":

> The Buddha land is separate from the three Realms [of Desire, Form and Non-Form], and is identical to the Dharma-realm. It is quiescent (*tannen* 湛然), undifferentiated (*byōdō* 平等) and eternal in past, present and future (*sanze jōjū* 三世常住). The *kami* deities manifest themselves in the world and mingle with its dust; they too are quiescent (*jakunen* 寂然), "one" (*ittai* 一体), and eternal. The two Ise shrines are also thus. The patterns that decorate the two shrines of Ise represent the shapes of [the twin] Mahābrahmās, the sun and the moon, and the [two] precious gems that contain the wondrous origin. Because they are traces containing the origin, they are the father and

the mother of all sentient beings. They are the form of that which
has never come and will never leave.

(Reikiki, p. 25)

This passage, replete with Tendai terminology, describes the Ise shrines
as the non-dual source of all existence, identical to the Dharma-realm
(*hokkai* 法界) that lies beyond samsara, "quiescent, undifferentiated and
eternal." In this same text (and many others in the same genre), gems,
patterns, objects (e.g. the one-pronged vajra), mountains, pillars and so
on are given the same status: the physical presence of the eternal
Dharma-body within the realm of samsara.

Here, we encounter a new type of secrecy that can be distinguished
from the "secret as a skill in means." In this discourse, the secret is that
which is mandalised. Mandalisation here means that the eternal
Dharma-body is "condensed" into material objects. It is this procedure of
condensation, rather than the idea of hiding something, that connects
the notion of *mitsu* ("dense; secret") with the concept of the mandala.
The keeper of esoteric knowledge reads objects, places, and texts as mandalas, "circles" of absolute reality that manifest themselves, unsoiled by
any kind of duality, in our conditioned world. Identifying objects and
places as mandalic, unlocking their secrets and manipulating them as
embodiments of the Dharma-body was at the core of what we may call
the esoteric Buddhist discourse on secrecy. This discourse does not
necessarily represent a break with the idea of the secret as a skill in
means. In both cases, the secret is conflated with the ultimate, the
domain of the buddhas. What has been added, however, is a mass of
concrete, secret "facts" on mandalic words, sites, and objects, and on
secret procedures for utilising them. Even more than before, secrets gave
access not only to higher truths, but also to greater powers.

Of course, the concept of the "secret as a mandala" was not limited to
the esoteric schools in a narrow sense – whatever categorisation we may
choose to adopt. Mandalised secrets of this kind were ubiquitous in
medieval Japan. They even spread beyond the Buddhist samgha, as the
mandalic secret was deployed widely to give new meanings to such
diverse cultural practices as poetry, theatre, and even carpentry.

3 *The secret as a violation of the public good*

In a striking contrast to the cultivation of the secret that characterised
the medieval world, negative comments on secrecy practices and secret
knowledge suddenly became ubiquitous in the seventeenth century. The
most common criticism of secrets was that they were counterfeits, manu-
factured "in a later age" to serve the interests of their inventors. Rapidly,
the older model that privileged secret texts over public texts was
exchanged for a new model that saw "secret" as the antonym of "canonical."

The canonical was true, sophisticated and orthodox; the secret was its opposite: fake, simplistic, and heretical. Matters became even worse when critics denounced secrecy as a trick to swindle people and make illegitimate profits.

What is perhaps most striking about this sudden critique of secrecy is its total disregard for the mystique of secrecy. Whether secrecy had been seen as a side effect of skill in means or as a mandalic manifestation of the Absolute, it had referred to the most profound wisdom and power of the buddhas. Not a trace of that fascination is left in a passage such as the following, from a text called *Yōfuku ki* 陽復記 (1650) by the Ise priest Deguchi Nobuyoshi 出口延佳 (1615–90):

> Q: Without old books, the methods of Japan cannot be known. What is the reason that people both in the capital and in the countryside keep old books secret?
>
> A: In most cases, it is for selfish reasons. There are, however, valid reasons for keeping some matters secret. At the Ise shrines, for example, texts about the divine objects or the shrines' central pillars are of no use to people of other Houses, and they concern very important matters. Therefore it is most reasonable that they are hidden away as profound secrets, and kept from people with other occupations. Moreover, many medieval books on the gods mix Buddhism and Shinto. Because they are products of particularly ignorant authors, they can easily lead people astray; therefore it is reasonable that they are kept secret. But it is very wrong to keep secret those books on the gods that should by rights be made widely available in the realm, especially books of law and national history. Buddhists do not hide their books but make them public. Therefore their books have spread throughout the realm. Our Land of the Gods has become a Buddhist land, and our people slaves of the Buddha. Is not this because the books about the gods and other old books of our land are falsely kept secret, so that people do not know them?
>
> (*Yōfuku ki*, pp. 109–10)

Nobuyoshi (who also played a central role in the founding of the Toyomiyazaki Bunko mentioned at the outset of this introduction) did not accept the notion that secret knowledge has a special status. In his view, what is secret is not necessarily particularly profound, nor does it offer a channel to a different realm or a different reality. To be sure, secrecy may be advisable in some cases. Not all professional knowledge of priests is relevant to others. For others to know it would not only be useless, it could even have an adverse (defiling?) effect. Technical knowledge is best reserved for those who have the expertise to filter the true from the false; others may be led astray and are best informed in more straightforward ways. But otherwise, Nobuyoshi has a negative view on secrecy. It is a barrier that prevents correct knowledge from reaching the people. Knowledge that is not in the public domain might as well not exist at all. Ironically, Nobuyoshi claims that his arch-enemies, the Buddhists, have understood this far better than his fellow shrine priests, and there-fore do *not* keep things secret.

In a later text (*Jingū zoku hiden mondō* 神宮続秘伝問答,1682), Nobuyoshi warns against secrecy as, at bottom, immoral. After all, "things one hides from others are mostly bad things":

> Secret matters (*mitsuji* 密事) erect a barrier between oneself and others, and they are mostly evil things, [arising from] an evil heart. One will never be able to act in accord with the will of the gods if one has an evil heart. The will of the gods is sincerity, like a bright mirror; an evil mind is insincerity, like rust.
>
> (*Jingū zoku hiden mondō*, p. 62)

Secrecy is a form of insincerity. What is hidden is suspect – why else should it be hidden? The act of hiding things has the effect of isolating one from others, and it damages the ties that hold society together. In that sense, secrecy is fundamentally destructive.

Nobuyoshi's perception of knowledge contrasts sharply with the views we discussed above, which valued secrecy positively. To Nobuyoshi, knowledge is about truth; it is something that must be spread for the betterment of all. Those who claim to "own" knowledge are either lying (for their secrets are false), or, even worse, they are selfishly damaging the common good. This view draws on a Confucian set of ethics that warned against private selfishness as the prime threat to the public common good. As the opposition "private (=selfish) vs. public (=righteous)" displaced the older "secret (=profound) vs. open (=shallow)," secrecy slipped from a positive into a negative set of associations.

Social practices of secrecy

Having identified three rather abstract discourses on secrecy, we must face the question how these relate to the history of more concrete *prac-tices* of secrecy. In a very general sense, we can discern a gradual change from a predominantly "Mahāyāna" conception of secrecy (as a skill in means), to a more markedly "esoteric" view (the mandalic secret), and finally to a negative view that resonated with Confucian ethics (the secret as a violation of the public good). These discourses were dominant in, respectively, the "classical" period (until the twelfth century), the medie-val period (until the seventeenth century), and the early modern period (from the seventeenth century onwards). However, this does not neces-sarily warrant the conclusion that the rise and fall of Japan's medieval culture of secrecy was *caused* by the emergence of new discourses on secrecy. In fact, the reverse would appear just as likely. Many of the essays in this book point at the importance of social and political change as a reason for instigating new secrecy practices. The first two (positive) discourses described here were important first of all as tools for legitimating forms of secrecy that were already in place, and the last (negative) one was used to denounce a system of secret transmissions that, as suggested in Chapters 8, 11 and 12, was already in decline.

To better understand the historical factors involved, we must look at the concrete *practices* of secrecy and their relationship to the respective forms of discourse. This leads us to a central question: Is the esoteric discourse on secrecy inherently tied up with a praxis that presupposes secrecy? Or is secrecy a secondary phenomenon that has little to do with the esoteric teachings *per se*? Robert Thurman (1988) and Ronald M. Davidson (2002) are two examples of scholars who have taken opposite positions on this question.

Based on an analysis of *anuttara yoga* tantras, Thurman has argued that the esoteric teachings in these texts are "by definition secret, occult, mysterious" (p. 125). Thurman posits that the aim of the Vajrayāna tantras is not the awakening of understanding, but the physical transformation of the adept into the Buddha-body. To achieve this aim, it is more productive to push the disciple beyond reason by the use of a "paradoxical expressions," than to help him "understand with superior clarity" – to quote Candrakīrti's words in the *Guhyasamāja*. In Thurman's analysis, the tantras appear as uniquely polysemic texts, conveying different levels of meaning to those who have attained different stages of enlightenment. The text can only be made to work by a vajra guru, who has mastered a complicated hermeneutical system traditionally termed "the seven ornaments" (identifying five preliminaries, four kinds of procedures, six parameters in elucidation, four kinds of interpretation, two types of teachings, five types of disciples, and two different aspects of the ultimate goal of practice) – all of which must be taken into consideration when applying the tantras in teaching disciples on various levels. By "teaching mysteriously," the buddhas create a multivocal expanse of meaning that radiates transformative powers on all levels; in that sense, the tantras are far superior to exoteric texts, which merely bring clarity to strictly limited matters by speaking with a single, easily interpretable voice. Thurman sees practices of secrecy (such as the necessity of initiation by a guru) as a function of the inner structure of the tantra texts themselves: only private interaction between a guru and a disciple can unlock the tantras. Since secret initiations are the only way for tantras to work, social practices of secrecy are inherent in and derived from the unique hermeneutics on which the tantra texts are based.

Where Thurman sees secrecy practice as rooted in the nature of the tantra texts themselves, Davidson argues in the opposite direction. He focuses on the historical and social circumstances that formed the context for the emergence of Tantra in India. Davidson posits that the Tantric movement evolved in response to the feudalisation of the Indian political realm after the fall of the Imperial Guptas in the late sixth and seventh centuries. In his view, Tantra "internalized, appropriated, reaffirmed, and rearranged the structures most closely associated with the systems of power relations, ritual authentication, aesthetics, gift-giving, clan associations, and sense of dominion that defined Post-Gupta polities" (p. 115). He proposes that Tantra (or Mantrayāna) was built around a central sustaining metaphor: that of an individual assuming kingship and exercising dominion. When monks gained entrance to the realm of the buddhas through an initiation or consecration (*abhiṣeka*), this was a metaphorical reference to the coronation (*abhiṣeka*) of a king (p. 122). Once consecrated, monks gained dominion over a circle of divinities (*maṇḍala*); again, the notion of the king's dominion over a circle of vassals (*maṇḍala*) hovered in the background. The monk manipulated secret spells (*guhyamantra*) as a king manipulated confidential counsel (*guhyamantra*), and showed his spiritual power by wielding symbols of royal power such as the vajra. Davidson sees the Tantric ritual system as a "consensual effort at sanctifying society" (p. 161): Indian esoteric Buddhism turned the political realities of the day into metaphors for the Buddhist path. This had the advantage both of making Buddhism more immediately understandable in a new social context and of opening up new channels of patronage.

Davidson's thesis on the origins of Tantra is also reflected in his view on the role of secrecy. He does not see secrecy as an early feature of Tantra; rather, he argues that secrecy became prominent first at a later stage (the eighth century), when sectarian friction and general militarisation became prevalent in Indian society. Davidson points at an early period when esoteric texts, including spells, were *not* kept secret. Even later, secrecy was applied to the specifics of ritual and meditative procedures, not to doctrine, as Thurman's analysis would lead us to expect. Davidson sees Tantric secrecy as an extension of the political and military espionage that was rife in the splintered society of eighth-century India: its primary aim was to trick and to exclude religious opponents, in order to prevent them from stealing one's own potent magical techniques.

The Japanese case appears to support Davidson's view of secrecy as a social dynamic, rather than Thurman's notion of a doctrinal hermeneutic of Tantric secrecy. In spite of Kūkai's esoteric rhetoric, even in the Shingon school secret initiations, rituals, and texts became prominent only several hundred years after Shingon's establishment, when Japan entered its own period of medieval feudalism. In Kūkai's own time, knowledge was first and foremost an imperial concern; Kūkai himself was sent to China as a court-sponsored student with the assignment to bring the court's expertise in Buddhist statesmanship up to date. Like Confucianism, Buddhism was a matter of state, pursued by the court to protect the imperial body and to bring peace and prosperity to the imperial realm. It was first after the central authority of the court had declined that knowledge of various kinds slipped from the official sphere of court institutions to the private sphere of lineages and aristocratic cloisters. Jacqueline Stone sums up the social context of medieval secret transmissions as follows:

> Politically, socially, and economically, the culture of secret transmissions was grounded in the privatization of land and power by *kenmon* [権門, ruling elites], in the aristocratization of the [Buddhist] clergy, and in the consequent transplanting of noble factions into the world of temple–shrine complexes. Its distinctive features included the primacy of the bond between master and disciple, sometimes reinforced by blood ties; Mikkyō-esque initiation rites; and secret transmissions that, even when written down, continued to be called *kuden* [口伝, oral transmissions], emphasizing their origins in private explanation given by the teacher to his chosen disciple, which others were not permitted to hear. Such conventions of secret transmission became normative for the dissemination of knowledge – not only in religious matters but in court ceremony, literature, the visual and performing arts, and many crafts – throughout the medieval period.
>
> (Stone 1999, p. 151)

This wide dissemination of secrecy, both in the form of concrete practices and as a more abstract discourse, is in itself a clear indication that secrecy was as much a product of the *context* as of the *contents* of secretive traditions.

The circumstances around the demise of this culture of secrecy point in the same direction. As we have already seen, Japan's medieval culture of secrecy fell victim to a radical epistemological shift in the second half of the seventeenth century. Before this shift, keepers of knowledge had derived their authority from secret "oral" transmissions, traced back to sacred origins through exclusive transmission lineages. Under the new epistemological regime, however, authority came to rest with (partly new) canons of sacred texts. As textual exegesis took over the role of lineage initiation, secret transmissions were marginalised, or even actively destroyed. This phenomenon was not peculiar to Buddhism but occurred almost simultaneously across the entire intellectual field: it was as prominent in schools of Confucianism, Shinto, and poetry (*kokugaku*). This fact alone suggests that it had a social rather than a purely doctrinal background.

It is hardly a coincidence that this shift coincided with the end of what we may call (with reference to Davidson) medieval feudalism. In the decades around 1600, Japan was transformed from a military culture of warfare not unlike that of medieval India into a hierarchical culture of order. In the short span of some sixty years (ca. 1570–1630), anarchy and opportunism gave way to a system of strong and pervasive state control.

Many historians have pointed out that the medieval temple complexes were among those who lost most in this transformation. These complexes had controlled a sizeable proportion of all agricultural land since the early medieval period; later, they had also dominated trade as patrons of guilds and markets. Central Japan was covered by a network of the so-called temple-precinct towns (*keidai toshi* 境内都市), which exerted considerable power due to their military, financial and, not least, spiritual expertise (Itō 1999, Adolphson 2000). However, these temple complexes began their slow decline already during the Ōnin war of 1467–77. In the ensuing turmoil they lost control over their landed goods, and were soon outperformed by local warlords in other fields as well. What remained of their old power was finally destroyed by Oda Nobunaga and Toyotomi Hideyoshi in the 1570s and 1580s. Milestones in this process were the destruction of the Tendai headquarters on Mount Hiei in 1571, the burning of the Shingon centre of Negoroji in 1585, and the capitulation of Kōyasan, also of the Shingon school, in that same year. The subjugation of the Ikkō movement in the so-called Ishiyama war of 1570–80 was another watershed in the breakdown of Buddhist secular power. As William Bodiford points out in his contribution to this book, the Buddhist institutions that were rebuilt in the ensuing decades were stripped of all political influence and placed under the strict control of the new Tokugawa shogunate.

To ensure that shogunal control extended to all temples, the third Tokugawa shogun, Iemitsu (r. 1623–51), forced all Buddhist temples to submit to central, sectarian head-temples. Further, Buddhist sects were ordered to establish head-temples in both the Kansai and the Kantō (in western and eastern Japan), an arrangement that diluted the powers of each head-temple. The education of monks and appointments to temple positions were coordinated centrally from these head-temples. Doctrinal study was strongly encouraged, and long training programmes diverted energy away from social and political activities. One result of this was that text-based study at central institutions increasingly displaced guru-led training within local, autonomous lineages – a trend that was further strengthened by the rapid spread of printed books.

This was not a process unique to Japan; parallels can be found both in China and further afield. In his analysis of the history of Tibetan Buddhism, Geoffrey Samuel (1993) suggests to distinguish between two broad types of Buddhism, which he terms "clerical" and "shamanic" Buddhism. Although Samuel's idiosyncratic use of the term "shamanic" has been widely criticised, his comments on the relations between state and religious culture are very suggestive with a view to developments in Japan. Samuel contrasts the Buddhism of the scholar-monk, whose main activities consist of "scholarship, philosophical analysis, and monastic discipline," to that of the Tantric lama, who "undergoes a prolonged retreat in order to gain the shamanic power of the Vajrayāna, and subsequently utilizes that power on behalf of a lay population" (pp. 9–10). He argues that the former could exist only in periods with a strong state, while the latter flourished in the many stateless periods of Tibetan history. Whenever effective state power was established, efforts were made to control and limit the movements of the Tantric lamas because "they represent an alternative source of power and authority" (p. 364).

Samuel's characterisation of Tantra as "shamanic" and therefore at odds with the state is in direct contradiction with Davidson's emphasis on the importance of royal metaphors in Indian Tantra. Also, Samuel's hypothesis does not help to explain why Tantra (or esoteric Buddhism) spread from one court to another throughout East- and South-Asia in a very short period of time, to become a major component of royal ritual wherever it took root. Yet, his point that text-based, institutionalised forms of authority tend to overrule practice-based, individual forms of authority in places and periods with strong states offers a striking parallel to developments in seventeenth-century Japan.

Both Davidson and Samuel argue that in the cases of Indian and Tibetan Tantra, secrecy was a product of social and political contexts, rather than a function of secret contents. The history of Japan's culture of secrecy as it emerges from this book is best explained in the same manner. This underlines the importance of analysing not only the discourses of secrecy that were current in different periods, but also the social structures that fostered them. The question remains, however, how far we can take such an analysis. If secrecy creates secrets rather than the reverse, what does that mean for our understanding of the actual contents of secret traditions, in as far as these can be traced in the sources? Is the tendency of secret teachings to trample on taboos and indulge in themes of sex and violence the *result* of their function as secret teachings, rather than the *reason* for their secret status? Moreover, did secrecy, over time, create a form of anti-orthodoxy that undermined the status of Buddhism as Japan's hegemonic discourse? Was the move away from secret traditions, which began well before the Tokugawa order was in place, to some degree a counter-reaction from within? When there were too many secrets, of a nature that was too "outrageous" and accessible to too many people, this would have caused inflation to set in. At the same time, the authority of Buddhism as a whole would have been adversely affected as contradictory statements about the nature of its teachings became ever more pervasive. Can a system of public secrets, combined with a Candomblé-like "secretism," work over a longer period of time? Or was such a state of affairs inherently unstable, inviting the rise of the "Confucian" discourse of secrecy? While the essays collected in this book do not answer these questions in a definite manner, they have at least enabled us to ask them, and given us some tools to begin considering their implications.

The essays in this book

The final part of this introduction will present the main arguments of the book's individual chapters and show how they relate to each other. The book is organised into three sections. Part I (Chapters 2–4) is concerned with secrecy outside Japan, and covers some necessary preliminaries for discussing the Japanese case. Part II (Chapters 5–12) addresses different aspects of Japan's medieval culture of secrecy, and Part III (Chapters 13–15) discusses the demise of this culture, while exploring alternative forms of secrecy that were prominent in the post-medieval or early modern period.

Part I: Prologue

The discussion is opened by *Albert de Jong*, who provides an overview of recent analyses of secrecy from the perspective of several different disciplines. De Jong begins by differentiating secrecy from related phenomena such as access restrictions, privacy, esotericism, and mysticism. For the case of Japan, the distinction between secrecy as "social secrets" on the one hand and esotericism or "divine secrets" on the other is particularly useful. As we have seen above, Buddhist discourses consistently conflated the social with the divine secret, tempting us to assume that esoteric interpretations were more secret, in a social sense, than exoteric ones. Many of the chapters in this book show that in fact much that was esoteric was not secret and vice versa. In the second part of his essay, De Jong summarises the main aspects of secrecy in the ancient Mediterranean world, focusing on secret knowledge, secret rituals, and secret identities. As a comparative touchstone, his account of secrecy in the Ancient World helps to bring the characteristics of Japan's culture of secrecy into focus. In the mystery cults of the Ancient World, the controlling of experience in the context of (lay) initiations emerges as a key function of secrecy; in Japan, authentication of the thaumaturgical powers of (professional) specialists appears to have been a more prominent concern.[15]

Ronald M. Davidson, whose work has already been discussed above, points out another important difference between the Hellenic mysteries and Tantric Buddhism: while the former typically left us very few texts (if any at all), the latter floods us with them. Tantric Buddhism emerges in the form of a proliferation of texts, produced in a short space of time and in a violent political environment where both Tantric and other religious groups faced the threat of obliteration. These facts go far towards explaining the difference between the types of secrecy in the Ancient World and India, as sketched by De Jong and Davidson. Davidson further contrasts Tantric secrecy to the Mahāyāna concept of skill in means: whereas in Mahāyāna, secrecy refers to temporary deception in the interest of bringing enlightenment to sentient beings, Tantric secrecy is almost exclusively concerned with aspects of ritual that are permanent and enduring. Tantric Buddhism, then, transformed secrecy from a provisional into a permanent attribute, pertaining to the "secret behaviors of the tantrika" rather than to doctrines. In Davidson's essay, this category of the permanently secret emerges as Tantra's main innovation in the Buddhist discourse on secrecy.

Martin Lehnert closes this section of the book with a discussion of the introduction of esoteric teachings (*mijiao*) to China and an analysis of the classical narrative about this transmission. The secret teachings were said to be based on scriptures that had been stored in the mythical Iron Stūpa of southern India. When Vajrabodhi, one of the Indian founders of Chinese esotericism, tried to bring them to China, they were lost at sea. According to Lehnert, this loss was an important aspect of the secret status of esoteric knowledge in China. In the absence of the "real texts" from the Iron Stūpa, authority came to be vested in their Indian transmitters, who "embodied" the lost wisdom. Even though these transmitters wrote summaries of the secret teachings, they downplayed their own writings as mere abstracts while emphasising ritual practice, especially consecration ceremonies (*abhiṣeka*, Chin. *guanding* 灌頂). It may be noted here that in medieval Japan, the Chinese scriptures (and even Japanese texts – cf. Susan Klein's essay) *did* attain the absolute status that Chinese esotericism reserved for the lost Indian originals. Lehnert further describes how Vajrabodhi's disciple Amoghavajra "accomplished what monks attempted less successfully in the warring feudal states of medieval India: to actualize Buddhism as a repository of state-related ritual services." By manipulating the absolute "words of truth" (mantras) known only to them, esoteric priests like Amoghavajra offered the embattled emperors of the Tang a new kind of authority, in the form of an "empowering liturgy of state protection." Their success, needless to say, was the foundation on which Japanese Mikkyō was built.

Part II: Analysing Japan's medieval culture of secrecy

The second part of the book sets out with an analysis by *Fabio Rambelli* of the epistemic characteristics of Japanese esoteric Buddhism and of the concrete ways in which it was taught and transmitted within Buddhist institutions. As a fundamental difference in perspective between Mahāyāna schools and Mikkyō, Rambelli points to the different ways in which they understand the Dharma-body. While Mahāyāna schools describe this absolute body as "devoid of signs and forms," Mikkyō sees it as "the totality of all signs," a living entity that speaks to all sentient beings about its own enlightenment in an absolute language, while generating its own form of semiotics. Esoteric knowledge is knowledge of the absolute and unconditioned nature of this language. The route from a "superficial view" of language (a view that sees language as provisional and referential) to an understanding of its absolute and unconditioned nature was envisioned as a progression from one level of "secrecy" to another. In spite of this rhetoric of secrecy, however, Rambelli shows that in actual praxis, doctrinal knowledge of this kind was not secret in a social sense. It was taught in classes rather than in one-to-one transmissions, and through texts rather than orally. Consecrations (*abhiṣeka*, Jap. *kanjō* 灌頂) were ceremonies marking the legitimate, unadulterated transmission of the esoteric signs, rather than occasions for the revelation of secrets. The exception was lineage-specific ritual knowledge, in which access to secrets was tied to questions of power and wealth. Rambelli shows quite plainly that the esoteric was not necessarily secret and that esoteric Buddhism should not be mistaken for a form of secretive occultism.

Where the focus in Rambelli's essay is on Shingon esotericism (Tōmitsu 東密), *Lucia Dolce* introduces us to Japan's other esoteric tradition, Tendai esotericism (Taimitsu 台密). While Shingon defined itself as entirely esoteric, Tendai combined the exoteric teaching of the Lotus sutra ("the perfect teaching," *engyō* 円教) with esoteric teachings (*mikkyō*). This confronted Tendai thinkers with the question of the relation between the exoteric and the esoteric in ways that did not arise in Shingon. Dolce shows how Tendai (and Tiantai) scholiasts reflected over the Mahāyāna concept of secrecy that is so prominent in the Lotus sutra, and how their interpretations reflect the esoteric (Tantric) discourse on secrecy. In the process, the boundary between esoteric and exoteric was redrawn, with the category of the esoteric becoming ever more comprehensive. In the second part of her essay, Dolce describes how a specifically Tendai form of esoteric practice was created by esoterising the Lotus sutra. This involved the mandalisation of the Lotus and the creation of an esoteric Lotus practice called *hokke hō* 法華法. While Tōmitsu was based on a set of two sutras with accompanying mandalas (called *ryōbu* 両部, "two parts"), Tendai preferred a set of three (*sanbu* 三部, "three parts"). Dolce traces how the Lotus sutra (rather than the *Suxidi jing*) was groomed to play the role of the third part in Tendai's own sectarian form of esotericism. At the same time she makes it clear that in actual practice, sectarian boundaries were more rhetorical than real, a point that is also stressed in other chapters (e.g. Chapter 8).

Shifting the focus away from doctrine, *Mark Teeuwen* investigates an essential feature of esoteric practice and its socio-economic context: transmission within lineages. Many of these lineages were based on institutions (cloisters, family lines) that had their own economic base, primarily in the form of land rights. In the late Heian period, possession of a lineage's secrets emerges as a precondition for appointments to leading positions within the institution to which that lineage was connected. Owning secrets was therefore a key not only to symbolic capital, but also to solidly economic capital. An important point here is that unknown secrets have no value; only famous ones do. This fact explains much of the complicated dynamic that reminds us of Johnson's secretism: tips of veils are forever being lifted as secrets are flaunted and stolen, lost and found. Teeuwen explores the dynamics of secret-making through a case study of the most renowned of all medieval secrets, the *sokui kanjō* 即位灌頂 (imperial enthronement unction). The history of the *sokui kanjō* demonstrates in concrete detail how "big" secrets were created at the centre (the court and the major temple complexes) and made famous with the help of all the tricks of secretism; how they soon were "stolen" and contested by various lineages, sub-lineages, and ambitious monks; and, finally, how they were dispersed into the periphery. Along this typical career track, the secret spawned countless sub-secrets as it interacted with other secrets. In this way, a secret could grow into an entire discourse of its own – or fall into oblivion, outshone by other, more exciting secrets. In this sense, we may recognise also in Japan some of the energy and the "outrageousness" that Davidson finds typical of medieval Indian Tantra.

Iyanaga Nobumi's essay takes us straight into the darkest depths of this "outrageous" realm. As in India, Japanese esoteric Buddhism invested much of its energy in text production. Iyanaga introduces us to a particular group that mass-produced "secret texts" in the late thirteenth century. This group (known to us only as "that school," *kano ryū* 彼の流, although it has been incorrectly identified with the notorious Tachikawa school until today) reportedly espoused the view that "intercourse with women is the most crucial thing in the Shingon teaching," and created hundreds of fascicles of scripture to prove this point – mainly by inserting sexual terms into assorted passages from Tantric sutras such as the *Yugikyō* and the *Rishukyō*. Iyanaga points at a wave of "dark" secrecy in the late thirteenth and fourteenth centuries. In this period, countless lineages concocted their own forms of "black magic," often playing on the twin themes of sex and imperial power. In the later medieval period, this "horror-like" realm of secrecy became "subject to inflation," as its contents gradually spilt out into the public realm. This sparked a movement within the Shingon school to denounce the most extreme texts and the most obvious apocrypha in lists of "heretical works." By the end of the medieval period, the secrets had become more trivial than dark, which suggests that they had already lost much of their allure by the time Japan's culture of secrecy went into its final decline in the Tokugawa period.

In the thirteenth century, esoteric and often sexual readings spread far beyond the confines of Buddhist groups. *Susan Blakeley Klein* has published previously on the esoterisation of *waka* poetry by Fujiwara Tameaki, who created a lineage of *waka* knowledge that featured its own *kanjō* initiations (Klein 2002). Like the "secret-makers" described by Teeuwen and Iyanaga, Tameaki was the losing figure in a struggle for influence within an existing lineage. All these persons, no matter whether they belonged to a family lineage or a Dharma lineage, created new secrets or even new lineages in response to a perceived lack of authority. In this sense, Tameaki is yet another example of the archetypical secret-maker in medieval Japan. In her essay, Klein goes on to look at another literary genre, that of Noh theatre, focusing on the troupe leader and author Konparu Zenchiku (1405–70?). Zenchiku, too, "lost the oral teachings that his father should have transmitted to him" when his father died suddenly, and in a typical move, he went on to create his own secret teachings on the basis of dream visions, revealed to him by the deity of poetry, Sumiyoshi. Klein shows that the notion of the "motivated sign" formed interpretive strategies such as etymological and numerological allegoresis, which were used to read literary texts on love and liaisons as esoteric revelations of the Dharma-body's salvific power through sex. In his treatise *Meishuku shū*, Zenchiku laid out a network of "continuously expanding and exfoliating identifications" which showed that his Konparu troupe was "grounded in a transcendent reality." Klein demonstrates how the same esoteric discourse marks one of Zenchiku's plays.

Bernard Faure introduces us to some of the central deities that inhabit the expansive networks spun by Zenchiku and others. Through a maze of identifications, he leads us from Vināyaka, through Yama, Ḍākinī, and Sarasvatī (Benzaiten) to more specifically Japanese divine figures such as Matarajin, Kōjin, and Shukujin. These deities blend into one another, to the extent of becoming variant names for a single divine cluster. This cluster displays clearly demonic features. Again, "black magic," sex and death feature prominently in the symbolic realm that these divinities personify; so do themes of procreation, incubation, and embryology. Faure proposes that deities from this group are thus archetypical hidden buddhas (*hibutsu*), "whose secret nature, symbolized by their withdrawal and concealment in the inner sanctum, evokes infinite power and potentiality." Setting aside questions of social context or doctrinal categorisation, Faure gives us a structural sketch of the divine figures that were thought to occupy the primordial secret space that lies beyond samsara, the realm of potentiality from which reality arises. In medieval Japanese Tantrism, this space was violent, unruly, and dynamic, and quite unlike the serene realm of Mahāvairocana's pure enlightenment that is associated with traditional Mahāyāna or, we may add, later forms of esoteric Buddhism.

Where sexual themes are prominent in the essays by Iyanaga, Faure, and Klein, *Kadoya Atsushi* takes us back to the other main axis of the world of medieval secrets: that of speculations on the nature of imperial power, as was also explored in Teeuwen's essay. Kadoya focuses on two lists of imperial regalia, the three and the ten Divine Treasures, and shows how these were portrayed in medieval apocrypha. In secret diagrams, these regalia were linked to cosmological characters in Kūkai's calligraphy, to patterns of studs in the gables of the two Ise shrines, and, again, to the *sokui kanjō* enthronement unction. Kadoya stresses the importance of non-textual forms of expression such as visual language (in illustrations and diagrams) and body language (in ritual) as constituents of the medieval discourse that were lost when the medieval culture of secrecy faded out in the seventeenth century. Comparing medieval understandings of the regalia with post-medieval ones, Kadoya describes the former as synthetic or integrative and the latter as analytical. Medieval writers were interested in weaving expansive webs of meaning, concretised in objects of supreme power such as the regalia; post-medieval writers, on the other hand, reduced these objects to mere symbols that they regarded as secondary to the abstract virtues of the Confucian classics. In the terminology of this introduction, we could say that in early modern Japan, the regalia ceased to function as "mandalic secrets." They were no longer recognised as "motivated signs," and, as a result, secret transmissions about them were no longer recognised as valuable or even valid.

In the final chapter of this section, *Bernhard Scheid* leads us back to the question of lineages. He takes up the medieval transmission of the *Nihon shoki* (720) as an example of what may be termed esoteric Shinto. The focus of Scheid's essay is on the difference between esoteric and non-esoteric forms of secret transmission. Specialist knowledge about the *Nihon shoki* was transmitted within the Urabe, a family of diviners at the imperial court, throughout the medieval period. In their transmission, both esoteric and non-esoteric forms were prominent at different historical stages. In a first phase, secrecy took the form of monopolistic exclusion, and did not inspire the Urabe to indulge in esoteric interpretations of the *Nihon shoki* text. Such esoteric explanations came into play only when the Urabe lineage faced an existential crisis (the Ōnin War, 1467–77) and lost its traditional hereditary position within the imperial court. This prompted Yoshida (Urabe) Kanetomo (1435–1511) to create a new teaching that eventually developed into Yoshida Shinto. The role of the *Nihon shoki* changed quite dramatically in the course of these events. During the first phase of Urabe history, the text had been treated as a historical source, and only its "possession" was protected by secrecy; now, it was interpreted as a religious revelation. Paradoxically, in this new role the text lost its secret status, since it was now used merely as a pointer towards much deeper ("mandalic") secrets, which were structurally identical with the concept of ultimate truth in esoteric Buddhism. Nevertheless, in the *Nihon shoki* commentaries of Kanetomo's successors Scheid notes a striking lack of "esoteric inspiration." Again, it becomes clear that the medieval culture of secrecy fell into decline well before it became the target of explicit criticism in the seventeenth century.

Part III: The demise of medieval secrecy

Often, the inner structure of a discourse is revealed most clearly as it unravels. Therefore, the last three chapters of this book address the question of how the medieval culture of secrecy came to an end. Also, they explore in what forms and shapes secrecy continued to play a role in post-medieval Japan.

William M. Bodiford presents us with a case study of the elimination of secret transmissions from Tendai by examining the so-called Anraku reforms in the last decades of the seventeenth century. Bodiford points at the central importance of these secret transmissions even in the early seventeenth century. Yet by the end of this century, these same transmissions were reviled as "devil's teachings," antinomian heresies that needed to be exterminated if Tendai Buddhism was to be restored to its classical glory. It is telling that the attack on secret transmissions occurred in the context of attempts to revive the rules of monastic discipline (*vinaya*). This reflects a more general trend to regard the secret teachings as a threat to social morality. The Anraku reforms replaced the secret transmissions of medieval Tendai with vinaya ordinations and textual studies. As factors that contributed to this outcome, Bodiford mentions the transformation of Tendai's institutional base and the new availability of printed books (including Ming dynasty works of Tiantai doctrine). At the same time, however, he underlines that the changes in Tendai were part of a much larger epistemological shift. This shift affected not only Buddhism but also Confucianism, and it occurred not only in Japan, but also had a close parallel in China, where Qing dynasty scholars began to cast doubt on received truths through "evidentiary learning" (*kaozheng xue* 考証学). In the end, Bodiford finds in the Anraku critique of secret transmissions "a moral choice between objective criteria based on authoritative scriptures, commentaries, and treatises versus subjective inner experience." As exemplified by Kadoya's analysis of the changing meaning of the regalia, this choice was at the same time also a choice between an exoteric discourse on virtue and an esoteric one on transformative power.

The connection between power and secrecy is also the main theme of *Anne Walthall's* essay. Her chapter stands out from the others in this book by focusing not on esoteric Buddhism, or even religion, but on questions of political authority. By focusing on shogunal ceremonial in the Tokugawa period, she introduces us to a consistent "iconography of absence" that was used to give expression to shogunal power. In contrast to European monarchs, the Tokugawa shoguns rarely allowed themselves to be seen. Walthall describes how shogunal audiences were designed for subordinates to be seen by the shogun, who remained invisible to them. On these occasions the shogun did not speak, or even move, and he expressed his authority by forcing others to expose themselves to his gaze. Walthall compares the shogun's "disembodied presence" in his castle in Edo to a "hidden buddha" in a temple. In both cases, a regime of concealment served to magnify the "secret, sacred power" of the figure that is kept from view. The few occasions on which the shogun did reveal his person, such as the annual *machi-iri* Noh performance, may be compared to Buddhist *kaichō* 開帳 ("curtain-opening") ceremonies, where statues that are normally hidden are displayed to the public for a limited period of time. In both cases, an elaborate "dialectic of disclosure and concealment" is employed to create power and authority. Walthall's essay demonstrates that secrecy continued to sustain authority in the early modern period, even if it was no longer connected with a discourse that privileged secrets over publicly accessible truths.

In the last chapter of this book, *Kate Wildman Nakai* takes us to the late Tokugawa period, when the medieval cult of secrecy was no more than a distant memory. Nakai shows us a sample of the new discourse that filled the empty space that had been left by the demise of medieval secret transmissions. Focusing on nineteenth-century thinkers of the late Mito school, she shows how these co-opted the texts that had been the mainstay of medieval esoteric exegesis for their own ideological agenda. In this school, the Japanese texts on the Age of the Gods (*kamiyo* 神代) were read as analogies to the Chinese classics. In this reading the focus was on the notion that the emperor, through the performance of public rituals, inspires the populace to feel "an instinctive readiness to assist and serve the ruler." In nineteenth-century Mito, this idea even inspired the distribution of a ritual calendar that encouraged villagers to "echo the rites performed at the court" through rituals that were appropriate to their status.

When we compare the understanding of imperial rituals in late Mito thought with the esoteric discourse on the *sokui kanjō* enthronement unction, the changed status of the secret versus the public becomes very clear. In late Mito thought, ritual served to extend the virtue of the emperor from the palace to the people, inspiring feelings of gratitude and awe. Where this early-modern view on imperial ritual emphasises the public promotion of virtue, the medieval discourse on the *sokui kanjō* looks at secret knowledge as a kind of "black magic." Such knowledge allowed the possessor of secrets to open up a channel between the absolute realm of the Dharma-body and the karmic realm of samsara. Both Walthall and Nakai show that in the Confucian world of the Tokugawa period, where ritual was about social order, there was no place for such dramatic ideas. This reflected a new conception of the emperor's significance: while the medieval emperor had embodied the Dharma-realm, his post-medieval counterpart had to be content with representing the Confucian notion of the public good.

Notes

1 Urban 1998, pp. 220–21. Urban refers here to Lamont Lindstrom, *Knowledge and Power in a South Pacific society* (Washington, DC: Smithsonian Institution Press, 1990), which makes the same point about the Tanna peoples of the South Pacific.

2 Another approach to secrecy, which will not be explored here but is certainly of great importance, is its psychological impact on those who keep secrets. For an insightful analysis, see Luhrmann 1989.

3 This is a reference to Henri-Georges Clouzot, an ethnographer who quite literally broke into a room said to contain Candomblé secrets – only to find that it contained nothing but "a powerful smell" (Johnson 2002, p. 3).

4 For a recent collection of essays on secrecy in Tokugawa Japan, see the recent issue of *Revue d'Études Japonaises du CEEJA* (CEEJA 2005), especially the case studies included in "Étude de l'époque d'Edo à travers les transmission secrètes (*hiden*) d'un art ou d'une pensée" (pp. 127–245).

5 *Śrāvakas* (auditors, listeners) are disciples of the Buddha; *pratyekabuddhas* are those who attain enlightenment independently. Both are contrasted to bodhisattvas, who seek buddhahood for the benefit of all sentient beings.

6 In Indian myth, *gandharvas* are celestial spirits who serve as the musicians of Indra.

7 This became clear to me through a search of this term in the *Thesaurus Linguae Sericae*. I would like to thank Christoph Harbsmeier for introducing me to the marvels of this database.

8 In fact, Tendai esotericism was most commonly referred to as Shingon, both by Tendai scholiasts themselves and by outsiders. Sectarian identities were extremely fluid in pre-Tokugawa Japan.

9 The impossibility of classifying Tendai doctrines of original enlightenment as either exoteric or esoteric is a good example of the fluid nature of these categories. See Stone 1999, pp. 363–64, and Abé 1999, p. 425.

10 Sharf 2002, p. 267. Chinese terms in this quotation have been changed to pinyin transcription, with apologies.

11 Abé 1999, "(No) traces of esoteric Buddhism."

12 See, e.g. Kūkai's *Ben kenmitsu nikyō ron* 弁顕密二教論 (On the difference between the exoteric and the esoteric teachings), pp. 474ff.; Hakeda 1972, pp. 151–57.

13 See Hakeda 1972, p. 155; Abé 1999, pp. 215–16.

14 Kūkai used this expression in *Hizō hōyaku* 秘蔵宝鑰 (The precious key to the secret treasury), pp. 418–19, to describe the concrete contents of the esoteric teachings as the most advanced of all doctrines. Translated in Hakeda 1972, p. 160.

15 Strikingly, the topic of secret identities is not raised in any of the chapters of this book. One reason for this is the fact that in Japan, state repression of religious groups (such as Fuju Fuse and hidden Christians) only became prominent in the post-medieval period.

References

Primary sources

Ben kenmitsu nikyō ron 弁顕密二教論. In KDZ 1 (1968).

Bunko reijō 文庫令条. In Jingū Bunko 神宮文庫 (comp.), *Jingū bunko enkaku shiryō* 神宮文庫沿革資料 (=Jingū Bunko sōsho 神宮文庫叢書 IV). Ise: Jingū Bunko, 1990 [¹ 1934].

Hizō hōyaku 秘蔵宝鑰. In KDZ 1 (1968).

Jingū zoku hiden mondō 神宮続秘伝問答. In Jingū Shichō 神宮司庁 (comp.), *Daijingū sōsho* 大神宮叢書, vol. *Watarai Shintō taisei kōhen* 度会神道大成後篇. Ise: Jingū Shichō, 1955.

Reikiki 麗気記. In Shinbutsu shūgō kenkyūkai 神仏習合研究会 (ed.), *Kōchū kaisetsu gendaigo-yaku Reikiki* I 校註解説現代語訳 麗気記 I. Kyoto: Hōzōkan, 2001.

Yōfuku ki 陽復記. In Taira Shigemichi 平重道 and Abe Akio 阿部秋生 (eds), *Kinsei Shintōron, zenki kokugaku* 近世神道論 41·前期国学 (=NST 39). Tokyo: Iwanami Shoten, 1972.

Modern sources

Abé, Ryūichi (1999), *The Weaving of Mantra: Kūkai and the Construction of the Esoteric Buddhist Discourse*. New York: Columbia University Press.

Adolphson, Mikael S. (2000), *The Gates of Power: Monks, Courtiers and Warriors in Premodern Japan*. Honolulu: University of Hawai'i Press.

Assmann, Jan (1995), "Unio Liturgica. Die kultische Einstimmung in götterweltlichen Lobpreis als Grundmotiv 'esoterischer' Überlieferung im alten Ägypten," in Kippenberg and Stroumsa 1995, pp. 37–60.

Bolle, K.W. (ed.) (1987), *Secrecy in Religion* (Studies in the History of Religions 49). Leiden: Brill.

CEEJA (2005), *Benkyōkai* (=*Revue d'Études Japonaises du CEEJA*). Strasbourg: Centre Européen d'Études Japonaises d'Alsace.

Davidson, Ronald M. (2002), *Indian Esoteric Buddhism: A Social History of the Tantric Movement*. New York: Columbia University Press.

Eco, Umberto (1976), *A Theory of Semiotics*. Bloomington, Ind.: Indiana University Press.

Eliade, Mircea (1958), *Rites and Symbols of Initiation: The Mysteries of Birth and Rebirth*, New York: Harper & Brothers.

Grapard, Allan G. (1987), "Linguistic Cubism: A Singularity of Pluralism in the Sannō Cult." *Japanese Journal of Religious Studies* 14/2–3, pp. 211–34.

Hakeda, Yoshito S. (1972), *Kūkai: Major Works. Translated, with an Account of his Life and a Study of his Thought* (=Unesco Collection of Representative Works, Japanese Series). New York: Columbia University Press.

Itō Masatoshi 伊藤正敏 (1999), *Chūsei no jisha seiryoku to keidai toshi* 中世の寺社勢力と境内都市. Tokyo: Yoshikawa Kōbunkan.

Johnson, Paul Christopher (2002), *Secrets, Gossip, and Gods: The Transformation of Brazilian Candomblé*. Oxford: Oxford University Press.

Katō, Bunnō, Yoshiro Tamura and Kojiro Miyasaka (tr.) (1975), *The Threefold Lotus Sutra*. New York and Tokyo: Weatherhill/Kosei.

Kippenberg, Hans G. and Guy G. Stroumsa (eds) (1995), *Secrecy and Concealment: Studies in the History of Mediterranian and Near Eastern Religions*. Leiden: E.J. Brill.

Klein, Susan Blakeley (2002), *Allegories of Desire: Esoteric Literary Commentaries of Medieval Japan*. Cambridge, MA: Harvard University Press.

Luhrmann, T.M. (1989), "The Magic of Secrecy." *Ethos* 17/2, pp. 131–65.

Martin, Luther H. (1995), "Secrecy in Hellenistic Religious Communities," in Kippenberg and Stroumsa (1995), pp. 101–22.

Misaki Ryōshū 三崎良周 (1988), *Taimitsu no kenkyū* 台密の研究. Tokyo: Sōbunsha.

Pye, Michael (1978), *Skilful Means: A Concept in Mahayana Buddhism*. London: Duckworth.

Rambelli, Fabio (2002), "Secret Buddhas: The Limits of Buddhist Representation." *Monumenta Nipponica* 57/3, pp. 271–306.

Samuel, Geoffrey (1993), *Civilized Shamans: Buddhism in Tibetan Societies*. Washington, DC: Smithsonian Institution Press.

Sharf, Robert H. (2002), *Coming to Terms with Chinese Buddhism*. Honolulu: University of Hawai'i Press.

Simmel, Georg (1906), "The Sociology of Secrecy and of Secret Societies." *American Journal of Sociology* 11, pp. 441–98.

Stone, Jacqueline I. (1999), *Original Enlightenment and the Transformation of Medieval Japanese Buddhism*. Honolulu: University of Hawai'i Press.

Tatz, Mark (1994), *The Skill in Means (Upāyakauśalya) Sūtra*. Delhi: Motilal Banarsidass.

Thurman, Robert A.F. (1988), "Vajra Hermeneutics," in Donald Lopez (ed.), *Buddhist Hermeneutics*. Honolulu: University of Hawai'i Press, pp. 119–48.

Urban, Hugh B. (1998), "The Torment of Secrecy: Ethical and Epistemological Problems in the Study of Esoteric Traditions." *History of Religions* 37/3, pp. 209–48.

Urban, Hugh B. (2001), *The Economics of Ecstasy: Tantra, Secrecy, and Power in Colonial Bengal*. New York: Oxford University Press.

Wolfson, Elliott R. (ed.) (1999), *Rending the Veil: Concealment and Secrecy in the History of Religions*. New York and London: Seven Bridges Press.

Part I
Prologue

2 Secrets and secrecy in the study of religion

Comparative views from the Ancient World

Albert de Jong

> "And you, Tat and Asclepius and Hammon,
> hide these divine mysteries among the secrets of your heart
> and shield them with silence."
> *Asclepius* 32[1]

The comparative study of religion(s)

From its inception in the nineteenth century to the present, the academic study of religion has been dominated by the comparative method.[2] Alongside the study of individual religious traditions, most often on the basis of textual evidence, scholars have explored ways of studying "religion" and "religions" by comparing fundamental elements and strategies found in various different traditions. The validity of this approach to the study of religion has often been questioned, but it seems that no viable alternative has yet been presented.[3] The comparative method in the study of religion is obviously fraught with difficulties. Power relations and ideology loom large in various stages of the process of comparison, for instance in the selection and naming of the subject, the selection of cultures or traditions to be compared, the description and contextualisation of the subject, and so on.[4] This is why opponents of comparativism have little difficulty in pointing out the many examples of projects that have gone haywire, often on a monumental scale.

The accusations against comparative approaches are varied, but they roughly fall into two categories. Many students of individual traditions (e.g. Biblical scholars or specialists in Islam or Buddhism) feel that comparative approaches are reductionist in nature, in that they take elements from each area of specialisation merely to illustrate a common human pattern or strategy (or a "universal"). This they consider to violate the unique nature or distinctiveness of the tradition they know intimately.

Such concerns are voiced both by representatives of the religions ("believers" and "theologians") themselves, and by scholars who have been influenced by the wave of post-modern theories and approaches.

This first objection is often coupled to the second objection that comparative approaches have an essentialist agenda, that they aim at constructing the universal, unchanging, and (almost) metaphysical "essence" of a given phenomenon. If that were the aim of the comparative study of religion, the risk of subsequently imposing that essential meaning or function onto the various religions of humankind would become distinctly real. In this way, scholars would be able to force culturally conditioned meanings onto religions, communities, or individuals who are no longer expected or allowed to respond. Such processes of disembodying or reification (or "epistemic violence") are often highlighted by post-modern scholars and by those working within the framework of post-colonial theory.[5]

This assortment of opponents to comparativism thus groups theologians (in the sense of those working explicitly from a religious perspective) and post-modern or post-colonial theorists together. None of them, however, have been able to escape the fact that classification and taxonomy are the most basic intellectual strategies of all humans, including scholars. To quote the famous statement by Jonathan Z. Smith:

> The process of comparison is a fundamental characteristic of human intelligence. Whether revealed in the logical grouping of classes, in poetic similes, in mimesis, or other like activities – comparison, the bringing together of two or more objects for the purpose of noting either similarity or dissimilarity, is the omnipresent substructure of human thought. Without it, we could not speak, perceive, learn, or reason.
> (Smith 1993, p. 240)

This is why, in recent contributions that aim to defend or re-establish the comparative method, one is showered by words such as "inevitable," "indispensable," "ineluctable," or "unavoidable."[6] The fact that comparison is the most important human way of learning forces us to pay it due attention in theoretical and methodological discussions. One cannot ignore, however, some of the issues raised by the opponents of comparativism: "power" and "politics" have had and continue to have a lasting impact on the development of scholarship and there is every reason to welcome analysis of this impact.

The point of departure for any comparative study of religious ideas and behaviour is given by human biology and sociobiology. There is, in other words, a certain level of unity in human experiences. Obvious subjects include food, kinship, sex, work, violence, competition, and death. These are aspects of the experience of all humans, and they always take place in social contexts because man is a social animal. Even though religion is found in all human cultures, "religion" does not seem to belong to this group of human activities and experiences. It has no obvious evolutionary function to fulfil, but it is a human "universal." In the introduction to his fascinating study of tracks of biology in early religions, Walter Burkert introduces in addition to the biologically grounded phenomena a second set of human universals:

> What is startling is the ubiquity of certain less trivial phenomena, which are culturally determined in every case and yet not generated nor explicable in isolation. They always appear integrated into specific cultures and take various shapes accordingly, but their unmistakable similarity makes them a general class transcending single culture systems. They must be presumed to fulfil basic functions for human social life in all its forms, even if it is easy to imagine alternatives. These universals include such disparate phenomena as the nuclear family with a marked role of the father and the special father–son relationship; the use of technology, especially of fire; interactions that include economic exchange but also warfare; and above all language, art, and religion. The last two mentioned may come as a surprise: what are in fact the functions of art and religion? They seem to be much less necessary for human life than the other items mentioned, yet they have been with us for all the time *homo sapiens* has been in existence.
>
> (Burkert 1996, p. 4)

If religion is, in that sense, a "second-order" human universal, one would expect it to be deeply involved with primary human activities and experiences, which it obviously is, and to use these in developing its symbolic systems of meaning. Secrecy, the subject of the present book, is a good example. It is undeniably a biologically programmed capacity that is characteristic of the behaviour of many animals, who hide themselves or their young, hide food or knowledge of where food can be found and divert attention by focusing intently on imagined dangers (Burkert 1996, p. 25). It is also, on a secondary level, one of the basic strategies in group formation and, in its wake, the generation of individuality (see below). In religious traditions, in particular, it has also fulfilled an important function that one could call the creation of a unity of experience. It is ideally suited, therefore, for comparative study, as long as we specify the ways in which we are going to approach it.

Definitions of secrecy

Like many other subjects in the comparative study of cultures and religions, secrecy has usually been discussed thematically by specialists of individual traditions. This has led to a number of conference volumes, in which the "phenomenon" of secrecy is discussed in the religious traditions of India,

the Ancient World, Judaism, Christianity, and Islam.[7] Although many of
the contributions to these volumes are excellent, they mainly provide
materials to illustrate particular points. Thorough analysis of the concept
of "secrecy" itself is remarkably absent from them. In fact, the various
scholars representing "the religions" differ markedly in their interpretation or demarcation of secrecy. There is, of course, no binding definition
of the concept; the statement that "secrecy has more often been defined
than understood" (Tefft 1980, p. 35) may be true, but at least in comparative analysis, some sort of definition must precede our attempts at
analysis and understanding.

Fortunately, the subject of secrecy has been explored and analysed in
recent works using the tools of psychology, philosophy/ethics, and
literary history.[8] The sociology of secrets has been dominated by the work
of Georg Simmel, which will be discussed separately below. On the basis of
these works, we can isolate certain requirements for a comparative study of
secrets and secrecy in religious contexts.

The two basic requirements are that a secret must be *intentional* and
that it must be *social*, that is to say it must include three parties: two who
share the secret and establish a bond to keep it, and the rest of humanity,
as a third party, which is to be excluded. The private secrets of individual
men and women of the past are not only most often lost to us (unless they
were committed to writing), but also do not provide us any possibilities
for comparative analysis. These are secrets that are governed either by the
(biological) programme of saving one's life or safeguarding its quality or
by mechanisms of modesty, shame, and so on. There are cultural constraints
on these mechanisms and these may have been influenced by religious
sensibilities, but this is not necessarily the case and our focus will therefore be on secrecy as a social institution.

The subsidiary requirement to the two mentioned is that the secrets must
be capable of being formulated and transmitted. These requirements can
be portrayed in four cases. We shall contrast secrecy with (1) other (types of)
restrictions, (2) privacy, (3) esotericism, and (4) mysticism.

1 *Secrecy versus other restrictions*

From our first condition, that a secret must be intentional (i.e. the "owner(s)"
of a secret must have the explicit intention not to reveal it, not keeping it
for themselves merely out of negligence), it follows that we have to put
aside a large set of data, as for instance restrictions on the grounds of
purity, that may appear as "secret" only to an outside observer. A good
illustration is provided by Parsi Zoroastrian fire-temples. Like some
Hindu temples (for instance the famous Jagannatha temple in Puri) and
like the two holy cities of Islam, Parsi Zoroastrian fire-temples may only
be entered by members of the community. There can be no mistake
about this: most fire-temples have plaques stating in Gujarati and English

(and sometimes Hindi) the fact that entrance is reserved solely to Parsis.[9] Certain parts of the fire-temples themselves are also off-limits to most Zoroastrians, being the exclusive reserve for consecrated priests. The reasons for these restrictions have nothing to do with secrecy, but are guided by the concept of purity: fire-temples are the dwelling-places of consecrated fires and a high state of ritual purity must be preserved in these sanctuaries. Non-believers are by definition ritually impure and therefore cannot enter a fire-temple as long as a consecrated fire is present. In fact, whenever the fire is temporarily removed, for instance when a temple is being repaired or redecorated, non-Parsis are allowed to enter.[10] The rituals in the fire-temples, moreover, are known in every minute detail, can be witnessed in schools for priests, and have been filmed and documented extensively.[11]

In addition to concerns for purity, there are other restrictions that may be in force for reasons other than secrecy: selection on the basis of gender, for instance. Most religions prescribe certain rituals in which only women or only men are allowed to participate. In some cases, such restrictions may be connected with secrecy, but in others other social codes or etiquette seem to be the dominant concern. Similarly, there may be class restrictions, financial barriers, or many other types of exclusivism. It is true, of course, that the excluded parties may frown upon such institutions, and because of their feeling of being excluded launch the accusation of secrecy against the excluding group. This would be a subject for analysis only if one wants to study the use of "secrecy" in polemical contexts, but as long as secrecy is not explicitly intended, such institutions should not be considered to be "secret."

2   *Secrecy versus privacy*

Although we tend to claim privacy as one of the great characteristics of modern Western civilization, a certain wish for privacy seems to be common to all humans of all times and places.[12] The distinction between secrecy and privacy is vital in modern Western civilisation, but only, in the present author's view, as *moral* categories. Sissela Bok distinguishes secrecy from privacy in the following manner: whereas secrecy is "intentional conceal-ment," privacy is "the condition of being protected from unwanted access by others – either physical access, personal information, or attention. Claims to privacy are claims to control access to what one takes – however grandiosely – to be one's personal domain" (Bok 1982, pp. 10–11).

In some Middle Eastern cultures, the concept of "modesty" would be roughly equated with Bok's definition of "privacy," but it is obvious that the backgrounds in both cases are thoroughly conditioned by cultural perceptions of individuality and social placement, and have a normative basis.[13] Apart from its normative foundations in Western culture, privacy barely fulfils the requirement of being a social secret. Although its scope can extend to the sphere of the family, the moment it leaves this domestic context, it immediately changes into "real" secrecy (or else, we would be forced to ponder the concept of privacy of any group of humans).

3   *Secrecy versus esotericism*

The terms "secret" and "esoteric" are almost interchangeable in common speech as well as in many modern studies of various religious traditions.[14] In recent years, the field of "Western esotericism" has made a Cinderella appearance on the stage of the academic study of religion.[15] The term is now used for a specific group of religious and spiritual movements that originated in the appropriation of certain types of knowledge and traditions from the Ancient World in the period of the Renaissance. As a consequence, the term "esoteric" can now be used in two distinct meanings: as a general term to refer to a system of interpretation focusing on finding extraordinary realities behind ordinary texts, persons, or objects, and in a special meaning referring to these European movements. In both meanings, the concept of secrecy is important. The movements themselves (spiritual alchemy, neo-Hermetism, Paracelsianism, theosophy, etc.) are often claimed or believed to be secret societies (which is by no means always the case). Also, in its general application, the term "esoteric" conjures up ideas of secrecy and concealment.[16]

It is crucial, however, to distinguish secrecy, as defined in social terms, from esotericism. Esoteric interpretations of texts and objects (including the cosmos) are found in many religions. They are also often claimed to be "secrets," but if they are, their "owner" is, to put it in squarely monotheist terms, God. Many of the branches of Islam, for example, are based on the distinction between *zāhir* ("manifest") and *bātin* ("inner, hidden") in their interpretation of the Qur'an, but they do not all keep the inner (and obviously more important) meaning hidden from others. What is there to penetrate, in most esoteric traditions, are the divine secrets, and those visionaries and others who have penetrated these secrets may choose to reveal them to all or to keep them within a limited circle.

Divine secrets, by definition, are not social secrets. Thus there is a split within the esoteric traditions: some of them are secret in that they restrict access to the keys for unlocking the hidden meanings, others are not, but share the knowledge gained freely and without reservation to those interested.

This can perhaps be illustrated by briefly discussing a little-noticed distinction in the Coptic texts that were found in 1945 in the vicinity of Nag Hammadi in Upper Egypt.[17] These texts, distributed over at least thirteen codices, twelve of which have been preserved along with some fragments of the thirteenth, form a collection of texts used by Egyptian Christian monks in the fourth century CE. Not all of the texts are Christian (the exceptions being a fragment from Plato's *Republic* and two Hermetic texts), and not all of the Christian texts are gnostic, but the collection includes an important number of texts that represent

Christian gnosticism, including texts that are reminiscent of the gnostic texts quoted in anti-gnostic polemics by the Christian theologian Irenaeus and the Neoplatonic philosopher Plotinus.[18] Several of the texts in the collection are "esoteric" in that they claim to give the "real" meaning of many biblical passages, often on the authority of a divine revelation.

Within the corpus, quite a few texts begin with an indication of secrecy (the opening words of the *Gospel according to Thomas*, for instance, are "These are the secret sayings which the living Jesus spoke and which Didymus Judas Thomas wrote down"), but many of these end with a doxology and an announcement that the truth is now finally revealed and made known to all.[19] The function of secrecy in these texts, apart from investing it with special importance by ascribing it as a divine (self-) revelation to important holy persons, is chiefly to give a reason for their sudden, unexpected appearance. This mechanism is well known from many ancient texts, which often claim to transmit knowledge or texts from before the flood (the books attributed to Enoch, for example, and certain parts of Mesopotamian literature), thus having to give a reason for the fact that these very ancient texts made their first appearance thousands of years after their alleged composition (Tromp 1993, p. 147).

Only a small number of texts, however, *end* with the command of keeping the text or the knowledge secret. Some texts stress the fact that the revealed knowledge is only destined for a select group ("the race of Seth") and others end with exhortations to silence and impressive oaths and threats (especially the *Apocryphon of John* and the *Discourse on the Eighth and the Ninth Sphere*). So, within this corpus of esoteric literature with secret origins, only a part continues to keep the texts or knowledge secret. This split in esoteric traditions can be observed in many different religions and systems. It is important, therefore, not to consider all esoteric literature secret in a social sense.

4 Secrecy versus mysticism

The final vital distinction is between secrecy and mysticism. Like gnosticism and magic, mysticism as a concept defies precise definition and is, therefore, problematic.[20] Several religions that originated in the Near East in late antiquity (Judaism, Christianity, Islam, and Hermetism) encapsulate traditions that stress the possibility of attaining unity with the divine. This unity is most often described, sometimes at length, as a process of melting, as loss of individuality, and as bliss and similar terms. The central aspect of it is the experience itself, which in most cases is described as ineffable. There literally are no words to describe what happens exactly, although this has not deterred many individual mystics to attempt to do just that. For our study, this implies that the mystical experience is not a "secret" because it cannot be transmitted or shared, nor shielded from outside inspection.

The pioneering efforts of Georg Simmel

No exploration of secrecy in the religious traditions of the Ancient World can be complete without a mention of the first and most influential theorist on the subject, the German sociologist and philosopher Georg Simmel (1858–1918).[21] The work of Georg Simmel is known as the most important example of formal sociology. He pioneered the construction of "social types," most famously the social type of the "stranger" in society. For Simmel, individuals are *produced* by society. To instantiate this, Simmel (notorious for his refusal to start from definitions) starts his portrayal of types of social structures by looking at the relations between two individuals, as the smallest possible social grouping, but particularly focuses on what happens once we move from a dyad – two individuals – to a triad, which in his analysis is the first "group" and therefore the first subject for the sociologist. This is because only a triad makes it possible for a group to display the basic characteristics of group behaviour that are impossible in unions of two: majority decisions overruling minority points of view, mediation, and the strategy of divide and rule.

The main part of his seminal study "The Sociology of Secrets and of Secret Societies" (Simmel 1906) is devoted to the idea of the "secret society," which, as we shall see, is only of limited relevance for the Ancient World. In the first part of his study, however, he sets out the basic rules of secrecy as a social phenomenon. Secrecy, first of all, is a "triadic" phenomenon in a double sense: it not only manifests itself in triads – consisting of two (or more) individuals who share the secret and the third party (the rest) from whom it must be shielded – but it also consists of three different operations, namely: concealing (initially), hiding (lasting), and revealing (spontaneous). These three options ("Interaktionstriade," Nedelmann 1995, p. 1) are of crucial importance for each and every individual because in choosing to hide or to reveal something of himself, an individual can create social proximity or social distance with respect to another person. To use a modern example, the minimum requirement for any real social interaction between two persons in contemporary Holland is knowledge of one's family name. All other items of knowledge, one's first name, professional position, address, phone number, marital status, religion, history, income, and so on may be revealed, but this is not necessary. By selectively "revealing" such items, one has the option of maximising or minimising social proximity. Revealing one's first name usually implies moving from formal to informal modes of address, showing pictures of one's children opens up the possibility of discussing private joys or sorrows, discussing one's research can provide a special limited field of proximity, a proximity which does not, however, necessitate the disclosure of one's political or religious position.

The process of hiding or revealing thus shapes the individual and enables every person to create an individual world of interaction.[22] This is not limited to processes between individuals; the same procedures can apply to groups of people, and in all cases secrecy plays a decisive role. This is why Simmel adamantly stressed the social productivity of secrecy. Secrecy as a social phenomenon was "one of the greatest accomplishments of humanity" (Simmel 1906, p. 462) and neither politics nor religion could exist without it. It is important to stress this point because especially in the fields of psychology and ethics, secrecy is often considered to be harmful. No one will deny that secrets can be terribly upsetting to the individual, but this chiefly belongs to the realm of individual psychology (Kelly 2002). Likewise, state secrecy is undoubtedly harmful for private interests and therefore a problem for ethicists.[23] It is possible that secrecy in religious communities can likewise cause harm to individuals, but as a rule, its benefits are greater than its drawbacks.

The Ancient World[24]

All ancient religions were characterised by a certain amount of secrecy. There were restrictions that applied to parts of the temple or the temple as a whole;[25] there were rituals without any human audience, featuring only the god and his priest or the king;[26] and knowledge and texts were kept out of reach from all but a few trusted ones.[27]

As a consequence, there are serious distortions in the evidence we have access to. On the one hand, one could say that we know more than most people in antiquity: we can excavate buildings that were off-limits to the vast majority of people in the Ancient World and we can study texts that were meant to be distributed only to those initiated, if we are fortunate enough to find them. If we take the Roman mysteries of Mithras as an example, we can study their various manifestations over a period of several centuries in a stunning variety of geographical and social settings: from Britain to Syria, from the traces of a modest wooden structure to richly decorated cave-like buildings. We have hundreds of works of art that can be compared and analysed, and inscriptions that offer the hope of drawing up social profiles as well as religious ideas and practices.[28] Almost none of these materials were available to the few authors in antiquity who attempted to write something about these mysteries and we can, in many cases, point out the distortions they introduced in their descriptions.

Unfortunately, we also know a lot less than most people in antiquity. The passage of time has removed from our collective memory and from the records of history and archaeology the overwhelming majority of "facts" that we would now be eager to know. This is true in general, of course, but it is particularly true if we want to study the secret traditions of the Ancient World. Since we have to rely on the records that have been preserved, we have lost everything that was transmitted orally, as well as most things that were written down. Our chief sources of information, the material records, are themselves often very difficult to interpret, and they remain silent, of course, about the majority of the secrets they once harboured. Writing on clay, it now turns out, is an excellent option if you want your records to be preserved over several millennia, but this was probably the least of the concerns of the scribes of Mesopotamia. Thanks to the scribal cultures of Mesopotamia, Egypt, and Greece, the particularities of the climate of Egypt (its extreme aridity, which favours the preservation of papyrus), the efforts of medieval monastic organisations where manuscripts in Greek and Latin were copied, and the diligence with which various other religious traditions (Judaism, the religion of the Samaritans, Zoroastrianism, Mandaeism) have preserved their literature, a lot of information has fortunately survived, but it is needless to say that Mesopotamia, Egypt, Greece, and Rome are documented in a much more substantial way than all other cultures. Any reconstruction of the spiritual worlds of antiquity is therefore by definition very provisional. With the data we have, we can discuss three different subjects: secret knowledge, secret rituals, and secret identities.

Secret knowledge

To be able to speak of secret knowledge, we must first tackle its opposite, the "public" nature of knowledge in antiquity. Here, fortunately, we have an excellent guide in Pamela Long's recent book on technical arts and the culture of knowledge from antiquity to the Renaissance (Long 2001). Long's book is, in effect, one of the first attempts to study manifestations of a very recent concept in not so recent cultures. The concept is *intellectual property*, a highly significant subject of a specialised section of law and jurisprudence in our times, since it involves such enormous quantities of money. To study the history of this concept in Western culture, Long has studied manuals on catapults, metallurgy, and many other technical subjects that are and were relevant for Western societies and especially for the military establishment. In her study, she distinguishes between this technical knowledge, which was usually guarded with secrecy, and religious knowledge that was equally secret. Long suggests that the secrecy of technical literature was guarded by guilds or families, because it was one of the foundations of their wealth and well-being, whereas the religious literature was kept secret because it was so "sacred" that to reveal it to others would be a case of "profaning" the mysteries. To quote from her introduction:

> If there is evidence for intentional concealment, what is the context and how does it function? Is it, to mention just two possibilities, the secrecy of a priest of a mystery cult, protecting sacred knowledge from defilement by the common rabble, or the secrecy of the medieval artisan, protecting craft knowledge in the interest of profit?
>
> (Long 2001, p. 7)

This distinction is actually questionable. One does not even have to introduce Bourdieu's notion of "symbolic capital," although we might, to show that there is not as much difference as Long seems to suggest. Apuleius' *Metamorphoses* clearly shows how expensive it could be to be initiated into mystery cults.[29] These movements did not just revolve around spiritual goods, but also controlled sums of more easily quantifiable goods. To hand out secret knowledge in that sense would also imply spoiling the market. But not all knowledge was for sale; some of it was simply to be had by those able to find it.

Estimates of literacy rates for any ancient culture rarely rise above 10 percent of the population (and hover around 1 percent for Mesopotamia). This means that "published" works in writing were inaccessible to the vast majority of the population. Political processes often excluded sizeable portions of the population: women, slaves, and peasants. Practical knowledge in crafts and trade was passed on in families or in guilds. Education was often neither public nor free, and in many cases was not considered desirable.

In religious matters, the situation was not very different. The primary *locus* of religious socialisation, of the transmission of religion, in most ancient cultures, was the family.[30] Children were brought up in the religion by taking part in domestic rituals, by taking part in festivals with their family members and by being taken to the temple by their parents or grandparents.[31]

Those who chose religion as their vocation or were destined for a job in a religious organisation were taught their rituals and other practical knowledge by their older colleagues in a style very similar to the transmission of craft knowledge. For this particular subject, there is a striking difference between the ancient cultures of the Near East and Egypt on the one hand and the institutions of the Greeks and Romans on the other. In Mesopotamia, in particular, priesthood was a lifelong vocation that involved vast amounts of study. The rituals that were performed were complicated and priests were expected to have a solid grounding in theology and literature; they were, as a consequence, literate and most of them were considered to be scholars (Bottéro 2001, pp. 119–25).

Among Greeks and Romans, most priesthoods were of a completely different nature. Priesthoods were chiefly honorary positions that could easily be combined with other professional careers. They were not associated with great learning (although priests could be required to radiate moral authority) and required little formal training (chiefly knowledge of the rituals themselves). Priests were not, in general, transmitters of sacred traditions.[32]

It is in these different modes of organisation that we can find the difference in "secret traditions" that meets the eye when Graeco-Roman and Mesopotamian cultures are compared. In both cultures, religion was very much a state affair and temples played an important role.[33] But the concept of secret knowledge in Mesopotamia, with its tradition of scholar-priests, was largely confined to the temples and is evidenced by ever more impressive "secrecy colophons" attached to tablets containing scholarly and religious texts (Beaulieu 1992). Among the Greeks, by contrast, secret traditions in their social sense were only rarely associated with temples. Several sanctuaries, it is true, were places of divine inspiration, and messages and information about the inner workings of these oracles were probably restricted to the personnel of these places (Johnston 2004a), but in general, temples were not houses of learning.

Among the Greeks, the concept of secret knowledge gained currency in small groups consisting of a teacher and his pupil(s). The paradigmatic examples of such teachers are Pythagoras and Empedocles.[34] In such small-scale settings, at least as transmitted in the traditions surrounding these teachers, knowledge that was believed to represent truths about reality that not every mortal was able or entitled to acquire was transmitted and developed. It required a conscious effort on the part of those interested to gain access to these traditions. In the many manifestations of these groups, there was a whole range of options to restrict access to these truths or to prepare the candidate properly. Common features were preparatory purifications, dietary and clothing rules (and similar prescriptions for the style of living), and formal or informal teaching. These options, which were almost never *all* present as far as we can now reconstruct, constituted a preparatory path following which the truths could be revealed to or perceived by the candidates.[35] One of the most important common features undoubtedly is the *regime* itself, regardless of its technical details, and the *time* it took. One of the things that can be perceived in most cultures is that there is a correlation between the raising of expectations, the promises made, the often strenuous demands of purification and mortification, and the resulting insight. The insight itself is culturally specific, but the preparatory programme shows striking cross-cultural similarities.[36]

The (obvious) question whether the knowledge that was accumulated in this setting was too sacred to be revealed to those without proper preparation or was to remain out of reach for such people is a very modern one. The connection between the two is the factor of experience: knowledge revealed in the proper setting transforms the person who receives it.[37] To hand it out to those without preparation was perhaps not necessarily seen as offensive, but rather it was considered to be pointless: there was no way it could be effective. Thus, in the development of Platonism as a religious tradition, the injunction against silence is often encountered for the stated reason that people may laugh at the knowledge that is passed on.[38]

What was handed down? In order to give a rough sketch of the contents of these secret, initiatory traditions, which are exemplified by Pythagoras and Empedocles, we need to rely on a much broader selection of sources than the small fragments of the writings that have been preserved of these early thinkers. The most important set of data, in this author's opinion, is presented by the *Corpus Hermeticum*, a collection of texts that was passed on under the name of the god Hermes Trismegistus, the Greek incarnation of the Egyptian god Thoth.[39] These are texts from roughly the first three or four centuries CE, separated by more than half a millennium from Pythagoras and Empedocles. This gap can be filled with several other movements and traditions, but the history of these traditions largely remains to be written. The connections between the earlier emblematic figures and the Hermetic movement were clearly pointed out by Peter Kingsley (1995, pp. 371–75). The Hermetic texts are favoured here because we can perceive the *system* of instruction and initiation through these texts.[40]

1   One common denominator in the content of such traditions seems to be the perception of living truths underlying ordinary things: well-known stories about the gods ("myths"), passages cited from early authorities (especially Homer) and similar texts that were read by everyone, and, of course, the cosmos itself. Under the right guidance and with the proper preparation, pondering these ordinary things could lead to other, better understandings of reality. We can see this, for example, in Porphyry's interpretation of the Homeric story of the Cave of the Nymphs.[41] A special case in this respect is, for example, alchemy in its "spiritual" form: working with metals, dye-stuffs, and furnaces could be a goal in itself, but was increasingly seen as a method of acquiring "saving knowledge," especially in the works of the Hermetic alchemist Zosimus of Panopolis.[42]

2   A second, related, element is what one could call the "defragmenta-tion" of reality or experience. Our common experience leads to a fragmented view of reality; various experiences or subjects are relevant to particular sections of our life, which we can store, so to speak, in different boxes. This is what Mary Douglas calls "boxing" or "framing" (Douglas 2002, pp. 78–79). Religion, work, family life, and leisure can be kept separate. Within these domains, further fragmentation is common: we can associate mathematics, for instance, not only with trade or practical uses, but also with philosophical or religious purposes, or we can develop it as a career. The hidden teachings most often stress the interrelatedness of all these things, of all human experiences.

Almost every aspect of human culture and experience could thus be presented or reinterpreted in the light of overarching themes that are not ordinarily associated with them. Typical subjects in this domain are theories about the organisation of the cosmos, the human soul, and the reality of the divine. In the interrelations between these subjects, reality could almost be reduced to a single unified domain. This simplification of experience was thought to reveal profound truths that would transform a person's life. This transformation should be connected with the whole preparatory path more than with the insight itself. The best example of this is the fact that in several religious systems of antiquity and later times, including Greeks, Jews, Christians, and Muslims, one could sum up the only truth that a person needed to embody and experience in a short phrase: "He who knows himself, knows All."[43] This Hermetic maxim was surely part of texts that circulated widely, and access to the idea was by no means restricted, but the path leading up to the experience of this truth was long and arduous.

3   A third element is the important subject of the power secret knowledge could bring. The experience of hidden truths not only changed a person's view of reality or transformed his life, but could also invest him (or her) with hidden powers. These claims can most obviously be associated with those elements of secret traditions that taught the hidden names of divine beings in order to enable the candidate to influence them; the formulas, words, and symbols with which his soul could find a path beyond this world. None of this knowledge was useful without a proper knowledge or understanding of its origins or of the workings of reality. Revealing them to the uninitiated could be perceived as dangerous, in their leading persons to places or stages for which they were unprepared, or as pointless, in their giving someone instruments he would be unable to use. It is clear that these claims cannot be tested empirically and should therefore be seen, first of all, as rhetoric or propaganda emanating from the circle of believers themselves.

The *Corpus Hermeticum* is one of the most extensive sources for this type of "secret knowledge." It reveals several of the characteristics mentioned above: the visionary setting of the *Poimandres* (**ch**. I), for instance, in which truths are revealed, initially, in visual experience, and then explained by a divine teacher. The texts of the *Corpus Hermeticum* and similar literature frequently use the language of silence: it is only in silence, in speechless words and soundless song, that the mind can access God. The most important Hermetic text on the subject of secrecy is **ch**. XIII, which contains a "secret hymn" that is said to be "a secret kept in silence" and may not be divulged. The reasons for this silence and secrecy are located in the "suppression of all the senses" (**ch**. X.5) that is considered necessary for true understanding. These techniques of guided meditation or contemplation ("mystagogy") are evidenced most impressively in the *Discourse on the Eighth and the Ninth* that is preserved in the Nag Hammadi codices. This text culminates in the vision of the self by the "ego" of the text. It is, probably, the closest we can get to the experience of rapture. Alongside these mystical elements, however, it also contains strings of vowels and hidden names of divine beings and thus combines the various elements of hidden teachings that were outlined above.[44]

Secret rituals

The language used in the section on secret knowledge comes very close to the language necessary for secret rituals, to the language of initiation and mystery cults. The Greek word *mystērion* itself, from which our word "mystery" derives, means "initiation." It is derived from the verb *myeō*, "to initiate," and it came to mean "(divine) secret," chiefly in early Christian literature.[45] Without any doubt the most important secret from the Ancient World was connected to the Mysteries of Eleusis (Burkert 1983, pp. 248–97). A large number of the citizens of Athens took part in these Mysteries at some stage of their lives and the "secret" of the initiation must, therefore, have been well known (Bremmer 1995b, pp. 70–78). It was, however, guarded and enforced with much energy. Profaning the secret by telling non-initiates about the Mysteries, even hinting at them, or acting them out in a public context was punishable by death. Several cases of such accusations have in fact been preserved. Thanks to some "revelations" in literary texts, modern scholarship has been able to reconstruct some elements of the Mysteries, but there remain some important gaps in our reconstructions.

There were, in the Ancient World, many other places where such local mysteries were celebrated. In one case, we even possess the "Rule" of the Mysteries, a long inscription that details many of the functions and rituals of the Mysteries of Andania on the Peloponnesus.[46] This text is important in that it shows us a lot of the "outer" workings of a traditional Greek initiation cult: it describes in detail the vestments to be worn, rules for hair and make-up, the order of the procession, and so on. It also gives us a hint of the less than solemn aspects of such rituals, which involved a large number of people. Among the officials of the cult were the rod-bearers, who had to discipline those in attendance, with force if necessary. What the inscription does not reveal, however, is the actual secret of the initiation.

Several of the other mystery cults of antiquity had different patterns of organisation. Alongside the local sanctuaries that did not even attempt to spread out geographically (the model set by Eleusis), there were mysteries associated with wandering priests (Dionysus, the Mother of the Gods), temples with personnel that replicated themselves all over the world (the Egyptian Isis) and clubs that had both social and religious aspects (the mysteries of Mithras).[47] In most of these, the rituals of the initiation were kept secret and in many cases they have remained secret: we do not know what went on (exactly). This has led generations of scholars to hunt for these secrets in the sense of hunting for their secret texts (*hieros logos*) and knowledge, but most scholars today agree that guarding the secret of initiation had little to do with secret theologies, that such theologies in fact probably never existed.

The secret of the Mysteries of Eleusis was said to have been based on the "awe" inspired by the goddess (Demeter). It was the reverence of the gods that kept people from talking about these rituals. This explanation has been deemed "fully satisfactory" (Bremmer 1995b, p. 72), but it is less than satisfactory to explain the similarities that can be observed in most of the other mystery cults.

There are, obviously, sociological mechanisms at work here: the secret around which the mysteries were (thought to be) centred was one of these cults' chief strategies to attract a new following (Johnston 2004b). But there may actually be more. One of the chief functions of secrecy in this initiatory context must have been the function of "control for experience." In all cases of initiation, the prime motivation for guarding the secret seems to have been the wish to safeguard the emotional impact of undergoing the ritual. Revealing the rituals and their symbols beforehand meant not only transgressing sacred institutions or betraying bonds, but also spoiling the effects the ritual was supposed to accomplish.

To give some examples: it is known especially from works of art, which are much less reticent than texts in displaying elements from the mystery cults, that initiations could culminate in a "hierophany," the revelation of a sacred object. In Eleusis, this was in all likelihood an ear of corn, and in Bacchic initiations, the cult of Dionysus, this was a replica of a phallus kept hidden under a veil in a winnowing basket (Burkert 1987, pp. 93–97). Neither the ear of corn nor the phallus were hidden symbols for the cults of Demeter and Dionysus; on the contrary, they clearly belong to the standard cult iconography of these deities. It is not likely that these objects were explained in the rituals as having some hidden symbolic meaning. It must have been the experience of revealing otherwise perfectly ordinary symbols as the culmination of rituals involving darkness, the swaying of torches, ritual shouts, dancing, and self-flagellation that was meant to produce a certain effect. If the whole sequence of the ritual was known beforehand and the candidate for initiation was simply biding her time until the penis in the basket was finally shown to her, the experience of the ritual would have been palpably different from a scenario in which the candidate did not know exactly what was going to happen. The materials we have are limited in this respect, but it seems likely that the strategy of concealment here, as well as in most other cases, was more significant than the "contents" of the secret. This should, however, not be pushed to its extreme. We know of several rituals in which the candidate at least knew *something* because he was expected to be prepared to do certain things. A good example is the initiation into the grade of *Miles* in the mysteries of Mithras, during which the candidate had to shake off a wreath placed on his head and proclaim solemnly that Mithras was his wreath.[48]

There thus are various options: in certain initiatory contexts, secrecy was most likely used as a control for experience, whereas the secrecy of rituals in regular meetings (ritual meals, for instance) lay more in the special significance these rituals were thought to have had and in the wish to celebrate these in a fitting manner with initiated members only.

Secret identities

The final subject to be discussed is the "secret identity," the existence of secret societies in the Ancient World. This is a problematic field for various reasons. The first of these is documentation. It belongs to the characteristics of secret societies that they can hide their existence completely, since they rely on a mutually agreed bond of concealment (Simmel 1906, pp. 469–72). In general, such secret societies do not manage to remain secret for a long period, but it is certainly possible that there were various secret societies in the Ancient World of which we remain wholly unaware for total lack of documentation.

In most cases this is not the case. Various religious movements in the Ancient World may have been elusive or secluded, but they were not altogether unknown. To remain entirely unknown creates difficulties in the area of recruitment. More often, concealment is attributed to various groups without a real foundation in the sources. This applies particularly to gnostic Christianity, which is habitually described as secretive.[49] This description, however, is an inextricable part of the fierce polemics against these Christians by other Christian authors and requires much more solid documentation than is usually offered.

In view of the structure of religious life in antiquity, characterised by the dominance of (polytheistic) civic cults and the absence of religious exclusivism, the emergence of real secret societies with a religious agenda is not really to be expected.

Participation in the so-called "mystery cults" did, however, offer those interested the option of enriching their life with something extra and secrecy added to this new identity. It is beyond doubt that the secrecy of certain groups was a major element in their attraction to outsiders.

Final considerations

Secrets and secrecy are annoying for scholars. There are many things we do not know and do not understand. There are many secrets from the Ancient World that were kept and remain as gaps in our knowledge. In those cases where we believe we *do* have the knowledge that was transmitted, however, it seems that the content of the secret traditions was less relevant than the secrecy of the traditions itself. We can attempt to reconstruct the main sociological and psychological mechanisms operative in the secret traditions.

Most importantly, secrecy ensured the social cohesion, attraction, and prestige of the movements and created a unity in experience. It fused private instruction, ritual, the manipulation of symbols, and above all time and expectation together. For comparative purposes that will have to do. Those who are still interested in the particulars of the ancient mysteries will have to reconcile themselves with the fact that many initiates in antiquity have, indeed, obeyed the commands of Hermes Trismegistus and have shielded the divine mysteries within themselves with eternal silence.

Notes

1 *Asclepius* 32 (Copenhaver 1992, p. 87).
2 For instructive overviews, see Sharpe 1986 and especially Kippenberg 2002.
3 For recent discussions, see, *inter multos alios*, Patton and Ray 2000, and the special issues of the journals *Numen* 48/3 (2001) and *Method & Theory in the Study of Religion* 16/1 (2004).
4 A landmark study of these dangers is Platvoet 1982.
5 For instance, see King 1999. See also Doniger 2000 for an elegant discussion of the issues.
6 These have all been taken from the contributions to *Numen* and *Method & Theory in the Study of Religion* referred to in n. 3, most often from their titles.
7 Bolle 1987; Kippenberg and Stroumsa 1995; Wolfson 1999. A collection of contributions from the social sciences can be found in Tefft 1980.
8 Psychology: Kelly 2002; ethics: Bok 1982; (literary) history: Long 2001.
9 See Hartman 1980, plates VII, VIII, IX, for illustrations.
10 This was told to the author of this essay by Professor Shaul Shaked, who was fortunate enough to be in Mumbai on such an occasion. The status of fire-temples in Iran is slightly different in that some of them do allow non-Zoroastrians restricted access; see Stausberg 2004, pp. 175–77.
11 See Stausberg 2004 for an impressive survey.
12 See the historical essays in Moore 1984.
13 This is not a critique of Bok's insistence on keeping the distinction between secrecy and privacy, since hers is a work on ethics, not a sociological inquiry.
14 One can also add "arcane," "occult," and similar terms to this inventory.
15 The names most commonly attached to this remarkable episode are those of Antoine Faivre (e.g. Faivre 1994) and Wouter Hanegraaff (e.g. Hanegraaff 1996).
16 An overview is given in Faivre 1999.
17 The Nag Hammadi texts have all been published in the series *The Coptic Gnostic Library. A Complete Edition of the Nag Hammadi Codices*, Leiden 2000 (5 vols).
18 For Irenaeus and Plotinus, see Broek 1996, pp. 57–66, 4–7 respectively, and, especially, Tardieu 1996.
19 These distinctions cannot be quantified because the beginning and end of too many texts have been lost.
20 The reasons for these problems are set out clearly in Shaked 2002, pp. 266–71.
21 For Simmel's life and an overview of his works, see Coser 1971, pp. 177–215; for Simmel's ideas on secrecy, see also Nedelmann 1995.

22 The most helpful analysis of Simmel's importance in this respect is Kippenberg 1991, pp. 419–20.
23 Bok 1982, ch. 8, which discusses accountability.
24 This part of the paper is partly based on De Jong 2005.
25 In general, temples were not places of communal worship, but the dwelling-places (homes) of the gods. In different traditions, they could fulfill different functions and they therefore show differences in the degree to which they let in the common people. In Mesopotamia, the common people as a rule did not enter the temple (Bottéro 2001, p. 118), whereas Greek temples appear to have been more easily accessible.
26 Most famously the ritual of the New Year in Babylon in the first millennium BCE: Toorn 1989.
27 The Mesopotamian evidence is discussed in Borger 1957–71.
28 The corpus of sites, monuments, and inscriptions of Vermaseren 1956–60 is seriously out of date, but has not been replaced. For a general introduction, see Clauss 2000; for a bibliography from 1984 to 2004, see Martens and de Boe 2004.
29 Apuleius, *Metamorphoses* (a.k.a *The Golden Ass*) 11.23, describes how the main character in the novel, Lucius, had to borrow money in order to acquire all that was necessary for his final initiation. See Griffiths 1975 for the text.
30 An excellent study of this process is Bremmer 1995a.
31 See Smith 2003, for a powerful presentation of the lasting importance of domestic religion in the Ancient World. A wide-ranging case study is given by Toorn 1996.
32 The variety of priesthoods is so enormous that it is virtually impossible to make general statements on the subject. The essays in Beard and North 1990 will provide the necessary corrections to the image sketched here.
33 Some scholars therefore refer to most religions of the ancient world (significantly with the exception of Iran) as being part of a "Near-Eastern-Mediterranean *koinē*" ("common speech or common culture"). See, most recently, Burkert 2004, pp. 1–15.
34 For Pythagoras, see Burkert 1972; for Empedocles, Kingsley 1995.
35 The writings of Kingsley 1999 (on Parmeneides) and 2003 (on Empedocles and Parmeneides) are extremely useful to gain a sense of what it *meant* to people in antiquity to be thus induced into important truths, but alongside the obvious historical scholarly merits of these works, they also consciously attempt to open ways of appropriating these truths for modern seekers.
36 Wulff 1991, pp. 61–88, is a good overview of the "deliberate facilitation of religious experience," but only tells half the story. For a very sensitive case-study, focusing on the concept of "appropriation," see Hijweege 2004.
37 See, for instance, the discussion of Empedocles' promise to his pupil Pausanias that he would teach him to control the weather and to bring the life-force of a dead man back from Hades (Empedocles, fragment 111) in Kingsley 1995, pp. 217–27.
38 Lamberton 1995; Stroumsa 1996, pp. 11–26. An instructive modern parallel can be found in Luhrmann 1989, which discusses the ways in which contemporary neo-pagan groups in London conceal the contents of their rituals and ideas in order to keep them from sceptical inquiry. Her interpretation is based on the notion that the "outside world" will by definition destroy the truth claims of the various groups because they do not live up to modern scientific reasoning. That scenario is not wholly applicable to the Ancient World, but it is not wholly unimaginable either, as the success of Christian attacks against "pagan" traditions and conventions shows. For a relevant critique of Luhrmann's approach to the subject, see Hutton 1999, pp. 374–76.

39 For introductions to this literature and to the Hermetic movement, see Copenhaver 1992 and Broek 1996, pp. 1–21.
40 Recent studies of the most likely social and ritual backgrounds of these texts are Södergård 2003 and Peste 2002.
41 Porphyrius, *De Antro Nympharum*.
42 See especially Fowden 1986, pp. 120–26, and Stolzenberg 1999.
43 The phrase was famously found in the Armenian *Definitions of Hermes Trismegistus to Asclepius* 9.4 (for which, see Mahé 2000).
44 See Broek 2000 for a good analysis.
45 Stroumsa 1996, pp. 147–68, with references.
46 For the text, see Meyer 1987, pp. 51–59.
47 For this typology, see Burkert 1987, pp. 30–53.
48 Tertullian, *De corona militis* 15; see Merkelbach 1984, pp. 95–96 for a discussion of the ritual.
49 The subject is critically discussed by Williams 1999; see also Williams 1996, pp. 96–115.

References

Beard, M. and J. North (eds) (1990), *Pagan Priests: Religion and Power in the Ancient World*. Ithaca: Cornell University Press.
Beaulieu, P.A. (1992), "New Light on Secret Knowledge in Late Babylonian Culture." *Zeitschrift für Assyriologie* 82, pp. 98–111.
Bok, S. (1982), *Secrets. On the Ethics of Concealment and Revelation*. New York: Pantheon.
Bolle, K.W. (ed.) (1987), *Secrecy in Religion* (Studies in the History of Religions 49). Leiden: Brill.
Borger, R. (1957–71), "Geheimwissen." *Reallexikon für Assyriologie* III, pp. 188–91.
Bottéro, J. (2001), *Religion in Ancient Mesopotamia*. Chicago: University of Chicago Press.
Bremmer, J.N. (1995a), "The Family and Other Centres of Religious Learning in Antiquity," in J.W. Drijvers and A.A. MacDonald (eds), *Centres of Learning: Learning and Location in Pre-Modern Europe and the Near East* (Brill's Studies in Intellectual History 61). Leiden: Brill, pp. 29–38.
Bremmer, J.N. (1995b), "Religious Secrets and Secrecy in Classical Greece," in H.G. Kippenberg and G.G. Stroumsa (eds), *Secrecy and Concealment: Studies in the History of Mediterranean and Near Eastern Religions* (Studies in the History of Religions 65). Leiden: Brill, pp. 61–78.
Broek, R. van den (1996), *Studies in Gnosticism and Alexandrian Christianity* (Nag Hammadi and Manichaean Studies 39). Leiden: Brill.
Broek, R. van den (2000), "Religious Practices in the Hermetic 'Lodge': New Light from Nag Hammadi," in R. van den Broek and C. van Heertum (eds), *From Poimandres to Jacob Böhme: Gnosis, Hermetism and the Christian Tradition* (Pimander. Texts and Studies published by the Bibliotheca Philosophica Hermetica 4). Amsterdam: In de Pelikaan, pp. 77–113.
Burkert, W. (1972), *Lore and Science in Ancient Pythagoreanism*. Cambridge, MA: Harvard University Press.
Burkert, W. (1983), *Homo Necans: The Anthropology of Ancient Greek Sacrificial Ritual and Myth*. Berkeley: University of California Press.

Burkert, W. (1987), *Ancient Mystery Cults*. Cambridge, MA: Harvard University Press.
Burkert, W. (1996), *Creation of the Sacred: Tracks of Biology in Early Religions*. Cambridge, MA: Harvard University Press.
Burkert, W. (2004), *Babylon, Memphis, Persepolis: Eastern Contexts of Greek Culture*. Cambridge, MA: Harvard University Press.
Clauss, M. (2000), *The Roman Cult of Mithras: The God and his Mysteries*. Edinburgh: Edinburgh University Press.
Copenhaver, B.P. (1992), *Hermetica: The Greek Corpus Hermeticum and the Latin Asclepius in a New English Translation with Notes and Introduction*. Cambridge: Cambridge University Press.
Coser, L.A. (1971), *Masters of Sociological Thought: Ideas in Historical and Social Context*. New York: Harcourt.
Doniger, W. (2000), "Post-modern and -colonial -structural Comparisons," in Patton and Ray 2000, pp. 63–74.
Douglas, M. (2002), *Purity and Danger: An Analysis of the Concepts of Pollution and Taboo*. London: Routledge.
Faivre, A. (1994), *Access to Western Esotericism*. Albany: SUNY Press.
Faivre, A. (1999), "The Notions of Concealment and Secrecy in Modern Esoteric Currents since the Renaissance (A Methodological Approach)," in E.R. Wolfson (ed.), *Rending the Veil: Concealment and Secrecy in the History of Religions*. New York & London: Seven Bridges Press, pp. 155–76.
Fowden, G. (1986), *The Egyptian Hermes: A Historical Approach to the Late Pagan Mind*. Princeton: Princeton University Press.
Griffiths, J.G. (1975), *Apuleius of Madauros: The Isis-Book (Metamorphoses, Book XI)* (Etudes préliminaires aux religions orientales dans l'Empire Romain 39). Leiden: Brill.
Hanegraaff, W. (1996), *New Age Religion and Western Culture: Esotericism in the Mirror of Secular Thought* (Studies in the History of Religions 72). Leiden: Brill.
Hartman, S.S. (1980), *Parsism: The Religion of Zoroaster* (Iconography of Religions XIV, 4). Leiden: Brill.
Hijweege, N.M. (2004), *Bekering in bevindelijk gereformeerde kring: een psychologische studie*. Kampen: Kok.
Hutton, R. (1999), *The Triumph of the Moon: A History of Modern Pagan Witchcraft*. Oxford: Oxford University Press.
Johnston, S.I. (2004a), "Divination and Prophecy. Greece," in S.I. Johnston (ed.), *Religions of the Ancient World: A Guide*. Cambridge, MA: Harvard University Press, pp. 383–86.
Johnston, S.I. (2004b), "Mysteries," in S.I. Johnston (ed.), *Religions of the Ancient World: A Guide*. Cambridge, MA: Harvard University Press, pp. 98–111.
De Jong, A. (2005), "Secrecy I. Antiquity," in W. Hanegraaff (ed.), *Dictionary of Gnosis and Western Esotericism*. Leiden: Brill, pp. 1050–54.
Kelly, A.E. (2002), *The Psychology of Secrets*. New York: Kluwer Academic/Plenum.
King, R. (1999), *Orientalism and Religion: Postcolonial Theory, India, and "the Mystic East"*. London: Routledge.
Kingsley, P. (1995), *Ancient Philosophy, Mystery, and Magic: Empedocles and Pythagorean Tradition*. Oxford: Oxford University Press.
Kingsley, P. (1999), *In the Dark Places of Wisdom*. Inverness: Golden Sufi Center.
Kingsley, P. (2003), *Reality*. Inverness: Golden Sufi Center.

Kippenberg, H.G. (1991), *Die vorderasiatischen Erlösungsreligionen in ihrem Zusammenhang mit der antiken Stadtherrschaft*. Frankfurt am Main: Suhrkamp.

Kippenberg, H.G. (2002), *Discovering Religious History in the Modern Age*. Princeton: Princeton University Press.

Kippenberg, H.G. and G.G. Stroumsa (eds) (1995), *Secrecy and Concealment: Studies in the History of Mediterranean and Near Eastern Religions* (Studies in the History of Religions 65). Leiden: Brill.

Lamberton, R. (1995), "The ΑΠΟΡΡΗΤΟΣΘΕΩΡΙΑ and the roles of Secrecy in the History of Platonism," in H.G. Kippenberg and G.G. Stroumsa (eds), *Secrecy and Concealment: Studies in the History of Mediterranean and Near Eastern Religions* (Studies in the History of Religions 65). Leiden: Brill, pp. 139–52.

Long, P.O. (2001), *Openness, Secrecy, Authorship: Technical Arts and the Culture of Knowledge from Antiquity to the Renaissance*. Baltimore and London: The Johns Hopkins University Press.

Luhrmann, T.M. (1989), "The Magic of Secrecy." *Ethos* 17, pp. 131–65.

Mahé, J.P. (2000), "The Definitions of Hermes Trismegistus to Asclepius," in C. Salaman, D. van Oyen, W.D. Wharton and J.P. Mahé (eds), *The Way of Hermes: New Translations of the Corpus Hermeticum and the Definitions of Hermes Trismegistus to Asclepius*. Rochester: Inner Traditions, pp. 99–122.

Martens, M. and G. de Boe (2004), "Bibliography of Mithraic Studies," in M. Martens and G. de Boe (eds), *Roman Mithraism: The Evidence of the Small Finds* (Archeologie in Vlaanderen. Monografie 4). Brussel: Instituut voor het Archeologisch Patrimonium, pp. 363–85.

Merkelbach, R. (1984), *Mithras*. Königstein: Hain.

Meyer, M.W. (1987), *The Ancient Mysteries: A Sourcebook. Sacred Texts of the Mystery Religions of the Ancient Mediterranean World*. San Francisco: Harper.

Moore, B. (1984), *Privacy: Studies in Social and Cultural History*. Armon, New York: Sharpe.

Nedelmann, B. (1995), "Geheimhaltung, Verheimlichung, Geheimnis – einige soziologische Vorüberlegungen," in H.G. Kippenberg and G.G. Stroumsa (eds), *Secrecy and Concealment: Studies in the History of Mediterranean and Near Eastern Religions* (Studies in the History of Religions 65). Leiden: Brill, pp. 1–16.

Patton, K.C. and B.C. Ray (eds) (2000), *A Magic Still Dwells: Comparative Religion in the Postmodern Age*. Berkeley: University of California Press.

Peste, J. (2002), *The Poimandres Group in Corpus Hermeticum: Myth, Mysticism and Gnosis in Late Antiquity* (Skrifter utgivna vid Institutionen för Religionsvetenskap, Göteborgs Universitet 26). Göteborg: Department of Religious Studies, University of Göteborg.

Platvoet, J.G. (1982), *Comparing Religions, a Limitative Approach: An Analysis of Akan, Para-Creole, and Ifo-Sananda Rites and Prayers* (Religion and Reason 24). The Hague: Mouton.

Shaked, S. (2002), "The Science of Religion in Israel with Notes on Interlocking Circles of Traditions," in G. Wiegers and J. Platvoet (eds), *Modern Societies & the Science of Religions: Studies in Honour of Lammert Leertouwer* (Studies in the History of Religions 95). Leiden: Brill, pp. 258–71.

Sharpe, E.J. (1986), *Comparative Religion: A History*. La Salle: Open Court.

Simmel, G. (1906), "The Sociology of Secrecy and of Secret Societies." *American Journal of Sociology* 11, pp. 441–98.

Smith, J.Z. (1993), *Map is not Territory: Studies in the History of Religions*. Chicago and London: University of Chicago Press.

Smith, J.Z. (2003), "Here, There, and Anywhere," in S. Noegel, J. Walker and B. Wheeler (eds), *Prayer, Magic, and the Stars in the Ancient and Late Antique World*. University Park, PA: The Pennsylvania State University Press, pp. 21–36.

Södergård, J.P. (2003), *The Hermetic Piety of the Mind: A Semiotic and Cognitive Study of the Discourse of Hermes Trismegistos* (Coniectanea Biblica. New Testament Series 41). Stockholm: Almqvist & Wiksell.

Stausberg, M. (2004), *Die Religion Zarathushtras: Geschichte – Gegenwart – Rituale, Band* III. Stuttgart: Kohlhammer.

Stolzenberg, D. (1999), "Unpropitious Tinctures: Alchemy, Astrology and Gnosis according to Zosimos of Panopolis." *Archives Internationales d'Histoire des Sciences* 49, pp. 3–31.

Stroumsa, G.G. (1996), *Hidden Wisdom: Esoteric Traditions and the Roots of Christian Mysticism* (Studies in the History of Religions 70). Leiden: Brill.

Tardieu, M. (1996), *Recherches sur la formation de l'Apocalypse de Zostrien et les sources de Marius Victorinus* (Res Orientales IX). Bures-sur-Yvette: Peeters.

Tefft, S.K. (ed.) (1980), *Secrecy: A Cross-Cultural Perspective*. New York: Human Sciences Press.

Toorn, K. van der (1989), "The Babylonian New Year Festival: New Insights from the Cuneiform Texts and their Bearing on Old Testament Study," in J.A. Emerton (ed.), *Congress Volume, Leuven 1989* (Supplements to Vetus Testamentum 43). Leiden: Brill, pp. 331–44.

Toorn, K. van der (1996), *Family Religion in Babylonia, Syria, and Israel: Continuity and Change in the Forms of Religious Life* (Studies in the History and Cultures of the Ancient Near East 7). Leiden: Brill.

Tromp, J. (1993), *The Assumption of Moses: A Critical Edition with Commentary* (Studia in Veteris Testamenti Pseudepigrapha 10). Leiden: Brill.

Vermaseren, M.J. (1956–60), *Corpus Inscriptionum et Monumentorum Religionis Mithriacae*. The Hague: Martinus Nijhoff.

Williams, M.A. (1996), *Rethinking "Gnosticism": An Argument for Dismantling a Dubious Category*. Princeton: Princeton University Press.

Williams, M.A. (1999), "Secrecy, Revelation, and Late Antique Demiurgical Myths," in Wolfson 1999, pp. 31–58.

Wolfson, E.R. (ed.) (1999), *Rending the Veil: Concealment and Secrecy in the History of Religions*. New York & London: Seven Bridges Press.

Wulff, D.M. (1991), *Psychology of Religion: Classic and Contemporary Views*. New York: John Wiley & Sons.

3 The problem of secrecy in Indian Tantric Buddhism

Ronald M. Davidson

The rigorous investigation of Indian Tantrism in general, and Indian Tantric Buddhism in particular, is still in its infancy. One of the more compelling areas in need of scrutiny is the issue of secrecy: what were the origins, dynamics, semantic fields, and specific idioms of secrecy in the early period of the esoteric movement and how did this change over time? I cannot suggest that I have solved many of the difficult issues embedded in this problem, but I have begun the examination of esoteric Buddhist literature in hope of exploring a few of the major questions relating to secrecy. This paper will propose that secrecy in Tantric Buddhism had much to do with the sectarian friction of India's early medieval period (sixth to twelfth century CE), exacerbated by the society's militarization. Tantric systems were both built on Mahāyānist mythologies and differentiated from them; the tantras ritualized the mythological episodes through the transmission from master to disciple and simultaneously imposed restrictions on the dissemination of Buddhist doctrine in a manner not previously witnessed.[1] The primary domains of secrecy were meditative ideology and ritual performance rather than philosophical or doctrinal development, even while the tantras made significant contributions to the latter. Consequently, secrecy became both a rubric for the unfoldment of new ritual or meditative horizons and a strategy for the restriction of these revelations to Buddhists, especially those initiated into the fold.

The difficult analysis of secrecy

The desirable nature of this enterprise can best be expressed by quoting from the late Edward Conze's classic text, *Buddhist Thought in India*, where he indicates his understanding of the basic problem of esoteric religion:

> In this field certainly those who know do not say and those who say do not know. There are two, and only two alternatives. Either the author of a book of this kind has *not* been initiated into a Tantra;

then what he says is not first-hand knowledge. Or he has been initiated. Then, if he were to divulge the secrets to all and sundry just to make a little profit or to increase his reputation, he has broken the trust placed in him and is morally so depraved as not to be worth listening to.

(Conze 1962, pp. 271–72)

I would have thought that such a statement was better left forgotten in the storeroom of inadequate academic analyses, particularly as it has already been questioned by Welbon and others.[2] However, it has been recently resurrected by Hugh Urban, in his work *The Economics of Ecstasy*, where he quotes this passage both with a degree of approval and as a challenge to others on the question of the ethics of studying Tantrism in the post-colonial period (Urban 2001, p. 19). Unfortunately, Urban neither acknowledges the multiple difficulties with this position nor adequately differentiates between the ethics of studying the historical circumstance of medieval Indian Buddhist Tantrism and the ethics of his own work with modern Bengali Tantrists. Indeed, we cannot presume that Tantric secrecy (or any religious secrecy) is an unchanging system or unambiguous phenomenon, for the rules and messages change both over time and from patron to patron. Urban (2001, pp. 15–16) in fact does point to conflicted statements by his own informants on whether Tantrism is actually to be withheld or broadcast and under what circumstances.

In terms of Buddhist materials, Conze's opinion is in some ways a good manifestation of the poor understanding of how Tantric secrecy is invoked, for Tantric Buddhism is not immediately comparable to the mystery religions, a supposition that is the basis for his assessment (Conze 1962, p. 272). The Hellenistic mystery religions operated with entirely different procedures, which is the reason that the evidence they left behind contrasts strongly with that of Tantric Buddhism. To cite but one example, the Mithraic cult lasted several centuries in a fairly narrow geographical area, encompassing perhaps two to three hundred distinctive sites or monuments. They collectively constitute its most extensive legacy, for the tradition produced no complete document known to us or surviving from that time.[3] In distinction, South Asian Tantric Buddhism, with its notorious paucity of archaeological remains, lasted from the seventh century to the present (continuing in Nepal) and has produced thousands of documents in many languages, which were widely translated and printed since the advent of Chinese printing in the Song dynasty.

Conze would have us believe that, because of secrecy, none of these documents means what it says. Consequently, if Conze's assessment were true, none of these documents would even be reliable, for all of them have been revealed to others, and therefore their authors may be suspected of moral depravity. The only conclusion, if we follow his logic, is that there was a real Tantric Buddhism unknown to anyone but a small body of adepts, who wrote nothing real, distinct from a false Tantric Buddhism that is encoded in actual documents. Yet, the treatment of documents in societies espousing esoteric Buddhism is the reverse of this: they are esteemed as the word of the Buddha and commented on word for word. Tantric texts are discussed, haggled over, bought and sold, copied, traded and challenged. They were hidden, revealed, forged and mythologized. In many of these textualized discourses, the author is invariably willing, even eager, to reveal the "opinion of the gurus" on such esoteric matters, so that esoteric language is always given a lexicon, even while individual yogins are on record as doubting the existence or utility of secret languages at all.[4] The extremely dubious nature of Conze's position should lead us to abandon facile analogies between esoteric Buddhism in its different societies, about which very much may be known, and the Hellenistic mystery religions, about which much less may be known, despite their common rhetoric of hiddenness and revelation.

Beyond Conze's questionable representation, we have the problem of cultural suppositions on secrecy. Culturally, we are – as are Indians themselves – disposed to believe that secrecy has a furtive goal, that all obfuscation is for nefarious purposes. This response is precipitated by the simple fact that secrecy is exclusionary, a restriction from information access to those deemed unfit, for whatever reasons, to be granted that information. However, secrecy is not necessarily deceptive, although deception requires that secrets be maintained and that secrecy be invoked among the conspirators. Some cultures and subcultures become so invested in suspicion and deception that they can only see the world through that lens, but, curiously, this implicates self-deception as well. A pathological mistrust of all apparent reality often stems from the conviction that there is a conspiracy to withhold the truth, which is forever being hidden. Such conspiracy convictions are perhaps not inconsistent with the pathology of a hypochondriac, who is consistently suspicious that his or her body is harboring secret diseases that doctors can never diagnose.

Subcultures of suspicion in turn feed off mainstream religious activity, for most religions require the suspension of philosophic doubt, and most religious scriptures have sources that have become occluded through the willing participation of communities invested in the secrecy of their scriptural origins. While the identity of scriptural authors is now unknown, at one time it was secret, both supported by knowing members of various communities and obscured from those outside of the immediate entourage. Here we encounter the consensual nature of scripture production: the reality that groups expect and desire to have sacred texts produced before their eyes and are willing to glance away when certain parts of the process do not fit the approved model of revelation. Such groups tend to keep unbelievers or those outside the pale at a distance, so that secrecy in most social worlds invokes exclusion, and patterns of segregation is one of the hallmarks of institutionalized secrecy. We might be wary, though, of interpreting all deception as nefarious, for certain aesthetic and religious sentiments appear unapproachable by the avenues of information transparency and its attendant sense of ordinariness. Thus, at least some of the subcultures of deception or secrecy engage in this behavior, not because there is something to hide, but because the final goal cannot be served by the rhetoric of self-evident truth.

Conversely, mysticism *per se* and secrecy cannot be directly conflated, even if the Greek *mysterion* of the New Testament is most often translated as a secret, as it comes from √*mua*, to shut one's eyes.[5] Mysteries may be actually secret or simply unanswerable, as the mysteries of Isis or the mystery of the Trinity. Mystics might keep secrets, but just as often mystics are missionaries using language in such a convoluted manner that its meaning is unapproachable without some interpretive key. Other mystics may simply talk about realms of perception inaccessible to ordinary consciousness, and so the category of "self-secret" (Tibetan: *rang gsang*) is sometimes encountered. It is a secret we keep from ourselves.

Finally, we should consider secrecy's alter ego – curiosity and the desire for knowledge. Without this continual obsession on the part of human beings, one's possession of secrets would simply be greeted with indifference. Thus, certain kinds of secrecy appear to require some method of revelation, for a secret not told is a secret that remains unknown – it remains actually secret. Those keeping such secrets do not reveal that they even have them, and absolute secrecy is better left entirely unspoken, for that is the method whereby such secrets are maintained absolutely. However, absolute secrecy is infertile and sterile. Instead, a secret or putative secret shared exclusively among a small body of individuals is a powerful psychological tool for group integration and an equally powerful method of proselyzation.

Classical Mahāyānist contributions

While the differentiation between Mahāyānist ritual openness and the restrictive rites of Tantric Buddhism emerged in the late seventh to early eighth century, Tantric systems built on Mahāyānist doctrinal developments. The clearest contribution of Mahāyānist monks to a theory of secrecy is in the bifurcation of perception into an appearance and reality model. This model is widely invoked throughout the Mahāyāna, whether one is discussing the relationship between the two truths, or the ideology of the *dharmakāya* (body of truth) and *rūpakāya* (body of form), or the distinction between apparent behavior and inner reality. Thus, Vimalakīrti is described as going to bars and brothels to teach their patrons the antidotes to desire, while maintaining vigilance and correct deportment for himself (*Vimalakīrtinirdeśa*, pp. 60–62). The model is also behind the well-known explanation of the Unique Vehicle (*ekayāna*) in the *Saddhar-mapuṇḍarīka-sūtra* (i.e. the Lotus sutra, pp. 72–80), where a householder offers his children toys of one variety to get them out of a burning house, only to bestow much better toys on them once they have left. Most impor-tantly, the sūtras discussing expedient means (*upāya*) employ this model, for they invoke an image of soteriological deception, in which one goal is described while there is actually another end to the path.[6] Conse-quently, when the Buddha proclaims the Śrāvaka-nirvāṇa (the disciples' nirvana), we are told that it was done so that the congregation will not become discouraged and abandon hope. It is like an illusory city created in the midst of a dense forest, so that travelers will not lose heart but be able to complete their journey to the real city of awakening (*Saddharma-puṇḍarīka-sūtra*, pp. 187–88). Essential to all of these is the idea that the seemingly deceptive process is based on an altruistic goal, so that the absolute reality eventually obtained is infinitely better than the illusory reality initially offered.

Within this perceptual differentiation, most Mahāyāna scriptures do not promote a rhetoric of secrecy or a practice of exclusion: the reality behind appearance has always been available, even if it is disconcerting to some. The description of the difference between a "secret Dharma" and the "clear Dharma" in the *Bodhisattvabhūmi* is exactly of this variety:

> Then, what is "teaching?" It is the teaching of the true Dharma, which is an accurate guide to correct accomplishment, to one who has not the ability to obtain his own goal by himself. It is also the teaching of the true Dharma for one able to obtain his goal, but the Dharma is conducive to quick super-cognition.

> Then, what is the explanation of the secret Dharma? It is the expla-nation of the Dharma to those of infantile intelligence for their easy entrance and joyful apprehension towards obvious reality, by occluding the very exalted and profound Dharma.

> So what is the explanation of the clear Dharma? It is the clear unfold-ment of the very exalted and profound Dharma to those beings of great intelligence, by whom the method of the Buddha's teaching has been joyfully entered.[7]

Here the "secret Dharma" must indicate a Dharma in which secrets are maintained – so that the clear Dharma remains secret to those of limited ability. While the apocryphal *Da zhidu lun* 大智度論 attributed to Nāgārjuna uses similar categories differently – the intentional Dharma is the Mahāyānist exaltation of the Bodhisattva path – the overall purpose is substantially the same.[8]

It may be useful to contrast such Mahāyānist positions with the two rhetorical statements about esoteric Buddhism widely cited in Tantric literature (Davidson 2002, p. 240). On one hand, it is said to be for those who are incapable of maintaining the procedures of normative Buddhism. Consequently, the Buddha is said to have preached the tantras to those fascinated by sex so that they will become Buddhists. Conversely, the opposite approach is equally claimed: Tantric Buddhism is so profound that it could not be revealed to the underdeveloped. Neither of these positions exactly fits the *Bodhisattvabhūmi* discussion, since the "secret" Dharma in the Yogācāra text actually means that the easily understood teachings of karma and human affairs are taught to the unintelligent, to whom the clear Dharma of the Mahāyānist path must remain secret. Thus, this appears another way of describing the *nītārtha/neyārtha* (scriptures of definitive meaning/provisional meaning) distinction already well known, with *nītārtha* hidden from those incapable of understanding it.

A somewhat different position on secrecy is found in the first several chapters of the *Tathāgatācintyaguhyaka-sūtra* (Sutra on the Tathāgatas' Inconceivable Secret), a sutra in need of much study. There is an early translation into Chinese by Dharmarakṣa, reputedly completed in November of 280 CE, perhaps a century before the composition of the *Bodhisattvabhūmi*. In the *Tathāgatācintyaguhyaka-sūtra*, the ideology of the difference between appearance and reality is fully developed into a doctrine of the secrets of the body, speech and mind of the bodhisattvas and the body, speech and mind of the buddhas. The body, speech and mind of the bodhisattvas and buddhas appear in various forms, while their realities represent the sources of these manifestations. So, the Buddha's speech never uttered a single syllable, while beings perceived the eighty-four thousand dharma doors.[9]

Such statements resonate with the Buddha's representation in the *Saddharmapuṇḍarīka*: the Buddha perceived in this world as performing the acts of the Buddha is actually a magical manifestation of the real Buddha, who obtained his awakening *niyutas* of kalpas in the past (pp. 315–26). Yet, this magical Buddha in the Sahālokadhātu (this universe) appears to send out further manifestations, so that we have another reality/appearance function based on the earlier one, even while the reality/appearance display in this world manifests further ones, *ad infinitum*. All such manifestations eventually fall under the rubric of "skill in means," so that another Mahāyāna scripture, the *Mahārahasyopāyakauśalya-sūtra*, will proclaim itself the scripture requested by the Bodhisattva Jñānottara, who wished to know about the secret expedient means (*mahārahasyopāyakauśalya*); the sutra proclaims that the manifestation of the Buddha's ability is in his unseen subtle intention to liberate beings.

The formulae of the *Tathāgatācintyaguhyaka-sūtra* will strike a chord with readers of the eighth-century Buddhist tantras, for we may note the similarity with, for example, the hermeneutic of the forty letters of the opening phrase of *Guhyasamāja* (Secret Congress), and so on, where the ideology of secrecy of body, speech and mind (*kāyavākcittaguhya*) is often mentioned.[10] That the third-century Mahāyānist *Tathāgatācintyaguhyaka* was read by at least some authors of eighth-century Tantric works is assured with the specific citation of the *Tathāgatācintyaguhyaka-sūtra* in the *Sarvamaṇḍalasāmānyavidhīnāṃ guhyatantra*. The *Guhyatantra* includes as part of its idiosyncratic ritual program the worship of four Mahāyāna sutras, one of which is the *Tathāgatācintyaguhyaka-sūtra*, the others being the *Prajñāpāramitā*, the *Gaṇḍavyūha*, and the *Suvarṇaprabhāsa*.[11] Moreover, I have been impressed by the position of Vajrapāṇi in the *Tathāgatācintyaguhyaka-sūtra* and by other factors that also may have contributed to later esoterism, where we see Vajrapāṇi as the reciter of the tantras and the primary enforcer of the will of the Buddha Vairocana.

However, the continuity between these Mahāyānist works and esoteric literature is more apparent than real, to employ the same model as a heuristic device. I have located no specifically Mahāyānist scripture that defines secrecy or that invokes it outside of a negligible rubric that is not revisited in the text. Scarcely found is any identification of a specific attribute, ritual or doctrine that is secret, or even how any of the above may be secret, since the scriptures themselves are not restricted. Secrecy here is a literary device for the introduction of the amazing ability of the buddhas and bodhisattvas to convert beings using various expedients for the purpose. When the *Saddharmapuṇḍarīka* rhetorically asks itself if this strategy is duplicitous, it answers that "No...it is not misleading!" because it is done for the welfare of beings (pp. 76–77).

We should note that the attribute of secret expedients does not, in my experience, necessarily extend to the magical phrases of *dhāraṇīs*, mantras or *vidyās*, all of which denote spells or mnemonic aids in the Mahāyānist literature. Having gone through many collections of these works, I have encountered no early invocation that such spells were secret in their moment of formulation or throughout much of their dissemination. Yes, they are powerful, but their power is to be spread about liberally, for they protect from snakes, spiders, demons and things that go bump in the night. That same description extends to the sutra literature that contains chapters on such elements, such as the *dhāraṇīmukha-parivarta*-s of the *Karuṇāpuṇḍarīka-sūtra* or of the *Saddharmapuṇḍarīka-sūtra*.[12] The reconstruction of these as part of the esoteric Buddhist tradition was an *ex post facto* event, and Skilling (1992) has conclusively demonstrated that such phrases were found throughout early Indian Buddhism. The eventual mystification of spells is rather late, such as found in the extensive *Dhāraṇīsaṃgraha* of Atikūṭa, translated into Chinese in 653–54. By then esoterism was gradually being formulated, however, and the preface of the text maintains that it is the secret of secrets.[13]

Esoteric Buddhist ritual

In distinction to these and other tangents, a thorough-going edifice of secrecy came to be invoked at least by the first half of the eighth century, and from this time onward we find a profusion of Tantric titles with the term "secret" involved, principally under the form *guhya* but also *rahasya*, *gupti, gupta, gopita* and so on, most denoting some variety of secrecy. So there is the *Guhya-tantra* (Secret Scripture), the *Guhya-garbha* (Secret Matrix), the *Guhya-samāja* (Secret Congress), the *Sarva-rahasya-tantra* (Scripture of Every Secret), and so forth. Moreover, other esoteric sutras, tantras, kalpas, and so on offer various definitions or uses of secrecy in ways that are extraordinary. We see names redefined, most certainly in the instance of Vajrapāṇi, who had often been described as *guhyakasenāpati*, the general of the *guhyaka* variety of *yakṣa spirits*. Now, however, Vajrapāṇi is the general of secrets, with *guhyaka* redefined to signify the emerging esoteric canon, which Vajrapāṇi is depicted as having recited and collected. For the rest of this paper, I would like to explore a few examples of the use of *guhya* and *rahasya* in eighth-century literature – as this material is positioned through translations into Chinese and Tibetan, or survives in extent Sanskrit recensions.

As I have proposed above, secrecy in Indian Tantric Buddhist documents is encountered in two core ways. First, there are procedures for secrecy found in the affirmation that a candidate for *abhiṣeka* is to maintain secrecy about certain items, rituals or ideas, so that others not so consecrated are not to be given certain kinds of information about the rites.[14] Second, there is a rhetoric of secrecy seen in the affirmation that a certain text or meditative/ritual practice is secret and is just now being revealed. The former variety of ritual restriction is closest to that indicated by Conze, and is frequently misunderstood, so it is well to begin with the exploration of such statements.

Restrictions on disseminating information about rites and their accompanying ritual texts are all the more curious in the Buddhist case, for we may recall that a common statement found in the Mahāyāna sutras is that the merit of copying or promoting this or that scripture exceeds imagination or is greater than all the sands of innumerable River Ganges.[15] This promotional strategy is appropriate for the earliest international missionary religion, and we often get the impression of Buddhist monks and nuns forcefully persuading others to write and propagate the sutras. We can see the uncomfortable transition between missionary dissemination and esoteric restriction in such early esoteric texts as the *Sarvadurgatipariśodhana-tantra* (Scripture on the Elimination of All Evil Destinies), which affirms both values. In places within the text, the reader is informed that if the text is written down, it is an excellent amulet, or the various worldly gods will protect anyone who will write down the tantra and expound its mantras to others.[16] Yet the beginnings of secrecy are also seen, so that the candidate should not reveal the vajra, bell and mudras to others not consecrated.[17] The text's ritual ambivalence is even evident in the discussion on who should be admitted: the *Sarvadurgatipariśodhana-tantra* maintains that all candidates should be consecrated without regard to their qualifications (p. 100), for any of them might become a buddha or receive any number of worldly benefits by being so initiated, and the lack of candidates' discrimination is found in the *Sarvatathāgata-tattvasaṃgraha* (Summation of the Reality of All Tathāgatas) as well.[18] In distinction to many later tantras, the *Sarvadurgatipariśodhana-tantra* has very modest vows that the candidate is to maintain, mostly concerning its regular practice but also extending to not ridiculing its ritual paraphernalia.[19] These modest requirements, most of which do not involve secrecy, are found in other early-eighth-century esoteric works and are reflected in the *Mañjuśrīmūlakalpa* (Mañjuśrī's Basic Rite) as well.[20]

In distinction, while the *Sarvatathāgata-tattvasaṃgraha* also agrees that the candidate not be examined, the restriction on the prospective disciple's behavior and the affirmation of secrecy are articulated throughout the text of this tantra. The instructions to the candidate are worth repeating, and are ritually enforced through the binding up of his face and vision until just after these instructions are given, whereupon the mandala is revealed.

[The *vajrācārya* (master) admonishes the disciple:]
"Today you have entered into the family of all Tathāgatas. I will generate the adamantine gnosis in you, whereby you will obtain the *siddhi* (accomplishment) of all the Tathāgatas, as well as other *siddhis*. Nor are you to speak to another who has not seen this mandala [about it], nor is the pledge to become lost to you."

Then the *vajrācārya*, binding his own [hands] into the *sattvavajramudrā* (adamantine gesture of the heroic being), with the opening turned toward the [disciple's] head, having placed it on the disciple's head, let him say:
"Let this *samayavajra* (pledge scepter) burst your head, if you should speak to anyone about this!"

Then with the *samayamudrā*, he impresses water with one recitation of the Cursing Heart-mantra, and then causes the disciple to drink it.

This is the Cursing Heart-mantra:
Vajrasattva himself has today entered into your heart.
Let him leave [your body], having split your heart, the moment you speak of this practice.
VAJRODAKAṬHAḤ

Then let him say to the disciple:
"Beginning from today, I am your Vajrapāṇi. If I say to you, 'Do this!' then you must do it, and I am not to be despised by you. Do not let it be that, by not shunning misfortune, you obtain an untimely death and fall into hell."[21]

So what has brought about the remarkable change in the vows associated with the *abhiṣeka*, so that in the space of a century a tradition goes from an active missionary stance to embracing a furtive system hiding itself from public explanation? In another section, the *Sarvatathāgata-tattvasaṃgraha* provides some reasons for its restrictions. It warns, "There are those with bad viewpoints, sinful actions, devoid of completeness, deficient in efforts, who do not have superior knowledge about visual representation (*citrakarma*)," and they are not to be included in the mandala because of their deficient efforts.[22] These evil people believe in other gods and do not believe in the all-penetrating gnosis of the Buddha.[23]

In this instance, as in all other Buddhist scriptural matters, our initial leads should come from the evidence in the commentaries, even though they must eventually be surpassed in a critical examination. However, in this instance the Indian commentaries, like that of Śākyamitra, are not helpful, and merely explain the words when they treat the section at all. Other indications, though, suggest that the politico-military and sectarian agonistic atmosphere of the first half of eighth-century India represents the generative matrix for these restrictions, which are principally focused on non-Buddhists gaining access to the *abhiṣeka*, ridiculing the teachers or their ritual implements and copying the mandala.

Indeed, this was the period when early medieval Śaiva and Vaiṣṇava scriptures also began to reflect the tension between missionary activity and secrecy, to espouse the rhetoric that they possess the revealed secrets and to articulate specific rules excluding Buddhists and other heretics from listening to their teachings. About this time, the earliest version of the *Skandapurāṇa* declared that it is to be revealed to none of these deceitful believers in the nāstika (nihilist = Buddhist) doctrine, for those doing so will go directly to hell.[24] Similarly, some relatively early Pāñcarātra works, like the *Jayākhyasaṃhitā*, required that its lore be hidden from Buddhists and others.[25] Examples could be multiplied, but the overall movement in India is clear: earlier *purāṇic* texts like the *Nīlamata* did not mention this restriction and earlier Buddhist works, like the *dhāraṇī sūtras*, did not seem to restrict Buddhist phrases from being revealed to those of other religious systems. Conversely, by the eighth century all traditions of Indian religion began to erect barriers against the appropriation of their proprietary rites by those of other traditions.

Eventually, the prohibitions on the discussion and verbal dissemination of the new material became part of the codified rules, and three rules became delineated.[26] Number seven of the "Root Transgressions" (*mūlāpatti*) indicates that one should not reveal secrets to the unprepared, which is virtually identical with rule eight of the "Gross Transgressions" (*sthūlāpatti*), while number four of the latter list prohibits showing secret Dharma. The redundancy in these rules was noticed by the most important exegete on them, Mañjuśrīkīrti.[27] This esteemed authority, who takes the sections of the *Sarvatathāgata-tattvasaṃgraha* that we have mentioned above as his canonical source, explains the issues under his comment on the first of these, number seven of the *mūlāpatti* prohibitions. He mentions that we are really dealing with transgressions appropriate to either the *vajrācārya* or the *vajraśiṣya*, i.e. master or disciple. His greatest concerns are about teaching the practices to those unprepared and using the sacraments for worldly purposes, such as taking a Tantric gathering (*gaṇacakra*) as a social venue for anyone to attend. Mañjuśrīkīrti's overall message is that these rules prohibit the defiling of intimacy and trust, the loss of control over the rituals, and have everything to do with restricting the revelation through verbal means and personal relationships.

In this light, I have not discovered any prohibition in the early esoteric works to writing down the content of the rites and instructions. As indicated above, the *Sarvadurgati* even proclaims that great merit accrues to those writing down the text. We do see that the circulation of the documents became a problem for some authorities by the ninth century, when Padmavajra complains that individuals would find a tantra and without authorization or consecration by another simply set themselves up as tantrika gurus.[28] Later, there occurs a prohibition to even displaying the tantra to others, and the *Hevajra-tantra* indicates that the text is to be hidden from all non-initiates.[29] Similarly, the *Caṇḍamahāroṣaṇa-tantra* admonishes that its text is not to be shown to one who has not entered into its mandala or even to one who has entered into another mandala, thus extending the sectarian prohibition to within the Vajrayāna Buddhist fold itself.[30]

So how might we understand these kinds of prohibition? First, we may see in the early statements the Buddhist acknowledgment that verbal transmission has been accorded the highest authority in India, where the written text was grudgingly granted secondary status. Consequently, the primary transgression is through verbal revelation rather than through written means. This means that eventually the restriction on dissemination became a constant struggle between those trying to organize the growing mass of Tantric statements into canonical or exegetical collections and those wanting to control the distribution of practices. Since early medieval sectarianism participated in both the appropriation of other traditions' doctrines and the exclusion of other followers from the ritual enclosure, the restrictions to access was in part a response to accelerated religious competition between emerging Tantric systems, each claiming supreme authority.

Second, it is necessary to acknowledge that Indians tend to extend suspicion both to those in positions of authority and often to each other, partially as a consequence of their stratified society. That sense of mistrust is the leitmotif of Śākyabhikṣu, the everyman-monk featured in the seventh-century farce, *Mattavilāsa*, where he wonders where he could find the true scriptures, the ones that the elders are hiding and that allow monks to enjoy booze and women.[31] We certainly find early medieval tantrikas employing subterfuge in the pattern of coded language (*sandhyābhāṣā*) and secret signs, both of which are known in the tantras as *chommā*, a Prakrit word not only indicating a mask, disguise or costume, but also signifying a masquerade or impersonation. Consequently, the Tantric yogins are to approach the *gaṇacakra* (Tantric feast) and be recognized by the knowledge of secret language and specific signs, which are not ostensibly known to others. These seemingly began in the eighth-century *Sarvabuddhasamāyoga* (All Buddhas' Consummation) with *chommāmudrā*, the physical gestures of secret signs – raising fingers or identifying marks on the body – but continued on to vocal symbols, which is the origin of the much misunderstood *sandhyābhāṣyā*, the "twilight language," which denotes coded words allowing entrance into a Tantric gathering. Such strategies speak of a society in which religious opponents are treated with suspicion, for it is expected that they will try to obtain the latest magical technologies for their own purposes.

Suspicion's darker relative is intentional deceit, such as that recommended by Padmavajra in his *Guhyasiddhi* (Secret Accomplishment), a work I am in the process of translating in conjunction with a monograph on secrecy in Tantric Buddhism. In the *Guhyasiddhi*, Padmavajra indicates that a Buddhist yogin should impersonate a Śaiva yogin and travel to a foreign land.[32] There, he should approach a family of outcastes and offer to provide them initiation (*dīkṣā*) into the Śaiva system of the *Kālottara* or the *Niśvāsa*. In return, the Buddhist should require that the outcaste's daughter be given to him as a sexual partner. This extreme recommendation is similar to the first section of the *Vyaktabhāvānugata-tattvasiddhi* (Accomplishment of the Reality Following the Apparent State), apparently written by a woman, yoginī Cintā, which provides a fairly straightforward seduction manual for yogins in need of a sexual partner.[33] The purpose is avowedly the yogin's liberation, not a reciprocal amorous relationship based on trust.

The rhetoric of secrecy

Although the above discussion barely begins treatment of the difficult questions of exclusiveness, furtiveness and related issues, we must now proceed on to the rhetoric of secrecy that permeates the tantras, and indeed much of Indian literature of the early medieval period. The rhetoric of secrecy actually extends from the bifurcation into reality and appearances, mentioned above. We have seen how the *Tathāgatācintyaguhyaka* describes that the secrets of the Buddha's body or speech or mind are displayed in a wide variety of apparent forms, most not immediately recognizable as belonging to the buddhas or bodhisattvas. The difference is that the items described as "secret" within the tantras are almost entirely ritual in nature, rather than an ephemeral activity that operates for the welfare of beings, only to disappear when its work is complete. Indeed, a sense of permanence and durability is implied or suggested for the ritual systems, much as was seen in the vows of the Bodhisattva and the Mahāyānist scriptures in earlier centuries. Analogously, the rites and mandalas described as secret in the tantras are depicted as enduring phenomena that occur irrespective of whether anyone practices them or not, much as the early tradition maintained that the *dharmatā* (reality) exists whether or not buddhas arise to discover it.

Moreover, like the *Tathāgatācintyaguhyaka*, the Tantric secrets are frequently organized into levels of the body, speech and mind of the Buddha. Consequently, the "guhya" of the *Guhyasamāja* is the secret assembly of the mandala, one so secret that it was unknown even to the buddhas and bodhisattvas.[34] This trope – how this or that tantra or teaching or rite or behavior is unknown to the buddhas themselves, because it is so secret – was observed as early as the Gilgit manuscript of the *Kāraṇḍavyūha-sūtra* (Scripture of the Array of Caskets) and remained a statement encountered sporadically within the tantras. I have yet to encounter a commentator who satisfactorily explains how, for example, the secret of the body of all the buddhas is unknown even to the buddhas themselves. Normally they try to explain it away with a combination of hermeneutical agility and simple denial of its literal import.

A few of the tantras inaugurate the process of describing secrecy, and the most philosophical of the several early definitions I have yet encountered is that of the *Guhyagarbha* (Secret Matrix). As in the case of the *Guhyasamāja*, the *Guhyagarbha* describes a series of events that are ostensibly secret in nature, but the *Guhyagarbha* also provides a definition of secrecy, beginning with traditional Mahāyānist category wordplay.

> Aho! The wonderful, miraculous Dharma is the secret of all Sambuddhas, and all dharmas are born from non-origination, for there is no birth within origination.

> Aho! The wonderful, miraculous Dharma is the secret of all Sambuddhas, and all dharmas cease from ceaselessness, for there is no eclipse in cessation.

> Aho! The wonderful, miraculous Dharma is the secret of all Sambuddhas, and all dharmas are stable from impermanence, for there is no stability within permanence.

> Aho! The wonderful, miraculous Dharma is the secret of all Sambuddhas, and all dharmas refer to nonreferentiality, for there is no reference in referentiality.

> Aho! The wonderful, miraculous Dharma is the secret of all Sambuddhas, and all dharmas come and go from neither coming nor going, for there is no coming and going in movement.

That having been stated [by Samantabhadra], all the Tathāgatas and the entire community of ladies became pervaded with satisfaction, and pronounced this pithy statement (*udāna*):

Aho! This Dharma that has been secret since the beginning, is the secret nature in all appearances, is very secret by its own proper nature, and is exceedingly secret, for it is not found elsewhere.[35]

This *udāna* (sacred phrase) is one of an entire class of *udānas* that were developed through the tantras and is an interesting redirection of a very early Buddhist literary form. In his comment on the text, the only assuredly Indian commentator available to us, Vilāsavajra, declares the term "secret" (*guhya*) in the title of the work, the *Guhyagarbha*, is of three varieties: naturally secret, hidden and obscure.[36] The first involves the nature of reality as indicated in the above *udāna*, the second, the secret behaviors of the tantrika, and the third is bestowed by the master.

The second of these actually goes to the heart of the matter, for the pattern of pronouncements in many of the *mahāyoga* and *yoginītantras* is to identify mandalas, sacramental rites and mantras as secret. Consequently, the most curious of all the Tantric formulae are signified with the terms *guhya* or *rahasya*, such as the secret *abhiṣeka* (*guhyābhiṣeka*) or the consistent pronouncement in the *Guhyasamāja* that the sacramental ingestion of feces and urine is the great secret of all the buddhas.[37]

Conclusion

Space prevents a further discussion of this most interesting question, although many other facets are in need of additional consideration: hermeneutics, coded language, secret signs, ritual behavior, secret sacraments, to mention but a few. So what conclusions might be drawn at this preliminary stage?

First, I would hope it is understood that, because of the very nature of the question, the precise contours of secrecy, both in breadth and in depth, remain unclear. However, I can assert with some certainty that esoteric Buddhism arose in a society given to the crossover between the political and the military world on the one hand, and the religious world on the other. The terms *mantra* and *mantrin*, for example, may mean both a sacred phrase and its keeper as well as state secrets and counselors of state. Both these uses of the terms mantra/mantrin are denoted as *guhya* or *rahasya* in their respective texts, and the paranomasia of the terms became a source of humor.[38] Consequently, there is always a public/social valence to secrecy in esoteric Buddhism, unsurprising since one must keep secrets from another, a quintessentially social act.

Second, its exclusive nature has allowed it to develop in unforeseen ways, for the initial rituals were neither sexual nor illicit in any sense, but entirely extensions of the rituals of kingship and dominion, of control and authority. Yet, the restriction of participants has allowed the small groups to operate on a different dynamic, so that the normative esoteric community in eighth- to ninth-century India was a small enclave at the margins of, or in proximity to, a larger Buddhist center. This is in some ways analogous to the development of language idioms and dialects, or the development of new species, for they exhibit a movement toward efflorescence in isolation. Consequently, I would conclude that the isolation enforced by Tantric secrecy allowed it to develop more quickly and with fewer restraints than would otherwise have been the case.

Finally, rather than strictly the independent revelation of an inspired yogin, Tantric Buddhism appears in part a series of religious strategies developed by communities to avoid obliteration in the militarized environment of the period. We see these attributes most definitively in the content described as secret, for the early statements seldom involve doctrinal or philosophical positions *per se*. When the *Guhyasamāja* goes on a lengthy *via negativa* description of ultimate reality, terms for secrecy are nowhere to be found.[39] Instead, the expressions of secrecy in some forty major pronouncements in the *Guhyasamāja* are almost exclusively identified with ritual or meditative agendas. Even the occasional philosophical discussions of secrecy – as in the *Guhyagarbha* section translated above – employs Ābhidharmika categories in a Madhyamaka manner, provides no new doctrinal formulae at all and principally employs secrecy to justify the revelation of a new mandala or novel meditative and yogic practices. Only later, perhaps in the ninth or tenth centuries, do we begin to see statements of secrecy extended to philosophical ideology.

In short, I would say that Indian Tantric secrecy is a self-disclosing idiom of scriptural development, a rubric that continues to require both self-emptying and self-filling, a kenotic process that discharges a horizon of expectations so that the real scriptures are continually being revealed, the new mandalas and new sacraments continually unfolding, while the yogins try to avoid suspicion by acting suspiciously themselves. The esotericness of Tantric Buddhism was a self-perpetuating strategy that ensured its continued independent maturation. Outside of India, neither the occlusive environment nor the scriptural proliferation was possible to the same degree, and consequently over time we see a decline of its rate of change and a concomitant decrease of its pure outrageousness.

Notes

1 The word "tantra" is a polysemic term in India, but as employed in Buddhism came to denote the esoteric scriptures, even though these often were identified with other terms in their titles, such as kalpa, sutra, and so on.

2 Guy R. Welbon "Secrecy in Indian Tradition," in Bolle 1987, p. 61.
3 Ulansey 1989, p. 3; Burkert 1987, p. 42. Maps of cult sites and monuments are found in Ulansey 1989, p. 5 and Cumont 1902, endpaper.
4 On these points, see Davidson 2002, pp. 257–69.
5 Kees W. Bolle 1987, p. 9.
6 A beginning to the discussion of this topic has been initiated by Pye 1978.
7 *Bodhisattvabhūmi* 82.16–21; To 4037, vol. wi, fols 44b7–45a2; T 1579.30.497b 28–c6; T 1581.30.900c9–14; Guṇaprabha's cy. To 4044, sems tsam 'i, fol. 168b4–5; Sāgaramegha's cy. Pe. 5548, sems tsam ri, fol. 126a4–126b6. The *Bodhisattvabhūmi* is the fifteenth part of the basic section of Asaṅga's *Yogācārabhūmi* and treats the Mahāyānist path for the Yogācāra monk.
8 *Da zhidu lun*, T 1509.25.84c (Lamotte 1944, vol. 1, p. 235); I thank Lucia Dolce for the reference.
9 This doctrine seems very close to the Jaina ideology of the *divyadhvani* of the Jinas, and may have been adapted from the Jaina model; cf. Jaini 1979, pp. 39, 42–43.
10 On this introduction, see Wayman 1977, pp. 1–22, Davidson 2002, pp. 236–57.
11 *Sarvamaṇḍalasāmānyavidhīnāṃ guhyatantra*, To 806, fol. 152b5–7.
12 *Karuṇāpuṇḍarīka-sūtra*, vol. 2, pp. 14–51; *Saddharmapuṇḍarīka-sūtra*, pp. 395–403.
13 *Dhāraṇīsaṃgraha*, T 901.18.785a5.
14 On the appropriation of Hindu coronation rites and the elaboration of the *abhiṣeka* ceremony in esoteric Buddhism, see Davidson 2002, pp. 123–31. Strickmann 1996, pp. 78–87, 98–100, 113–23, 330–32, discusses the early Chinese evidence on the rite.
15 Schopen's well-known 1975 article on this question is in need of re-evaluation.
16 *Sarvadurgatipariśodhana-tantra*, pp. 10, 72.
17 *Sarvadurgatipariśodhana-tantra*, p. 106.
18 *Sarvatathāgata-tattvasaṃgraha*, p. 21.
19 *Sarvadurgatipariśodhana-tantra*, p. 106.
20 See the discussion in Davidson 2002, p. 165.
21 *Sarvatathāgata-tattvasaṃgraha*, p. 22; To 479, fol. 27a7–27b4. The term *mūdhvāmukhī* is translated by the Tibetan as "facing inward," (*kha nang na bstan pa*; fol. 27b2), where I would have interpreted it as facing upward. *Viṣamāparihāreṇa* is poorly examined in our lexicons; I have adapted the Tibetan translator's *mi bde ba ma spangs pas*, (fol. 27b4).
22 *Sarvatathāgata-tattvasaṃgraha*, p. 49; reading "*vaikalyarahita.*"
23 *Sarvatathāgata-tattvasaṃgraha*, p. 93.
24 *Skandapurāṇa* III. 2, p. 121.
25 *Jayākhya-saṃhitā* VII.113; *Ahirbudhnya-saṃhitā* LIX. 71.
26 See Davidson 2002, pp. 322–27, for these rules.
27 *Vajrayānamūlāpatti-ṭīkā*, fols 213b1–214b1.
28 *Guhyasiddhi* I.46–47.
29 *Hevajra-tantra* II.vii.3–4.
30 *Caṇḍamahāroṣaṇa-tantra* I. 28–29, III. 64–71; pp. 46–47, 55–56.
31 *Mattavilāsa prahasana*, pp. 42–43.
32 *Guhyasiddhi* VIII. 2–15.
33 *Vyaktabhāvānugata-tattvasiddhi*, pp. 169–72.
34 On this point, see the discussion in Davidson 2002, pp. 252–57.
35 *Guhyagarbha-tattvaviniścaya*, fol. 12a2–12b1; in the last verse, I have followed the Rumtek edition (fol. 6a4) reading *gzhan du min las*.
36 *Guhyagarbha-ṭīkā*, pp. 397.2–398.5.
37 For example, *Guhyasamāja* VI.19–27, p. 19.
38 This point is discussed in Davidson 2002, pp. 143–44.
39 *Guhyasamāja*, pp. 83–85, the prose section at the end of ch. XV.

76   *Ronald M. Davidson*

References

Primary sources

Ahirbudhnya-saṃhitā. In Pandit V. Krishnamacharya (ed.), *Ahirbudhnya-saṃhitā of the Pancaratragama*, 2 vols. Madras: Adyar Library and Research Centre, 1986.

Bodhisattvabhūmi. In Unrai Wogihara (ed.), *Bodhisattvabhūmi: A Statement of Whole Course of the Bodhisattva (Being Fifteenth Section of Yogācārabhūmi).* Reprinted in Tokyo: Sankibo Buddhist Book Store, 1971. (To 4037; T 1579)

Caṇḍamahāroṣaṇa-tantra. In Christopher S. George (ed. and tr.), *The Caṇḍamahāroṣaṇa Tantra. A Critical Edition and English Translation, Chapters I–VIII.* New Haven: American Oriental Society, 1974.

Da zhidu lun 大智度論, attrib. Nāgārjuna. T 1509.25.57–757.

Dhāraṇīsaṃgraha, *Atikūṭa (tr. 653–54). T 901.18.785a–897b.

Guhyagarbha-tattvaviniścaya. To 832. *Bka' 'gyur*, Rnying rgyud, kha, fols 110b1–132a1.

Guhyagarbha-ṭīkā, fasc. Vilāsavajra. In Bdud-'joms Jigs-bras ye-shes rdo-rje (ed.), *Rnying ma bka' ma rgyas pa*, vol. 23. Kalimpong, WB: Dubjung Lama, 1982, pp. 389–620.

Guhyasamāja. In Yukei Matsunaga (ed.), *The Guhyasamāja-tantra.* Osaka: Toho Shuppan, 1978.

Guhyasiddhi, fasc. Padmavajra. In Samdhong Rinpoche and Vrajvallabh Dwivedi (eds), *Guhyādi-Aṣṭasiddhi-Saṅgraha* (Rare Buddhist Text Series 1). Sarnath, Varanasi: Central Institute of Higher Tibetan Studies, 1987, pp. 5–62.

Hevajra-tantra. In David Snellgrove (ed. and tr.), *The Hevajra Tantra: A Critical Study* (London Oriental Series vol. 6). Oxford: Oxford University Press, 1959.

Jayākhya-saṃhitā. In Embar Krishnamacharya (ed.), *Jayākhyasaṃhitā, crit. ed. with an introduction in sanskrit, indices, etc.* (Gaekwad's Oriental Series 54). Baroda: Oriental Institute, 1967.

Karuṇāpuṇḍarīka-sūtra. In Isshi Yamada (ed.), *Karuṇāpuṇḍarīka: The White Lotus of Compassion*, 2 vols. London: School of Oriental & African Studies, 1968.

Mahārahasyopāyakauśalya-sūtra. To 82. *Bka' 'gyur*, dkon brtsegs, cha, fols 30a1–70b7. (T 310 (38); T 345, 346).

Mattavilāsa prahasana. In Michael Lockwood and A. Vishnu Bhat (ed. and tr.), *Mattavilāsa Prahasana ("The Farce of the Drunken Sport") by King Mahendravikramavarma Pallava.* Madras: The Christian Literature Society, 1981.

Nīlamatapurāṇa. In K. de Vreese (ed.), *Nīlamata or Teachings of Nīla.* Leiden: Brill, 1936.

Saddharmapuṇḍarīka-sūtra. In H. Kern and Bunyiu Nanjio (eds), *Saddharmapuṇḍarīka* (Bibliotheca Buddhica X). St. Petersburg: Imperial Academy of Sciences, 1908–12.

Sarvadurgatipariśodhana-tantra. In Tadeusz Skorupski (ed. and tr.), *The Sarvadurgatipariśodhana Tantra: Elimination of All Evil Destinies.* Delhi: Motilal Banarsidass, 1983.

Sarvamaṇḍalasāmānyavidhīnāṃ guhyatantra. To 806. *Bka' 'gyur*, rgyud 'bum, wa, fols 141a1–167b7.

Sarvatathāgata-tattvasaṃgraha. In Lokesh Chandra (ed.), *Sarva-Tathāgata-Tattva-Saṅgraha.* Delhi: Motilal Banarsidass, 1987. (To 479).

Skandapurāṇa. In R. Adriaensen, H.T. Bakker, and H. Isaacson (eds), *The Skandapurāṇa. Volume I. Adhyāyas 1–25. Critically edited with a Prolegomena and English Synopsis.* Groningen: Egbert Forsten, 1998.

Tathāgatācintyaguhyaka-sūtra. To 47. *Bka' 'gyur*, Dkon brtsegs, ka, fols 100a1–203a7. (T 310(3).11.42b–80c; T 312.11.504b–751b).

Vajrayānamūlāpatti-ṭīkā, fasc. Mañjuśrīkīrti. To 2488. *Bstan gyur*, rgyud, zi, fols 197b7–231b7.

Vimalakīrtinirdeśa. Study Group on Buddhist Sanskrit Literature (ed.), *Vimalakīrtinirdeśa: Transliterated Sanskrit Text Collated with Tibetan and Chinese Translations.* Tokyo: Taisho University Press, 2004.

Vyaktabhāvānugata-tattvasiddhi, fasc. yoginī Cintā. In *Guhyasiddhi*, pp. 169–79.

Modern sources

Bolle, Kees W. (1987), *Secrecy in Religion* (Studies in the History of Religions 49). Leiden: Brill.

Burkert, Walter (1987), *Ancient Mystery Cults.* Cambridge, MA and London: Harvard University Press.

Conze, Edward (1962), *Buddhist Thought in India: Three Phases of Buddhist Philosophy.* Reprinted in Ann Arbor: University of Michigan Press, 1973.

Cumont, Franz (1902), Thomas J. McCormack (tr.), *The Mysteries of Mithra.* Reprinted in New York: Dover Publications, 1956.

Davidson, Ronald M. (2002), *Indian Esoteric Buddhism: A Social History of the Tantric Movement.* New York: Columbia University Press.

Jaini, Padmanabh S. (1979), *The Jaina Path of Purification.* Berkeley: University of California Press.

Lamotte, Étienne (1944), *Le Traité de la grande vertu de sagesse*, vol. 1. Reprinted in Louvain-la-Neuve: Institut Orientaliste, 1981.

Pye, Michael (1978), *Skilful Means: A concept in Mahayana Buddhism.* London: Gerald Duckworth & Co.

Schopen, Gregory (1975), "The Phrase '*sa pṛthivīpradeśaś caityabhūto bhavet*' in the *Vajracchedikā*: Notes on the Cult of the book in Mahāyāna." *Indo-Iranian Journal* 17, pp. 147–81.

Skilling, Peter (1992), "The *Rakṣā* Literature of the Śrāvakayāna." *Journal of the Pali Text Society* 16, pp. 109–82.

Strickmann, Michel (1996), *Mantras et mandarins: Le bouddhisme tantrique en Chine.* Paris: Gallimard (Bibliothèque de Sciences humaines).

Ulansey, David (1989), *The Origins of the Mithraic Mysteries: Cosmology and Salvation in the Ancient World.* New York and Oxford: Oxford University Press.

Urban, Hugh B. (2001), *The Economics of Ecstasy.* Oxford and New York: Oxford University Press.

Wayman, Alex (1977), *Yoga of the Guhyasamājatantra: The Arcane Lore of Forty Verses, a Buddhist Tantric Commentary.* Delhi: Motilal Banarsidass.

4 Myth and secrecy in Tang-period Tantric Buddhism

Martin Lehnert

Esoterism or secrecy?

"Esoterism" is an ambivalent concept with regard to the hybrid formation of Buddhism traditionally referred to by the term *mijiao* 密教. For reasons which I will discuss in the following, *mijiao* is in itself an ambiguous term that may be best translated as "secret teachings." Generally, it denotes Buddhist practices that were closely related to Tantric ritual pragmatics, though it did not designate a self-contained Tantric tradition in China; a Chinese equivalent of the Sanskrit term *tantra* did not even exist.[1] Moreover, the prevalence of Tantric scriptures, ritual manuals, and practices during the eighth century of the Tang (618–907) neither presupposed a denominational dichotomy between two groups of schools – one esoteric, the other exoteric[2] – nor is it to be understood in terms of social division or lineages of esoteric doctrine (which are often considered to be precursors of Tōmitsu 東密 and Taimitsu 台密 classifications of Japanese esoterism).[3]

At first sight, the Chinese term *mijiao* suggests a self-defined Buddhist esoterism intended for an inner circle of advanced disciples, a teaching so demanding and subtle that it has to be kept secret in order to prevent its vulgarization. Analogous to the Greek concept of *esoterikòs, mijiao* seems to denote a doctrine that implies social division by exclusion from and initiation into hidden contents supposedly of divine origin too arcane to be disseminated among the unworthy.[4] Hence, the very term *mijiao* involves the question how the practices it was used to designate were introduced and validated as meaningful acts, beliefs, and forms of ultimate truth. As expressions of reciprocal discursive relations and social functions, the phenomena in question are open to further discourse analysis.

From the late 720s, the term *mijiao* came to denote practices and related scriptures that had been introduced by Śubhakarasiṃha (Chin. Shanwuwei 善無畏, 637–735), and was subsequently used by Vajrabodhi (Chin. Jingangzhi 金剛智, 671–741) and his disciples to designate their own activities in the field of Buddhist praxis. The scholar-monk Yixing

(一行, 673–727), who became an assistant of Śubhakarasiṃha and Vajrabodhi, defined *mijiao* as that which "cannot be promulgated directly" (*bu ke zhi xuan* 不可直宣).[5] Amoghavajra (Chin. Bukong 不空, 705–74), the main disciple of Vajrabodhi, professed that it was his aim "to carry forward the secret teachings" (*hong mijiao* 弘密教).[6]

This use of the term *mijiao* by Yixing and Amoghavajra confronts us with an ambivalent concept of promulgation: on the one hand, the teachings it designates cannot (or should not) "be promulgated directly"; on the other hand, it applies to a mission "to carry forward" these teachings. Over two centuries later, the issue of promulgation had retained its significance, as seen for example in the "Song [Dynasty Edition of the] Biographies of Eminent Monks" (*Song gaoseng zhuan* 宋高僧傳, d. 983–88) compiled by the scholar-monk Zanning 贊寧 (919–1001).[7] Zanning divided Buddhism into three branches of teaching, depending on their respective mode of transmission: (1) "explicit teachings" (Chin. *xianjiao* 顯教) that are constituted by the three divisions of sutra, vinaya, and abhidharma, transmitted through written and spoken language; (2) "secret teachings" (Chin. *mijiao*) consisting of the methods of yoga, consecration, the five divisions, fire rituals (*homa*), the three mysteries, and mandala, which are transmitted secretly; (3) "heart teachings" (Chin. *xinjiao* 心教), i.e. Chan praxis transmitted directly from mind to mind.[8]

Later historical records and chronologies such as the "True Succession of Śākyamuni's Teaching" (*Shimen zhengtong* 釋門正統, d. 1237) or the "Chronicle of Buddhas and Patriarchs" (*Fozu tongji* 佛祖統紀, d. 1269) referred to a similar conception of *mijiao*, and listed Śubhakarasiṃha, Vajrabodhi, Amoghavajra, Yixing, and Huilang (慧朗, n.d.) as prominent promulgators of Tang-period "secret teachings."[9] Hagiographic literature represented these individual monks less in terms of esoteric lineages than in descriptions of ritual services and apotropaic wizardry for which they were renowned and appreciated at the court.[10] While the designation *mijiao* alludes to pragmatics of promulgation and transmission allegedly shrouded in secrecy, doctrinal, or sectarian esoterism does not seem to be a characteristic issue of the "secret teachings," as Robert Sharf concludes, "...there is little evidence that esoterism was viewed as an independent school, lineage, teaching, or bibliographic category in the T'ang" (Sharf 2002, p. 275).

Disregarding the question as to what the compound *mijiao* actually meant (or connoted),[11] its usage as outlined above raises the question of the function of secrecy as an expedient of promulgation. If we free our view from the problems of tenet classification, lineages of esoterism and sectarian history (which have dominated the discussion so far), it becomes evident that secrecy took on a ubiquitous yet multifarious status as an organizing policy. It goes without further saying that the purely heuristic approach to secrecy proposed in this essay does not intend to exhaust the semantic field of the term *mijiao* nor to assert any "most essential" aspect of it in the Chinese context. Bearing these premises in mind, the textual corpus and the related praxis introduced to China by Śubhakarasiṃha, Vajrabodhi, Amoghavajra *et al.* will be referred to with the expression "secret teachings" for Chin. *mijiao* in a purely etic sense and as a matter of convention.

What made the "secret teachings" secret?

The "Treatise on the Grand Prajñāpāramitā" (*Da zhidu lun* 大智度論 , d. 402–05), a standard exegesis of the "Grand Prajñāpāramitā-sūtra,"[12] introduced the discrimination between "explicit" (Chin. *xian* 顯, resp. *xianshi* 顯示) and "secret" or "concealed" (Chin. *mi* 密, resp. *bimi* 秘密) teachings.[13] This discrimination refers to the notion that there are different techniques of salvation, and that a bodhisattva's or buddha's didactic takes the mental faculties of their audience into account, responding to the situation under which a salvific expedient is implemented. Hence, particular teachings appear to be secret or concealed (Chin. *bimifa* 秘密法) due to individual limitations of thaumaturgic perceptiveness and comprehensibility. Furthermore, in monastic as well as lay practice, access, progress, and authorization are mainly based on ritualized curricula, master–disciple hierarchies, procedures of initiation and exclusion. These criteria, however, are also supposed to correspond to the respective individual's mental faculties. In either respect, hierarchies founded on the ability to access transcendent insight (Skt. *prajñā*) and (knowledge of) related "skill in means" (Chin. *fangbian shanqiao* 方便善巧, Skt. *upāya-kauśalya*) constitute discrimination perceived in terms of exclusion and secrecy in the field of promotional pragmatics, techniques of conversion, and salvific attainment in general. Conceived as provisional and instrumental because of the respective karmic situation in which a salvific operation takes place, "secrecy" refers at best to a weak notion of esoterism inasmuch as the Buddhist community is structured according to the mental and thaumaturgic capacities of disciples into outer and more advanced inner circles centered around the realization of complete awakening to reality as such (Skt. *anuttara-samyak-saṃbodhi*).

Posing the problem of realization, one has to consider the Buddhist concept of a twofold truth, namely the mediating conventional truth (Chin. *su di* 俗諦, Skt. *saṃvṛti-satya*) and the intrinsic ultimate truth (Chin. *zhen di* 真諦, Skt. *paramārtha-satya*): The former points to the *hermeneutic* problem that any possibility of (processual) realization is defined by its specific conditions and perspective,[14] whereas the latter is only accessible to sages who are able to transcend the *ontologic* confines of conditioned language, reason, and constructions of reality.[15] This bifurcation implies a hierarchy that refers to the confines of language and divides the community into those who are able to grasp this division as a matter of pragmatics and those who are not yet able to realize liberation beyond reason and language.[16] Such duplicity constitutes and mediates a difference "between true discourse and 'the discourse of truth,' the latter being no more than a form of ideology that has to be discovered behind grand ideals" (Faure 2004, p. 140).

Being a function of hierarchy, secrecy turns out to be both a pragmatic and a doctrinal or "ideological" problem of Buddhist praxis: It is part of a twofold perspective on truth which is on the one hand delimited by concealment and on the other hand conceived in terms of realization. Therefore, secrecy may be addressed as being inscribed into a soteriologic process that embraces both concealment and the perception of concealment. This process finds an eloquent expression in the metaphor of the perceptibility of the new moon by daylight, formulated by Amoghavajra in his "Treatise on the Production of the Thought of Anuttara Samyaksaṃbodhi in the Vajra Pinnacle Yoga" (*Jingangding yujia zhong fa anouduoluo sanmiao sanputi xin lun* 金剛頂瑜伽中發阿耨多羅三貌三菩提心論, d. between 746 and 774). Complete awakening is depicted as the annihilation of obstruction, an obstruction that paradoxically turns out to be caused by the brightness of the sunlight outshining the alternating phases of the moon – a metaphor of processual attainment:

> Generally the bright feature of each division of the moon seems to stand in conjunction with the time of night, but actually it is the sunlight which eclipses its brightness. That is why it is not visible. After the new moon has arisen, it is getting gradually fuller day by day until the fifteenth day when it is round and full without obstruction.[17]

This metaphor comprehends "visibility" as the perception of that which appears to be concealed, and at the same time it proposes a dialectical relationship between the realization and the concealed evidence constitutive of secrecy: If it is true that secrecy precedes a concealed content, it is because a secret may lack any content; without disclosing the secret one cannot decide whether the secret is a hidden content or a disguise without content. Because the secret has to be perceived as a secret in order to be disclosed, there have to be signs oozing out of the secret, referring back to it. The perception of a secret results from the secretive manner of acting on the part of those who create and guard the secret. This may also simply be playing make-believe in the sense of the children's game: "I see something you don't see...". In this regard, Amoghavajra's metaphor proposes the idea of secrecy as an organizing function which comprehends a dialectic of ultimate realization in terms of concealment and its subsequent *aufhebung* ("sublation"). It does not refer to a hidden content to be disclosed and then grasped by the practitioner; rather, it is conceived as an adjustment of perception and insight into a natural process.

But what is implied by linking concealment and insight in this way? Once a secret is disclosed, it is annihilated, and what remains is the secret's content – or rather the perception of disclosure and insight. To conclude that a secret is therefore merely a game of deception policies that instigates a struggle for disclosure does not reach far enough. In the case of the "secret teachings," secrecy is first of all performative. The secret as concealment (with or without content) is superseded by the perception of the secret that refers neither to a content nor to a disguising form: To perceive that the brightness of the moon is outshined by sunlight presupposes an observer who is able to realize the relation between shades of light, transparency, and visibility. In this way, secrecy – merely a transparent veil – modifies perception in order to enable reali-zation. As a modifier of perception, secrecy further constitutes modes of interaction and interpersonal bonds of exclusiveness between those who are able to perceive and to *realize*; secrecy sets free and ties together.[18]

The traditional narrative of transmission gives a comprehensive as well as self-referential expression of the problems outlined above. As we will see, the narrative neither speaks in terms of esoterism nor follows any plot of seclusion, obscurantism, and mysticism. Instead, it frankly admits that there was not much left to be hidden. Therefore, the emphasis of this essay does not concern questions such as whether there was a doctrinal esoterism prevalent during the eighth-century Tang dynasty, what kind of knowledge was hidden or transmitted secretly, and what social circumstances might have effectuated a "need to hide." Instead, secrecy will be discussed as being concomitant of an ultimate truth claim in relation to promotional pragmatics and recognition of authority.

"...not to lose words..." – a story of loss

During the eighth century, the cauldron of conditions and interests – historical, social, political – as well as individual endeavor and personal relations at the court fostered the rise of the "secret teachings" to their status as a ritual "technology" of state-protection. Their prominent promulgators – Śubhakarasiṃha, Vajrabodhi, and Amoghavajra[19] – were expected to verify the authenticity of texts they had to translate, and to legitimize a related form of knowledge they had set out to introduce to an initially hostile environment. In short, they were faced with the problem of validating their system of thought. Accordingly, self-representation and self-promotion were central concerns.

In this regard, the traditional narrative about the divine status and transmission of the "secret teachings" is quite revealing as it portrays secrecy in multifarious ways. It is documented in a commentary composed by Amoghavajra, the "Instructions on the Gate of Teaching about the Secret State of Mind of the Great Yoga, the Vajra Pinnacle Scripture" (*Jingangding jing da yujia bimi xindi famen yijue* 金剛頂經大瑜伽秘密心地法門義訣, d. between 746 and 74). This text describes the circumstances under which essential scriptures of the "secret teachings" were transmitted in India, brought to China and finally translated. To construct the narrative, Amoghavajra chooses a somewhat ambivalent approach. Referring to his master Vajrabodhi's oral account, he maintains the mythic origin of the "Vajra Pinnacle Scripture" (*Jingangding jing* 金剛頂經, Skt. *Vajraśekhara-sūtra*) and stresses the unconditioned, invariable truth expressed therein, countering the then widespread notion that the Dharma had entered its age of decline.[20] On the other hand, Amoghavajra represents the process of textual transmission and translation as a story of loss – loss of textual completeness and authenticity. The narrative opens with a rather blunt statement:

> This scripture [which] has one hundred thousand verses in its expansive text, is unknown in this land [China].[21]

Furthermore, ritual practices are likely to be incomplete and to have technical deficiencies, according to Amoghavajra. He states that even in India the textual transmission is fragmentary (in order to demonstrate that it would be a vain effort to seek anew for a complete transmission or any further evidence):

> This land's two-volume Scripture of Brahma's Net (*Brahmajāla-sūtra*) [contains] the abridged performances from this scripture, but in it the expanded signs and roots are inadequately [treated]. Now, as for this abridged yoga, those in the Western Land [India] who obtain consecration (*guanding* 灌頂, Sanskrit *abhiṣeka*) expound it and confer it on one another. But when it comes to the expanded text, they still do not transmit it.[22]

The legitimacy of such fragmentary transmission is confirmed by the consecration and exclusive initiation into ritual duties.[23] In order to validate authority, exclusiveness is given priority to evidence. Consequently, secretion[24] precedes textual transmission as a means to establish exclusiveness:

> This one-hundred-thousand-verse text is, moreover, just the outline of the great treasure scripture of the bodhisattvas, [and] this great scripture is the scripture the teacher (*ācārya*, that is, Vajrabodhi) spoke of bringing [here]. Broad and long like a bed, and four or five feet thick, it has innumerable verses. It was enclosed in an iron stūpa in south India and during several hundred years after the Buddha's extinction, no one was able to open the stūpa, [because] iron gates and locks were used to secure it.[25]

At first, the object of secrecy is presented as a concealed content, epitomized in the motif of the iron stūpa: The complete teaching is known to be locked inside; it was not hidden away in some inconspicuous or undiscoverable place in order to let it sink into oblivion. Enclosed in the stūpa, its presence remained perceptible, becoming an object of worship and ritual practice, a myth within the myth. The motif of the iron stūpa relates myth and ritual, on the one hand defining the status of the "secret teachings" as a sacred relic of the Buddha, and on the other hand representing their authenticity, which is thereby protected from the constant threat of (life-worldly) decay and dilution:

> In this country of central India the Buddhist teaching had gradually decayed. At that time there was a great worthy (*dade*, Sanskrit *bhadanta*) [who had] first recited and held the mantra of Mahāvairocana, and attained Vairocana Buddha who manifested his body and a multitude of bodily forms. In mid-air, [Vairocana] expounded this teaching together with its textual passages and lines. He had [the great worthy] write them down in sequence. When it was finished [he] vanished. It is in fact the present *Essential Rites for Vairocana* [*Taishō* 849], in one volume.[26]

To open the stūpa, technical perfection (Chin. *chengjiu* 成就, Skt. *siddhi*)[27] is required, which is neither readily available nor could be attained by individual human efforts such as altruistic or yogic practice. As an act of divine grace, a corresponding ritual knowledge is bestowed on the chosen "worthy" by a manifestation of the Vairocana Buddha, and its efficacy depends on divine empowerment (Chin. *shenbian jiachi* 神變加持, Skt. *vikurvitādhiṣṭhāna*). Similar to a key that fits a lock mechanically, *siddhi* relates to ritual practice and thereby serves a definite purpose: to authenticate its possessor (which is why keys as well as rituals confer the perception of exclusiveness and symbolize legitimacy).

> At that time this great worthy held and chanted the "technique" [*chengjiu*, Sanskrit *siddhi*, detailed in the scripture] vowing to open the stūpa. For seven days [he] circumambulated the stūpa chanting, and taking seven grains of white mustard seed [he] threw them against the stūpa door and it opened. Within the stūpa a multitude of spirits at once leaped forward, angrily barring [his] entry. [...] Then the great worthy sincerely confessed [his] sins and, giving rise to the great vow, thereafter gained entry into the stūpa. Once [he] was inside, the stūpa closed.[28]

Albeit being technically enabled by the Vairocana Buddha to enter the stūpa, the worthy has to prove his legitimacy to an authority hidden behind the authority: a group of spirits guarding the secret who are responsible for exclusion and initiation. To gain access to the secret content, authentication by ritual technique is apparently deemed insufficient. A demonologic aspect typical for Tantric imagery is introduced. It implies the dialectics of repentance and recognition which unfold between the empowered hierophant[29] and the spirits that succumb to his empowerment as soon as he has qualified himself in moral terms through confessions and vows. The secret content becomes a sacred object of redemption. The narrative demonstrates that ritual practice is both a matter of the (technical) quality of performance and a matter of the (moral) quality of the performer who has prepared himself to face divine forces. In other words, to be initiated into the secret, two conditions are to be fulfilled, namely (1) to be granted authentication, and (2) the moral qualification confirmed by confessions and vows.

> During the course of several days he [chanted] the praises of the expansive text of this scripture king, and each recitation was done [as if] in the space of a single meal. He obtained the instruction of all the buddhas and bodhisattvas and these [he] remembered and held and did not forget. Then he was commanded to go forth from the stūpa and the stūpa gate once again closed as of old.[30]

The vow includes the command of being a guardian of the secret: while the secret becomes a means of tacit exclusion and social division, it determines a specific mode to transmit the ritual knowledge allegedly shrouded in secrecy. Consequently, the narrative turns to the issue of the preservation and transmission of the sacred content.

> At that time the transcription of the methods that were recorded and held consisted of one hundred thousand verses. This is the [scripture] entitled *The Scripture of the Diamond's Tip* and it is the expansive text preserved in the great treasury stūpa of the bodhisattvas that was cut off and missing from the world. [...] This scripture – the one-hundred-thousand-verse text – is not yet available in this country. [As for] the arrival of this superficial text in this land, it was recounted by the ācārya [teacher] Vajrabodhi Tripiṭaka at the beginning of the Kaiyuan ("Opened Prime," December 713–February 742) period: [...][31]

Once removed from the authenticity of the iron stūpa, the textual transmission is conceived – parallel to the transition of the secret from the sphere of divine forces to the life-world of imperial order – as a conversion of myth into history, indicated by the explicit referral to the era name "Opened Prime."[32] This transition is depicted as resulting from a coincidence of natural forces and (collective) human endeavor. Both are related to an act of wizardry which demonstrates the "secret teachings"' potential to become a pacifying, apotropaic "technology" to preserve the social order. This finds expression in the realistic account of the "fleet of more than thirty great ships" in a typhoon:

> [. . .] I (i.e. Vajrabodhi) set forth from the western country to cross the southern ocean in a fleet of more than thirty great ships, each one carrying more than five or six hundred persons. Once, when all were crossing in convoy in the very middle of the great ocean we ran into a typhoon. All the ships were tossed about, and the ship I was on was about to be inundated. At that time I always kept the two scriptures I was bringing nearby so that I could receive and keep them and do the offerings. Now, when the captain saw that the ship was about to sink, everything on board was cast into the ocean, and in a moment of fright the one-hundred-thousand-verse text was flung into the ocean, and only the superficial text was saved. At that time I aroused my mind in meditation. Doing the technique for eliminating disasters, and the typhoon abated, and for perhaps more than a quarter mile around the ship, wind and water did not move. All on board took refuge in me, and bit by bit we got to the shore and arrived in this country.[33]

The salient point of this part of the narrative is not so much the naturalization of the "secret teachings" *per se* as the testimony of the loss of evidence, which implies – despite its vivid description of wizardry – the imposition of rational thought on the mythic framework.

To better understand what is supposed to have happened, one should ask why Vajrabodhi did not apply his "technique for eliminating disasters" until the one-hundred-thousand-verse text was already flung into the ocean. For Amoghavajra there were two motives for relating this story of loss in which Vajrabodhi appears to be a failure, unable to protect the integrity of the sacred scripture:

1   The narrative represents Vajrabodhi's occult skills in order to demonstrate his potential to become a refuge for "all on board" whereas the motif of a fleet in distress allegorizes (social) disorder and the threatened Dharma. In this way, it not only anticipates the close relationship between Buddhist ritual technique and imperial order typical for the "secret teachings," but also attributes greater importance to the master of transmission (and his occult skills) than to the transmission of the sacred scriptures. The deliberate focus on the individual master and the recognition of his competence will become a crucial aspect of Amoghavajra's own promotional strategy to be discussed below.

2   The disaster of having lost the text in a typhoon also renders possible the declaration that the extant scripture (the "superficial text" known in China) is merely an abridged version (Chin. *lüeben* 略本).[34] As if to amplify this loss, Amoghavajra composed the "Indications of the Goals of the 18 Assemblies of the Yoga of the Vajra Pinnacle Scripture"

(*Jingangding jing yujia shiba hui zhigui* 金剛頂經瑜伽十八會指歸, d. between 746 and 774), a synopsis of the "Vajra Pinnacle Scripture" (*Jingangding jing* 金剛頂經, Skt. *Vajraśekhara-sūtra*), that is the "one-hundred-thousand-verse text" supposedly flung into the ocean.[35] Thus, a myth of absence is established, defining the status of the transmitted "superficial text" with reference to the sacred text kept secret in the iron stūpa.

In the following passage of Amoghavajra's narrative (i.e. his "Instructions on the Gate of Teachings..."), another significant turn takes place. Here Vajrabodhi, the main protagonist, raises the question to what degree truth and meaning of the "superficial text" could be preserved in a Chinese translation:

> In the seventh year of the reign period Opened Prime (CE 721) [I] arrived in the Western Capital (Changan) and the Chan master Yixing sought consecration from me. When it became known that [I had] this extraordinary Gate of the Teaching, [he] commanded Iśvara to help translate it into Chinese. Yixing and the others, as it turns out, personally transcribed it. First [we] relied upon the order of the Sanskrit text and then [we] discussed its meaning so as not to lose words. [Yet] its meaning has not yet been [fully] explained.[36]

Instead of claiming fidelity to the original text, Vajrabodhi frankly admits deficiencies and does not attempt to defend his work or to validate the unconditional claim of ultimate truth therein.[37] The ultimate truth is conceived extrinsic to the Chinese translations, which are regarded to be contingent[38] and consequently fallible interpretations: "We related its (the Sanskrit text) intent so as not to lose words, though the meaning has not yet been fully explained" (*shu qi yi, bu shi ju, yi wei yuan* 述其意, 不失句, 義未圓).[39] In the case of the Chinese text, truth could be only of an indirect, mediated nature.

As the process of transmission necessarily depends on human labor, translation and exegesis are understood in terms of contingency: In medieval China, scholar-monks critically discussed problems of textual transmission, translation, and equivalence; due to different methodical approaches to translation work and the developments of terminology, an almost philological awareness for the evident lack of conceptual as well as grammatological equivalence between Sanskrit and Chinese culminated in textual as well as hermeneutic criticism.[40] Because any authority founded on textual transmission and any truth claim based upon textual evidence could justifiably be questioned, it would be inadequate to base authority exclusively on translated texts, claiming that these were equally authentic expressions of the absolute as for instance the scripture kept in the iron stūpa.

Consequently, linguistic problems of translation and interpretation had to become part of the narrative. Instead of trying to substantiate the authenticity of the extant scripture, a critical distinction was introduced between the complete text that was lost and an abridged contingent version that had been transmitted to China.

Mediating between divine origin and historical circumstances under which scriptures and ritual practices were transmitted, Vajrabodhi's and Amoghavajra's skilfully construed narrative serves to justify a ritual praxis in terms of exclusion and secrecy. Its alleged aim being to define the life-worldly status of the translated scriptures, it starts as a myth that disguises itself step by step as a historical record; the narrative follows the intent to mythologize, but the story of the text's loss actually "demythologizes" the very myth it has set out to establish. This "demythologizing" tendency within the myth follows a dialectic of secrecy: The secret moves from the definite and localized content of the iron stūpa to a non-localizable loss of evidence that has happened incidentally. Thereby, secrecy changes its own mode of expression. Attaining imperceptibility, the secret turns into secretion as an infinite form of secrecy referring to an ultimate truth impossible to validate. Guarded by Vajrabodhi, Amoghavajra, and their chosen initiates,[41] the secret has become a personalized indication of exclusiveness and sacral "prestige": no one can ever expect to verify or to falsify it through textual evidence or factual knowledge; hence, legitimacy is ultimately confirmed by consecration (Chin. *guanding* 灌頂, Skt. *abhiṣeka*), while the function of secretion is to insinuate a hidden content or secret knowledge.[42] In practice, this dialectical process of secrecy led to a sacra-lization of the imperial and social order.

"...*all on board took refuge in me*..." – exclusiveness and secretion

The traditional narrative about the transmission of the "secret teachings" reaches its climax by representing Vajrabodhi as a refuge. Performing an apotropaic ritual, he pacifies a typhoon to save "all on board." To be recognized as a refuge, a priest needs special skills and protective power, spiritual as well as actual. Accordingly, the "secret teachings" stress apotropaic ritual services and assign an exclusive status to the priest/hierophant.

In China, Buddhism was perceived as a sacral "ideology," supportive as well as potentially subversive with regard to the imperial and social order. With the arrival of Śubhakarasiṃha in 716 and, four years later, of Vajrabodhi and Amoghavajra in Chang'an, the ritual function of Buddhism at the court, which so far had not transgressed the limits of liturgy, started to evolve into a ritual "technology" and thus assumed a new quality.

Initially, Emperor Xuanzong 玄宗 (r. 712–56) inclined to Daoist learning and showed hostility toward Buddhism in general (see Twitchett 1979, p. 412). Hence, as the "Record of Śākyamuni's Teachings from the Era Opened Prime" (*Kaiyuan shijiao lu* 開元釋教録, d. 730; T 2154) indicates, Śubhakarasiṃha, having presented his first translation to Emperor

Xuanzong, was not allowed to continue his work and to translate further manuscripts.[43] But the efficiency promise of the newly introduced ritual praxis and its occult aesthetics reminiscent of Daoist rituals might have been the reason why the emperor changed his hostile attitude.[44] Śubhakarasiṃha also depended on the efforts of the prominent Chan-monk Yixing, who became his assistant and whose broad learning as well as eminent genealogical ancestry had fostered his rise to political power.[45] Trusted by the emperor, Yixing became in charge of supervising the process of translation and of formulating a doctrinal expression consistent with acknowledged conceptions, and thus sustained the development of "secret teachings" as a Buddhist court liturgy.

From the early 720s, the growing acceptance of the "secret teachings" was further consolidated by the translations and apotropaic ritual services introduced by Vajrabodhi, who was also joined by Yixing.[46] A real breakthrough, however, was achieved two decades later, when Amoghavajra came back from India and started his prolific activities as translator, compiler, and exegete.[47]

During his stay in India (741–46), Amoghavajra came in touch with the current developments of religious praxis and experienced the ongoing displacement of Buddhism of that period. He gained insight into its political and economic constraints, and thereby also came to understand the potential of Tantric practices for promotional ends. As indicated by Ronald Davidson (2002), these practices had been adopted by Buddhism in response to the actual trends of thought and the unstable social order of medieval India after the disintegration of the old imperial order and the emergence of warring feudal states. For a better understanding of Amoghavajra's ritual practice at least four characteristic features of Indian Tantric Buddhism deserve special attention:

1   The Tantric Buddhist purificatory ceremony of consecration (Skt. *abhiṣeka*) emulated the function of the Brahmanic coronation ritual that confirmed the divinity of the king and bestowed sanctity upon him (Davidson 2002, pp. 126–31).
2   The implementation of *siddha* occultism allowed Buddhist institutions to address the demand of the ruling and military class for the sacralization of the political sphere.[48] In addition, *siddhas* were considered to be ideal mediums of deception and espionage.[49]
3   Mandalas iconized the administrative grid of sāmanta-feudalism[50] as a domain (Skt. *kṣetra*) of sanctifying power relations, accessible to the hierophant who is charged by divine forces with "numinous empowerment" (Skt. *vikurvitādhiṣṭhāna*).[51]
4   As a means of ultimate realization of truth, mantric speech acts overrode the complexities of scholastic debates that proved to be detrimental to the acceptance of Buddhist teachings among the political and military elite (Davidson 2002, pp. 99–105).

After returning to Chang'an, Amoghavajra systematically adopted such Tantric practices to alleviate a crisis of imperial power he encountered at the Tang-court (Orzech 1998, pp. 140–46) and accomplished with much more success what Buddhist monks had attempted in the warring feudal states of medieval India: to actualize Buddhism as a repository of state-related ritual services, thereby justifying its privileged position which in turn enabled Buddhism to influence and exploit imperial power.

Pursuing his ritual duties under Emperor Xuanzong, Amoghavajra slowly gained influence, blending religious, administrative, and political expertise into a praxis of apotropaic ritual and a liturgy of state protection. His rise to actual power as a trusted agent of the imperial family, however, was a result of the military revolt of General An Lushan 安祿山 (703–57) and the subsequent crisis of imperial order in the years between 756 and 63 which initiated the gradual decline of the Tang.[52] While Xuanzong and his court fled the rebel army, Amoghavajra was captured in the capital. After the emperor's abdication, he became active as a spy in service of the heir apparent Li Heng 李恒 (i.e. Suzong 肅宗, r. 756–62), who entered into an alliance with Tibetan and Uigur forces to recapture lost territory and his imperial authority. To extirpate the usurpers, Amoghavajra performed rituals evoking the Vidyārāja Acala (Chin. Budong mingwang 不動明王), a Tantric deity, to support the Tang loyalists.[53] In 759, soon after the restoration of Tang imperial order, Amoghavajra was called upon to consecrate Emperor Suzong as "universal overlord" (Chin. *lunwang* 輪王, Skt. *cakravartin*), sacralizing a social order that already belonged to the past; outside the walls of the imperial court, disorder spread across an impoverished land that had been devastated by the rebellion.[54]

The next emperor, Daizong 代宗 (r. 762–79), found himself without much real power. Being dependent on the support of his military leaders and rival warlords, he sought spiritual support to confirm his legitimacy and political expertise, circumstances that turned out to be auspicious for Amoghavajra, who was ready to serve the new emperor and to become his trusted "refuge."[55] Ritual services at the court allowed Amoghavajra to redefine his status in respect of both the "secret teachings" and the imperial order. He expanded the traditional sphere of action of a Master of Dharma (Chin. *fashi* 法師) by introducing new areas of sacral responsibility centered on his person as an enforcer of apotropaic techniques. The manner in which Amoghavajra presented himself as an imperial servant and thereby succeeded in becoming an institution himself depended on a generic relation between the warring state, its social disorder and secrecy: Associating imperial power with Buddhist soteriology, the rule of the Son of Heaven (Chin. *tianzi* 天子) with the spiritual sovereignty of a "teacher" (Chin. *asheli* 阿闍梨, Skt. *ācārya*) and a *siddha*'s skill in wizardry and deception, Amoghavajra was able to monopolize three functions of religious authority, namely (1) the master who is the authority of transmission of the Dharma and guarantor of its authenticity, (2) the priest who is the director of liturgy and its doctrinal representation, and (3) the hierophant who presents himself as a mediator of the divine sphere, of numinous empowerment and ultimate realization of truth. These three functions came into operation by means of secrecy in terms of exclusiveness, aesthetics, and mythologization:

1   Amoghavajra presented the Chinese scriptures as contingent expressions of ultimate truth. Therefore he did not need to scruple at textual authenticity as a critical problem of legitimacy. Introducing a ritual praxis accessible only to a selected audience, he concentrated on the exclusive transmission of a performative knowledge for which he relied on a corpus of ritual manuals he had (assumedly) brought back from India (Strickmann 1996, pp. 80–81). Arranged for particular occasions, these rituals were mostly either purificatory or apotropaic in nature, and were used to sacralize imperial power.

    Amoghavajra's policy also aimed at the possibility to conduct textual transmission and exegesis exclusively and independently. It directed audience and ritual performers to "take refuge" in the very person of the Master of Dharma as an exclusive link to the true teaching. As epitomized in the traditional narrative of transmission in which a fleet in distress was saved by Vajrabodhi's wizardry, Amoghavajra gained the exclusive status of a Master of Dharma while textual evidence had been lost.

2   The next step was to become a director of liturgy. The linguistic obscurity of Buddhist tantras as well as the imagery and iconography of their ritual implementation surely did not fail to intensify a feeling of mystery and awe among the courtiers, who were taking part in the representation of the princely household as a sacral environment. Linking performative practice to his own person, Amoghavajra determined his proper field of liturgical display and created an aesthetic of empowerment evoked during the ritual.[56] Stressing sacral performance as a matter of exclusive transmission, he gained the authority to elevate a chosen congregation of initiates. As their status depended on Amoghavajra's authority, they were tied together through ritual self-sacralization. In this way, the Master of Dharma became the director of liturgy, a high priest in the service of the state (Chin. *guoshi* 國師), who advanced the faith in a Buddhist praxis centered on the ritual aesthetics he had created.[57]

3   In turn, performance of rituals in the presence of a distinguished audience of Tang aristocrats and military leaders conscious of having the privilege to share a sanctifying experience was fundamental for the prominent status of Amoghavajra in relation to the imperial order. By the choice of events or incidents that could be interpreted as the object of apotropaic ritual performance, he was able to relate

social reality to mythical order. An opportunity to mythologize his own person of this type was given to Amoghavajra at the latest in the summer of 765, when he was asked by Emperor Daizong to prepare a new version of the "Scripture on Perfect Insight for Benevolent Kings" (*Renwang boreboluomi jing* 仁王般若波羅蜜經; late fifth century).[58] Authorized to serve as a thaumaturge for a "benevolent king," Amoghavajra finally became an imperial hierophant qualified for the mediation between social order and divine force.

The new version stressed governmental norms of state protection in Tantric terms: ritual practice devoted to the Vidyārāja Acala promised destruction to the enemy, divine empowerment, and control over social disorder (Orzech 1998, pp. 187–91). Charles Orzech has analyzed in detail how the new version[59] corresponded to the political circumstances of Emperor Daizong's reign. The former Tibetan–Uigur allies of Emperor Suzong had become a serious threat. In the winter of 765, Pugu Huai'en, a leading Uigur military commander, suddenly died and the alliance broke apart.[60] The fact that good fortune repeatedly stood by the Tang was interpreted as a result of Amoghavajra's liturgy based on the new version (Dalby 1979, p. 579). Subsequently, in 767, Amoghavajra initiated the ordination of thirty-seven monks for repeated ritual perform-ances on Mt. Wutai to "establish the state as a field of merit," referring to the *Vajradhātu-maṇḍala* and its thirty-seven central deities.[61]

By then, the circle of demythologization and remythologization between myth and secrecy had been completed. While the legend of the iron stūpa represented the introduction of the "secret teachings" to the Tang-court as a process of demythologization and intrusion of contingency into a teaching of mythic origin, the promotional pragmatics by which teaching and praxis actually spread worked the other way round, namely as a ritual aesthetics that reinscribed imperial and social order into myth and sacrality. The mandala of which the thirty-seven deities were ritually invoked emulated an ideal imperial order as the domain of sanctified power relations supervised by the hierophant. On the one hand the ritual sacralized the state as an administrative grid of salvific functions, on the other hand it conferred authority upon the hierophant as well as upon the emperor: In a quasi symbiotic interaction the former gained actual power and influence, the latter was granted sanctity.[62]

Amoghavajra's career followed a self-referential progress; he started as scholar-monk, turned into a "secret agent" in service of the emperor, and finally managed to remythologize himself in terms of the imperial order he had ritually sacralized. Because the ritual manuals were no longer considered to be direct expressions of divine origin but a means of mediation or contingent descriptions of ritual "technology," their implementation amounted to a "power of attorney" conferred upon the hierophant by divine force. Having presented secret transmission as a story of lost evidence, Amoghavajra was able to transfer the authority of the teaching onto his own person. By paying close attention to techniques and pragmatics, and by shrouding seemingly trivial details of ritual performance in a limpid rhetoric, he sublated the hidden "meaning" of a practice to a performative secrecy without any reference to secret content.[63] The conception of secrecy he put into practice constituted a process operating through transparency and concealment: Emphasizing practice, he himself became the secret that in turn made his performance appear authentic and sacral.

"... *it is called secret signs* ..." – recognition and words of truth

The case of Śubhakarasiṃha, who was initially not allowed to continue his activities of promulgation, exemplifies a situation in which actual power collides with the claim of spiritual sovereignty. Mutual recognition becomes a critical issue as soon as the hierophant – facing the emperor – has presented himself to be an authority in his own right: On the one hand, he claims to have mastered a secret knowledge by which divine forces superior to imperial power can be instrumentalized, on the other hand he presents himself as an instrument of imperial power, offering his services to the emperor. Hence he defines his role as a mediator between divine force and imperial power, presupposing that the latter needs (and is inferior to) the former, a precarious situation that implies – as was the case in medieval India – a crisis of imperial and social order.

At first, the hierophant derives his authority to mediate from a circular concept of empowerment,[64] secretion and exclusion: The praxis he aims to validate is his *raison d'être*, which in turn implies a claim of truth that justifies his authority (as opposed to the actual power embodied by the emperor). In order to make his authority unassailable, possession of truth is claimed on behalf of an exclusively realized absolute (cf. Sanderson 1995, p. 47), depicted as the myth of the *dharmakāya* Buddha (Vairocana) who is the central source of all Tathāgatas' attainment and skill in means, and who confers empowerment upon the hierophant. Subsequently, it is in the performative process itself that a law-like connection between the divine force and the hierophant is supposed to become perceptible, evident, and true. Implementing ritual sequences of gestures and speech acts, empowerment is represented as the perception of divine semiosis, suggesting that the world signifies before anyone knows what it signifies: secretion again. In ritual, the soteriologic signification of mundane reality is expressed by secret signs that evoke a sacral hierarchy in which the hierophant represents divine authority and truth. The function of language to convey meaning in ritual praxis[65] is deliberately limited by the use of mantric speech acts. Explicitly referring to the perception of secret signs, Śubhakarasiṃha and Yixing addressed mantric speech as *zhenyan* 真言:

> In Sanskrit called *mantra*, it is the sound of speech of truth, speech of suchness (Chin. *ru yu* 如語), not vain, invariable. In the treatise of Nāgārjuna it is called "secret signs" (Chin. *bimi hao* 秘密號). Obsolete translations read it "spell" (Chin. *zhou* 呪) which is an improper translation.[66]

Discussing the subjectification of ritual speech in his "General Explanation of the Meaning and Praise of Dhāraṇī" (*Zongshi tuoluoni yizan* 總釋陀羅尼 義讚, d. between 746 and 74), Amoghavajra concluded that mantric speech acts do not represent the absolute but are intrinsic expressions of the *dharmadhātu*, the "pure field of dharma" (Chin. *qing jing fajie* 清浄 法界; *nota bene*: not of the *dharmakāya* Buddha Vairocana).[67] To better understand this comprehension of the concept of *zhenyan* the subject of mantric speech should be considered first. Amoghavajra put it this way:

> Truth: that which is related to suchness.
> Words: purport of evidence of truth.[68]

As the statement by Śubhakarasiṃha and Yixing suggests, the Chinese term *zhenyan* was not conventionally interpreted in the sense of "true words." Instead, *zhenyan* should be read as *genitivus subjectivus*: "words of truth," which means words spoken *by* truth. There is no individual enunciation anymore, not even a self of enunciation; it is ritually personified truth that speaks. *Zhenyan* are words spoken by the absolute that reifies itself in speech as truth. Reified in ritual, the absolute has become phenomenal and the world is changed into a salvific field of religious praxis, the "field of dharma" (Chin. *fajie* 法界, Skt. *dharmadhātu*).

At first sight, this explanation appears to be a sophism. But if the ritual context is taken into account, "words of truth" operate as quotations embedded into illocutionary conglomerations of conditioned, translated, or compiled scriptures and ritual manuals; they are phenomenal incidences of the absolute. As a subject implementing "words of truth" ritually, the hierophant attains the unconditioned "pure field of dharma." Thereby, the self becomes the limit of reality, *bhūtakoṭi*, constituted by "words of truth": What appears to be a sophist conception of ultimate truth turns out to be a solipsism that marks the limits of signifiance. Therefore, in ritual praxis, "words of truth" mark the limitation of meaning; in other words, when claiming to remain true to the absolute, rituals inevitably have to retain their proper form of meaninglessness. In ritual performance, the hierophant mediates and – by the same act – divides the phenomenal and the absolute, drawing a line of demarcation between imperial power and divine force: Beyond any further need of epistemic justification, he makes himself the absolute secret. In this way – as a master of "words of truth" – the hierophant embodies an authenticity preceeding the imperial order, representing sovereignty as a matter of unconditional recognition, a recognition that no longer refers to any meaning.

Such conceptions of supra-human signifiance were not unknown to the Chinese and, in particular, to Emperor Xuanzong, who was trained in Daoist practice. Around the early sixth century, the Daoist Lingbao 靈寶 tradition had invented a somewhat similar approach relating a pseudo-Sanskrit to the divine sphere, though the mythical field of reference is set in a different way. In Lingbao, ritual speech operates through the linguistic indeterminacy of a "Hidden Language of the Great Brahmā" (Chin. *da fan yin yu* 大梵陰語), having located the origin of divine signifiers in a "Sanskritic" context by using graphs chosen by Buddhist translators to transcribe Sanskrit terms and spells. The result was a sort of Sanskrit-sounding hierolalia that was conceived to be a divine language transmitted down to the human realm.[69]

In the case of the "secret teachings," the argument that the Chinese translations were either abridged versions or fragments separated them from the very myth they served to establish and helped to promote the notion that the absolute remained authentic in unintelligible signifiers of the ultimate truth. It was well understood that mantric speech acts – although complying with Sanskrit words and syllables[70] – could not be subject to interpretation, nor was there a provision of genuine Chinese *zhenyan*.[71] Apart from the syllabic Siddham script, a specific set of Chinese graphs containing the "mouth" radical (Chin. *kou* 口) was alternatively used, indicating that both reproduce – as was the case in Sanskrit practice – syllables to be uttered without a contingent meaning to be interpreted (cf. van Gulik 1980, p. 72–79). Consequently, the gap between ordinary language and mantric speech is felt more thoroughly in the Chinese texts than in Sanskrit. In terms of justification, the use of Siddham syllables and their Chinese transcriptions further emphasized the principal distinction between an ordinary language such as Chinese that can be understood, and – on the other hand – something ultimately secret and authenticating: the signifying regime of unintelligible signs of the absolute, to which the hierophant claims to have exclusive access.

Concluding remarks

By now, it should have become clear, why it makes sense to distinguish the Greek concept of *esoterikòs* referred to at the beginning from the functions of secrecy presented on the following pages. From the perspective of transmission and social distinction, the "secret teachings" seem to build on a similar concept of secrecy as the Chan/Zen-Buddhist transmission of sudden enlightenment: both depend largely on orally transmitted knowledge and subtle techniques that were exclusively shared between master and disciple, creating a thread of legitimacy with regard to their succession.

However, this would underestimate the epistemic aspects of the "secret teachings," which relate social functions and imperial order in a mythical framework. Similar to the brahmin in the ancient Vedic social order, where secrecy played a significant role in the transmission and ritual practice of the Veda, the masters of the "secret teachings" at the Tang-court presented themselves as mediators of sacrality, tying together Buddhist soteriology and imperial order in ritual performance. As a performative expression of secrecy, secretion was vital for the spread of certain practices through the imperial order: Buddhist rituals of state protection performed by meticulously chosen initiates at the Tang-court established new hierarchies of sacral inclusion and exclusion by radiating signs and coded speech. Validated by initiation suggesting sanctity, legitimatized by consecration, these practices helped to establish an authority free of the confines of institutionalized denominations, which surpassed imperial and administrative power.

Amoghavajra's outstanding success – as compared to his predecessors – was the result of his ability to turn the historical and social circumstances to his advantage and to convince the Tang-court that the hermeneutic shroud he had skilfully woven around his person constituted an empowering liturgy of state protection. The related praxis was not only part of a legitimatizing strategy that was implemented in order to deal with imperial power and to promote the Dharma; it was also concomitant to a solipsistic concept of ultimate truth. Facing imperial power, the "secret teachings" resulted in a dialectical reversal of the impossibility to verify an unconditional truth claim dependent on the inherent solipsism of Buddhism. The Chinese term *zhenyan*, "words of truth," epitomized the whole paradoxon.

If we conclude that the dialectic relation between secretion and myth created a movement of mythologization by demythologization and remythologization, this does not imply that we are trapped in a vicious circle. Rather, such a conclusion highlights a self-referential progress of ritual expressivenenss beyond the confines of tenet classification, doctrines of esoterism, and sectarian history: Assuming an ubiquitous yet multiple status as organizing policy, secrecy was a functional part of the conceptual scheme; it passed through the narrative of transmission, the linguistics of translation, and the epistemic concept of language; even the authority of individual promulgators was based on secrecy. This "blind spot" of soteriologic perspective – the ultimate secretion so to speak – may have been the final clue that made this religious praxis appear meaningful, until new foundations of ritual praxis and social order were conceived by Confucian scholars during the Song-period.

Notes

1 Some formative patterns common to most Tantric practices were determined by White 2000, pp. 7–18 and pp. 24–34. For a detailed historical account of the conception of "Tantrism" as a western phantasm, see the work of Hugh B. Urban (2003). For a discussion on the foundations of esoteric Buddhism in eighth- to tenth-century China and Japan, see Orzech 1998, pp. 125–28, 191–206; Abé 1999, pp. 202–04; Sharf 2002, pp. 263–78.

Questions, as to which practices or doctrines belong to Tantric Buddhism, or whether they can be distinguished from "standard" Mahāyāna or "sinified Buddhism" at all, depend on the respective research strategy. Such questions tend to become bothersome as soon as they refer to essentialist categories, the self-institution of a religion, or the foundations of orthodoxy, since these problems inevitably involve metaphysical considerations. To acknowledge the relativity of categories, on the other hand, does not mean to subscribe to nihilism but to question different accounts of meaning, validation, and justification with regard to their discursive, social, and historical circumstances; cf. Vasilache 2003, pp. 84–88. Besides, the reproof of nihilism in turn depends on the notion of a preconceived authentic (if not transcendent) truth; cf. Rorty 2001, p. 35.

2 Cf. the Buddhologic representation by Tajima 1992, pp. 215–16, 218–19, as well as Wayman's comment, Wayman 1992, pp. 351–54. The traditional *ken-mitsu* 顯密-paradigm as a way to integrate different schools of Buddhism in a normative exoteric/esoteric-taxonomy seems to be a Japanese phenomenon which does not fit the Chinese situation. Even the Japanese case is still not well understood with regard to its historical status, as the recent discussions on Kuroda Toshio's approach to medieval Japanese Buddhism indicate; see the brief review by Abé 1999, pp. 416–28.

3 For details, see Petzold 1995, pp. 493–500, 523, 527–28, 551, 557–62 (for Tōmitsu), and pp. 573–74, 582–94 (for Taimitsu).

4 The imposition of social division on a distinct community is the central purpose of esoterism; e.g. the social division established between the esoteric and the exoteric Pythagoreans was based on such a functionalist understanding of esoterism; cf. Gorman 1979, pp. 120–24.

5 *Da Piluzhena chengfo jing shu* 大毘盧遮那成佛經疏, T 1796.39.579c29.

6 *Daizong chao zeng sikong dabianzheng guangzhi sanzang heshang biaozhi ji* 代宗朝贈司空大辨正廣智三藏和上表制集, T 2120.52.827c28.

7 On Zanning and his systematizing as well as for an apologetic historiography of Buddhism, see Welter, 1999, pp. 21–61; cf. Guo 1981, pp. 151–56. Zanning himself tried to construe a Chinese Buddhist antiquity to prove its validity and commensurability with Confucian and Daoist beliefs. His systematization served exegetical aims and was not meant to document historical developments in a strict sense. On Zanning's approach to Buddhist scriptures, literature, and translation, see Wang 1984, pp. 277–89.

8 *Song gaoseng zhuan*, T 2061.50.724b16–19; cf. Sharf 2002, p. 271.

9 *Fozu tongji*, T 2035.49.295b11–14, 373b26–c25; *Shimen zhengtong*, DNBZ 130.460c–462c; Sharf 2002, p. 276.

10 Kieschnick 1997, pp. 76–77, 80, 89.

11 See the historical survey by McBride 2004, pp. 332–54.

12 Traditionally attributed to Nāgārjuna, it is only preserved in a Chinese version composed by Kumārajīva (350–413); French tr. Lamotte (1944–80). The text refers to Kumārajīva's translation of the *Pañcaviṃśati-sāhasrikā-prajñāpāramitā* (*Da pin boreboluomi jing* 大品般若波羅蜜經, d. 403–04; T 223). Kumārajīva's activities as translator and exegete in general as well as this

commentary in particular were of seminal importance for the foundation of Mahāyāna and Buddhist scholasticism in China; see Demiéville 1973, pp. 470–90.

13 *Da zhidu lun*, T 1509.25.84c19–85b6, 517a29–b20, 597b16–22, 754b15–26; cf. Sharf 2002, p. 340, nn. 20, 21.

14 On this problem of Buddhist praxis, see Obert 2000, pp. 239–42.

15 Significantly, Charles Orzech interprets the problem of the twofold truth in cosmologic terms, see Orzech 1998, pp. 48–50.

16 This in turn establishes definite relations between the practicing subject and a concept of truth which is constituted differently in the religious, mystic, and magic aspects of the "secret teachings," see Lehnert 2001, pp. 997–1001.

17 *Jingangding yujia zhong fa anouduoluo sanmiao sanputi xin lun*, T 1665.39. 574a18–20.

18 Cf. the discussion on the secret in Deleuze/Guattari 1987, pp. 286–87, 299, 544 n. 79.

19 Śubhakarasiṃha was born in 637 as a royal descendant in a country located in today's Orissa. He abdicated the throne and became a Buddhist monk. He stayed at Nālandā monastery, a famous center of Buddhist learning, and undertook several pilgrimages. Finally, he left for China, and in 716 he arrived in the Tang capital Chang'an, bringing with him a collection of manuscripts of which he was able to translate only a few. In 732, his request to return to India was declined by the emperor. Śubhakarasiṃha died in 735, in his ninety-ninth year.

Vajrabodhi was born in 671 in South India as the son of a brahmin. At the age of sixteen he became a monk and studied at Nālandā. He went to China by the sea route, and in 720 arrived in Chang'an. The emperor came to have confidence in Vajrabodhis's thaumaturgical skills, and ordered the translation of several texts in 723. In 741, his seventy-first year, Vajrabodhi was allowed to return to India, but he died en route during a stay at Luoyang.

Amoghavajra was born in 705 in North India; his father, a brahmin, died early. In his childhood, Amoghavajra visited China together with his uncle; in 718, during a stay in Java, Amoghavajra became a disciple of Vajrabodhi. Together they reached Chang'an in 720. At the age of twenty he was fully ordained and became an expert in monastic discipline. Because of his linguistic skills, he assisted his master with translation work, and finally Vajrabodhi agreed to initiate him into the practices of the "secret teachings." After Vajrabodhi's death in 741, Amoghavajra went to Ceylon and India, as his master had ordered him to do, to collect texts and to further pursue his studies. After his return to the Tang in 746 he made an exceptional career and gained strong support at the court. He died in 774, in his seventieth year, honored by the imperial family.

For further biographical as well as historical details, see Chou 1945, pp. 251–72, 272–84, 284–307, 321–22.

20 Later, a modified version of Vajrabodhi's/Amoghavajra's narrative was related by Kūkai (空海, 774–835). He referred to an oral transmission of his teacher Huiguo (惠果, 746–805), in Japan revered as the disciple and successor of Amoghavajra. This story is of great significance for the construction of a transmission lineage of "secret teachings" from India to Japan and adds further details to authenticate and validate Kūkai's status; see Tajima 1992, pp. 237–40; cf. Orzech 1995, pp. 314–15; on Huiguo and Kūkai, see Abé 1999, pp. 120–27, cf. Orzech 1998, pp. 146, 150, 201; Sharf 2002, p. 272.

21 *Jingangding jing da yujia bimi xindi famen yijue*, T 1798.39.808a18–19; tr. Orzech 1995, p. 316.

22 Ibid., T 1798.39.808a21–24; tr. Orzech 1995, p. 316. In China, the apocryphal "Scripture of Brahma's Net" (*Fanwangjing* 梵王經; mid-fifth century; T 1484) became a source book of bodhisattva precepts and lay Buddhist praxis; the scripture condemns thaumaturgic and divinatory practices for profit-making purposes in particular; Strickmann 1996, pp. 324–26.

23 In medieval India, the Tantric ceremony of consecration alluded to the exclusiveness of the Brahmanic priest to ritually confirm the divinity of the king and bestow legitimacy upon him by means of ritual unction (Skt. *abhiṣeka*); see Davidson 2002, pp. 122–31. The earliest source for an employment of this Tantric Buddhist ritual, however, was written in China. The apocryphal "Consecration Scripture" (*Guanding jing* 灌頂經, fifth century) conceived the consecration of an initiate similar to the investiture of a prince into state-affairs. Parts of this scripture are influenced by Daoist initiation documents (Chin. *lu* 録), suggesting a rather pragmatic interchangeability of Daoist and Buddhist rituals; see Strickmann 1996, pp. 82–85, Kuo 1994, pp. 160–62; for the original description of the consecration ritual, see *Fo shuo guanding jing* 佛説灌頂經, T 1331.21.497b5–24.

24 By using the term "secretion," I would like to emphasize the very act by which concealment is established. "Secretion," therefore, also applies to secrets without content, i.e. where one cannot speak of concealed contents in a strict sense.

25 *Jingangding jing [...] yijue*, T 1798.39.808a24–28; tr. Orzech 1995, p. 316.

26 Ibid., T 1798.39.808a28–b3; tr. Orzech 1995, p. 316. The text mentioned is the "Scripture of Essential Recitations Expounded by the Great Vairocana Buddha" (*Da Piluzhena fo shuo yaolüe niansong jing* 大毘盧遮那佛説要略念誦經; d. between 723 and 736; T 849), translated by Vajrabodhi.

27 The term *siddhi* (lit. "perfection") refers to occult techniques implemented in order to achieve mundane benefit as well as accomplishment on a larger soteriologic scale up to enlightenment; dealing with *siddhi*, the "Scripture on What is Good to Produce Success" (*Susiddhikara-sūtra*, Chin. *Suxidijieluo jing* 蘇悉地羯羅經, d. 726; T 893) consequently places a bearer of *siddhi*, the *siddha*, on the same hierarchic level as the "Three Jewels" (i.e. Buddha, Dharma, Samgha), and with regard to his (occult) skills compares him to a bodhisattva or buddha; see T 893.18.605a4–7; tr. Giebel 2001, p. 136.

28 *Jingangding jing [...] yijue*, T 1798.39.808b3–6, b8–9; tr. Orzech 1995, pp. 316–17.

29 The term "hierophant" is used in an etic sense emphasizing principal functions of the *ācārya* ("teacher") and *siddha*. Being part of a divine hierarchy, the hierophant has access to and interprets secret/sacred knowledge; he appoints and initiates chosen disciples to fulfill sacral duties. In this way, a hierophant creates and represents hierarchically structured groups that follow secret rules and sacred roles, often displayed in ritual practice. The environment he creates imposes belief systems that foster an awareness of exclusiveness and group identity.

30 *Jingangding jing [...] yijue*, T 1798.39.808b9–11; tr. Orzech 1995, p. 317.

31 Ibid., T 1798.39.808b11–16; tr. Orzech 1995, p. 317.

32 On such transitions of myth in relation to the state and to history, see Clastres 1977, p. 169.

33 *Jingangding jing [...] yijue*, T 1798.39.808b16–25; tr. Orzech 1995, p. 317.

34 Ibid., T 1798.39.808b22; tr. Orzech 1995, p. 317.

35 The *lüeben* presents itself as a condensed version of the first part of the "one-hundred-thousand-verse text" whereas the "Indications" outline the structure and central contents of that lost text. About the "Indications ..." (T 869), see Giebel 1995, pp. 107–17; cf. T 869.18.284–87.

36 *Jingangding jing [. . .] yijue*, T 1798.39.808b25–28; tr. Orzech 1995, p. 317.
37 Cf. Xuanzang's (玄奘; 600–64) quest for complete translations, textual fidelity and equivalence between the Sanskrit and the Chinese wording, and his criticism of earlier translations that did not match his standards; Lehnert 1999, pp. 109–15; see *Da Ciensi sanzang fashi zhuan* 大慈恩寺三藏法師傳, T 2053.50.259a13–28.
38 A contingent event is one that does not necessarily take place, i.e. that may happen if something else happens; the problem here is that scriptures which claim to be unconditioned expressions of the absolute, but may have suffered changes due to contingent events, can no longer be taken as true whatever the circumstances.
39 Note that my translation differs from Orzech's rendered above; on the Chinese key terms *yi* 意 and *yi* 義 denoting intent and meaning, cf. Andersen 2001, p. 172.
40 See the general survey by Wang 1984, pp. 203–96.
41 The number of advanced students allowed for full initiation by Amoghavajra was very limited, "Many are the disciples who have entered the altar to receive the *Dharma*. Eight of them have been nurtured and established in the [Yoga of the] Five Sections [. . .], and two of these died, leaving six persons [so trained]." *Daizong chao [. . .] biaozhi ji*, T 2120.52.844a28–29; tr. Orzech 1998, p. 150.
42 Nevertheless, it would be inappropriate to regard secrecy in ritual praxis merely as obscurantism, since this would insinuate that the ritual act was deliberately conceived to be devoid of (intrinsic) meaning and content; cf. Staal 1975, p. 66.
43 T 2154.55.572a12–15; cf. Chou 1945, p. 265, n. 78.
44 Cf. Weinstein 1987, pp. 54–55; Orzech 1998, p. 139.
45 See Chen 2000, pp. 1–38; cf. Weinstein 1987, pp. 55–56.
46 On the relationship between Xuanzong and Vajrabodhi, see Weinstein 1987, p. 55; Kieschnick 1997, pp. 77, 89.
47 On Amoghavajra's practice of translation, compilation, and composition of scriptures supposedly of Indian origin, see Strickmann 1996, pp. 80–81.
48 *Siddhas* (lit. "Perfected Ones") being in possession of *siddhi* (cf. note 27) were considered to embody divine sovereignty; as such they represent a Buddhist notion of "cosmocracy." See Orzech 1998, pp. 50–53.
49 Davidson 2002, pp. 160–68, 174–75, 187–90, 194–201.
50 On "sāmanta-feudalism" as a system of administrative and political order in medieval India, see Chattotpadhyaya 1994.
51 Davidson 2002, pp. 131–44. For a buddhologic interpretation of the term *maṇḍala* in terms of *adhiṣṭhāna*, see Wayman 1999, pp. 24–28.
52 On An Lushan, see Dalby 1979, pp. 561–71.
53 *Daizong chao [. . .] biaozhi ji*, T 2120.52.827c24–828a24, 849a1–5; see Chou 1945, pp. 294–95; Orzech 1998, pp. 141–42, 201.
54 Dalby 1979, p. 579; Peterson 1979, pp. 484–86.
55 On the reign of Daizong, see Dalby 1979, pp. 571–80; on the relationship between Daizong and Amoghavajra; cf. Weinstein 1987, pp. 77–89.
56 In his "Indications . . .," Amoghavajra explicitly refers to the "nine tastes" (Chin. *jiu wei* 九味, Skt. *navarasa*), a central concept of Indian dramaturgy, when describing the ninth assembly of the *Vajraśekhara-sūtra* the following way:

> "Herein is explained the *yoga* whereby one makes of one's own person the chief deity, and it criticizes the *yogin* who makes of images outside the body [the chief deity]. It expounds extensively the principle of reality, as well as explaining the methods of *yoga*, which are endowed with nine

tastes, namely, 'splendour' (Vajrasattva), 'valour' (Vairocana), 'great compassion' (Vajradhara), 'mirth' (Avalokiteśvara), 'anger' (Vajrateja), 'terror' (Trailokyavijaya), 'disgust'" (Śākyamuni Buddha), 'wonder' (Vajrahāsa), and 'tranquillity' (Vairocana in *yoga*). *Jingangding [. . .] zhigui*, T 869.18.286c10–14; tr. Giebel 1995, pp. 179–82.

57 Since rituals appear to be techniques of auto-suggestion, one might conclude that Amoghavajra and his disciples were themselves taken in by their own acting, implying that they conceived the rituals as exercises in aesthetic imagination and that they allowed themselves to be affected as if that imagination were real; cf. Staal 1975, p. 149. However, one should resist the temptation to regard ritual practice as a simulation deliberately implemented to delude the court, as one would run the risk of interpreting this religious praxis according to modern concepts, presupposing a prevalence of rational criticism. Whether one maintains that such experience is created by divine empowerment or merely by a hysteric imagination effectuated by ritual aesthetics, as soon as it is accepted as meaningful for the person in question, one has to acknowledge that this person is in possession of objects of belief, that must not be understood in terms of mere conceptions that the intellect accepts as true. In fact, one can only assume that the ritual praxis was focused on religious experience in the sense of an inner self-attestation of divine force in a framework of myth and pragmatic teaching.

58 The former version, *Renwang boreboluomi jing*, traditionally attributed to Kumārajīva, was suspected to be an "apocryphal scripture" (*yijing* 疑經) or a Chinese "forgery" (*weijing* 偽經); it is of late-fifth-century origin (Orzech 1998, pp. 125–33, 289–91). Emperor Daizong wrote an imperial foreword to Amoghavajra's version *Renwang huguo boreboluomiduo jing* (T 246.8.834a10–b25). On the imperial commission for an actualization of the text, see also *Daizong chao [. . .] biaozhi ji*, T 2120.52.831b20–c4.

59 *Renwang huguo boreboluomiduo jing*. English translation in Orzech 1998, pp. 209–74.

60 Peterson 1979, pp. 489–92; Weinstein 1987, pp. 77–79.

61 *Daizong chao [. . .] biaozhi ji*, T 2120.52.835b17–c9; Orzech 1998, p. 161.

62 Michel Strickmann understood the self-referential structure outlined above as reciprocity between royal power and religious authority: "La participation royale au rituel tantrique est un thème qui imprègne la littérature tout entière, et ce n'est pas par accident que le mystère central du tantrisme, la consécration, a été modelé à partir de l'ancien rituel indien de l'investiture royale. Il n'a pas seulement transformé les moines en rois tantriques, mais également les rois en maîtres tantriques." Strickmann 1996, p. 40.

63 Cf. Poul Andersen's discussion of theoretical approaches to "meaning" in Daoist ritual praxis, Andersen 2001, pp. 162–71; cf. Sharf 2003, pp. 51–55, 85.

64 Similar in Śaiva Tantric ritual; Sanderson 1995, p. 49.

65 See Andersen 2001, pp. 162–66.

66 *Da Piluzhena chengfo jing shu*, T 1796.39.579b19–21.

67 *Zongshi tuoluoni yizan*, T 902.18.898a24; cf. also the Buddhologic representation of this topic according to the *Vairocanābhisaṃbodhi* by Wayman 1992, pp. 62–64. Kūkai, on the other hand, remythologized mantric speech as specific utterance of Vairocana, the *dharmakāya* Buddha, a notion that refers to the Mahāyāna soteriology of the preaching *dharmakāya*. The *dharmakāya* is the absolute reified as a salvific plan of meaning and becoming, to which the manifold levels of Buddhist praxis correspond. Consequently, Kūkai claimed that the texts of *mikkyō* were self-reifications of the absolute. The world is the primal text, then there is the mythical scripture which was transmitted by Vajrasattva to Nāgārjuna in the iron stūpa. Finally, there is the abridged

version of this scripture, transmitted to China and translated into Chinese; see Abé 1999, pp. 213–23; cf. Wayman 1992, pp. 61, 79 n. 15.

68　*Zongshi tuoluoni yizan*, T 902.18.898a23.

69　Bokenkamp 1997a, pp. 63–67; 1997b, pp. 8, 385–92. Pointing out this analogy does not mean to construe some sort of conceptual continuity; it refers to the ritual function of speech acts as quotations of unintelligible signifiers that allude to Sanskrit without being conceived as elements of ordinary language.

70　*Zongshi tuoluoni yizan*, T 902.18.898b21.

71　Xuanzang refused to translate *dhāraṇī* because he considered them to be secret signs beyond the possibility of interpretation. Their expressiveness is limited to effectiveness (Wang 1984, p. 266).

References

Primary sources

Da Ciensi sanzang fashi zhuan 大慈恩寺三藏法師傳, by Huili 慧立. T 2053.50. 220–80.

Da Piluzhena chengfo jing shu 大毘盧遮那成佛經疏, by Yixing 一行. T 1796.39. 579–790.

Da Piluzhena fo shuo yaolüe niansong jing 大毘盧遮那佛説要略念誦經, Vajrabodhi (tr.). T 849.18.55–65.

Da zhidu lun 大智度論, Kumārajīva (tr.). T 1509.25.57–757.

Daizong chao zeng sikong dabianzheng guangzhi sanzang heshang biaozhi ji 代宗朝贈司空大辨正廣智三藏和上表制集, by Yuanzhao 圓照. T 2120.52.826–60.

Fo shuo guanding jing 佛説灌頂經, Śrīmitra (tr.). T 1331.21.495–536.

Fozu tongji 佛祖統紀, by Zhipan 志磐. T 2035.49.129–475.

Jingangding jing da yujia bimi xindi famen yijue 金剛頂經大瑜伽秘密心地法門義訣, Amoghavajra. T 1798.39.808–23.

Jingangding jing yujia shiba hui zhigui 金剛頂經瑜伽十八會指歸, Amoghavajra. T 869.18.284–87.

Jingangding yujia zhong fa anouduoluo sanmiao sanputi xin lun 金剛頂瑜伽中發阿耨多羅三藐三菩提心論, Amoghavajra. T 1665.39.572–75.

Kaiyuan shijiao lu 開元釋教録, by Zhisheng 智昇. T 2154.55.372–723.

Renwang boreboluomi jing 仁王般若波羅蜜經, attributed to Kumārajīva (tr.). T 245.8.825–34.

Renwang huguo boreboluomiduo jing 仁王護國般若波羅蜜多經, Amoghavajra (tr.). T 246.8.834–45.

Shimen zhengtong 釋門正統, by Zongjian 宗鑑. DNZ 130.357–463.

Song gaoseng zhuan 宋高僧傳, by Zanning 贊寧. T 2061.50.709–901.

Suxidijieluo jing 蘇悉地羯羅經 (Skt. *Susiddhikara-sūtra*), Śubhakarasiṃha (tr.). T 893.18.603–92.

Zongshi tuoluoni yizan 總釋陀羅尼義讚, Amoghavajra. T 902.18.898.

Modern Sources

Abé, Ryūichi (1999), *The Weaving of Mantra: Kūkai and the Construction of Esoteric Buddhist Discourse*. New York: Columbia University Press.

Andersen, Poul (2001), "Concepts of Meaning in Chinese Ritual." *Cahiers d'Extrême-Asie* 12, pp. 155–83.

Bokenkamp, Stephen R. (1997a), "The Yao Boduo Stele as Evidence for the 'Dao-Buddhism' of the Early Lingbao Scriptures." *Cahiers d'Extrême-Asie* 9, pp. 55–67.

Bokenkamp, Stephen R. (1997b), *Early Daoist Scriptures*. Berkeley and Los Angeles: University of California Press.

Chattotpadhyaya, Brajadulal (1994), *The Making of Early Medieval India*. New Delhi: Oxford University Press.

Chen, Jinhua (2000), "The Birth of a Polymath: The Genealogical Background of the Tang Monk-Scientist Yixing (673–727)." *T'ang Studies* 18/19, pp. 1–39.

Chou, I-liang (1945), "Tantrism in China." *Harvard Journal of Asiatic Studies* 8, pp. 241–332.

Clastres, Pierre (1977), Robert Hurley (tr.), *Society against the State*. New York: Urizen.

Dalby, Michael T. (1979), "Court Politics in Late T'ang Times," in Denis Twitchett and John K. Fairbank (eds), *The Cambridge History of China* vol. 3, part 1. Cambridge: Cambridge University Press, pp. 561–681.

Davidson, Ronald M. (2002), *Indian Esoteric Buddhism: A Social History of the Tantric Movement*. New York: Columbia University Press.

Deleuze, Gilles and Félix Guattari (1987), Brian Massumi (tr.), *A Thousand Plateaus: Capitalism and Schizophrenia*. Minneapolis: University of Minnesota Press.

Demiéville, Paul (1973), *Choix d'Études Bouddhiques (1929–1970)*. Leiden: E.J. Brill.

Faure, Bernard (2004), Janet Lloyd (tr.), *Double Exposure: Cutting Across Buddhist and Western Discourses*. Stanford: Stanford University Press.

Giebel, Rolf W. (1995), "The Chin-kang-ting ching yü-ch'ieh shih-pa-hui chih-kuei: An Annotated Translation." *Journal of Naritasan Institute for Buddhist Studies* 18, pp. 107–201.

Giebel, Rolf W. (tr.) (2001), *Two Esoteric Sutras*. Berkeley: Numata Center for Buddhist Translation and Research.

Gorman, Peter (1979), *Pythagoras: A Life*. London: Routledge & Kegan Paul.

Guo Peng 郭朋 (1981), *Song Yuan Fojiao* 宋元佛教. Fuzhou: Fujian renmin chubanshe 福建人民出版社.

Kieschnick, John (1997), *The Eminent Monk: Buddhist Ideals in Medieval Chinese Hagiography*. Honolulu: University of Hawai'i Press.

Kuo, Li-ying (1994), *Confession et Contrition dans le Bouddhisme Chinois du Ve aux Xe siècle*. Paris: Publications de l'École Française d'Extrême-Orient.

Lamotte, Étienne (tr.) (1944–80), *Le Traité de la grande vertu de sagesse de Nāgārjuna*, 6 vols. Louvain: Institut Orientaliste.

Lehnert, Martin (1999), *Die Strategie eines Kommentars zum Diamand-Sūtra (Jingang-boruo-boluomi-jing Zhujie, T. 1703)*. Wiesbaden: Harrassowitz.

Lehnert, Martin (2001), "Anmerkungen zum wissenschaftlichen Umgang mit Texten des Esoterischen Buddhismus (mijiao)." *Asiatische Studien/Etudes Asiatiques* LV.4, pp. 995–1006.

McBride, Richard D, II. (2004), "Is there really 'Esoteric' Buddhism?" *Journal of the International Association of Buddhist Studies* 27/2, pp. 329–56.

Obert, Mathias (2000), *Sinndeutung und Zeitlichkeit*. München: Meiner.

Orzech, Charles D. (1995), "The Legend of the Iron Stūpa," in Donald S. Lopez, Jr. (ed.), *Buddhism in Practice*. Princeton: Princeton University Press, pp. 314–17.

Orzech, Charles D. (1998), *Politics and Transcendent Wisdom: The Scripture for Humane Kings in the Creation of Chinese Buddhism*. University Park: The Pennsylvania State University Press.

Peterson, C.A. (1979), "Court and Province in Mid- and Late T'ang," in Denis Twitchett and John K. Fairbank (eds), *The Cambridge History of China* vol. 3, part 1. Cambridge: Cambridge University Press, pp. 464–560.

Petzold, Bruno (1995), *The Classification of Buddhism: Bukkyō Kyōhan*. Wiesbaden: Harrassowitz.

Rorty, Richard (2001), "Sein, das verstanden werden kann, ist Sprache," in Rüdiger Bubner (ed.), *Sein, das verstanden werden kann, ist Sprache: Hommage an Hans-Georg Gadamer*. Frankfurt am Main: Suhrkamp, pp. 30–49.

Sanderson, Alexis (1995), "Meaning and Tantric Ritual," in Anne-Marie Blondeau and Kristofer Schipper (eds), *Essais sur le Rituel*, vol. 3. Louvain, Paris: Peeters, pp. 15–95.

Sharf, Robert H. (2002), *Coming to Terms with Chinese Buddhism: A Reading of the Treasure Store Treatise*. Honolulu: University of Hawai'i Press.

Sharf, Robert H. (2003), "Thinking Through Shingon Ritual." *Journal of the International Association of Buddhist Studies* 26/1, pp. 51–96.

Staal, Frits (1975), *Exploring Mysticism: A Methodological Essay*. Berkeley and Los Angeles: University of California Press.

Strickmann, Michel (1996), *Mantras et Mandarins: Le Bouddhisme Tantrique en Chine*. Paris: Editions Gallimard.

Tajima Ryūjun (1992), "Study of the Mahāvairocana-sūtra (Dainichikyō)," in Alex Wayman (ed. and tr.), *The Enlightenment of Vairocana*. Delhi: Motilal Banarsidass, pp. 207–347.

Twitchett, Denis (1979), "Hsüan-tsung (r. 712–56)," in Denis Twitchett and John K. Fairbank (eds), *The Cambridge History of China* vol. 3, part 1. Cambridge: Cambridge University Press, pp. 333–463.

Urban, Hugh B. (2003), *Tantra: Sex, Secrecy, Politics, and Power in the Study of Religion*. Berkeley and Los Angeles: University of California Press.

van Gulik, Robert H. (1980), *Siddham* (Śata-Piṭaka Series vol. 247). New Delhi: Aditya Prakashan.

Vasilache, Andreas (2003), *Interkulturelles Verstehen nach Gadamer und Foucault*. Frankfurt, New York: Campus.

Wang Wenyan 王文顔 (1984), *Fodian hanyi zhi yanjiu* 佛典漢譯之研究. Taibei: Tianhua chuban shiye 天華出版事業.

Wayman, Alex (1992), "Study of the Vairocanābhisaṃbodhitantra," in Alex Wayman (ed.), *The Enlightenment of Vairocana*. Delhi: Motilal Banarsidass, pp. 1–205.

Wayman, Alex (1999), "The Maṇḍa and the -la of the Term Maṇḍala," in N.N. Bhattacharyya and Amartya Ghosh (eds), *Tantric Buddhism. Centennial Tribute to Dr. Benoytosh Bhattacharyya*. New Delhi: Manohar, pp. 23–30.

Weinstein, Stanley (1987), *Buddhism under the T'ang*. Cambridge: Cambridge University Press.

Welter, Albert (1999), "A Buddhist Response to the Confucian Revival: Tsan-ning and the Debate over Wen in the Early Sung," in Peter N. Gregory and Daniel A. Getz, Jr. (eds), *Buddhism in the Sung*. Honolulu: University of Hawai'i Press, pp. 21–61.

White, David Gordon (2000), "Introduction, Tantra in Practice: Mapping a Tradition," in David Gordon White (ed.), *Tantra in Practice*. Princeton: Princeton University Press, pp. 3–38.

Part II
Japan's medieval culture of secrecy

5 Secrecy in Japanese esoteric Buddhism

Fabio Rambelli

In this essay I will address the issue of secrecy from the standpoint of the esoteric episteme and esoteric rituals. In addition, I will discuss the education process of Shingon initiates in which these rituals were transmitted. In particular, I will outline the main features of the epistemic field of medieval esoteric Buddhism in which the Japanese discourse of secrecy originated, the nature of the semiotic entities it employed, and the multileveled structure of meaning within which the esoteric signs were organized. By contextualizing the nature of secret knowledge within the ways in which the esoteric episteme was stored in texts and transmitted, it is possible to avoid the risk of reducing the teachings of esoteric Buddhism to a vague and ineffable mysticism.

The status of the "secret" in esoteric Buddhism

The discourse of Japanese esoteric Buddhism (in the following, Mikkyō 密教, lit. "secret teachings," "hidden doctrines"), particularly the Shingon tradition, developed in conjunction with the emergence of a distinctive form of philosophical reflection on signs and the formation of a corpus of practices relating to the production of meaning. In fact, esoteric Buddhism can be understood as a discursive formation that presupposes a particular cosmology, a particular attitude towards reality, and a particular episteme. It can be seen, in other words, as a system of knowledge and practices concerned with the interpretation of reality as well as with the production, selection, conservation, and transmission of knowledge. Like every discourse, that of esoteric Buddhism determines (and is determined by) distinctive institutions, ideologies, rituals, and power relations.

Mikkyō divides the Buddhist teachings into two general kinds: superficial (*kengyō* 顕教) and secret (*mikkyō*). Superficial teachings are the provisional doctrines that were taught by Śākyamuni, or, more generally, by lower, provisional manifestations of the Buddha: the *nirmāṇakāya* (the shape of the Buddha as he appears to ordinary sentient beings) and the *sambhoghakāya* (the sublime Buddha-body as it manifests itself to the bodhisattvas). The meaning of these teachings is clear and easy to comprehend. Secret teachings are "most profound doctrines that are beyond the faculties of sentient beings, dealing with the ultimate secrets of all buddhas' enlightenment."[1] As an unconditioned discourse spoken by the *dharmakāya* (Jap. *hosshin* 法身, lit. "Dharma-body," i.e. the absolute and unconditioned modality of existence of the Buddha) to himself for the pure pleasure of the Dharma, these teachings are envisioned as permanent and immutable. They are composed of "truth words" (*shinjitsugo* 真実語) that are free of all communicative, pragmatic, and contextual constraints.

Since Mikkyō claims to teach the contents of the Buddha's enlightenment (something which, according to other forms of Buddhism, is beyond representation and understanding), it would seem to *reveal* secret and hidden things and not to conceal them. This is the first and the most obvious problem we face when we translate the Sino-Japanese term *himitsu* 秘密 ("secret"). A possible clue to solve this paradox is that in the Buddhist tradition, secret is essentially contextual: it refers to something that is unknown to someone, but known to someone else. From the perspective of a self-defined "profound" doctrine, its content is "secret" (e.g. unknown) from the standpoint of a more superficial doctrine. Thus, the Buddhist precepts are "secret" for the non-Buddhists, in the same way as the Lotus sutra is "secret" for the members of the Lesser Vehicle. What is "secret" (unknown) to one tradition is the actual content of the teachings of another tradition. It is the duty of the depositaries of this "secret" knowledge to reveal it to people they consider worthy. In this way, we have two different regimes of secrecy: one that defines Shingon vis-à-vis the outside (what it knows in relation to whom), and one that organizes internal levels of instruction and attainment.

Kūkai 空海, in the *Ben kenmitsu nikyō ron* 弁顕密二教論 (On the distinctions between exoteric and esoteric teachings), defined two fundamental forms of secrecy: the "secret of sentient beings" (*shujō himitsu* 衆生秘密) and the "secret of the Tathāgata" (*nyorai himitsu* 如来秘密). Sentient beings are part of the twofold mandala and are innately endowed with its principles (*ri* 理) and with the wisdom (*chi* 智) to realize it; however, being hindered by ignorance, they do not know this. This is the "secret of the sentient beings" – or, more accurately, what is "unknown to sentient beings." In contrast, Mahāvairocana preaches the superficial teachings as skilful means according to the capacities and the situation of the audience, and therefore he does not reveal the most profound doctrines concerning his enlightenment: this is the "secret of the Tathāgata." However, Mahāvairocana does transmit the profound teachings to people with the right capacities to whom such secret teachings are no longer "secret."[2] In Kūkai's treatment, "secret" is the unknown, the unthought-of, that which is ignored – the outside of an intellectual system. The opposite of "secret" is that which is "revealed," "made-known," rather than that which is "evident." Secrecy is organized along a downward vertical axis – or, more precisely, a reversed pyramid. At the wide top are the evident truths, the exoteric teachings; secret teachings are situated deeper and deeper, and access to them is more and more limited. Thus, the secret of the Tathāgata is revealed to some, but kept secret from most; the secret being held from sentient beings has been revealed to all, but is unknown to most.

The Tendai monk Annen 安然 (841–95?) developed two more detailed typologies of secrecy, consisting respectively of four and six elements. The *Shingonshū kyōji gi* 真言宗教時義 (On the phases of the [development of the Buddhist] doctrines according to the Shingon ([i.e. Tendai]) school) describes four kinds of secrets:

1 Things kept hidden by the buddhas: buddhas preach only doctrines that can be understood by their audience as a strategy to spread Buddhism. This secret corresponds to Kūkai's secret of the Tathāgata.

2 Things secret to sentient beings: for example, ordinary people do not know that all sounds are mantras, but their ignorance is not due to the fact that the Buddha hides this truth from them: their limited capacities prevent them from knowing what is in this case self-evident. This secret corresponds to Kūkai's secret of sentient beings.

3 Linguistic secrets: words spoken by the buddhas have meanings that are deeper than they appear; "if one interprets them according to their written expression (*mon* 文), the intention of the Buddha (*butsui* 仏意) is lost." This is a reference to linguistic intension, in particular to the connotative aspects of signs, and to the existence of different levels of meaning (isotopies).

4 The secret of the Dharma-substance (*hottai* 法体): the enlightenment of the buddhas exceeds the capacities of people exposed only to exoteric teachings – even bodhisattvas can only experience this form of enlightenment through empowerment (*kaji* 加持), but do not experience it directly. This is a sort of ontological dimension of secrecy: only those who have undergone a certain training and have achieved the consequent bodily and cognitive transformations can understand this secret.[3]

This is a development of Kūkai's ideas on the subject. Two elements are relevant here, namely the recognition of semantic isotopies in language, so that each expression has several meanings that are usually unknown and, thus, "secret"; and the positing of a fundamental "secret" that is related to the ontological nature of the Dharma itself and that can be known only to those who have attained enlightenment.

In the *Bodaishingi* 菩提心義 (The meaning of *bodhicitta*), Annen puts forward a different typology, consisting of six kinds of secrets:

1   The subtle secret of the Dharma-substance (*hottai* 法体): this is the fact that the three secrets of the Tathāgata and those of sentient beings are originally one and the same. This is the basis of the doctrines of original enlightenment (*hongaku shisō* 本覚思想); of course, ordinary people are not aware of their innately enlightened nature and therefore do not know this secret.
2   The content of the enlightenment of the buddhas: this is the basis of the distinction between exoteric and esoteric teachings. As we have seen before, while the exoteric Buddha does not explain the content of his enlightenment, which thus remains a secret for his followers, Dainichi 大日 (Mahāvairocana) teaches his enlightenment (albeit only to some).
3   Things that cannot be taught to lowly, unworthy people: this kind of secret presupposes a sociology of esoteric transmission; "under-classes" (*hisen no hito* 卑賎ノ人) may have no access to it.
4   Things that ordinary people cannot comprehend because of their lack of enlightenment (or awareness): this level posits the existence of epistemological limits; even if they were taught something of this order, they would not understand it. This corresponds to Kūkai's secret of sentient beings.
5   Things that cannot be transmitted to those who have not yet practiced meditation (*samādhi*): this category presupposes steps in the education process; at each stage, the following stages are unknown, thus "secret."
6   Things that the practitioners keep secret (violations being a very serious sin): rules related to the management of initiatory knowledge and lineages.[4]

In this typology, Annen emphasizes the rules and presuppositions of initiatory lineages – issues related to the social control of meaning. Thus, there are things that cannot be revealed openly, not only because they would not be understood but also because of the social status or the level of the curriculum of some among the possible recipients; accordingly, the initiated should internalize this policing attitude toward "secret" meanings.

To summarize, the esoteric "secret" refers to a particular transmission from the Buddha, namely teachings revealed by the supreme Buddha, Mahāvairocana, to particularly worthy people. This is related to the definition of the esoteric Buddhist tradition, but it also implies procedures to establish who can be initiated into these doctrines. Moreover, these teachings are organized on several levels – which requires procedures to move from one level to the other.

The esoteric Buddhist episteme

What is the relation between the above definitions of secrecy, as related to a special transmission from the Buddha, and the actual contents of the esoteric teachings? An important element to emphasize in this regard is that esoteric Buddhism, far from ignoring the other traditions, is in fact based on them – but reverses or radically transforms the contents of their "exoteric" teachings. Accordingly, access to esoteric Buddhism presupposes an understanding of the classical Mahāyāna. A second element is that the esoteric teachings gradually came to be organized on two or four levels, each with its own characteristics. These two elements are in fact related to the basic features of the episteme of esoteric Buddhism and its semiotic system in particular.

While the Mahāyāna schools describe the Dharma-body – the absolute, the kernel of Buddhist ontology and soteriology – as devoid of signs and forms, Mikkyō describes it as the totality of all possible signs. The Dharma-body is thus able to "speak" and explain its own enlightenment to all beings – an absolute language exists that in some way is able to convey the ultimate reality. A particular semiotics governs such absolute language. In fact, within Mikkyō it is possible to recognize three different modes of semiotic knowledge and interpretive practice of reality. I will call these, respectively, semiosophia, semiognosis, and semiopietas.

Semiosophia refers to the various forms of semiotics developed by exoteric Buddhism (essentially, Abhidharma, Mādhyamika, and Yogācāra), according to which language and signs are arbitrary and illusory, but nevertheless usable as *upāya* ("skillful means") in order to indicate the supreme truth. Since esoteric semiotics presupposes forms of exoteric semiotics, semiosophia constitutes the superficial level (what exegetes called *senryakushaku* 浅略釈, lit. "abbreviated interpretation") on which the esoteric interpretive structure (*jinpishaku* 深秘釈, lit. "profound interpretation") is built; I call this next level *semiognosis*. *Semiognosis* denotes the discursive practices about signs typical of esoteric Buddhism. Predominantly ritual in character, semiognosis maintains that the initiatory knowledge concerning the structure, function, and power of esoteric symbols (especially mantric expressions and their graphic forms, the Siddhaṃ script) is the seed of enlightenment and the key to becoming a buddha in this very body (*sokushin jōbutsu* 即身成仏). In other words, esoteric Buddhism claims that salvation (and also various kinds of supernatural powers) can be extracted from signs, as they embody the general structure and power of the cosmos – which is none other than the Buddha Mahāvairocana himself. Finally, *semiopietas* concerns various forms of relating oneself to expressions of the sacred, such as diffuse beliefs and non-specialized practices of the uninitiated concerning such esoteric objects as sacred images, texts, amulets, and talismans.

Mikkyō exegetes operated at the level of semiognosis, on language and signs with the aim to "re-motivate" them, that is, to overcome their arbitrariness (as defined on the level of semiosophia) by finding a special "natural" relation between expression, meaning and the referential object. Re-motivation is accomplished by reorganizing each expression's semantic structure and thereby making the expression "identical" to its meaning. In this process, an esoteric symbol becomes a kind of replica of its object, and the practice in which it occurs is deemed identical to its goal. Mikkyō salvific practices consist mainly in visualization and manipulation of mantric signs – *shingon-darani* 真言陀羅尼 utterances and *shittan* 悉曇 (Skt. Siddhaṃ) characters – as well as other complex symbols of various kinds, whose very structure, organized on superficial and deep levels, appears to the initiated person as the inscription of the path to salvation and the attainment of mundane supernatural powers (*siddhi*). I would like to emphasize here that by signs I do not mean only linguistic expressions, but any form of representation (tools, icons, etc.).

The relation between semiosophia and semiognosis is represented by the two-level semantic structure of esoteric signs. The superficial level is called *jisō* 字相, and the deep, esoteric level is called *jigi* 字義. *Jisō* refers to a signification based on appearances, the shape of a sign: the primary meaning at this level is usually a term that begins with the same sound as its expression. For example, the *jisō* of the expression *va* is *vāc*, that is, "word, language." In this way, the syllable *va* is treated as the condensation of another sign that it stands for, namely *vāc*, whose meaning is illustrated according to mainstream exoteric teachings.

The structure of the true meaning, *jigi*, on the deep, esoteric level, is very complex. The *jigi* can be the opposite of the superficial meaning: in the case of the syllable *ha*, whereas the *jisō* is "cause" (from the Skt. *hetu*, "cause"), the *jigi* is "no causation" or "uncausedness." *Jigi* can also be – and this is more interesting from a semiotic viewpoint – a meta-term transcending the dichotomy (fallacious because it results from attachment to false ideas) between *jisō* and its contradictory. This meta-term is defined as "unobtainable" (*fukatoku* 不可得), an expression defining a situation of conceptual nondualism: the real meaning is "not obtainable" (unattainable) within ordinary language (since any concept can be denied by its contradictory), whose dichotomic nature it transcends. Once one reaches the semantic level of "unobtainability," one realizes the real nature of language and therefore reaches enlightenment. In the case of the mantric seed *ha*, the ultimate *jigi* is "cause is unobtainable." One should note that unobtainability is not the result of a process of negation as in the Buddhist traditional strategy established by Nāgārjuna. On the contrary, "unobtainability" presupposes the coexistence of all terms and concepts related to the original expression being analyzed as the ultimate consequence of esoteric polysemy. In other words, "unobtainability" renders the concepts it applies to not "empty" (as in Nāgārjuna's Mādhyamaka), but absolute, as elements of the unconditioned Dharma realm. Unobtainability can thus be understood as the ultimate goal of the interpretation process. It is situated outside semiosis, and it corresponds to the point at which a sign ceases to be a sign. An unattainable term transcends the articulations of sense and resists interpretation, situating itself at the level of nondualism.

This esoteric semantic structure was first defined by Kūkai in his *Bonmōkyō kaidai* 梵網経開題 (Explanation of the title of the *Brahmajāla-sūtra*), in which he associated *jisō* with exoteric Buddhism (*kengyō*) and *jigi* with esoteric Buddhism (*mikkyō*). However, Kūkai also put forth another interpretation, according to which *jisō* refers to the idea that each character (sign) has only one specific meaning, whereas *jigi* refers to the idea that each character (sign) has countless meanings. For example, in the case of the syllable *ha*, the *jisō* is "operation" (a synonym here of the previously mentioned "cause"), whereas the *jigi* is the unobtainability of operation (*sagō* 作業 *fukatoku*). *Fukatoku* is here a synonym of the Middle Path (*chūdō* 中道). Kūkai wrote, "When one contemplates un-obtainability [one sees that] all characters have penetrated the profound principle of the Dharma-nature; being all undifferentiated and homogeneous, one does not see individual meanings or features/signs" (quoted in *Mikkyō daijiten*, p. 959a). Whereas the theoretical basis for this doctrine can be found in the *Shōji jissō gi* (On the meaning of language and reality), similar arguments are made in many other texts, such as the *Unjigi* (On the meaning of the [mantra] *hūṃ*) and the *Bonji shittan jimo narabini shakugi* (On the Siddhaṃ Sanskrit letters and their meanings).

In this way, the pair *jisō/jigi* is almost interchangeable with another pair, *senryakushaku* (superficial meaning) and *jinpishaku* (profound meaning). Raihō 頼宝 (1279–1330?) gives the following definition of these two levels of meaning:

> Superficial [meaning] is like that of provisional words provisionally uttered by common folks and saintly people [i.e., monks]. When one interprets them, their meaning is shallow; sentences are long but their meaning is simple. [...] Profound [meaning] refers to the external manifestation of profound matters by the mind. Since these matters cannot be transmitted to unworthy people, they are called profound and secret.[5]

This definition presupposes that different cognitive attitudes toward language and signs result in different semiotic practices. Those for whom language is merely a conventional means of communication can only say and understand "shallow things" (obviously, from an ontological and soteriological point of view). However, in the case of those who understand the ontology of language and its role in the process of salvation, their utterances and semiotic activity in general constitutes "the external manifestation of profound matters by the mind." This is a form of unconditioned activity in which the enlightened mind, essentially identical with Mahāvairocana's mind, free of conditionings, puts forth micro-cosmic semiotic formations that embody the structure and the power of the universe. Levels of sense give a soteriological value to words, concepts, and phenomena, and therefore play a fundamental role in esoteric Buddhism as representations of its soteriologic trajectory.

Some medieval authors, most notably Raihō and Gōhō 杲宝 (1306–62), developed a fourfold system of semantic levels known as *shijū hishaku* 四重秘釈 (lit., "four levels of secret interpretation"). By expanding on the double structure of meaning (superficial/deep) discussed above, these authors envisioned each sign as endowed with four levels of sense: a superficial one (*senryakushaku*) and three secret ones (resp. *jinpishaku*, *hichū* 秘中 *jinpishaku* and *hihichū* 秘々中 *jinpishaku*). By following the interpretive process from one level to the other, the practitioner is able to realize the absolute and unconditioned nature of signs and, consequently, their salvific power. This is a connotative semiotics, in which each signified becomes the signifier of the sign on the next level. Let us look at this in more detail.

The superficial level (*senryakushaku* or *jisō*) is related to the shape or the sound of a Sanskrit character and is in any case part of the received, non-esoteric Buddhist conceptual system. The deep, or secret, level (*jinpishaku*, or *jigi*) constitutes a radical negation of the previous meaning. As we have already seen, if the superficial meaning of *vāc* is speech, its deep meaning is the unobtainability (*fukatoku*) of speech; if the superficial meaning of the Siddhaṃ character *ha* is "operation," its deep meaning is the unobtainability of operation. Unobtainability refers here to the fact that at this level signs are beyond dualistic distinctions. The third level is the secret within the secret meanings (*hichū jinpishaku*). The unobtainabillty we reached in the previous level is defined at this level as the superficial meaning (*jisō*), and the deep meaning (*jigi*) here is "perfect and luminous" (*enmyō* 円明). At the previous stage, we learned that the profound meaning of each sign is unobtainable; however, the idea remained that there might be something to obtain (such as the meaning or a referent) that is separate from the means of obtaining it (the sign); in other words, a distinction remained between signifier (*nōsen* 能詮) and signified (*shosen* 所詮). Thus, this is still a superficial meaning (*jisō*). The profound meaning is attained when one contemplates that there is no signified outside the signifier and that the sign as it stands is perfect and clear (*kyotai enmyō* 挙体円明). At the third level of sense, the distinction between signifier and signified has been surmounted and we reach a stage in which a sign is a "pure and perfect circle containing all virtues" (*rinnen shutoku* 輪円衆徳, *shōjō muku* 清浄無垢), that is, a sort of mandalic formation (see also Rambelli 1991). This is the level of emptiness (Skt. *śūnyatā*, Jap. *kūshō* 空性), in which there is nothing to obtain (*mushotoku* 無所得).

The fourth and last level is the most secret of the secret meanings (*hihichū jinpishaku*). The previous meaning, "perfect and clear" (*enmyō*) is the superficial level (*jisō*) of this stage, and a different distinction between signifier and signified is the new and ultimate deep meaning (*jigi*). At the previous level, the distinction between signifier and signified was abolished by a return to the homogeneous perfect purity of the one-mind (*isshin* 一心). The third level corresponds to the stage of eliminating delusions (*shajō* 遮情) in order to realize the principle of the single Dharma realm (*ichi hokkai* 一法界). However, characters are signifiers; the principles they signify are the substance (*tai* 体) of the universe; within perfect purity there is still another signifier and signified pair, and the three mysteries (*sanmitsu* 三密) are evident. This is the true meaning that expresses the virtues (*hyōtoku* 表徳) of the multiple Dharma realm (*ta hokkai* 多法界). Accordingly, at this ultimate level the superficial meaning (*jisō*) is the provisional doctrine of the single Dharma realm (*ichi hokkai*); the deep meaning (*jigi*) is the ultimate doctrine of the multiple Dharma realm (*ta hokkai*).

We can summarize the fourfold isotopic structure in the following way:

1   First level (*senryakushaku*): denotative meaning (common sense, or received Buddhist meaning).
2   Second level (*jinpishaku*): beginning of esoteric connotations – underlying doctrinal principles of a certain sign, concept, or object; "unobtainability" (*fukatoku*).
3   Third level (*hichū jinpishaku*): beyond the opposition of semioticity and signlessness (*usō* 有相 and *musō* 無相), this level indicates a fundamental principle of the Dharma as indicated by a specific sign, concept, or object; the sign embodies the single Dharma realm (*ichi hokkai*).
4   Fourth level (*hihichū jinpishaku*): the essence of the Dharma does not exist separately from each concept and object – this is, the level at which each sign is realized as being absolute and unconditioned; its distinctiveness is absolute and unconditioned, and it is part of the multiple Dharma realm (*ta hokkai*); this is the ultimate meaning of unobtainability.

A concrete example from the *Mikkyō daijiten* (p. 931c), namely the meanings of the offering of flowers and incense to the Buddha, helps us clarify this interpretive structure further:

1   Superficial level: offerings are made to please the Buddha.
2   Secret level: flowers represent the sum of all good deeds, and incense represents earnest devotion (*shōjin* 精進).
3   Secret within secrets level: each flower and each incense stick are produced by the combination of the six cosmic elements and are therefore differentiated aspects of Mahāvairocana and the Dharma realm.
4   Most secret level: there is no all-pervasive Dharma realm beyond each individual flower and incense stick; accordingly, offering one to a buddha means to offer it to the entire Dharma realm.

It is worth noting that the above fourfold structure was mostly employed to interpret concepts and objects, rather than for the contemplative analysis of mantric expressions. Mantras were subject to analogous processes of proliferation and dissolution of meaning that did not necessarily involve a systematic fourfold typology. Rather, the absolute nature of Siddhaṃ graphs was attained through vertiginous raids across the entire semantic encyclopaedia of the esoteric episteme.

Transmitting the secrets: The education process of Shingon scholar-monks

The esoteric episteme outlined above was transmitted and diffused in a particular educational process that became the primary paradigm for the transmission of knowledge in medieval Japan. The education of monks was finely tuned according to the class background and the specific hierarchical rank, position, and duties of each student. It ranged from semi-literacy, to memorization (more or less accurate) of scriptures and mantras, to highly sophisticated technical skills and philosophical learning. For example, the educational curriculum for children at the Ninnaji in the late Heian period consisted of the worship of the temple's guardian kami, reading short scriptures such as the Heart sutra, and chanting a *dhāraṇī* ("*Kujaku myōō*" 孔雀明王) and an invocation to Kūkai ("*Namu Henjō kongō*" 南無遍照金剛). Education proper consisted of learning to read and write, to compose prose and poetry, and to sing and make music. Children also learned how to play *go*, *sugoroku* (a board game), and *kemari* (kickball), and to practice archery.[6]

We can catch a glimpse of more specialized training through the regulations of the Kyōō Jōjūin 教王常住院, a centre of advanced studies in esoteric Buddhism founded by the retired emperor Go-Uda (1267–1324) at Daikakuji in the years following 1280. These regulations prescribed three major areas of study, each to be mastered in one year, for a total of three years. These areas were, respectively, the *Kongōchō-gyō* 金剛頂経, the *Dainichi-kyō* 大日経, and Buddhist chanting (*shōmyō* 声明) along with Sanskrit writing (*shittan*). Education consisted of listening to the lectures of scholar-monks for three months followed by an individual study period of three months, and at the end of these six months the student would receive the consecration (*kanjō* 灌頂) by an esoteric Buddhist master (*ajari* 阿闍梨).[7] Classes were usually held in a lecture–discussion format. The text constituting the main study material was addressed at the pace of one fascicle every ten days. For each assigned fascicle, the master first read the text and indicated its pronunciation, intonation, and punctuation. He then proposed an interpretation of relevant terms and sentences by referring to previous scholarship. At this point, first beginners and then more advanced students asked questions.[8] The fundamental form of higher learning in medieval Japan was a dialogic model known as *dangi* 談義 or *rongi* 論議, in which young scholar-monks were asked to illustrate a doctrinal theme and respond to questions from senior monks, who often upheld unorthodox views. In fact, many medieval texts were written in the context of such educational processes; this explains not only these texts' fragmentary nature but also their polyphony of voices and ideas as well as their freshness.

Strictly speaking, esoteric knowledge was transmitted not in a single operation, but in a number of separate transmission steps. In fact, transmission was not something that was achieved once and for all, but was a shifting element in an ongoing process that combined study, education, teaching, and ritual activities, leading one from the status of disciple to that of master. Because of the nature of such knowledge, not everyone was entitled to receive it; specific sacred rituals of initiation and/or consecration called *kanjō* were performed at the end of a specific training that involved taking classes, studying, and performing rituals. With their strict regulations, consecration rituals functioned as devices to control the meaning of and limit access to knowledge; they were also a means to control legitimacy.

Consecration (Jap. *kanjō*, Skt. *abhiṣeka*, often translated as "unction") is a ritual in which a master (Jap. *ajari*, Skt. *ācārya*) sanctions the transmission of the essence of esoteric Buddhism to a disciple. Literally, the term means "pouring (water) on (someone's) head" and stems from the central part of the ritual. Originally, *abhiṣeka* was performed in India as the enthronement ceremony for a new king or for the proclamation of the heir to the throne. Water especially drawn from the four oceans was sprinkled on the head of the new ruler (or the prince), symbolizing his legitimate control over the entire world. The adoption of this ritual within the esoteric tradition to signify the transmission of doctrines and practices reveals the constant circulation of religious and imperial imageries in Buddhism. In Japan, Saichō 最澄 (767 [or 766]–822) performed the first *kanjō* ceremony at Takaosanji 高雄山寺 in 805, and the first complete *kanjō* of the two mandalas was carried out by Kūkai (774–835) at the same temple in 812.

There are several forms of *kanjō*, classified in a number of ways and levels in various texts (see *Mikkyō daijiten*, pp. 409c–410c). The most common typology consists of five categories (*goshu sanmaiya* 五種三昧耶, "five kinds of *samaya* [symbolic activities leading to salvation]"). The first *samaya* is the worship of and giving of offerings to a mandala. This category corresponds to the rituals performed to a mandala (such as the *mandaraku* 曼荼羅供), and is not, properly speaking, a form of initiation. The second *samaya* is an initiation in which a karmic relationship with an aspect of esoteric Buddhism is established (*kechien kanjō* 結縁灌頂). In this rite, the initiand, with his (more rarely, her) eyes covered, is brought in front of a mandala, throws a flower on it, and on the basis of the deity upon which it lands the master teaches him/her a mantra and a mudra. The third *samaya* is performed when one becomes a disciple of a master (*jumyō kanjō* 受明灌頂, lit. "initiation in which a formula is bestowed [upon the disciple]"); in this *samaya*, a specific meditation object (mantra, mudra, and a visualization), among other things, is taught to the initiand. The second and the third *samaya* are, properly speaking, "initiations" – since they initialize a person's contact with Buddhism through a specific ritual practice. The fourth *samaya* is the most important called *denbō kanjō* 伝法灌頂 ("consecration ritual of the transmission of the Dharma"): it takes place after the disciple has completed a certain curriculum of study and religious practice and becomes thereupon a master himself. As such, this is not an "initiation," the training that precedes the change of status, but rather a "finalization" or "consecration" – a ritual of completion and attainment which follows a period of training (including both general education and religious practice) and constitutes the official sanctioning of knowledge/status that has been acquired through this study and practice. In rites of passage, described by Van Gennep and later by Victor Turner as divided into three stages, *kanjō* corresponds to the third stage, that of "reintegration" into the clergy as a master, and into the mythical/ritual world of esoteric Buddhism as a "double" or an embodiment of the first master. A fifth *samaya* also exists, a "secret initiation" (*himitsu kanjō*) performed on particular occasions and for special recipients; it leaves open the theoretical possibility of a spontaneous and innate realization of the esoteric truth (*jinenchi* 自然智) – a transmission without master that constitutes the ideal form of esoteric enlightenment. However, since the fourth *samaya*, the *denbō kanjō*, is the most systematic and complete, let us examine it more in detail.

The consecration proper is preceded by a phase of purification of body and mind that is articulated in four kinds of rituals (*shido kegyō* 四度加行, lit. "four additional practices"), which can last from one week to a hundred days. These four activities are the *jūhachidō hō* 十八道法, the *kongōkai hō* 金剛界法, the *taizōkai hō* 胎蔵界法, and the *goma hō* 護摩法. The *jūhachidō hō* consists of the basic practical concepts concerning the performance of esoteric worship (*kuyō* 供養). The *kongōkai hō* and the *taizōkai hō* are ceremonies based on the two fundamental Shingon mandalas. Finally, the *goma hō* is the esoteric sacrifice ritual. After these four propaedeutic rituals have been completed, consecration (*denbō kanjō*) is performed.

At the time of consecration, the initiand cleanses his/her body by bathing in perfumed holy water and then maintains its purity by donning a white robe. The mind is purified by receiving the *samaya* precepts (*sanmaiyakai* 三昧耶戒), by taking refuge in the three jewels, and by pledging allegiance to a number of Buddhist ethical propositions.

The location where the consecration ceremony takes place is divided into an outer and an inner area (respectively, *gejin* 外陣 and *naijin* 内陣). In the inner area there are two altars on which are placed the Vajra and the Womb mandalas used for the flower-throwing ritual already described above; there is also another altar, called "altar of true awakening" (*shōgakudan* 正覚壇), where the *kanjō* proper is performed. Hung on the eastern and western walls of the inner area are the portraits of the eight Shingon human patriarchs: Nāgārjuna, Nāgabodhi, Vajrabodhi, Amoghavajra (Bukong 不空), Śubhakarasiṃha (Shanwuwei 善無畏), Yixing 一行, Huiguo 恵果, and Kūkai. The setting is thus a replica of the entire Shingon tradition; the ritual aims at putting the initiand on the same level as these patriarchs in a process that denies history and instead emphasizes unchanging continuity.

The initiand enters the inner area with his face covered, reaches one of the mandala altars and throws a flower onto it to determine the deity to whom he is karmically related. After this the cloth covering his face is removed, in a gesture representing the final separation from the delusory world of everyday reality and the opening of the eye of wisdom to the absolute realm of the mandala. The initiand is then led to the altar of true awakening (*shōgakudan*), where the initiation proper is to take place. He/she sits on a mat representing an eight-petaled flower – Mahāvairocana's own seat in the mandala – and receives the initiation from the master. The actual initiation contents vary, but in general they consist of very specific and practical instructions on how to perform certain rituals and how to interpret certain texts (which mudras to employ, the succession of mantric formulae, etc.). The master also gives the disciple a series of sacred objects (a crown, a vajra club, a *horagai* 法螺貝 shell trumpet, a mirror, etc.) to certify the successful completion of the initiation. These objects symbolize the transformation of the initiand into Mahāvairocana's adamantine body-mind. The initiated then pays homage to the images of the patriarchs to inform them of his newly attained initiation. Finally, the master hails the former disciple as a newborn master and shades him under his parasol to signify respect and equality. The ritual ends here.

Kanjō rituals were a natural complement to the semiotics of esoteric Buddhism, which considers itself to be a form of salvific knowledge extracted directly from the signs. A semiognosis of consecration is indicated in the *Keiran shūyōshū* 渓嵐拾葉集, a Tendai encyclopaedia composed in the late Kamakura period by the priest Kōshū 光宗 (or Kōjū). As in all semiognosis exegeses, the meaning of the event or object (in this case, transmission) is envisioned as being inscribed in its name. In this case, the first character, *kan* 潅 ("pouring water") refers to wisdom attained through practice; the second character, *chō* 頂 ("top of the head") refers to the realm of the eternal principle (*ri* 理) of original enlightenment. Together, these two characters mean that the wisdom of the past buddhas, in the form of water, is poured on the head of the new buddha in the initiation ceremony (*Keiran shūyōshū*, p. 609b). In other words, consecration rituals made practice and original enlightenment coincide.

It is important to emphasize that, contrary to common understanding, consecrations (also as they are still performed today) did not generally reveal occult doctrines or "esoteric" truths. These are (and were also in the past) available relatively easily in texts studied before the performance of *kanjō*. What the master reveals at the consecration are (from the point of view of an outsider, such as the intellectual historian) *details* such as the order of the utterance of a series of mantras, specific pronunciations or intonations, which mudras to perform and when: indeed, the kind of *knowledge* that distinguishes a true certified professional from the amateur. What this ritual enacts is the sanctioning of the initiand's legitimate membership in a certain lineage and his/her capacity to teach certain doctrines and to perform certain rituals. It also guarantees the soteriological attainment of the initiated, which was often related to his/her social position in the hierarchy of religious institutions. Thus, consecration rituals control the structuring and the reproduction of the Buddhist esoteric system – a system both of knowledge and of power.

Around the end of the Heian period, and more frequently from the Kamakura period, different forms of *kanjō* began to appear; they included secret transmissions (*kuden* 口伝 or *hiden* 秘伝) concerning esoteric texts, doctrines, and rituals, often of a heterodoxical and extra-canonical nature (such as those associated with the so-called Tachikawa-ryū 立川流 and *genshi kimyōdan* 玄旨帰命壇, and those related to ideas and practices concerning the kami). Gradually, consecration rituals also began to be performed in order to transmit knowledge concerning literary texts such as poetry collections and the *Ise monogatari* 伊勢物語 (*waka kanjō* 和歌潅頂), performing arts (Noh, music), and professional tools and crafts. The attainment of secret knowledge transmitted through initiation rituals was a soteriological goal, since it was equivalent to the attainment of salvation (becoming a buddha or, in the case of *shintō kanjō* 神道潅頂, the identification of oneself with the kami) and involved a promise of worldly benefits (outside of the religious world, this translated into professional and artistic success); it was also a moral obligation as the understanding of the essential principles and duties of a specific craft or profession (and, at the same time, the acquisition of the "trade secrets" of a specific family lineage). It is not by chance, then, that in medieval Japan, *kanjō* became the general template for procedures to transmit legitimate knowledge as part of certain hierarchical systems, such as family lineages that dealt with specific literary or artistic texts, with technologies, and with extra-canonical teachings such as matters related to the kami. The reason for the development of such a wide range of initiation rituals is not clear. I believe it was a consequence of the systematic conceptual "mandalisation" that was carried out in medieval Japan by esoteric Buddhism as a way to establish a sort of cultural hegemony among the intellectual elites. In such a framework, each text or each cultural artefact, including non-religious ones, was understood as a potential esoteric symbol endowed with several levels of secret meanings.

Shittan study and transmission rituals

After this general outline of the transmission process of esoteric Buddhism and the paradigmatic form of consecration (*denbō kanjō*), let us turn our attention to a specific ritual, the *shittan kanjō*, performed to sanction the acquisition of knowledge concerning the *shittan* 悉曇 characters, an important component of the esoteric episteme.

The study of *shittan* consists in mastering the Sanskrit syllabary (*mata taimon* 摩多体文) and the most common ligatures as listed in manuals called *Shittan jūhasshō* 悉曇十八章. The actual study ends with the transmission of the *Jūhasshō*; however, the acquisition of the status of "master" (*ajari*) of *shittan* learning is sanctioned by the *shittan* consecration (*shittan kanjō*), in which the deep meaning of these characters is handed down to a disciple (who thus becomes a new master). This ritual is modelled after the *denbō kanjō* and began in medieval Japan (it does not seem to have existed in India or in China). Today, *shittan kanjō* is a specialized ritual for those interested in *shittan*; it is performed based on the procedures of the Kojima-ryū 小島流 lineage (a.k.a Tsubosaka-ryū 壺坂流), which was established by Shingō 真興 (934–1004). The ritual consists of a propaedeutic stage (*shittan kegyō* 悉曇加行) that has two main sections and the consecration proper.

- Propaedeutic Stage A: The preliminary rituals (*shittan zen-gyōhō* 悉曇前行法) consist of making offerings to the main deity (*honzon* 本尊), bowing twenty-five times, performing mudras and mantras as prescribed in ritual manuals, a protection ritual (*goshinhō* 護身法, in which the practitioner purifies himself and protects himself with mantras and mudras), mantras to the main deity (five times), chanting the complete list of the fifty-one basic *shittan* syllables from *A* to *kṣa* (five times) and making a final bow (five times). All this is performed three times a day for a seven-day period. This period ends with making a vow (*kechigan* 結願). Then, the ritual to Fudō Myōō (*Fudō-hō* 不動法) is performed, again three times a day for seven days. Fudō's protection is invoked upon to secure a smooth performance of the consecration without interference from demonic forces.
- Propaedeutic Stage B: The preparation for the *shittan* consecration (*shittan kanjō kegyō* 悉曇灌頂加行) consists of memorizing and writing down the entire *Jūhasshō* once a day for seven days. In detail, the rituals of stage B consist of making offerings to the main deity, the protection ritual, performing mudras and mantras, chanting the complete list of the fifty-one basic *shittan* syllables from *A* to *kṣa* (seven times), chanting mantras to the main deity (three times), and chanting

the Heart sutra (seven times). Also in this case, all these rituals are performed three times a day for a seven-day period.

• Consecration: The consecration hall is adorned with special versions of the two basic Shingon mandalas represented by *shittan* seeds (*shuji* 種字) as well as hanging scrolls with the names of the Shingon patriarchs written in *shittan* characters and the mantras of bodhisattvas such as Kannon to the west and Monju to the east. The presence of these two deities is not by chance. Kannon is associated with the syllable *si-* (and is also associated with compassion, principle, nirvana, and the Womb mandala), while Monju is associated with the syllable *-ddhaṃ* (and is also associated with wisdom, enlightenment, and the Vajra mandala).[9] Thus, the term *siddhaṃ* is envisioned in the context of the consecration ritual as a representation of the twofold mandala, enlightenment and the principal virtues of Buddhism, embodied iconographically by the couple Kannon and Monju.

The Vajra realm is synthesized by a version of the *jōjinne* 成身会 section of the Vajra mandala, with the *shittan* seeds of the five buddhas at the centre, surrounded by those of the four *pāramitā* bodhisattvas and the sixteen great bodhisattvas – all portrayed within a lunar disk (*gachirin* 月輪). This hanging scroll is placed in the west. The Womb mandala contains the vowels (*mata*) in the upper part and the consonants (*taimon*) in the lower part. The five *mata* are structured according to a square with A at the centre, whereas the *taimon* are presented as based on Dainichi's eight-petal lotus with the syllable *ma* at the centre. This hanging scroll is placed in the east.

During the ritual, the master transmits these *shittan* seeds to the disciple orally. Then the disciple performs a meditation called *fujikan* 布字観 ("spreading the syllables"). The disciple visualizes *shittan* covering his body and meditates on their esoteric meanings in order to embody the deities through their seeds. For example, in the *fujikan* based on Fudō Myōō, the practitioner, in order to identify himself with the deity, visualizes nineteen *shittan* seeds on various parts of his body, which are dispersed from the top of the head to his feet. In this meditation, the *shittan* characters clearly function as symbolic shifters performing the transformation of the disciple into the deity.

At this point the consecration proper takes place. The master imparts certain instructions to the disciple in the form of transmission documents (*injin* 印信), which are collected in a document in twelve parts entitled *Shittan jūnitsū kirigami daiji* 悉曇十二通切紙大事 (Twelve essential documents concenring the *shittan*). These instructions concern issues such as the pronunciation of *shittan*, ligatures, variant writing styles, portions of their esoteric meanings, and the origin of the graphs (see Kushida 1979, pp. 565–79). Importantly, the master also gives the disciple a lineage chart that follows the transmission of *shittan* from Dainichi Nyorai down to the disciple being consecrated.

The *Shittan jūnitsū kirigami daiji* contains a section entitled *Shittan jū fuka no koto* 悉曇十不可ノ事 (Ten prohibitions of *shittan*), which indicates the basic position of *shittan* students and masters:

1 Do not burn Sanskrit letters. This action results in the destruction of one's Buddha seeds.
2 Do not write (*shittan* characters) on impure wood, stone, paper, or other impure materials.
3 As is also the case for Chinese characters, do not write over other characters and do not erase or omit characters.
4 Do not write Sanskrit characters in non-Buddhist texts.
5 Do not copy or explain *shittan* letters if you do not know how to write them. They will not be effective.
6 Do not copy or chant *shittan* characters if you do not wear a clerical robe (*kesa* 袈裟).
7 Do not explain the wondrous meanings of Sanskrit characters to people who will not believe them.
8 Do not begrudge teaching *shittan* to those who are worthy of it.
9 Do not turn your back on your master. Do not raise doubts on writing methods, pronunciation, and the ligatures (as taught by your master).
10 Do not create your own personal interpretation of what has been written in the texts by past authorities and in the teachings of the masters.[10]

In other words, this document defines, literally, the *discipline* of *shittan*. It construes these graphs as sacred entities of a specifically Buddhist nature that entail particular rituals (instruction n. 6) and have soteriological power (1). Thus, they should be treated with respect (1, 2), they should not be mixed up with non-Buddhist writings (4), and in general they should not be fuddled with (5). The document also attempts to enforce a strict control of *shittan* learning (7), also in order to prevent the development of new interpretations and of different ways to write and use these characters (9, 10). Finally, it stresses the fundamental moral attitude toward *shittan*: one of both caution (7) and generosity (8), and of respect toward the discipline (especially 3).

Transmission lineages of the esoteric episteme

Section 10 of the *Shittan jūnitsū kirigami daiji* contains four explications about the origin of the *shittan* characters. The first states that in the initial kalpa (*jōgō* 成劫) after the creation of this universe, the deities of the Light–Sound Heaven (Skt. *ābhāsvara*, Jap. *kōonten* 光音天: the highest heaven of *dhyāna* in the Realm of Forms) descended to the earth, taking the names of Brahmā, Śaṅkara, and Maheśvara, and revealed forty-seven Sanskrit syllables. The reference to the Ābhāsvara Heaven is interesting, since the language (Skt. *svara*) of the deities residing there was believed to consist in modulations of light (Skt. *ābhā*) that they put forth by their mouths. The second explanation states that twelve centuries after the death of Śākyamuni, Nāgārjuna entered the Dragon Palace (*ryūgū* 龍宮) on the bottom of the ocean and gained access to many Mahāyāna scriptures. The *shittan* was also included among the various subjects he later taught in Central India, and it was called the "writing of the Dragon Palace." The third explanation says that Śākyamuni himself taught the *shittan* toward the end of his life: first, he taught the fifty syllables in the *Monju mon-gyō* 文殊聞経, then the forty-two syllables in the *Kegon-kyō* 華厳経, and finally the forty-six syllables in the *Daishōgon-kyō* 大荘厳経. The fourth and last explanation says that Mahāvairocana in person, after attaining enlightenment in the Akaniṣṭha Heaven, taught the *Kongōchō-gyō*, in which one chapter, the *Shaku jimo bon* 釈字母品, lists fifty syllables that were transmitted to Vajrapāṇi (Kongōshu 金剛手); these syllables are the origin of the esoteric scriptures and the mantric seeds known in our world. This lineage seems to have been the most influential, since it was the basis of lineage charts given to disciples at *shittan* consecrations. By the Muromachi period there seem to have been two different types of such lineage charts (see Kushida 1979, pp. 566–67). One contains the following series:

> Mahāvairocana → Vajrasattva → Nāgārjuna → Nāgabodhi → Śubhaka-rasiṃha → Yuanchao 玄超 → Huiguo 恵果 → Kūkai → Shinga 真雅 → Gennin 源仁 → Shōbō 聖宝 and further to Eizon 叡尊 and Raiken 頼験.

Another chart, dated 1503, contains the following series:

> Mahāvairocana → Vajrasattva → Nāgārjuna → Nāgabodhi → Amogha-vajra → Huiguo → Kūkai → Shinga → Gennin → Yakushin 益信 and further to Saisen 済暹, Jōson 定尊 all the way down to Seison 勢尊.

Like all lineage charts of this kind, the two examples above embrace several insights. They connect the transcendent and the immanent; the original moment beyond ordinary space–time in which Mahāvairocana trans-mitted his enlightenment to Vajrasattva is connected to the specific historical space–time location in which transmission occurs in the present. They reproduce and re-enact historical narratives of the propa-gation of Buddhism through the Three Countries (India, China, and Japan). They create a communion between venerated patriarchs of the past and contemporary monks. They also point to the existence of a continuous and unbroken chain of signification, in which signifiers, signifieds, and pragmatic instructions for their interpretation and use have been transmitted from one generation to another, from one country to another, from one ontological dimension to another.

The continuous and unbroken nature of the transmission line connecting masters to disciples is also underscored by the root metaphor for esoteric transmission rituals, namely decanting (Jap. *shabyō* 写瓶, lit. "decanting a bottle"), that is, the act of pouring the contents of one bottle into another. Its scriptural source is a passage from the Nirvana sutra:

> Ānanda has been with me for more than twenty years. [...] Since he joined me, he has memorized the twelve-division teachings I have taught; once a teaching entered his ear, he did not ask [to be reminded about it] any more. It has been like pouring the content of one bottle into another.[11]

Kūkai also used this metaphor in his *Fuhōden*, a work on the Shingon lineage: "receiving the transmission is not different from decanting a bottle."[12] This metaphor serves to emphasize continuity going all the way back to the original transmission by the Buddha. In this sense, transmission rituals do more than transmit teachings: they sanction that the transmission is complete and has been unaltered (unadulterated).

This kind of transmission is obviously related to the nature of the esoteric Buddhist episteme. From an *internal* point of view (i.e. from the perspective of the exegetes who have developed the semiotic field of esoteric Buddhism), esoteric signs are not arbitrary but microcosms, unconditioned condensations of the universe and the soteriological processes that take place within it; as such, no arbitrary act of interpretation changes their innate and absolute signification. Their transmission from master to disciple avoids conventions stipulated for ordinary semiotic acts, and the transmission is secret and subject to initiation. The first link of this initiatory chain is Mahāvairocana: signs and practices related to his teachings have been born in the self-presence of the Unconditioned. The myth of the appearance in the sky of *shittan* texts and mandalas to Nāgārjuna and Śubhakarasiṃha, and the unconditioned transmission in the Iron Stupa are part of this general framework. It is not by chance that esoteric teachings were copied by these two patriarchs: Nāgārjuna is positioned at the junction between the transcendent and the immanent, between the mythical and the historical chronotopes, while Śubhakarasiṃha, who brought the esoteric teachings to China, connects the Indian mythological past with the East Asian historical present. The teachings they faithfully transcribed and transmitted to their disciples were subsequently brought to Japan and constituted the foundations of the Shingon and esoteric Tendai traditions. The *shittan* characters play an important role in this portrayal of the transmission, similar to that of the "original" mandalas known as *genzu* 現図. Even today, *genzu* mandalas are considered to be perfect copies of the original and unconditional mandala, whose images and meaning are strictly transmitted by means of a causal chain. Furthermore, the connection between the mythical and the historical dimensions of the transmission makes a claim such as that of Kūkai possible, according to which Mahāvairocana is still preaching his doctrines (*hosshin seppō*) with true words (*shinjitsugo, nyogigo* 如義語), whereas the lineage of Śākyamuni became *de facto* extinct with the Buddha's entrance into nirvana.[13] Thus, esoteric consecration rituals re-enact the original and eternal utterance of Mahāvairocana in our historical time-space. These traditions and legends further reinforce the idea that esoteric expressions are unconditioned entities that transcend the arbitrariness of signs, cultural codes, or everyday semiotic strategies.

An important element in this characterization of esoteric expressions is the emphasis on the fidelity and accuracy of initiatory knowledge – thus, on the fidelity and accuracy of everything that concerns signs. According to the esoteric episteme, its initiatory signs cannot lie and cannot be used to lie. We find here the paradoxical idea of an absolute sign that is directly and ontologically connected to the object or the event for which it should stand. The problematic of absolute signs is developed on three different levels: the internal structure, as motivated and analogical; the power with which these signs are endowed; their transmission by way of a rigid causal chain. As we have seen, esoteric signs are semiotic modalities of the Dharma realm's being, and their direct ties with reality are envisioned as an intrinsic, ontological property. The active power over reality with which the esoteric signs are endowed derives from this direct connection with the Unconditional. The non-initiated, uninformed use of esoteric signs as amulets or talismans, use that disregards meaning, is based on the secret nature of these signs, on the weight of tradition, and on an unchanging transmission.

Conclusion

Contrary to popular understanding, esoteric Buddhism is (was) not a form of occultism, in which its adepts receive secret initiations to abstruse doctrines through curious rituals, as is reported to be happening in some strange sects today. Moreover, extant documents seem to indicate that current ideas about the paramount importance of the one-to-one, master–disciple transmission are overstated. The training of Shingon clergy (in particular its intellectual elites, the scholar-monks) in the Middle Ages took place within the context of institutions for higher education. Young monks sat in classes with a lecture–discussion format and studied assigned texts individually or in groups. They engaged in practical activities (ritual, meditation, etc.). At the end, they received a diploma of attainment in a ceremony called "consecration" (*kanjō*), which often gave the recipient the right to teach the subject he had been initiated in, and thus to establish his own group of disciples. A few of these students inherited their teacher's position and, in some cases, also the teacher's possessions. Emphasis on a personal, master–disciple relation seems to be the result of literalist readings of the esoteric education rhetoric (which to an extent does stress master–disciple relations) and, more directly, of the impact of Zen modernist ideas propounded, for example, by D.T. Suzuki (see Sharf 1995).

In fact, esoteric Buddhist monks received a specialized training (most often, in a collective setting) in a number of philosophical issues and ritual matters related to the world view of esoteric Buddhism – primarily in topics we would today consider as part of semiotics. An analysis of medieval and early modern "secret transmissions" (*hiden* or *kuden*) shows that they often took place within a ritual context: they were part of processes of transmission of knowledge originating in esoteric Buddhism. When the training in a particular subject was concluded, the student went through a consecration ritual known as *kanjō*, which sanctioned the level of education that had been attained. Consecration rituals were not ends in themselves, but important elements in the more general process of the transmission of esoteric teachings – which in some cases went beyond the original religious setting and influenced important aspects of the economy and the arts.

The discourse of secrecy, in which most of esoteric Buddhism was and still is wrapped, served several functions. It was useful to define esoteric Buddhism in comparison to other Buddhist traditions; to determine levels of meaning and degrees of education/transmission within the esoteric schools; to establish and legitimate a sociology of the initiated (by distinguishing social groups who were "worthy" of receiving the esoteric teachings from those who were not); and to control access to prized knowledge (which was necessary for the establishment of lineages, and therefore had important social and economic connotations). What is particularly significant is that "secrecy" was defined in terms of a specific set of teachings concerning the supposedly real meaning of languages and signs as related to the nature of Mahāvairocana as the absolute form of the Buddha (*dharmakāya*).

Notes

1 Raihō, *Shingon myōmoku*, pp. 734c–735a.
2 Kūkai, *Ben kenmitsu nikyō ron*, p. 381c; Hakeda 1972, pp. 156–57.
3 Annen, *Shingonshū kyōji gi*, p. 449b.
4 Annen, *Taizō kongō bodaishingi ryaku mondō shō*, p. 492b.
5 *Shingon myōmoku*, p. 734b.
6 Shukaku (1150–1202), *Uki* 右記, pp. 601–04.
7 *Go-Uda hōō goyuigō* 後宇多法皇御遺告, quoted in Saitō 1978, pp. 64–67; see also *Mikkyō daijiten*, pp. 290b–291a.
8 Saitō 1978, p. 68; see also Tanaka 1999, pp. 78–83.
9 See Jōgon, *Shittan sanmitsu shō*, p. 722a.
10 This translation is based on Kushida 1979, p. 578 and Kodama 2002, pp. 21–22.
11 *Nehan-gyō* 涅槃経, p. 601b–c.
12 Kūkai, *Himitsu mandarakyō fuhōden*, p. 112.
13 Ibid., pp. 66–67.

References

Primary sources

Ben kenmitsu nikyō ron 弁顕密二教論, by Kūkai 空海 . T 77 n. 2427. (English translation in Hakeda 1972, pp. 151–57.)

Bonji shittan jimo narabini shakugi 梵字悉曇字母並釈義, by Kūkai. T 84 n. 2701.

Bonmōkyō kaidai 梵網経開題, by Kūkai. In Kōbō Daishi chosaku kenkyūkai 弘法大師著作研究会 (ed.), *Teihon Kōbō daishi zenshū* 定本弘法大師全集 vol. 4. Kōyasan: Mikkyō Bunka Kenkyūjo, 1995.

Dainichi-kyō 大日経 (*Da Piluzhena chengfo shenbian jiachi jing* 大毘廬遮那成仏神変加持経). T 18 n. 848.

Daishōgon-kyō 大荘厳経 (*Da zhuangyan lun jing* 大荘厳論経). T 4 n. 201.

Himitsu mandarakyō fuhōden 秘密曼荼羅教付法伝, by Kūkai. KDZ 1.

Kegon-kyō 華厳経 (*Da fanghuang fo huayan jing* 大方廣仏華厳経). T 9 n. 278.

Keiran shūyōshū 渓嵐拾葉集, by Kōshū (or Kōjū) 光宗. T 76 n. 2410.

Kongōchō-gyō 金剛頂経 (*Jingangding yiqie rulai zhenshi she dasheng xian zheng da jiaowang jing* 金剛頂一切如来真実摂大乗現証大教王経). T 18 n. 865.

Monju mon-gyō 文殊聞経 (*Wenzhushili wen jing* 文殊師利聞経). T 14 n. 468.

Nehan-gyō 涅槃経 (*Dabanniepan jing* 大般涅槃経). T 12 n. 374.

Shingon myōmoku 真言名目, by Raihō 頼宝. T 77 n. 2449.

Shingonshū kyōji gi 真言宗教時義, by Annen 安然. T 75 n. 2396.

Shittan sanmitsu shō 悉曇三密鈔, by Jōgon 浄厳. T 84 n. 2710.

Shōji jissō gi 声字実相義, by Kūkai. T 77 n. 2429. (Partial English translation in Hakeda 1972, pp. 234–46.)

Taizō kongō Bodaishingi ryaku mondō shō 胎蔵金剛菩提心義略問答抄, by Annen. T 75 n. 2397.

Uki 右記 , by Shukaku 守覚. T 78 n. 2491.

Unjigi 吽字義, by Kūkai. T 77 n. 2430. (Partial English translation in Hakeda 1972, pp. 246–62.)

Modern sources

Hakeda, Yoshito S. (1972), *Kūkai. Major Works*. New York: Columbia University Press.

Kodama Giryū 児玉義隆 (2002), *Bonji de miru mikkyō* 梵字でみる密教. Tokyo: Daihōrinkaku.

Kushida Ryōkō 櫛田良洪 (1979), *Zoku shingon mikkyō seiritsu katei no kenkyū* 続真言密教成立過程の研究. Tokyo: Sankibō Busshorin.

Mikkyō daijiten 密教大辞典, revised edition by Chishakuin Daigaku Mikkyō Gakkainai Mikkyō daijiten saihan iinkai 智積院大学密教学会内密教大辞典再版委員会 (ed.). Kyoto: Hōzōkan, 1983 [reduced size reprint]. (Full size version, 1970; original edition by Mikkyō daijiten hensankai 密教大辞典編纂会, 1931).

Rambelli, Fabio (1991), "Re-inscribing Mandala. Semiotic Operations on a Word and Its Object." *Studies in Central and East Asian Religions* 4, pp. 1–24.

Saitō Akitoshi 斎藤昭俊 (1978), *Nihon bukkyō kyōikushi kenkyū* 日本仏教教育史研. Tokyo: Kokusho Kankōkai.

Sharf, Robert H. (1995), "The Zen of Japanese Nationalism," in Donald S. Lopez, Jr. (ed.), *Curators of the Buddha: The Study of Buddhism under Colonialism*. Chicago: University of Chicago Press, pp. 107–60.
Tanaka Takako 田中貴子 (1999), *Muromachi obōsan monogatari* 室町お坊さん物語. Tokyo: Kōdansha.

6 Reconsidering the taxonomy of the esoteric

Hermeneutical and ritual practices of the Lotus sutra

Lucia Dolce

The distinction between "revealed teachings" (*kengyō* 顕教) and "secret teachings" (*mikkyō* 密教) is often assumed to be a crucial element in the classification of currents of Japanese Buddhism. Undoubtedly such a division was historically made, and the positioning of *mikkyō* as a category apart was the hermeneutical strategy that allowed it to pronounce the esoteric (or Tantric)[1] teaching as a superior form of Buddhism. This operation may arguably be the starting point of a process of "esoterization" of Japanese religion, which took place beyond the sectarian and doctrinal dimensions, and which became a characteristic of Japanese culture *vis-à-vis* other East Asian contexts, where the esoteric model was apparently not prominent. Yet, if we were to sketch the relation of "esoteric Buddhism" to its other, that is, "non-esoteric" Buddhism, we would find ourselves representing an idiom of intersection and reciprocal borrowing rather than opposition. After Kūkai 空海 (774–835) established *mikkyō* as a "bibliographic category,"[2] throughout the mid-Heian period and well into the mediaeval era Buddhist scholiasts often referred to the distinction between *kengyō* and *mikkyō* as a basic taxonomy of Buddhism, similar to the division Mahāyāna/Hīnayāna. This suggests that the term "secret teaching" was not so much used in the sense of hermetic knowledge reserved for a few, but rather more broadly, to indicate one type of mainstream Buddhism available to practitioners, albeit with its own principles and conventions. Moreover, in the mediaeval period, while the two categories continued to be used, the distinction between them seems to have rested on rhetorical grounds, losing strength at both the doctrinal and the liturgical levels, where more parallels were argued and more interactions occurred.

Thus, the mediaeval period may be discerned as the climax of a progressive affirmation of Tantric Buddhism, which eventually resulted in the exportation and exploitation of the esoteric model in various religious contexts. At the same time, however, the ideological context in which such a process took place makes the meaning of esoteric problematic and brings to the fore a number of questions concerning the content and the significance of the category itself. What were the defining elements of esoteric Buddhism? Is it correct to consider it, as often happens, to be a monolithic category that remained static through the centuries and supposedly continued to be demarcated by the characteristics that the putative father of Tantric Buddhism in Japan, Kūkai, had established for it? Or was the concept of the esoteric subject to transformations and evolutions, affecting the very understanding of the boundaries between *kengyō* and *mikkyō*? Within Buddhism itself, the establishment of esoteric lineages prompted not only the creation of new ritual practices, but also a rethinking of the nature of the esoteric. Since the formal beginning of the Tantric traditions in Japan in the early Heian period, extensive discussions existed within Buddhist circles about which teachings possessed "esoteric" qualities; in this sense doctrines and practices deemed to be "secret" always remained within the realm of theological and scholastic concern.

This chapter addresses the technical definition of the "esoteric," as grounded in, but not limited to, the notion of "secrecy." It explores aspects of the (re)formulation of the category *mikkyō* carried out by the Tendai 天台 lineages of scholar-ritualists who were interested in Tantric knowledge, and whom I shall for convenience's sake call Taimitsu 台密. (The sense in which this term can be applied to the ritualists of the Heian and mediaeval periods depends on our understanding of the sectarian awareness among pre-modern practitioners.) One distinctive characteristic of the Taimitsu discourse was the "esoterization" of the Lotus sutra, a non-esoteric scripture that was among the most popular Buddhist texts in East Asia. It was a semantic and hermeneutical operation that occurred at both the doctrinal and the liturgical levels, and it seems to reflect a specifically Japanese development of the esoteric discourse. The Lotus sutra, however, belonged to an exegetical (non-esoteric) tradition that had already imparted the sutra the status of "secret teaching." Before looking at the Japanese evolution of the concept of the esoteric, it is therefore crucial to consider the terms of the pre-esoteric appreciation of "secret" and the extent to which teachings defined as being secret were not the exclusive prerogative of Tantric Buddhism. Taimitsu thinkers were concerned with demonstrating the identity of the perfect teaching (i.e. the continental interpretation of the Lotus sutra) and the esoteric teachings, and therefore they re-evaluated the connotation of "secret" that already existed, in particular, in the Chinese Tiantai tradition, eventually incorporating it into their own understanding of "esoteric teachings." It is my contention that, in doing so, they transformed *mikkyō* into a more sophisticated and complex concept in which the distinction esoteric/exoteric was less clear-cut than is usually assumed. Chinese non-esoteric thought, moreover, greatly influenced the major texts of East Asian Tantrism even before Taimitsu, and a reassessment of the context of tropes and texts that would become representative of esoteric Buddhism may be useful to measure the degree of the Japanese innovations.

The chapter thus consists of two parts. The first section explores interpretations of the "secret" as presented first in the Tiantai continental tradition and then in its Japanese esoteric offspring. The multiplicity of textual references that address this issue cannot be properly reviewed here, and I shall only point to major canonical sources that served as a direct theoretical background for Taimitsu writers and, on the Japanese side, to the synthesis undertaken by the representative Taimitsu scholar-monk Annen 安然 (841–903?). The second part looks at concrete examples of the esoterization of the Lotus sutra as it took place in mediaeval Japan through a specific rite called *hokke hō* 法華法. The transformation of the non-esoteric scripture involved the reuse of images and idioms that had been established in continental exegetical works of the Lotus sutra as well as of the esoteric tradition, filtered through the interpretations of early Taimitsu writers. My analysis centres on the mandala of the Lotus sutra, on the assumption that a mandala is the element that, more than any other, distinguishes esoteric Buddhism. I also address the question of the mandala's use in a sectarian framework.

Non-esoteric notions of the "secret" in Chinese Buddhism

Canonical Tiantai texts include elaborate discussions of the meaning of "secret" (*bimi* 秘密), suggesting that the topic was a significant one in the doctrinal perspective of Sui and Tang Buddhism. To Zhiyi 智顗 (538–97), the putative founder of Tiantai, and other scholar-monks of his time a number of scriptural sources were available to propound the "secret" qualities of certain teachings of the Buddha and at the same time to argue for the special status that these teachings should hold within the canon. The Lotus sutra was easily the most appropriate material to draw from, in that it repeatedly self-evaluated its contents as the secret quintessence of the buddhas, the epitome of the Buddhist discourse, which the Tathāgatas had preserved and protected from those who could not grasp its meaning.[3] In Chapter 10 of Kumārajīva's translation, "The Teacher of the Dharma," for instance, the scripture defines itself as "the most difficult to believe and understand" (最為難信難解), "the storehouse of the buddhas' secret essence (諸仏秘要之蔵), which may not be distributed nor given to people at random" (不可分布妄授与人; T 9, p. 31b, Hurvitz 1976, p. 178), "profound, firm, obscure and remote from the ordinary" (深固幽遠無人到; T 9, p. 31c, Hurvitz, p. 179). Zhiyi made use of these expressions to articulate the connotations of a secret doctrine and, at the same time, to emphasize the uniqueness of the Lotus sutra. In the *Fahua wenju*, a line-by-line commentary on the Lotus sutra, he elucidated the above passage in the following way:

As for [the expression] "storehouse of the secret essence" (*biyao zhi zang* 秘要之蔵), it is [called] secret (*bi* 秘) because it is hidden and it is not explained; it is [called] essence (*yao* 要) because it brings everything together; it is [called] storehouse because it envelops the true aspects of reality (*zhenru shixiang* 眞如実相). It cannot be propagated bit by bit [because] the subtlety of the dharma is difficult to believe. [Only] profound wisdom can give rewards, [while] ignorance increases error; this is why one cannot explain it indiscriminately. Since long ago it has never been revealed and explained. In the *Tripitaka* it is not explained that the two vehicles [*śrāvakas* and *pratyekabuddhas*] attained liberation (*ersheng zuofo* 二乗作仏), nor is it explained that the teacher [of the dharma] and his disciples are related, as origin and traces [are] (*shidi benji* 師弟本迹). In the *Vaipulya* and *Prajñāpāramitā* scriptures, the storehouse of the true reality (*shixiang zhi zang* 実相之蔵) is expounded, but the enlightenment of the five vehicles is not, nor [is it explained that] the traces reveal the origin (*faji xianben* 発迹顕本). None of the sutras [that speak of] sudden and gradual [enlightenment] comprehend this [truth], and therefore it is called secret. This [Lotus] sutra comprehensively explains the dharma that in the past remained secret. That is to say, this [sutra] opens the treasure house of the secret and mysterious (*bimizang*). Namely, this [sutra] is the treasure house of the secret and mysterious. Accordingly, the secret storehouse (*bizang*) has not yet been revealed.

(T 34, p. 110b)

Zhiyi's exegesis identifies the secret with a specific type of reality: an existence or truth that is the essence of all things, is all-comprehensive, cannot be divided, and therefore needs to be propagated as it is, in its entirety and in all its complexity. Such a level of comprehensiveness implies that this reality encompasses everything: there is nothing but perfect buddhahood. In this context, the liberation of *śrāvakas* and *pratyekabuddhas* is presented as a concrete example of how the ultimate reality expresses itself: they are beings who do not belong to the world of comprehensive buddhahood (the Mahāyāna ideal) and therefore would not be able to attain liberation were it not for the all-encompassing, inclusive power of the "secret" truth. Zhiyi also uses other key concepts of Tiantai doctrine, such as the relation between trace and origin and between teacher and disciple, to articulate the nature of the ultimate reality and create the image of a perfectly rounded world of enlightenment. The process by which the inclusiveness comes about is said to be mysterious, secret, and is not explained in any Buddhist scripture other than the Lotus sutra. The *Fahua wenju* also addresses the question of the propagation of this doctrine, continuously shifting the emphasis from a general definition of secrecy as the expression of an ideal truth to specific patterns of the realization of this truth. In this way, Zhiyi presented the Lotus sutra as the embodiment *par excellence* of secret teachings.

However, the Lotus sutra was not alone in offering a basis for the definition of secret. The *Mahāparinirvāna-sūtra*, another fundamental Mahāyāna scripture and an important canonical basis in the formulation of Tiantai doctrine, also claimed to contain the "secret teachings" of the Tathāgatas. This scripture speaks of itself and of its representative doctrine, the idea of an all-pervading buddha-nature, as the secret storehouse of all buddhas (*bimizang* 秘密蔵).[4] It was therefore necessary for Zhiyi to resolve the differences between the *Mahāparinirvāna* and the Lotus scriptures, and he did so by arguing that although the *Mahāparinirvāna* implied the possibility of inclusive liberation in its concept of a buddha-nature which is present in all beings, this possibility remained theoretical and incomplete insofar as the text did not supply actual instances of its practical application. In this sense, Chinese Tiantai deemed the abstract notion of an omnipresent buddha-nature not sufficiently compelling to give the scripture that upholds it the status of a secret teaching. The concern with the concrete actualization of a principle, a point that would become extremely important in Japanese Buddhism, is worth noting. Towards the end of another of his major works, the *Fahua xuanyi*, Zhiyi characterized the Lotus sutra as secret in contrast to yet another category of canonical literature, the *Prajñāpāramitā* scriptures. Once again the argument focused on the assertion contained in the Lotus sutra that not only bodhisattvas but also *śrāvakas* and *pratyekabuddhas* attain buddhahood. According to Zhiyi, this was a less obvious teaching that people could not easily understand, and hence it was secret (T 33, p. 811c).

While these interpretations aimed at disclosing the ontological and epistemological dimensions of the "secret," the discussion on the nature of the Lotus sutra in contrast to other important scriptures of Chinese Buddhism added a sectarian accretion to the discourse on secrecy. This would remain a crucial feature in the development of the trope, and would similarly be a constitutive element in the definition of esoteric lineages as distinct from other forms of Buddhism. I shall come back to the sectarian dimension of the esoteric. Here it is relevant to note that Zhiyi's reinterpretation of the Lotus sutra versus the *Prajñāpāramitā* sutras was not entirely innovative, nor was it solely motivated by Zhiyi's desire to elevate the Lotus as part of a self-legitimation strategy. It followed instead an interpretative rubric put forward in another major work of Chinese Buddhism, the *Da zhidu lun*, which had already set the two texts in opposition. This massive commentary on the *Mahāprajñāpāramitā-sūtra* did not explicitly identify the Lotus with secret teachings, but it claimed that

> The *Prajñāpāramitā[-sutra]* is not a secret and mysterious dharma (*bimifa* 秘密法). On the other hand, sutras such as the Lotus explain that the *arhats* will attain [buddhahood].

(T 25, p. 754b)

This passage is quite controversial in that it uses the enlightenment of the *śrāvakas* in a polemic way, to differentiate between teachings within the Mahāyāna. Elsewhere, however, the treatise seems to discuss the explicit and the secret in terms that correspond respectively to Hīnayāna and Mahāyāna.[5] The *Da zhidu lun*, which may be considered an encyclopaedic compendium of Chinese Buddhist thought, is thus one of the earliest sources that repeatedly classifies the Buddhist doctrine into two categories, secret and non-secret teachings:

> There are two types of dharma: one is the secret and mysterious (*bimi* 秘密), the other is the explicit (*xianshi* 現示).
>
> (T 25, p. 84c)

> The buddhas' actions (*zhufo shi* 諸仏事) are of two kinds: one is mysterious (*mi* 密) the other is explicit (*xian* 現).
>
> (T 25, p. 517a–b)

The idiom exo-esoteric (*xianmi*, Jap. *kenmitsu* 顕密), which was to play a considerable role in the construction of esoteric Buddhism in Japan, emerges from this exegetical context. Drawing from the *Da zhidu lun*, Zhiyi employed it to indicate the two modalities in which the Buddha reveals his teaching. He contrasted the term *mijiao* (Jap. *mikkyō*) 密教 with *xianshi* 顕示 and used the two categories of *xian* 顕 and *mi* 密 to underline a temporal progression in the teaching of the Buddha, from the sutras expounded before the Lotus sutra to the Lotus itself (T 34, p. 48a, exegesis of Chapter 2 of the Lotus sutra, "Skilful Means"). Here the terms *xian* and *mi* can be translated as exoteric and esoteric, but *mijiao* obviously does not indicate a particular (esoteric) lineage of Buddhism.[6] It rather continues to denote the most profound and unexpected disclosure of the Buddhist truth, in contrast to a course of instruction that can be easily understood by anyone because it follows common-sense logic. The concern of Tiantai exegetes hence rested mainly with how the Buddha's teaching is delivered and accessed. Yet, by associating the two epistemological categories with specific scriptures, they also pointed to a "bibliographic" meaning of the taxonomy, whereby specific classes of teachings were embodied in specific texts. As the scripture(s) containing the most hidden, secret doctrine was (were) evaluated as the uppermost scripture within the canon, this interpretative stance becomes a factor in the creation of a hierarchy of texts and, eventually, of the lineages that upheld them – again, a sectarian outcome. The pattern would be reproduced in the construction of Japanese esoteric Buddhism, and may be contextualized within the framework of the classification of doctrines (*panjiao* 判教), which characterized Sino-Japanese scholasticism.

Zhiyi's commentaries on the Lotus sutra contain other arguments related to the definition of secret, which would later be re-used by Taimitsu writers. The *Fahua wenju*, for instance, discusses the activity of the Buddha in these terms:

> As for [what is] secret and mysterious (*bimi*), [the notion that] "one body is identical with the three bodies" is called secret (*bi*), [the notion that] "the three bodies are one body" is called mysterious (*mi*). Again, what was not revealed in the past is called *bi*, [the concept that] "only a Buddha knows by himself" is called *mi*. The power of supernatural permeation (*shentong* 神通) is the activity of the three bodies [of the buddhas]... The buddhas in the three existences [past, present and future] have three bodies. In the various teachings this is secret and is not transmitted."
>
> (T 34, p. 129c)

This passage again employs key expressions of Tiantai doctrine, in turn originating from the narrative of the Lotus sutra, as catch phrases for conveying the real nature of the Buddha's being. While the question of the modes of propagation of the Buddhist truth is important, here it is clear that "secrecy" at the same time concerns the essence of buddhahood, since it indicates the process by which a buddha can maintain an immovable essence that knows by itself and at the same time abide in the world. What constitutes the (mysterious) unfolding of the Buddha's existence seems to be ontologically different from what is commonly perceived as the Buddhist preaching and therefore it can be transmitted to only a few discerning practitioners. Other passages from the Tiantai corpus highlight this double focus on the nature of the Buddha and the ability of the listeners to access it:

> The secret teaching (*bimijiao* 秘密教) means that, within the previous four periods [of the Buddha's preaching before the Lotus sutra], the three activities (*sanlun* 三輪, i.e., bodily, verbal and mental activity) of the Tathāgata were beyond comprehension. Therefore, [the Buddha] expounded the sudden [method] for some people and the gradual for others. Because they reciprocally did not realize that the other could receive the benefits [of the Buddha's teaching], this is called secret teaching.
>
> (*Tiantai sijiao yi*, T 46, p. 775b)[7]

The texts so far surveyed do not elaborate on the type of practitioner that can receive the secret teachings. In his introduction to another major work of Tiantai doctrine, the *Mohe zhiguan*, Zhiyi distinguished between two types of contemplative practice, the "explicit" (*xianguan* 顯観), related to openly revealed teachings (*xianjiao* 顯教) and the "esoteric" (*miguan* 密観), related to the secret teachings (*mijiao* 密教) (T 46, p. 3c). When questioned on whether the esoteric contemplation could be explained, he pointed out that this was a practice that ordinary people (*fan* 凡) could neither perform nor transmit, and that was limited to saintly beings (*sheng* 聖) and to people who had an advanced level of training. The similarities that these notions bear to later esoteric elaborations should be kept in mind. It is also interesting to note that the Tiantai terms used to describe the caution of the Buddha to deliver his secret teachings only to appropriate people would be re-used in the esoteric context. For instance, the expression "the Buddha does not expound at random," which appears in the Lotus sutra and was elaborated upon by Zhiyi, would also employed in the *Commentary to the Dari jing* with reference to the revelation of the secret signs (mudra) of the buddhas (Misaki 1988, pp. 30–33).

A number of conclusions may be drawn from the material examined above. First, it seems clear that the connotation of "secret" as the truth that has finally been revealed, explained and embodied pertains not only to what we are used to consider properly esoteric teachings, that is Tantric Buddhism, but also to non-Tantric doctrines. Second, Chinese textual sources suggest that the term "secret" contains a multiplicity of connotations, which may be interpreted at an ontological, epistemological or classificatory level, referring to different aspects of the Buddhist truth, the status of the listeners or the nature of the Buddha. Finally, linguistically esoteric Buddhism appears to use a number of idioms coined in Tiantai. This is an important point to which I shall now turn. It is not only the case that expressions from the Lotus sutra on which Zhiyi's interpretation is based would remain crucial in the later identification of the Lotus sutra as an esoteric text. They also played an important role in the formation of the esoteric discourse, as they were included in the Chinese exegesis of canonical Tantric sources, such as the *Commentary to the Dari jing*.

The non-esoteric nature of quintessential Tantric concepts

The correspondence between non-esoteric and esoteric notions, and the alterations that Tantric Buddhism effected on what we may consider mainstream Mahāyāna ideas (in their East Asian formulation), are perhaps best pinpointed by exploring concepts that are commonly regarded as axiomatic of esoteric Buddhism. Two such notions, the "three secrets" and the "preaching of the dharmakāya" are particularly pertinent to the argument here.

The three secrets

The term "three secrets" (Jap. *sanmitsu* 三密) is often treated as a catchword for esoteric Buddhism, subsuming the ritual elements specific to the esoteric practice, namely mantras, mudras, and mandalas. The expression itself, however, may be found in several Chinese non-esoteric sources, where it singles out the qualities proper of a buddha. The *Da zhidu lun*, for instance, argues,

> As expounded in the *Miji jingang jing* 密迹金剛経, the Buddha has three secrets: the secret of the body, the secret of the word and the secret of the mind. None of the heavenly and human beings understand or know [them].[8]

Canonical texts interpreted the activity of the Buddha and his preaching as "secret" and denoted this mysterious movement in a threefold way, albeit with varying idioms. The passage from the *Tiantai sijiaoyi* cited in the previous section drew on such a trope. Following, once again, the *Da zhidu lun*, the Tiantai commentarial tradition on the Lotus sutra explained the term *sanmitsu* as "the secrets of body, word and mind" (*shenkouyi mi* 身口意密) and glossed it as the three wheels (*sanlun* 三輪) or the three activities (*sanye* 三業) of the Buddha.[9] In other words, the three secrets were the modes through which a buddha expressed himself and communicated. This point is exemplified in Zhiyi's *Fahua wenju*, where the threefold secret action of the Buddha is identified with a karmic process, of which the result is inexplicable:

> The cause [of enlightenment] is called the three activities, the result is called the three secrets. When the cause [is at work], [the Buddha's] compassion guides the three activities and benefits others. When the result [is produced], it is called the mysterious transformation of the three wheels (*sanlun busiyihua* 三輪不思議化).
>
> (T 34, p. 118c)

It should be noted that both buddhas and sentient beings perform actions, which the textual tradition characterized as threefold, but only those of the buddhas are labelled as secret. Indeed, whereas the term *sanye* 三業 is used for both, *sanmi* never refers to sentient beings. Here one finds the common background with the esoteric formulation of the concept as well as the discrepancies. While esoteric and non-esoteric sources seem to agree in their understanding of the Buddha's "secret life," it is with regard to the status of sentient beings that their positions diverge. The exegetical material calls forth several considerations. To begin with, one may note that esoteric sources also attribute secret modes to the activities of sentient beings, and yet still distinguish them from the action of the buddhas. Kūkai for instance, in his treatise on the differences between esoteric and exoteric, *Ben kenmitsu nikyō ron*, argued that

> There are two meanings of secret (*himitsu*). The first is the secret of human beings; the second is the secret of the Tathāgata.
>
> (T 77, p. 381c)[10]

The same point would be made and elaborated upon by Annen. But what does the secret of sentient beings consist of, and how is it related to the secret of the buddhas? The lack of awareness of the essence of reality is what makes the truth (which is, at the same time, the Buddha's mode of existence) a secret for common beings. It is questionable whether the esoteric concept is different from mainstream Mahāyāna. What is interesting here, however, is that esoteric sources offer a clue as to how to unveil such a secret by introducing another term, *sanmitsugyō*, meaning the practice of the three secrets. This is the practice that allows human beings to identify their threefold karmic action with the three mysterious acts of the Buddha. One of the crucial passages in the *Commentary to the Dari jing* explains,

> To enter the gate of mantras, in short, there are three things (*shi* 事): the first is the gate of the bodily secret, the second is the gate of the verbal secret, the third is the gate of the secret of the mind.... The practitioner, through these three skilful means (*sanfangbian* 三方便), purifies his three activities (*sanye*) and therefore is at once empowered (*jiachi* 加持) with the three secrets (*sanmi* 三密) of the Tathāgatas.
>
> (*Shu*, p. 579b, *Yishi*, p. 4a.)

The basic difference between secrecy as applied to human beings and secrecy as referred to the buddhas appears to be that while the buddhas intrinsically pertain to the secret (i.e. the essence of reality), sentient beings can know and penetrate it, but in order to achieve this they need to perform a particular practice.[11]

The identification of the three secrets with mantric utterances, specific hand gestures and mandalas has its *locus classicus* in the *Putixin lun*, a Chinese treatise traditionally regarded as Amogavajra's translation of an Indic text. Here it is explicitly asserted that those who train in the contemplative practice of yoga perform the three secret practices (*sanmixing* 三密行) and attain the body of Mahāvairocana through a fivefold meditation (*wuxiang chengshen* 五相成身). The three practices consist in forming mudras (the secret of the body), reciting mantras (the verbal secret) and "contemplating the mind aspiring to enlightenment" (the secret of the mind).[12]

These passages seemingly establish an unambiguous difference between the esoteric and the non-esoteric traditions. The textual material, however, raises a number of questions. First of all, it suggests that Chinese esoteric Buddhism rested on the understanding of the practice of *sanmitsu* as being skillful means expressed through concrete forms (*youxiang fanbian* 有相方便). In this it followed a tendency to emphasize the abstract principle of enlightenment as the ultimate truth, which appears to have been common to much of Chinese thought of the Tang period. The *Dari jing* itself repeatedly asserts that ritual forms, being physical marks (*shixiang* 事相) of the identity with the absolute, led to inferior forms of knowledge (*liehui* 劣慧) (see T 18, pp. 4c–5a and T 18, p. 54c). A most important canonical scripture of the esoteric traditions thus remained consonant with the interpretation of non-esoteric Buddhism. The terminology that identified the nature of the Buddha and of the practitioner in the *Commentary*, and the notion that ritual activity is an expedient means, echoed traditional Tiantai understandings of the topic.[13] The *Commentary* also quoted extensively from the Lotus sutra to explain that skilful means were necessary in order to enter the reality embodied in the *Dari jing*, and that through these means it was possible to attain enlightenment during a single life-time (*yisheng kecheng* 一生可成) (*Shu*, p. 613a; *Yishi*, p. 90a). Significantly, Japanese Buddhism would be ill at ease with this interpretation of the three secret practices and both Tōmitsu (i.e. Kūkai's lineages) and Taimitsu lineages would engage in complex debates on whether the three practices should be given a relative or absolute status. This has led scholars to suggest that it was only in Japanese Tantrism, more prominently in Annen's writings, that the importance of ritual practices (*usō* 有相) as the expression of the ultimate reality was unequivocally argued and validated.[14]

A second issue at stake is the meaning of the "secret of the mind." This feature of esoteric praxis is usually explained as the visualization/contemplation of a mandalic object of worship (*honzon* 本尊), and indeed the mandala may be regarded as the single element that sets esoteric doctrine and practice apart from its non-esoteric equivalent. The *Commentary to the Dari jing* emphasizes the visualization of the *honzon* as a practice that on its own allows the practitioner to enter the dharma world (*Shu*, p. 582a; *Yishi*, p. 10c). However, another fundamental text of the esoteric tradition, the *Putixin lun*, explains the third secret as being a conceptual contemplation of the *bodhicitta* (*guan putixin* 観菩提心) rather than the visualization of a concrete object. In other words, the emphasis is still on an abstract mode, resonating with more conventional Mahāyāna positions. Unless the focus of visualization (for instance, the seed-letter A) is specified, the secret practice of the mind remains the same activity as that advocated in non-esoteric traditions – meditation is after all a fundamental Buddhist practice.

These different elements have prompted scholars to suggest that the idiom related to the three secrets does not come from Indic Tantric texts; as with its use in *Fahua xuanyi*, its textual origin must be sought in Chinese thought, first of all in the *Da zhidu lun* (Misaki 1988, pp. 39–40). The *Putixin lun* itself cites several passages of the *Commentary to the Dari jing*, indicating that it may have been compiled in China after Amogavajra and under the influence of Tiantai notions.[15]

The preaching of the dharmakāya

Another crucial standpoint of Japanese esoteric Buddhism is the claim that all three bodies of the Buddha, including his eternal dharma body, perform a threefold action. This is what is known as "the preaching of the *dharmakāya*" (*hosshin seppō* 法身説法). Kūkai argued that the active nature of the dharma body was not properly clarified in non-esoteric texts. Furthermore he posited esoteric teachings to be scriptures which, by definition, had been preached by the *dharmakāya*.

While the motionless character of the Buddha's dharma body is asserted in several sources of mainstream Mahāyāna, Kūkai cannot be completely credited with the invention of a new concept of the dharma body, nor did this originate in Japan. Let us turn again to the hermeneutical tradition of the Lotus sutra. The "Medicinal Herbs" Chapter of the Lotus speaks of the Buddha's teaching as a dense cloud (*miyun* 密雲) that spreads out in the sky and lets rain fall over various types of plants and grass, allowing each of them to grow in a different way. The exegesis of the chapter that Zhiyi presented in his *Fahua wenju* interpreted the cloud as a metaphor for the three mysteries: its spreading over all the plants (symbol of the compassion of the Buddha), its form and colours, and the roar of the thunder that comes out of the cloud are said to be respectively the secret of the mind, the secret of the body and the verbal secret of the Buddha. Zhiyi identified the element of the voice with the preaching of the Buddha in his transformation body (*ōjin seppō* 応身説法) and thus associated the production of sound (i.e. the preaching) to the *nirmāṇakāya* and not to the two other bodies of the Buddha (T 34, p. 92b; cf. T 9, p. 19b–c). Contrary to this perspective, however, other Chinese interpretations of the Lotus sutra argued that the cloud represented the dharma body's actions. One case in point is the *Fahua jingshu* 法華経疏 by Daosheng 道生 (d. 434), which explicitly asserts that the preaching of the *dharmakāya* is embodied by the "Medicinal Herbs" Chapter of the Lotus sutra (Ōkubo 2004, pp. 65–66). Ōkubo Ryōshun has pointed out that the preaching of the dharma body was an important issue in continental Tiantai. The term itself already appeared in Zhiyi's commentaries on the *Vimalakīrti-sūtra* and was elaborated upon by Zhanran 湛然 (711–782) (Cf. *Weimo jing lueshu*, T 38, p. 566c). One may question whether the concept was fully developed in China, but these sources are relevant in the Buddhist intellectual history, also because they closely influenced esoteric formulations in Japan, at least within the Tendai lineages. Annen's interpretation of the "preaching of the *dharmakāya*," for instance, drew extensively on continental Tiantai, and Zhiyi's *Commentary to the Vimalakīrti-sūtra* constituted a major textual source for him. Interestingly, although Annen was greatly influenced by Kūkai's writings, in this context especially by the treatise on reality as sound and letters, *Shōji jissōgi* 聲字実相義, he did not refer to the text that is today regarded as the *locus classicus* of Shingon's concept of the *dharmakāya*, Kūkai's *Ben kenmitsu nikyō ron*.[16]

Annen may have been particularly interested in associating and comparing non-esoteric and esoteric sources, but in fact the textual grounds on which Kūkai himself constructed his interpretation of *hosshin seppō* included non-esoteric sutras. In *Ben kenmitsu nikyō ron*, for instance, Kūkai extensively cited the *Laṅkāvatāra-sūtra* as evidence for the preaching of the *dharmakāya*

(T 77, p. 370a–b; cf. *Lankāvatāra-sūtra*, T 16, no. 671, p. 525b).[17] Thus Kūkai, too, did not find it problematic to use non-esoteric sources to prove concepts that, by definition, should have belonged to esoteric Buddhism. Tantric thinkers were well aware of the extent to which the concept of *hosshin seppō* was present, at least as an idiom, in non-esoteric sources. Kūkai argued that previous interpreters had not fully understood the meaning of the concept. Annen explained that the way in which previous schools (i.e. non-esoteric interpretations) presented the *hosshin seppō* was different from the way in which "Shingon-shū" (i.e. Japanese Tantric lineages) understood it. One can therefore conclude that the notion of *hosshin seppō* may be a characteristic of the esoteric schools if considered in its full development and in its emphasis on the *dharmakāya*, not in its origins: the *Lankāvatāra-sūtra* had presented the idea that all three bodies of the Buddha preach, but Tantric thinkers highlighted that the preaching of the *dharmakāya* is the only preaching that is significant, since this action only can express the most profound reality of the Buddha world.

Two elements of traditional Mahāyāna doctrine are thus renewed and revamped in the esoteric system: first, the notion of a threefold action is applied to the two supreme bodies of the Buddha, the *dharmakāya* and the self-oriented *samboghakāya*, and from here the concept of the preaching of the *dharmakāya* is enunciated; second, the three activities performed by sentient beings are posited as being identical to the threefold secret action of the Buddha, at least within the ritual context. In this sense they can be called the "three secret activities" (*sanmitsugyō*). While the notion of the "three mysteries" existed in non-esoteric Buddhist thought, as diversely as it was defined, the idea that the practitioner performs three secret activities remains specific to esotericism and serves as the *trait d'union* between the threefold secret of the Buddha and the three activities of human beings. This concept is ultimately related to the notion of *sokushin jōbutsu* 即身成仏, the attainment of buddhahood with one's own body, another fundamental concept in esoteric Buddhism, which cannot be addressed here.[18]

The esoteric–exoteric secret according to Annen: A Taimitsu synthesis?

To conclude the conceptual analysis undertaken so far it is valuable to revisit the connection between the esoteric and the non-esoteric meaning of *himitsu* by turning to Japan. The question of esoteric Buddhism's relation to other streams of Chinese Buddhism seems to have been particularly relevant for Taimitsu writers, who had to make sense of two elaborate and apparently competing systems of doctrine and practice: the esoteric system created by Kūkai, and the Lotus-based Tiantai system. In spite of the established connections between the two, which the material surveyed above demonstrates, the sectarian tendency that I have noted in the designation of a teaching as "secret" became definitive in Japan with Kūkai. Taimitsu thinkers responded in various ways to the challenge of rearticulating the esoteric with the help of its matching category, the "exoteric." Annen is perhaps the most fascinating of these scholiasts, as he systematized earlier and contemporary doctrines held by both Japanese esoteric lineages. He is often identified as the thinker responsible for the formal "esoterization" of Japanese Tendai, which he designated "Shingon," in this way stressing the importance of the esoteric mode for his school. At the same time, he was a follower and a critic of Kūkai, and therefore his thought represents a crucial step in the permutations that the understanding of the esoteric underwent in the Heian period.

There seems to be a conscious, reflective effort in Annen's analysis of the use of the notion of "secret" in Buddhism. His *Bodaishingi shō*, an extended commentary on the *Putixin lun* and a compendium of the esoteric knowledge that existed in Japan in the early Heian period, offers good examples for his hermeneutics. While discussing the three esoteric secrets of body, word and mind, Annen questions whether the term *himitsu*, as it was used in exoteric canonical literature, had the same meaning as the term that appears in two major esoteric sutras, the *Dari jing* and the *Jinggangding jing* (T 75, p. 492a–c). These two sutras are the textual source for the twofold esoteric system created by Kūkai, otherwise known as the mandalic tradition of the womb and diamond worlds (*taizō-kongōkai* 胎蔵·金剛界). To explore the question, Annen first looked into six possible meanings of *himitsu* that can be found in the scriptural body associated with the two esoteric sutras, first in the *Commentary to the Dari jing*, which he held to represent the *taizōkai* tradition, and then in different texts of the *kongōkai* lineage. Secondly, he compared these esoteric expressions with other occurrences of the word *himitsu* in the Buddhist intellectual tradition, in sutras and śāstras such as the Lotus, the *Mahāparinirvāna-sūtra* and the *Da zhidu lun*. He addressed the meaning of *himitsu* in both semantic and philosophical terms. His final aim was to demonstrate that there is no difference between the concept of *himitsu* formulated in esoteric sources and that elaborated on in the Tiantai/ Tendai tradition. On the other hand, he argued that the interpretation that both Lotus and esoteric teachings give of the "secret" (*hokke shingon himitsu* 法華真言秘密) is not the same as the "secret" of other Buddhist traditions, for instance, the tradition of the Hossō School (T 75, p. 493b).[19]

The taxonomy included in *Bodaishingi shō* summarizes the various levels and connotations of the concept of secret that have been discussed in this chapter, and it may be useful to enumerate the six meanings while pointing out the textual sources Annen used as evidence, although these cannot be examined in more detail here.[20]

The first meaning, the secret of the true essence of the dharma (*hottai* 法体), equates the threefold secret of the Buddha and the threefold secret of sentient beings. Textual passages from Vasubandhu's *Treatise on the*

Lotus sutra illustrate the *taizōkai* position, while the *Hongaku san* 本覚賛 (the initial strophe of the spurious *Rengezanmai-kyō* 蓮華三昧経) represents the *kongōkai* line. The second meaning, the inner awareness of all buddhas (*shobutsu naishō* 諸仏内証), is defined as a secret that cannot be known by the bodhisattvas emerging from the earth, sentient beings or beings belonging to non-Buddhist traditions (*gedō* 外道). It draws on the *Commentary to the Dari jing* and the *Yuqi jing* 瑜祇経, another scripture that played an important role in the Taimitsu lineages. The third meaning is the secret that cannot be transmitted to those who do not have the capacity (*hikifuju* 非機不授 to receive it. This point readdresses the question of the predisposition of the audience of the Buddha along traditional terms. Annen corroborates it with a long quotation from a famous passage of the *Commentary to the Dari jing*, which explains the highest enlightenment offered by the practice of the three secrets with images and notions borrowed from the Lotus sutra.[21] The fourth meaning is the secret of which sentient beings are part although they are not yet aware of it. This point seems to be self-evident and does not receive much attention. The fifth meaning is a secret that cannot be perceived by those who have not entered the practice of meditation. Quotations from the *Commentary to the Dari jing* and the *Moheyan lun* 摩訶衍論 emphasize the need to keep the precepts and "enter the mandala" in order to possess this secret. Finally, the sixth meaning of secret concerns the contents of the ritual practice, which cannot be revealed to outsiders.

Several themes can be highlighted from this taxonomy. First of all, Annen made a distinction between what is *ontologically* secret and what is *ritually* secret. Second, he differentiated between buddhas and sentient beings, but put emphasis on the perspective of sentient beings. Third, he considered different steps of the process through which sentient beings can enter esoteric practice. The latter is interesting in that it seems to indicate a move from beings who do not have the capacity to grasp and share the enlightenment of the Buddha at all (that is, have an innate hindrance), to those who are not yet awakened to it (that is, have yet to implement their potentiality), to those who are not yet initiated (i.e., have not ritually accessed the truth). Annen thus seems to shift the focus from an epistemological concern for the most profound doctrine, to which access is gained on the basis of capacity, to an understanding of the doctrine being dependant on training. In other words, the emphasis is no longer, or not exclusively, on the content of the secret teaching, which may change, but on the method to reach it. In separating the perspective of the Buddha from the perspective of human beings, Annen stressed the aspects involved in the endeavour of sentient beings entering esoteric practice. In this sense, he dealt with the question by addressing not only the ontological dimension of secrecy, but also the training needed to grasp and partake in such secrecy. Finally, the textual sources that Annen used suggest a new semantic dimension of the esoteric landscape. The fluctuation of vocabulary and imagery that occurs between the esoteric and the non-esoteric provides an example of the difficulty of setting clear-cut demarcations between the two, since from the beginning they shared much of the technical language and continued to borrow from each other during their development.

From secret teaching to esoteric teaching: The esoterization of the Lotus sutra

The interaction between the esoteric and its "other" is crystallized in the process of esoterization of the Lotus sutra. This was a development that amplified the significance of the esoteric through the comprehensive transformation of a non-esoteric source. It exemplifies the way in which the taxonomic categories and buddhological notions outlined above were applied to a specific case, and, at the same time, it supplies a wealth of material that sheds light on the practice of mandalization from a different point of view. In this, it challenges the monolithic definition of the esoteric shaped by contemporary Shingon orthodoxy.

A new taxonomy of esoteric scriptures

The first step towards the transformation of the Lotus sutra into an esoteric scripture proper is arguably a taxonomic inclusion of the scripture in the category of *mikkyō*. Kūkai presented the esoteric scriptures as the teachings of the *dharmakāya* Mahāvairocana and claimed that, as such, they were of a completely different nature than the exoteric scriptures that had been preached by the *nirmāṇakāya* Śākyamuni. The Lotus sutra clearly fell under this rubric of exoteric. Nevertheless Kūkai credited it with a degree of "esoteric" status, as conveyed at the end of his most extensive sectarian writing the *Jūjūshin ron*. Here an imaginary interlocutor questions the use of the term *himitsu* as exclusively indicating the teachings expounded by Mahāvairocana, on the ground that the terms *shingon* and *himitsu* were also recurrent among the teachings of Śākyamuni. Kūkai defends his position, arguing for two types of "secret" (*himitsu*):

> In various sutras such as the Lotus and the Nirvana, or the Vinaya canon, secret (*hi*) [teachings] are mentioned.... In the Lotus sutra this term is used in reference to the enlightenment of the two vehicles [*śrāvakas* and *pratyekabuddhas*].... This is a small secret (*shōmitsu* 小密), which does not explain the ultimate. The *Dari jing* states:

The continuously existent marks of the mind, which is the place of the superior Mahāyāna, are the great secret of all buddhas (*shobutsu dai himitsu* 諸仏大秘密). Those outside the path (*gedō*) cannot perceive it.

Therefore, as for "secret," there is the great and the small. Of Shingon, too, there is the great and the small. This is why in the *Putichang jing* 菩提場経 it is said: "I name [some teachings] Shingon, and I name [others] Great Shingon." The Shingon of the beginning is the Shingon expounded by the *nirmāṇakāya*. The Great Shingon is the Shingon expounded by the ultimate *dharmakāya*.

Question: How are Shingon and Great Shingon distinct?

Answer: It is, for instance, like [the difference] between Mahāyāna and Hīnayāna.[22]

Kūkai thus acknowledged that certain elements of the Lotus sutra, which the tradition had regarded to be typical of a secret teaching, would qualify the scripture as esoteric (if one takes the meaning of Shingon in this passage to be that of esoteric teachings in a broad, non-sectarian sense); meanwhile he maintained an irreducible difference with the esoteric teachings proper, embodied in the two sutras, *Dari jing* and *Jinggangding jing*.[23]

Ninth-century Taimitsu scholar-monks reformulated this hermeneutical model and, drawing from notions of the "secret" that had been put forward in the continental tradition of the Lotus, created a new definition of *mikkyō*. They set aside the dichotomy based on the preacher of the scriptures in favour of other aspects of the Buddhist doctrine. Ennin 円仁 (794–864), for instance, emphasized that Mahāyāna sutras were esoteric (*mikkyō*) and equated exoteric teachings (*kengyō*) with Hīnayāna – a position that reiterated the Chinese discourse on the secret as expressed in the *Da zhidu lun* and in other treatises on the Lotus sutra.[24] He classified the scriptures that contained the notion of "three vehicles" (namely, the existence of different paths for *śrāvakas*, *pratyekabuddhas* and bodhisattvas) as exoteric, and considered the notion of the "one vehicle" to constitute the category of the esoteric (*Soshijjikyō shō*, pp. 388a–b, 408b). In this way, Ennin was able to add the Lotus sutra (and other sutras as well) to the *Dari jing* and *Jinggangding jing* in order to form a new taxonomy of *mikkyō*: he eliminated the original distinction between exoteric and esoteric set-up by Kūkai and expanded the category of *mikkyō*, including scriptures that Kūkai had classified as exoteric. This operation implied a more complex articulation of the category of the esoteric. Ennin and his successors Enchin 円珍 (814–91) and Annen maintained a nuanced understanding of the esoteric, within which distinctions were made between different *classes* of *mikkyō*. Ennin introduced two types of esoteric teachings: those that only contain the principle of esoteric Buddhism (*rimitsu* 理密) and those that also reveal the practice of esoteric Buddhism (*riji gumitsu* 理事倶密) (*Soshijjikyō shō*, p. 388; *Kongōchōkyō shō*, p. 133). This classification, which again borrowed from the continental distinction of *li* 理 and *shi* 事, was an important contribution of Taimitsu to the history of esoteric Buddhism in Japan, and was developed within the lineage in various ways. Annen, for instance, using the *Commentary to the Dari jing* as textual evidence, characterized the Lotus sutra as an "abbreviated explanation" (*ryakusetsu* 略説) that, accordingly, elucidated only the principle of esotericism; the esoteric scriptures, on the contrary, were "comprehensive explanations" (*kōsetsu* 広説) that clarified both the practice and the principle (*jiri* 事理) (*Bodaishingi shō*, p. 590).

These theories emphasize that the exoteric and the esoteric are equivalent in their understanding of the ultimate reality; at the same time they maintain the superiority of the esoteric practice (*ji* can be here glossed with *sanmitsu*), which is seen as a privileged access to the ultimate. Such a limitation notwithstanding, Taimitsu was successful in establishing a taxonomic understanding of the Lotus sutra as an esoteric scripture. By being inserted into a formal classificatory system, the Lotus was thus elevated to the status of a "proper esoteric" text, albeit in a less complete form.[25] If one takes into account the role played by scriptural classifications (*panjiao*) in shaping the meaning of a sutra in pre-modern Buddhism, one realizes to what extent the hermeneutical strategy put forward in Taimitsu was a crucial step in the process of esoterization of the Lotus.

The preacher(s) of esoteric scriptures

Although the new classifications of the esoteric devised by the Tendai lineages seem to overshadow the role of Mahāvairocana in determining the esoteric status of scriptures, Taimitsu scholiasts were extremely concerned with reassessing the figure of the Buddha and re-evaluated the position of Śākyamuni *vis-à-vis* Mahāvairocana as the preacher of the esoteric teachings. The esoterization of the Lotus sutra was also carried out at the ontological level, through a reconfiguration of the Buddhist reality embodied by the scripture. This was a complex operation in which specific aspects of the preaching of Śākyamuni were equated with characteristics of the esoteric Buddha. Taimitsu monks stressed the imagery of the eternal assembly of the Vulture Peak, the place where Śākyamuni had preached the Lotus, and drew from different interpretations of the sixteenth chapter of the Lotus sutra – the chapter where Śākyamuni proclaims his "eternity" – to substantiate the absolute dimension of the spatio-temporal identity of Śākyamuni. As a result, the Buddha who preached the Lotus sutra could be conclusively characterized as a counterpart of the Buddha Mahāvairocana in his (eternally preaching) dharma body. Enchin turned to the *Commentary to the Dari jing*, which had presented Mahāvairocana's "body of the original ground" as "the deepest and most secret abode of the Lotus" (the passage mentioned in the previous section), and reformulated this phrase to assert that "the original ground that attained enlightenment in the remote past" (*kujō honji*), that is, the Buddha of the sixteenth chapter of the Lotus sutra, was "the ground of the mind of the dharma world" (*hokkai shinji*) explained in the *Dari jing* (*Daibirushanakyō shiki*, p. 665).

The relation of the *Commentary to the Dari jing* to the Lotus sutra needs to be underlined here, as both texts played a crucial role in defining the multi-layered connections between the esoteric and the exoteric. Taimitsu thinkers exploited the *Commentary* to propound the esoteric aspects of the Lotus sutra, since the *Commentary* was an established and important canonical source of esoteric Buddhism. In doing so they replicated, in the reverse direction, the hermeneutical strategy deployed in the *Commentary*, which had made use of the Lotus sutra and its exegetical tradition (a major stream of intellectual thought in Chinese Buddhism of the Tang period) to convey the special character of Mahāvairocana. The associations made by Enchin have their precedent in the *Commentary* itself. Yixing, the compiler of the *Commentary*, who had trained as a Tiantai monk before becoming a disciple of Śubhakarasiṃha, had borrowed the idea of the immeasurable lifespan of Śākyamuni to "translate" the eternal existence of Mahāvairocana. He had explained the Womb mandala (*taizōkai*) as the "pure land" of the Lotus sutra, and had also described visions of Śākyamuni and the bodhisattvas of the Lotus as the result of esoteric practice. The strategy at issue is clear in a passage such as this:

> When the practitioner attains this mind [of enlightenment], he knows that the pure land of Śākyamuni will not be destroyed; he sees that the Buddha's life span extends into the very distant [past] (*changyuan* 長遠) and that [this] body of the original ground (*bendishen* 本地身) sits in one assembly together with Visistacāritra and the other bodhisattvas who have emerged from the earth.[26]

The assimilation of lexicon, images and concepts derived from the Lotus sutra thus had crucial consequences for the reformulation of the category of the esoteric carried out in Taimitsu; further, it affected the esoteric ritualization of the Lotus that was accomplished in Japan. It may be suggested that although the early Taimitsu thinkers posited the Lotus as a "lower class *mikkyō*," they did open up the possibility of constructing an esoteric system for the Lotus. In order to accomplish this, the scripture needed to be furnished with proper esoteric accessories, the mudras, mantras and mandalas that defined the threefold esoteric practice (*sanmitsu*) – in other words, the Lotus identity in principle with the esoteric teachings (*rimitsu*) needed to be changed into an identity of praxis (*jimitsu*). This is what took place with the development of the esoteric rituals of the Lotus.

Esoteric liturgies of the Lotus (*hokke hō*)

The analysis of the liturgical transformation of the Lotus according to esoteric patterns is a complex task, as the documents related to it have been little studied and their origins and contexts are in many cases still problematic. The first description of an esoteric Lotus rite is in the *Fahua guanzhi yigui*, a Chinese manual that explains a method to realize the identity of the three mysteries (Jap. *sanmitsu yuga* 三密瑜伽) by using the Lotus sutra. Traditionally this text was thought to be an Indian manual translated by Amoghavajra, but scholars are now more inclined to regard it as a work compiled in China by someone within Amoghavajra's entourage – once again the presence in the text of several elements derived from the Tiantai interpretation of the Lotus sutra points to a Chinese, rather than Indian, origin. The liturgy described in the *Fahua guanzhi yigui* unfolds in several steps, comprising hymns of praise for each chapter of the Lotus sutra, the construction of a ritual platform and of a mandala of the Lotus, the recitation of mantras (some of which are taken from the scripture itself) and the recitation of chapters of the Lotus sutra. I shall focus my analysis on the mandala qua representative element of the adoption of an esoteric pattern, and on its concurrent connections to the two major esoteric mandalas and to the Lotus sutra imagery.[27]

The mandala of the Lotus sutra

The *Fahua guanzhi yigui* gives a brief description of the mandala, while another short, apocryphal sutra known as *Weiyi xingse jing* supplies its iconographic details. The basic structure of the Lotus mandala derives from the central hall of the *taizōkai* mandala. It consists of an eight-petalled lotus flower, inscribed in the centre of which is a jewelled stupa, with the two Buddhas of the Lotus, Śākyamuni and Prabhūtaratna, seated inside. On the eight petals of the flower, eight bodhisattvas that appear in the Lotus sutra are installed (Maitreya, Mañjuśri, Bhaiṣajyarāja, Gadgadasvara, Nityodyukta, Akṣayamati, Avalokiteśvara and Samantabhadra) and four *śrāvakas* are placed in the corners of this first hall (Mahākāśyapa, Subhuti, Śāriputra and Maudgalyāyana). The other two layers of the Lotus mandala include deities borrowed from the two major esoteric mandalas: the offering bodhisattvas in the second hall, and a cohort of protective deities, including the Four Heavenly Kings, dragons and other demonic beings, in the external hall (Fig. 6.1). The basic principle of the mandalization of the Lotus scripture seems thus to be to construct a recognizable mandalic structure and to inscribe deities directly connected to sections or chapters of the sutra in its central section. The central placement of the stupa is noteworthy: the precious stupa is a fundamental element of the narrative of the Lotus sutra and was predominant in non-esoteric representations of the scripture; at the same time it invited associations with an important constituent of mythological accounts of the transmission of esoteric teachings, the iron stupa wherein their transmission took place. Probably because the stupa alone is a clear semantic referent, some representations visualize only the central part of the mandala focusing on the stupa (Fig. 6.2).[28] In the liturgical material of the *hokke hō*, the two Buddhas of the Lotus sutra, Śākyamuni and Prabhūtaratna, are conceived as embodiments of the two aspects of Mahāvairocana, Mahāvairocana of the *kongōkai* and Mahāvairocana of the *taizōkai*. This is clearly indicated in documents that prescribe the practitioner to visualize the two Buddhas through a progressive transformation of images, first their seed-letters, then esoteric objects and finally the two Mahāvairocana. Some icons also show this identity, the two Buddhas of the Lotus being represented with the mudras specific to each aspect of Mahāvairocana: Prabhūtaratna forming the wisdom fist mudra (*chiken-in* 智拳印), which is the signifier of Mahāvairocana of the *kongōkai*, and Śākyamuni forming the meditation mudra (*jō-in* 定印), which identifies Mahāvairocana of the *taizōkai* (Fig. 6.3).[29] Not only does this double connection accentuate the identification of Mahāvairocana and Śākyamuni; at the same time it highlights the nature of the *hokke hō* as a rite aiming at the unification of the two worlds of esoteric Buddhism.

Further mandalic associations

An expansion of the mandalic pattern occurred later in the history of the esoterization of the Lotus sutra. Japanese exegetes devised a more articulated combination of the world of the Lotus and the twofold system of esotericism (*ryōbu* 両部), producing multiple "mandalizations." For example, the two parts in which the Lotus sutra had been divided by the Tendai exegeses, the *honmon* 本門 and the *shakumon* 迹門 sections, were identified with the two mandalas *taizōkai* and *kongokai*; and individual chapters of the Lotus sutra were made to correspond with each part of the mandalic pattern, according to different principles of distribution. In *Hokekyō ryōkai wagōgi*, an apocryphal writing attributed to Enchin, the two most important chapters of the Lotus sutra were associated with the two major esoteric mandalas: Chapter 16, "The long life span of the Tathāgata," was associated to the Mahāvairocana of the main assembly of the *kongōkai* mandala, the *jōjinne* 成身会, and Chapter 2, "Skilful Means," was associated to the central hall of the *taizokai* mandala (CDZ 3, pp. 945–50). In this way more correlations were established between smaller segments of the scripture and the esoteric visual structure. Other combinations centred on the title of the Lotus sutra. In *Kōen hokke gi*, another Heian period text controversially attributed to Enchin, the characters of the Sino-Japanese title of the Lotus sutra, *Myō-hō-ren-ge*, are associated to the two esoteric mandalas: the two characters of *myō-hō* are said to embody the *taizōkai* mandala, and the two characters of *ren-ge* the *kongōkai* mandala; eventually the title in its entirety is conceived to be a symbol of the non-dual nature of the esoteric mandalas (CDZ 3, pp. 920–21). These hermeneutical practices point to a more advanced stage of the process of esoterization that was carried out in Japan, where the appropriation and incorporation of elements external to the Chinese Lotus ritual manual were accomplished through associative sequences *ad infinitum.*

Esoterizing the kami of the Tendai school

Since the late Heian period, several *kuden* 口伝 were produced that integrated Tendai doctrines in multiple ways and gave manifold shapes to each fundamental element of the Lotus ritual. Both liturgical expressions and interpretative positions were highly diverse and seem never to have been standardized. A case in point is the continuous shifting of the *honzon* from the canonical mandala of the Lotus to other Lotus-related objects, such as the stupa, a copy of the scripture itself, and even the *sarīra* (Dolce 2002). Similarly, the choice of deities to venerate during the liturgy attests to a great degree of variability.

An interesting example of this process of absorption of external elements, Tantric and otherwise, that characterized the Japanese practice is a document by Jien 慈円 (1155–1225), simply known as *Hokke betchō*. It consists of a detailed as well as peculiar version of the Lotus ritual, which must be regarded as Jien's personal interpretation of the liturgical tradition of the esoteric Lotus and its *kenmitsu* character. Among other features, the inclusion of two deities that were not part of the original set of venerables worshipped during the ritual is remarkable: Ichijikinrin 一字金輪 and the kami of Mount Hiei. The name of Ichijikinrin appears in some of the invocatory sections of the rite included in anthologies such as the *Asabashō* and the *Kakuzenshō*. In his *Hokke betchō*, however, Jien discussed the connections of this deity with the Lotus sutra in a more comprehensive way. He identified Ichijikinrin with Śākyamuni of the Lotus sutra and, accordingly, employed the seed-letter of Ichijikinrin, *bhrūm*, in the visualization stages of the Lotus ritual – for instance, he prescribed to the practitioner to imagine this seed-letter inside the mandala he would create in his mind. Jien's manual also attests to the association of the Sannō 山王 kami to Ichijikinrin. According to Misaki Ryōshū, this ritual text is one of the earliest examples of such association. Jien elucidated it both by arguing the personal identity of Sannō with Ichijikinrin and, more specifically, by using Ichijikinrin's seed-letter as the *honji* 本地 of the Sannō kami (Misaki 1992b). Further, Jien listed the name of Mount Hiei's kami among the deities to be venerated in different sections of his ritual manual, included the recitation of their mantras (*sannō shingon*), and stated that "when the Lotus ritual is performed at the [Hiei] shrines (*onsha* 御社) this ritual programme should be used" (ZTZ, p. 260). These instructions give evidence that the *hokke hō* was used as a distinct liturgy for the Sannō deities.

Jien apparently was very interested in the esoteric Lotus ritual, and from 1205 performed it every year for seven days and nights at the Daizanbō-in of Shōrenji (the residence of the Tendai *zasu*) for the benefit of the Retired

Emperor Go-Toba. The tradition of using the *hokke hō* for the Sannō kami was continued within Jien's lineage, and it is attested until the early Tokugawa period. Tenkai 天海 (1536–1643) commissioned a Lotus mandala as the *honzon* for a ritual to be performed for the Sannō Gongen 山王権現, the deified Tokugawa Ieyasu, at the Tōshōgū in Nikkō. Although there are no details on how the liturgy itself was performed, the mandala that was presumably used in the occasion has been preserved (Fig. 6.4).[30] In fact three Lotus mandalas are among the holdings of the Treasure Hall of Rinnōji 輪王寺 in Nikkō.[31] Scholars have also suggested that the construction of a "Lotus stupa" (*tahōtō* 多宝塔) in Nikkō, which Tenkai sponsored, was part of his programme to reiterate, *mutatis mutandi*, the process that had taken place in mediaeval Japan (Misaki 1992b).

The integration of deities that were important within the Tendai lineages into the distinctively Tendai esoteric liturgy of the Lotus, a conspicuously Japanese development of the practice of the Lotus, points to a sectarian use of the Lotus ritual. Other examples of Lotus mandala also shed light on this hypothesis.

The Lotus mandala and Taimitsu "threefold Tantrism": An alternative system of the esoteric?

The liturgical material offers ample ground to assess the construction of the *hokke hō* as a rite that unifies the two worlds of esoteric Buddhism. The nature of the *hokke hō* as a combinatory practice already emerges in Chinese canonical sources such as the *Fahua guanzhi yigui*, and according to scholars of Chinese esotericism it may have represented a stream of esoteric interpretation that existed in Tang China. In Japan, however, it took on a comprehensive format, supported as it was by the theoretical elaborations of Taimitsu thinkers, and, I believe, it crucially affected the development of the esoteric paradigm along lines different from those set by Kūkai.

The distinctive configuration of esoteric Buddhism put forward by Taimitsu scholiasts was a "threefold system of Tantric Buddhism" (*sanbu mikkyō* 三部密教), in which the ultimate reality was explained and represented according to a threefold pattern. This mode, clearly triggered by the exegetical pattern developed in continental Tiantai, contrasted with the system developed by Kūkai, where the esoteric reality of enlightenment was embodied in two mandalas, *taizōkai* and *kongōkai*, based respectively on the *Dari jing* and the *Jinggangdingjing*, and considered to be non-dual in their distinct forms. In the Taimitsu interpretation, the two mandalas continued to represent the two symbiotic aspects of buddhahood, but its accomplishment, embodied in the non-duality of the *taizōkai* and *kongōkai* mandalas, was thought to be achieved only in a third element, which functioned as the unifying core of the two worlds. This third component was epitomized in the *Suxidi jing* 蘇悉地経, a text that played an important role in Chinese Buddhism but not in Kūkai's system.[32] Pertinent to our argument is that this text included mantras and mudras of certain relevance in the history of esoteric Buddhism, but a proper mandala based on it was never produced.[33] It is not clear, thus, how the *Suxidi jing* could fulfil such a fundamental function within the threefold system, when its ritual use lacked one of the three essential components (*sanmitsu*): the mandala, focus of the practice of the secret of the mind. In this sense it is questionable whether the triple structure consisting of *taizō, kongō* and *soshijji* 蘇悉地 (Chin. *suxidi*) worked beyond the basic theoretical (hermeneutical) level. This anomaly in the system also means that there are no concrete representations of the specific type of Tantrism put forward by Taimitsu.

It may be suggested, however, that the Lotus mandala functioned as the missing third element, since it offered a tangible illustration of the unity of the worlds of the two mandalas, and consequently may have been used instead of a "soshijji mandala." In this sense, the Lotus mandala again played a role in the sectarian construction of the esoteric that took place in Japan.

Threefold mandala sets

The most important evidence for this hypothesis comes from iconographic material from the late Heian to the mediaeval period, to which scholars have thus far paid no attention: threefold sets of mandalas where the two major esoteric mandalas are associated with the Lotus mandala. I have to date identified three examples of this curious iconographic group.

The first set consists of three *shuji* mandalas on silk, representing the venerables of the *taizōkai, kongōkai* and Lotus mandalas with their seed-letters. It is dated 1052 according to an inscription on the reverse side of the *kongōkai* mandala (Fig. 6.5). They were found in a sutra container that was excavated, together with other objects, from the area around the Oku no In on Mount Kōya.[34] The container, dated 1113, is inscribed with the name of a certain Bikuni Hōyaku, probably the woman who sponsored the reproduction of the mandalas as a personal vow. More about the circumstance of this set may perhaps be learnt by analysing the *ganmon* and the list of pious activities of the patron, which are among the buried items. Interestingly, the mandalic icons were buried together with a copy of the Threefold Lotus sutra preciously written in indigo and gold. This combination with (non-esoteric) material related to the cultic practices of the Lotus sutra points to the diffusion of the Lotus mandala as an established representation of the sutra, defying the distinctions between esoteric and exoteric.

The second instance is a set of three "three thousand buddha images" (*sanzenbutsu zu* 三千仏図) on silk, dated from the Muromachi period, and held at Shōsanji 焼山寺, one of the eighty-eight temples in the Shikoku pilgrimage circuit. Each of these three paintings depicts in its centre one of the three mandalas, or rather their representative sections: the *jōjinne* of the *kongōkai*, the central hall of the *taizōkai* and the central hall of the Lotus mandala (Fig. 6.6).[35]

The final example is a portable altar (*zushi*厨子) enshrining a *taizōkai* mandala that was carved in wood in Tang China and is now among the holdings of the Kongōbuji 金剛峰寺, also on Mount Kōya. The mandala is thought to have been brought to Japan in the early eighth century, since it represents a version of the *taizōkai* older than that transmitted by Kūkai, and it is known to have been at Kōya-san already in the second half of the thirteenth century. The *zushi*, however, was made in Japan in the Kamakura period. The inner sides of its doors represent two seed-letter mandalas: on the left, the *jōjinne* of the *kongōkai*, and on the right, a Lotus mandala. In this way, the *zushi*, when it was opened, showed a threefold mandalic icon (Fig. 6.7).[36] This is a most intriguing example because it suggests a conscious attempt to operate a visual transformation of the Chinese model by combining the two great esoteric mandalas with the Lotus mandala.

Constructing a new type of "esoteric" through the Lotus

Not much is known of the context in which these threefold mandala sets were conceived and spread in mediaeval Japan, but their existence points to a concrete possibility that the Lotus mandala constituted a viable representation of the (originally Taimitsu) attempt to construct an alternative system of *mikkyō*. Early Taimitsu sources do not discuss a substitute mandala for the *Suxidi jing*. Yet mediaeval works present some textual evidence of the attempt to insert the esoteric Lotus within a threefold structure.

The *Keiran shūyōshū*, a fourteenth-century doctrinal and liturgical collection of the Tendai school, by Kōshū 光宗, includes an articulate examination of the issue, which decodes the canonical source of the Lotus mandala, the *Fahua guanzhi yigui*, and the mandala itself, in order to demonstrate that it embodies the *Suxidi jing* and therefore can play the middle role in the threefold system. The text distinguishes between the interpretations of the Tōji 東寺 lineages (Tōmitsu) and of the Sanmon 山門 and Jimon 寺門 lineages (Taimitsu), and explicitly asserts that "by adding the Lotus ritual [to the practice of the two mandalas], the Sanmon lineages concretely symbolized the integration of the three parts (*sanbu gusoku* 三部具足)." (T 76, p. 593b).[37] Kōshū draws attention to Śākyamuni as a crucial link between the esoteric Lotus and the *Suxidi jing*, since Śākyamuni is the central buddha in both (T 76, p. 593b). Even more significant is his analysis of the stupa of the Lotus mandala. He reiterates the identification of the central section of the Lotus mandala with the *taizōkai*, on the grounds that both are arranged in the same eight-petalled flower pattern; he links the second hall of the Lotus mandala with the *kongōkai* because the offering bodhisattvas that are installed in it are figures from the *kongōkai*; and finally he considers the stupa at the centre of the Lotus mandala to signify the *soshijji* (T 76, pp. 608b, 609c). To validate this connection, the *Keiran shūyōshū* discusses the differences and similarities between the precious stupa that appears in the narrative of the Lotus sutra and the iron stupa where the esoteric teachings were found, and here the text asserts the sameness of the exoteric and the esoteric (*kenmitsu funi*) (T 76, p. 607b). This position is of great consequence for the reassessment of the relation between *ken* and *mitsu*, and in several places the ritual anthology alludes to a different meaning of the esoteric. For instance, borrowing from other exegetes of this liturgical tradition, it presents the content of the *Fahua guanzhiyigui*, that is, the esoteric liturgies of the Lotus sutra, as the "secret within the exoteric-esoteric [system]" (*kenmitsu chū himitsu* 顕密中秘密) (T 76, p. 592).

Mediaeval iconographic and doctrinal materials thus suggest that the attempt to construct an alternative system of *mikkyō*, initiated within Taimitsu circles, was crystallized in the *hokke hō* in a multi-faceted manner. The ritual embodied the Taimitsu ideal of the unity of the exoteric and esoteric (*enmitsu itchi*); the mandala and its multiple combinations with the *taizōkai* and *kongōkai* realms presented a concrete example of a threefold esoterization of reality. Did this process of esoterization truly help form a sectarian identity, Taimitsu *versus* Tōmitsu? The distinctive discourse on the esoteric carried on in the *Keiran shūyōshū* seems to imply so. On the other hand, the provenance of the iconographic examples of a threefold interpretative pattern from locations that unambiguously represent Kūkai's lineages (Mount Kōya, for instance) suggests the possibility that the structure devised by Taimitsu thinkers spread beyond the sectarian confines of Tendai. Similarly, one may object to the simple narrative of antagonistic systems, the twofold and threefold esotericism, by noting that their opposition was not absolute: on the one hand, the *Suxidi jing* was used not only in Taimitsu, but transmissions based on it are attested also in Tōmitsu lineages such as the Ono-ryū;[38] on the other hand, the two major mandalas, *taizōkai* and *kongōkai*, maintained a central role in the practice of both Tōmitsu and Taimitsu lineages, since the fundamental ritual of ordination of all schools of Japanese esotericism (*shidokegyō*) was (and still is) based on them. Such convoluted relationships intimate that it is more pertinent to speak of alternative, rather than competing, types of *mikkyō*. These were not the exclusive possession of one school, but may have been shared by different lineages having a common interest in reinterpreting the esoteric system.

The esoteric impasse: Sectarian hermeneutics and intersectarian performance

The significance of the esoteric Lotus ritual in a sectarian context is a controversial subject, and more historical sources are necessary to shed light on it.

One of the first Japanese documents which mentions the *hokke hō* is the diary that the Tendai monk Jōjin 成尋 (1011–81) kept during his journey in China, *San Tendai godaisan ki*. Jōjin recounts having performed the Lotus ritual to pray for rain. The monks who attended the liturgy, however, saw the rite as a novelty, and questioned Jōjin as to why he did not use a more common esoteric rite for rain-making. Jōjin's responses seem to imply a sectarian use of the *hokke hō*: he advocated it as a practice used by the Tendai lineages for different purposes, including prayers for rain; he also admitted his inability to perform the rain-making ritual used by Shingon monks, because he had not been initiated in it.[39] This answer may have been prompted by the particular situation in which Jōjin found himself, a foreign monk who had to justify his actions. To be true to the text, he spoke of the specific application of the rite as upheld within his own lineage (Enchin's lineage), rather than of an exclusive monopoly of the *hokke hō* by the Tendai school (DNBZ, p. 134b). Nevertheless he was obviously aware that a sectarian reason had prevented him from using the Shingon school's rite for rain.

Yet, a glance at ritual compilations of the Shingon school from the Insei period (1086–1192) onwards proves that the *hokke hō* had been adopted by several Taimitsu and Tōmitsu lineages, and for disparate uses. A handful of titles can be named that include sections on the Lotus ritual: the *Shijūjō ketsu* of Chōen 長宴 (1016–81), a contemporary of Jōjin, but belonging to the Sanmon lineage of Tendai; Genkai's 元海 (1094–1157) *Atsuzōshi*, of the Sanbōin branch of Tōmitsu; the *Denjushū* by Kanjin 寛信 (1084–1153), of the Kajūji branch of the Ōno school; Kenni's 兼意 (1072–after 1145) *Jōrenshō* 成蓮抄, of the other major Tōmitsu school, the Hirosawa, Ōmuro branch; and, finally, the *Kakuzenshō*, compiled by a monk of the Ōno-ryū between 1183 and 1213 and considered to be the representative anthology of Shingon liturgies, which devotes three ample sections to the rite. Thus, by the Insei period the *hokke hō* had acquired popularity among all branches of esoteric Buddhism, regardless of sectarian affiliations.

This intersectarian use of the *hokke hō* may be taken as evidence of the interest of mediaeval ritualists in all sorts of esoteric liturgies, in particular rituals devoted to the worship of an individual deity (*besson* 別尊), a rubric that also comprises rites centred on a single specific sutra (*kyōhō* 経法). It calls for a non-sectarian approach to ritual, in particular esoteric ritual, but at the same time it brings to the fore the problem of the countless sectarian subdivisions that exist in Japanese esotericism. This impasse is not only of concern to the modern academic. Esoteric masters, too, had to deal with it, although at times it seems that they regarded it as a question of form, not preventing the actual exchange of ritual knowledge. The beginning of the *Hokke hiketsu* section of the *Kakuzenshō* contains an interesting discussion of the canonical texts of the Lotus mandala, which relates to this issue as it addresses the legitimacy of sources that were not transmitted within a specific lineage. A monk casts doubts on whether the *Weiyi xingse jing*, the text that contains the iconographic details of the Lotus mandala, should be used by Shingon lineages even though it had not been transmitted by Kūkai. The position of the master here is that "it is wrong to maintain that one cannot use what has been transmitted by other lineages." He explains that the *Weiyi xingse jing* has authority in any case, since it was translated by Amoghavajra, one of the patriarchs of esoteric Buddhism. As with other rituals, Kūkai did not transmit all related texts and manuals. He passed on the essence (*kanjin* 肝心) of the various practices, and this became the foundation of their liturgies; the details are secondary, and therefore there is no problem with using sources that were imported later by monks of other lineages (DNBZ, p. 644a–b). This argument thus suggests that even the notion of a privileged transmission within one lineage, which is often considered to be a decisive factor in the construction of the esoteric, is not undisputed.

A final comparative consideration is necessary to put the esoteric Lotus into the larger picture of Sino-Japanese Buddhism. Jōjin's diary proves that the *hokke hō* was of no concern to Tiantai circles in twelfth-century China. Monks were keen to receive its transmission, and Jōjin also claimed to have reintroduced the textual sources of the ritual to China.[40] In spite of its deep roots in the Chinese esoteric discourse, the *hokke hō* had left no traces in Chinese Buddhism, while a full-fledged and diversified development took place in Japan through the centuries. Is it possible to deduce from this that the accomplished esoterization of the Lotus sutra was a truly Japanese phenomenon, triggered and sustained by the predominance of the esoteric model in the mediaeval period? And, was this esoterization different from the transformation that other non-esoteric scriptures had undergone in China? Amoghavajra's re-reading of the *Renwang jing* 仁王経 may be taken as a good example of another non-esoteric scripture that was altered by the inclusion of *dhāraṇī* and mandalas so that it could be used for esoteric rites of empowerment (Orzech 1998). The ritual based on the *Renwang jing* (*ninnōkyō hō* 仁王経法) and its mandalas continued to be used in Japan, but the liturgical anthologies do not offer evidence of elaborate doctrinal interpretations of this rite, nor of big variations in the ritual procedures. At one level this seems to indicate that the *Renwang jing* did not play a role in the reformulation of the category of the esoteric, as the esoteric Lotus did. In this sense, the esoterization of the Lotus sutra may have been different: it was part and parcel of a larger context in which different agents were involved in the taxonomic invention of the esoteric.

"The secret of the *kenmitsu*": Closing remarks

The meaning of the esoteric is usually articulated according to the doctrinal and ritual orthodoxy of today's Shingon school, a tendency that has led to essentialize the reality of Japanese Tantric Buddhism with a few catchwords, and to emphasize the uniqueness of the Tantric experience *vis-à-vis* the other Mahāyāna traditions active in Japan. Yet the findings discussed in this chapter reveal that the esoteric was diversely defined in Japanese Buddhism of the Heian and mediaeval periods. Moreover, the category of the "esoteric" included meanings which had already been formulated in (non-esoteric) Mahāyāna teachings; likewise, when new rituals or concepts of the esoteric were constructed, they were also informed by non-esoteric meanings. These features highlight the need for a less dichotomous and sectarian understanding of both the esoteric and the notion on which it is based, secrecy.

The focus on the Lotus sutra allows valuable insights into this issue, because it draws attention to the permutations of the notion of the secret into the notion of the esoteric and to the significance (and contradictions) of setting the esoteric apart from the rest of Buddhism. The esoteric liturgy of the Lotus and its related iconography may be seen as the climax of the process of "mandalization" of the Lotus. However, since the *hokke hō* was a ritual based on the Lotus sutra, not only did it rely on existing esoteric interpretations of the scripture, converting core elements of these interpretations into a proper ritual, it also incorporated non-esoteric hermeneutical and ritual practices of the Lotus, drawing in particular on the Tiantai tradition. Because the Lotus sutra was considered to be the fundamental text of the Tendai lineages, in scholastic terms it played a distinctive role in their sectarian legitimation, and this function was carried on into the esoteric Lotus, with the contradictions it may have had in a context of pan-sectarian use of rituals such as that of mediaeval Japan. To a certain extent, this purpose was also accomplished in political terms, by associating the kami of Mount Hiei and later of Nikkō to the liturgy.

The material related to the esoteric Lotus has raised as many questions as it has answered. Of these the most pressing, and the crucial one for understanding the nature of the esoterization process itself, remains the question of whether, and to what extent, the opposition esoteric/exoteric was an absolute and founding distinction. The ritual programmes and the different *honzon* and mantras used during the *hokke hō* reveal a continuous shift between esoteric and exoteric which, as I have pointed out elsewhere (Dolce 1999), in part already existed at the beginning of the tradition in China and greatly increased in the implementation of the practice during the mediaeval period in Japan. The same fluctuation can be detected in the scholastic technique of using both esoteric and non-esoteric sources as evidence for the esoteric, and in the discussions on the taxonomic position of the Lotus analysed in this chapter. The clerics who articulated the esoteric were well read in both esoteric and exoteric Mahāyāna texts, and their ritual and hermeneutical strategies indicate that, in spite of the rhetoric of the superiority of the esoteric, they acknowledged a degree of identity of the esoteric and the exoteric at various theoretical and practical levels. By the mediaeval period in Japan, this appreciation produced an ambiguous discourse of compatibility and differentiation. The corpus of esoteric knowledge reviewed here seems to intimate that, to paraphrase the words of the *Keiran shūyōshū*, the secret (i.e. real) meaning of the esoteric is to be found only within the multiple combinations of the esoteric and the non-esoteric.

Figure 6.1 Lotus mandala, *Kakuzenshō*. (Reproduction by courtesy from a
photographic replica of the Kajūji manuscript, Kakuzenshō
kenkyūkai (ed.) *Kajūji zenpon eiin shūsei* 勧修寺善本影印集成, vol. 4
Kōya city: Shinnōin Gyōei Bunkō, 2000.)

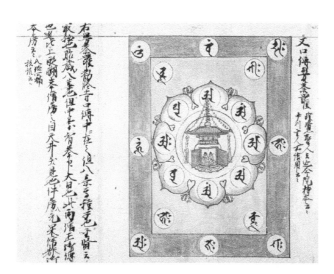

Figure 6.2 Lotus mandala, *Kakuzenshō*. (Reproduction by courtesy from a
photographic replica of the Kajūji manuscript, Kakuzenshō
kenkyūkai (ed.) *Kajūji zenpon eiin shūsei* 勧修寺善本影印集成, vol. 4.
Kōya city: Shinnōin Gyōei Bunkō, 2000.)

Figure 6.3 Details of a Lotus mandala showing the mudras of two Buddhas of the Lotus sutra. Colours on silk. Early Edo period. (Reproduction by courtesy of the Treasure Hall of Rinnōji, Nikkō.)

Figure 6.4 Lotus mandala. Colours on silk. Dated Kan'ei 17 (1640). (Reproduction by courtesy of the Treasure Hall of Rinnōji, Nikkō.)

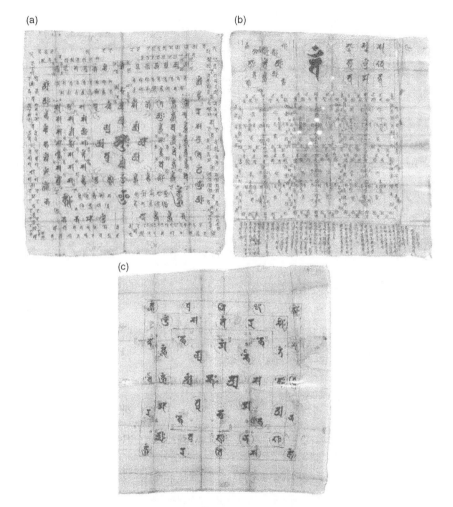

Figure 6.5a–c Taizōkai, kongōkai and Lotus mandalas in *shuji*. Ink on silk. Eleventh century. Important cultural property. (Reproduction by courtesy of Kongōbuji, Mt. Kōya.)

Figure 6.6a–c Set of three *sanzenbutsu zu* with *kongōkai, taizōkai* and Lotus mandalas inscribed at the centre. Colours on silk. Muromachi period. (Reproduction by courtesy of Shōsanji, Tokushima prefecture.)

(b)

Figure 6.6a–c (Continued)

(c)

Figure 6.6a–c (Continued)

Figure 6.7 Taizōkai mandala carved in wood. China, Tang period. Portable shrine (*zushi*). *Makie* gold decoration on lacquered wood. Kamakura period. Important cultural property (Reproduction by courtesy of Kongōbuji, Mt. Kōya.)

Notes

Research for this study was made possible by two generous grants of Canon Foundation in Europe and the Japan Foundation Endowment Committee, and the support of the British Academy.

The author would like to thank the following institutions for graciously giving permission to publish these images: Kongōbu Temple at Mt. Kōya, Wakayama prefecture; Treasure hall of Rinnō Temple, Nikkō, Tochigi prefecture; Shōsan Temple, Tokushima prefecture; Shinnōin Gyōei Archives, Wakayama prefecture.

1 Throughout this chapter, I use esoteric Buddhism and Tantrism as synonyms.
2 This is the insightful way in which Ryūichi Abé (1999) has described Kūkai's contributions to Japanese Buddhism.
3 See for instance Ch. 2 ("Skilful Means"): "This subtle dharma is the secret essence of all the Buddhas" (T 9, p. 10b); Ch. 4 ("Faith and Discernment"): "[This sutra is] the dharma of the secret storehouse of all buddhas" (T 9, p. 18b); Ch. 14 ("Peaceful Practices"): "This Lotus sutra is the storehouse of the secret essence of the buddhas and Tathāgatas. Among the diverse sutras it is placed at the very top. [The Buddha] guarded [it] through the long night [of time] and did not expound [on it] at random." (T 9, p. 39a)
4 See for instance T 12, p. 616b. The term *bimi* is recurrent in all translations of the *Mahāparinirvāna-sutra*.
5 Cf. T 25, p. 84c–85a, where it is stated that "explicit" refers to those teachings which exemplify that both buddhas and the two vehicles attain buddhahood by completely eliminating their defilements, while "secret" refers to teachings which explicate that the bodhisattvas bring all their defilements to an end and attain the six supernatural powers in order to benefit all sentient beings. Here obviously the difference corresponds to that between Hinayāna and Mahāyāna. A similar understanding appears also in T 25, p. 517a–b.
6 For a discussion of other Chinese sources that use the term in a sectarian sense see Sharf (2002), Appendix I.
7 Here, "secret" is one of the four methods of conversion (sudden, gradual, secret and variable) in which Buddhist teachings are classified. The implication of this taxonomy is that what can be understood depends on the level of capacity (a bodhisattva perceives more than a monk). In the *Sijiao yi*, however, the category of secret is defined in ambiguous terms, and eventually all four types of doctrines of conversion are said to be potentially secret. Moreover here the Lotus sutra, together with the Nirvana sutra, is said to be beyond the fourfold taxonomy, neither sudden nor gradual, neither secret nor invariable. The explanations in the *Sijiao yi* obviously contrast with the extensive explanations offered by Zhiyi in other treatises to qualify the Lotus scripture as a "secret teaching," and in fact the *Sijiaoyi* does not seem to have been used later in the tradition to elucidate this point.
8 T 25, p. 127c. This passage would later be an important piece of textual evidence for Kūkai, who cited it in his *Ben kenmitsu nikyō ron* (T 77, p. 381a). The *Miji jingang jing* (T 11, no. 310, p. 53b) is also mentioned in the *Commentary to the Dari jing* (T 39, p. 736a (*Shu*) and ZTZ 1, p. 520a (*Yishi*).
9 Zhanran, for instance, in his interpretation of Zhiyi's *Fahua wenju*, asserted that "the three activities, the three secrets, the three wheels and the three virtues are all different names [for the same thing]." (*Fahua wenju ji*, T 34, pp. 317). Misaki (1988, p. 38) notes that the expression *shenkouyi sanye* appeared in several canonical scriptures, including the Agon sutras.
10 A similar distinction is made in *Sokushin jōbutsugi* (T 77, p. 383), where it is explained that the three secrets of the *dharmakāya* (*hōbutsu*) are called "secret"

(*mitsu*) in virtue of their profoundness, subtleness, and impenetrability even to bodhisattvas of the highest degree; for the three secrets of sentient beings, on the other hand, the term *sanmitsu kaji* should be used. The text argues that the practitioner can match and be empowered with the three secrets of the Tathāgata (*sanmitsu sōōkaji* 三密相応加持) through mudras, mantras and meditation.

11 The phrases "to enter the secret" and "to know the secret" have a long exegetical history. They originate from a passage in the Nirvana sutra, which asserts that those who are endowed with the nature of delusion can know the storehouse of the Tathāgatas" secret. See Ōkubo 2004, pp. 199ff.

12 T 32, p. 574b. The expression "to attain the body of Mahāvairocana through the five marks" refers to the diamond body of the Buddha as attained through a series of meditative steps. Mantras are rendered here as "true words" (*zenyan*, Jap. *shingon*).

13 *Shi* in the sense of ritual activity carried out through expedient means was a category of practice, which was contrasted with the contemplation of the principle also in the *Mohe zhiguan*. See Dolce 2002, p. 38.

14 On the notions of *usō* and *musō*, see Fukuda 1995, pp. 384–90; Asai 1973, pp. 339–43. A very useful analysis of the debates between Taimitsu and Tōmitsu lineages is in Ōkubo 2004, pp. 81–98.

15 Misaki (1988, pp. 38–39) draws attention to this hypothesis in his discussion of the problems arising from a textual analysis of the *Putixin lun*. The authorship of the treatise had already been object of lengthy enquiries in the Taimitsu tradition. See Asai 1973, pp. 581–87, and Dolce 2002, p. 84.

16 Annen did not use Daosheng's interpretation of the Lotus sutra either, as Ōkubo has pointed out, perhaps because it was not part of the Tendai tradition and because that tradition offered other textual evidence to assert the preaching of the dharmakāya. Annen articulated his theory of *hosshin seppō* by dissecting the general concept of the preaching of the dharma-body into different types, and applying each type to one aspect of the representation of the *dharmakāya* (for instance, the body of the four mandalas). On the development of *hosshin seppō* in Taimitsu, see Asai 1973, in particular pp. 318–26 (on Ennin), and Ōkubo 2004, pp. 150–90.

17 Besides this well-known scripture, Kūkai also used other non-esoteric sources as evidence for the *hosshin seppō*. For a detailed analysis of this point in English, see Abè 1999, pp. 215–19.

18 It should be noted, however, that the major ritual activities directed towards the achievement of worldly benefits are also called *sanmitsugyō*, and this bears some consequences for the definition of *sokushin jōbutsu*.

19 In the *Bodaishingi shō*, Annen seems to have reorganized and perhaps systematized the principles outlined in the *Kyōjigi*, where he distinguished between four meanings of "secret." (T 75, p. 449b). The two analyses, however, are in neither conceptual nor temporal sequence, and although the two sets of definitions of *himitsu* seem to correspond roughly, they are not exactly the same. Furthermore, the textual sources used as evidence are different, and *Kyōji mondo* does not address the issue of training. For an overview of these relationships, and a detailed analysis of the passages, see Misaki 1988a, pp. 59–76.

20 The six meanings of the secret are also discussed by Fabio Rambelli in this book.

21 "This sutra [*Dari jing*] is the secret gem of the King of the Law; it is not revealed indiscriminately to ignoble people. Śākyamuni, forty and more years after he appeared in the world, because Śāriputra and the others implored him three times, briefly expounded the meaning of the Lotus of the Wonderful Law to them. Likewise, now this body of the original ground (本地之身) is the

tranquil, deep and secret abode of the Lotus of the Wonderful Law. Therefore in the chapter "The Life-span of the Tathāgata" it is said, "I live forever on the Vulture Peak and in every other abode. My pure land will never be destroyed, although people see it as burning up." The meaning of the *yoga* 瑜伽 of this school is just this." (T 39, p. 658a)

22 T 77, p. 362b–c; cf. *Dari jing*, T 18, p. 2a; *Putichang jing*, T 19, p. 207c.

23 It should be added that Kūkai compiled the earliest Japanese esoteric commentaries on the Lotus scripture. Most of them are *kaidai* 開題, and outline the esoteric principles expressed in the text through an analysis of its title, according to the modalities of this traditional Chinese exegetical genre. Cf. KDZ 1, pp. 756–808, 855–56, and KDZ 4, pp. 99–115. An overview of these short works is in Dolce 2002, pp. 311–13.

24 Among the treatises not belonging to the Tiantai tradition, Jizang's *Fahua youyi* 法華遊意, for instance, explicitly mentions two types of doctrines, the secret and the non-secret (*bimi/fei bimi*), and calls the Mahāyāna secret because it was the most profound teaching that could not be transmitted at random. T 34, p. 645c.

25 For more details on how early Taimitsu scholiasts reconstructed the classical Tiantai hermeneutics to make space for the category of esoteric teachings see Dolce 2002, Ch. 2.

26 *Shu*, p. 603c; *Yishi*, p. 34. Yixing here rephrased the well-known idiom of *jiuyuan* 久遠 as *changyuan* 長遠, this, too, a term from the Lotus sutra.

27 I have discussed the ritual and its textual sources at some length in Dolce 2002, pp. 215–84. See also Dolce 1999, pp. 369–76.

28 Figure 2 shows a *shuji* mandala from the *Kakuzenshō*. This icon combines two types of representation, anthropomorphic and that consisting of seed-letters.

29 In mediaeval transmissions, however, the association between the two Buddhas of the Lotus and the two Mahāvairocanas was also made in the reverse order, with complex explanations of the rational for the associations. For examples see Dolce 2002, pp. 288–89.

30 Holding of the Treasure Hall of Rinnōji in Nikkō. Tochigi Kenritsu Hakubutsukan 1996, p. 19. For a record of the liturgy, see *Tokugawa jikki* 3, p. 184a.

31 Tochigi Kenritsu Hakubutsukan 1996, pp. 15, 19, and 27. The first of these *hokke mandara* is of great interest to revisit the demarcation between exoteric and esoteric. The museum curator and Professor Sugahara Shinkai regard it to be an icon contemporary to the mandala recorded in *Tokugawa jikki* and used during another *hokke hō*. (Personal communication. In some catalogues the two mandalas are indeed confused.) However, iconographically the painting appears to be a curious mix of elements of specific (exoteric) representations of the Vulture Peak assembly and the format of the esoteric mandala. See Dolce (forthcoming).

32 This text is not concerned with doctrinal matters but with the ritual rules for a successful performance. Misaki, 1988, discusses the controversial aspects of this scripture. For an excellent analysis in English of the Sino-Japanese transmission of the text, see Hunter 2004.

33 The *Mikkyō daijiten* (pp. 1414–16) includes the drawings of a "soshijjikyō mandala." These were not based on material examples, rather they were made by the famous *mikkyō* scholar Ōmura Seigai following the descriptions in the sutra. See Ōkubo 2001, p. 112.

34 Holding of Kongōbuji, important cultural property. Kyōto Kokuritsu Hakubutsukan 2003, p. 69, exhibit no. 26/11 and 26/12.

35 Mainichi Shinbunsha 2002, pp. 32–33. *Senbutsu zu* were used as the *honzon* for repentance practices based on the recitation of the names of the buddhas of the past, present, and future (*butsumyō kekae*).

36 Kyōto Kokuritsu Hakubutsukan 2003, p. 72.
37 The association is based on the initial characters of the full title of the (*Fahua guanzhi yigui* 法華観智儀軌, *Chengjiu miaofa lianhua jingwang yuqie guanzhi yigui*, 成就妙法蓮華経王瑜伽観智儀軌), as *chengjiu* 成就 means "accomplishment" and is therefore tantamount to the supernatural attainments, *susiddhi* (Chin. *suxidi*), to which the *Suxidi jing* is devoted. *Keiran shūyōshū* also draws on Kūkai's Lotus commentaries to explain the meaning of the rest of the title. T 76, p. 593c.
38 Misaki 1988, pp. 606–33; Ōkubo 2001, p. 112. It is also important to consider how the identity of esoteric Buddhism was perceived in the mediaeval period. Ōkubo notes that in the thirteenth century *Hasshū koyō* 八宗綱要 (a popular outline of the eight Japanese Buddhist schools), the entry on esoteric Buddhism starts by explaining that it is the "secret doctrine of mantras" of the *Dari jing* and *Suxidi jing*, without mentioning the second sutra of the twofold esotericism, the *Jinggangding jing*, at all. Thus, although this entry generally reflects Kūkai's system, the author of the *Hasshū koyō* centres its definition on a sutra that had no hermeneutical relevance for Kūkai.
39 I am grateful to Robert Borgen for drawing my attention to this point. Jōjin's understanding of the purpose of the *hokke hō*, however, may have been his personal interpretation, not shared by his contemporaries. Perhaps Jōjin had a particular predilection for the *hokke hō* and charged it ideologically. Misaki Ryōshū (1992a) also points out that Jōjin's performance of the rite was quite eclectic.
40 The transmission of the rite and the list of related texts is recorded in the sixth volume of the diary. Jōjin says to have brought to China a copy of the *Fahua guanzhi yigui*, two fascicles of ritual procedures (*shidai* 次第), the "Gyōzō giki" (which must have been the *Weiyi xingse jing*) and a copy of the Lotus mandala in seed-letters.

References

Primary sources

Asabashō 阿娑縛抄, by Shōchō 承澄. DNBZ 57–60.
Atsuzōshi 厚造紙, by Genkai 元海. T 78, no. 2483, pp. 258–288.
Ben kenmitsu nikyō ron 弁顕密二教論, by Kūkai 空海. T 77, no. 2427, pp. 374–81.
Bodaishingi shō 菩提心義抄, by Annen 安然. T 75, no. 2397, pp. 451–560.
Da zhidu lun 大智度論. T 25, no. 1509, pp. 57–756.
Daibirushanakyō shiki, by Enchin 円珍. CDZ 2, pp. 656–74.
Dainichikyōsho shō 大日経疏抄, by Enchin. CDZ 2, pp. 675–83.
Dari jing 大日経. T 18, no. 848, pp. 1–55.
Dari jing yishi 大日経義釈, ZTZ, *Mikkyō* 1.
Dari jingshu 大日経疏. T 39, no. 1796, pp. 579–789.
Denjushū 伝受集, by Kanjin 寛信. T 78, no. 2482, pp. 224–58.
Fahua guanzhi yigui 法華観智儀軌. T 19, no. 1000, pp. 594–602.
Fahua wenju 法華文句, by Zhiyi. T 34, no. 1718, pp. 1–149.
Fahua wenju ji 法華文句記, by Zhanran 湛然. T 34, no. 1719, pp. 151–361.
Fahua xuanyi 法華玄義, by Zhiyi 智顗. T 33, no. 1716, pp. 681–814.
Fahua youyi 法華遊意, by Jizang 吉蔵. T 34, no. 1722, pp. 633–50.
Hokekyō ryōkai wagōgi 法華経両界和合義, by Enchin (attrib.). CDZ 3, pp. 945–50.
Hokke betchō 法華・別帖, by Jien 慈円. ZTZ, *Mikkyō* 3, pp. 257–90.
Hokke mandara shobon haishaku 法華曼陀羅諸品配釈, by Enchin (attrib.). CDZ 3, pp. 941–44.

Jinggangding jing 金剛頂経. T 18, no. 865, pp. 207–23.

Jūjūshin ron 十住心論, by Kūkai. T 77, no. 2425, pp. 303–62.

Kakuzenshō 覚禅抄, by *Kakuzen* 覚禅. DNBZ 53–56.

Keiranshūyōshū 渓嵐捨葉集, by Kōshū 光宗. T 76, no. 2410, pp. 503–888.

Kōen hokkegi 講演法華義, by Enchin (attrib.). CDZ 3, pp. 911–40.

Kongochōkyō sho 金剛頂経疏, by Ennin 円仁. NDZ 18, pp. 129–376.

Kyōjigi 教時義, by Annen. T 75, no. 2396, pp. 374–450.

Lankāvatāra-sūtra (*Lengqie abatuoluo baojing* 楞伽阿跋佗羅寶経). T 16, no. 670, pp. 479–513.

Lotus sutra (*Saddharmapuṇḍarīka-sūtra*) see *Miaofa lianhua jing.*

Mahāparinirvāna-sūtra (*Da banniepan jing* 大般涅槃経). T 12, no. 375, pp. 605–852.

Miaofa lianhua jing 妙法蓮華経. T 9, no. 262, pp. 1–62.

Mohe zhiguan 摩訶止観, by Zhiyi. T 46, no. 1911, pp. 1–140.

Putichang jing 菩提場経. T 19, no. 950, pp. 193–224.

Putixin lun 菩提心論. T 32, no. 1665, pp. 572–74.

San Tendai godaisan ki 参天台五台山記, by Jōjin 成尋. DNBZ 115, pp. 321–490.

Shijūjō ketsu 四十帖決, by Chōen 長宴. T 75, no. 2408, pp. 425–460.

Sokushin jōbutsugi 即身成仏義, by Kūkai. T 77, no. 2428, pp. 381–84.

Soshijjikyō shō 蘇悉地経疏, by Ennin. NDZ 18, pp. 377–640.

Suxidi jing 蘇悉地経. T 18, no. 893, pp. 603–33.

Tiantai sijiao yi 天台四教儀, by Chegwan 諦観. T 46, no. 1931, pp. 773–80.

Tokugawa jikki 徳川実紀, 10 vols. In Kuroita Katsumi 黒板勝美 (ed.), *Kokushi taikei (Shintei zōho)* 国史大系 (新訂増補). Tokyo: Yoshikawa Kōbunkan, 1976.

Weimo jing lueshu 維摩経略疏, by Zhanran. T 38, no. 1778, pp. 562–711.

Weiyi xingse jing 威儀形色経. T 19, no. 1001, pp. 602–06.

Modern sources

Abé, Ryūchi (1999), *The Weaving of Mantra*. New York: Columbia University Press.

Asai Endō 浅井円道 (1973), *Jōko Nihon tendai honmon shisōshi* 上古日本天台本門思想史. Kyoto: Heirakuji Shoten.

Dolce, Lucia D. (1999), "Criticism and Appropriation. Nichiren's Attitude toward Esoteric Buddhism." *Japanese Journal of Religious Studies* (special issue "Revisiting Nichiren") 26/3–4, pp. 349–82.

Dolce, Lucia D. (2002), *Esoteric Patterns in Nichiren's Interpretation of the Lotus Sutra*. PhD dissertation, Leiden University.

Dolce, Lucia D. (forthcoming), "Taimitsu ni okeru hokekyō kaishaku to girei: hokke hō to hokke mandara ni tsuite" 台密における法華経解釈と儀礼：法華法と法華曼荼羅について. In Tendai gakkai (ed.), *Tendai kyōgaku no kenkyū* 天台教学の研究. Tokyo: Sankibo Shoten.

Fukuda Gyōei 福田堯穎 (1995), *Tendaigaku gairon* 天台学概論. Tokyo: Nakayama Shobō Busshorin [rev. ed. [1]1954].

Hunter, Harriett (2004), "Faquan's Transmission of the *Susiddhi* Category of the Esoteric Buddhist Teachings." *Journal of the International College for Advanced Buddhist Studies* 8, pp. 43–93.

Hurvitz, Leon (1976), *The Lotus Sutra. Scripture of the Lotus Blossom of the Fine Dharma*. New York: Columbia University Press.

Kyōto Kokuritsu Hakubutsukan 京都国立博物館 (ed.) (2003), *Kūkai to Kōyasan* 空海と高野山. Osaka: NHK Ōsaka Hōsōyoku.

Mainichi Shinbunsha 毎日新聞社 (ed.) (2002), *Kūkai to henro bunkaten* 空海と遍路文化展. Tokyo: Mainichi Shinbunsha.

Mikkyō daijiten 密教大辞典. Mikkyō jiten hensankai 密教辞典編纂会 (ed.), 6 vols. Kyoto: Hōzōkan, 1970. (Rev. ed.).

Misaki Ryōshū 三崎良周 (1988), *Taimitsu no kenkyū* 台密の研究. Tokyo: Sōbunsha.

Misaki Ryōshū (1992a), "Jōjin ajari to hokusō no mikkyō 成尋阿闍梨と北宋の密教." *Mikkyō to jingi shisō* 密教と神祇思想. Tokyo: Sōbunsha, pp. 65–97.

Misaki Ryōshū (1992b), "Shōrenin Yoshimizu-zō *Hokke betchō* yori mita Jien no mikkyō shisō" 青蓮院吉水蔵『法華・別帖』より見た慈円の密教思想. In Misaki Ryōshū (ed.), *Nihon chūgoku bukkyō shisō to sono tenkai*. Tokyo: Sankibō Shoten, pp. 3–36.

Misaki Ryōshū (1994), *Taimitsu no riron to jissen* 台密の理論と実践. Tokyo: Sōbunsha.

Ōkubo Ryōshun 大久保良峻 (1998), *Tendai kyōgakū to hongaku shisō* 天台教学と本覚思想. Kyoto: Hōzōkan.

Ōkubo Ryōshun (2001), "Shingonshū" 真言宗. In Ōkubo Ryōshun (ed.), *Shin Hasshū kōyō* 新・八宗綱要. Kyoto: Hōzōkan, pp. 111–39.

Ōkubo Ryōshun (2004), *Taimitsu kyōgaku no kenkyū* 台密教学の研究. Kyoto: Hōzōkan.

Orzech, Charles (1998), *Politics and Transcendent Wisdom: The Scripture for Humane Kings in the Creation of Chinese Buddhism*. University Park, PA: Pennsylvania State University Press.

Sharf, Robert H. (2002), "On Esoteric Buddhism in China." *Coming to Terms with Chinese Buddhism: A Reading of the Treasure Store Treatise*. Honolulu: University of Hawai'i Press, pp. 263–78 (Appendix I).

Tochigi Kenritsu Hakubutsukan 栃木県立博物館 (ed.) (1996), *Nikkōsan Rinnōji no butsuga* 日光山輪王寺の仏画. Utsunomiya: Tochigi Kenritsu Hakubutsukan.

7 Knowing vs. owning a secret

Secrecy in medieval Japan, as seen through the *sokui kanjō* enthronement unction

Mark Teeuwen

Introduction

When we take a closer look at practices of concealing and disclosing secrets in Japanese Buddhism, we soon realise that secrecy in this context is a very ambiguous concept. The word "secret" (*hi-* 秘, as in *hiden* 秘伝 "secret transmission," *hiki* 秘記, "secret record," *hihō* 秘法 "secret method," etc.) certainly should not be taken at face value, as classified information that must never be revealed. Today, a visit to the library is enough to find written documentation of many of the secrets of temple lineages in various periods of Japanese history. The collected secret transmissions of Tōmitsu 東密 (Shingon) lineages, for example, are readily accessible to anyone who is curious enough to plough through the twenty-two volumes of the *Tōmitsu shohōryū injin ruijū* ("Assorted initiation documents of the various Dharma lineages of Tōmitsu"), compiled by Wada Daien and published in Osaka between 1988 and 1991. Here, one can find detailed documentation of the secret knowledge that for centuries has been passed down from teacher to disciple under strict vows of secrecy – and that in many cases is still being transmitted in this way today.

The first document in this large collection closes in a typical fashion: "This teaching is the ultimate secret (*saigoku no himitsu* 最極の秘密). You must not reveal it to anyone before [the day of] your death, and even then only to one single person."[1] Leafing through this compilation, one is left with the impression that such admonitions (sometimes accompanied with the threat of divine punishment and rebirth in the Hell of Uninterrupted Suffering[2]) were the rule rather than the exception. Intriguingly, these materials have been published, while at the same time the same institutions that must have at least cooperated with this publication have continued to transmit the same secrets by means of time-honoured rituals of initiation. Clearly, the secrets have somehow remained secrets, even while they are out in the open. What does secrecy mean in this context? How can revealed secrets retain their status as secret knowledge?

A number of possible explanations come to mind. The injunctions against revelation could be mere stock phrases, without any real meaning. They may be understood as a rhetorical device, used to emphasise the importance of the information that is contained in the documents. Perhaps, publication is thought unproblematic because it is assumed that the technical nature of the material makes it incomprehensible to those who are not part of the tradition. Or the material is simply thought to be uninteresting and irrelevant for those who do not engage in Tōmitsu ritual – while for those who do, it is not detailed enough to enable them to perform the practices that the material is about because it reveals only a few crucial details. It is true that the written material in itself is insufficient for anyone who would want to put it into practice. It must be accompanied by training and the oral transmission of a teacher to become useful. Yet, it would seem to me that such pragmatic considerations cannot fully explain the ambiguities of secrecy in this context. In this essay, I will argue that such secrets are a function of a complicated set of official rules of transmission. These rules signalise that the secret in question is the property of a specific lineage. "Secret" appears here to mean "that which is to be transmitted within a lineage," rather than "that which is to be hidden." Even when the knowledge that is declared secret is not physically removed from the public realm, it still retains a special status in the sense that only those who have gained it in the "proper" way, through an initiation within the right lineage, have the authority to use it. A person who has studied the Tōmitsu secrets in the library, or who has overheard them in a temple, has no legitimacy as a priest – just as a person who has read a medical handbook is not allowed to practise as a medical doctor.

The paradox of non-secret secrets is not a recent phenomenon. Even in the medieval sources that will be the focus of this essay, the status of secrets is filled with contradictions. On the one hand, secrets are fenced in by dire threats against all who dare to reveal them. On the other hand, we encounter the same "secret" knowledge across a broad sweep of lineages, settings and texts, and across large swaths of territory. Is it possible to find out more about the regimes of concealment and disclosure that have produced this result? Can an analysis of the creation and dispersal of secret transmissions tell us more about the dynamics behind the proliferation of secret teachings and practices in medieval Japan? Who created new secrets, under what circumstances and why? How was it done? How was a secret used? How was a secret transmission transformed into a piece of active capital? How did the success of one secret trigger the creation of new secrets?

Above all, we need to address the historical circumstances under which secrecy practices flourished. Many authors have stressed that secrecy in Japan was first and foremost a medieval phenomenon. Hazama Jikō (1953, pp. 11–94) has shown that in Tendai traditions, orally transmitted secrets took a high flight in the Insei period (1086–1192). Kamikawa

Michio has pointed out that at Tōji, one of the main centres of Shingon, appeals to secret teachings also began to appear in the historical record around this time.[3] Hayami Tasuku (1975) has discussed the sudden interest, also during the same period, among courtiers in what he terms "secret rituals" (*himitsu shuhō* 秘密修法). From another angle, Kikuchi Hitoshi (1997) confirms these findings by tracing the appearance of terms like "secret matters" (*hiji* 秘事) and "secret transmissions" (*hiji kuden* 秘事口伝, *hikuden* 秘口伝, *hiden* 秘伝) in the diaries of court aristocrats from the Insei period onwards. What happened in the Insei period that caused this sudden predilection for secrecy?

The Insei period saw a fusion of two types of lineages: "scholarly" or "religious" lineages (called "Dharma lineages," *hōryū* 法流) concerned with the transmission of teachings and rituals on the one hand, and secular, familial lineages concerned with the management of hereditary property (notably lands) on the other. A range of scholars have pointed out that the rise of secrecy coincided with this fusion. Hazama describes how the secret transmissions of Tendai Dharma lineages came to be regarded as familial private property in the Insei period. He notes that these transmissions were sold at a high price to those who were interested in them, especially in those cases where Dharma lineages were handed down from father to son (Hazama Jikō 1953, pp. 73–86). Kamikawa argues that the proliferation of secret transmissions at Tōji can be explained as a side effect of Tōji's development from a classical, court-controlled and court-funded institution into a medieval, more independent one. The eleventh century saw the development of major religious institutions into semi-autonomous power blocs that had their own economic base in a portfolio of lands (*shōen* 荘園) and sub-temples (*matsuji* 末寺), and even kept their own military forces. What distinguished these religious institutions from other power blocs was their religious identity, which consisted first and foremost of their possession of the ritual means to control the invisible realm of deities and demons (Kuroda Toshio 1996, pp. 233–69). Kamikawa points out that in struggles for positions of power within these institutions, monks frequently claimed to have inherited secret knowledge from previous incumbents. In the new, "privatised" temples of this period, the possession of secret transmissions was understood as an essential requirement for those who aspired to important posts within the temple hierarchy. This phenomenon can be traced back to the second half of the eleventh century, around the time of the beginning of the Insei period. Kamikawa mentions a 1076 conflict in which the headship of the Ono Mandaraji was disputed in exactly this fashion. It would seem, then, that there was a close relation between the control of lands by family lineages and the control of secret transmissions by Buddhist Dharma lineages.

In this essay, I will follow up on these findings. In order to analyse the relationship between the struggles within lineages (both at temples and at the court) and the creation of secrets, I shall take a closer look at the *sokui kanjō* 即位灌頂 or "enthronement unction," as a case study of the production and management of secrets. This ritual is particularly suitable for my purposes for several reasons. The *sokui kanjō* was created and implemented at the court, in an environment where every detail of ceremonial change was recorded. This enables us to trace the circumstances under which this ritual was conceived in great detail. Moreover, secret transmissions about the *sokui kanjō* spread to all parts of the Japanese religious world with astonishing speed. Temples and shrines both at the centre and in the periphery handed down teachings about the *sokui kanjō* in their secret transmissions, and in some cases even performed their own versions of the ritual. These temple transmissions were called *sokui hō* 即位法 , "enthronement methods." They were claimed to be identical to actual imperial practice (with some resembling this practice more closely than others), but they were intended for a different stage: that of temples and their Dharma lineages. Below, I will first describe the circumstances around the creation of the *sokui kanjō* at the imperial court. Then I shall trace the invention and proliferation of a particular *sokui hō* transmission that was associated with a particular Shingon lineage. My aim is to analyse the invention and management of a secret, first within its original setting, and then to describe and explain its dispersal as a secret belonging to a variety of different lineages. The rich source material on *sokui kanjō* and *sokui hō* is ideally suited for delving into the reasons that lineages of various descriptions have had for creating, collecting, stealing, protecting and advertising secrets.

The Nijō lineage and the *sokui kanjō*

In a narrow sense, the term *sokui kanjō* refers to a ritual that was performed by emperors when they ascended the throne. The history of its performance stretches back to 1288, when it was first introduced into the enthronement ceremonies of Emperor Fushimi, and continued until 1847, when it was performed for the last time by Emperor Kōmei.[4] Before the enthronement ceremony of *sokui no gi* 即位の儀, the imperial regent (*sesshō* 摂政 or *kanpaku* 関白) taught the emperor a mudra and a mantra. On the day of the enthronement itself, the emperor then performed this mudra and mantra while walking towards, or (later?), while seated on the enthronement platform.[5]

In spite of the fact that the *sokui kanjō* had a history of more than five hundred years of fairly consistent performance, it has attracted the attention of historians only quite recently. Arguably, the ritual first became a focus of attention in 1981, when Itō Masayoshi published a long article exploring various legends concerning its origin (Itō 1981). In 1989, Kamikawa Michio published a groundbreaking article in which he not only established the basic facts about the history of the *sokui kanjō*, but also stressed its importance as a new source of imperial authority in an age when this authority was under threat (Kamikawa 1989, 1990). He pointed out that the origin of this new ritual coincided in time with the conflict between two imperial lineages (the Daikakuji and Jimyōin lineages), and that its practice became standardised during the Nanbokuchō period (1337–92), when two imperial courts battled for supremacy. After these discussions, the *sokui kanjō* has been primarily examined in the context of recent debates about the historical changes in the nature of the authority of the imperial house.

More recently, however, Ogawa Takeo (1997) has looked at the *sokui kanjō* from a different angle. Using medieval court diaries, Ogawa succeeds in giving us a much more concrete understanding of the circumstances that led to the introduction of this rite into court ceremonies. Most importantly, he points to the fact that while the *sokui kanjō* did indeed contribute to the mystification of the emperor's reign, the main actors in its history were the regents. From the beginning, the secrets of the *sokui kanjō* were transmitted to each emperor by a specific lineage of regents, the Nijō. It was the Nijō lineage that acted as the guardians of this transmission, not the imperial house. Ogawa convincingly shows that the history of the *sokui kanjō* was closely connected with the fortunes of the Nijō house and with the Nijō's relations with other lineages of imperial regents.

Before delving into the concrete circumstances that occasioned the creation of the *sokui kanjō*, a few words need to be said about its more indirect sources. The institutionalisation of this rite was made possible by the existence of references in Buddhist scriptures to the investiture of kings in India. In central Mikkyō texts such as *Darijing shu* 大日経疏, Śubhakarasiṃha's commentary on the *Mahāvairocana-sūtra*, the origin of the Tantric procedure of initiation by unction (*kanjō*, from the Sanskrit *abhiṣeka*) is related to older royal enthronement rituals. Among "lay people in the West," we learn, kings were sprinkled with water from the four seas or from the rivers in their territory before they ascended the throne. Precious herbs and grains were laid out, a map was made of the land under their rule, and their subjects offered their services to the throne (T 39, p. 1798a).[6] Through references such as this, the notion of enthronement by means of a *kanjō* must have been well known in Japan already from classical times, at least as a theoretical possibility.

However, the actual performance of *sokui kanjo* by Japanese emperors does not go back further than the thirteenth century. In spite of its name, the *sokui kanjō* does not conform to the royal *kanjō* described in Buddhist scriptures. In fact, it does not even include the rite of pouring (*kan* 潅) water on the king's head (*jō* 頂) that gives the procedure its name. There is little in the *sokui kanjō* that reminds us of the *kanjō* described by Fabio Rambelli in this book. This reflects the fact that the *sokui kanjō* had a very different function from *kanjō* as they were used by temple lineages. Most strikingly, in contrast to all other types of *kanjō* it did not serve to incorporate the recipient (in this case, the emperor) into the lineage of the transmitter (his regent). The *sokui kanjō* was designed to serve the interests of a lay court lineage (the Nijō regents), not a Buddhist institution.

Who were these regents, and whence their interest in introducing this new kind of imperial ritual at this point in history? In the early days of the regency (the ninth century), regents were maternal relatives – fathers-in-law – of the emperors they served. However, already in the late eleventh century this was no longer necessarily the case. The post of regent remained hereditary within the so-called *sekkanke* lineage(s)[7] established by Fujiwara Michinaga (966–1027), but the regents no longer enjoyed the monopoly of offering consorts to the imperial line. This left their regency under constant threat from contenders from other lineages – especially those whose daughters had become imperial consorts and mothers of imperial princes. This situation inspired a search for alternative ways of legitimising their position as the emperor's closest aids. The monk Jien 慈円 (1155–1225), himself the son of a regent, addressed this problem by redefining the relationship between emperor and regent as an ancient divine pact between the ancestors of their lineages, the imperial ancestor Amaterasu and the Fujiwara ancestor Ame no Koyane.[8] In this way, Jien transformed the shifting relationship between each particular regent and his particular emperor into an eternal bond, a pact between two equally divine institutions: the imperial dynasty on the one hand, and the *sekkanke* dynasty of regents on the other.

Ogawa (1997, p. 3) reveals that this special relationship was also given new expression in court ritual, on no less an occasion than the *daijōe* 大嘗会 or "Great Tasting" ceremony. This was the first harvest ritual performed by a new emperor, often a year or more after his enthronement. The *daijōe* reached its climax in a rite called *shinzen no gi* 神膳の儀 ("rite of divine offerings"), in which the emperor shared rice and sake with the deities. This rite was performed in great secrecy by the emperor himself, assisted only by his regent and a court lady (*uneme* 釆女). It was an important task of the regent to teach the new emperor, who was often still a child, how this rite was to be performed and to make sure that no lapses occurred. At some point – it is unclear now exactly when – regents began to claim that they possessed oral traditions on the correct performance of this *shinzen no gi*, and even a secret text on this matter (called the *Gyokurinshō* 玉林抄).[9] These traditions were said to have been transmitted by Ame no Koyane, the Fujiwara ancestor, to his descendants. In this way the *shinzen no gi* symbolised the sacred cooperation between emperor and regent on the basis of ancient precedents that were traced back all the way to the Age of the Gods.

The introduction of a secret tradition into the *shinzen no gi* is an example of secret-making as a means of securing a position of power. In this case, it was claimed that to qualify as a regent, one had to have access to both a secret text and the oral knowledge transmitted within a particular lineage. No regent could function as such if there were any doubts concerning his command over these secrets. But what was one to do if one had not inherited any such secrets? The answer was to create new secret procedures and introduce them – if one was creative and powerful enough to do so. It was in this manner that the *sokui kanjō* came about.

Ogawa makes clear that the *sokui kanjō* was created and implemented by two brothers, the Regent Nijō Morotada and the monk Dōgen (see Table 7.1). Morotada's problem was that in spite of being *kanpaku*, he had not inherited the secrets of the *shinzen no gi* from his father, Yoshizane. Due to a conflict between Morotada's father and grandfather (Yoshizane and Michiie), both the family secrets and the family lands had been passed on to Morotada's uncle, Ichijō Sanetsune. This conflict led to a split in the Kujō house of regents, which gave rise to the Ichijō and Nijō lineages. These developments left his Morotada's own Nijō lineage without any expertise in the necessary secrets. And indeed, his Ichijō rival, Sanetsune's son Ietsune, did not hesitate to point out this fact. According to *Fushimi-in shinki* 伏見院宸記, Ietsune complained that it was wrong for Morotada to perform the ritual tasks of a *kanpaku* without knowledge of the sacred text that was in the possession of the Ichijō.[10] Certainly, Ietsune objected, Morotada would not know the spell that was to be uttered at the *shinzen no gi*!

Table 7.1 An abbreviated table of lineages of regents

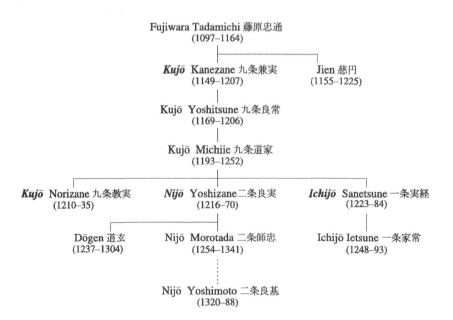

Jien had already theorised about the possibility of performing a *kanjō* as part of the enthronement procedures. In a work entitled *Jichin kashō musōki* 慈鎮和尚夢想記 (1203–9), he had even hinted at the possibility that Emperor Go-Sanjō had already done so in 1068 – a claim that few historians accept today.[11] Dōgen (who is not to be confused with his namesake, the famous founder of Sōtō Zen) received the teachings of Jien as a disciple of Dōkaku 道覚, one of Jien's favourite disciples; he would also have had easy access to them as the abbot of the Shōren'in 青蓮院, a Tendai temple that had been developed into one of the main imperial cloisters in the capital by Jien himself.[12] Drawing on Dōgen's knowledge of Jien's work, Morotada took the radical step of turning theory into practice. The occasion was Emperor Fushimi's enthronement in 1288; the ritual setting was Fushimi's *sokui no gi*. In Fushimi's diary, we can read that he was taught "a secret mudra and other things" two days before the *sokui no gi*. On the day of the enthronement he himself, "formed a mudra and intoned a mantra" as he "entered the main hall from the room at the back."[13]

What can we learn about secret transmissions in medieval Japan through the lens of the history of the *sokui kanjō*, as traced by Ogawa Takeo? We are reminded of Hazama's point that the proliferation of secrets was prompted by the emergence of privatised, hereditary lineages. Likewise, we recognise Kamikawa's argument that the possession of secrets rapidly became an essential requirement for those who aspired to important positions, whether at the court or in the Buddhist Samgha. It is clear that secrecy of this kind was closely tied to with the notion of hereditary power. The secrets of the *sokui kanjō* were handed down within the Nijō lineage from one generation to another, in much the same way as other forms of capital, such as land rights. As with land rights, it was preferable for the secret to be old and well attested. But if need be, a powerful figure could use his influence to override such concerns, overcome the scepticism and resistance of others and introduce quite radical innovations. Since secrets functioned as a form of hereditary capital, conflicts that caused lineages to split and new lineages to be established could lead to a struggle over the secrets of the original lineage. The ownership of the transmission was contested in much the same way as other forms of family capital. In the case of the *sokui kanjō*, the Nijō realised that their loss of the secrets of the *shinzen no gi* represented a real problem, and they solved it by establishing the *sokui kanjō* in its stead.

Another important point is that in order to use a secret with authority, it was necessary to establish the legitimacy of its transmission. As we shall see below, there are numerous references to the *sokui kanjō* in a number of writings that have nothing to do with the Nijō house, the Shōren'in or even the other regent houses. It would seem that the secret mudra and mantra were soon known to many, both in the capital and elsewhere. But knowing a secret and having the authority to use it are two very different things. Morotada, too, was confronted with this fact in his capacity of *kanpaku*. He claimed to know about the *shinzen no gi* from his father Yoshizane, who had indeed taught its procedures to an earlier emperor (Go-Saga, in 1242), but since everybody knew that not Morotada but his Ichijō rival Ietsune had inherited the tradition, his authority was questioned nonetheless.

The essential condition for turning a secret into an active form of capital, then, was to establish one's exclusive authority to use it. We can trace the efforts of the Nijō to acquire such authority over the *sokui kanjō* in documents of the period. Initially, in Morotada's time, the validity and credibility of the *sokui kanjō* depended at least in part on the Buddhist expertise that was involved in its creation. In actual fact, the transmission was kept not at a Nijō villa, but at the imperial cloister Shōren'in, where it was conveyed to the Nijō regent prior to each enthronement. It is not even certain whether the transmission was a Nijō monopoly from the beginning, or whether this monopoly was established only two generations later, during the regency of Morotada's grandson, the *kanpaku* Nijō Michihira.[14] Michihira himself admitted quite frankly that "since medieval times" (*chūko* 中古) "the *sokui kanjō* had been carried out in consultation with the monastic lineage of the Jūrakuin (i.e. the Shōren'in)."[15] But in the same breath, Michihira also claimed that this had not been the case in ancient times (*jōko* 上古). The core of the secret, he maintained, was an ancient family tradition and owed nothing to any Buddhist institutions. A few generations later, Yoshimoto went even further in this direction. Through a later text (Hayashi Razan's *Shintō denju* 神道伝授, 1640s) we can glean that Yoshimoto stressed the fact that the *sokui kanjō* had been transmitted in the Fujiwara family from the days of Amaterasu and Kasuga Myōjin (i.e. Ame no Koyane), and that no Shingon lineages (*shingon ke* 真言家) know anything about it whatsoever.[16]

Of course, the reason for the necessity of stressing the non-Buddhist nature of the "real" *sokui kanjō* of the Nijō was that many Buddhist lineages claimed otherwise. On occasion, emperors would look for an alternative channel to acquire the *sokui kanjō*; at such times, the Shōren'in was the most obvious place to turn to. Emperor Go-En'yū (r. 1371–82) of the Northern Dynasty (the Southern Dynasty never performed the *sokui kanjō*) is a rare example of such an occasion. For political reasons, Go-En'yū was wary of Yoshimoto's influence and refused to receive the *sokui kanjō* from Yoshimoto's son, who held the post of *kanpaku* at the time of Go-En'yū's *sokui no gi* in 1374. Instead, he appears to have gained knowledge of the mudra and mantra directly from Sondō 尊道, the prince-abbot of the Shōren'in.[17]

Yoshimoto's reaction to this challenge may serve as a striking example of the flexibility that was inherent in the system of ritualised secrecy. In a meeting with Urabe Kanehiro 卜部兼熙, the court diviner (*miyaji* 宮主)

who was responsible for the preparation of the Great Tasting (*daijōe*), Yoshimoto revealed that the Nijō house possessed the secret transmission of an "imperial unction" (*tenshi on-kanjō* 天子御灌頂) that should be performed during this ritual.[18] He claimed that the imperial lineage had lost this secret, and argued that it should be reintroduced on the basis of the transmission of the Nijō. The fact that his main rivals, the Ichijō lineage, had just been taken over by his own son (due to a lack of Ichijō sons) made it all the easier for Yoshimoto to make such claims. The result was that in 1375, Emperor Go-En'yū performed a mudra and a mantra as part of the *shinzen no gi* and thus introduced a Nijō "imperial unction" into this ritual. After this the Nijō lineage boasted possession of the innermost secrets of both *sokui kanjō* and *shinzen no gi* (i.e. both the enthronement ceremony of *sokui no gi* and the Great Tasting). We have seen that the loss of the *shinzen no gi* secrets occasioned the introduction of the *sokui kanjō* into the *sokui no gi*; now, the same secret was used to reclaim the *shinzen no gi*. With this bold move, Yoshimoto had finally solved the problem that had troubled the Nijō regents from the time of Morotada.

It would appear that the Nijō managed their transmission with great skill. There are only very few cases (in my understanding, four) in which the *sokui kanjō* transmission was conducted by a lineage other than the Nijō. When the regency was in the hands of one of the other *sekkanke* lineages, either the *sokui kanjō* was not performed or someone from the Nijō lineage was called upon to carry out the transmission in the regent's place. The Nijō was by far the most successful of the five lineages that shared the regency (Nijō, Takatsukasa, Konoe, Ichijō and Kujō); of the 330 years that these five lineages occupied the regency in the late medieval period (between 1252 and 1585), the regent came from the Nijō house for all of 116 years, more than twice as long as their closest rivals. The Nijō lineage's skill in establishing and managing secret knowledge must have contributed to this fact, if only as one of many aspects behind their success.

Secret documents and Dharma lineages

From the above it is easy to gain the impression that the secrets of the *sokui kanjō* were jealously guarded and never revealed to outsiders. In fact, however, secrets about the *sokui kanjō* figured prominently among the secret documents preserved at numerous Buddhist institutions, where they were transmitted under the name of *sokui hō*. This is clearly another case in which the rhetoric of secrecy should not be taken too literally. What is unique about the *sokui kanjō* is that, thanks to the existence of a wide historical record, Japanese scholars have been able to trace some of the routes along which its secrets spread. An analysis of these routes could help us to understand more about the dynamics of secrecy in

medieval Japan. But first, let me make a few more general points about
the world of medieval temples as the institutional context in which secret
transmissions thrived.

The Buddhist world of medieval Japan can only be described as
chaotic. It was conventionally portrayed as a conglomerate of different
schools (*shū* 宗), such as Tendai, Shingon and the six Nara schools, but
these schools were little more than nebulous networks of competing
lineages, concentrated in competing temple complexes. In the case of
the Shingon school, the Tōji, Kōya-san, Tōdaiji, Ninnaji and Daigoji
temple complexes were the most important. However, even these individual
temple complexes were decentralised in structure. Daigoji, for example,
contained within its precincts more than sixty private cloisters known as
in 院 (Nagamura Makoto 1991). Some of these (the Hōon'in 報恩院, for
example) were founded by Daigoji monks, who in this way set up their
own "shop," while others (such as the most powerful of them all, the
Sanbōin 三宝院) were founded by aristocratic lineages from outside the
temple.

Each of these *in* had its own buildings, monks and other staff, as well as
an economic base in the form of land rights, which were either bought
(as in the case of the Hōon'in) or donated (as for the Sanbōin). But what
was perhaps most central to the existence of an *in* was its unique Dharma
lineage. Each *in* had its own secret ritual manuals, statues, mandalas and
ritual implements, often referred to collectively as the lineage's "sacred
teachings" (*shōgyō* 聖教). Most of these *shōgyō* concerned the so-called
shosonbō 諸尊法 rituals, specialised rituals focusing on *shoson*, "various
divinities" outside the standard curriculum. It was these rituals that
formed the *in*'s specialised expertise and that defined the *in*'s position
within the ritual market place. Therefore the exclusive possession of
these *shōgyō* constituted the *raison d'être* of each *in*. Transmission of all of
the secret *shōgyō* of the *in* was reserved for a single favourite disciple, who
with this initiation also inherited the headship over the *in* and the control
over its resources. Such a transmission was called a *shabyō sōjō* 瀉瓶相承
or "transmission of pouring [the teachings] into a new bottle" (see also
Fabio Rambelli, Chapter 5). A *shabyō* transmission had both religious and
secular significance.

In medieval Japanese cloisters, religious and secular authorities were
closely linked: those to whom the secrets of a Dharma lineage were transmitted thereby gained a claim to control over the corresponding cloister,
its staff and its lands. This meant that whenever more than one disciple
received a complete initiation, a conflict over the control of the lineage
and its cloister could be the result. This was by no means rare. Jien, for
example, left many conflicts in his wake by giving full transmissions to no
less than six disciples, many of whom challenged Jien's *shabyō* disciple
after Jien's death. Such conflicts could lead to the founding of new lineages and new cloisters. This process can be traced back to the late ninth

century, when Shōbō 聖宝 (832–909) and Yakushin 益信 (827–906) laid the foundations for the two main branches of Shingon, the Ono and Hirosawa branches. The fragmentation of lineages peaked in the decades around the year 1100, when the Ono and Hirosawa branches split into six lineages each. In the course of the medieval period, these lineages splintered further into more than seventy sub-lineages.

As sub-lineages multiplied, so did *shosonbō* rituals and secret transmissions. The establishment of a new sub-lineage required the creation of a new ritual repertoire if the lineage was to survive beyond the lifetime of its original patrons. The system of transmitting such rituals and their theological explanations in great secrecy, often at least in part orally, facilitated innovation. New practices were routinely attributed to early patriarchs, and the fact that they were not attested in the canonical, "open" writings of these authoritative figures only underlined their exclusiveness and effectiveness. Inaccessibility heightened rather than lowered their status. It is against this background that the proliferation of new teachings and practices in medieval Mikkyō must be understood.

There are many parallels between the way in which the Nijō managed their *sokui kanjō* secrets and the management of *shōgyō* by temple lineages. The oral traditions and secret texts of the *sokui kanjō* were the *shōgyō* of the Nijō. They were acquired and/or created in order to supply the Nijō with a ritual specialisation and secret expertise that made them indispensable at court. *Shōgyō* were as a rule attributed to famous founders not only of the specific sub-lineage that possessed them, but of a wider circle – in the case of Shingon lineages, patriarchs such as Kūkai, Shōbō, Gyōki etc. and in the case of the Nijō, the Fujiwara ancestor Kamatari: all figures that rival sub-lineages also had to relate to. Moreover, the *shōgyō* were not thought to have been "invented" by these founding figures, but to have been revealed to them by sacred entities such as Ame no Koyane, Amaterasu and Dainichi. When lineages split, possession of the secrets was contested. On such occasions new secrets tended to be discovered, which made room for new specialisations and new sub-lineages. This is what occurred in Morotada's time when the Kujō house of regents split into three lineages, the Kujō, the Ichijō and the Nijō, inspiring the disinherited Nijō to create new secrets.

In this sense, the culture of secrecy that was represented by temple *shōgyō* was not exclusive to Mikkyō. It was a product of the social and economic circumstances in the medieval period (including the Insei period), rather than a phenomenon that was inherent in Mikkyō from the start. As Jacqueline Stone has pointed out, the pattern of rival lineages each guarding their own secret transmissions was not necessarily an echo of the classical Tantric guru–disciple relationship (Stone 1999, pp. 113–14). Aristocratic families at the court had a long tradition of transmitting specialised knowledge of court protocol (*yūsoku kojitsu* 有職故実) from father to son, forming lineages called *denke* 伝家 ("transmission houses").

These lineages produced and handed down texts, ranging from diaries and "oral transmissions" (*kuden* 口伝, by the tenth century for the most part oral in name only) to rubricated handbooks that contained detailed information on all kinds of ceremonial precedents. The history of these houses of court protocol, such as the Kujō, Ono-no-miya and Midō lineages, has been mapped by Takeuchi Rizō (1940). He traces their origins back to the tenth and eleventh centuries; but he notes that their expertise took the form of secret transmissions (*hiji kuden*) only after the time of Fujiwara Michinaga, at the beginning of the Insei period.

Of course, there are important differences between the transmissions of *denke* and Dharma lineages. The *denke* derived their importance from their ability to advise the court on procedures that were not performed by the *denke* themselves. It was considered their duty as court families to provide information, and, in a sense, their knowledge was supposed to be public. Even while their records were kept in the family as "oral transmissions on secret matters," the information they contained derived its value from its usefulness in the public domain. This stands in contrast to the secrets of Dharma lineages, which mostly concern ritual specialisations that were performed by the keepers of the secrets themselves. Another obvious and vital difference is that *denke* transmissions did not involve any kind of initiation ritual.

Nevertheless, in spite of these differences it is worth pointing out that oral transmissions had already been an important source of political authority at the court before they became prominent in the temple world of Mount Hiei. Nakanishi Zuikō (1981) has argued that the pattern of transmitting knowledge in closed-off family lineages was transplanted to Mount Hiei when large numbers of cloisters were founded there by court aristocrats in the Insei period. This assessment helps us to recognise that the emergence of secret transmissions such as the *sokui kanjō* was not a one-way process in which aristocratic traditions took on a Mikkyō format. Rather, it was a result of the crisscrossing of lay and temple lineages, as seen in the founding of aristocratic and imperial cloisters at central temple complexes. In one sense, there was perhaps some truth to the Nijō claim that their secret transmission was pre-Buddhist after all: their creation of the *sokui kanjō* occurred as another step in the long court tradition of creating and transmitting court protocol.

It was in this landscape of crossing Buddhist and lay lineages that a new dynamic arose between Buddhism on the one hand, and the lay corpus of imperial mythology and ritual on the other. We have already seen how the Nijō lineage tended to play down the Buddhist nature of the *sokui kanjō*, and did so more and more categorically over time. Whenever possible, they related the *sokui kanjō* to imperial kami mythology, a mythology that they reinterpreted and rewrote to suit their new transmissions. This practice was echoed by temple lineages, which responded by creating *shōgyō* related to imperial mythology – a topic that was obviously of interest to the court lineages with which they were connected or would like to have been connected. It was this process that produced the tangle of Buddhist kami lore we know today as "medieval Shinto."

Daigoji and its shōgyō

As I have already mentioned, secret transmissions about real or imagined imperial enthronement rituals (*sokui hō*) spread quickly and widely through the world of Japanese temples and shrines from the late thirteenth century onwards. It has been customary to divide these transmissions into two groups, associated respectively with Tendai and Shingon. Recently, however, Matsumoto Ikuyo (2004b) has pointed out that within the Shingon school alone, there were at least four radically different types of *sokui hō*. In addition, *sokui hō* also spread to other Buddhist schools and even to kami shrines. It is of course impossible to map all of these transmissions within the limitations of this essay, or indeed of my abilities. Rather, I shall trace a concrete case of the dissemination of *sokui* secrets and try to draw some conclusions about the mechanisms behind their concealment and disclosure.

To this end, let me return to the Daigoji temple complex, which was an important centre from which *sokui hō* spread to other places. Daigoji was founded in the ninth century by Shōbō, whom we encountered above as the patriarch of the Ono branch, and flourished early on thanks to the sponsorship of Emperor Daigo (r. 897–930). As we have already seen, in the twelfth and thirteenth centuries a great number of *in* were founded here, in which the main lineages of the Ono branch were based. All this made the Daigoji a true breeding ground of secret transmissions. In fact, reliance on oral transmissions is often cited as a characteristic of the Ono branch, in contrast to the more scripturally biased Hirosawa branch of Ninnaji. Daigoji was also the stage where some of the most famous conflicts over the ownership of *shōgyō* were fought. These conflicts reveal much about the importance that was attached to *shōgyō*, and about the ways in which they were managed. Also, we shall see that the creation of *sokui hō* secrets at Daigoji was closely connected to these conflicts.

The period's most famous battle over *shōgyō* was triggered by an ambitious project that Emperor Go-Uda (1267–1324, r. 1274–87) had set himself after his retirement: to restore the temple Tōji in Kyōto as the governing institution of the Shingon school.[19] Go-Uda wanted to use his authority as retired emperor for the "unification of the Dharma lineages" (*hōryū ikki* 法流一揆) within Shingon. Needless to say, if his plan succeeded it would affect all lineages dramatically. It would mean the end of their exclusive ownership of secret transmissions, and the autonomy of the various *in* would lose much of its religious legitimacy.

Go-Uda took the tonsure in 1307. Shortly after, in the first month of 1308, he became an *ācārya* (a fully initiated master) by receiving the *denbō*

Table 7.2 The conflict over the *shōgyō* of the Hōon'in

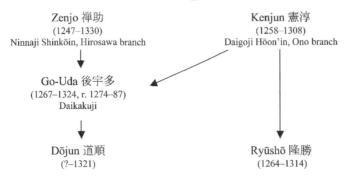

kanjō 伝法灌頂 initiation at Tōji. Zenjo of Ninnaji served as his initiating master (Table 7.2). Zenjo initiated Go-Uda in the Hirosawa branch and was rewarded with the (new) post of Tōji abbot (*Tōji chōja* 東寺長者).In the second month, Go-Uda then approached Kenjun of the Hōon'in at Daigoji, with the request to be initiated by him in the Ono branch. Go-Uda's messenger was one of Kenjun's disciples, a monk named Dōjun who will play an important role in the rest of this essay.[20]

The rewards of a close relationship with the retired emperor were enormous. Kenjun, too, could expect to be appointed as a Tōji abbot, and the Hōon'in would prosper under imperial protection. However, Kenjun was afraid that his initiation of Go-Uda would lead to the loss of the most important *shōgyō* of the Ono branch, which at this time were kept at Hōon'in (as the Sanbōin, the main *in* of Daigoji, had burnt down). With good reason, Kenjun feared that Go-Uda's plan to "unify all Dharma lineages" would cause the Ono and Hirosawa branches to be combined. He agreed to initiate Go-Uda only under strict conditions, seven in all, of which the following are particularly relevant to our topic of secrecy:

- The innermost secrets (*hiō* 秘奥) of the Dharma transmission of [Kōbō] Daishi are to be kept at this temple. Therefore you must adopt Ono as your main lineage (*honryū* 本流), in accordance with the regulations of the [Ono] founders.
- Neither at this time nor at any time in the future are you to allow a single matter to pass into the hands of the Hirosawa branch or any other Houses.
- The main objects of worship (*honzon* 本尊), such as the ritual utensils, etc., are not to leave the temple House. From one generation to the next, the founders [of the Ono branch] have passed down an oath to this effect. Other lineages tend to split up, and [their secrets] have been scattered, but as yet not a single scroll has been lost from this lineage.

• Not a single divinity or mudra may be revealed to one who has not yet received the transmission (*denju* 伝受). This is due to the *samaya* precept against spilling the Dharma (*oppō* 越法). Therefore, it is not possible to give you access to matters that have not been [formally] transmitted to you. [. . .]. (*Kamakura ibun* 30, no. 23212)

The term *oppō* refers (among other things) to the crimes of receiving secret methods (*hihō*) without being properly initiated, reading secret texts without the right preparation, revealing secret matters to uninitiated persons etc.

From these restrictions, it is clear that Kenjun was of no mind to contribute in any way to Go-Uda's grand plan. Uniting the Shingon branches or lineages (both translate the Japanese *ryū* 流) under the aegis of Tōji was to him the same as breaking the sacred oath of the founders of his lineage. Yet when Go-Uda agreed to all his conditions, Kenjun had no other choice but to travel to Kyoto and grant Go-Uda the *denbō kanjō* of the Ono branch (1308/4/14). Nonetheless, in the initiation document presented to Go-Uda on this occasion, Kenjun stressed that the Ono secrets were to remain at Daigoji:

On secret buddhas, secret mandalas, important scriptures, ritual implements and the matters of the in

According to an oath of the founders [of the Ono branch], the important scriptures, ritual implements etc. mentioned above must never be surrendered to persons of other lineages or other Houses, and may not leave our temple House. This oath is particularly firm and strict. Also I, Kenjun, will observe this ancient law and I have written a pledge to that effect. I will select a disciple who resides in the temple and leave my pledge with him. Emperor Uda[21] was able to learn the secrets of Ninna[ji] because he used that temple as his imperial palace; now you must make Daigo[ji] your residence and adopt our lineage as your main lineage. [. . .] Many *in* at our temple were reduced to ruins while they were administered from another temple. Therefore, persons who hold positions at other temples will not be allowed access to a single statue or scroll, even if they hold the title of a monk of [our] temple.

(*Kamakura ibun* 30, no. 23242)

After his initiation by Kenjun, Go-Uda was handed a list of the *shōgyō* that were kept at the Hōon'in. This list gave Go-Uda the right to take possession of these *shōgyō* – but only when he adhered to Kenjun's conditions. The whole situation adds yet another twist to the question of knowing vs. owning: through his initiation, Go-Uda became the owner of secrets that he was not (yet) allowed to know.

Go-Uda's next step was to put pressure on Kenjun to allow him to pass on his own initiation to Dōjun, and to make Dōjun the *shabyō* heir of Kenjun's lineage. Kenjun protested, but was soon forced to hand over a part of the *shōgyō* to Dōjun. However, he deposited the most valuable secret texts and implements with the *shabyō* disciple of his own choice, Ryūshō. Kenjun died that same summer (1308/8/23), after having instructed Ryūshō once more not to surrender the remainder of the *shōgyō* to Dōjun and Go-Uda.

This set the scene for new battles. Ryūshō soon realised that it would be impossible to deny Go-Uda and Dōjun access to the rest of the *shōgyō*. When Go-Uda sent Dōjun to Daigoji to collect them, Ryūshō resisted and fled to Kamakura with a portion of them (1309/2). Even so, Dōjun did manage to obtain some of the most important of the *shōgyō*, including a lacquered bamboo box (*kawago*) containing secret documents and a ritual implement called the *tenpōrin-zutsu* 転法輪筒. This was a cylindrical object that was placed on the altar for the performance of the *tenpōrin hō* 転法輪法, allegedly the most powerful of all esoteric rituals of exorcism (Sawa 1993, p. 12). Ryūshō appealed to the Kamakura shogunate to have the *shōgyō* returned to the Hōon'in. From this point on, the case escalated rapidly: now it was not only Ryūshō against Dōjun, but also Kamakura against Go-Uda, and Go-Uda's Daikakuji 大覚寺 line against the competing Jimyōin 持明院 line. This conflict dragged on over many years, with fortunes shifting as the imperial throne alternated between the Daikakuji and the Jimyōin lines. In the end, Kenjun's fears proved well founded. Among the victims of the affair were the *shōgyō* that Dōjun had taken away from the Hōon'in. They passed into the hands of Go-Uda, and were eventually lost in a fire during the fighting that accompanied Go-Daigo's Kenmu restoration (*Daigoji shin yōroku*, p. 749).

The failure of Go-Uda's plans amply illustrates the supreme importance that was attached to *shōgyō*. Sawa Hirokatsu emphasises strongly that in the struggle between Go-Uda/Dōjun and Kenjun/Ryūshō, the *shōgyō* were valued highly for their own sake, and not only as entry tickets to abbotships and material gains. Sawa points out that the only reason Go-Uda approached Kenjun of the Hōon'in was that this was the *in* where the *shōgyō* of the Ono Sanbōin lineage were kept; if he had been after the Daigoji abbotship or after more lands, he would have chosen someone else (Sawa 1993, pp. 11–12). Indeed, Kenjun himself never gained the title of Daigoji abbot, a fact that reminds us that holding the *shōgyō* in itself was not enough to attain positions of power. Yet, there is plenty of evidence to suggest that the struggle between Dōjun and Ryūshō was also a struggle about the abbotship and about control over the lands of the Hōon'in. Within months of receiving his initiation, Go-Uda used it to claim the Hōon'in for Dōjun. Even in this case, the *shōgyō* were thought to qualify their holders for great things, both in the religious and in the secular realm.

Also, we see once more that simply "finding out" a secret was not enough to claim it as one's own. The focus of the conflict between Dōjun and Ryūshō was on the question of accreditation. The question was not who *knew* the secret, but who was its rightful owner. To acquire such ownership, it was vital to gain possession of material *objects* such as manuscripts and ritual implements; just getting hold of secret *information* did not achieve much in this respect.

Dōjun and the sokui hō

As a major player in the ritual politics of the court, Daigoji naturally developed its own *sokui hō*. Matsumoto (2004b) has shown that at least three different kinds of *sokui hō* were transmitted at Daigoji, two within the Sanbōin lineage (at the Jizōin 地蔵院 and Hōon'in branches), and yet another within the Kongōōin 金剛王院 lineage. Among these three, Dōjun played a central role in the creation of the *sokui hō* of the Hōon'in. A text with the obscure title *Bikisho* 鼻帰書 (1324) allows us to trace Dōjun's efforts in creating this *sokui hō* in great detail, and gives us a very rare opportunity to witness the inception of a secret transmission.

Bikisho is a collection of Buddhist interpretations of the Ise shrines and their main deity, Amaterasu or Tenshō Daijin.[22] Its compilation became possible due to a string of encounters between an unusual constellation of religious figures (Table 7.3): Dōjun, presented here as the abbot of Daigoji; Watarai Tsuneyoshi, the headpriest (*chōkan* 長官) of the Ise Outer Shrine; a monk named Jibu Risshi, who was connected to the Watarai clan temple of Sekidera; and finally another monk by the name of Chien, who is the author of the text. In *Bikisho*, Chien explains how Jibu came to learn about the *sokui hō* from Dōjun and about a set of secret diagrams from Watarai Tsuneyoshi. He then recounts how Jibu came to reveal these matters to him.

Table 7.3 Dōjun in Ise

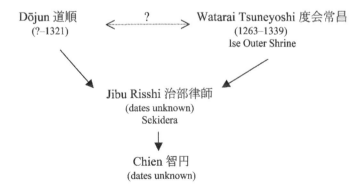

How did these figures, all from very different backgrounds, happen to meet in Ise? Chien states that Dōjun was sent to Ise by Go-Uda, on a mission to pray that the imperial succession be passed on to Go-Uda's son, the later Go-Daigo (a wish that would take many years and intervening emperors to be realised). This suggests that Dōjun was in Ise on orders from Go-Uda. Although no such meeting is specifically mentioned by Chien, it is natural to assume that this would have brought Dōjun into contact with another fervent supporter of Go-Uda, Watarai Tsuneyoshi, in whose clan temple Dōjun was staying. Brought together by such circumstances, Dōjun and Tsuneyoshi would have used the opportunity to exchange information about how to develop their own caches of secret knowledge. Through Jibu's report, Chien allows us to listen in on their conversation.

Interestingly, Chien begins his tale about Dōjun's visit with the *sokui kanjō*, which here is called *shikai ryōshō no hō* 四海領掌ノ法, "the method of ruling over the four seas":

> When Lord Daikakuji (Go-Uda) first received [the *shikai ryōshō no hō*] from his regent he did not think it strange, but much later, when he met Shinkōin Zenjo and became well versed in Shingon,[23] he was puzzled by it and said: "I thought that what was handed down to me at the Mandokoro (the regents' office) at the time of my enthronement was the Shingon of [Kōbō] Daishi, but what the regents transmit in these days is only a mudra of sorts, and not a mantra (*myō* 明). Is this a Shingon method from which one of the Three Secrets [of body, speech and mind] is missing?"
>
> Zenjo made enquiries among other high-ranking monks of the Hirosawa branch, but nobody knew the answer. Then [Go-Uda] asked Dōjun, the holder of the Ono branch of the Sanbōin. Dōjun found an old diary in a lacquered bamboo box of [the Ono patriarch] Shōbō and presented it to Go-Uda. Go-Uda thought it a miracle [and said]: "In Japan this very ritual must be the secret method of [Tenshō] Daijin [天照] 大神, the essence of the imperial house." Convinced that there could be none wiser than [Dōjun], he planned to appoint him to the post of abbot of the Sanbōin at Daigoji. When he heard that Kenjo 賢助, the [current] abbot of Daigoji, was opposed to this, Go-Uda suppressed [his protests] and pushed through Dōjun's appointment. [Kenjo] was so aggrieved by this that he set fire to the Sanbōin and fled to Tanabashi in Ise[24] in the dark of night. Then Go-Uda appointed Dōjun as abbot, as was his wish.
>
> (*Shingon shintō* 2, p. 511)

Kenjo (1280–1333?) served as Daigoji abbot from the twelfth month of 1314 until some time in 1318. Daigoji records show that most of the Sanbōin burnt down in the second month of 1318.[25] Dōjun's visit to Ise must therefore have occurred either in 1318 or shortly afterwards, in the years before his death in 1321.

In Chien's account, the box that we already encountered among the *shōgyō* of the Hōon'in takes centre stage. Dōjun must have told Jibu (and/ or Tsuneyoshi?) that he had reached his elevated position thanks to his access to a secret transmission about the *sokui kanjō* (*shikai ryōshō no hō*) that Shōbō, the founder of both the Ono lineage and the Daigoji, had deposited in this box. Let it be said that this story can hardly be true. Go-Uda never received the *sokui kanjō* from a regent; as we have already seen, the first emperor to do so was his successor, Emperor Fushimi. The reality behind this tale will have to remain obscure.[26] What we do know is that at this time, two competing lines of emperors were disputing the throne: Fushimi of the Jimyōin line and Go-Uda of the competing Daikakuji line. It may be imagined that Go-Uda would have been interested in learning more about the secret initiation that his rival had acquired. Whatever Go-Uda may or may not have known, Dōjun appears to have grasped at the opportunity to show Go-Uda the true value of the *shōgyō* from the Hōon'in. He produced a secret document written in the hand of Shōbō himself, supposedly found in the lacquered box that he had commandeered from Ryūshō. Obviously, Shōbō, who died in 909, had nothing to do with the *sokui kanjō*.

Was Dōjun's sojourn in Ise in any way related to his bluff about the *sokui kanjō*? Was one of Dōjun's objectives for this trip to flesh out his own transmission on the "method of ruling the four seas"? It would certainly seem that Dōjun acquired a lot of novel information during his stay in Ise. In *Bikisho*, Chien writes that Dōjun transmitted his *shikai ryōshō no hō* to Jibu. In his conversation with Jibu, Dōjun identified the *shikai ryōshō no hō* with a rite that was performed by shrine maidens at the Ise Outer Shrine. In a daily ritual, these young girls, called *kora* 子良, offered food to the deities of both Ise shrines at the Mike hall in the Outer Shrine precincts. Dōjun explained that this ritual dated from before the arrival of Buddhism. Only later, "after Amaterasu had manifested himself as Kōbō Daishi," was the true esoteric meaning of the rite revealed:

> In ancient times, [before Buddhism arrived,] people simply had faith in animals with special powers, and prayed to them to increase their worldly treasures. It is on the basis of this [ancient practice] that at these [Ise] shrines, the shrine maidens practise the method of the dragon-fox (*shinko no hō* 辰狐ノ法) after they have presented the divine food. Its meaning is to show that the promise that was made in ancient times has not been forgotten. Therefore, the emperors, who are descendants of the Great Deity [of Ise], are initiated in this method as part of their enthronement. When Kōbō Daishi reappeared in this world as a rebirth (*saitan* 再誕) of these shrines, he gave a detailed interpretation of this ritual, renaming it the "method of

ruling the four seas" (*shikai ryōshō no hō*). In ancient times, [the emperors] gained authority and power by practising this method and became kings of men in this way; therefore this method is handed down to this day for the benefit of the kings of men.

(Shingon shintō 2, p. 511)

Here, information from Ise and Daigoji is woven together to create a new secret transmission. We learn about an ancient tradition preserved by the shrine maidens at the Outer Shrine: a ritual gesture that signifies faith in the "dragon-fox."[27] It is not a mudra; it involves putting one's hands on one's shoulders and "turning them inwards" (?). Then we are told about two more elaborate *sokui* procedures, allegedly introduced by Kōbō Daishi. One retains the gesture of the *kora* maidens and adds a mantra of Ḍākinī ("put your right hand on your left shoulder, say *dagini*; put your left hand on your right shoulder, say *gyachi* . . .");[28] the other consists of three "proper" mudras with accompanying mantras. Dōjun links the *kora* gesture to the Tantric *shikai ryōshō no hō* by stating that the recognisably Buddhist versions of the rite, those with mantras, were introduced by Kōbō Daishi, as a more sophisticated variant. None of the variants should be seen as superior to any of the others; Dōjun claims that they are all used by the regents in their *sokui* transmission to the emperors. He argues,

Before the Dharma had been transmitted, the variant without a mantra was good. [Kōbō] Daishi was not some stranger; he came [to Japan] as a transformation of [Tenshō] Daijin to spread the Dharma. How could an ordinary worldling assess the merits [of these different versions]?.

(Shingon shintō 2, p. 513)

How can we interpret this exchange? Has Dōjun taken on board the Nijō position that the *sokui kanjō* was transmitted to their Fujiwara ancestors by Amaterasu (Tenshō Daijin) and Ame no Koyane, and that it is not part of "Shingon lineages"? Is he using his trip to Ise to find out more about this transmission from Amaterasu, and, at the same time, to spread the message that since the founder of Shingon, Kōbō Daishi Kūkai, was a "rebirth" of Amaterasu, his lineage does indeed have its own expertise on these matters?[29]

Dōjun's sokui hō and its proliferation

We can only speculate about the intentions and strategies that Dōjun pursued in Ise. What can be established as a fact, however, is that his idea of combining the *kora* maidens' gesture with a Ḍākinī mantra spread widely after his death.[30]

Matsumoto Ikuyo (2004a, 2004b) has made it clear that Dōjun's "Ise version" of the *sokui hō* lived on as a transmission of the Hōon'in at Daigoji. The "twelfth box" of the Daigoji archives contains a document with the title *Tōji sokui hō ki* 東寺即位法記 and a copying date of 1394.[31] In no more than nine short lines, it describes a *sokui hō* procedure that combines the gesture of the *kora* maidens and the mantra of Ḍākinī in the same way as Dōjun had. It then concludes with a short explanation of the origin of this procedure, stating, like Dōjun in *Bikisho*, that the "mudra" of the *kora* maidens was first revealed by Tenshō Daijin. Both of these elements are clearly different from the *sokui hō* of other Dharma lineages, and are characteristic of the Hōon'in transmission. Matsumoto also introduces a document that appears to be a more complete version of the same text. It carries the title *Tōji gosokui hō* 東寺御即位法 and is preserved at the Kanchiin 観智院 of Tōji.[32] In addition to the *kora*/Ḍākinī procedure, this version contains a number of new elements, most notably a variant in which the *kora* gesture is accompanied by the seed syllable *bhrūṃ*.[33]

From the perspective of secrecy practices, the Kanchiin is another interesting institution that deserves a closer look. Founded in 1359, it served as a general archive of Shingon transmissions. Its collection contains copies of *shōgyō* texts from all lineages, brought together by the Kanchiin heads Gōhō 杲宝 (1306–62) and Kenpō 賢宝 (1333–98) in the course of the fourteenth century. The knowledge of the different Dharma lineages of Shingon was collected (or should we say deposited?) at Tōji, as the main centre of Shingon doctrinal studies. This means that the contents of the secret transmissions of the different Dharma lineages were not in a strict sense secret: knowledge of them was shared, at least with the scholars of Tōji. Yet this did not in any way subtract from their status as exclusive property of the lineages in which they were formally transmitted. At Kanchiin, no such transmissions took place. In contrast to the *injin* 印信 (transmission documents) of Dharma lineages, the documents that are kept in the Kanchiin do not include information about the identity of the transmitter and the receiver of their contents. Therefore, it was only the *knowledge* of the transmission that was stored at the Kanchiin, not the *ownership*. Again, we notice the importance of the difference between knowing and owning a secret.

This difference is vital if we are to understand the dynamics behind the dispersal of secrets. Because of this difference, Dōjun was able to reveal secret knowledge without losing its ownership. We have already seen that Dōjun was ready to share his knowledge with Jibu. From Dōjun's perspective, Jibu was a figure of incomparably low status – but he was also a person with access to local knowledge that was of interest to Dōjun. Dōjun's "initiation" of Jibu can be seen as an example of the trading of secrets, a process that must have been going on in many places, but that is only very rarely depicted in any detail in the period documents.

Chien describes the transmissions that led to his compilation of *Bikisho* as follows:

> [Dōjun] said to [Jibu] Risshi: "I am prevented from initiating you directly into the important matters of the Sanbō[in] of Shingon (*Shingon Sanbō no daiji* 真言三宝ノ大事), but I will make an exception for you to enhance the Buddhist services (*hōraku* 法楽) to the Great Deity [of Ise]." Then he initiated [Jibu Risshi] in many layers of important matters (*jūjū no daiji* 重々ノ大事). Among them was the method of the dragon-fox performed at the emperor's enthronement (that is, the *shikai ryōshō no hō* – MT). This is a secret practice of the emperor, and also a secret method of these [Ise shrines], from times immemorial to this day. [Dōjun] told [Jibu] Risshi that the *kora* maidens perform this method every day after the offering of divine food has finished, and he transmitted it to him.
>
> At this time, Chien Risshi had come to Ise to pray at the Great Shrines. He was staying at Jibu Risshi's temple quarters. [Chien] initiated Jibu Risshi in the important matters (*daiji*) of the Hirosawa branch [of Shingon]. Jibu Risshi was elated with joy, and told [Chien] about various methods that had been revealed to him – among others, the secret practice of the emperor's enthronement. Chien wished to learn about this method, so he became [Jibu's] disciple and was initiated in it.
>
> (*Shingon shintō* 2, p. 512)

What strikes us in this passage is how eager the possessors of secrets appear to share them with others – any others, it would seem, who had something interesting to offer in exchange. The rhetoric of secrecy has not disappeared, but it appears to be taken very lightly. One "important matter" (*daiji*) is exchanged for another, without any regard for the lineages or even schools to which the other belongs.

We can even follow this process beyond the *Bikisho*. Only three years after *Bikisho* was written, Chien passed his knowledge on to a monk of the Ritsu school named Kakujō 覚乗 (ca. 1273–1363), who wrote it down in a text entitled *Tenshō daijin kuketsu* 天照太神口決 ("Oral explanations on Tenshō Daijin," 1327). Here we find more information about the *sokui kanjō* and its relation to the rite of the *kora* maidens at Ise; among other things, we discover more about the relationship between Ḍākinī, Tenshō Daijin and the Fujiwara ancestor Kamatari. Of special interest here is a passage claiming that the *shikai ryōshō no hō* "is not limited to kings; those who possess of this method, from temple monastics to lay people, will all in their own ways attain high positions."[34] This shows that within a decade of Dōjun's visit to Ise, his *sokui hō* was already finding new applications, not only outside the Hōon'in, but even outside the Shingon school.

Discussion

At this point, we can pause and look back on the striking career of a particular secret: that of the imperial enthronement unction. The story began with Nijō Morotada, an imperial regent who had failed to inherit any secret traditions from his father and became the target of criticism from his court rivals for that reason. Drawing on the research of Ogawa Takeo, I have argued that the creation of the *sokui kanjō* and its implementation in 1288 show that access to secret traditions was an essential requirement for those who aspired to high positions at the court. The history of the *sokui kanjō* illustrates how knowledge, especially knowledge about ritual and protocol, could be transformed into power. Morotada, who lacked formalised ritual expertise, used his influence to create new knowledge that he passed on to his descendants. This knowledge was cherished by the Nijō lineage as a secret transmission. By monopolising on this transmission, the Nijō succeeded in carving out a permanent role for themselves as the guardians of the innermost secret of imperial authority.

From here, we turned to the tale of Go-Uda and Dōjun and their struggle to acquire the secret transmissions of the Ono branch that were handed down within the Hōon'in lineage at Daigoji. This famous battle illustrates the importance of *shōgyō*, the "sacred teachings" (a term that includes not only texts, but also statues and ritual objects) of *in* cloisters and their Dharma lineages. Although the context is very different from the case of the Nijō and their *sokui kanjō*, it is clear that also in the world of temples, access to secret transmissions had by this time become a prerequisite for success. The *shōgyō* were not to be shown, let alone handed over to anyone with connections outside of the *in* and its Dharma lineage. Possession of the *shōgyō* was identical with possession of the lineage, the *in* where it was based, and all the *in*'s wealth and resources. As soon as Dōjun was able to claim possession of a good cache of Ono *shōgyō*, he began a long battle to win control over the Hōon'in, where the Ono *shōgyō* had been kept, and even over the Ono headquarters, the temple complex of Daigoji.

However, in order to achieve this goal Dōjun had to establish not only that he had access to the secrets of the lineage, but also that he was their rightful owner. Here, a central characteristic of the secrecy of Dharma lineages comes to light. A secret was not lost to its original keepers when others had discovered its contents; it was lost only when others could prove that they were the ones who had acquired it in the correct way: through an initiation (preferably an exclusive one) by the previous rightful owner of the transmission. Due to the ambiguity of the transmission from Kenjun to Go-Uda (and by extension, from Go-Uda to Dōjun), Dōjun had great trouble in establishing his own legitimacy as heir to Kenjun's transmission. Of course, the fact that he was closely associated with the political battle between Go-Uda's Daikakuji line and the opposing Jimyōin line (backed by the shogunate) did not help.

Next, we saw that in ca. 1318, Dōjun appeared in Ise, where he revealed secrets about the *sokui kanjō* to a monk called Jibu. He claimed to have found these secrets among the *shōgyō* of the Ono lineage, which had been kept at the Hōon'in. Again, we encounter a concrete instance of the creation of a new secret. As in the case of Morotada, the secret was construed to deal with a real crisis. It is worth noting that in both cases, claiming to possess secrets nobody had heard of before was a way to deal with an acute lack of legitimacy. We can discern a pattern here: when one's credentials were put into doubt, one could reply by producing a convincing secret.

Buddhist transmissions on the *sokui kanjō* are differentiated from actual imperial (Nijō) practice and are known as *sokui hō*. Dōjun's *sokui hō* resembles the *sokui kanjō* of the Nijō in that it focuses on Ḍākinī, but that is where the similarity stops. The main characteristic of Dōjun's *sokui hō* is that it incorporated secret knowledge from Ise, both in the procedure itself and in its explanation. In Ise, Dōjun seems to have traded secrets with a range of other religious figures. In his wake, the *sokui hō* that he had generated spread widely and rapidly to other schools and lineages, taking on ever more elaborate forms.

Only thirty years had passed between 1288, when the *sokui kanjō* was first performed at the court, and 1318, when Dōjun created his *sokui hō*. By 1327, this *sokui hō* was already being advertised by a provincial Ritsu monk as a method for all who wished to attain "high positions," whether monk or layman. This otherwise unknown monk had, within a very short period, been able to gain access to both Dōjun's transmission and at least one other kind of *sokui hō*. This would suggest that the Go-Uda–Dōjun route was only one of many trajectories along which *sokui* secrets were leaked into the periphery; some others are mentioned by Iyanaga Nobumi in this book (Chapter 8).

What do these events tell us about the concept of secrecy? There appears to be a blatant contradiction between the strict rhetoric of secrecy that we encountered in the conflict over the *shōgyō* of the Hōon'in on the one hand, and the casual or even eager exchange of secrets depicted in *Bikishō* on the other. Both the *sokui kanjō* and the *sokui hō* were supposed to be the ultimate secrets of the lineages that transmitted them, and yet, knowledge of them appears to have spread across the country with astonishing speed. How was this possible? What does this fact reveal about the dynamics of medieval secrecy?

Conclusion

It seems to me that there are two keys to understanding the realm of secrecy that has been explored in this essay: the twin concepts of *transmission* (*fuhō* 付法, *denju* 伝授/伝受) and *lineage* (*ryū* 流, *monryū* 門流

etc.). Secret knowledge was knowledge that required a formal transmission. Formal transmission meant incorporation into a lineage. Therefore, those who received a transmission were at the same time allowed membership in a lineage. Secrets acquired without proper transmission did not qualify one as such a member. Lineages (especially Dharma lineages) existed in order to transmit secrets: without such transmissions, the lineage would have no function at all. The importance of the lineage was equal to the importance of its transmissions. When these transmissions were said to be secret, that did not mean that no one should be aware of their existence. Quite to the contrary, a lineage that transmitted unknown secrets would not have had much appeal. It was preferable for the secrets of one's lineage to be famous: only then did they acquire value. The fact that there was a difference between disclosing (parts of) a secret and formally transmitting it created a playing field in which secrets could be hinted at and even exchanged without destroying their value as the hereditary capital of particular lineages.

However, both of our two key concepts are disconcertingly vague. To start with *transmission*: what is a "true" transmission, and what is a mere exchange of information? What stops an enterprising person from claiming a transmission and beginning his own lineage? In the case of Go-Uda, who challenged the principle of the exclusivity of Dharma transmissions itself, the conditions set by his transmitter Kenjun were very strict. His transmission was to be recognised only if he settled in the right cloister (*in*) and cut his ties with all other lineages. But we need not go far into the periphery for the line between a transmission and a casual exchange of information to become blurred. There is clearly a large difference between Kenjun's transmission of the Ono branch to Go-Uda, and Chien's transmission of the Hirosawa branch to Jibu. The contrast between these two cases indicates the wide span of meanings that was covered by the single term *transmission*.

The same is true of the concept of a lineage. What is one to think of, for example, the so-called "Kanpaku lineage" (*kanpaku-ryū* 関白流), which was active in the Kantō region in the late medieval period?[35] This lineage claimed that its secrets had their source in "Ise Tenshō Daijin," and that by way of a person they called "the *kanpaku* Saneo," (Tōin Saneo 洞院実雄, 1217–73, who never was a *kanpaku*), they had been transmitted to a Hirosawa sub-lineage that was active in the Kantō area at that time. Obviously, this Kanpaku lineage belonged to a different dimension than, for example, the Nijō lineage at the court. It may serve as one example of a peripheral lineage with roots in some informal spilling out of secrets – in this case, secrets about the *sokui* in particular. At some point, material acquired through an informal exchange of knowledge must have crystallised into a "formalised" lineage that claimed ownership of the knowledge of the *kanpaku* regents, performed ritual initiations and handed out lineage documents called "diplomas of the Shinto Kanpaku lineage" (*Shintō kanpaku-ryū menkyojō* 神道関白流免許状).

In the range between powerful court lineages at the centre and pioneering rural lineages in the provinces, secrets large and small were invented and exchanged, flaunted and concealed, transmitted and contested, stolen and reclaimed, documented and stored, forgotten and rediscovered. It is clear that this crisscrossing of secret transmissions constituted a large part of religious activity in medieval Japan. It is doubtful whether we will ever have the means, or the patience, to lay bare the whole picture of this chaotic world of medieval secret transmissions. I imagine it as a tangle of live wires, where new ideas and practices flew like sparks from one circuit to another, setting off instantaneous, unpredictable chain reactions, triggered by historical circumstances that (with the exception of special cases like those of Nijō Morotada and Dōjun) are no longer accessible to us. In its endless complexity, this world of secrets will probably continue to defy our powers of analysis and understanding, but at least the mass of sources that it produced allows us to discern some of its structural characteristics, and gives us a taste of the bold imagination and relentless energy that pervaded this medieval realm.

Notes

1 *Tōmitsu shohōryū injin ruijū* 1, p. 10.
2 Ibid. 4, p. 256.
3 Kamikawa Michio 1985, pp. 48–68 (esp. 2, "Tōji no hōe to shishi sōshō," pp. 56–61).
4 For lists of all *sokui kanjō*, see Hashimoto Masanobu 1998, pp. 100–101 and Matsumoto Ikuyo 2004b, p. 45. An earlier list, which is somewhat different from the lists of Hashimoto and Matsumoto, can be found in Ogawa Takeo 1997, pp. 8–9.
5 The oldest record, in the diary of Emperor Fushimi, suggests that the mantra and mudra were performed while the emperor moved towards the enthronement platform. However, Matsumoto Ikuyo has shown that at least by the time of Ichijō Kaneyoshi (1402–81) a central point of the ritual was the fact that it was performed on the enthronement platform itself. Matsumoto Ikuyo 2004b, pp. 42–73, especially pp. 47–48.
6 Here Śubhakarasiṃha explains the difference between the *kanjō* used by secular kings, Vedic brahmins and Buddhists. Also in Japanese texts one often encounters references to the origin of *kanjō* as an Indian enthronement rite; see for example *Hikyō yōryaku shō* 秘教要略抄 (1303), entry "*kanjō*," in *Tendaishū zensho* 7, p. 5.
7 *Sekkanke* 摂関家 means "House of *sesshō* and *kanpaku* regents." *Sekkan* is short for *sesshō* and *kanpaku*, regents for child and adult emperors.
8 Most famously so in *Gukanshō* 愚管抄 (p. 140) written in 1220; Delmer Brown and Ishida Ichiro 1979, pp. 29–30.
9 It was thought that this text was written by the regent Fujiwara Tadamichi 藤原忠通, who had participated in the *shinzen no gi* of Emperor Sutoku. Sutoku, who was five years old at the time, had proven unable to perform his ritual duties, and Tadamichi had been forced to step in. It would seem that in retrospect, this was interpreted as a sign of Tadamichi's profound knowledge of the ritual. Ogawa relies on *Go-Fushimi in shinki* 後伏見院宸記 and *Ōei daijōe ki* 応永大嘗会記.

10 *Fushimi-in shinki*, entry Shōō 1 (1288)/11/14. See Ogawa 1997, p. 6. Ietsune had initiated Emperor Go-Uda in the *shinzen no gi* procedure in 1274.

11 See Kamikawa 1989, pp. 111–12.

12 Dōgen served as abbot of both Jūrakuin 十楽院 and Shōren'in. These two cloisters were closely connected with each other already in Jien's time. After Dōgen, it became common for the abbotships of these two cloisters to be combined. They were finally merged under the abbotship of Prince Sondō 尊道 (1332–1403). On Jien and the Shōren'in, see Itō Toshikazu 1991.

13 *Fushimi tennō nikki* 伏見天皇日記, entries Shōō 1 (1288)/3/13 and 15.

14 There is some evidence to suggest that Emperor Go-Fushimi received the *sokui kanjō* from his Takatsukasa regent Kanetada (in 1298), and that Emperor Hanazono acquired his initiation (which occurred nine years after his enthronement, in the midst of mounting pressures to give up the throne) from the retired regent Kujō Moronori (in 1317).

15 In Michihira's diary *Go-Kōmyō Shōin kanpaku ki* 後光明照院関白記, entry Genkō 4 (1324)/5/3, quoted in Ogawa 1997, p. 7. On the Jūrakuin and the Shōren'in, see n. 12.

16 In his *Shintō denju* (*tsuika* 75), Razan refers to a text that he calls *Nijō kanpaku Yoshimoto hiki* 二条関白良基秘記, where this point is made.

17 Ogawa (1997, p. 10) suggests that a few generations earlier, Emperor Kōmyō received the *sokui kanjō* directly from Son'en, also at the Shōren'in, but as pointed out by Hashimoto Masanobu (1998, p. 99) this view is based on a misreading. Kōmyō received the transmission from Nijō Yoshimoto. Hashimoto further indicates in his table of *sokui kanjō* performances (p. 100) that Go-En'yū received the transmission from *kanpaku* Nijō Moroyoshi, but at the same time he also quotes evidence that clearly supports Ogawa's reading of events (*Go-Komatsu in gyoki* 後小松院御記).

18 Ogawa 1997, p. 11. The source is a record of Go-En'yū's *daijōe*, entitled *Daijōe mi no koku shidai, u no hi* 大嘗会巳剋次第卯日, preserved at Tenri Toshokan.

19 See Tsuji Zennosuke 1931 and Nagamura Makoto 1993.

20 On Dōjun, see also Iyanaga Nobumi's essay in this book.

21 Uda (867–931) was the first retired emperor to receive the *denbō kanjō* (901, in the Tōji). Go-Uda was very conscious of Uda's legacy and referred to him on many occasions as an example and a precedent.

22 Tenshō Daijin is the Sino-Japanese reading of 天照大神, which had the Japanese reading Amateru Ōngami in medieval Japan and Amaterasu Ōmikami from the mid-Tokugawa period onwards. The medieval Tenshō Daijin was a rather different and much more complicated figure than the ancient Sun Goddess or her early-modern and modern incarnations. See Teeuwen 2003 for a discussion of the medieval transformation of this deity.

23 As noted above, Zenjo served as Go-Uda's precept master when Go-Uda took the tonsure in 1307, and also initiated him into the Hirosawa lineage.

24 Tanabashi, a few kilometres west of the Ise shrines, was the location of Rengeji, later Daijingū Hōrakuji, an old Nakatomi clan temple that Tsūkai 通海 (1234–1305) had brought under the control of Daigoji. The fact that Kenjo was staying in this temple explains why Dōjun had to resort to the much more modest Sekidera.

25 *Daigoji shin yōroku*, pp. 917, 591. See Kadoya 1993, p. 89.

26 Terai Hikaru (2001, p. 58) reads this passage in *Bikisho* as evidence that Go-Uda had been taught this mudra when he was initiated into the secrets of the *shinzen no gi* by Ichijō Ietsune in 1274. However, as noted above, Ietsune mentioned only a secret spell, while in *Bikisho* Go-Uda (allegedly) claimed to have received a mudra without a spell.

27 On the meaning of this fox, see Yamamoto Hiroko 1993 (in the chapter "Irui to sōshin") and Mark Teeuwen 2000.

28 The mantra is, *On dakini kyachi kyaka neiei sowaka*. On the role of Ḍākinī in the *sokui kanjō*, see Yamamoto Hiroko 1993, Tanaka Takako 1993, Iyanaga Nobumi 1999, Mark Teeuwen 2000.

29 Itō Satoshi (1995) points to Dōjun as the author of a range of other "secret teachings" about Tenshō Daijin. He argues that Dōjun (or a person close to him) was the likely author of *Daijingū honji* 太神宮本地, a text that identifies Kūkai with the Ise shrines, and that uses this identification to explain the significance of the secret Sanbōin-ryū ritual of *sanson gōhō* 三尊合法. Interestingly, Itō refers to Dōjun's conflict with Ryūshō over the headship of the Sanbōin as Dōjun's reason for creating these secret teachings, and to explain their later transmission within Go-Uda's Hirosawa (Miwa) lineage rather than at the Sanbōin itself.

30 There is some evidence to show that this *sokui hō* was indeed understood to have begun with Dōjun. A document from 1420, entitled "oral explanation on the transmission of the enthronement" (*Gosokui injin kuketsu*) and preserved at the Shingon temple of Kongōji in modern Kawachi-Nagano (south of Osaka), explains the relationship between the *kora*, Tenshō Daijin and Ḍākinī; it then recounts how Dōjun showed Go-Uda an "old diary" as the source of this "secret method of Tenshō Daijin." *Kawachi-Nagano-shi shi* vol. 5, p. 221.

31 *Daigoji monjo* vol. 8, no. 1927, p. 264.

32 Matsumoto Ikuyo 2004a, pp. 94–96 and 2004b, pp. 62–63.

33 Matsumoto (2004b, p. 59) traces the use of this syllable to another type of *sokui hō* that she terms the "Kanjuji (or Kajūji) 勧修寺 type," and that was not otherwise represented at Daigoji. *Bhrūṃ* represents Ichijikinrinnō (Ekākṣara-uṣṇīṣa-cakra), who takes the place of Ḍākinī as the central figure in this type of *sokui hō*.

34 *Shingon shintō* 2, p. 500. The practice of praying to Ḍākinī for promotion to a higher position is well attested in such sources as *Kokon chomonjū, Heike monogatari, Genpei seisuiki, Taiheiki* and *Keiran shūyōshū*; see Terai 2001, p. 60.

35 Cf. Itō Satoshi 1999.

References

Primary sources

Daigoji monjo 醍醐寺文書, 8 vols. (= *Dainihon komonjo, iewake* 大日本古文書、家わけ 19). Tōkyō Daigaku Shiryō Hensanjo (comp.). Tokyo: Tokyō Daigaku Shuppankai, 1971–81.

Daigoji shin yōroku 醍醐寺新要録, by Gien 義演 (1558–1626), 3 vols. Kyoto: Kyōto-fu Kyōiku Iinkai, 1951–53.

Kamakura ibun 鎌倉遺文, 42 vols. Takeuchi Rizō (comp.), Tokyo: Tōkyōdō shuppan, 1971–91.

Kawachi-Nagano-shi shi 河内長野市史, 10 vols. Kawachi-Nagano-shi Shi Henshū Iinkai 河内長野市史編修委員会 (comp.). Kawachi-Nagano: Kawachi-Nagano-shi, 1972–98.

Gukanshō 愚管抄, Okami Masao and Akamatsu Toshihide (eds), NKBT 86 (1967).

Shingon shintō 真言神道, vol. 2 (= ST, *Ronsetsu-hen* 論説篇 2), Murayama Shūichi 村山修 (annot.). Tokyo: Shintō Taikei Hensankai, 1993.

Tendaishū zensho 天台宗全書, Tendaishūten Kankōkai 天台宗典刊行会 (comp.). Tokyo: Daiichi Shobō, 1973–74.

Tōmitsu shohōryū injin ruijū 東密諸法流印信類聚, 22 vols. Wada Daien 和田大円 (ed.). Osaka: Tōhō Shuppan, 1988–91.

Modern sources

Abé, Ryuichi (1999), *The weaving of mantra: Kūkai and the construction of esoteric Buddhist discourse*. New York: Columbia University Press.

Brown, Delmer and Ishida Ichiro (1979), *The future and the past: A translation and study of the Gukansho, an interpretative history of Japan written in 1219*. Berkeley: University of California Press.

Grapard, Allan G. (2002–03), "Of Emperors and Foxy Ladies." *Cahiers d'Extrême-Asie* 13, pp. 127–49.

Hashimoto Masanobu 橋本政宣 (1998), "Sokui kanjō to Nijō-ke (jō)" 即位灌頂と二条家（上）. *Tōkyō Daigaku Shiryō Hensanjo Kenkyū Kiyō* 東京大学史料編纂所研究紀要 8, pp. 85–107.

Hashimoto Masanobu 橋本政宣 (1999), "Sokui kanjō to Nijō-ke (ge)" 即位灌頂と二条家（下）. *Tōkyō Daigaku Shiryō Hensanjo Kenkyū Kiyō* 東京大学史料編纂所研究紀要 9, pp. 53–72.

Hayami Tasuku 速水侑 (1975), "Insei-ki ni okeru himitsu shuhō" 院政期における秘密修法, in *Heian kizoku shakai to bukkyō* 平安貴族社会と仏教. Tokyo: Yoshikawa Kōbunkan.

Hazama Jikō 硲慈弘 (1953), "Edan ryōryū no hassei oyobi hattatsu ni kansuru kenkyū" 恵檀両流の発生及び発達に関する研究, in *Nihon bukkyō no kaiten to sono kichō* 日本仏教の開展とその基調 vol. 2. Tokyo: Sanseidō, pp. 11–94.

Itō Masayoshi 伊藤正義 (1981), "Jidō setsuwa kō" 慈童説話考. *Kokugo kokubun* 国語国文 49/11, pp. 1–32.

Itō Satoshi 伊藤聡 (1995), "Tenshō daijin – Kūkai dōtaisetsu o megutte: toku ni Sanbōin-ryū o chūshin to shite" 天照大神・空海同体説を巡って—特に三宝院流を中心として. *Tōyō no shisō to shūkyō* 東洋の思想と宗教 12, pp. 112–31.

Itō Satoshi 伊藤聡 (1999), "Kanpaku-ryū shintō ni tsuite" 関白流神道について. *Kanazawa Bunko Kenkyū* 金沢文庫研究 303, pp. 1–12.

Itō Toshikazu 伊藤俊一 (1991), "Shōren'in monzeki no keisei to bō mandokoro" 青蓮院門跡の形成と坊政所. *Komonjo kenkyū* 古文書研究 35, pp. 11–29.

Iyanaga Nobumi (1999), "Ḍākinī et l'Empereur: Mystique bouddhique de la royauté dans le Japon médiéval." *VS (Versus)* 83/84, pp. 41–111.

Kadoya Atsushi 門屋温 (1993), "Ryōbu shintō shiron: *Bikisho* no seiritsu o megutte" 両部神道試論 —『鼻帰書』の成立をめぐって. *Tōyō no shisō to shūkyō* 東洋の思想と宗教 10, pp. 80–96.

Kamikawa Michio 上川通夫 (1985), "Heian kōki no Tōji: gusō to hōe" 平安後期の東寺—供僧と法会. *Komonjo kenkyū* 古文書研究 24, pp. 48–68.

Kamikawa Michio 上川通夫 (1989), "Chūsei no sokui girei to bukkyō" 中世の即位儀礼と仏教, in Iwai Tadakuma 岩井忠熊 and Okada Seishi 岡田精司 (eds), *Tennō daigawari gishiki no rekishiteki tenkai* 天皇代替り儀式の歴史的展開. Tokyo: Kashiwa Shobō, pp. 106–39.

Kamikawa Michio 上川通夫 (1990), "Accession rituals and Buddhism in medieval Japan." *Japanese Journal of Religious Studies* 17/2–3, pp. 243–80.

Kikuchi Hitoshi 菊池仁 (1997), "Kuden, hiden, kikigaki: chūshaku to iu media" 口伝・秘伝・聞き書き — 注釈というメディア, in Mitani Kuniaki 三谷邦明 and Komine Kazuaki 小峯和明 (eds), *Chūsei no chi to gaku: chūshaku o yomu* 中世の知と学—注釈を読む. Tokyo: Shinwasha, pp. 271–95.

Kuroda Toshio, James C. Dobbins (tr.) (1996), "The development of the *kenmitsu* system as Japan's medieval orthodoxy." *Japanese Journal of Religious Studies* 23/3–4, pp. 233–69.

Maki Takayuki 真木隆行 (1998), "Go-Uda tennō no mikkyō juhō" 後宇多天皇の密教受法, in Ōsaka Daigaku Bungakubu Nihonshi Kenkyūshitsu (comp.), *Kodai chūsei no shakai to kokka* 古代中世の社会と国家. Osaka: Seibundō, pp. 479–98.

Matsumoto Ikuyo 松本郁代 (2001), "Chūsei Tōji o meguru rekishi jojutsu to ōken shinwa" 中世東寺をめぐる歴史叙述と王権神話. *Nihon bungaku* 日本文学 50–59, pp. 11–19.

Matsumoto Ikuyo 松本郁代 (2004a), "Daigoji Sanbōin-ryū no sokui hō to ōtō bunritsu" 醍醐寺三宝院流の即位法と王統分立. *Bukkyō bungaku* 仏教文学 28, pp. 90–100.

Matsumoto Ikuyo 松本郁代 (2004b), "Chūsei no sokui kanjō to 'tennō': Shingon-kata sokui hō ni okeru sokui inmyō no kōsō" 中世の即位灌頂と「天皇」—真言方即位法における即位印明の構想. *Ritsumeikan Bungaku* 立命館文学 585, pp. 42–73.

Nagamura Makoto 永村眞 (1991), "Inke to hōryū: Omo ni Daigoji Hōon'in o tōshite" 「院家」と「法流」—主に醍醐寺報恩院を通して, in Inagaki Eizō 稲垣栄三 (ed.), *Daigoji no mikkyō to shakai* 醍醐寺の密教と社会. Tokyo: Sankibō, pp. 235–71.

Nagamura Makoto 永村眞 (1993), "Jiin to tennō" 寺院と天皇, in Nagamura Makoto *et al.* (eds), *Tennō to shakai shoshūdan* 天皇と社会諸集団 (*Kōza: Zenkindai no tennō* 講座 前近代の天皇 3). Tokyo: Aoki Shoten, pp. 189–216.

Nakanishi Zuikō 中西随功 (1981), "Kuden hōmon seiritsu no shakai kiban" 口伝法門成立の社会基盤. *Indogaku bukkyōgaku kenkyū* 印度学仏教学研究 29/2, pp. 142–43.

Ogawa Takeo 小川剛生 (1997), "Sokui kanjō to sekkanke: Nijō-ke no 'Tenshi on-kanjō' no rekishi" 即位灌頂と摂関家 — 二条家の「天子御灌頂」の歴史 *Mita Kokubun* 三田国文 25, pp. 1–16.

Sawa Hirokatsu 沢博勝 (1993), "Ryōryū tetsuritsuki no ōken to bukkyō: Shōren'in to Daigoji o tsūshin ni" 両流迭立期の王権と仏教—青蓮院と醍醐寺を中心に. *Rekishigaku kenkyū* 歴史学研究 648, pp. 1–17, 31.

Stone, Jacqueline I. (1999), *Original enlightenment and the transformation of medieval Japanese Buddhism*. Honolulu: University of Hawai'i Press.

Takeuchi Rizō 竹内理三 (1940), "Kuden to kyōmei: kugyōgaku keifu (hiji kuden seiritsu izen)" 口伝と教命—公卿学系譜（秘事口伝成立以前). *Rekishi chiri* 歴史地理 75/3, pp. 1–15 and 75/4, pp. 27–42.

Tanaka Takako 田中貴子 (1993), *Gehō to aihō no chūsei* 外法と愛法の中世. Tokyo: Sunakoya Shobō.

Teeuwen, Mark (2000), "The kami in esoteric Buddhist thought and practice," in John Breen and Mark Teeuwen (eds), *Shinto in history: Ways of the kami*. Richmond, Surrey: Curzon Press, pp. 95–116.

Teeuwen, Mark (2003), "The creation of a *honji suijaku* deity: Amaterasu as the judge of the dead," in Mark Teeuwen and Fabio Rambelli (eds), *Buddhas and kami in Japan: Honji Suijaku as a combinatory paradigm*. London: RoutledgeCurzon, pp. 115–144.

Terai Hikaru 寺井光 (2001), "Tennō sokui higisetsu no keisei ni tsuite: sokui kanjō to shikai ryōshō hō" 天皇即位秘儀説の形成について—即位灌頂と四海領掌法, in Uwayokote Masataka 上横手雅敬 (ed.), *Chūsei no jisha to shinkō* 中世の寺社と信仰. Tokyo: Yoshikawa Kōbunkan, pp. 50–71.

Tsuji Zennosuke 辻善之助 (1931), "Ryōtō tairitsu no han'ei to shite no Sanbōin-ryū chakusho no arasoi" 両統対立の反映としての三宝院流嫡庶の争, in *Nihon bukkyōshi no kenkyū zokuhen* 日本仏教史之研究続編. Tokyo: Kinkōdō Shoseki, pp. 147–68.

Yamamoto Hiroko 山本ひろ子 (1993), *Henjōfu: chūsei shinbutsu shūgō no sekai* 変成譜 — 中世神仏習合の世界. Tokyo: Shunjūsha.

8 Secrecy, sex and apocrypha

Remarks on some paradoxical phenomena

Nobumi Iyanaga

Introduction

Let me begin this essay with some general remarks on the nature of secrecy in esoteric Buddhism. In order to make clear what this type of secrecy entails, it seems useful to consider it in contrast with the ordinary personal secret. Unlike the personal secret, which ideally should be kept secret during the entire lifetime of the concerned person, the secret teachings in esoteric Buddhism must be transmitted to at least one disciple.[1] In other words, the secret teachings in esoteric Buddhism have the paradoxical nature of having to be spread for them to have any value; however, if they are spread too widely, they lose their value. The difficult thing is to keep the "golden mean." In addition, whereas for the personal secret it is ideal if even the fact that it exists remains totally unknown, a secret teaching gains in value when its existence is made known as widely as possible (this may be compared to advertising in our consumer society) while its contents are kept concealed. The secret in esoteric Buddhism is a kind of commodity that, at the same time, is a source of power and authority. In this sense, I would argue that it functions very much like treasures that fulfill wishes or relics of the Buddha.

That said, we may wonder why esoteric teachings must be kept secret. In fact, it seems that in earlier Chinese traditions of esoteric Buddhism, the need for secret transmission was almost never evident.[2] Osabe Kazuo (1963, p. 269), who devotes some interesting pages to this issue, points at the following passage from the "Dhāraṇī sutra of the Bodhisattva Avalokiteśvara in the form of Amoghapāśa" (*Bukong juansuo tuoluoni jing* 不空羂索陀羅尼経):

> The practitioner of this spell will want to confer benefit on all beings, and, putting on the armor of zeal, will not conceal this teaching, but teach it in detail according to its literal meaning (*wenyi* 文義).
>
> (T 20.415a10–12)

This sutra presents a similar attitude to that of classical Mahāyāna sutras: the Dharma should be spread as widely as possible, for the benefit of all beings. At first glance, the *Commentary on the Mahāvairocana-sūtra* (*Darijing shu* 大日経疏) exhibits a somehow different attitude, since we find passages such as "These essentials of teaching are very difficult to understand; they should be protected all together, and should not be propagated recklessly (*bu wang xuanchuang* 不妄宣伝)."[3] But in the same text it is also written that "if a person is willing to purify himself, nothing should be concealed from him, and [everything] should be transmitted to him."[4] In contrast to these ambiguous statements, there is the following remark typical for a ritual text translated by Amoghavajra:

> This teaching is the most excellent among the teachings of Garuḍa; it is secret and difficult to obtain. You must choose a worthy recipient able to receive it and transmit it to him. If he is a person who is not worthy, it will hurt him, and afterwards, the rite will not succeed. This is why it must be kept most secret and one must not transmit it recklessly.[5]

In fact, this is one of very few occurrences in Chinese esoteric texts of the phrase "most secret" (*jimi* 極秘, Jap. *gokuhi* or *jimimi* 極秘密, Jap. *gokuhimitsu*) that can be traced back to an Indian origin with certainty.[6] A search in the esoteric section of the CBETA files[7] (vol. 18–21) reveals an interesting fact: many texts in which one finds this phrase are either of Chinese origin, or Japanese apocrypha.[8]

Compared to Japanese ritual texts, the difference is striking. For example, in a single passage on the ritual of Aizen Myōō 愛染明王 in the *Shikan* 四巻 by Kōzen 興然 (1120–1203), we find many occurrences of terms meaning "most secret," such as *saigokuhi* 最極秘 (T 79.773b19), *saihi* 最秘 (T 79.773b20, b25; 774a10; 775b9), *saihimitsu* 最秘密 (T 79.775a4), *kukyō hiji* 究竟秘事 (T 79.776c22), and so on. Thus, we can say with certainty that while in the early Indian and Chinese esoteric tradition the need for secrecy in the transmission of teaching was ambiguous, it became more and more prominent over time, especially in medieval Japanese Mikkyō. This result fits in neatly with Jacqueline Stone's analysis of the evolution of secret transmissions in Japan, in particular in the medieval Tendai tradition. In her *Original Enlightenment and the Transformation of Medieval Japanese Buddhism*, Jacquline Stone (1999, pp. 92–152) shows that the "culture of secret transmission" became increasingly important from the late Heian period (794–1192) onward, and continued to expand throughout the medieval period. She explains this phenomenon by several factors: the "privatization of land and power" by people belonging to "influential houses or ruling elites" (*kenmon* 権門), "the aristocratization of the clergy," and "the consequent transplanting of noble factions into the world of the temple-shrine complexes" (pp. 150–51). More concretely, the increase of esoteric rites sponsored by individual nobles in the Insei period (1086–1192) resulted in a "growing elaborateness and complexity of ritual performance," and

> knowledge, as well as land, wealth, and political power, was becoming privatized. For example, this period witnessed the emergence of hereditary schools of poetry (*waka no ie*)... This phenomenon was in turn related to the rise of the idea of *michi*, or 'Way' – the pursuit, as a vocation, of some specialized art or knowledge that was transmitted through a lineage, from father to son, or master to disciple.
>
> (Stone 1999, pp. 108–09)

Stone's discussion of this aspect of Japanese medieval culture is very well documented, and her explanation seems very plausible. Nevertheless, it appears to me that many of the factors that she lists are external to the development of Japanese esoteric Buddhism itself. It is true that esoteric Buddhism was imported to Japan at a relatively early stage of its evolution, but at that time it was already named the "school of secrecy" (*mimizong* 秘密宗) in China. This name is found in the very authoritative *Commentary on the Mahāvairocana-sūtra* (T 39.602a2, 666c10), and some texts (especially after Amoghavajra) stipulate that they be treated as "ultimate secrets" (*jimi*). We know that in later Indo-Tibetan Buddhist Tantrism, the guru–disciple relationship was most important (Snellgrove 1987, pp. 176–80), and in the transmission of magical formulae, even financial transactions became a common practice (Masaki 2002, pp. 63, 70–71) – just as in Japan, where "there is evidence that master–disciple transmissions sometimes involved some form of financial transaction" (Stone 1999, pp. 144–48).[9] Thus, in the broader perspective of the history of Buddhist Tantrism in general, the increasing importance of secret transmissions in medieval Japanese Mikkyō seems a rather natural evolution, even though it was a particular characteristic of Japanese culture that this mode of transmitting knowledge also spread to such a wide range of other fields (all Buddhist schools, Shugendō, Onmyōdō, Shinto, court protocol, poetry, calligraphy, Noh drama, *biwa* recitation, flower arranging, the tea ceremony, martial arts, etc.). If we use "esotericism" as a term for *secret* doctrines, we can say that medieval Japanese culture *in toto* was an "esotericized" culture. Thus, it is possible to raise the question whether the social changes that were noted by Stone as possible factors behind the growing importance of secrecy in Japan were not rather the result of the "natural" evolution of Mikkyō secrecy instead of its cause. In any case, I think that it is safe to say that the influences were mutual and came from both sides.

To return to the question that opened this discussion on the reason and evolution of secret transmission of esoteric teaching, it seems to me that it was not so much secrecy itself that was important, but rather the direct transmission from master to disciple, which goes back in a unique lineage to the transcendental Buddha Vairocana (Dainichi). This lineage impressed on the disciple not only that he was receiving authentic teachings, but also, and most importantly, that he belonged to the "mystical family" of the Buddha, in short, that he was sacralized. This would have been the reason why the authentication of documents such as *kechimyaku* 血脉 (lit. "[document attesting] a blood lineage") became so important. Many of the teachings that were transmitted in this way may have consisted of no more than a mantra and a mudrā, without much doctrinal meaning; but by the very fact that they were assumed to have been transmitted directly from the Buddha Vairocana, they could confer supreme authority on the disciple by transforming him into a sacralized being. The expression "blood lineage" may have a literal meaning: those who received documents attesting such a blood lineage belonged to the sacred family of the Buddha Vairocana and hence, they usually called themselves *kongō busshi* 金剛仏子, "Buddha's child in vajra." It is possible that this "familialization" of religion was one of the stimuli for the increasing privatization of the society. The medieval semiotic world was based on this kind of sacrality; this may explain why the secret transmission of knowledge became so crucial and omnipresent in Japanese medieval culture.

Juhō yōjin-shū and Tachikawa-ryū: What Tachikawa-ryū is not

After this general introduction, let me go to the "heart" of the medieval Mikkyō world and discuss a specific text: a work entitled *Juhō yōjin-shū* 受法用心集 ("Notes on precautions to be taken when receiving teaching"), written by a Shingon monk named Shinjō 心定 in 1268. As we shall see later, this text contains interesting passages with regard to the notion of secrecy in Mikkyō and to the "heretical teachings." But before coming to this point, we should try to characterize this curious document.

Juhō yōjin-shū is a well-known text describing a rather eccentric sexual ritual known as the "skull ritual," which has commonly been attributed to the so-called Tachikawa-ryū 立川流. The Tachikawa-ryū is a branch of the Shingon school, famous, or rather infamous, because it was thought to have taught a sexual doctrine and ritual. From the late fourteenth century onward, it was considered as the most important "heresy" within the Shingon school. In fact, as will be discussed below, almost nothing about it is known with certainty. Until very recently, the *Juhō yōjin-shū* was assumed to be one of very few (or perhaps even the only) original sources to give any details about the teachings of this lineage. However, if one reads the *Juhō yōjin-shū* without preconceived ideas about the Tachikawa-ryū, it becomes clear that the ritual described in this text is *not* a ritual of the Tachikawa-ryū. The author never names the school that teaches the "skull ritual." He consistently calls it "this teaching" or "that teaching" (*kono hō* 此の法, *kano hō* 彼の法) and also uses the term "evil teaching" (*jahō* 邪法 or *jakyō* 邪教).[10]

It is true that Shinjō does mention the name of Tachikawa-ryū: it occurs twice in the introductory part of this work, which recounts the curriculum of his studies in different Shingon branches. First, he says that at the age of twenty-five, "around the summer season of the first year of Ennō" (1239), he received the three *abhiṣeka* of the "Secret *Yugikyō*," the "[Body of the] natural outcome," and the "Body of the Dharma" (*himitsu yugi tōru-hosshin sanshu no kanjō* 秘密瑜祇等流法身三種の灌頂) from the *ācārya* Ashō 阿聖 of Hosono in the country of Etchū. On that occasion, he "copied all the secret works of the Tachikawa-ryū."[11] In the second passage, Shinjō writes that at the age of thirty-six, around the summer of 1250, a monk named Kōamidabutsu 弘阿弥陀仏, of the monastery Shin-Zenkōji 新善光寺 of Akasaka in the country of Echizen, came to his cell[12] and stayed there some days. He told Shinjō about the different places of pilgrimage that he had visited and about the masters with whom he had become acquainted and how they were practicing. After several days, he asked Shinjō for a teaching on the *Bodaishin ron* 菩提心論 (Treatise on the Bodhicitta). Shinjō gave him a lecture on the main teaching of this treatise for four or five days; then he left Shinjō's cell. After some time, Shinjō had an opportunity to go to Shin-Zenkōji. Kōamidabutsu invited him repeatedly to his cell, and there he found a big bag full of books on the desk of sutras. Kōamidabutsu opened it and took out many fascicles, more than a hundred in all. Shinjō discovered that they were mainly *orikami* 折紙 (folded pieces of paper containing secret ritual texts) of the Tachikawa-ryū, which were in circulation in Etchū. However, among these fascicles, there were seven or eight containing what Shinjō referred to as "those Three Inner Sutras (*kano nai-sanbukyō* 彼の内三部経) and oral traditions of Kikuran 菊蘭の口伝" (Shinjō writes "*those* Three Inner Sutras" because his work begins with a question about the nature of these "Three Inner Sutras"; see below). Shinjō writes that he saw these texts for the first time and found them very unusual. He borrowed these fascicles to bring them back to his room and copy them, but there were details in them that were not clear to him (Moriyama 1965, p. 532).[13]

These two passages show that many texts of the Tachikawa-ryū circulated in the Echizen and Etchū regions (modern Fukui and Toyama) around the middle of the thirteenth century. Among them, one could occasionally find some famous texts of "that school" (*kano ryū*), but Shinjō does not confound the texts of the Tachikawa-ryū with those of what he calls "that school." Shinjō found the Three Inner Sutras and the oral traditions of Kikuran odd or unusual, in spite of the fact that he had copied "all the secret works of the Tachikawa-ryū" ten years earlier.

One year after these events, in the spring of 1251, Shinjō went to Kyoto. At the Jizōdō of Gojōbōmon he followed a course on Kūkai's *Sokushin jōbutsu gi* 即身成仏義 (Principle of Attaining Buddhahood within the Present Body), given by an important monk of Kōya-san named Kaiken 快賢. According to Kōda Yūun, this Kaiken received an *injin* 印信 (initiation document) called *Gonyūjō daihō* 御入定大法 (Great formula of entering into *dhyāna*) from Myōchō 明澄 of Kongōin 金剛院 in 1252; this Myōchō is portrayed as a "heretic" in the *Shōryū jō jaryū ji* 正流成邪流事 of Kaijō 快成 (?–1367).[14] Moreover, Mizuhara Gyōei has pointed out that Kaiken would also have received the *yugi kanjō* 瑜祇灌頂 of the Tachikawa-ryū from Dōhan 道範 (1184–1252).[15] Shinjō spent about a month attending this course. One day, he reports, there was a visitor before him in the cell of Kaiken, and he had to wait for his master in the Jizōdō chapel. A monk appeared, and they talked together. The monk (Shinjō does not mention his name) asked what he was doing, and Shinjō replied that he was receiving a teaching on the *Sokushin jōbutsu gi*, Kūkai's teachings on attaining buddhahood within the present body. Then the monk replied that the most secret teachings on this topic were revealed completely in the Three Inner Sutras; without receiving these teachings, it would be impossible to grasp the deepest meaning of Kūkai's work. Shinjō asked about the contents of these sutras, but the monk said that they could not be easily understood. He told that if Shinjō was really interested, he should come to his lodging close to Hitotsubashi near Hosshōji 法性寺 (Hosshōji is located slightly to the south of the present-day Tōfukuji, in Kyoto's Higashiyama ward). There he would be willing to initiate him into these teachings. Shinjō felt it would be a pity not to take the opportunity, and he went with the monk to his lodging. He spent the night there, and the next morning he again asked the monk about the teachings. Then the monk said that Shinjō would have to receive a special *abhiṣeka* in order to receive them. Since Shinjō was serious in his wish to learn these teachings, he received the necessary *abhiṣeka* with sincerity, and the monk granted him all the sutras and the secret oral teachings (Moriyama 1965, pp. 533–34).

It was on this occasion that Shinjō learned the actual contents of the teachings of "that school" for the first time. In the *Juhō yōjin-shū* we find a list of the titles of works that Shinjō received after his initiation into "that school" in 1251 (Moriyama 1965, p. 534). All the titles on this list are unusual. For example, the *Gozō kōteikyō* 五臓皇帝経 (Sutra of the Emperor of Five Visceral Organs?), a text said to be a "translation" by Yixing 一行 , sounds much like a title of some Chinese medical or Daoist work.[16] Other titles are clearly erotic or sexual, for example *Shaku rengekyō* 赤蓮花経 (Sutra of the Red Lotus) and *Bōnai fudōkyō* 房内不動経 (Sutra of Immobility *or* Acala of the Inner Chamber).[17] The title *Kikuran dōjikyō* 菊蘭童子経 (Sutra of the Youth of the Chrysanthemum-Orchid) seems to contain an allusion to homosexuality. Characteristic of the texts of "that school" seem to be rare words such as *tenteki* 甜滴, "sweet drops" in the title *Shichi tenteki henge jizai daranikyō* 七甜滴変化自在陀羅尼経 (Sutra of the Spell of the Omnipotent Transformation of Seven Sweet Drops).[18] Another typical word is *henjōju* 変成就, "odd *siddhi* or accomplishment," in the title *Henjōju daranikyō* 変成就陀羅尼経 (Sutra of the Spell of Odd Accomplishments). This word appears in two texts by Mujū 無住 (1226–1312), the famous *Shasekishū* 沙石集 (1283)[19] and the *Shōzaishū* 聖財集 (1299). (See Itō 1996, pp. 88–89.) It is also mentioned in a work by the Tendai monk Ejin 恵尋 entitled *Endonkai kikigaki* 円頓戒聞書 (ca. 1263).[20] In these texts, *henjōju* is used to designate a sexual practice that seems similar to the one described in the *Juhō yōjin-shū*. On the other hand, as I wrote above, there was an oral tradition about *Kikuran* in one of the *orikami* of the Tachikawa-ryū that Shinjō saw in the cell of Kōamidabutsu. The word *kikuran* also occurs in a passage of the *Byakuhō kushō* 白宝口抄 by Ryōzen and Ryōson 亮禅述・亮尊記 (composed before 1341). They mention a "Kikuran-ryū" lineage that possessed (produced?) many apocryphical texts on Aizen Myōō rituals.[21]

In the same paragraph, Shinjō gives the numbers of fascicles that he received. Included were eighty fascicles for the works belonging to the category of "Three Inner Sutras" (containing three series of three sutras and other sutras, and one treatise), one hundred and twenty-six for the secret oral traditions related to these sutras and this treatise, a non-specified number of fascicles for *kanjō injin kechimyaku* 灌頂印信血脈 (certificates and lineage documents of the *abhiṣeka*) and a "journal of transmission" (*sōden no nikki* 相伝の日記), as well as three fascicles of personal notes on the practice of the *abhiṣeka*. All together, that makes more than two-hundred and ten fascicles. Further in the same text, in the second fascicle, Shinjō says that he had been able to collect even more works belonging to "that school" on other occasions; in all, there would have been more than five hundred fascicles that he kept in six boxes (Moriyama 1965, pp. 561–62). Even if there is some exaggeration, and even if many "fascicles" may have been very short documents, all this gives the impression of a considerable number of works. We can say that the group that constituted "that school" of Shinjō was surprisingly productive in composing apocryphal texts.

We know practically nothing about the contents of these texts. However, Shinjō gives two short quotations from a text entitled *Tentekikyo* 甜滴経 (Sutra of Sweet Drops) or *Sen-tentekikyō* 染甜滴経 (Sutra of the Lust of Sweet Drops), which consisted of at least two fascicles (Moriyama 1965, pp. 545–46). This title seems to refer to one of the "Three Inner Sutras," the *Shichi tenteki henge jizai daranikyō* – but in the list of works that Shinjō received, it is said that this text had only one fascicle, so we cannot be sure that they are indeed the same work. In any case, Shinjō states that the principal sutra of "that school" was nothing more than a plagiarized version of the *Yugikyō* 瑜祇経 and the *Rishukyō* 理趣経, in which the original meaning of these sutras was greatly distorted. From the first fascicle of the *Tentekikyō* (very probably the beginning of the sutra), he quotes a passage that is a clear imitation of the beginning of the *Rishukyō* (T 8.784a19–22, b1–5); then he quotes a passage from the second fascicle that obviously plagiarizes the *Yugikyō* (T 18.254a22–b1).

Comparing the passages quoted by Shinjō with the original sutras, we can see that certain terms of the *Rishukyō* and the *Yugikyō* have been replaced by some characteristic expressions. For example, "Sen-tenteki Nyorai" 染甜滴如来 (Tathāgata of the Lust of Sweet Drops) replaces the words *myōteki shōjō ku* 妙適清浄句 (pure words of [sexual] pleasure) of the *Rishukyō*, and the same word replaces the name "Kongōshu bosatsu" 金剛手菩薩 (Bodhisattva Vajrapāṇi) of the *Yugikyō*. Similarly, the expression *issai shujō gozō* 一切衆生五臓 (five visceral organs of all beings) is used instead of *gobu kongō* 五峯金剛 (vajra with five prongs) of the *Yugikyō*, *chō* 頂 (sinciput, the upper half of the cranium) replaces *kō* 鈎 (elephant-driver's hook, Skt. *aṅkuśa*) or *mani* 摩尼 (jewel), and so forth. If indeed the group of "that school" described by Shinjō created their "sutras" in this manner – that is, taking a model text and replacing certain words with other typical words here and there – then it would have been easy to produce many texts.

There may be other quotations from texts of "that school" in the *Juhō yōjin-shū*. Reading the *Juhō yōjin-shū*, we soon notice that the author follows a particular pattern when he gives quotations. Nearly throughout, he first names the title or the nature of the text from which he is going to quote; then he gives the quotation itself; then he writes, "...thus it was said."[22] However, when it comes to quotations from texts of "that school," he does not mention the title of the source. He merely writes, for instance, "It is said in the compendium of oral traditions of that [school]:..., thus it was said," and "It is said in a text of that teaching:..., thus it was said."[23] The long description of the skull ritual in the second fascicle of the *Juhō yōjin-shū* is also most likely a quotation from texts of "that school," since it begins with the sentence "As to the practice of this evil teaching, it is said in a secret oral tradition of that [school]..."[24]

The first "question" with which the whole work begins may contain one of the very rare doctrinal overviews of "that school":

Question: Recently, felicitous sutras called the "Three Inner Sutras" have spread in the world. In earlier times, these sutras used to be transmitted only among the abbots of [the Shingon center of] Tōji and the Tendai school, but these days, they have spread so widely that everyone trifles with them in the capital as well as in the countryside. In these sutras it is said that intercourse with women is the most crucial thing in the Shingon teaching, and that it is the highest among the [practices for] attaining buddhahood within the present body. If one avoids it, then the path to the accomplishment of the buddhahood is said to be distant. [It is also said that] eating meat is the inner attestation of all buddhas and bodhisattvas, and that it is the most profound foundation of the [practices of] skillful means for the benefit of beings. If one dislikes it, then one will lose the way to escape from transmigration. This is why one should not choose between the pure and the impure, one must not dislike intercourse with women and eating meat. All the dharmas are altogether pure, so one will quickly attain buddhahood within the present body. This appears to be the main theme of these [Three Inner Sutras]. People also say that if one practices the ritual taught in these sutras, then the principal deity will suddenly appear, who will teach one about all matters of the three worlds [of the past, present and future] clearly. The deity will grant one fortune, wisdom and a high official rank, so that it will appear as though one has obtained a miraculous power in one's present body. One will be endowed with wisdom and eloquence, and will gain any amount of wealth at one's will. [These sutras even claim] that the virtue of the great masters and worthy men of earlier times, who had such power that they could make flying birds fall, reverse the course of flowing water, make dead people come back to life and make poor people rich, was altogether due to the efficacy of this ritual. How about all this?

(Moriyama 1965, pp. 530–31)

This passage is of a particular importance because part of it seems to have been quoted by Yūkai 宥快 (1345–1416) in his *Hōkyōshō* 宝鏡鈔 (Compendium of the precious mirror, composed in 1375) as being the main doctrinal feature of the Tachikawa-ryū (Moriyama 1965, pp. 574–75). In this work Yūkai claims that the Tachikawa-ryū, allegedly founded by Ninkan 仁寛, taught that the "path of Yin and Yang between men and women" is the secret art for attaining buddhahood within the present body, and that there is no other way to attain buddhahood and obtain the way.[25] It is worth mentioning that in the same passage, Yūkai refers to the *Juhō yōjin-shū* for a detailed description of the Tachikawa-ryū. Yūkai's identification of the teaching of "that school" (the teaching of Shinjō's Three Inner Sutras) with the Tachikawa-ryū was decisive for the later reputation of Tachikawa-ryū as the heresy *par excellence* – especially because Yūkai became the highest authority in the doctrine of the Kogi branch of Shingon.

It may be useful to summarize here what we can say for now about the Tachikawa-ryū and the sexual doctrines and rituals of medieval Mikkyō. Although the name Tachikawa-ryū was rarely used before the time of Yūkai (the later fourteenth century), it does occur in some thirteenth-century documents, one of the earliest being the *Juhō yōjin-shū*.[26] At the same time, there exist *injin* which, albeit not mentioning the name Tachikawa-ryū, contain *kechimyaku* lineage lists that include figures who are closely associated with that lineage: Shōkaku 勝覚 (1057–1129) of the Sanbōin-ryū 三宝院流, Rennen 蓮念 (which is said to be another name of Ninkan, a younger brother of Shōkaku, assumed after he was exiled to Izu in 1113), and Kenren 見蓮 (dates unknown). These *injin* have been studied by Kushida (1964, pp. 344–62) and Kōda (1981b), who say that they could find nothing particularly "heretical" or sexual in them.[27] On the other hand, as I showed above, the ritual described by the *Juhō yōjin-shū* does *not* belong to the Tachikawa-ryū. Because what Yūkai writes about the Tachikawa-ryū in his *Hōkyōshō* is almost entirely based on the *Juhō yōjin-shū*, his work cannot be used as a source for a description of the Tachikawa-ryū. Thus, we can draw the conclusion that the infamous reputation of the Tachikawa-ryū as a lineage that taught heretical and sexual doctrines and rituals is without any foundation.

On the other hand, we know that many Mikkyō schools and lineages had some sexual teachings. One of the most important was the Sanbōin-ryū, where in particular there is evidence of a teaching called the "doctrine of the five positions [of the embryo] in the womb" (*tainai goi setsu* 胎内五位説), which had a lasting influence on pre-modern thought.[28] However, as far as I know, there appears to be no clear evidence in extant documents of any actual practice of sexual rituals. "That school" described by Shinjō was probably a very special group, not belonging to any "official" school (Shingon or Tendai), but rather a kind of popular religious movement. We should note that all the testimonies that may be related to "that school" are from the later thirteenth or the early fourteenth century. Finally, strongly sexualized doctrines were advocated within a certain school of *waka* exegesis, which produced various works of *waka* interpretation that were of an esoteric nature (see Klein's essay in this book). This school is usually named Tameaki-ryū 為顕流 from the name of its initiator, Fujiwara no Tameaki (ca. 1230s to after 1295), and one of its most representative texts is the *Ise monogatari zuinō* 伊勢物語髄脳 (author unknown, early fourteenth century?).[29] This very special group set forth a kind of new religion in that period and was most likely made up primarily of aristocrat poets or scholars. It is *possible* that they actually practiced sexual rituals.

Secrecy and forgery according to the Juhō yōjin-shū

Another interesting aspect of the *Juhō yōjin-shū* is the view on secrecy in Mikkyō as presented by the author. As quoted also above, Shinjō wrote,

> Recently, felicitous sutras called the "Three Inner Sutras" have spread in the world. In earlier times, these sutras used to be transmitted only among the abbots of Tōji and the Tendai school, but these days, they have spread so widely that everyone trifles with them in the capital as well as in the countryside.

This would imply that "in earlier times," this teaching had been a great secret shared only among the most eminent prelates of the Mikkyō schools, but now it had spread and become a common teaching that everybody knows. Since the *Juhō yōjin-shū* is written in a question-and-answer form (*mondō* 問答), and since this statement is part of a "question," we cannot know whether this was Shinjō's personal opinion. However, throughout the work we find similar statements that express the dialectic between secret teachings and their dissemination. In one passage, Shinjō writes that although nobody among the people of the correct schools of the main temples talks about this teaching, nine out of ten Shingon masters in the countryside believe that this is the essence of Mikkyō (Moriyama 1965, p. 555). Shinjō repeatedly states that everybody – especially in the countryside – knows these teachings, although none of the learned monks of the main temples are aware of this. He continues by stating that he has asked every learned monk he has encountered about these teachings, but they all replied that they had never even heard of its name.

Shinjō also argues that however secret a teaching is, if it is a real teaching at least its name should be known by learned persons, even if there are only very few people who actually receive its transmission. It is incomprehensible, he writes, that the monks of the main schools have never even heard the name of these teachings, while ignorant people of the countryside know it so well. In one passage, he notes that he once asked his master in these teachings about his doubts on this point. The latter replied that in the main temples, the teachings must have been kept so secret that even their name had been lost, whereas in the countryside the secret could not be kept so strictly, and thus everybody now knows it (Moriyama 1965, pp. 542–43). Shinjō repeatedly criticizes the teaching of the Three Inner Sutras on the grounds that it is so widely spread among common people, but not known by learned monks.

All these arguments may appear somewhat contradictory. First we must recognize that there is certainly some exaggeration in Shinjō's statements. We can easily imagine that the "eminent monks" to whom Shinjō asked his questions replied that they knew nothing, simply because they were afraid of being implicated in the scandal of these "heretical" teachings. We can also imagine that "ignorant monks" were tempted to say that they knew these teachings, without knowing them concretely. On the other hand, these statements seem to be somehow inconsistent with what Shinjō himself writes about how he came to know these teachings: he had made all possible efforts to obtain them, and yet it was a chance encounter with the monk at the Jizōdō of Gojōbōmon that enabled his initiation in them. Despite this, Shinjō reveals his skepticism with the clear purpose of discrediting these teachings. Nevertheless, we can understand that this situation appeared strange or suspect to Shinjō. Normally, the "eminent monks" should at least know the names of secret teachings, and "ignorant people" should be unaware of them. This view confirms that secrecy in Mikkyō is closely related to authority.

Shinjō also reports on other traditions related to the secrecy of these teachings. For example, he quotes a text of "that school" (again without giving a name), claiming that the statue of Yakushi Nyorai (Tathāgata Bhaiṣajyaguru) in the main hall on Mount Hiei was created through the skull ritual, and that its most important secrets were stored in the so-called First Box of the Tendai school (*Tendai no ichi no hako* 天台の一の箱) (Moriyama 1965, p. 538). According to what Shinjō writes, it seems that there was a legend about this mysterious box, which was said to contain the most secret teachings of the Tendai school. It was said to have been transmitted from one Tendai abbot to the next, and these abbots had allegedly been virgins all their lives (*isshō fubon* 一生不犯).[30] In another passage, Shinjō quotes another text on the transmission lineage of the 'Three Inner Sutras' (Moriyama 1965, p. 537). According to this text, Kōbō Daishi (Kūkai) imported these sutras to Japan, but having found no worthy disciple to whom he could transmit them, he entered into *dhyāna* (i.e. passed away) while keeping the sutras in a box around his neck. Five generations of disciples after Kūkai, a master called Kangen 観賢 (853–925) went to Kūkai's mausoleum and shaved his head there. On that occasion these sutras were given to him (note that there is another legend saying that Kangen was the first person to have gone to Kūkai's mausoleum and to have seen his mummy). Of course, none of this is true, and Shinjō reports these traditions only to criticize them. But these legends give us some idea of the way in which apocryphal works were produced in this kind of milieu.

Heresy, forgery and secrecy

Up to this point, I have used the word "apocrypha" without any definition. But as soon as we try to define what an apocryphal work is, we encounter insoluble problems. Depending on one's point of view, one could say that in one sense, almost all the Buddhist texts are apocryphal – and indeed, the Edo-period Nativist Hirata Atsutane 平田篤胤 (1776–1843) claimed that all Buddhist scriptures are forgeries. Nearer to our topic, one could say that two-thirds or three-quarters of the so-called "translations" of esoteric works by Amoghavajra are in fact his own compositions. Of course, this can be doctrinally justified: a Tantric master can be said to be ritually identical to the Buddha Vairocana, and thus he can utter or write words on behalf of the Buddha himself. On the other hand, as Satō Hiroo has shown in a recent book (Satō 2002), medieval Japan was inundated by a flood of apocryphal works of all kinds.

Here I am more specifically interested in the apocryphal works of Mikkyō schools and their relation to secrecy. There is a very large number of apocryphal works in Mikkyō if by "apocryphal work" we mean all

216 *Nobumi Iyanaga*

works that have been falsely attributed to an author, but I would propose to distinguish between different degrees of "obviousness" in the manner of their falsification. Some works, such as the Three Inner Sutras of "that school" described by Shinjō, are false in a very obvious way, while other texts are more subtle forgeries (for example, the *Renge sanmaikyō* 蓮華三昧経, studied by Mizukami 2003). On the other hand, there are also works that have been denounced as falsifications by various authors. A number of what we could call "heresiological works" exist in the Shingon school, these works listing books accused of being forgeries. The *Juhō yōjin-shū* is one of the earliest; the famous *Hōkyōshō* by Yūkai denouncing the Tachikawa-ryū is another. Yūkai's *Tachikawa shōgyō mokuroku* 立河聖教目録 (Catalogue of the Scriptures of Tachikawa-ryū) contains a list of about three hundred and sixty titles of apocryphal works. This is by far the most comprehensive list of this kind. There is also a work entitled *Gisho ron* 偽書論 (Treatise on Apocryphal Works) written by Kyōi 恭畏 (1565–1630) in the early seventeenth century, criticizing mainly works of the Sanbōin-ryū (edited in T 78.915c–917a; see Itō 2002, pp. 199, 213–215, 228, n. 3). The works denounced in these texts may or may not be actual falsified works. Since these "heresiological works" reflect factional struggles between different branches of the Shingon school, they are all tendentious, and should not be taken at face value. One interesting thing is that, although there are certainly accusations of falsification here and there in earlier texts, these works specializing in "heresiology" or apocrypha seem generally to have been composed in the late Middle Ages, or even later. We can assume that in this period there was a movement to purify the Shingon school that attempted to eliminate all spurious or suspicious traditions from it. This movement may have reflected a change of mentality toward a more "rational" attitude with regard to earlier traditions.

A closer examination of these heresiological works and the texts listed in them is quite interesting. For example, Yūkai's *Hōkyōshō* (Moriyama 1965, p. 575) mentions the lineage of Myōchō (active in the middle of the thirteenth century) and Kenzei 賢誓 (active in the later half of the thirteenth century) as belonging to the "evil teaching." In *Hōkyōshō*, Yūkai gives the titles of several *injin* that originated within this lineage.[31] The listed works are

- *Kusshutsu hō* 堀出法 (Formula of Unearthing)
- *Hikō jizai hō* 飛行自在法 (Formula for Flying at One's Will)
- *Toten daiji* 渡天大事 (Essentials for Going to India [or Heaven])
- *Shusoku funi-daiji* 手足不二大事 (Essentials of Non-Dual Hands and Feet)
- *Sanze jōgō hō* 三世常恒法 (Formula for Permanently Existing in the Three Worlds [of the Past, Present and Future])
- *Gonyūjō kajū daiji* 御入定何重大事 (Essentials, in Several Depths, of [Kūkai's] Entrance into Dhyāna)

At first sight, these titles may look like magical formulas more or less related to Shugendō practice. However, this lineage has been studied in detail by Kōda Yūun, who has actually located some of these texts and quotes them in his article (Kōda 1981a). First, the word *kusshutsu hō* is apparently not the title of a work, but designates teachings that have been miraculously "unearthed." According to one of the texts quoted by Kōda (*Gisho mokuroku narabini jagi kyōron* 偽書目録并邪義経論; Kōda 1981a, p. 21a–b), these *injin* were allegedly unearthed by Myōsan 明算 (1021–1106) in the Inner Hall (Oku no In 奥の院) of Kōya-san, probably the site of Kūkai's mausoleum. Myōsan had a miraculous dream that enabled him to locate the spot where these texts were buried. When he unearthed them, the monk Shinnen 真然 (one of Kūkai's nephews who had passed away much earlier) appeared to Myōsan and confirmed that these teachings had been transmitted to him (i.e. to Myōsan).[32]

Kōda also quotes from the *Gonyūjō daihō* and *Hikō jizai injin*, which are included in this list (Kōda 1981a, pp. 25a–27a). It seems that they actually contain nothing in particular that could qualify as an "evil teaching." The Formula for Flying at One's Will says for example that the practitioner, without abandoning his present body, must form a mudra called *musho fushi in* 無所不至印 (mudra that leaves no places unattained), and with the letter *A* as the substance of the self-nature, the letter *VAM* as the body of enjoyment, and so on he will gain the ability to walk in the air. Even so, it is true that this "Formula for Flying at One's Will" does have something unusual to it, since the entire text is interspersed with passages from the *Mahāvairocana-sūtra* (T 18.21a10–11, 9b25–c1, 9c4–8) without indicating them as quotations.[33] This shows clearly that it is a falsified text.

At the conclusion of his article, Kōda raises the problem of why this Genshō-Myōchō-Kenzei lineage had to produce such apocryphal traditions. He proposes the following hypothesis. After Myōsan, the Chūin-ryū was divided into two branches. The branch to which Genshō belonged (the Ryūkōin 龍光院 branch) was, although the more legitimate, somehow inferior in strength to its rival (the Hokushitsuin 北室院 branch). To improve this situation, Genshō would have had to find traditions that were both unique to his branch *and* backed up by the authority of Myōsan. This would have been his main motive for "inventing" these forgeries. (Kōda 1981a, pp. 33a–35a)

I find this hypothesis very convincing. Religious authority, based on the secret transmission of special teachings, was the aim and motive of most of the apocryphal traditions. Moreover, secrecy is also at work in the process of producing these traditions: according to Genshō, the *injin* that were transmitted to Myōsan were so secret that they initially had to be buried. In the same way, the apocryphal Three Inner Sutras of the teaching described by Shinjō were so secret that they were transmitted in the First Box of the Abbots of Mount Hiei, or in a box that hung around the neck of Kūkai's mummy, and so on. The temporary disappearance of a text is a good sign that very probably it is a forgery.

Even though Kōda's article shows that we must be cautious when conjecturing the actual contents of works only from their titles, I think we can safely say that some of the titles listed in the *Tachikawa shōgyō mokuroku* are related to the ritual of the *abhiṣeka* of enthronement (*sokui kanjō* 即位灌頂). Most obviously this is the case with *Gosokui* 御即位 and *Gosokui bō ichi* 御即位某一 (both meaning "Enthronement"), or *Tōji gosokui inmyō* 東寺御即位印明 (Mudra and *vidyā* [spells] of the enthronement according to the Tōji [Shingon] tradition). There are also some works that seem to refer to the legend of King Kalmāṣapāda (Jap. Hanzoku-ō 斑足王), and they too are very probably connected to the Ḍākinī ritual and the *abhiṣeka* of enthronement.[34] Other titles in the *Tachikawa shōgyō mokuroku* have close parallels to titles found in the Shugendō collection *Shugen seiten* 修験聖典, for example:

- "Essentials for the Prolongation [of Life] by Six Months" (*Nōen roku-gatsu daiji [jū]* 能延六月大事 [十])
- "Ritual Sequences of the Cult of the Great Kōjin" (*Daikōjin ku shidai [hi]* 大荒神供次第 [秘])[35]

Of these titles, several are directly related to the ritual of Ḍākinī:

- "Sutra of the King of the Gleaming Fox with the Wish-Fulfilling Wheel" (*Shinko-ō nyoirinkyō* 辰狐王如意輪経)
- "Sutra of the King of the Gleaming Fox who produces the Wish-Fulfilling Jewel" (*Shinko-ō jō nyoihōjukyō* 辰狐王成如意宝珠経) – which is glossed with the note "According to one opinion, this sutra belongs to the Three Inner Sutras"
- "Secret Transmission of Secret Magic of One Hundred and Eight Spells of the Deva Ḍākinī" (*Dakiniten hyakuhachijū hijutsu hiden* 吒枳尼天百八呪秘術秘伝)
- "Secret Formula of the Deva Ḍākinī" (*Dakiniten hihō* 吒枳尼天秘法)

Shugen seiten also includes a work called *Dakiniten hihō* 吒枳尼天秘法 (pp. 492b–500a) that contains two formulas for obtaining the wish-fulfilling jewel.[36] Finally, the *Tachikawa shōgyō mokuroku* mentions a work entitled *Sanzon gōgyō* 三尊合行 (Ritual of Three Deities Combined), which is very probably related to the ritual of Nyorin Kannon (Avalokiteśvara with the Wish-Fulfilling Wheel), flanked by Aizen Myōō and Fudō Myōō. This ritual seems to have been created by monks of the Sanbōin-ryū such as Dōjun 道順 (?–1321) and Monkan 文観 (1278–1357) (see Abe 1989, pp. 152–53).

These are only a few examples of the numerous works listed in the *Tachikawa shōgyō mokuroku*, but from them it is possible to form a picture of the kinds of texts that were condemned by Yūkai and others similar to him. The texts related to the *abhiṣeka* of enthronement are representative of one of the most secret and powerful traditions of medieval Buddhism. On the one hand, this *abhiṣeka* was connected to imperial power, and on the other hand, it was closely related to the popular cult of Dakiniten, as the various apocryphal sutras on the "King of the Gleaming Fox" illustrate. The Ritual of the Prolongation [of Life] by Six Months may be one of the sources for the popular cult of Dakiniten, and also of the skull ritual of "that school" described by Shinjō. Within the same tradition, the Ritual of Three Deities Combined was a set of secret teachings elaborated on in the Sanbōin-ryū and associated with the names of Dōjun and Monkan, monks who played a prominent role in the "revolution" of Emperor Go-Daigo (1288–1339, r. 1318–39). Finally, the texts related to the Ritual of Kōjin may be related to the festival of Kōjin, or to a popular cult of this deity.

In Yūkai's Tachikawa-ryū list, the cult of Kōjin described by Bernard Faure in this book and the *abhiṣeka* of enthronement discussed in Mark Teeuwen's essay are brought together into a single category: heretical "black magic" that manipulates sex to create "imperial" power. This gives us a revealing perspective on the medieval world of secrecy, at least as it looked from Yūkai's point of view.

Cross-transmission and the spread of secrecy

Another intriguing question about the secret transmission of teachings in Mikkyō is to what degree these teachings were *really* secret. This is a very difficult question, but since a master usually transmitted a teaching to more than one disciple, and since each disciple often received teachings from more than one master, we can logically presume that rules of secrecy could not be kept very strictly.

We can call this kind of transmissions "cross-transmissions": transmissions in which different master–disciple lineages cross. Here again, let me give some examples from the *Juhō yōjin-shū*. In the introductory part of this work, there is a kind of autobiographical account in which the author, Shinjō, gives a detailed curriculum of his Mikkyō studies. According to this narrative, Shinjō began his studies at the age of eighteen and received the final *abhiṣeka* at the age of forty-seven. This would mean that his studies continued for twenty-nine years. He says that he studied with at least eight masters. He names the Chūin-ryū, Shōchiin-ryū 正智院流, Hojuin-ryū 保寿院流, Kezōin-ryū 華蔵院流 and also other sub-lineages; as I mentioned earlier, it is possible that he also learned some teachings of the Tachikawa-ryū from a monk named Ashō in Etchū. Moreover, he lists different transmissions that his main and final master, Nyojitsu 如実, received from different masters: these are, for example, the Sanbōin-ryū, Kongōōin-ryū 金剛王院流 and Kōmyōsan-ryū 光明山流 from Jikken 実賢 (1176–1249)

of the Kongōōin 金剛王院 , Anjōji-ryū Zonnen-gata 安祥寺流尊念方 from Dōhan, the "Essentials of the Ono branch" (Ono no daiji 小野の大事) from Rendō 蓮道 (1189 [or 1187?] – after 1233), and so on. It is worth mentioning that in many of these transmissions we find traces of lineages that were regarded as "heretical" in later traditions. Dōhan received the *abhiṣeka* of the *Yugikyō* of the Tachikawa-ryū; Jikken continued the lineage of Shinkyō 真慶 and Zōyu 増瑜 , condemned by Kaijō (Moriyama 1965, p. 588); and Rendō is the author of the *Kakugenshō* 覚源鈔 (edited in the *Shingonshū zensho*, vol. 36), a work well known for its sexual teachings.

Such cross-transmissions were not at all uncommon. We know for example that Shukaku 守覚 (1150–1202) and Jien 慈円 (1155–1225) gathered a considerable number of transmissions of every branch of their schools, Shingon and Taimitsu, thus constituting "nodes" in the history of Mikkyō transmissions. In the same way, the libraries of Shōmyōji 称名寺 at Kanazawa 金沢 (Yokohama) and Shinpukuji 真福寺 in Owari (Nagoya) collected an impressive number of transmissions of all kinds. On the other hand, it seems that transmissions occurred not only between different branches or lineages within one school, but even between monks of different schools. For example, the monk Mujū first studied the Hossō and the Ritsu schools, became a Zen monk, and also studied Shingon. There were many cases of this kind. We can note also that Shōmyōji itself was not a Shingon temple, but a Shingon–Ritsu temple.

Moreover, in many Tendai ritual works, such as *Gyōrin* 行林 or *Keiran shūyōshū* 渓嵐拾葉集, we find a number of references to "Tōji teachings," in other words to Shingon. In *Keiran shūyōshū*, for example, there is an account on the making of wish-fulfilling jewels, attributed to a "master of Shingon of Tōji" who allegedly had been initiated into both the Ono and the Hirosawa 広沢 branches.[37] In a similar way, in the *Sōjishō* the Tendai author Chōgō reports a complete version of the myth of the *abhiṣeka* of enthronement of the Shingon school (which differed from the myth of the Tendai school). This myth should have been very secret within Shingon lineages, and yet we encounter it here in a Tendai work, with no reference at all to the Shingon school![38] I should note here that in general there are fewer references in Shingon texts to Tendai teachings than the other way around.

Even more interesting is the question of how these teachings were spread to a wider public, including the secular world. One of the most striking examples of such scattering is the Tendai school's myth of the *abhiṣeka* of enthronement, which was quoted very accurately in the warrior epic *Taiheiki* 太平記, although its ritual context was omitted entirely (Iyanaga 1999, pp. 92–93). Another interesting case is that of the interpretation of the word Ise 伊勢 in a certain "esoteric" tradition of *waka* studies, where the character *i* 伊 is explained as representing the female and the *Garbhadhātu-maṇḍala*, and the character *se* 勢 as representing the male and the *Vajradhātu-maṇḍala*.

For this problem of increasing circulation we must study each case in detail,[39] but it is perhaps possible to propose a few more general clues for this research. It would be fruitful to begin by mapping the environments and the personal relationships between monks who were in possession of secret teachings. An interesting example is that of the Prince Shukaku, the abbot of Ninnaji and son of Emperor Go-Shirakawa. As I already noted, Shukaku collected the secret teachings not only of the Hirosawa-ryū to which he belonged, but also those of the Ono-ryū. He was moreover a very cultivated and erudite aristocrat of the period. He left two works, *Shinzoku kōdan ki* 真俗交談記 (Account of a Conversation between Monks and Laymen) and *Shinzoku tekkin ki* 真俗擲金記 (Account of Throwing Gold [i.e., teachings] between Monks and Laymen), in which he reports on a kind of open symposia, where high-ranked monks and aristocrats had cultured discussions on various topics, both secular (Chinese literature and poetry) and esoteric (various rituals). Yamazaki Makoto (1981) has shown that the historicity of these symposia cannot be proven, but it is certainly true that Shukaku had a circle of erudite aristocrats and monks around him, and that they could meet and freely discuss topics that interested them. Fora of this kind would have allowed secrets of esoteric teachings to leak out.

Another interesting person is Tsūkai 通海 (1234–1305). He was a son of a high priest of the Ise shrines and a disciple of Kenjin 憲深 (1192–1263), one of the most prominent monks of the Sanbōin-ryū lineage. He founded the Hōrakuji 法楽寺 in Ise, and implanted a Sanbōin-ryū mentality (as well as doctrines and practices) into the Ise environment. Yet another interesting monk is Dōjun (who also plays a central role in Mark Teeuwen's essay in this book). Dōjun had close relations with the Emperors Go-Uda and Go-Daigo, who were so interested in Mikkyō that they received the "*Abhiṣeka* of the Dharma Transmission" (*denbō kanjō* 伝法灌頂). Dōjun also knew Watarai Tsuneyoshi 度会常良 (1263–1339), who was the high priest of the Outer Shrine of Ise, and he was very active in producing apocryphal works of Ryōbu Shinto.[40] Personal relationships of this kind must have constituted important channels through which secret Mikkyō teachings were able leak out into the secular world.

Conclusion

In *Fūshi kaden* 風姿花伝 (ca. 1400), the Noh playwright Zeami famously wrote, "Hidden is the flower" (*hi sureba hana* 秘すれば花 , NKBT 65, p. 394). Although I have no evidence for this, it seems to me that the system of secret transmissions in Mikkyō, formed from the end of the Heian period onward, gradually disintegrated in the course of the Middle Ages, reaching a kind of dead end around the beginning of the Edo period. Zeami, who was a contemporary of Yūkai, understood the meaning and the functioning of the system of secrecy very well. As I wrote in the beginning of this essay, secrecy in Mikkyō functioned much like buddha relics; just like these relics, secret teachings soon became subject to "inflation" which caused their value to fall. The "hidden" meaning of Zeami's saying would be that what appears as a beautiful flower when it is hidden becomes trivial when it is manifested. Similarly, Mikkyō teachings could maintain an aura of supreme power and sacred authority while they were secret, but when they were diffused too widely they began to appear as petty doctrines and rituals.

It is my impression that the contents of secrets also changed when the system of secret transmission began to disintegrate. The dark and horror-like tone that prevailed at the outset changed into something more trivial in the end. In an earlier work, I wrote that it is possible to find an echo of the "graveyard aesthetics" of medieval Tantrism in some popular art products of the Edo period, which manifest a very particular taste for the macabre and the grotesque, a taste that may be described as *"eros and thanatos"* (Iyanaga 2004a, pp. 21–22). We can probably find a similar relationship between sexual elements in medieval secret teachings and certain sexual discourses in the Edo period.

Many unanswered questions remain. For example, I do not know what the concrete conditions of secret transmissions were – were there always only one master and one disciple facing each other? What were the criteria by which the master chose his disciple? It would also be interesting to examine the emotional aspects of secret transmission: was there a loving relationship between the master and his disciple? Was there any jealousy between disciples? These and other questions impress on us that the problem of secret transmissions in medieval Mikkyō has yet to be studied in depth.

Notes

I am most grateful to Fabio Rambelli and Mark Teeuwen, who helped me to improve the contents and the form of this paper.

1 It would be interesting to compare this notion of "secret to be communicated" to the modern usage of the Japanese word *naisho* 内証 or *naisho-banashi* 内証話. *Naisho-banashi* may be translated as a "talk in whispers" or a "confidential talk." *Naisho-banashi* can constitute a kind of exclusive "circle of confidence" from which others are excluded. It may also be noted that the word *naisho/naishō* is a Buddhist word originally meaning "inner attestation/enlightenment"; the history of this word would make still another interesting topic of study.
2 This point is also stressed by Martin Lehnert in this book.
3 T 39.745c5–6. See also 592a10, 614c17–18, 620b22.
4 *Darijing shu*, T 39.616a24. See Osabe 1963, p. 262.
5 *Suji liyan Moxishouluo-tian shuo aweishe-fa* 速疾立験魔醯首羅天説阿尾奢法, T 21.330b18–21. See Osabe 1963, p. 263.
6 Although Osabe (1963, p. 263) thinks that this passage was interpolated.

7 Electronic texts of the Indian and Chinese sections of the Taishō canon, created and distributed by the Chinese Buddhist Electronic Text Association (CBETA, www.cbeta.org).

8 Here is a list of references, in a roughly chronological order: T 20.791c19–20 (a translation by Bodhiruci); T 20.798b8–9 (another translation by Bodhiruci); T 39.750b10 (the *Commentary on the Mahāvairocana-sūtra* by Yixing 一行); T 21.330b21 (a translation by Amoghavajra; see n. 5); T 20.525c16 (another translation by Amoghavajra); T 18.267b12 (an apocryphal ritual later than Amoghavajra); T 20.532b22 (a translation by anonymous translator); T 21.57b4 (a translation by anonymous translator); T 20.607b2 (Chinese or Japanese apocrypha); T 21.101a14 (a work by Kongqi 空蕃 of the Tang, date unknown); T 21.243c11, 248a12–13 (Chinese, or more probably Japanese apocrypha); T 21.356c15 (Japanese apocrypha of the mid-tenth century); T 19.333a17–18, c12–13, 334b23–25 (Japanese apocrypha of the mid-tenth century); T 18.203a22 (Japanese apocrypha, probably later than the mid-eleventh century).

9 Stone (1999 pp. 142, 144–45) points out the "warnings in transmission texts that they are not to be passed on inappropriately, 'not even for a thousand in gold'" (p. 142). The first occurrence of such an expression (*senkin makuden* 千金莫伝) seems to be found in the ritual of Mahākāla, *Daikokutenjin hō* 大黒天神法 (T 21.355c9, 356c16), which is a Japanese apocryphal text written between the later half of the tenth century and earlier half of the eleventh century, probably by a Shingon author. See Iyanaga 2002, pp. 353–54.

10 I have written about this problem in more detail in Iyanaga 2004b. I have used the text of the *Juhō yōjin-shū* edited in Moriyama 1965, pp. 530–71.

11 Moriyama 1965, p. 531. It is possible that on this occasion, he received a teaching of the Tachikawa-ryū itself, since there is a *yugi kanjō* 瑜祇灌頂 ritual in the Tachikawa-ryū.

12 Shinjō signs his name as Seiganbō Shinjō of Toyohara of the country of Echizen (越前国豊原誓願房心定). There is a place named Toyohara in modern Fukui prefecture (Sakai district, Maruoka-machi Toyohara); but I could not verify whether this is the place where Shinjō lived. On the other hand, Miyasaka Yūshō (1958, p. 38a, n. 2) writes that his name is Shōjō 正定, and that he lived in Muryōju-in 無量寿院 (probably the Muryōju-in of Mount Kōya). This name may be correct (Iyanaga 2004b, p. 17b, n. 22), but here I will nevertheless use Shinjō, which is more commonly used.

13 It is interesting to note that the two monks mentioned in Shinjō's text in relation to the Tachikawa-ryū have names that evoke the Pure Land schools, as they contain the elements *a* 阿 or *amida* 阿弥陀.

14 According to Itō (1996, p. 87), Kaijō was the master of the master of Yūkai (1345–1416), the author of the *Hōkyōshō* and the *Tachikawa shōgyō mokuroku* (Catalogue of sacred books of the Tachikawa-ryū) discussed below. The *Shōryū jō jaryū ji* is quoted in the *Tachikawa shōgyō mokuroku*, edited in Moriyama 1965, pp. 588–89. For more on Myōchō, see n. 31.

15 Kōda 1981a, pp. 25a–26a; Mizuhara 1923, pp. 52–53, 153–59.

16 One is reminded, for instance, of the famous medical work entitled *Huangdi neijing* 黄帝内経 (Internal Book of the Yellow Emperor), or of Daoist titles such as *Wuzang liufu zhenren wang yu jing* 五臓六府真人王軸経 (Book of the Axis of the King of the True Man's Five Visceral Organs and Six Bowels) and *Wudi neizhen jing* 五帝内真経 (Book of Internal Truth of Five Emperors).

17 The famous Chinese medical work *Yixin fang* 医心方 has a chapter entitled *Fangnei pian* 房内篇 which deals with sexuality. *Fangnei* means "sexual cultivation."

18 In the whole CBETA database, there is only one occurrence of the expression *qidi tianshui* 七渧甜水, "seven drops of sweet water," and it is clearly related to the ideas of "that school." It occurs in the *Guanyin yishu* 観音義疏 by Zheyi 智顗: "In the human heart there are seven drops of sweet water mixed with the pneuma and the spirit. When a demon eats one drop, this gives [its host] a headache" 人心中有七渧甜水和氣精神。鬼噉一渧令頭痛 (T 34.925c18). This passage is certainly related to Jizang's 吉藏 *Fahua yishu* 法華義疏: "The [tenth demoness is named] Sarvasattvojahārī, 'Eater of the vigor of all the beings.' In the hearts of living beings, there are seven drops of sweet water. When that demoness takes one or two drops, it gives a man a headache. If three drops are taken, his heart will suffer. If four, five or more drops are taken, he will die" 奪一切衆生 精気衆生心中有七滴甜水。 取一滴二滴令人頭痛。三滴令人心悶。 四滴五滴已下則死 (T 34.630b14–16). In these passages, Zheyi and Jizang comment on the name of the last of the Ten Rākṣasī (*jū rasetsunyo* 十羅刹女) listed in the Dhāraṇī chapter of the Lotus sutra: Datsu Issai Shujō Shōki 奪一切衆生精気 (Skt. Sarvasattvojahārī). See T 9.59a25.

19 NKBT 85 1966, pp. 285, 497a; see also Kushida 1964, p. 343, n. 2. Caroline Hirasawa pointed out to me that Morrell 1985, p. 194, "interprets" the word *henjōju* as "Tachikawa sect." This is an unfortunate error.

20 *Zoku-Tendaishū zensho, Enkai* I, 240b; see also Tanaka 1993, pp. 274–75, n. 11.

21 In the chapter on the *Aizen myōō hō*, it is said that "there exist ritual treatises on Aizen, but they are all apocryphal texts that should not be used; it seems that the Kikuran-ryū had many of them." *Byakuhō kushō*, T *zuzō* 7.95b6–7.

22 For example: *Goyuigō ni iwaku:...to ieri* (It is said in the *Testaments* of Kūkai: [...], thus it was said), or *Giki ni iwaku:...to ieri* (It is said in a ritual: [...], thus it was said). Moriyama 1965, pp. 537, 552.

23 *Kano kudenshū ni iwaku:...to ieri* (Moriyama 1965, p. 539); and *Kono hō no ki ni iwaku:...to ieri* (Moriyama 1965, p. 538).

24 *Kano hikuden ni iwaku...*, (Moriyama 1965, pp. 555–58).

25 Compare this passage of the *Juhō yōjin-shū* ...

女犯は真言一宗の肝心、即身成仏の至極なり。若し女犯をへだつる念をなさば成仏みちとをかるべし

It is said that intercourse with women is the most crucial thing in the Shingon teaching, and that it is the highest among the [practices for] attaining buddhahood within the present body. If one avoids it, then the path to the accomplishment of the buddhahood is said to be distant.

... with the following passage from the *Hōkyōshō*:

其宗義者、以二男女陰陽之道一爲二即身成仏之秘術一、成仏得道之法無二此外一

Their doctrine is that the secret art of attaining buddhahood within the present body is the path of Yin and Yang between men and women; there is no other [way] to attain buddhahood and obtain the path.

26 However, Kushida 1964, p. 342 quotes a document dating back to 1211.

27 See also Köck 2000 (this is the first article to have made this point clear). However, these manuscripts are not yet edited in printed form, and a more extensive study must be done on them.

28 For a recent bibliography on the subject, see Itō 2002, p. 229, n. 11. See also Faure 2003, pp. 81–90.

29 For an English translation and commentary, see Klein 1997, 1998, and 2002, pp. 273–91. See also Itō 1996. Some of the most important texts of this

school, among them the *Ise monogatari zuinō*, have newly been published in a new annotated edition by Ogawa (2005). Note that in the *Ise monogatari zuinō*, we find a mention of the Three Inner Sutras (Ogawa 2005, p. 141). This refers very probably to the same Three Inner Sutras as those of "that school" in the *Juhō yōjin-shū*.

30 In *Heike monogatari* 平家物語, we find a legend about a box in the treasure house of the main hall of Mt. Hiei that was said to contain a scroll by Saichō 最澄, in which the names of all future abbots were listed. Each abbot could open it and read the list just until the point where his name was written. *Heike monoga-tari*, NKBT 32 (1959), p. 143. This passage is quoted in Komine 2003, pp. 20–21.

31 This lineage, belonging to the Chūin-ryū 中院流 , is mentioned earlier by Kaijō in his *Shōryū jo jaryū ji* (quoted in the *Tachikawa shōgyō mokuroku*) as an "evil teaching." It begins with Genshō 源照 (active in the early thirteenth century), who is followed by Myōchō. See Moriyama 1965, p. 588.

32 We encounter the same term *kusshutsu kyō* in the *Gisho ron* of Kyōi. Here it is said that the sutra entitled *Hōshitsu daranikyō* 宝悉陀羅尼経 is an apocryphal work because it is a *kusshutsu kyō*: T 78.915c25. On this work, see also T 78.750a26–b27.

33 Here is an example:

				[逮得神境通力]
<u>不捨於此身</u>	無所不至印	A字自性体	挙手動足歳	辺得□□也
神反合掌印	VAM 字受用身	天地和合月	<u>遊歩大空位</u>	加持独古印

> <u>Without abandoning his present body,</u> [the practitioner will form] the mudra that leaves no places unattained; the letter *A* is the substance of the self-nature; he will move his hands up, and his feet [in the direction of the Star of] the year (?); <u>then he will attain…. [or: he will quickly attain magical powers]</u>; reversing the spirit (?), he will form the mudrā of *añjali* [joining his palms]; the letter *VAM* is the body of enjoyment; the union of the Heaven and the Earth [forms] the Moon; <u>he will attain the position of walking [at his will] in the air</u>; he will apply the magical power to the mudrā of the vajra with one prong….
>
> The underlined verses are quoted from the *Mahāvairocana-sūtra* (T 18.21a10–11); see also Hodge 2003, p. 194, n. B.

34 These are *Ri hanzoku hō* 利班足法 (Formula of Sharp Kalmāṣapāda?) and *Hanzoku gyōhō* 半足行法 (Formula of Walking with Half Steps?). On the rela-tion of the legend of the King Kalmāṣapāda (a king who ate children's flesh and later became a flying *rākṣasa*) with the *abhiṣeka* of enthronement, see Iyanaga 1999, pp. 42–43, 66–67, 103.

35 In the *Shugen seiten* the respective texts are entitled *Nōen rokugatsu hō* 能延六月法 (pp. 408b–09a) and *Kōjin ku shidai* 荒神供次第 (pp. 484b–88a). Note that *Nōen rokugatsu hō* in the *Shugen seiten* contains only four ordinary mudras and four ordinary *vidyā* spells. But there is a section entitled *Nōen rokugatsu ji* 能延六月事 in the *Sōjishō* 総持抄 of the Tendai monk Chōgō 澄豪 (1259–1350), which recounts the myth of the subjugation of Ḍākinī by the Buddha Mahāvairocana (T 77.76a3–21) that goes back to the *Commentary of the Mahāvairocana-sūtra* (T 39.687b18–c11); see Iyanaga 1999, pp. 51–54. The work entitled *Nōen rokugatsu daiji*, which is mentioned in the *Tachikawa shōgyō mokuroku*, may have been similar to this section of the *Sōjishō*. See also Iyanaga (forthcoming).

36 These formulas are named *Tonjō shijji nyoihōju hō* 頓成悉地如意宝珠法 (Formula of the Sudden Attainment of the Wish-fulfilling Jewel) and *Shinko-ō bosatsu hō* 辰狐王菩薩法 (Formula of the Bodhisattva King of the Gleaming Fox).

37 T 76.545b–c. About Sanbōin-ryū traditions on the making of artificial wish-fulfilling jewels, see Itō 2002. Making the wish-fulfilling jewels was one of the most secret rituals of the Sanbōin-ryū. In fact, this account does not seem to be very well informed about the details of this ritual. By the way, the *Juhō yōjin-shū* writes that according to an oral tradition of "that school," its principal deity (which is a skull) is no less than the wish-fulfilling jewel created by Kōbō Daishi (Moriyama 1965, pp. 539–40).

38 T 77.89b14–90a22; see Iyanaga 1999, pp. 90–91.

39 For the two examples just mentioned there are already good studies: Abe Yasurō (1984) on the myth of the *abhiṣeka* of enthronement in Tendai, and Itō Satoshi (1996) and Susan Klein (1997, 1998, and 2002) on the word Ise in *waka* traditions.

40 The "salon" of Emperor Go-Uda has been studied very thoroughly by Kadoya Atsushi (1992, 1993).

References

Abe Yasurō 阿部泰郎 (1984), "Jidō setsuwa no keisei" 慈童説話の形成 I, II. *Kokugo kokubun* 国語国文 600 and 601, pp. 1–56.

Abe Yasurō (1989), "Hōju to ōken – Chūsei-ōken to mikkyō-girei" 宝珠と王権 — 中世王権と密教儀礼. In *Nihon shisō* 日本思想 2 (= Iwanami-kōza Tōyō-shisō 岩波講座　東洋思想, vol. 16). Tokyo: Iwanami-shoten, pp. 115–69.

Faure, Bernard (2003), *The Power of Denial: Buddhism, Purity, and Gender*. Princeton: Princeton University Press.

Hodge, Stephen (tr.) (2003), *The Mahā-vairocana-abhisaṃbodhi-tantra with Buddhaguhya's Commentary*. London: Routledge Curzon.

Itō Satoshi 伊藤聡 (1996), "Ise ni-ji wo megutte – Kokin-chū, Ise-chū to mikkyō-setsu, shintō-setsu no kōshō" 伊勢二字を巡って — 古今注・伊勢注と密教説・神道説の交渉, in Sugahara Shinkai 菅原信海 (ed.), *Shinbutsu shūgō shisō no tenkai* 神仏習合思想の展開. Tokyo: Kyūko shoin, pp. 77–122.

Itō Satoshi (2002), "Chōgen to hōju" 重源と宝珠. *Bukkyō Bungaku* 仏教文学 26, pp. 10–26.

Iyanaga Nobumi 彌永信美 (1999), "Ḍākinī et l'Empereur – Mystique bouddhique de la royauté dans le Japon médiéval." In Fabio Rambelli and Patrizia Violi (eds), *Reconfiguring Cultural Semiotics: The Construction of Japanese Identity*. Special issue of *Versus: Quaderni di studi semiotici* 83–84, pp. 41–111.

Iyanaga Nobumi (2002), *Daikokuten hensō: Bukkyō shinwa-gaku* 大黒天変相 — 仏教神話学 1. Kyoto: Hōzōkan.

Iyanaga, Nobumi (2004a), "Tantrism and Reactionary Ideologies in Eastern Asia: Some Hypotheses and Questions." *Cahiers d'Extrême-Asie* 13 (2002–03 [published in 2004]), pp. 1–33.

Iyanaga Nobumi (2004b), "Tachikawa-ryū to Shinjō *Juhō yōjin-shū*" 立川流と心定「受法用心集」. *Nihon bukkyō sōgō kenkyū* 日本仏教綜合研究 2 (2003 [published in 2004]), pp. 13a–31b.

Iyanaga, Nobumi (forthcoming), "Le «Jaune d'homme» et le pouvoir magique dans le tantrisme et la culture du Japon médiéval."

Kadoya Atsushi 門屋温 (1992), "*Ryōgū honzei rishu makaen* kō: Chūsei shintō ronsho kenkyū 1"『両宮本誓理趣摩訶衍』考 — 中世神道論書研究 1. *Tōyō tetsugaku ronsō* 東洋哲学論叢 1, pp. 76–99.

Kadoya Atsushi (1993), "Ryōbu shintō shiron: *Bikisho* no seiritsu o megutte" 両部
神道試論 —『鼻帰書』の成立をめぐって. *Tōyō no shisō to shūkyō* 東洋の思想と
宗教 10, pp. 80–96.

Klein, Susan (1997), "Allegories of Desire. Poetry and Eroticism in Ise Monogatari
Zuinō." *Monumenta Nipponica* 52/4, pp. 441–65.

Klein, Susan (1998), "Ise Monogatari Zuinō. An Annotated Translation."
Monumenta Nipponica 53/1, pp. 13–43.

Klein, Susan (2002), *Allegories of Desire: Esoteric Literary Commenatries of Medieval
Japan* (Harvard-Yenching Institute Monograph Series). Cambridge, MA: Harvard
University Press.

Köck, Stephen (2000), "The Dissemination of the Tachikawa-ryū and the Problem
of Orthodox and Heretic Teaching in Shingon Buddhism," in Tōkyō Daigaku
Daigaku-in Jinbun-shakaikei Kenkyū-ka Bungaku-bu Indo Tetsugaku
Bukkyōgaku Kenkyū-shitsu 東京大学大学院人文社会系研究科・文学部・インド
哲学仏教学研究室 (ed.), *Indo tetsugaku bukkyōgaku kenkyū* インド哲学仏教学研究
7, pp. 69–83.

Kōda Yūun 甲田宥吽 (1981a), "Chūin-ryū no jaryū o tsutaeta hitobito" 中院流の
邪流を伝えた人々. *Mikkyō bunka* 密教文化 135, pp. 19–37.

Kōda Yūun (1981b), "Dōhan ajari no jagi-sōden ni tsuite" 道範阿闍梨の邪義相伝
について. *Mikkyōgaku kaihō* 密教学会報 19/20, pp. 66–70.

Komine Kazuaki 小峯和明 (2003), "Gokibun to iu na no mirai-ki" 御記文という名
の未来記, in Nishiki Hitoshi 錦仁, Ogawa Toyoo 小川豊生 and Itō Satoshi 伊藤
聡 (eds), *Gisho no Seisei*「偽書」の生成. Tokyo: Shinwasha, pp. 5–28.

Kushida Ryōkō 櫛田良洪 (1964), *Shingon mikkyō seiritsu-katei no kenkyū* 真言密教成
立過程の研究. Tokyo: Sankibō Busshorin.

Masaki Akira 正木晃 (2002), *Sei to jusatsu no mikkyō: Kaisō dorujetaku no yami to hikari*
性と呪殺の密教 — 怪僧ドルジェタクの闇と光. Tokyo: Kōdansha. (Kōdansha
Sensho Metier 講談社選書メチエ).

Miyasaka Yūshō 宮坂宥勝 (1958), "Mikkyō kana-hōgo no shiryō, II" 密教仮名法
語の資料(二). *Mikkyō bunka* 密教文化 43–44, pp. 32–48.

Mizuhara Gyōei 水原堯榮 (1923), *Jakyō Tachikawa-ryū no kenkyū* 邪教立川流の研究.
Tokyo: Fuzanbō Shoten (reprinted 1968).

Mizukami Fumiyoshi 水上文義 (2003), "*Renge sanmai-kyō* no kisoteki kōsatsu"『蓮
華三昧経』の基礎的考察, in Nishiki Hitoshi 錦仁, Ogawa Toyoo 小川豊生 and
Itō Satoshi 伊藤聡 (eds), *Gisho no seisei*「偽書」の生成. Tokyo: Shinwa-sha,
pp. 233–84.

Moriyama Shōshin 守山聖真 (1965), *Tachikawa jakyō to sono shakaiteki haikei no
kenkyū* 立川邪教とその社会的背景の研究. Tokyo: Rokuyaen.

Morrell, Robert E. (tr.) (1985), *Sand and Pebbles (Shasekishu): The Tales of Muju
Ichien, A Voice for Pluralism in Kamakura Buddhism*. New York: State University of
New York Press. (SUNY Series in Buddhist Studies).

Ogawa Toyoo 小川豊生 (ed.) (2005), *Waka kokin kanjō no maki, Gyokuden jinpi no
maki, Ise monogatari zuinō* 和歌古今灌頂巻・玉伝深秘巻・伊勢物語髄脳 (=*Nihon koten
gisho sōkan* 日本古典偽書叢刊 1). Tokyo: Gendai Shichōsha.

Osabe Kazuo 長部和雄 (1963), *Ichigyō zenshi no kenkyū* 一行禅師の研究 (= Kenkyū
sōsho 研究叢書 3). Kōbe: Kōbe Shōka Daigaku Gakujutsu Kenkyūkai.

Satō Hiroo 佐藤弘夫 (2002), *Gisho no seishin-shi: Shinbutsu/ikai to kōkan suru chūsei*
偽書の精神史. Tokyo: Kōdansha. (Kōdansha sensho metier).

Shugen seiten hensan-kai (Daigoji Sanbōin nai) 修験聖典編纂会 (醍醐寺三宝院内) (ed.)
(1977), *Shugen seiten* 修験聖典. Kyoto: Sanmitsu-dō Shoten.

Snellgrove, David (1987), *Indo-Tibetan Buddhism: Indian Buddhists & Their Tibetan Successors*. London: Serindia Publications.

Stone, Jacqueline (1999), *Original Enlightenment and the Transformation of Medieval Japanese Buddhism* (Kuroda Institute Studies in East Asian Buddhism 12). Honolulu: University of Hawai'i Press.

Tanaka Takako 田中貴子 (1993), *Gehō to aihō no chūsei* 外法と愛法の中世. Tokyo: Sunakoya Shobō.

Yamazaki Makoto 山崎誠 (1981), "Shinzoku kōdan-ki kō: Ninna-ji bun'en no ichi-kōsatsu" 真俗交談記考 ── 仁和寺文苑の一考察. *Kokugo to kokubungaku* 国語と国文学 58/1, pp. 13–27.

9 Esotericism in Noh commentaries and plays

Konparu Zenchiku's *Meishuku shū* and *Kakitsubata*

Susan Blakeley Klein

Introduction

Most of the chapters in this book examine facets of the culture of secrecy in medieval and early modern Japanese religious phenomena and institutions. But if we look at medieval artistic institutions we find that similar forms of esotericism were widely practiced. The simultaneous development of a culture of secrecy in both religious and artistic institutions is not, of course, unrelated, and is not a simple matter of religion "influencing" art. For one thing, the same social, economic, and political forces that encouraged the development of secrecy within religious institutions were at work in artistic traditions as well.[1] And in medieval Japan, religion and the arts were by no means separate areas. Much artistic production was in the service of religious institutions. On a personal level, it was common for artists to have taken religious vows of some kind; a number of the foremost medieval poets also held high-ranking ecclesiastic positions. Not surprisingly, therefore, the issue of how the path of artistic creation might mesh with the path of religious vocation was of vital concern.

Another shared factor is what might be called the "episteme" of the medieval Japanese, that is, their attitude toward the signifying power of signs. A grounding assumption of the medieval episteme was that the linguistic/symbolic relation of signifier and signified is not arbitrary, as we believe today, but motivated (ultimately non-dual). This meant that the surface "meaning" of practically any linguistic or material signifier (Sino-Japanese characters, poetry, icons, clothing/costumes, sacred spaces, etc.) could be analyzed productively to show profound truths about phenomenal (and even absolute) reality, particularly hidden identities. On a popular level, this understanding of the symbolic relation enabled the medieval ideology of *honji suijaku*, in which kami and Buddhist deities were enmeshed in a complex pattern of associational identification. We can see a more elite version of this episteme at work in medieval Shingon

Buddhism's multi-leveled pedagogical system, in which initiates were introduced to progressively more sophisticated levels of semiosis.[2] In the secret texts and commentaries related to artistic production, on the other hand, the level of semiotic sophistication varies quite a bit from text to text, depending on authorship and audience. It is clear, however, that for all of these texts, both religious and artistic, the notion of the ultimate non-duality of signifier and signified transformed the material world into a virtually unlimited field of semiotic play.

My book *Allegories of Desire: Esoteric Literary Commentaries of Medieval Japan* (Klein 2002) examines one example of the culture of secrecy as it appeared in the court tradition of waka poetry in the late thirteenth century. The book focuses on the development of a pedagogical system of initiations into the secrets of waka poetry, modeled on the esoteric initiation (*kanjō* 灌頂) system used in medieval Shingon esoteric Buddhism. As I demonstrated in *Allegories*, the commentaries and initiation system were mainly the creation of an obscure poet named Fujiwara Tameaki 藤原為顕 (ca. 1240s–1290s).[3] Tameaki was a member of the Mikohidari 御子左 poetry family, founded by his great-grandfather Fujiwara Shunzei 藤原俊成 (1114–1204), which dominated the teaching of poetry composition in the capital. But for a variety of reasons[4] Tameaki was shut out of his poetic patrimony, so sometime in the early 1270s he took orders as a Shingon priest and moved to Kamakura, where he developed a strong following among samurai and court officials attached to the shogunate, Buddhist and Yin Yang (onmyōdō 陰陽道) priests, and shrine officials. It seems clear that his development of the waka *kanjō* initiation system and the manuscripts, commentaries, images, poetic mantras, and mudras, as well as legitimating transmission genealogies (*kechimyakufu* 血脈譜) were meant to produce a family lineage that could be used as a form of cultural capital in the competitive field of court poetry. Other, more "orthodox" Mikohidari poets quickly understood the usefulness of this kind of initiation system, and within a very short time all the major schools of poetry were producing their own waka *kanjō* as well as esoteric commentaries to be transmitted within the initiations.

In my current project, a companion book to the first, I am exploring the relationship of these esoteric literary commentaries (mainly on the tenth-century prose-poem collection *Ise monogatari* [*The Tales of Ise*] and on the first imperial poetry anthology, *Kokinshū*) to the composition of Noh plays as well as secret commentaries by Noh actors. On one level, I am interested in how the content of the earlier literary commentaries appears in the Noh: identifications of the anonymous poems in the *Kokinshū* and generic *otoko* (men) and *onna* (women) in *Tales of Ise* with various "historical" personages, including the court poet Ariwara no Narihira 在原業平 (825–80), along with supplementary anecdotal material used as the basis (*honsetsu* 本説) for the plots of plays. But this can all too quickly devolve into simple identification of material – this line quotes *Waka chikenshū*, that line quotes the Reizei lineage *Ise monogatari shō*.[5] The more interesting approach is, I believe, to understand how this commentary material is being used to provide not only content, but also a form of rhetorical structure for those Noh plays influenced by the material.

Thus, on a more profound level, I am interested in the commentaries' methodology, which I have termed "etymological and numerological allegoresis": reading metaphorical associations, punning identifications, paronomasia (the analysis of Sino-Japanese characters into their component parts), and numerological homologies into and onto linguistic or material signifiers so as to provide insight into a hidden reality. This allegorical reading strategy, which could be considered the practical application of the medieval epistemic understanding of the symbolic relationship, is ubiquitous in medieval Japanese religious texts, particularly those encountered at the conceptual intersection of esoteric Buddhism and kami shrines.[6] Fujiwara Tameaki, however, appears to have been the first to apply the methodology to the interpretation of literary texts.[7]

My basic argument is that this epistemic belief in motivated signs, and its accompanying methodology of allegoresis, might also be at work in certain Noh plays, especially those composed by Konparu Zenchiku Ujinobu 金春禅竹氏信 (1405–70?). I am encouraged in this pursuit by the fact that Zenchiku's treatise *Meishuku shū* 明宿集 (or *Myōshuku shū*, "Collected Writings Illuminating the Indwelling Deity") uses the same method of argument and makes the same assumptions about the nature of reality as the medieval commentaries I have been working on, although I should note that I have my doubts about whether Zenchiku understood what he was doing in any kind of systematic way.[8] At any rate, as we shall see, Zenchiku's argument in *Meishuku shū* is supported by an interconnected web of metaphorical associations, punning identifications, and paronomasia. Zenchiku assumes that such associative identifications, when properly understood, tell us something important about the true nature of reality; specifically, that they are the legitimating basis for the efficacy of rituals performed in connection with *sarugaku* 猿楽 Noh. The question is whether he might have used a similar approach in creating his plays. I am even interested in whether paronomasia used both in the esoteric literary commentaries and in Zenchiku's commentaries might be working somehow in the composition of his plays (although this is highly speculative and probably not provable). In providing a case study of a secret commentary that arose in a somewhat different context than the world of religious culture, that is, within the world of Noh theater, I will touch on a number of issues that are raised in other essays in this book, thus revealing a wider range of facets in the culture of secrecy in medieval Japan.

The scholarship on secret Noh treatises

Having prefaced this essay, I want to briefly provide another preface, a discussion of some problems with the typical approach taken by both

Japanese and Western scholars to these secret Noh commentaries. In so doing, I am building on research by Noel Pinnington on how Zenchiku's commentaries are symptomatic of his historical context, focusing particularly on the patronage relationships of the Konparu troupe, which Zenchiku led.

Pinnington notes that until recently, scholars of *sarugaku* Noh have treated the secret texts written by playwrights such as Kanze Zeami Motokiyo 観世世阿弥元清 (ca. 1364–1443) and Konparu Zenchiku as theoretical discussions of the art of Noh (*nōgakuron* 能楽論) which can be grouped with other discussions of the arts such as discussions on poetry (*karon* 歌論), on linked verse (*rengaron* 連歌論), and on *haikai* 俳諧 verse (*hairon* 俳論).[9] As Pinnington points out,

> [The term *ron* 論] is associated with detached philosophical or academic discussions, and seems deliberately chosen to resist social purposes. [...] Any adequate investigation of these works needs to integrate both approaches, taking account of their social roles as well as their intellectual positions. [...] There seems, however, to have been almost a convention among twentieth-century scholars of *nōgakuron* to ignore these aspects, and to present the works as detached disquisitions on aesthetics and metaphysics.
>
> (Pinnington, forthcoming, p. 5)

On this level, the texts are idealized, floating free of their historical context, and are very nearly treated as though they were public documents. In fact, however, most of these texts were not available for public (scholarly) scrutiny until the twentieth century, and probably had an extremely limited circulation.

I suspect one reason why scholars would like to ignore that these texts were transmitted as family secrets is that when such texts are treated as *hidensho* 秘伝書 (writings of secret transmission) the treatises become aligned with the *kadensho* 家伝書 (writings transmitted in poetry houses), and such an alignment tends to provoke a hermeneutic of suspicion. First, a number of the *kadensho* are clearly spurious – that is, they are not written by the authors to whom they are attributed. Second, there is a definite bias among scholars against texts that were put to social uses, and enabled their owners to accrue material benefits. We have evidence that the pedagogical system of waka *kanjō*, along with its attendant transmission of manuscripts, commentaries, genealogies, and so on was quite lucrative. This has counted against it. Third, much of the content of the esoteric literary commentaries was based on discredited sects of Shingon and esoteric Shinto, and so by the twentieth century had become esoteric in the metaphorical sense of being completely obscure to anyone but specialists in the field. For all of these reasons, it is likely that Noh scholars would have wanted to avoid the contamination of the heterodox and the spurious that taints so much of the *hidensho* and *kadensho*. They have therefore concentrated most of their energy on commentaries such as the various *Rokurin ichiro* 六輪一露 (Six Wheels, One Dewdrop) texts, whose methodology is close enough to contemporary notions of what is deemed appropriate in a theoretical treatise on aesthetics that scholars have been able to ignore any aspects, whether religious and social, with which they might be uncomfortable. In fact, however, even those commentaries that to us seem devoted to aesthetic issues were meant to produce effects that went well beyond the aesthetic, that is, they were meant to do more than simply enable the recipient to compose and perform plays of superior quality.

Zenchiku argues quite overtly in *Meishuku shū*, for example, that receiving the secret writings is necessary for the artist to produce performances that have religious efficacy. He uses the interpretive methodology of etymological and numerological allegoresis found in the *kadensho* as well as numerous other kinds of religious documents of the time, but which no contemporary scholar would touch. And Zenchiku implicitly argues for the commentaries' production of what might be called material efficacy, in that they were meant to help the actor and his family accrue real material benefits, particularly in the fierce competition for patronage with the other three Yamato *sarugaku* troupes. Within this polemical struggle for patronage, Zenchiku found it expedient, perhaps because of his connections to the poets Shōtetsu 正徹 (1381–1459) and Regent Ichijō Kaneyoshi 一条兼良 (1402–81), to constantly reiterate the non-dual relationship between poetry and dance. Thus, if we are to understand what these texts meant to their authors and their audience, it seems obvious we need to take account not only of their intellectual positions, but of the social and religious purposes to which these texts were put as well.

The historical context

In order to understand the historical position that Konparu Zenchiku and the Konparu troupe of actors found themselves in, let me start with a comparison to Zeami Motokiyo of the Kanze troupe. Zeami, along with his father Kan'ami 観阿弥 (d. 1384), is considered to have created the basic form of Noh theater as it is practiced today, and wrote many of the most famous plays in the current repertoire. At the age of twelve Zeami managed to obtain the patronage of the most powerful man in the country, the Shogun Ashikaga Yoshimitsu (d. 1408), when he appeared with his father Kan'ami in a command performance before the eighteen-year-old shogun, his father dancing the role of the Okina 翁 deity in the ritual performance piece, *Shikisanban* 式三番.[10] Zeami's father was an enormously popular actor and playwright, who performed before a very wide range of audiences. Zeami, however, appears to have focused his attention on gaining the patronage of the elite of Muromachi society. His writings focus fairly narrowly on transmitting a body of secret performance techniques that will enable the Kanze actor to succeed in the highly competitive capital. In this sense, while there is a certain amount of what we might term "religious mystification" present in Zeami's work, his treatises follow the pattern of a kind of technical knowledge whose secrecy enables a family to sustain an economic living.

The circumstances facing Zenchiku growing up and inheriting the Konparu troupe were quite different, and his secret commentaries are symptomatic of those differences.[11] The Konparu troupe was tied to the Nara area, and in particular to the Kōfukuji–Kasuga temple–shrine complex. The Konparu troupe had no chance of competing with the Kanze in the capital, who had the shogunate patronage sewn up. Zenchiku lost his father at a very young age, and with that death he also appears to have lost the oral teachings (*kuden* 口伝) that his father should have transmitted to him as the heir of the Konparu troupe. Perhaps in an attempt to remedy this extremely problematic loss of secret technical knowledge, as a young man Zenchiku married Zeami's daughter, and was thus able to receive a certain number of Zeami's treatises and play manuscripts. But even in possession of this kind of apparent symbolic capital, and despite the fact that Zenchiku was by all accounts one of the most respected actors of his generation, he was unable to break into the elite patronage circles of the capital. Given the increasingly unstable character of the time, and the very unstable personality of the Ashikaga Shogun Yoshinori (d. 1441), who followed Yoshimitsu's son Yochimochi, Zenchiku might have felt this was just as well. At any rate, Zenchiku instead concentrated on the Konparu family connections to the Kōfukuji–Kasuga complex in Nara. For example, we see in texts such as *Meishuku shū* an emphasis on anecdotal genealogies that trace the Konparu family's descent from participants in the legendary beginnings of *Okina sarugaku* at the Kasuga shrine. Unlike Zeami, Zenchiku puts very little attention on audience response, and we find little in the way of secret technical information that might have proved useful in competition with other troupes. Instead, a great deal of attention is placed on the cultivation of *sarugaku* Noh's spiritual efficacy.

I should note that the Kōfukuji–Kasuga complex was not just a temple, but had the rights of the *shugo* (constable) of Yamato province, as well as being the clan temple of the Fujiwara. So it was a very powerful force and would have been a patron worth cultivating. In terms of other kinds of patronage relationships, Zenchiku studied poetry under Ichijō Kaneyoshi, also known as Kanera, the imperial regent and leading poet of the day. One of Kaneyoshi's sons, Jinson 尋尊, was the superintendent of Kōfukuji. Zenchiku also studied with Shōtetsu, a Reizei school poet who had lost the favor of the shogun Yoshinori but was patronized by Kaneyoshi. Zenchiku sought to identify Reizei poetic traditions with his own particular style of *sarugaku* plays.[12] It is likely that Kaneyoshi and

Shōtetsu served as Zenchiku's sources for the secret literary commentaries that formed the basis for his treatise *Meishuku shū* and the play *Kakitsubata* 杜若.

Esoteric allegoresis in Zenchiku's treatises on Noh

There is more I could say about the historical context but now I want to turn to Zenchiku's commentaries. First, I want to think about the role of oracular revelation in the production of secret commentaries, because Zenchiku's case is rather different from the case of the esoteric commentaries I wrote about in *Allegories of Desire*. Zenchiku claimed that two of his texts, *Rokurin ichiro* (Six Wheels, One Dewdrop) and *Meishuku shū* were, at least in part, the product of oracular revelation. The vision of six circular diagrams and a sword described in various versions of the *Rokurin Ichiro* treatises appears to have been vouchsafed to Zenchiku while meditating at the Kanzeon temple in Hasedera.[13] In *Meishuku shū* Zenchiku claims he received an oracular revelation from the Sumiyoshi deity when he visited the Sumiyoshi Shrine on the thirteenth day of the ninth month (*meigetsu* 明月). At first glance this date might not seem particularly important, but in fact this place, deity, and date were all carefully chosen as part of Zenchiku's legitimating strategy for the text, since there are important poetic precedents for those dates in the poetic tradition.

For example, *Waka chikenshū* 和歌智顕集 (Revealed Knowledge of Poetry), a commentary associated with Fujiwara Tameaki, claims that on the thirteenth day of the ninth month, the poet Minamoto Tsunenobu 源経信 (1016–97) received an oracular revelation on the secrets of *The Tales of Ise* from the Sumiyoshi Shrine deity appearing as a rather disreputable but nevertheless godly old man, that is, as Okina.[14] And a text by Shōtetsu, with whom Zenchiku studied, quotes a secret treatise supposedly by Fujiwara Teika that claims he received an oracular revelation from the Sumiyoshi deity on the unity of the path of poetry and the path of enlightenment. Shōtetsu asserts that the revelation occurred on the thirteenth day of the ninth month.[15] There are other examples in the various esoteric literary commentaries, so it is undoubtedly not coincidental that Zenchiku's dream vision came on that day.[16] We know that Zenchiku, like Shōtetsu, was a fan of Teika; on one level he was probably simply retracing the steps of a revered master.[17] But there was another goal as well. In the case of Tsunenobu and Teika the revelation was meant to demonstrate the non-dualism of the paths of Buddhism and waka poetry; in Zenchiku's case, the dream vision reveals the non-dualism of waka and *sarugaku* Noh, a concept dear to his heart.

One major difference between *Rokurin ichiro* and *Meishuku shū* and earlier secret commentaries such as *Waka chikenshū* that claimed oracular revelation as the origin of their secrets is that the earlier commentaries always (1) claimed the reception of those secrets had actually occurred back in the Heian period, and then (2) created a spurious genealogy of transmission to authenticate the transmission of those secret texts to the present. Obviously, this was also a very common strategy in the creation of apocryphal sutras and spurious esoteric material. None of the anonymous authors of these earlier secret texts felt confident enough to claim that the dream vision was vouchsafed to himself or herself – they instead claimed that the oracular revelation had occurred at a much earlier time and used such legitimating strategies as "expedient means" (*hōben* 方便) to explain why the text had not appeared until now.[18] So it is striking that Zenchiku did not feel it necessary to do this. It seems to demonstrate enormous confidence on his part; an assumption that he was just as likely a candidate for oracular revelation about the unity of Buddhist enlightenment and artistic endeavor as Teika. Perhaps because Zenchiku was a highly revered actor himself, he was able to carry it off. Nevertheless, a personal revelation alone could not provide the kind of legitimating authority that he needed, particularly to prove the non-dualism of poetry and dance.

As we see in other cases discussed in this book, Zenchiku needed to do at least two things to transform this oracular revelation into cultural capital. First, he had to make it known. Secrets that are personal are simply not useful; they have to be known *as* secrets (with the content hidden) to function as cultural capital. Second, Zenchiku had to find some other form of authority to back it up. Although he did not have outside authorities comment on *Meishuku shū* (perhaps because it was written so late in life),[19] he did so with *Rokurin ichiro*, and not surprisingly, *Rokurin ichiro* was both more widely disseminated (there are twelve known copies) and has been the focus of much more intense scrutiny within Noh scholarship. Zenchiku showed versions of *Rokurin ichiro*, in turn, to Shigyoku 志玉 (1384–1468), abbot of the Kaidan-in at Tōdaiji in Nara and a Kegon Buddhist scholar; to the Regent Ichijō Kaneyoshi, a leading poet with a strong connection to Kōfukuji; and to Nankō Sōgen 南江宗沅, a Zen monk and poet. Each of them wrote comments on it and returned it to Zenchiku, whereupon it was transformed into a treasured secret of the Konparu lineage that, of course, was not to be shown to outsiders.

Another point is that unlike the earlier secret poetic commentaries, which clearly fabricate their origins in oracular revelation, it seems possible that Zenchiku's dream visions are genuine – they are certainly cryptic enough. In the same way, as far as I can tell, Zenchiku did not produce any spurious texts, or make claims based on texts that he must have known were nonexistent, both quite common methods of generating "authority" in secret commentaries. He quoted from and adapted texts that were transmitted to him by Zeami and others, and created complex interpretative commentaries involving etymological allegoresis, but we do not have the feeling about him that we have about Fujiwara

Tameaki for example, that he was in the business of creating spurious texts and lineage documents. And although he mentions that initiation into certain secrets should be treated as an esoteric initiation (*kanjō*), there seems to have been almost no concerted effort to create anything in the way of systematic pedagogy.

One last point about *Rokurin ichiro* before I turn to *Meishuku shū*. A striking feature of the *Rokurin ichiro* texts is how abstract they are, and how resistant to interpretation – or rather how easy it is to project a variety of quite different interpretations onto them. Here is a sample:

> Now, the way of the household task of *sarugaku* is to exhaust beauty with the body and to "create pattern with the voice." Hereby "unwittingly the hands gesture and the feet tread." Consequently, this must surely be the mysterious operation (*myōyū* 妙用) of what is fundamentally without master and without phenomena. That is why the forms of the six circles and the dewdrop have been provisionally attained; the first is called the circle of life (*jurin* 寿輪), the second is called the circle of the vertical (*shurin* 竪輪, the third is called the circle of abiding (*jūrin* 住輪), the fourth is called the circle of images (*zōrin* 像輪), the fifth is called the circle of breaking (*harin* 破輪), the sixth the circle of emptiness (*kūrin* 空輪), the dewdrop (*ichiro* 一露) is the highest, most important stage.[20]

Because it is *not* tied into local myths about sacred names and places or into any larger concrete sacred context, Zenchiku's material on the "six circles, one dewdrop" never develops the kind of "thick description" that seems to be a feature of the various origin stories (*engi* 縁起), oral transmissions (*kuden*), secret transmissions (*hidensho*), and so on that we see in the wider religious field of medieval Japan. What this also means is that it has been quite receptive to completely ahistorical readings, fitting all too easily into the category of "aesthetic" treatise.[21]

The main theme of Zenchiku's second oracular text, *Meishuku shū*, is the explication of the nature and significance of the Okina deity, who appears in the *Shikisanban* ritual (the originating ritual of *sarugaku* Noh) as a benevolent old man dispensing blessings of fertility and longevity. It is a long, rambling, disorganized text, which may be one reason *Meishuku shū* has been given relatively little attention within Noh scholarship. It was also only discovered relatively recently; it was first published in 1969. There are two known manuscripts of *Meishuku shū*, the original in Zenchiku's hand and one copy. Both were discovered in an archive (*bunko*) of a Konparu actor; there is no record of it having been disseminated in the Edo period. Although it was undoubtedly written by Zenchiku for his son and heir, it had apparently fallen into neglect only a generation or two after Zenchiku's death, and so it is unlikely to have been influential on the later development of Noh.

A second problem is the method of argument, which is nearly the opposite of *Rokurin ichiro*. At first glance *Meishuku shū* appears to be nothing but "thick description" – there is so much density of detail that the reader rapidly feels overwhelmed and disoriented. And the methodology of associational identification used to generate that detail is difficult for contemporary scholars to accept as appropriate in an aesthetic treatise on *sarugaku* Noh. Arthur Thornhill is typical of Noh scholars when he notes, "This work is of limited interest in the study of *nōgakuron* or aesthetics, but it provides a wealth of fascinating, although often obscure, material for scholars of ethnology and Japanese religion" (Thornhill 1993, p. 198). Finally, there is the fact that it is clearly in draft form, as attested by numerous erasures, emendations, and notes on areas that need further clarification. All of these issues have militated against *Meishuku shū* being taken seriously as a means to understand how Zenchiku might have understood his role as actor and composer of plays, as well as leader of the Konparu school.[22]

Meishuku shū apparently originated in a dream vision revelation to Zenchiku from the Sumiyoshi Daimyōjin that was both brief and (of course) obscure: "The sun, the moon, and the constellations harbor the reflection [of Okina]" (*hi tsuki hoshiyado, kage o yadosu zo* 日・月・星宿、影ヲヤドスゾ).[23] Given that the Sumiyoshi deity was the patron deity of *waka*, it makes sense that the revelation came in the form of the last two lines of a *waka* poem. According to Mark Nearman (1984, p. 40), the phrase relates to a common medieval invocation of longevity: "the sun, the moon, the stellar constellations" (日月星宿). Zenchiku's title, *Meishuku shū* 明宿集, is an abbreviation (a reverse paronomasia if you will) of both the oracular revelation and the invocation: the character for *mei* 明 is a combination of the characters for sun and moon, and the character for *shuku* 宿 is an abbreviation for "stellar constellation" 星宿. In *Meishuku shū* Zenchiku takes this cryptic revelation and uses every possible interpretive means to expand it into a religio-aesthetic polemic supporting the Konparu troupe as the pre-eminent performers of *Okina* in the *Shikisanban* dance ritual.

Fairly early on in the text Zenchiku claims that Yamato *sarugaku* Noh descended directly from an ancestor of the Konparu family, a Nara period performer/divinity named Hada no Kōkatsu 秦河勝.[24] According to legend, Prince Shōtoku commanded Kōkatsu to create sixty-six public entertainments, which became known as *sarugaku*. Later one of Kōkatsu's descendants, Hada no Ujiyasu 秦氏安, and Ujiyasu's brother-in-law, Ki no Gonnokami 紀権守, selected three representative pieces from the sixty-six. These three became known as *Shikisanban* (The Three Ceremonial Pieces), and it is from these pieces that the present *Okina* performance is said to derive.[25] One way *Meishuku shū* can be read is as an explication of the performance of this *Okina Shikisanban* ritual. It apparently needed some explication because already by Zenchiku's time entire sections of the libretto had become unintelligible, even to the performers. For Zenchiku, however, such difficulties served as triggers for interpretation, enabling wide-ranging associational identifications supported by etymological and numerological allegoresis.

In the course of the text Zenchiku identifies the rather generic Okina deity with Shukujin (or Shukushin 宿神), an even more generic celestial deity of primordial creativity that was an object of cult worship for medieval performers. Reading the characters for Shukujin as "indwelling deity" and treating it as the clan deity of the Konparu, he identifies it with the raging spirit (*kōjin* 荒神) of Hada no Kōkatsu.[26] This Shukujin thus manifests in both a benevolent and a raging form: as Okina he is the benevolent deity of song and dance, but he also manifests as the raging spirit of Kōkatsu, who apparently provides the creative energy. We can see at work here the concept of non-dualism omnipresent in medieval religious culture: *bonnō soku bodai* 煩悩即菩提, that passion is the *necessary* flipside to enlightenment. Zenchiku then goes on to identify Okina/Shukujin with virtually every Buddhist and shrine deity you can imagine, using the methodology of etymological allegoresis. In order to explicate Zenchiku's methodology, I will first give two examples from other sources: (1) an example from the wider medieval religious context, taken from a hagiographic biography; (2) an example from *Ise monogatari shō*, a secret esoteric literary commentary.

Toward the end of the Heian period and throughout the Kamakura a number of documents offering rationales for combinatory identifications between kami and Buddhist deities and/or principles were produced on Mt. Hiei, the center of Tendai esoteric Buddhism. As Allan Grapard has written about in some detail, "the result was a single but complex multi-layered entity to which the name Sannō (Mountain King 山王) was given" (Grapard 1987, p. 215). The following example of identification, which is typical in its use of allegoresis, is taken from a medieval biography of the Tendai priest Gyōen 行円 (?–1047). According to the biographer, the Sannō deity appeared to Gyōen and told him the following:

> Do you know why I am called Sannō 山王? I signify the three truths [*santai* 三諦] are one. The three [vertical] strokes of *san* 山 denote emptiness [*kū* 究], temporariness [*ke* 假], and the mean [*chū* 中]. The underlying stroke signifies oneness. *Ō* 王 consists of three [horizontal] strokes standing for the three truths while the center stroke symbolizes oneness. Both characters have three strokes and one common stroke. That is why I am called Sannō Myōjin. In other words, [my name represents] the three-fold contemplation in one mind, the three thousand [existences contained in] one thought. Therefore I protect my Tendai and give peace to the country. There is no name without body and no body without name. There is no Dharma without name and there is no name without Dharma. Body

is Dharma – Dharma is name. This is called one vehicle. This is the meaning of my name.[27]

This example of etymological allegoresis involves paronomasia: breaking down the grapheme (Sino-Japanese character) into its component parts and then rearranging those parts to reveal a hidden meaning. The graphemes for Sannō are analyzed to reveal a hidden correspondence with the fundamental three-part Tendai doctrine (*santai*) of emptiness (all dharmas are empty), temporariness (they appear to have provisional existence), and the middle path which unites the other two. These three ways of viewing existence stand in a relation of conditional interdependence, a relation summed up in the phrase *santai ichijitsu* 三諦一実 (three relative truths, one absolute truth). The two graphemes in the name "Sannō" are shown to be made up of three parallel strokes combined with a third unifying stroke, thus graphically symbolizing this relation. The last part of the passage is particularly noteworthy: "There is no name without body, and no body without name. There is no Dharma without name and there is no name without Dharma. Body is Dharma – Dharma is name." These lines illustrate the philosophical basis for how punning word play garnered persuasive authority in religious contexts. The body, the dharmas which go to make up that body, and the name attached to the body are indivisibly related; thus correct analysis of a name provides insight into the essence of what is named and, by extension, into the nature of reality. Puns and visual rebuses are therefore not mere accidents of language but apertures for the initiated.

This basic assumption also underlies the esoteric literary commentaries with which Zenchiku was familiar, such as *Waka chikenshū*. *Waka chikenshū*'s opening discussion of the meaning of the title of *Tales of Ise* explains why a correct understanding of names and graphemes is so important: "The myriad things arise from their names, in accordance with the principle that the name is the result of the essential nature of the grapheme."[28] For the esoteric literary commentaries in particular, this principle is fundamental; as noted at the outset of this chapter their approach to textual analysis depends on a non-arbitrary relationship between linguistic signs and both absolute and phenomenal reality.

For example, take the phrase *mukashi otoko* 昔男, loosely translated "the man of old," which opens a number of the episodes in *Tales of Ise*. First of all, medieval readers of *Tales of Ise* assumed that repetition is meaningful: they used what might be called a "rule of correspondence," that each and every one of these *mukashi otoko* must be subtended by the same persona, assumed to be the ninth-century poet Ariwara no Narihira. But then the commentaries go a step further to reveal the deep, esoteric meaning of the phrase. The Reizei school commentary *Ise monogatari shō* (Selected comments on *Ise monogatari*) analyzes the grapheme for *mukashi* 昔 as follows:

When [the primordial deities] Izanagi and Izanami had sex [thereby creating the country of Japan], one female and three males were born in twenty-one days. As this was the origin of Yin and Yang, when Narihira wrote of eroticism (*irogonomi* 色好み) he used the word *mukashi* 昔 because that graph is written with the elements for "twenty-one days" 廿一日.[29]

Here, the repetitive use of the phrase *mukashi otoko* (the man of old) in *Tales of Ise* is understood to be a clue left deliberately by Narihira as author. When properly analyzed this clue reveals that the *Tales of Ise*, although superficially appearing to be about Narihira's passionate love affairs (and his exile to the Eastern Provinces because of one of them), is actually grounded in something much more profound: the origin of Japan through the sexual act of Izanagi and Izanami, an act which serves as a model for enlightened sex.[30]

In *Meishuku shū* Zenchiku uses this same rule of correspondence to argue that any and all mentions of the term *okina* are to be identified with Okina as the primordial deity of dance and, ultimately, with Shukujin as the primordial essence of creativity. He backs this thesis up with paronomasia. For example, he analyzes the first grapheme of Kasuga 春日 into its component parts, 二大日 (two-great-suns), and uses it to identify Kasuga with Dainichi 大日 (Great Sun), the principal Buddha of esoteric Buddhism who manifests himself in two different forms in the Womb and Vajra mandalas.[31] He then makes a further connection to his own family through the grapheme of *haru* 春 which appears in both Kasuga 春日 and Konparu 金春. He ends by saying, "As it is a case of a name expressing the innate nature, this name of Konparu is likewise something that does not simply designate a person. You should have confidence that it is a wondrous effect of Okina since Okina and Kasuga are one and the same substance" (Omote and Itō 1969, p. 295). Here Zenchiku espouses the same attitude toward the analysis of written characters that we saw above in the allegoresis of the characters of *Sannō* and of *mukashi otoko*.

Zenchiku uses the rule of correspondence right from the start in *Meishuku shū*, to show how the sacred old man who manifests in the *Okina* ritual performed at Kasuga shrine is identical with the Sumiyoshi Daimyōjin's manifestation as an *okina*, as well as Ariwara no Narihira in *Tales of Ise*:

As for the origins of the marvelous substance of Okina, he first appeared when the heaven and earth were opened; from that time to the present he has protected the sovereigns, ordered the country, and saved the people. His "original ground" (*honji* 本地) is Dainichi Nyorai [...] who unites the three Buddha bodies (the dharma body, enjoyment body and accommodative body); the provisional separation of these three bodies is revealed in *Okina Shikisanban* (The Three

Rituals of Okina). His "manifest trace" (*suijaku* 垂迹) forms can be analyzed historically. First he is the Sumiyoshi Daimyōjin [...names a number of other deities]. The profound secret is that all these *honji suijaku* manifestations are one body/substance (*ittai* 一体)[32]; not increasing, not decreasing, eternal, unperishing, the one body/substance of the marvelous kami. [...]

When we come to the age of human beings, the author of *Tales of Ise*, the Middle Captain Narihira, was born the fifth son in a family versed in poetry (歌道の家); referred to as *katai okina* (the humble old man) he guided foolish women and taught them the Way of Yin and Yang (*onmyō no michi* 陰陽の道). He is named as one of the sages of poetry (*kasen* 哥仙) and one of the three *okina* (*mitari okina* 三人翁) of the *Kokinshū*; revealed as an incarnation (*bunshin* 分身) of the one substance [of Dainichi Nyorai], he composed poems about birth, old age, illness and death.[33]

You can see here that Zenchiku has been reading the esoteric literary commentaries: a number of important pieces are being fit together. The Kasuga Okina's *honji* (Buddhist identities) include Dainichi Nyorai, his *suijaku* (kami identities) include Sumiyoshi Daimyōjin, and his mortal incarnations include Ariwara no Narihira. As I have mentioned above, one of Zenchiku's most consistent arguments is that the path of waka and the path of *sarugaku* Noh are one, so it would make some sense that he would collapse the Sumiyoshi Okina patron deity of poetry and the Kasuga Okina patron deity of dance into one figure. Furthermore, here Zenchiku specifically identifies the poet Narihira as Okina because he is referred to by the epithet *katai okina* かたい翁, "old beggar," in *Tales of Ise*.[34] This process of continuously expanding and exfoliating identifications based on correspondences, which Zenchiku uses to legitimate his argument, is the same method used in syncretic Buddhist texts and in esoteric literary commentaries influenced by Tameaki. In addition, Zenchiku's identification of the three *okina* in the *Kokinshū* is connected to the Fujiwara Tameaki affiliated commentary *Gyokuden jinpi no maki* 玉伝深秘巻 (Jeweled Transmission of Deep Secrets), where we are told that "the phrase [the three *okina*] is said to signify that [Sumiyoshi] Daimyōjin, Hitomaro, and Narihira are apparently three, but in reality one substance."[35] For Zenchiku the rule of correspondence proves that the identifications made between the Konparu troupe, the Kasuga shrine, Okina as the founding deity of *sarugaku* Noh, and Shukujin as the primordial deity of creativity are grounded in a transcendent reality and thus beyond contestation.

Allegoresis in a Zenchiku play

The play *Kakitsubata* 杜若 (The iris) assumes, like *Meishuku shū*, the identification of the ninth-century poet Ariwara no Narihira with a variety of deities. First, he is the Bodhisattva of Song and Dance, a common medieval identification of poets; second, a manifestation of the kami of Yin and Yang, Izanami and Izanagi, whose originary act of procreation is understood as a model for enlightened sex; and third, Dainichi Nyorai, the central Buddha of Shingon esoteric Buddhism and the embodiment of absolute reality (*shinnyo* 真如, also translated as true thusness) of the universe. These multiple identifications in turn generate multiple levels of meaning, progressively revealed in an ever-widening exfoliation of associations via punning imagery that create a complex set of parallels between, for example, the *waki* (supporting) character as a wandering monk; the "historical" Narihira, wandering in exile from the Heian capital for his illicit relationship with the Emperor's consort; and the sacred, transcendent Narihira, who as "the heavenly Bodhisattva of Song and Dance made mortal left Buddha's Capital of Tranquil Light to bring salvation and blessings to all."[36]

As an example of how these multiple levels are produced through associative identification, we might begin with the *waki*-priest's entrance scene. In Noh plays the entrance of the *waki* is often an extremely stereotyped section, with little or no thematic connection to the rest of the play. In the case of *Kakitsubata*, however, even this relatively unimportant scene is carefully constructed:

> WAKI   I am a monk, taking a look at the various provinces. Not too long ago I was in the capital and while there I left no famous spot or historical site unseen. Now I have set my heart on a pilgrimage to the Eastern provinces.

ageuta (taking a few steps to indicate travel)

> WAKI   Night after night on pillows transient,
> night after night on pillows transient,
> the lodgings diverse and oft-changing,
> yet the same body, fated to drift in
> uneasy slumber – Mino, Owari,
> Mikawa at last I've reached,
> Mikawa at last I've reached.

tsukizerifu

> WAKI   I have traveled so quickly that in no time at all I have reached Mikawa, land of "Three Rivers." Here along the edge of the marsh I see the *kakitsubata* irises are just now in full bloom. I believe I'll go a bit closer to take a better look.

sashi

WAKI   Truly, time never tarries:
        spring slips by, summer's at hand;
        the artless trees and grass mind not,
        we say, yet mindful of the season
        these flowers arrayed in color –
        are they not also called "sweet faces"?
        Ah, these *kakitsubata* are so beautiful!

(*Kakitsubata*, pp. 259–60)

To begin with, the *waki*'s travel poem (*michiyuki*) contains hints and fore-shadowings important for the development of our understanding of Narihira's persona as presented in the play. In it a parallel is set up between the priest and Narihira that will allow for implicit comparisons between them. The *waki* has been sightseeing in the capital, and is now making a pilgrimage to the Eastern Provinces. His journey follows the same path taken by Narihira (the Man of Old) as described in the later *kuse* (expository) scene, based on episodes 7 through 9 of the original *Tales of Ise*:

In search of a place to live,
eastward he drifts [like] the clouds
to Ise and Owari[37]

Instead of Ise, however, the *waki* stops at Mino, which allows for some complex word play:

yet the same body, fated to drift in uneasy slumber – Mino, Owari, Mikawa at last I've reached

onaji ukine no Mino Owari   同じ憂き寝のみのをはり
Mikawa no kuni ni tsukinikeri   三河の国に着きにけり

(*Kakitsubata*, p. 259)

Here *ukine* means both "sad/weary sleep" (憂き寝) and "floating river-weed" (浮き根); *mi no owari* indicates "the body's end/one's fate" (身の終り) and "Mino, Owari" (美濃、尾張), two provinces in what are now Gifu and Aichi prefectures. The path that the *waki* follows thus introduces an important allegorical image in the play: the *michi* 道 (path) as a triple-layered trope for the path through life. This journey is understood at three parallel but deeply interconnected levels: for the *waki* (a priest whose endless traveling is part of his religious vocation), the secular Narihira (whose journey is seen as an exile from the capital and thus in terms of a fall in social position), and the sacred Narihira (identified as the Bodhisattva of Song and Dance, the kami of Yin and Yang, and

Dainichi Nyorai). As an incarnation of the Bodhisattva of Song and Dance, Narihira leaves the Buddha's Capital of Tranquil Light and travels far, far along the mortal path to bring salvation and blessings to all living beings through his poetry, which has the soteriological efficacy of sutras. As in incarnation of the kami of Yin and Yang, Narihira uses the expedient means of sex to bring the women he loves to enlightenment. This is the path hinted at in the later expository section, which incorporates a phrase from the Kunaichō *Waka chikenshū*:

> Now as to this story, who was it about and why did his passionate thoughts, tearful as the dew on Mt. Shinobu, secretly travel along this grassy path without end or beginning?[38]

On one level the "grassy path" is that of life, a cyclical journey that inevitably leads to death and then reincarnation (thus having no beginning or end). On this level *Tales of Ise* is understood as being about the secular Narihira, caught in the endless karmic cycle of reincarnation by his amatory attachments. According to the esoteric commentaries, however, Narihira as Bodhisattva was born into this degenerate world as a poetic sage and wrote *Tales of Ise* in order to reveal the nondual path of eroticism (*irogonomi*) and poetry that will help us transcend the path of reincarnation.

This understanding of "the path" as both secular and transcendent is reinforced by the trope *omoi no tsuyu* 思ひの露 (the dew of passion) which also works on at least two different levels. Dew is a standard epithet for tears; the tears that the secular Narihira shed when forced to take the Eastern Sea Road to Azuma, leaving his lover Fujiwara no Kōshi 藤原高子 behind in the capital. However, given the reading of Mt. Shinobu as "Faithful Spouse Mountain" (信夫山) and the meaning of *shinobite kayou* 忍びて通ふ (to secretly visit a lover), I suspect that the "dew of passion" may well have a secondary meaning of "sexual fluids," again pointing to Narihira as the kami of Harmonious Union between the sexes.[39]

In addition, certain key words in the *waki*'s travel song subtly parallel Narihira's path of sexual enlightenment. The terms *karimakura* 仮枕 (borrowed/temporary pillows), *yado* 宿 (inn), and *ukine* 浮き寝 (floating sleep) each have strong connotations of a temporary tryst with a woman; the kind of one-night stand one might have with a prostitute at an inn. The priest's attraction to the beauty of the *kakitsubata* and his description of it as a "pretty-faced flower" would also indicate a certain susceptibility, not to mention his willingness to accept the offer of a night spent in her hut later on in the play. In other words, the priest may already be following the path of Yin and Yang. In addition, the *waki*'s opening poem, with its image of pillows and lodgings changing while the weary body remains the same, parallels and thus foreshadows the play's use of Narihira's

famous *tsuki ya aranu* 月やあらぬ poem from *Tales of Ise* episode 4
(*Kokinshū* 747), in which the spring and the moon change, but his body
alone remains the same:

> Isn't this the same moon, isn't this spring, the spring of old?
> Or has my body alone remained the same body as before.[40]

This poem represents the culminating instance of the use of natural
imagery as an allegorical trope for the secular Narihira's emotional state.
According to the prose section attached to the poem in episode 4 of *Tales
of Ise*, it was composed as a reaction to the loss of a loved one. The typical
medieval reading of this poem assumed the man was Narihira and the
woman was Fujiwara no Kōshi, and understood the poem as
commenting on how the change in Narihira's situation from last year to
this year has affected his attitude toward his surroundings: "Last year
when I had her with me, the world reflected my happiness – now that
she is gone, the moon and the spring seem joyless – how then can they be
the same moon and spring?" In the last two lines the poem was understood to stress the man's sense of bodily continuity over time: it is
because the moon and spring depart, only to return again, that he is able
to delude himself that they must have changed while they were gone. In
contrast, his awareness of his embodied self has continued unabated –
the same sense of self that he had a year ago he still has now.

This interpretation (one of at least four possible ones) depends on
Buddhist dialectical logic. The experience of a self-identical consciousness
grounded in bodily continuity directly contradicts a Buddhist conception
of true reality: that the spring and moon as natural phenomena
are eternally the same, whereas the experience of our "self" as a self-
identical consciousness is illusory. In this reading, Narihira's lovesick
suffering was so powerful that it could force him (at least ironically) to
disregard one of the most basic of Buddhist principles, a principle that
could be seen underpinning a number of other poems attributed to
Narihira.[41]

Obviously for the esoteric literary commentaries this version of the
Narihira persona – an ordinary man whose passionate attachment causes
him to question basic Buddhist truths – was untenable, and in response
we find a truly remarkable rewriting of this poem into a complex religious
allegory. The most pertinent commentary to my discussion here is probably that found in *Ise monogatari engi* 伊勢物語縁起 (a fragmentary text
which seems to be a variant of *Gyokuden jinpi no maki*):

> The phrase *tsuki ya aranu* signifies that "I [Narihira] am an avatar of
> the dharma body of [Dainichi] Nyorai. For the purpose of trans-
> forming and benefiting all living beings I have come to this country."
> However, because so many of these living beings are difficult to

transform, [Narihira] recited "does the moon of original enlightenment of long ago no longer exist?" The phrase *haru ya mukashi no
haru naranu* (is this spring not the spring of old?) refers to the fact
that having departed from the Pure Land of Tranquil Light we have
forgotten the path by which to return there, and so the phrase
means "has the spring of original enlightenment been forgotten?"
The phrase *waga mi hitotsu wa moto no mi ni shite* (my body alone
remains as it was originally) means "my body alone is the Bodhisattva
of original enlightenment."[42]

Embedded within the context of the play, the meaning of the poem
comes very close to the meaning given to it in *Ise monogatari engi*:

Is this moon not the dawning moon whose light enlightens all? Is
this spring not the spring of old? [Or does] my body alone remain
unchanged as an incarnation (*mi o wake* 身を分け) of originally
enlightened absolute reality (*hongaku shinnyo* 本覚真如, i.e. Dainichi
Nyorai) and the kami of Yin and Yang, as Narihira is also called.[43]

Compare this line to the section of Zenchiku's treatise *Meishuku shū*,
already quoted once in this Chapter, that identifies Narihira and Okina:

When we come to the age of human beings, the author of *Tales of Ise*,
the Middle Captain Narihira, was born the fifth son in a family
versed in poetry; referred to as *katai okina* (the humble old man) he
guided foolish women and taught them the Way of Yin and Yang.
He is named as one of the three *okina*, and one of the sages of poetry
of the *Kokinshū*; revealed as an incarnation (*bunshin*) of the one
substance [of Dainichi Nyorai], he composed poems about birth, old
age, illness and death.[44]

This passage alone might serve as a strong basis for arguing that Zenchiku
wrote *Kakitsubata*, particularly the shared use of the term "incarnation" (身を
分け and 身分 respectively); it clearly indicates his familiarity and
substantial agreement with the commentary's interpretation of the poem.[45]

Within the original *Tale of Ise* context the poem depended for its effect
on our knowledge that Narihira had neatly reversed the whole idea of
what is real and what is appearance. Recontextualized within the Noh
play, however, it is no illusion that there are two moons and two springs.
There is the secular spring and moon, intimately related to the mortal
Narihira's lively youth in the capital; the loss of these reveals the delusion
of attachment to worldly love and success. But the moon and spring are
also understood via the esoteric literary commentaries as emblematic of
original enlightenment. Because we have forgotten the spring and moon
of original enlightenment the Bodhisattva had to depart Buddha's

Capital of the Original Ground of Tranquil Light (*honji jakkō no miyako* 本地寂光の都).   Appearing here on earth as Narihira, he traveled the path of transforming and benefiting all living beings so that we all may eventually find our way back to our "home" of original enlightenment. Interpreted this way, the poem becomes an expression of the essential identity of Narihira's Buddha nature with the unchanging ground of being. As "the incarnation of originally enlightened absolute reality" he *is* himself the law which governs both the fateful changes of man's destiny and the cyclical change of the seasons – it is no wonder that in his secular form his life should play out that very law.

Through the use of the *tsuki ya aranu* poem, then, two main thematic and imagistic strands are brought to final fruition: Narihira's journey is transformed from a secular exile because of a covert love affair, into the self-exile of a bodhisattva for the salvation of all people. The sensitivity toward nature that the "historical" Narihira displays in his secular poems, especially his awareness of how nature's cycles could be used to reflect allegorically his own emotional state and social position, is supplemented by a new transcendent meaning.

Conclusion

My argument here has been that to understand how a Noh play like *Kakitsubata* was constructed, one needs to understand the interpretive method that underlies it, an interpretive method that also underlies *Meishuku shū*, and which in turn was taken directly from the secret culture of esoteric literary commentaries first developed by Fujiwara Tameaki in the thirteenth century. Although such use of etymological allegoresis has been discounted by contemporary scholars as unbelievable and even inappropriate in a "proper" aesthetic treatise, *Meishuku shū* provides a unique aperture into Zenchiku's worldview, his *modus operandi*, that needs to be given more careful consideration. This is the case for its content as well. Like *Meishuku shū*, *Kakitsubata* makes a passionate claim for the potent power of words to affect phenomenal reality: Narihira, as the Bodhisattva of Song and Dance incarnate, "leaves inscribed in sheaves of poetry miraculous sermons on the Buddha's Dharma. When drenched in the blessed dew, even trees and grasses bear forth in fruitful enlightenment" (*Kakitsubata*, p. 262). In this worldview, poetry is not merely rhetoric, and dance is not simply movement: both have the power to bring us to enlightenment if they are correctly interpreted.

I would like to go further to argue that one can find etymological allegoresis actually embedded in Noh plays, but because of the vagaries of reception and transmission, it is hard to sustain that kind of claim. I know that when I was translating *Kakitsubata* for the first time, I was very struck by the way that in the first half of the play the grapheme 身 (*shin*, body) appears again and again, and then from a certain point in the second half suddenly 身 disappears and 心 (*shin*, heart/mind/consciousness) is everywhere. When I brought it up, I was told that it was unlikely to be meaningful, but it has stuck in my head since then. If I pushed this kind of analysis too far, of course, I could be accused of taking on the mindset of the object of my study – a kind of transference if you will – that there is no such thing as coincidences and that metaphorical associations *must* point to higher-order identities. This mindset, which underlies contemporary conspiracy theories such as those behind popular novels such as *The Da Vinci Code*, is all too likely to devolve into tautological nonsense. Nevertheless, I still think it makes sense to treat the influence of the rhetorical strategy of the esoteric commentaries on Noh seriously, on their own terms; Konparu Zenchiku certainly did.

Notes

1 For a succinct discussion in English of the development of the culture of secrecy in the court poetic tradition and its relationship to the culture of secrecy in religious institutions, see Klein 2003, pp. 193–203.
2 See Fabio Rambelli's chapter in this book, in which he describes the three main levels of semiotics as understood in esoteric Buddhism: one exoteric (semiosophia) and two esoteric (semiognosis and semiopietas). All the texts discussed here implicitly assume an esoteric understanding of the semiotic relation.
3 See Klein 2002, particularly chapters 6 and 8.
4 Tameaki, the son of Fujiwara Tameie 藤原為家 (1198–1275) by an unknown lady-in-waiting, appears to have gotten little economic or social support from his father.
5 This is not to say that making the initial identifications was easy; I am indebted to Itō Masayoshi's three-volume collection of Noh plays (SNKS 57–59), the first annotated collection that identified allusions to the esoteric commentaries.
6 See my discussion in Klein 2002, particularly pp. 135–50, of why allegoresis should have arisen in this context. Allan Grapard was the first scholar in English to discuss what he terms "paronomasia" in his essay on the Sannō cult of Mt. Hiei; he also suggests it as one of several organizing principles for the creation of associations between buddhas and kami in the Kasuga Shrine. See Grapard 1987 and 1992, particularly pp. 81–82. See also Jacqueline Stone's discussion of "*kanjin*-style interpretation" in relation to medieval Tendai Buddhism in Stone 1999, pp. 156–67.
7 An explicit warning that a commentary should not be revealed to anyone but a *kanjō no hito* 潅頂の人 appears in Fujiwara [Rokujō] Kiyosuke's *Ōgishō* 奥義抄 (Poetic Profundities, ca. 1130s), cited in Miwa 1994, p. 11, and there is some possibility that the Rokujō family may have developed a *kanjō* initiation in connection with their memorial ceremony (*eigu* 影供) for the poet Kakinomoto no Hitomaro 柿本人麻呂. However, the first documented evidence we have for a waka *kanjō*, and the first consistent use of etymological allegoresis as an interpretive technique to analyze literary texts, is found in commentaries associated with Fujiwara Tameaki. See Miwa 1967 and Klein 2002, pp. 166–76.
8 It is clear that Zenchiku did not have access to the kind of carefully graded levels of instruction in the esoteric Buddhist understanding of language discussed by Fabio Rambelli in this book.

 9 See ch. 1 of Noel Pinnington (forthcoming), *Traces of the Way: Michi and the Writings of Komparu Zenchiku*. I am grateful to Noel Pinnington for letting me read his unpublished manuscript.

10 In the rest of the essay, in order to distinguish between the various uses of the term *okina* 翁, I use "Okina" to refer to the deity manifesting as a benevolent old man, "*Okina*" to refer to the ritual dance performance, and "*okina*" when I simply mean the term itself, in its most general sense of "old man."

11 For a more thorough discussion of the effects of patronage on both Zeami and Zenchiku, see Pinnington (1997) as well as his discussion in chapters 1 and 2 of Pinnington (forthcoming). For a summary biography of Zenchiku's life, see Thornhill 1993, pp. 12–19. In Japanese, documentary information concerning the life of Konparu Zenchiku is summarized in Omote and Itō 1969, pp. 56–63, and Itō 1970, pp. 11–45.

12 See, for example, the discussion of Zenchiku's use of Fujiwara Teika's "demon-quelling style" in Atkins 2003.

13 Noel Pinnington (forthcoming) argues that the diagrams existed prior to Zenchiku and that his "revelation" at Hasedera was how those diagrams might intersect with the practice of Noh.

14 *Waka chikenshū* (b) in Katagiri 1969, p. 207.

15 *Maigetsu shō*, p. 352. In fact, Teika probably did not go on a pilgrimage to Sumiyoshi Shrine; it seems more likely that this was a fabrication inserted into the semi-spurious commentary *Maigetsu shō* 毎月抄. See Brower 1985, pp. 404–5. The anecdote was retold by Shōtetsu, Zenchiku's poetry teacher, in *Shōtetsu monogatari* 正徹物語. See Brower 1992, pp. 89–90.

16 See my longer discussion of this point in Klein 2002, pp. 195–97, 203.

17 Evidence of Zenchiku's reverence for Teika includes the fact that the only two Noh plays in the current canon that allude to Teika's poetry, *Teika* 定家 and *Oshio* 小塩, are by Zenchiku.

18 That is, at the time of the revelation people were not ready yet for its insights and so it was kept hidden; but now a select few have attained the necessary level of enlightenment.

19 Itō Masayoshi (1970, pp. 141–44) argues that it was written sometime after Zenchiku's retirement at age sixty. Note that Pinnington (*Traces of the Way*, chapter 6) points out that Zenchiku uses the "three treasures" of the Konparu house (a demon [*oni*] mask, an image of the Kasuga deity, and some Buddha relics) as a material basis for the Konparu lineage's origin and transmission narrative as presented in *Meishuku shū*. Perhaps because of the lineage's possession of these physical objects, the legitimating commentary of outside authorities was not felt to be necessary.

20 Konparu Zenchiku, *Rokurin ichiro* in Omote and Itō 1969, p. 197; translation Pinnington, *Traces of the Way*, ch. 5, pp. 25, 32. For an example of how differently the same section can be translated, see Nearman 1995–96, p. 1, p. 240.

21 In English, while both Mark Nearman and Arthur Thornhill attempt to place the *Rokurin ichiro* texts within their aesthetic and religious context, neither goes further to fully historicize the text. See Nearman 1995–96 and Thornhill 1993.

22 In English, Mark Nearman has translated one section from *Meishuku shū* and provided a commentary meant to remove the "surface obscurities" of the text (i.e. its esoteric and allegorical aspects) to reveal the hidden "expression of the goals and ideals of mask wearing that still pervade the modern tradition of Nō acting" (Nearman 1984, p. 40). In his accompanying essay Nearman makes a good case for the meaningfulness of Zenchiku's notion of creativity to contemporary actors. But chapter 6 of Noel Pinnington's *Traces of the Way*

presents a much more persuasive analysis of what the text would have meant to Zenchiku himself by attending precisely to those "surface obscurities."

23 *Meishuku shū*, cf. Omote and Itō 1969, p. 283.

24 The medieval pronunciation; contemporary scholars favor Hata no Kawakatsu.

25 Omote and Itō 1969, pp. 283–84, 289. For Zeami's more detailed version of the origin story, see Rimer and Yamazaki 1984, pp. 3, 31–35.

26 See also Bernard Faure's essay in this book, which discusses how the dead spirit of Kōkatsu becomes a *kōjin*.

27 *Honchō kōsōden*, p. 680. Translation modified from Matsunaga 1969, pp. 190–91. Gyōen's biography is found in a collection compiled in the early Edo period from a number of medieval sources, so it is difficult to date. It is unlikely, however, that this kind of etymological analysis would have been produced during Gyōen's life-time. The similarity of content with a text written by the Tendai monk Shinga 心賀 (1329–?) makes it more probable that the story was produced sometime in the Kamakura period. For Shinga's version of this analysis see Kojima and Takayoshi 1976, p. 202; in English see Grapard 1987, p. 226.

28 *Waka chikenshū* (a), in Katagiri 1969, p. 117.

29 *Ise monogatari shō*, in Katagiri 1969, p. 193.

30 For a fuller analysis of how the esoteric commentaries conflated the path of poetry and path of sexuality as paths to enlightenment, Izanagi and Izanami were understood as the originary deities of both paths, and Narihira was identified as their incarnation, see Klein 2002, especially pp. 153–57.

31 "When two of the three horizontal strokes are raised up and the character is pulled apart, the phrase 'the two great suns' is created. These are none other than the dual Womb and Vajra mandalas, which are symbolic representations of Dainichi Nyorai." Konparu Zenchiku, *Meishuku shū* in Omote and Itō 1969, p. 294. Translation is mine.

32 The *honji suijaku* theory of hypostasis claimed that kami were "manifest traces" (*suijaku*) of Buddhist deities who formed their "original ground" (*honji*). It was initially understood that the Buddhist deities temporarily took the form of kami to prepare the Japanese for the arrival of the more advanced teachings of Buddhism. By the Kamakura period, however, non-dualism was being used to argue that the Buddhist deities and kami were "not two, but one in nature" (*funi ittai* 不二一体), and so neither took precedence.

33 Omote and Itō 1969, pp. 279–80.

34 The designation of the man of old as *okina* occurs in episodes 76, 77, 79, 81, 83, and 97.

35 *Gyokuden jinpi no maki*, p. 528. The phrase *mitari okina* was used to refer to three poems from the *Kokinshū* (893, 894, 895) whose anonymous authors lament their old age.

36 *Kakitsubata*, in SNKS 57, p. 263. All following translations of *Kakitsubata* are mine, slightly modified from my previously published translation (Klein 1988).

37   *sumidokoro motomu tote*　　　　住み所求むとて
　　 Azuma no kata ni yuku kumo no　東の方に行く雲の
　　 Ise ya Owari　　　　　　　　　いせや尾張

　　　　　　　　　　　　　　　　　　　　　　　　　　　（*Kakitsubata*, p. 264)

38   *somosomo kono monogatari wa*　　　　　そもそもこの物語は
　　 ikanaru hito no nanigoto ni yotte　　　いかなる人の何事によって
　　 omoi no tsuyu no Shinobuyama　　　　思ひの露の信夫山
　　 shinobite kayou michishiba no　　　　忍びて通ふ道芝の
　　 hajime mo naku owari mo nashi　　　　はじめもなく終りもなし

　　　　　　　　　　　　　　　　　　　　　　　　　　　（*Kakitsubata*, p. 263)

Cf. *Waka chikenshū*: "*Somosomo, mazu kono monogatari wa, ikanarikeru hito no, nanigoto o sen to shite, kakitarikeru mono zo*" そもそも、まづこのものがたりは、いかなりける人の、なに事を詮として、かきたりけるものぞ. (*Waka chikenshū* [a] in Katagiri 1969, p. 105). Itō Masayoshi (1967) made the preliminary identifications of specific commentaries alluded to in *Kakitsubata*.

39 And as we will see, at the climax of the play (pun intended), Narihira's poetry is compared to the blessings of dew (*tsuyu no megumi* 露の恵み) bestowed by the Buddha onto flowers and grasses, allowing them to acquire the fruit of enlightenment.

40   *tsuki ya aranu / haru ya mukashi no / haru*   月やあらぬ春や昔の春ならぬ
      naranu /
      waga mi hitotsu wa / moto no mi ni shite   わが身一つはもとの身にして

The following analysis of the *tsuki ya aranu* poem is indebted to the following discussions in English: McCullough 1985, pp. 211–12; McCullough 1968, pp. 52–53; Brower and Miner 1961, pp. 193, 290, and 476; and Okada 1991, pp. 144–46. In Japanese, see NKBT 9, p. 113, n. 28, and p. 191, n. 18; and SNKS 2, pp. 16–17.

41 McCullough (1968, p. 53) argues that *tsuki ya aranu* is typical of a group of poems including *Kokinshū* 476, 616, 644, and 646 in which Narihira uses a dialectical rhetoric of negation to explore the nature of illusion and reality. Whether or not their author intended them that way, it is certainly clear that in the Kamakura period these poems were read in terms of a specifically Buddhist framework. In making this point, however, I do not mean to claim that the poem in its original context was not capable of being interpreted in several contradictory ways; what is interesting to me is how the poem's ambiguity was already being stabilized within medieval Japanese interpretation. See Richard Okada's discussion of the "radical undecidability" of the *tsuki ya aranu* poem in Okada 1991, pp. 144–46.

42 *Ise monogatari engi*, in Katagiri 1968, p. 581. Translation is mine.

43 Since Dainichi Nyorai is identified with True Thusness, Narihira is here being identified as an avatar of the Nyorai. (*Kakitsubata*, p. 265, n. 19.)

44 See *Kakitsubata*, p. 261.

45 Itō Masayoshi bases his argument that Zenchiku was the author of *Kakitsubata* on a comparison with *Meishuku shū*, as well as the use of certain idiosyncratic phrases that appear in other plays more securely attributed to him. See Itō 1989, pp. 65–69.

References

Primary sources

Gyokuden jinpi no maki 玉伝深秘巻. In Katagiri Yōichi 片桐洋一 (ed.), *Chūsei Kokinshū chūshakusho kaidai* 中世古今集注釈書解題, vol. 5. Kyoto: Akao Shobundō 1986, pp. 521–87.

Honchō kōsōden (shidenbu) 本朝高僧伝, by Shiban 師蠻. In Bussho Kankōkai 仏書刊行会 (ed.), DNBZ vol. 103. Tokyo: Meichō Fukyūkai, 1979.

Ise monogatari 伊勢物語, see NKBT 9; SNKS 2.

Ise monogatari engi 伊勢物語縁起, in Katagiri 1968, pp. 579–82.

Ise monogatari shō 伊勢物語抄 (=Kunaichō Shoryōbu shozō, Reizei-ke ryū *Ise monogatari shō* 宮内庁書陵部所蔵、冷泉家流伊勢物語抄), in Katagiri 1969, pp. 287–400.

Kakitsubata 杜若, in SNKS 57, pp. 257–66. (English tr. Klein 1988)

Maigetsu shō 毎月抄, attrib. Fujiwara Teika 藤原定家. In Sasaki Nobutsuna 佐々木信綱 (ed.), *Nihon kagaku taikei* 日本歌学大系, vol. 3. Tokyo: Kazama Shobō 1973, pp. 346–54.

Meishuku shū 明宿集, by Konparu Zenchiku 金春禅竹, in Omote and Itō 1969, pp. 279–307.

NKBT 9. Sakakura Atsuyoshi 阪倉篤義, et al. (eds), *Taketori monogatari, Ise monogatari, Yamato monogatari* 竹取物語・伊勢物語・大和物語. Tokyo: Iwanami Shoten 1959.

Rokurin ichiro 六輪一露 (various versions) by Konparu Zenchiku 金春禅竹, in Omote and Itō 1969, pp. 197–262. (English tr. Nearman 1995–96)

SNKS 2. Watanabe Minoru 渡辺実 (ed.), *Ise monogatari* 伊勢物語. Tokyo: Shinchōsha 1976.

SNKS 57. Itō Masayoshi 伊藤正義 (ed.), *Yōkyokushū* 謡曲集. Tokyo: Shinchōsha 1983–86.

Waka chikenshū 和歌智顕集
   (a) Kunaichō Shoryōbu shozō, den Tameuji hitsu *Waka chikenshū* 宮内庁書陵部所蔵、伝為氏筆和歌智顕集, in Katagiri 1969, pp. 96–195.
   (b) Shimabara Kōminkan Matsuhira Bunko shozō *Waka chikenshū* 島原公民館松平文庫所蔵和歌知顕集, in Katagiri 1969, pp. 197–286.

Modern sources

Atkins, Paul (2003), "The Demon-Quelling Style in Medieval Japanese Poetic and Dramatic Theory." *Monumenta Nipponica* 58/4, pp. 317–46.

Brower, Robert H. (1985), "Fujiwara Teika's *Maigetsushō*." *Monumenta Nipponica* 40/4, pp. 399–425.

Brower, Robert H. (tr.) (1992), *Conversations with Shōtetsu*. With introduction and notes by Steven D. Carter. Ann Arbor: Center for Japanese Studies, University of Michigan.

Brower, Robert H. and Earl Miner (1961), *Japanese Court Poetry*. Stanford, CA: Stanford University Press.

Grapard, Allan G. (1987), "Linguistic Cubism: A Singularity of Pluralism in the Sannō Cult." *Japanese Journal of Religious Studies* 14/2–3, pp. 211–34.

Grapard, Allan G. (1992), *The Protocol of the Gods: A Study of the Kasuga Cult in Japanese History*. Berkeley, CA: University of California Press.

Itō Masayoshi 伊藤正義 (1967), "*Yōkyoku Kakitsubata* kō" 謡曲「杜若」考. *Bunrin* 文林 no. 2 (December), pp. 61–83.

Itō Masayoshi (1970), *Konparu Zenchiku no kenkyū* 金春禅竹の研究. Kyoto: Akao Shōbundō.

Itō Masayoshi (1989), *Yōkyoku zakki* 謡曲雑記. Osaka: Izumi Shoin.

Katagiri Yōichi 片桐洋一 (1968), *Ise monogatari no kenkyū* 伊勢物語の研究, vol. Kenkyūhen 研究篇. Tokyo: Meiji Shoin.

Katagiri Yōichi (1969), *Ise monogatari no kenkyū* 伊勢物語の研究, vol. Shiryōhen 資料篇. Tokyo: Meiji Shoin.

Klein, Susan (tr.) (1988), "*Kakitsubata*," in Karen Brazell (ed.), *Twelve Plays of the Noh and Kyōgen Theaters*. Ithaca, NY: Cornell East Asia Series, pp. 63–79.

Klein, Susan (2002), *Allegories of Desire: Esoteric Literary Commentaries of Medieval Japan*. Cambridge, MA: Harvard University Press.

Klein, Susan (2003), "Wild words and syncretic deities. *Kyōgen kigo* and *honji suijaku* in medieval literary allegoresis," in Teeuwen and Rambelli (eds),

Buddhas and Kami in Japan: Honji Suijaku as a combinatori paradigm. London: RoutledgeCurzon, pp. 177–203.

Kojima Michimasa 小島通正 and Fukuhara Takayoshi 福原隆喜 (1976), "Tendai kuden hōmon no kyōdō kenkyū" 天台口伝法門の共同研究. *Bukkyō shisō ronshū* 仏教思想論集. Kyoto: Heiraku-ji Shoten.

McCullough, Helen Craig (tr.) (1968), *Tales of Ise*. Stanford, CA: Stanford University Press.

McCullough, Helen Craig (1985), *Brocade by Night*. Stanford, CA: Stanford University Press.

Matsunaga, Alicia (1969), *The Buddhist Philosophy of Assimilation*. Tokyo: Sophia University.

Miwa Masatane 三輪正胤 (1967), "Chūsei kadō ni okeru kanjō denju ni tsuite" 中世歌道における潅頂伝授について. *Chūsei bungaku* 中世文学 12, pp. 28–32.

Miwa Masatane (1994), *Kagaku hiden no kenkyū* 歌学秘伝の研究. Tokyo: Kazama Shobō.

Nearman, Mark J. (1984), "Behind the Mask of Nō," in Rebecca Teele (ed.), *Nō/Kyōgen Masks and Performance* (=*Mime Journal* 1984). Claremont, CA: Pomona College Theater Department, pp. 20–64.

Nearman, Mark J. (1995–96), "The Visions of a Creative Artist: Zenchiku's *Rokurin Ichiro* Treatises" (parts 1–4). *Monumenta Nipponica* 50:2 (1995), pp. 235–61; 50:3, pp. 281–303; 50:4, pp. 485–521; 51:1 (1996), pp. 17–33.

Okada, Richard (1991), *Figures of Resistance*. Durham, NC: Duke University Press.

Omote Akira 表章 and Itō Masayoshi 伊藤正義 (eds) (1969), *Konparu kodensho shūsei* 金春古伝書集成. Tokyo: Wan'ya Shoten.

Pinnington, Noel (1997), "Crossed Paths: Zeami's Transmission to Zenchiku." *Monumenta Nipponica* 52/2, pp. 201–34.

Pinnington, Noel (forthcoming), *Traces of the Way: Michi and the Writings of Konparu Zenchiku*. Ithaca, NY: Cornell East Asia Series.

Rimer, Thomas J. and Masakazu Yamazaki (tr.) (1984), *On the Art of Nō Drama: The Major Treatises of Zeami*. Princeton, NJ: Princeton University Press.

Stone, Jacqueline I. (1999), *Original Enlightenment and the Transformation of Medieval Japanese Buddhism* (Kuroda Institute, Studies in East Asian Buddhism vol. 12). Honolulu: University of Hawai'i Press.

Thornhill, Arthur (1993), *Six Circles, One Dewdrop: The Religio-Aesthetic World of Konparu Zenchiku*. Princeton, NJ: Princeton University Press.

10 The elephant in the room

The cult of secrecy in Japanese Tantrism

Bernard Faure

There are many kinds of secrecy and many motivations for them. I have discussed the political and sectarian implications of secrecy in the particular case of relic worship elsewhere (Faure 1999 and 2004), and other contributions to this book examine the relationships of secrecy and power in other areas of pre-modern Japanese society. In medieval Japan, secrecy characterized above all the tradition of esoteric Buddhism. By privileging the secret over the manifest, esoteric Buddhism was led, paradoxically, to privilege certain figures of the sacred, in particular mysterious deities that took precedence over the traditional symbols of Buddhism. As Yamaori Tetsuo (1991, pp. 113–20) has noted, Japanese deities (*kami*) were initially compared to the Indian buddhas as being symbols of the invisible in contrast to figures of the visible. Whatever one may think of the so-called aniconism of early Buddhism and of the inconceivable transcendence of the Buddha himself, in the concrete reality of the cult, the buddhas are eminently visible, and the main characteristic of their anthropomorphic manifestation is their aura, which symbolizes a world of light. In order to call attention to their transcendence, medieval Japanese Buddhism tended to conceal them, and this led to the notion of "hidden buddhas" (*hibutsu* 秘仏), whose secret nature, symbolized by their removal and concealment in the inner sanctum, evokes infinite power and potentiality. Japanese art historians, who have often monopolized the concept of *hibutsu*, have not always been able to distinguish between the circumstantial and the structural factors that led to the development of that ragbag category, nor to discuss its theological and mythological premises.[1]

One of the paradigmatic cases of *hibutsu* is probably that of the elephant-headed Vināyaka, also known as Shōten 聖天 (the "Saintly Deva") or Kangiten 歓喜天 (the "Deva of Bliss"). Under the latter name in particular, the highly sexual "dual-body" (*sōshin* 双身) Vināyaka has attracted the attention of a number of scholars.[2] The sexual element, however, is only one aspect of this figure. More broadly, Kangiten's case sheds light on the notion of secrecy in medieval Buddhism. The Japanese Vināyaka is not only a sexual god like the *yab-yum* deities of Tibetan Buddhism. He is also a *kōjin* 荒神, literally a "wild" or "raging" deity, a god or demon of obstacles, and, by extension, a deity that controls human destiny. But above all, the underlying structure that determines his figure seems to be that of secrecy. Not only is he worshiped in a secret, hidden place, but this secrecy is also defined by various symbolic factors – including his unbridled sexuality and the belief in his "evil eye," from which humans must be shielded. In the last analysis, it is essentially the pervading symbolism of embryonic gestation that explains his transformation from a mere demon into a blissful deva and ultimately into the primordial, secret *kōjin*, the "hidden god" of medieval Japan.

Vināyaka's origins are usually traced back to the Hindu god Gaṇeśa, himself a protector of secrecy – in this case the privacy of his mother Pārvatī. According to the Hindu myth, because of his attempt to prevent Śiva from entering the room in which his mother was taking her bath, Gaṇeśa incurred his father's wrath. Śiva's looks can kill, but in this case they merely burnt Gaṇeśa's head, which was eventually replaced by that of an elephant. The myth also emphasizes the impure origins of Gaṇeśa, who is said to have been created by Pārvatī from the secretions of her body. Likewise, his brother Skanda was born from Śiva's semen, without sexual intercourse. This puts the two brothers in the category of gods who were not born from a mother's womb.

Gaṇeśa was therefore not always the jovial, child-like deity he has become in later Hinduism, the Lord of Beginnings who removes all obstacles. As Paul Courtright puts it: "The Purāṇic texts are uncomfortably aware of the discrepancy between the malevolent, obstacle-creating powers of Vināyaka and the positive, obstacle-removing actions of Gaṇeśa, and they attempt to disguise Gaṇeśa's demon background through the clever use of false etymologies for the name 'Vināyaka.'" (Courtright 1985, p. 134.) As a demon, Gaṇeśa's image fuses with those of Nīla and Andhaka, the elephant-demons killed by Śiva.[3] In Buddhist iconography, the motif is repeated in the elephant-skin held by Mahākāla (or other similar figures) above his head.[4] This motif is important, for reasons to be explained later.

Vināyaka represents the demonic aspect of the Gaṇeśa, an aspect played down in devotional Hinduism. The dark side of Gaṇeśa (or Vināyaka) appears clearly in some early Indian representations, for instance in the Ellora caves, where he is represented in the company of a group of pestilence deities, the so-called "Seven Mothers" (Saptamātṛkā). This representation was well known to the Buddhists who lived side by side with the Hindus and the Jains at Ellora during the sixth and seventh centuries. A Buddhist version of Gaṇeśa (Vināyaka) can be found for instance in one of the Aurangabad caves, where he is represented on the back wall with a group of female deities on the left wall and two buddhas on the right.[5]

Vināyaka/Shōten as demon/deva

In Buddhism, Vināyaka is a powerful demon who has been ordered by Maheśvara to steal the vital breath of living beings and to create obstacles. Although his name initially meant "remover of obstacles," Buddhists reinterpreted him as the cause of all demonic obstacles. Indeed, he is the god of obstacles *par excellence*. He is eventually tamed by the bodhisattva Avalokiteśvara, who assumes his same form, but of female sex, to seduce him.[6] However, despite his taming, the Japanese Vināyaka/Shōten remains an ambivalent figure that needs to be coerced or propitiated again and again.

Even when subdued and converted, Vināyaka remains a dark, cruel god, invoked in black magical rites. In 1329, Emperor Go-Daigo (r. 1318–39) performed a subjugation ritual during which he poured oil over a statue of Shōten. The ritual was intended to "quickly dispel evil men and evil acts" – in other words, to get rid of the shogunate.[7] In this episode, in which a ruler resorts to black magic to defeat his political opponents, Amino Yoshihiko sees an illustration of the "weird" or "heteromorphic" (*igyō* 異形) nature of Go-Daigo and of medieval kingship (Amino 1993, pp. 221–23). Of course, black magic is in the eye of the beholder, and Go-Daigo saw himself as perfectly justified in trying to subjugate demon-like warriors.

This was by no means the first Shōten ritual performed at court. From the end of the Heian period, Shōten had occupied a privileged seat in the imperial chapel, owing to his perceived efficacy in curbing enemies.[8] A case in point is the ritual of subjugation performed by the Tendai priest Son'i 尊意 at the time of Taira no Masakado's rebellion in 940. Although the central deity (*honzon* 本尊) of that ritual was actually Fudō Myōō 不動明王 , we are told that, at one point, a Shōten statuette standing on a lateral altar suddenly flew away, and Masakado's head fell on the main altar.[9] Son'i also attempted to subjugate the vengeful spirit (*onryō* 怨霊) of Sugawara no Michizane with the help of Shōten. As is well known, Michizane died in exile after being accused of a plot, and the calamities that struck the palace and the capital after his death attributed to his vengeful spirit, led to his placation and his deification as an "august spirit" (*goryō* 御霊) and eventually as a "heavenly deity" (Tenjin 天神).[10] Interestingly, Michizane is said to have been a devotee of Shōten, and the *Tenjin engi*, one of the origin stories (*engi* 縁起) that describe his apotheosis as Tenjin, also includes an account of Shōten's miraculous powers.[11] Perhaps the demonic power attributed to Shōten explains why the latter came to be associated with, and at some point also equated to, Michizane.[12] Whatever the case may be, in Japan Shōten seems to have been associated with powerful malevolent spirits (*onryō*, or *goryō*) that were victims of an untimely death. Initially he may have been perceived as one of these resentful spirits, whose wrath could cause various calamities such as epidemics.

In Japanese sources, Vināyaka is often referred to as the demon that "constantly follows individuals, like the shadow follows the body."[13] This characterization is important for my purpose. As noted earlier, he is above all a powerful demon-king, the leader of a horde of demons also called vināyakas. These demons are responsible for everything that goes wrong in our lives, and in particular they are the cause of our nightmares. According to the *Kakuzenshō*, a text by Kakuzen 覚禅 (1143–1213), "one calls vināyakas [those] who cause obstacles to all dharmas. All these obstacles come from false thinking." (*Kakuzenshō*, vol. 6, p. 107.)

Vināyaka is further associated with King Yama (Jap. Enmaten 閻魔天), who is the judge of the dead, and he appears in Yama's mandala, the so-called *Enmaten mandara* 閻魔天曼荼羅 Among Yama's retinue, we find various scavenger-types such as ḍākinīs and mātṛkās, as well as a pair of scribes called *gushōjin* 倶生神, "twin deities," to which I will return shortly.

Vināyaka/Shōten is also often included in a divine triad, together with Dakiniten 荼枳尼天 (a deity derived from the Indian ḍākinī, associated with the fox) and Benzaiten 弁才天 (a deity derived from the Indian goddess Sarasvatī). Sometimes this triad becomes a single, three-headed deity. A case in point is the image of one of the former protecting deities of the Shingon temple Tōji 東寺, called Matarajin 摩多羅神. This name, often taken as a personal name, can also be interpreted as "god of the *matara*," in other words, a leader of the mātṛkās (Mothers), deities of pestilence, and devourers/protectors of fetuses and children. The Matarajin of Tōji was a three-headed deity whose central, golden face was that of Vināyaka/Shōten, and whose right and left faces, red and white, were those of Dakiniten and Benzaiten. Here, the color symbolism has embryological connotations, referring to the red female blood and the white male semen – the Yin and Yang fluids – that form the golden embryo. As the Shingon master Kakuban 覚鑁 (1095–1143) put it, "Vināyaka (Daishō Kangiten 大聖歓喜天) is the root of Yin and Yang, from which the ten thousand forms are born."[14]

A painted scroll entitled "Three Devas" shows a three-headed, winged deity, riding a fox (the usual mount of Dakiniten). Here again, the central face is that of Vināyaka, although the color symbolism is missing.[15] The Three Devas even entered some sites of Shinto worship, for instance at Inariyama 稲荷山 (the cultic center of the deity Inari, in the southern part of Kyoto), where the Lower Shrine was said to correspond to Dakiniten, the Middle Shrine to Benzaiten, and the Upper Shrine to Shōten/Vināyaka.[16]

Vināyaka as Kōjin, lord of obstacles

In the *Chōseiden* 窕誓伝, a work by the priest Ikū 以空 (d. 1670), Vināyaka is described as a *kōjin* – or is identified with the deity named

Kōjin.[17] The term *kōjin* refers to a category of "wild" or "rough" gods or spirits, whose wrathful appearance is meant to instill fear in unbelievers. They create obstacles for those who do not worship them, even as they protect their followers. As an individual deity, however, Kōjin appears in Buddhist garb as Sanbō Kōjin 三宝荒神. This elusive figure played a crucial role in the development of medieval Japanese religion, being a kind of symbolic shifter that allowed easy passage between Buddhism and other religious movements such as Onmyōdō 陰陽道, Sukuyōdō 宿曜道, Shugendō 修験道, and Shinto.

I cannot dwell further on (Sanbō) Kōjin here; I will merely remark on two aspects that are related to the etymology of *kōjin* 荒神 (also read *araburu kami*). The term connotes either a specific violent deity or a class of deities, in both cases of demoniac, violent, and unruly nature. However, *ara* 荒 also connotes the foundation, the virgin, untouched aspect of reality, as well as the intrinsic violence of being and its manifestations. As Suzuki Masataka (2001, pp. 7–10, *passim*) and Simone Mauclaire (1992) have shown, the *kōjin* is in this sense the god of uncleared, virginal land, the accursed (or blessed) share of reality that remains impenetrable to any kind of symbolic intrusion. From there to making it the symbol of fundamental ignorance (*mumyō* 無明), and thence to the form *par excellence* of ultimate reality, the primordial chaos, was only a small step, gladly taken by the advocates of the Tendai notion of innate awakening (*hongaku* 本覚), with its equation of awakening and defilement or ignorance.[18]

As a "god of obstacles," Vināyaka needs to be propitiated at the beginning of all rituals. He thus becomes a "god of beginnings," and this chronological priority tends to become a precedence in rank, helping him to move to the central position and become the main object of worship (*honzon* 本尊). This characteristic explains in part how he eventually became a "hidden buddha," a transcendent being worshiped in the inner sanctum, away from profane view.

According to the *shibu Binayaka hō* 四部毘那夜迦法 (Ritual of Vināyaka in Four Sections, attributed to the Tendai priest Annen 安然, ca. 841–915), the foundation of the Jetavana monastery had been prevented by a series of calamities.[19] As Śāriputra, perplexed, meditates to find the cause of such ill-luck, a monstrous being with eight faces appears to him and claims to be the "Raging King of the Three Jewels," also called Nagyō Tosajin 那行都佐神. The text comments, "This is Kōjin, or Vināyaka." (*Kakuzenshō*, vol. 6, p. 135.) The demon, who refers to himself as a deva, adds that those who do not worship him will suffer all kinds of calamities, and that Śāriputra, in order to avoid these calamities, must produce an image of him and make offerings to it.

The story reappears in another source, the *Shintō zōzōshū* 神道雑々集. Here, the description of Kōjin is a little more specific: his gigantic size is described, and he appears with a retinue of eight deities. He identifies himself as Sanbō Kōjin Vināyaka and as Nagyō Tosajin. But what is new, and particularly significant, is that he claims to be "the elder brother of the Buddha" and to have a fabulous number of followers – 9 billion 43 thousand and 490 *kōjin* to be exact.[20] Śāriputra, baffled, avows that he did not know of his existence, and promises to worship him. Vināyaka's claim sounds like hubris. However, assuming that the Buddha himself went through a human birth, his placenta could be conceived as his divine twin – in other words, an elder brother. If the *kōjin* Vināyaka is, as I will argue, a "placenta deity," his claim seems to make sense (at least in this particular context).

The name Nagyō Tosajin seems at times to refer to a single deity (Vināyaka), at others to designate a pair of demonic beings, Nagyō 那行 and Tosa 都佐.[21] All sources emphasize the equivalence between Kōjin, Vināyaka, and Nagyō Tosajin – whether the latter is a single or a dual god. We should note in passing that Shōten himself can be seen as either a dual-bodied god (Kangiten), or as a couple formed of Vināyaka and his female partner (Avalokiteśvara). The latent twin nature of the *kōjin* Vināyaka as Nagyō Tosa and his definition as the demon that follows beings like their shadow, the silent witness of all their acts, point toward another function: that of the placenta deity, to which I now turn.

Vināyaka as placenta deity (*ena kōjin*)

One of the most characteristic forms of Kōjin is the so-called "placenta *kōjin*" (*ena kōjin* 胞衣荒神), a deity that is identified with the placenta, and that protects the fetus (and the child, once it is born). With the work of scholars such as François Bizot and James Sanford, the importance of Buddhist embryology, and in particular the fascination of Tantric Buddhists for the process of gestation, has become clear.[22] Gestation belongs by essence to the symbolic realm of secrecy. And as we will see, at least two of the deities considered here are, precisely, embryological deities, gods of the placenta.

We recall that Vināyaka was said to "always follow beings like their shadow." This definition is precisely that of the so-called *ena kōjin*, or, more broadly, of all placenta deities. The placenta has in many cultures been perceived as a double of the child, and it was (and still is sometimes) buried carefully. Even after its burial, it was believed to watch over the destiny of the child. Many beliefs concerning twins (and in particular, the divine nature of a dead twin) were also applied to the placenta.

A number of Japanese texts describe the placenta as a deity that constantly watches and protects the individual, from the initial moment of conception to the final moment of death. This deity, for which we find no specific cult or shrine, can be found in one form or another in all spheres of Japanese life and religion. Let me present, for instance, the detailed description given in a document entitled *Kōjin kōshiki* 荒神講式:

When [a person] receives the breaths of heaven and earth, and its *hun* 魂 (Jap. *kon*) and *po* 魄 (Jap. *haku*) spirits dwell in the womb, above her head is a canopy (gai 蓋) called *ubugami*. After her birth, and up to the age of seven, it becomes the *tatemashigami* 立増神.[23] Dwelling above her head, it protects her carefully day and night. When she reaches the age of eight, it becomes the *shutakujin* 守宅神 (god protecting the house), and day and night, ensures her growth. When she dies, it becomes a numinous demon and watches over her bones. After her skeleton and bones have disappeared, it becomes a god of the grave, and it is the *ujigami* 氏神 (god of the clan) that protects her descendents. Thus, just like the shadow follows the body, its compassion envelops us, from the moment of our conception onward, in a way that surpasses the nurturing provided by our father and mother.[24]

A similar description is applied to Vināyaka/Shōten in *Asabashō*, a commentary on the *Hu zhu tongzi tuoluoni jing* 護諸童子陀羅尼經 (T 19.1028a; better known in Japanese as *Dōjikyō* 童子経):

When [the individual is] in the womb, Shōten becomes the placenta (*ena*). When [it comes] out of the womb, he is the hood (*kasa* 笠). When [the individual] becomes a buddha, [Shōten] is the heavenly canopy (*tengai* 天蓋). From the moment of conception to that of buddha-hood, one is never distant from Shōten.

(*Asabashō*, vol. 9, p. 219b)

In the Shingon mandalas, we find four directional vināyakas. One of them, Sangai Binayaka 傘蓋毘那夜迦, holds a parasol, and we are told that this parasol means that he covers and protects all beings.[25] Another is called Kongōeten 金剛衣天 (Skt. Vajra-vāsin, the Deva with the Vajra Robe), and his name is said to derive from the fact that the placenta protects the fetus from the cold or heat generated by the mother's food (Mochizuki, p. 1311). The motif of the parasol is related to that of the "heavenly canopy," which occupied a central place in Buddhist rituals. All these can be seen as metaphors for the placenta (and its god).[26] This symbolism was particularly developed in Shugendō 修験道, a form of mountain asceticism strongly influenced by esoteric Buddhism.

In a text entitled *Kōjin saimon* 荒神祭文,[27] we read that when the Buddha asks the identity of the demon who has been preventing the construction of the Jetavana monastery (apparently unaware that this demon is or claims to be his elder brother), the latter (Vināyaka) answers that his name is Kōjin (alias Tosa Nagyō), and that he is the *ubugami* 産神 (god of childbirth) in the womb, the *enagami* 胞衣神 (placenta god) at the time of birth, the earth-deity after birth, and the Buddha that precedes the three stages of human life.[28]

All the sources agree that the *ena kōjin* constantly follows human beings, from their first moment to their last, like a shadow following the body. This is also, we recall, the characteristic of Vināyaka. We must keep in mind, however, the demonic origins of that *kōjin*, closely associated with demons like the mātṛkās and the ḍākinīs, whose main function was to attack the fetus in the womb. Before becoming a protector of the fetus, he has to be duly propitiated.

We have seen that Vināyaka was also called Tosa Nagyō. In the *Shugen seiten* 修験聖典 (Sacred Scriptures of Shugendō), the twin gods Tosa and Nagyō are described as personifications of the "obstacles born at the same time as the individual" (*Shugen seiten*, pp. 484–88). I need to say a few words about the gods "born together" or "at the same time" as an individual, in Japanese *gushōjin* 倶生神 (also translated as "twin-devas").

The notion of twin-devas can be traced back to the couple Yama and Yamī, the lord of the underworld and his sister. The very name Yama means "twin." The "gods born together" are two spirits, born at the same time as the individual and reporting on all his or her actions, both good and bad. The belief that these two deities dwell above the shoulders of each individual seems to have originated in India, and was also popular in Tibet (Stein 1962, pp. 246–48).

In the bureaucratic conception of the underworld that characterizes Chinese religion, these two deities turn into infernal scribes who present their report when an individual faces King Yama's judgment. In Chinese Buddhist iconography, they are often equated with the acolytes of the God of Taishan (Jap. Taizan Fukun 泰山府君), the Controller of Life (Chin. Siming, Jap. Shimei 司命), and the Controller of Registers (Chin. Silu, Jap. Shiroku 司禄). Two variants are the so-called *daṇḍa* staff of King Yama, the top of which being formed of two talking heads that report good and evil; and the acolytes of the Bodhisattva Dizang 地藏 (Kṣitigarbha, Jap. Jizō), the so-called Lads of Good and Evil.[29] The Chinese have known other similar conceptions of invisible spirits, like that of the Three Worms or of the Stove God, that report on the (bad) deeds of the individual, who as a result sees his life shortened in punishment. In some sources, the dual Vināyaka is clearly identified with these twin-devas.

Finally, Vināyaka appears as a placenta deity in the *Shinkō musōki* 真興夢想記 (Shinkō's Record of Dreams) by the Shingon priest Shinkō (934–1004). The text first describes the union of the two principles (Yin and Yang) through the fusion of the two – red and white – drops, that is, the male and female essences semen and blood. That fusion results in the conception of a new being, formed of the Five Elements (and therefore described symbolically as a five-wheel stupa [*gorintō* 五輪塔]). This stupa is covered by two vināyakas, represented by a double elephant-head and an elephant's skin. This skin forms a kind of placenta covering the fetus (the stupa). It calls to mind the elephant-skin in representations of the god Mahākāla (Śiva). These two vināyakas also correspond to the dual-body Kangiten. They are described as the *hun* (Jap. *kon*) and *po* (*haku*) spirits of the individual. The *po* spirit on the right is called the Buddha-body, it corresponds to the individual; the *hun* spirit on the left corresponds to the placenta (*ena*), that is, the placenta deity. A gloss says, "This deva corresponds to the placenta; this is why it is identical with Shōten, the wisdom god of Tōji."[30]

This is a rather strange document about which much remains obscure, but in any case it confirms that Vināyaka was perceived in medieval Japan as a form of the *ena kōjin*, a deity governing human destiny. The henotheistic interpretation of Vināyaka/Shōten is particularly evident in the *Bikisho* 鼻帰書:

> Shōten is King Yama in the nether-world, he is Shōten among the devas, he is the "god(s) born at the same time" (*gushōjin*) among men, and he is Susanoo no mikoto among the kami. All these are transformations of Shōten.[31]

Here, the name Shōten no longer simply designates a particularly powerful deva (and former demon-king), but he has become a transcendent god, the source of all other gods.

In his multivalent role, Vināyaka calls to mind the mysterious god called *shukujin* 宿神 (god of destiny, astral deity). The notion of such a primordial, cosmic deity that includes all the various gods of Japan could have developed into a form of monotheism. However, this kind of deity was promoted by Buddhist monks interested in local culture and by marginal groups like blind singer-monks and *sarugaku* 猿楽 actors, inhabitants of the so-called *shuku* 宿 (relay station; and in this sense, the *shukujin* is also the "god of the *shuku*"). This perhaps explains why, despite his popularity, he never occupied the front-stage of the Japanese pantheon. Another, more structural reason has to do with his shadowy and secret nature, which explains why Vināyaka, till today, remains a "hidden buddha." He remains, as it should be, the elephant that is in the room but that nobody seems to see, whose presence nevertheless affects everyone.

Toward the end of the medieval period, as shown in a text by the Noh playwright Zenchiku in a work entitled *Meishuku shū* 明宿集 (Record on the Shukujin deity), the figure of Okina 翁 takes on cosmic proportions as a kind of demiurge who controls human destinies, and who is the source of all the buddhas and gods.[32] This Okina is also fundamentally ambivalent and is identified with Kōjin. As Hattori Yukio has shown, Okina and Kōjin are two aspects of the Shukujin, which is not only a stellar deity, but also a god of destiny (*shuku* means both an astral constellation and fate).[33] The same seems true of Vināyaka, who counted Zenchiku among his devotees. Indeed the latter, noting Vināyaka's identity with Kōjin, draws the conclusion that he is also identical with Okina (*Meishuku shū*, p. 414).

Incidentally, *shukujin* is also sometimes written *shugūjin* 守宮神 (god protecting the Palace). The "Palace" (*miya* 宮) in question may be the Imperial Palace, but the term could also refer to a constellation, or to the womb. Thus, the connotation of placenta deity seems plausible. At any rate, the Shukujin remains an elusive, hidden god, and it is only natural that he hides his true nature behind a mask (in the case of Okina) or behind closed doors (in the case of Vināyaka). He dwells not only in secrecy, in the deepest recesses of living beings and things, in the darkness of the womb, in the inner sanctum, behind the stage, or in the basement of temples – but also in the deepest recesses of space (the Palace of the Northern Dipper) or of the earth (the court of King Yama, where we find Vināyaka and the twin-devas controlling human destiny). All these places are structurally analogous, dark abodes of secret gods that only dark and secret rituals can reach.

Obviously, the notion of secrecy at work here exceeds the limits of esoteric Buddhism in a strict sense. Esoteric Buddhism did not have a monopoly on secrecy, even though, by its very esoteric nature and its elaborate discussion of the *kenmitsu* (exoteric vs. esoteric) paradigm, it contributed significantly to the development of secrecy practices. It helped to expose (and therefore perhaps also to kill, or at least to trivialize) a notion that, like Laozi's fish, should never have left the depths; in a word, it illuminated the belief that, prior to the process of emanation that creates the manifest and manifold reality, there is a secret space at the origin of things, a hidden realm of pure potentiality. This is of course the realm of the Buddha Mahāvairocana (Dainichi 大日). However, it is not simply the serene reality of traditional Mahāyāna, but rather the violent, unruly dynamism of pure potentiality.

As the guardian of the threshold between being and non-being, Vināyaka is also the first manifestation of that reality and the god who controls access to it. His "evil eye" is the third eye that opens onto that realm of secrecy, or that brings its intrinsic violence out into the open. On a more serene note, that realm is also described in metonymic fashion and in embryological terms as the secret, womb-like world in which incubation takes place. As the power that rules over that hidden world, Vināyaka, the "secret Buddha," is even more secret than Dainichi himself (in this sense too, he is the "elder brother" of the Buddha). He was also perceived as a placenta deity, a god who protects human life during gestation's threshold between human consciousness in the invisible and the visible world.

Notes

1 For a recent study of *hibutsu* from the standpoint of Religious Studies, see Rambelli 2002.
2 See for instance Getty 1936, especially, ch. 7, "Gaṇeśa in China," and ch. 8, "Gaṇeśa in Japan"; Sanford 1991, pp. 287–335; Kabanoff 1984; and Sasama 1989.

3 In a variant, Śiva kills the elephant-headed demon Andhaka by trampling him under foot. The Seven Mothers (Saptamatṛkā) are also created on that occasion in order to drink the blood of the murdered demon. Andhaka eventually repents and takes refuge in Śiva. The latter gives him to Pārvatī as a son, and Andhaka becomes the leader of Śiva's troupe, the Gaṇa (in other words, he is reborn as Gaṇeśa). These myths explain the birth of the Seven Mothers and their relation to Vināyaka, as well as the motif of the elephant skin with which Śiva (or his Buddhist version, Mahākāla) covers himself. On the relationship between Gaṇeśa and the "Mothers," see Yadav 1997, pp. 159–67.

4 On this question, see Iyanaga 1994, p. 866b.

5 See Berkson 1986, pp. 115–21 and 226–28.

6 On this myth, see Sanford 1991. In *Kakuzenshō* 覚禅鈔, vol. 6, p. 121, the two figures are said to represent a female deva (Vināyaka as the Mother of Demons, Kishimo 鬼子母) and a bodhisattva (Avalokiteśvara/Kannon 観音). See also *Keiran shūyōshū* 渓嵐拾葉集, p. 526a. The dual-bodied Kangiten represents taming through seduction, rather than mere sexuality. This legend illustrates the Tantric notion of the "revolution by coupling" (*maithunasya parāvṛtti*), as described for instance in the *Mahāyānasūtrālaṃkāra* (T 1604.605a).

7 Shōten was by no means the only supernatural ally invoked against the bakufu. Using the pretext of the pregnancy of the imperial consort, Go-Daigo had rituals performed to Butsugen Butsumo 仏眼仏母 and Ichiji Kinrin 一字金輪, to the five great Myōō 五大明王, to Kujaku Myōō 孔雀明王, the Seven Yakushi 七薬師, the Five Kokūzō 五虚空蔵, the Six-Letter Kannon 六字観音, the Eight-Letter Monju 八字文殊, Fugen 普賢, and Kongō Dōji 金剛童子. See *Taiheiki* 太平記, translation McCullough 1979, p. 12.

8 See for instance de Visser 1935, p. 518.

9 This statuette is said to be the same one that the Tendai priest Ennin 円仁 (794–864) had placed at the front of the boat to placate demons and appease a storm during his return trip from China in 847. It was finally enshrined at Zentōin 前唐院 on Mt. Hiei. See Nanri 1996, pp. 47–52; and Iyanaga 2003.

10 On this question, see Iyanaga 1983.

11 See *Tenjin engi* 天神縁起 (a.k.a. *Kangiten reigenki* 歓喜天霊験記), quoted in Nanri 1996, pp. 47–52.

12 Nanri Michiko argues that Michizane was a devotee of Vināyaka by emphasizing his relationship with the Tantric master Annen. See Nanri 1996, p. 49.

13 See for instance *Kakuzenshō*, vol. 6, p. 110b:

> He is called the "Demon who always follows" (*jōzuima*) because, unlike heavenly or earthly demons, he always follows sentient beings and looks for their weaknesses.

14 See Miyasaka 1977, vol. 2, pp. 27–31, quoted in Sanford 1991, p. 301.

15 See Kōyasan Reihōkan 2002, pp. 105, 168. See also Kōyasan Reihōkan 1994 (*Tenbu no shoson* 天部の諸尊, English title: Divine Figures in the Realm of Deva), Ill. 48. This painting is strikingly similar to a representation of Dakiniten riding a fox, in which one of the deity's lateral faces is that of Shōten (Ill. 41). See also *Keiran shūyōshū*, p. 853a.

16 According to tradition, the "Three Peaks" were the places where the Shingon priest Kūkai 空海 had borrowed the "wish-fulfilling jewels" (*nyoi hōju* 如意宝珠, Skt. *cintāmaṇi*). See *Keiran shūyōshū* (p. 631c) and Yamamoto 1993, p. 360. The Three Devas were also said to be the "traces" (*suijaku* 垂迹) or manifestations of the *cintāmaṇi* (*Keiran shūyōshū*, p. 853a). The fact that the Upper Shrine was formerly identified with Shōten may be related with the existence, today,

of a "Kōjin mound" (Kōjin-zuka 荒神塚) near the top of Mount Inari. On the
Three Devas in Shinto, see also *Jingi hishō* 神祇秘抄, pp. 394–95; Yamamoto
1993, p. 359; and Iyanaga 2002, p. 605.

17 See Seki 1987 (I owe this reference to the kindness of Robert Duquenne.)
See also *Shiojiri* 塩尻, p. 51.
18 On this notion, see Stone 1999.
19 Unfortunately, this text is no longer extant, but the passage in question is
quoted in *Kakuzenshō*, vol. 6, p. 135; *Asabashō*, vol. 9, p.174a. See also *Kangiten
reigenki*, quoted in Nanri 1996, pp. 47–52; and Iyanaga 2003, p. 155.
20 See "Kōjin engi" 荒神縁起 in *Shintō zōzōshū* (ms. of the Yamada Collection,
Tenri Library), text quoted in Yamamoto 1998, p. 345.
21 On this deity (or pair of deities), see Yamamoto 1998, pp. 345–47, 544–45.
22 See Bizot 1976 and 1992; and Sanford 1994.
23 This term remains unclear to me. Literally, the characters mean the "god who
stands and increases," a possible reference to a phallic deity, but they may also
be *ateji* being used to transcribed a Japanese name.
24 Text in the Sanzen-in Enjubō Collection, quoted in Yamamoto 1998, p. 352.
25 This Vināyaka is also called Kongōzai suiten 金剛摧碎天. See Mochizuki,
Bukkyō daijiten, p. 1325.
26 For an explicit identification, see Hattori Nyojitsu 1972, p. 98.
27 Cf. *Shugen shuyō hiketsu shū* 修験主要秘訣集, p. 368.
28 The normal sequence of *ubugami* and *enagami* seems reversed here.
29 On these Lads of Good and Evil, see Soymié 1966; on the *daṇḍa* staff, see
Seidel 2003, pp. 1113–22.
30 See Manabe 1999, pp. 157–82; and Manabe 2000, pp. 110–17.
31 See *Bikisho*, p. 509. Incidentally, Susanoo, the tumultuous brother of the sun-
goddess Amaterasu, is another paradigmatic manifestation of Kōjin.
32 On this text, see Pinnington 1998; Nakazawa 2003; and Susan Klein's
contribution to this book.
33 See Hattori 1974–75. It is perhaps relevant to note in this respect that in
India, Gaṇeśa is often represented with the Navagrahās (the Nine Planets).
On this point, see Yadav 1997, pp. 167–71.

References

Primary sources

Asabashō 阿娑縛抄, by Shōchō 承澄 (1205–82). In TZ, vols 8–9.
Bikisho 鼻帰書. In 眞言神道 2 (=ST, *Ronsetsu-hen* 2), 1993, pp. 505–21.
Jingi hishō 神祇秘抄. In Kokubungaku kenkyū shiryōkan 国文学研究資料館 (ed.),
  Shinpukuji zenpon sōkan 真福寺善本叢刊 (=*Chūsei Nihongi shū* 中世日本紀集, vol. 7).
  Tokyo: Rinsen Shoten, 1999.
Kakuzenshō 覚禅鈔, by Kakuzen 覚禅 (1143–1213), 7 vols. DNBZ 45–51.
Keiran shūyōshū 渓嵐拾葉集, by Kōshū 光宗 (1276–1350). In T 76.2410.
Meishuku shū 明宿集, by Konparu Zenchiku 金春禅竹. In Omote Akira 表章 and Katō
  Shūichi 加藤周一 (eds), *Zeami, Zenchiku* 世阿弥・禅竹 (=NST 24). 1974, pp. 399–416.
Shiojiri 塩尻, by Amano Sadakage 天野信景 (1661–1733). In *Nihon zuihitsu taisei*
  日本随筆大成, vol. 10. Tokyo: Kawase shoten, 1930.
Shugen seiten 修験聖典. In Shugen seiten hensankai 修験聖典編纂会 (ed.). Kyoto:
  Sanmitsudō Shoten, 1927.
Shugen shuyō hiketsu shū 修験主要秘訣集, in *Shugendō shōso* 修験道章疏, vol. 2.
  Tokyo: Meicho Shuppan, 1985. [[1]1917]

Modern sources

Amino Yoshihiko 網野善彦 (1993), *Igyō no ōken* 異形の王権. Tokyo: Heibonsha.

Berkson, Carmel (1986), *The Caves of Aurangabad: Early Buddhist Tantric Art in India*. New York: Mapin Internationala.

Bizot, François (1976), *Le Figuier à cinq branches: Recherche sur le bouddhisme khmer 1*. Paris: Ecole Française d'Extrême-Orient.

Bizot, François (1992), *Le Chemin de Lanka* (=Textes bouddhiques du Cambodge, 1). Paris: Ecole Française d'Extrême-Orient.

Courtright, Paul B. (1985), *Gaṇeśa: Lord of Obstacles, Lord of Beginnings*. New York: Oxford University Press.

de Visser, Marinus Willem (1935), *Ancient Buddhism in Japan: Sutras and Ceremonies*, 2 vols. Leyden-Paris.

Faure, Bernard (1999), "Relics, Regalia, and the Dynamics of Secrecy," in Eliot R. Wolfson (ed.), *Rending the Veil: Concealment and Secrecy in the History of Religions*. New York and London: Seven Bridges Press, pp. 271–88.

Faure, Bernard (2004), "Buddhist Relics and Japanese Regalia," in David Germano and Kevin Trainor (eds), *Embodying the Dharma: Buddhist Relic Veneration in Asia*. Albany: State University of New York Press, pp. 93–116.

Getty, Alice (1936), *Gaṇeśa: A Monograph on the Elephant-faced God*. Oxford: Clarendon Press.

Hattori Nyojitsu 服部如実 (ed.) (1972), *Shugendō yōten* 修験道要典. Kyoto: Sanmitsudō Shoten.

Hattori Yukio 服部幸雄 (1974–75), "Shukujin ron: geinōshin shinkō no kongen ni aru mono" 宿神論 – 芸能神信仰の根源に在るもの. *Bungaku* 文学 42/10 (1974), pp. 64–79; 43/1 (1975), pp. 54–63; 43/2 (1975), pp. 76–97.

Iyanaga Nobumi 彌永信美 (1983), "Daijizaiten" 大自在天. In *Hōbōgirin: Dictionnaire encyclopédique du bouddhisme d'après les sources chinoises et japonaises*, vol. 6. Paris: Adrien Maisonneuve, pp. 713–65.

Iyanaga Nobumi (1994), "Daikokuten" 大黒天. In *Hōbōgirin: Dictionaire encyclopédique du bouddhisme d'après les sources chinoises et japonaises*, vol. 7. Paris: Adrien Maisonneuve, pp. 839–920.

Iyanaga Nobumi (2002), *Daikokuten hensō* 大黒天変相. Kyoto: Hōzōkan.

Iyanaga Nobumi (2003), "The Logic of Combinatory Deities: Two Case Studies," in Mark Teeuwen and Fabio Rambelli (eds), *Buddhas and Kami in Japan: Honji suijaku as a Combinatory Paradigm*. London and New York: RoutledgeCurzon, pp. 153–55.

Kabanoff, Alexander (1984), "The Kangi-ten (Gaṇapati) Cult in Medieval Japanese Mikkyō," in Ian Astley (ed.), *Esoteric Buddhism in Japan*. Copenhagen and Aarus: The Seminar for Buddhist Studies 1, pp. 99–126.

Kōyasan Reihōkan 高野山霊宝館 (ed.) (1994), *Tenbu no shoson* 天部の諸尊. Kōya-machi: Kōyasan Reihōkan.

Kōyasan Reihōkan (ed.) (2002), *Sacred Treasures of Mount Koya: The Art of Japanese Shingon Buddhism*. Honolulu: Honolulu Academy of Arts.

McCullough, Helen Craig (tr.) (1979), *The Taiheiki: A Chronicle of Medieval Japan*. Rutland, Vermont and Tokyo: Charles E. Tuttle Company.

Manabe Shunshō 真鍋俊照 (1999), *Jakyō, Tachikawa-ryū* 邪教·立川流. Tokyo: Chikuma Shobō.

Manabe Shunshō (2000), "Shingon mikkyō to jakyō Tachikawa-ryū" 真言密教と邪教立川流. *Kokubungaku* 国文学 10, pp. 110–17.

Mauclaire, Simone (1992), "L'être, l'illusion et le pouvoir: Le complexe kōjin/ misaki selon un rituel de l'Ecole d'Izanagi, Tosa, Japon." *Journal Asiatique* 280/3-4, pp. 307-400.

Miyasaka Yūshō 宮坂宥勝 (1977), *Kōgyō daishi senjutsu shū* 興教大師撰述集, 2 vols. Tokyo: Sankibō Busshorin.

Mochizuki Shinkō 望月信亨 (ed.), *Bukkyō daijiten* 仏教大辞典 (3rd ed.). Tokyo: Sekai Seiten Kankōkai, 1958-63. [¹1909-12]

Nakazawa Shin'ichi 中沢新一 (2003), *Seirei no ō* 精霊の王. Tokyo: Kōdansha.

Nanri Michiko 南里みち子 (1996), *Onryō to shugen no setsuwa* 怨霊と修験の説話. Tokyo: Perikansha.

Pinnington, Noël (1998), "Invented Origins: Muromachi Interpretations of *Okina sarugaku.*" *Bulletin of the School of Oriental and African Studies* 61/3, pp. 492-518.

Rambelli, Fabio (2002), "Secret Buddhas: The Limits of Buddhist Representation." *Monumenta Nipponica* 57/3, pp. 271-307.

Sanford, James H. (1991), "Literary Aspects of Japan's Dual-Gaṇeśa Cult," in Robert L. Brown (ed.), *Ganesh: Studies of an Asian God*. Albany: State University of New York Press, pp. 287-335.

Sanford, James H. (1994), "Wind, Waters, Stupas, Mandalas: Fetal Buddhahood in Shingon." *Japanese Journal of Religious Studies* 24/1-2, pp. 1-38.

Sasama Yoshihiko 笹間良彦 (1989), *Kangiten (Shōten) shinkō to zokushin* 歓喜天(聖天) 信仰と俗信. Tokyo: Yūzankaku.

Seidel, Anna K. (2003), "Danda." In *Hōbōgirin: Dictionnaire encyclopédique du bouddhisme d'après les sources chinoises et japonaises* vol. 8. Paris: Adrien Maison-neuve, pp. 1113-22.

Seki Shōdō 關尚道 (1987), *Waga kuni ni okeru shōten shinkō* わが国における聖天信仰. Tokyo: Tōmyōji.

Soymié, Michel (1966), "Notes d'iconographie chinoise: les acolytes de Ti-tsang (1)." *Arts Asiatiques* 14, pp. 45-73.

Stein, Rolf (1962), *La civilisation tibétaine*. Paris: Dunod.

Stone, Jacqueline (1999), *Original Enlightenment and the Transformation of Medieval Japanese Buddhism* (=Kuroda Institute, Studies in East Asian Buddhism 12). Honolulu: University of Hawai'i Press.

Suzuki Masataka 鈴木正崇 (2001), *Kami to hotoke no minzokugaku* 神と仏の民俗学. Tokyo: Yoshikawa Kōbunkan.

Yadav, Nirmala (1997), *Gaṇeśa in Indian Art and Literature*. Jaipur: Publication Scheme.

Yamamoto Hiroko 山本ひろ子 (1993), *Henjōfu: chūsei shinbutsu shūgo no sekai* 変成譜 – 中世神仏習合の世界. Tokyo: Shunjūsha.

Yamamoto Hiroko (1998), *Ijin: chūsei Nihon no hikyō-teki sekai* 異神 – 中世日本の秘教的世界. Tokyo: Heibonsha.

Yamaori Tetsuo 山折哲雄 (1991), *Kami to okina no minzokugaku* 神と翁の民俗学. Tokyo: Kōdansha.

11 Myths, rites, and icons
Three views of a secret

Kadoya Atsushi

Introduction

From a modern viewpoint, based on rationalism and "objective" verification, medieval mythical narratives may seem illogical and invalid. Since people today are unfamiliar with the line of reasoning in such narratives, they criticize them as distorted. The works of medieval authors followed their own special logic or rationality. One of the reasons medieval texts are so difficult to understand is that they employ not only language, but also diagrams and descriptions of ceremonies. The figures and colors of the illustrations and the sounds and actions of the rituals stimulated the imagination. In order to understand the intentions of medieval authors, therefore, their writings must be examined imaginatively. Resemblance of form or similarity of sound was readily taken as an indication of common properties. Today, this kind of reasoning may seem like sophistry or mere punning, but to medieval authors it served as the most convincing means of rhetoric methodology. This paper will examine the "Ten Sacred Treasures," a set of imaginary objects of political and religious significance, to illustrate this type of medieval logic and to reveal some of the mechanisms that stood behind esoteric logic in medieval Shinto thought.

The Three Sacred Regalia

Almost everyone in Japan knows that the emperor (*tennō*) possesses Three Sacred Regalia (*sanshu no jingi* 三種神器), but nobody has seen them, perhaps not even the emperor himself. These Regalia prove the legitimacy of the emperor's sovereign power. They consist of the Yata no kagami (a mirror), the Kusanagi no tsurugi (a sword), and the Yasakani no magatama (a jewel). The *Nihon shoki* (720) records that the deity Amaterasu conferred these sacred treasures upon her grandson Ninigi, a forefather of the legendary first emperor Jinmu (*Nihon shoki* 1, p. 146). It is believed that they have since been passed down through generations of emperors and that these same objects are currently stored in the Imperial Palace. In ancient Japan, however, there was no clear notion of the *sanshu no jingi* as regalia. Moreover, the number of regalia was not clearly defined, some sources claiming two (mirror and sword; *Kogoshūi*, p. 27) and others claiming three (mirror, sword, and jewel; *Kojiki*, p. 127). It is also unknown what role the regalia played in ancient enthronement ceremonies. Documents of the period do not indicate a consensus that the Three Sacred Regalia proved the legitimacy of an emperor's sovereign power. In addition to the misconceptions in contemporary beliefs concerning the historical function of the regalia, documents also indicate that the surviving objects are actually not the originals supposedly entrusted to Emperor Jinmu. Over the centuries, the mirror was destroyed in a palace fire and the sword was lost in a sea battle. Both were replaced with replicas long before our modern era.

The term *sanshu no jingi* first appeared in medieval sources.[1] Specifically, the Three Regalia were referred to as *shinji* 神璽 (the jewel), *hōken* 宝劔 (the sword), and *naishidokoro* 内侍所 (the mirror). The characters *shinji* mean "holy jewel" or "holy seal," *hōken* means "precious sword," and *naishidokoro* is the name of the room where the mirror was enshrined. Debates about the *shinji*, *hōken*, and *naishidokoro* increased dramatically at the end of the Heian period (794–1192), when they began to be regarded as symbols of imperial legitimacy. It is certainly no coincidence that this was a time of crisis in the imperial rule. Thus, the sword's whereabouts became a problem after it sank into the sea with the young Emperor Antoku at the end of the Genpei wars (1180–85).[2] Likewise, in the Nanbokuchō era (1336–92), the possession of the Three Regalia was deemed critical in a dispute between two imperial lines over imperial legitimacy (*Jinnō shōtōki*, pp. 59–61). These events illustrate how in the medieval period, during which the sovereignty of the emperor was challenged by the rise of the warrior class and by conflicts over succession, the Three Sacred Regalia drew a great deal of attention.

On the other hand, during the periods in ancient times when imperial power enjoyed relative stability – and also during the Edo period (1600–1868), when emperors virtually disappeared from the stage of politics – the existence of the Three Sacred Regalia was of no particular significance, nor was their location. In other words, discussions about the Three Sacred Regalia are specific to the unstable medieval period. Although they became objects of great political import, in this essay I am interested in the "theological" proposition of the Sacred Regalia in the medieval period. To this end, I shall shift my attention to another set of regalia, related to the Three Regalia just discussed, that also occupied the medieval Shinto imagination.

The Ten Sacred Treasures

In tandem with the rise of the Three Regalia to political importance, a set of "Ten Sacred Treasures" (*jisshu shinpō* 十種神宝) was used to explain the legitimacy of Shinto. The concepts concerning these treasures are emblematic of medieval thought. However, neither of Japan's ancient mytho-historical texts, the *Kojiki* (712) and the *Nihon shoki* (720), contain descriptions of these Ten Treasures. They first appear in a tenth-century text called the *Sendai kuji hongi* 先代旧事本紀 (hereafter *Kuji hongi*).[3] In the medieval period, this text was believed to have been compiled by the prince Shōtoku Taishi (574–622),[4] and since he lived a hundred years before the compilation of the

Kojiki or *Nihon shoki*, people believed the *Kuji hongi* to be the first national history and to have more authority than the other texts.[5] While the *Kojiki* states that Sacred Regalia were passed down from Amaterasu to her grand-child Ninigi when he assumed the throne, the *Kuji hongi* claims that she gave Ten Sacred Treasures to her grandson Nigihayahi.[6] Nigihayahi is an ancestor of the house of Mononobe 物部. The *Kuji hongi*, therefore, places the Mononobe house at the beginning of the line of imperial succession, according it extreme import and honor. It is therefore assumed that this text was actually authored by a member of the Mononobe house.

In any event, the Ten Sacred Treasures undeniably derive from the Three Sacred Regalia. The stories about the origins of both the Treasures and the Regalia are nearly identical, but the characteristics of the Treasures and the Regalia differ. According to the *Kojiki* and *Nihon shoki*, Amaterasu bestowed two or three Sacred Regalia upon Ninigi. The texts provide no further details concerning their use or function.[7] The Ten Sacred Treas-ures, on the other hand, are described as magical implements given to the imperial house by *kami* deities, and as possessing or imparting magical powers. According to the *Kuji hongi* (ch. 3, p. 25) for example, one can revive the dead by shaking the treasures while reciting the spell *furue furue, yura yura to furue* ("shake, shake, sway, sway"). According to the same text, the *chinkonsai* 鎮魂祭 rite of the imperial court also originates from the treasures' magical function. The *chinkonsai* was held in the eleventh month (the winter solstice) in order to revive the spirits of the emperor and empress. In this ceremony, the Sarume no Kimi 猿女君 performs a *kagura* 神楽 dance and sings the words "one, two, three, four, five, six, seven, eight, nine, ten!" The *Kuji hongi* (ch. 5, pp. 58–59) claims that, since this spell is also recited during a ritual related to the Ten Treasures, the *kagura* performed during the *chinkonsai* derives from the tradition of the Ten Sacred Treasures. Thus the Mononobe author of the *Kuji hongi* used an actual ritual to add realistic attributes to his fictitious treasures, and his apocryphical myth increased the ritual's authority. When the Sarume no Kimi recited the sacred counting to ten, the invisible treasures performed their magic.

Safely stowed away in the court, the Three Sacred Regalia became, for all intents and purposes, invisible. The Ten Sacred Treasures, however, were so mysterious that nobody had ever seen them. Other than in the *Kuji hongi*, no testimony or evidence survives stating that the Ten Sacred Treasures actually existed anywhere. Although the Three Sacred Regalia may once have existed, from their inception the Ten Sacred Treasures were imaginary regalia, their substance being purely textual.

Diagrams of the Ten Sacred Treasures

The Ten Sacred Treasures consist of the following:

1   Oki tsu kagami 瀛都鏡
2   He tsu kagami 辺都鏡

3 Yatsuka no tsurugi 八握劔
4 Iku tama 生玉
5 Makaru tama 死玉
6 Taru tama 足玉
7 Chikaeshi no tama 道反玉
8 Hebi no hire 蛇比礼
9 Hachi no hire 蜂比礼
10 Shinamono no hire 品物比礼

(*Sendai kuji hongi* 3, p. 25)

Judging by the names of the treasures, we can visualize some of them as resembling mirrors (*kagami*) or jewels (*tama*), but the nature and shape of the *hire* is less evident. A *hire* is thought to be a scarf-like piece of cloth used for sweeping away poisonous vermin such as snakes or hornets.[8] The

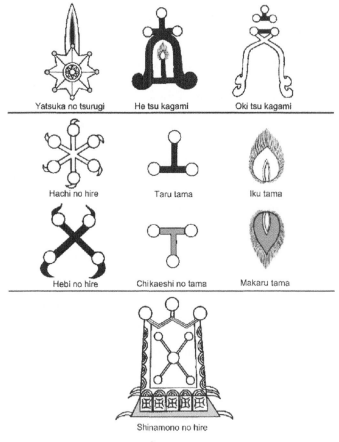

Figure 11.1 Jisshu shinpō zu[9] (Reproduction by courtesy of the Shibunkaku Suppansha, Kyoto.)

fourteenth-century Tendai priest Jihen 慈遍, in his *Kogo ruiyō shū* 古語類要集, also seems to have interpreted the *hire* as a kind of cloth. His text contains illustrations that depict the Hebi no hire and Hachi no hire as objects made of sashes or ribbons (see fig. 11.4). However, the true form of the Ten Treasures cannot be ascertained, for nobody has ever seen them.

In addition to Jihen's text, in the medieval period various other explanations of the Ten Sacred Treasures evolved, many treating the treasures as if they had material substance. The source of these interpretations is thought to be the *Jisshu shinpō zu* 十種神宝図 (Diagrams of the Ten Sacred Treasures), which also includes diagrams of the Sacred Treasures (Fig. 11.1).[10] While the traditional attribution to Kūkai 空海 (774–835) is certainly apocryphal, it is not clear exactly when the *Jisshu shinpō zu* was written or who authored it. We may assume, however, that it originated in the late twelfth or early thirteenth century. At the end of the text a colophon claims that Kūkai sketched the diagrams directly from the original Ten Sacred Treasures in the treasure house of the Ise shrine. A variant explanation was that Kūkai drew the diagrams based on Shōtoku Taishi's *Kuji hongi*. The apocryphal *Jisshu shinpō zu* bases its authority upon another apocryphal text, the *Kuji hongi*. Thus, two texts with highly improbable origin hypotheses record and authenticate the existence of the Ten Treasures. In their legacy, large numbers of counterfeit texts and documents were composed during the medieval period. Among the various supposed authors of these works, Kūkai and Shōtoku Taishi were by far the most popular and authoritative.

The Sacred Treasures as characters

The meaning contained in the graphic representations of the Ten Treasures can only be understood if we relate them to the mysterious descriptions of the individual objects, which further stress their symbolic importance. To decipher their meaning, we must consult medieval explanations. Two important annotations of the *Reikiki* 麗気記,[11] the *Tenchi reiki furoku* 天地麗気府録[12] and the *Reiki kikigaki* 麗気聞書,[13] describe the Ten Sacred Treasures in detail. According to these texts, the two mirrors, two jewels, and two *hire* express the meanings of certain Chinese characters. *Tenchi reiki furoku* writes,

> Oki tsu kagami represents the character for "heaven" 天. He tsu kagami represents "large" 大 or, alternately, "earth" [地 in the *Reiki kikigaki*]. Taru tama represents the "father's body," and is also indicated by the character "upwards" 上. Chikaeshi no tama represents the mother's body, and is also indicated by the character for "downwards" 下. Hebi no hire becomes the character "water" 水 and represents purity, based on the color white. Hachi no hire originates from the character for "fire" 火 and is of red hue.
>
> (*Tenchi reiki furoku*, pp. 130–31)

The Chinese characters for "heaven," "large," "upwards," "downwards," "water," and "fire" are all ideographs rather than mere symbols. In these texts, they are purported to represent essences. For example, the graphical form of the Hebi no hire resembles the character for "water," indicating that this treasure enables access to water in all of its manifestations: its cooling properties, its tendency to pour downwards, its protean qualities, and so on. The forms of such Chinese characters as "heaven" or "water" do not express concrete objects as much as abstract principles. Moreover, the characters associated with the Ten Treasures come in matched sets with opposing attributes: heaven and earth, upwards and downwards, and water and fire.

Intriguingly, the shapes of these treasures do indeed resemble examples of Kūkai's writing. Famous as a master calligrapher, Kūkai had learned various styles of handwriting that could express, he felt, the inner essence of certain characters. The generic name he assigned to these styles was *zattaisho* 雑体書 (miscellaneous writing styles). They include scripts derived from such forms as birds' footprints, cranes' heads, dragons' talons, and so on. Characters in an inscription on a monument at Masuda pond 益田池 (Fig. 11.2), written in Kūkai's hand, closely resemble the shapes of Oki tsu kagami and He tsu kagami as represented in the *Jisshu shinpō zu* (Fig. 11.1). Thus we can see how diagrams of the Ten Sacred Treasures achieved symbolic meaning and function through their association with calligraphic forms. The person who drew these diagrams must have known the calligraphy of Kūkai. As mentioned above, legend relates that the *Jisshu shinpō zu* was authored by Kūkai. His putative authorship lent the text authority, as with so many other medieval texts, but in this case it also increased the power assigned to the "magical" characters illustrated therein. Although nonexistent, by utilizing the potency of the Chinese characters of the elements, the Ten Sacred Treasures acquired universal, transcendent qualities.

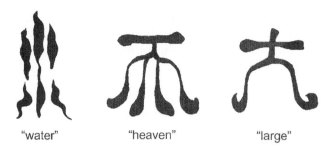

"water"　　　　　"heaven"　　　　　"large"

Figure 11.2 Kūkai's calligraphy in the inscription on a monument at Masuda pond[14] (Reproduction by courtesy of the Kyoto National Museum.)

The Ten Sacred Treasures and the Three Sacred Regalia

The relationship between the Three Sacred Regalia and the Ten Sacred Treasures was also an important theme in medieval Shinto thought. Of the Ten Treasures, the *tsurugi* (sword) seems to correspond to one of the Three Regalia, but as the Ten Treasures include more than one *kagami* (mirror) and *tama* (jewel), questions inevitably arose about the correlations between the two sets of regalia. The priest Jihen tackled this problem in his *Kuji hongi gengi* 旧事本紀玄義 (a commentary on the *Kuji hongi* from ca. 1332). According to this text, the Ten Sacred Treasures are transformations of the Three Sacred Regalia: the Yasakani no magatama was divided into four jewels, namely Ikutama, Makarutama, Tarutama, Chikaeshi no tama; the Kusanagi no tsurugi transformed into the Yatsuka no tsurugi and the two *hire*, Hachi no hire and Hebi no hire; and the Yata no kagami was manifested in the two mirrors, Oki tsu kagami and He tsu kagami (*Kuji hongi gengi* 9, p. 75–96). Jihen explained that *hire* was a synonym for *hari* (stinger or needle), so these were transformations of the sword.

Where did the idea of equating *hire* with *hari* come from? This part of our puzzle can only be solved by locating similar equations in other texts. In fact, another work dealing with the Ten Sacred Treasures, the *Shinpō zugyō shinpi sho* 神宝図形神秘書 (Secret Book of Diagrams of the Sacred Treasures) depicts the Hebi no hire and Hachi no hire as resembling spearheads (Fig. 11.3). This diagram suggests that Jihen's interpretation of the *hire* as a *hari* became a means to reconcile the two systems. It is not clear exactly when the *Shinpō zugyō shinpi sho* was written,[15] and other books illustrating the diagrams of the *hire* and *hari* in the same manner have not surfaced. Without further research we cannot, therefore, determine which came first, the diagrams or Jihen's text, but a relationship between these diagrams and texts is undeniable. The sword-like image of the *hire* puts the two sets of regalia or treasures into perfect mutual correspondence. As Jihen wrote, "although the Three and the Ten are different, they unite and disunite flexibly." (*Kuji hongi gengi*, p. 83.) This kind of logic is typical of medieval thought; nothing hinders the transformation, multiplication, or division of these objects.

Shinamono no hire   Hachi no hire   Hebi no hire

Figure 11.3 Hire in the *Shinpō zugyō shinpi sho*[16] (Reproduction by courtesy of Kōgakkan University, Mie Prefecture.)

There remains, however, a problem with the last of the ten treasures, the Shinamono no hire. According to Jihen, it incorporates the other nine treasures, and as they are transformations of the Three Sacred Regalia (*Kuji hongi gengi*, p. 83), his conclusion is that the Shinamono no hire represents the Three Regalia. This view is repeated in the *Reiki kikigaki* (p. 237), which states in its definition of the Shinamono no hire: "This is a supreme secret: the first nine [treasures] compose one [crown]. The emperor wears [this crown] when he ascends the throne." Likewise, Jihen wrote: "Using the Shinamono no hire, the emperor governs the three realms [of heaven, earth, and human beings] vertically. He also rules everything in the seas of the four directions [i.e. the entire world] horizontally." (*Kuji hongi gengi*, p. 85.). We can see that the Shinamono no hire became a symbol of sovereignty, conceived as a kind of super-regalia that transcended the original Three Sacred Regalia. Thus, medieval Shinto apparently created a "Fourth Regale" pertaining to the throne.

The Sacred Treasures in the enthronement initiation

The above discussion leads to reflection upon why the Shinamono no hire took the shape of a crown. Medieval Shinto accorded special significance to the Shinamono no hire during the imperial enthronement initiation rites called *sokui kanjō* 即位潅頂.[17] Emperors performed this esoteric Buddhist rite from the late Heian through the Edo periods. The Emperor formed a mudra with his hands and recited a mantra while seated on the throne, and was thus bestowed sovereignty by Buddha Mahāvairocana (Dainichi). There are, however, differences concerning the mudra and mantra depending on the transmission lineage of this rite. A description kept at the Shingon temple Tōji, for example, states that the wisdom-fist mudra (*chiken-in* 智拳印) and the Ḍākinī mantra are to be employed, while other Shingon lineages used the mudra of "rule over the four seas" (*shikai ryōshō-in* 四海領掌印). According to a legend associated with a lineage of the Daigoji temple (which is discussed in more detail in Mark Teeuwen's essay in this book), the wisdom-fist mudra was introduced by Kūkai, while the mudra of rule over the four seas was bequeathed by Amaterasu.[18] The *sokui kanjō* enthronement initiation was therefore alternatively known as "the method of rule over the four seas" (*shikai ryōshō hō* 四海領掌法). This explains Jihen's statement that "the Shinamono no hire rules the seas of the four directions" (*Kuji hongi gengi*, p. 83). Moreover, as we saw in the *Reiki kikigaki* passage cited before, the emperor was said to "wear [the Shinamono no hire] when he ascends the throne" (*Reiki kikigaki*, p. 237). The Shinamono no hire, therefore, clearly symbolized the emperor's enthronement.

Buddhist consecration rituals purportedly originated from the enthronement ceremonies of ancient Indian kings. We shall now explore how medieval Japanese enthronement ceremonies restored this imperial function to such Buddhist rituals. In diagrams the Shinamono no hire resembles a crown, but there is no documentary evidence indicating that Japanese emperors actually wore any such headdresses during enthronement ceremonies. There are, however, crowns used in pre-modern esoteric Buddhist initiation rituals that closely resemble illustrations of the Shinamono no hire.[19] The Shinamono no hire is illustrated with three round mirrors (indicating the heavenly, earthly, and human realms) on the top, and has a fin-like trimming on the sides. It is quite possible that this shape of the Shinamono no hire was based on that of crowns used in esoteric Buddhist initiations. The Shinamono no hire was connected with the emperor's sovereignty by the imperial enthronement initiation rites.

The Sacred Treasures as a mandala

The design of the Shinamono no hire contains yet another layer of meaning; the decorative patterns on the crown resemble the so-called *gogyōmon* 御形文 patterns that adorn the shrines of Ise.

In Jihen's drawings in the *Kogo ruiyō shū* (pp. 395–96, Fig. 11.4), captions for the particular patterns inside the Shinamono no hire read: "Gekū 外宮 *gogyōmon*, Naikū 内宮 *gogyōmon*." Gekū is Ise's Outer Shrine and Naikū is Ise's Inner Shrine, so there is an explicit connection to Ise. The *gogyōmon* are decorative patterns made by studs nailed into the gables of both Ise shrines (cf. Kadoya 1996). According to legend, when Yamato-hime 倭姫 first built the shrines in Ise, she carved "a symbol of the Brahmā Palace (Bongū 梵宮) in the Plain of High Heaven (Takamagahara 高天原)" on the gables (*Shinkō jitsuroku*, p. 167). This symbol of the Heavenly Brahma Palace can be nothing else than the *gogyōmon* patterns indicating that the Ise

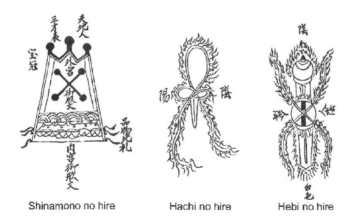

Shinamono no hire   Hachi no hire   Hebi no hire

Figure 11.4 Hire Treasures according to Jihen's *Kogo ruiyō shū* (Reproduction by courtesy of Shintōtaikei hensan kai.)

shrine is Amaterasu's palace on earth. Their symmetrical designs decorate T-shaped square planks on both sides of the central pillars. There are two types of *gogyōmon*, one for each shrine. Both consist of square units, but at the Outer Shrine these are composed of five studs arranged like the number five on a domino or a dice, while at the Inner Shrine they are composed of two crescent shapes, arranged back to back (Figs 11.5 and 11.6). If we compare these designs to those decorating the Shinamono no hire (Figs 11.1 and 11.4), we can see the dice-like five dots in the middle of the crown and the double arcs along its edges. This is what Jihen's captions indicate. By conjecture we may say that the Shinamono no hire represents both shrines of Ise.

Furthermore, according to the esoteric interpretations of Ryōbu Shinto 両部神道, the Inner and Outer Shrines of Ise correspond to the mandala representations of the universe, the Womb and Vajra mandalas respectively. In this theoretical system, Amaterasu is identified with the Buddha Mahāvairocana (Dainichi), the main deity of both mandalas. Consequently, the shrines of Ise represent the two esoteric mandalas, the universal Buddha Mahāvairocana and the palace of Amaterasu. An emperor who wears the Shinamono no hire crown with its *gogyōmon* patterns places both Ise shrines on his head, enabling him to reign over the entire universe. The wearer of the crown becomes both the universal Buddha Mahāvairocana

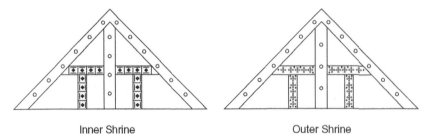

Inner Shrine   Outer Shrine

Figure 11.5 The two *gogyōmon*[20] patterns of Ise shrine (Adapted from drawings by the author.)

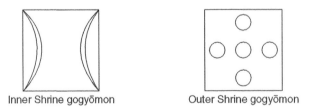

Inner Shrine gogyōmon   Outer Shrine gogyōmon

Figure 11.6 The units of the *gogyōmon* (Adapted from drawings by the author.)

and Amaterasu. According to this layer of meaning, the Shinamono no hire becomes a symbol of the medieval throne as authorized by both the buddhas and the kami.

The end of the Sacred Treasures

In the fifteenth century, the Shinto polemicist Yoshida Kanetomo 吉田兼俱 (1435–1511) discussed the Three Sacred Regalia and the Ten Sacred Treasures in his work *Yuiitsu shintō myōbō yōshū* 唯一神道名法要集. He argued,

> There is a distinction between the provisional (*gon* 権) and the real (*jitsu* 実), but there is no distinction between superior (*shō* 勝) and inferior (*retsu* 劣) [...] The Ten Sacred Treasures are the provisional but represent the real. The Three Sacred Regalia are the real and acquire the provisional.[21]

In this treatise, he did not declare the "three" to be superior to the "ten," but he made a clear distinction between the two sets of regalia/treasures. Since he defined the "ten" as "provisional," he laid the foundations for a debate about the materiality of the Ten Treasures. After the fifteenth century, the power assigned to the Ten Treasures declined. Kanetomo reorganized the theoretical framework of Shinto as it had developed during the medieval period. He systematized the various Shinto rituals and adjusted them to accord with his new theories – including those about the provisional quality of the Ten Treasures. As a result, the Ten Sacred Treasures were divorced from the legends of Amaterasu and dissociated from the symbolism we have been examining.

In the early modern period, complicated esoteric explanations of the Ten Treasures ceased. While the logic in operation during the medieval period was one of integration, later ages were more concerned with analysis. For example, in a seventeenth-century text of Miwa-ryū Shinto (*Miwa-ryū shintō kanjō hoshin shō* 三輪流神道灌頂補真抄, written in 1673), each of the Three Regalia was split into three objects, belonging to one of three abstract categories: wisdom (*chi* 智), principle (*ri* 理), and phenomenon (*ji* 事). As a result of this analysis, the Sacred Regalia were divided into material and spiritual categories, the material regalia being assigned no more value than that of ordinary objects. For example, the jewel corresponding to the category of "wisdom" was determined to be that mentioned in the legend of *Nihon shoki*: the jewel that Amaterasu gave to her grandson Ninigi. The jewel of "principle" had a religious nature. It was defined as that which nurtured all living things and was represented by a one-pronged vajra (*tokko* 独鈷). A picture of this jewel was hung on the wall during Miwa-ryū initiation rituals. Lastly, the jewel of the category "phenomenon" was the real, physical jewel that had been passed down through generations of emperors and was stored at the imperial court. Thus the wisdom jewel represented mythology, the principle jewel represented doctrine, and the phenomenon jewel represented the material object. The author then compared the Three Sacred Regalia to the Ten Sacred Treasures and concluded that the former were superior. When the son of Nigihayahi and Emperor Jinmu fought over the throne, they compared their sacred treasures with the result that the Three Sacred Regalia ultimately defeated the Ten Sacred Treasures. Therefore, Amaterasu summoned the deities and poured water from the four seas onto the Emperor Jinmu's head.

Likewise, in the seventeenth century *Miwa monogatari* 三輪物語, the famous Confucianist Kumazawa Banzan 熊沢蕃山 (1619–91) described the mirror, jewel, and sword as symbols of wisdom (*chi* 智), humanity (*jin* 仁), and courage (*yū* 勇), respectively. In these explanations, the emperor does not have legitimacy to rule merely because he possesses the regalia; rather, he is qualified to receive the regalia because he is equipped with the attributes of a king: wisdom, virtue, and courage (*Miwa monogatari* 3, p. 55). For Banzan, the Sacred Regalia were simply symbols of Confucian ethics.

As a result, in the early modern and modern eras the regalia themselves came to be worth less than their corresponding virtues. Accordingly, the Ten Sacred Treasures – creations of "irrational" medieval logic – were completely forgotten. The Three Sacred Regalia, on the other hand, were reduced to merely symbolic objects, no longer of vital interest to the public or even to people involved in matters of imperial legitimacy.

Conclusion: Myth, rite, and icon

As we have seen, the Ten Sacred Treasures were linked to various factors in the medieval period. These included myths about the enthronement of Amaterasu's grandson, the symbolism of Chinese characters, the establishment of sovereign power through imperial initiation rituals, and symbolic representations of the palace of Amaterasu. These mythological, symbolic, and ritual elements were woven into a complicated tapestry that gave rise to various explanations. This paper demonstrates how only a close examination of the intersection of myth, rite, and icon in the medieval religious imagination makes the unraveling of secrets that surrounded the Ten Sacred Treasures possible.

I have attempted to explain the logic behind certain medieval explanations of mystical matters. This logic was constructed using a range of different languages. In the case we have examined, "language" refers not only to words, but also to the language of movement (the actions performed during rituals), visual language (illustrations and schemas), and symbolic language (signs or spells). These various languages were connected and used to formulate arguments. In this synthetic logic, objects were not necessarily substantial; the world was also composed of and affected by imaginary things. The Ten Sacred Treasures were imaginary objects produced by language that then became the basis for a new logic and new ideas.

Speaking metaphorically, where modern thought is carved into stone, medieval thought was built up from clay. Modern people reveal the "truth" from extant materials. We analyze, dissect, and compare those materials, working to isolate and cast away falsehoods, counterfeits, and fictions. Medieval thinkers, however, connected, integrated, and superimposed, as if adding clay to a sculpture. Words were connected to other words by sounds, and images were superimposed upon other images by rituals. In the creative technologies of medieval thought, all "languages" were of equal value in understanding the world.[22]

Notes

1 In the *Nihon shoki* (vol. 1, p. 146) they are called simply *mikusa no takara* 三種宝物 (three treasures).
2 See for instance *Gukanshō* 5, pp. 263–66.
3 *Sendai kuji hongi*, ch. 3 "Tenjin hongi" 天神本紀, in SZKT 7, p. 25.
4 According to the preface of *Kuji hongi*, Shōtoku Taishi commanded Soga no Umako to compile old documents to a history.
5 *Kuji hongi* was believed to be the first text of national history until the eighteenth century.
6 In the *Nihon shoki*, Nigihayahi is not the grandson of Amaterasu. He descended from heaven before Ninigi and married a sister of Nagasunehiko. *Nihon shoki* 1, pp. 208–10.
7 In the *Nihon shoki*, Amaterasu told her son to "look at the mirror as you look at me." *Nihon shoki* 1, p. 152.
8 In the *Kojiki*, Ōkuninushi used *hire* to sweep away snakes, centipedes, and hornets (*Kojiki*, p. 97).
9 *Jiun Sonja zenshū* 10, pp. 772–78. These illustrations are based on an Edo period manuscript.
10 *Kōbō daishi zenshū* 5, pp. 183–87. The version of *Jisshu shinpō zu* published in the *Kōbō daishi zenshū* is based on an Edo-period print that is in poor condition. I therefore consulted the plates in the *Jiun Sonja zenshū* instead.
11 For research on the *Reikiki*, see Shinbutsu Shūgō Kenkyukai 2001.
12 This text was written before 1320.
13 This text is a transcription of lectures on the *Reikiki* by Ryōhen 良遍, held in 1419.
14 The inscription on the monument at Masuda pond in Yamato survived as a copy from the eleventh century, now stored at Shakabun-in on Mt. Kōya. This was shown in a special exhibition "Treasures of a Sacred Mountain: Kukai and Mount Koya" (Kyoto National Museum, 2003). The pictures here are taken from the catalogue of this exhibition.
15 For an in-depth discussion on the authorship and dating of this text, see Mure Hitoshi (2000). Though Mure accepts the dating of 1176 given in a notation at the end of the document, I have my doubts. This explanation for *hari* seems anachronistic for this early date.

16 Cf. Mure 2000, p. 191.
17 On the imperial enthronement initiation ceremony, see Kamikawa Michio 1989, Matsumoto Ikuyo 2001, 2004a, 2004b, and 2004c, or Mark Teeuwen's essay in this book.
18 For a detailed description of the respective mudras and mantras see Matsumoto 2004c.
19 For example, among the implements used in consecration rituals (*kanjō*) in the Ryūkoin 龍光院 monastery's collection, there is a collapsible square crown composed of four metal plates. The top of the front plate is engraved with an image of the Buddha Mahāvairocana and ribbons are attached to both sides of the crown. See the catalogue of the special exhibition "Treasures of a Sacred Mountain: Kukai and Mount Koya" (2003).
20 See Kadoya 1996.
21 *Yuiitsu shintō myōbō yōshū*, pp. 219–20. For a further discussion of the text, see Scheid 2000.
22 Bernard Faure called this "correlative thinking" in his resume in the Evans–Wentz Lectureship "Buddhist Priests, Kings, and Marginals" at Stanford University, 1999. A translation of the resume into Japanese can be found on Nobumi Iyanaga's website: Bernard Faure, "Nyoini to gyokunyo" (http://www.bekkoame.ne.jp/~n-iyanag/articles/Faure_paper_resume.html, 04/12/20). Also see Faure 2002–03.

References

Primary sources

Gukanshō 愚管抄, by Jien 慈円. NKBT 86, 1967.
Jinnō shōtōki 神皇正統記, by Kitabatake Chikafusa 北畠親房. NKBT 87, 1965.
Jisshu shinpō zu 十種神宝図, attrib. Kūkai. In KDZ 5, pp. 183–87; *Jiun Sonja zenshū* 慈雲尊者全集, vol. 10. Kyoto: Shibunkaku Suppan, 1976, pp. 772–78.
Kogo ruiyō shū 古語類要集, by Jihen 慈遍. In *Tendai shintō* 天台神道 1 (=ST, *Ronsetsu-hen* 3), 1990.
Kogoshūi 古語拾遺, by Inbe no Hironari 斎部広成. In Nishimiya Kazutami 西宮一民 (ed.). Tokyo: Iwanami Shoten (Iwanami bunko), 1985.
Kojiki 古事記. NKBT 1, 1958.
Kuji hongi gengi 旧事本紀玄義, by Jihen 慈遍. In *Tendai shintō* 1 (=ST, *Ronsetsu-hen* 3), 1990, pp. 3–98.
Miwa monogatari 三輪物語, by Kumazawa Banzan (1619–91). In *Kumazawa Banzan* 熊沢蕃山 (=ST, *Ronsetsu-hen* 21), 1992.
Miwa-ryū shintō kanjō hoshin shō 三輪流神道潅頂補真抄. In *Shingon shintō* 真言神道 2 (=ST, *Ronsetsu-hen* 2), 1993, pp. 130–33.
Nihon shoki 日本書紀, vol. 1. NKBT 67, 1967.
Reiki kikigaki 麗気聞書, by Ryōhen 良遍. In *Shingon shintō* 1 (=ST, *Ronsetsu-hen* 1), 1992, pp. 213–74.
Reikiki 麗気記. In *Shingon shintō* 1 (=ST, *Ronsetsu-hen* 1), 1992, pp. 3–117.
Sendai kuji hongi 先代旧事本紀, SZKT 7.
Shinkō jitsuroku 神皇実録. In *Ise shintō* 1 (=ST, *Ronsetsu-hen* 5), 1982.

Tenchi reiki furoku 天地麗気府録. In *Shingon shintō* 1 (=ST, *Ronsetsu-hen* 1), 1992, pp. 121–50.

Yuiitsu shintō myōbō yōshū 唯一神道名法要集, by Yoshida Kanetomo 吉田兼倶. In *Chūsei shintō ron* 中世神道論 (=NST 19), 1967, pp. 210–51.

Modern sources

Faure, Bernard (2002–03), "Une perle rare: la 'nonne' Nyoi et l'ideologie medievale." *Cahiers d'Extrême-Asie* 13, pp. 177–96.

Kadoya Atsushi 門屋温 (1996), "Ise *gogyōmon kō* 伊勢「御形文」考, in Sugahara Shinkai 菅原信海 (ed.), *Shinbutsu shūgō shisō no tenkai* 神仏習合思想の展開. Tokyo: Kyūko Shoin.

Kamikawa Michio 上川通夫 (1989), "Chūsei no sokui girei to bukkyō" 中世の即位儀礼と佛教, in *Tennō daigawari gishiki no rekishiteki tenkai* 天皇代替り儀式の歴史的展開. Tokyo: Kashiwa shobō.

Kyoto National Museum (2003), *Treasures of a Sacred Mountain: Kukai and Mount Koya*. Osaka: NHK Ōsaka Hōsōkyoku.

Matsumoto Ikuyo 松本郁代 (2001), "Chūsei Tōji o meguru rekishi jojutsu to ōken shinwa" 中世東寺をめぐる歴史叙述と王権神話. *Nihon bungaku* 50/9 (579), pp. 11–19.

Matsumoto Ikuyo (2004a), "Shingon mikkyōkai ni okeru 'teiō' no isō – shingon-kata sokui hō o megutte" 真言密教界における「帝王」の位相－真言方即位法をめぐって. *Nihon bungaku* 53/2 (608).

Matsumoto Ikuyo (2004b), "Daigoji sanpōinryū sokuihō to ōtō no bunritsu" 醍醐寺三宝院流の即位法と王統分立. *Bukkyō bungaku* 28, pp. 90–100.

Matsumoto Ikuyo (2004c), "Chūsei no sokuikanjō to 'tennō' – shingon-kata sokui hō ni okeru sokui inmyō no kōsō" 中世の即位灌頂と「天皇」－真言方即位法における即位印明の構想. *Ritsumeikan bungaku* 585, pp. 42–73.

Mure Hitoshi 牟礼仁 (2000), *Chūsei shintō setsu keiseiron kō* 中世神道説形成論考, Mie: Kōgakkan Daigaku Shuppanbu.

Scheid, Bernhard (2000), "Reading the *Yuiitsu Shintō myōbō yōshū*," in John Breen and Mark Teeuwen (eds), *Shinto in History: Ways of the Kami*. Richmond: Curzon Press, pp. 117–43.

Shinbutsu Shūgō Kenkyūkai 神仏習合研究会 (2001), *Reikiki – Kōchū, kaishaku, gendaigoyaku* 麗気記—校註・解釈・現代語訳. Tokyo: Hōzōkan.

12 Two modes of secrecy in the *Nihon shoki* transmission

Bernhard Scheid

In this essay, I will focus on the transmission of one of the most treasured sources of Japanese mythology that is, at the same time, one of the oldest extant written texts of Japan, the *Nihon shoki* 日本書紀 (Chronicles of Japan), also known as *Nihongi* 日本紀, compiled by Prince Toneri and Ō no Yasumaru in 720. The text was already translated into German and English in the late nineteenth century, and it has been meticulously studied by both Japanese and Western scholars. However, my attention will not be directed to the text itself, but to its fate in the so-called medieval period. In particular, I shall focus on the *textpflege*[1] of this mytho-historical document, that is the manner in which it was kept alive and meaningful in spite of changing cultural and linguistic conditions. This *textpflege* of the *Nihon shoki* shall serve as a paradigmatic case of the relationship between secrecy and knowledge in medieval Japan.

I will first discuss a stage at the beginning of the medieval period when the *Nihon shoki* was embedded in a "philological" transmission that not only saved it from falling into oblivion but also "protected" it from unwanted readership. Studying and teaching the *Nihon shoki* became the responsibility of scholar-priests, who were at the same time careful to keep their knowledge within the confines of their own family. They monopolized the "possession" of the text and tried to ensure that almost no one else had access to the original manuscripts nor learned the "correct" way to read them. This monopolization of knowledge will be the first type of secrecy to be analyzed in this essay.

The second type refers to what may be called the esoteric exegesis of mythology. As we will see, there was much more secrecy on the rhetoric level in this case, but on the practice level, the confinement to a single lineage was actually more loose. Thus, while there was more talking about secrecy, the purpose was no longer only to exclude others from a valuable source of symbolic capital, but to increase the symbolic capital by creating an ever-growing community of insiders, consisting of those who were initiated into the secret. In other words, secrecy became important as a means of religious propaganda, in contrast to its older function as a kind of "copyright protection."

In the main body of the essay, I will demonstrate how this shift can be detected within a certain genre of texts in one priestly lineage by analyzing this lineage's discourse on mythology. To introduce this analysis, I shall briefly describe the historical setting of this priestly lineage, the *Nihon shoki* and its *textpflege*.

Historical setting

As is commonly known, one of the unique features of Japanese history lies in the fact that the dynasty of the Tenno continued to hold an exalted rank even after it lost political authority at the beginning of the medieval period. In fact, not only the Tenno but also the courtiers (*kuge*) around him upheld their hereditary roles and kept their courtly functions, while the court as a whole gradually shifted from the execution of political power to the management of ritual and symbolic signification. The bestowment of titles on the new ruling elites of the "warrior houses" (*buke*) is perhaps the most telling example of the enduring imperial authority in this respect, but this authority can be seen also in the regulation of the calendar and the establishment of era names (*nengō*), which were still the task of the court. Last but not least, a good deal of scholarship, particularly on historical and ritual matters, remained the prerogative of several *kuge* lineages. The transmission of the *Nihon shoki* was one example of this kind of court expertise.

In the medieval period, the *Nihon shoki* was considered the last of the three ancient chronicles of the country. The other two were the *Kojiki* 古事記 (Chronicles of Ancient Matters, 712) and the *Kuji hongi* 旧事本紀 (Original Chronicles of Ancient Matters, also known by its full title *Sendai kuji hongi*, or as *Kujiki*), which came to be regarded as apocryphal only in the Edo period.[2] Before the Edo period, however, the *Kuji hongi*'s attribution to Shōtoku Taishi (d. 622) went uncontested. While the *Nihon shoki* appeared therefore newer than the other texts, it was, at least by some, considered more important than the other two. In the first place, this was due to its position as the first of six imperial histories (*rikkokushi*), thus granting it official appeal. Moreover, while all three texts cover similar subjects, the *Nihon shoki* is more extensive than the other two and in many respects closer to Chinese models of imperial historiography. It is for this reason that many Nativist scholars of the Edo period, as for instance Motoori Norinaga (1730–1801), preferred the *Kojiki* because they considered it more authentic than the *Nihon shoki* text. Before the Nativist movement (*kokugaku* 国学), however, both the *Nihon shoki* and the *Kuji hongi* were given preference over the *Kojiki*. Much of the transmitted knowledge about the *Nihon shoki* was based on the scholarly tradition of the Urabe 卜部 family members, who established themselves as experts on ancient native philology at some point in the thirteenth century.

Two phases of Urabe history

The long history of the courtly lineage of the Urabe can be divided into two distinct phases. The first phase starts in the mid-Heian period and covers the family's slow but steady rise from comparatively low-ranking diviners at the Heian court to the main executors of religious court ceremony in the Kamakura and Muromachi periods. This development is illustrated by the increase in court rank of family members within the Jingi-kan 神祇官, the office for matters concerning kami, at the imperial court.[3] The apex of this phase was reached in the early fifteenth century. It seems that by that time, the Urabe of the Jingi-kan were only surpassed by nominal supervisors of imperial pedigree. The other two families involved in Jingi-kan business, the Nakatomi 中臣 and the Inbe 忌部, were still active as well, but the Urabe outranked them in terms of ritual expertise. In this capacity, they also came into "possession" of the *Nihon shoki* transmission, which certainly meant a great increase in status when compared to their original standing as court diviners. In both roles, literary experts and diviners, they employed secrecy to protect their "possession": knowledge of divination techniques as well as knowledge about the correct readings and meanings of the *Nihon shoki* text gradually took the form of a secret canon that was kept strictly within the confines of the lineage. Under the regime of the Urabe, the original text of the *Nihon shoki* was therefore only disclosed to specific members of the nobility in the form of special lectures.

This phase of Urabe history ended with the physical destruction of the imperial palace during the violent disturbances of the Ōnin and Bunmei eras (1467–77), which marked the beginning of the "warring states" period and at the same time the nadir of imperial authority.

Faced with the utter obliteration of his family tradition and its cultural environment (in particular the Jingi-kan), Yoshida Kanetomo 吉田兼倶 (1435–1511), the most famous scion of the Urabe lineage, set out to restore his family's body of transmissions and thereby initiated the second phase of Urabe history. In particular, he directed his energies to the restoration of the Jingi-kan. Much of the new theological system that Kanetomo created can be explained as an attempt to base the Jingi-kan exclusively on the traditions of the Urabe and to present it as the business of only this family. The result was a new Shinto school – Yuiitsu Shinto 唯一神道, the "One and Only Way of the Kami," which is now known as Yoshida Shinto.[4] Indeed, Yoshida Shinto managed to recover many functions of the old Jingi-kan and became the most influential Shinto lineage in the early Edo period. In particular, it appropriated the Jingi-kan's prerogative to distribute court ranks to Shrine deities in the name of the Tenno, and this became a major source of income for Yoshida priests (Maeda 2002).

Admittedly, the Yoshida-Urabe never succeeded in overruling all claims of other aristocratic *kuge* families (notably the Shirakawa 白川, who in time recalled their former hereditary positions as the heads of the

Jingi-kan). From the point of view of these other families, the Yoshida were simply upstarts who had achieved their privileges through fraud and political manipulation. While such objections certainly did not lack historical justification, they nevertheless did not prevent the Yoshida priests from spreading their new concept of Shinto on a countrywide level. At least in terms of quantity the Yoshida were indeed quite successful. By the Edo period, they were officially acknowledged as supervisors of all shrines that had had no previous connections to the imperial court.[5] Thus the Yoshida became the main agent to judge on the status of shrines especially on the village level, and to intervene in all kinds of conflicts regarding shrine matters – between local groups as well as between villages and the government (Maeda 2003, ch. 3–5).

Apart from this historical role, Yoshida Shinto is also a good example of medieval Shinto theology, which was deeply rooted in the conceptual framework of esoteric Buddhism. Yoshida Shinto is therefore in itself a prominent representative of the medieval culture of secrecy. In the following, I will take a closer look at Urabe philology in order to show how the historical phases sketched above are reflected in the Urabe discourse on the kami, and how the changes within this discourse relate to different modes of secrecy.

The Urabe philology of Japanese myths

Judging from their contents alone it is quite clear that both *Kojiki* and *Nihon shoki* were not merely anthologies of mythological stories, but that existing myths had been rewritten and redesigned in order to produce a historical narrative that testified to the primordial importance of imperial rule by the descendents of the sun deity. In accordance with these highly political connotations, there are traces of an early, stately sponsored *text-pflege*. We know of scattered ceremonial lectures during the first half of the Heian period, in which the *Nihon shoki* was read and explained.[6] These events were typical for the classical period, when knowledge, while not plainly accessible, was administrated and taught in an official framework provided by stately institutions. Such ceremonial lectures, however, are no longer mentioned from the mid-tenth century onward. As a famous anecdote from the early eleventh century illustrates, knowledge about the *Nihongi* was by then considered to be extraordinary: Lady Murasaki, the author of the *Genji monogatari*, was praised by Emperor Ichijō for her command of the ancient chronicle and became therefore known as the "court lady of the *Nihongi*" (*Nihongi no o-tsubone*).[7] Another hundred years later, the eminent court scholar Ōe Masafusa 大江正房 (1041–1111) revealed in his diary that he had read the *Nihongi* only in part and that it was "hard to understand."[8]

Yoshihara Hiroto (1999, p. 44) infers from these facts that in the late Heian period even the educated elite of court society was not acquainted with the details of ancient Japanese history, not to mention the *Nihon shoki* proper. The reasons for this development may partly be due to linguistic and orthographic difficulties: as one of the first Japanese texts written in Chinese characters, the *Nihon shoki* was probably never readable without special expertise, and with the natural changes in language, even those who could read it gradually lacked an understanding of the ancient words. Already in the official lectures on the text, mentioned before, the language of the *Nihon shoki* was explained as different from ordinary speech, deriving from the age of the gods, and the pronunciation of certain words became an important topic (Abe 1999, p. 6). A more specific reason for the increasing lack of knowledge on these matters in late Heian court society is the general decline of official, state-sponsored scholarship and stately ritualism that went hand in hand with political decentralization. At the end of the Heian period, however, there is some evidence of a new interest in the *Nihon shoki* by members of the dominant court clan, the Fujiwara, the first extant commentary on the text having been written by a member of this family.[9]

It is probably by way of the Ichijō – one of the leading branch families of the Fujiwara – that the Urabe eventually came into possession of the *Nihon shoki*, enabling their monopoly of its transmission. Some evidence for such a relationship can be found in what Okada Shōji (1999, p. 77) calls "*Nihongi* study-groups" (*benkyōkai*) organized by Urabe Kanefumi 卜部兼文 (n.d.) for members of the Ichijō in the 1270s. More informal intellectual contacts between the Urabe and branches of the Fujiwara are already mentioned in court documents of the late twelfth century (Okada 1984a, p. 710).[10] The interest of the Ichijō in the lesser-ranking masters of court ritualism is probably explained by the growing import-ance of ritual knowledge in the early medieval period. As discussed in detail by Mark Teeuwen in this book, knowledge on ritual precedence became essential in the competition among the five leading branches of the Fujiwara for the highest offices at court. Since the Urabe were too low in status to participate in this competition actively, they were ideally suited as experts or tutors for members of the Fujiwara.[11] This may have been the reason why the Urabe were allowed to deal with historical and ritual texts that were originally collected by members of the Fujiwara themselves.

I am not sure to what extent there were exceptions to the Urabe monopoly of the *Nihon shoki*, but it seems safe to say that during the medieval period it was nearly impossible to gain access to the original text – not to mention its "correct" reading – other than by way of the Urabe family. This did not exclude the possibility to gain access to other versions of the mythological accounts. As already mentioned (note 7), in the medieval period the term "*Nihongi*" did not necessarily refer to a particular text, but to many spurious versions of the text that circulated in religious circles. Nevertheless, the Urabe enjoyed a particular status within these mythological traditions, as evidenced by the fact that they were even mentioned in the classic medieval warrior epic *Taiheiki* as *Nihongi no ie* 日本紀 – "the house of the *Nihongi*."

For a member of the Urabe family, the usual way to get acquainted with the *Nihon shoki* text was probably the act of copying it. Copying can therefore be seen as the basic training in philological expertise. As in the case of other literary traditions, this kind of *textpflege* was not necessarily confined to simple reproduction, but also included interlinear annotations referring to difficult expressions and related passages in other works. Annotations by former copyists were also reproduced in this way. As the corpus of annotations grew larger, extensively annotated versions of the original text became independent works of their own, evolving into a further secret family tradition within the Urabe lineage. The first extant evidence of this kind of Urabe commentary literature is a text called *Shaku nihongi* 釈日本紀 ("Explaining the *Nihon shoki*"), composed around 1300 by Urabe Kanekata 卜部兼方 (dates unknown). *Shaku nihongi* is a kind of synopsis of Urabe scholarship on the *Nihon shoki*. It served for centuries as the basis for in-house education as well as for lecturing on the *Nihon shoki* to outsiders. Needless to say, the transmission of this text was almost as precious as that of the *Nihon shoki* itself.

During the second phase of Urabe history, starting with Yoshida Kanetomo's expounding of Yuiitsu Shinto in the late fifteenth century, the *Nihon shoki* remained central to the Urabe tradition but the way to comment on it changed. Kanetomo initiated a new genre of commentaries called *Nihon shoki shō* 日本書紀抄 or *Jindai no maki shō* 神代巻抄 (Commentaries on the Divine Age section [of *Nihon shoki*]). Here, the emphasis was put on the cosmological aspects of the text – that is the mythological stories about the world's creation covered in the "Divine Age section" (*jindai no maki*) – and religious truth was given precedence over historiographical or philological detail. It is only at this point, therefore, that "religious commentaries," as identified in Susan Klein's typology of medieval commentary literature,[12] entered the Urabe tradition. As we shall see below, the discourse of this genre is characterized by a high degree of esoteric terminology and "allegorical" interpretation alien to previous Urabe works. Therefore, the new role of the Urabe (Yoshida) as the priests of an all-encompassing Shinto theology mentioned above is clearly reflected on the level of discourse.

In the main body of this essay, I will illustrate these differences by analyzing the treatment of a particular mythological account in Urabe commentaries. This account lends itself particularly well to the topic of secrecy, since it deals with the "hiding" of a deity. Although it seems therefore predestined for all kinds of esoteric interpretations, only the later group of commentaries effectively made use of this possibility.

Text analysis

Ōkuninushi's "yielding the land"

The mythical story that I will take as an example is known as the *kuni-yuzuri* 国譲 or "yielding the land" episode. It appears in slightly differing versions in the two chronicles, the *Kojiki* and the *Nihon shoki*, as well as in the apocryphal *Kuji hongi*. The *kuniyuzuri* episode is part of the politically most important narrative in classical Japanese myths: the Heavenly Gods' descent to earth and their subsequent establishment of a permanent government. Today, the historical basis of this narrative is generally seen in the conquest and the unification of the central parts of the Japanese archipelago by the ancestors of the Yamato clan, which led to the formation of the first Japanese state. In mythical language, however, what may have been a conflict of rival clans is presented as a contest between two kinds of divine beings, the kami of heaven (*ama tsu kami* 天神) and the kami of earth (*tsuchi tsu kami* 土神). The climax of this narrative is the triumphant procession of Ninigi, the heavenly grandson of the sun goddess Amaterasu, and his entourage, who are presented as the ancestors of the Tenno and the families of the imperial court.

The *kuniyuzuri* episode covers the preliminaries of this climactic descent. Two heavenly gods have been sent to Ōkuninushi 大国主, the chief deity of the earth, to prepare the way for his "yielding the land" to Ninigi. They appear in front of Ōkuninushi, impress him by a demonstration of magical power (they seat themselves on the tips of their swords, pointing upright from the ground), and ask him whether he is willing to surrender to the kami of Heaven or not. Ōkuninushi, after consulting his eldest son, agrees to surrender. He yields the symbols of his power – in one version a spear, in another version the *magatama* 勾玉 jewels – to the Gods of Heaven and disappears from the scene.

This account is not only rendered differently in *Kojiki* and *Nihon shoki*, but the *Nihon shoki* contains a total of three different versions. Most notably, the very name of the chief deity of the earth differs. In the *Kojiki* version, he is known as Ōkuninushi, the Great Lord of the Land, while the *Nihon shoki* calls him Ōanamuchi 大己貴 (rendered sometimes as "He who possesses a Great Name").[13] According to both chronicles, Ōkuninushi or Ōanamuchi is a descendent of Susanoo, the wicked brother of Amaterasu, who was expelled from heaven and became the Lord of the Netherworld after spending some time on earth and leaving many children. Just as Susanoo is, the kami of earth are generally presented as "wicked" and "unruly," thus justifying the fact that the kami of heaven must take control over them. Ōkuninushi, however, appears as a distinguished ruler whose surrender is presented as an act of superior wisdom and insight. According to some versions, he even receives a beautiful palace as a reward for his cooperation. As soon as he retires, however, there is no further mention of his actual whereabouts.

Since this is quite important for later interpretations of this story, we have to look at a few key passages in more detail:

According to the *Kojiki*, Ōkuninushi demands a palace in the style of the imperial line, with "crossbeams raising up to the High Fields of Heaven." A heavenly palace (*ame no miaraka* 天之御舎) is eventually built for him near Tagishi beach in Izumo. He then announces his retirement to the "less-than-one-hundred eighty windings" (*momo tarazu yaso kumade* 百足不八十手) (*Kojiki*, p. 93; Philippi 1968, pp. 134–35).

This mysterious phrase is also found in the main *Nihon shoki* account. In this version, however, no palace is mentioned. After announcing his retirement to the less-than-one-hundred eighty windings, Ōanamuchi, as he is called in the *Nihon shoki*, simply surrenders the insignia of his power and "conceals himself."[14] An additional variant account in the *Nihon shoki*, however, describes these events in much more detail. In this version, Ōanamuchi is not immediately willing to surrender, and his discussion with the heavenly messengers leads to a kind of compromise. Ōanamuchi will renounce his political power, but shall remain in command of some secret or mysterious power. This compromise is rendered in the words of the chief supervisor of Ninigi's descent to earth, his maternal grandfather Takamimusubi:

> Let the visible matters (*arawani no koto* 顕露事), which you have charge of, be conducted by my grandchild, and do you rule the matters of the kami (*kami no koto* 神事).

To this, Ōanamuchi answers,

> Let the August Grandchild direct the visible matters, of which I have charge. I will retire and direct the hidden matters (*kakuretaru koto* 隠事).[15]

We should note that while Takamimusubi's words are nearly parallel to those of Ōanamuchi, there is also a puzzling difference: "kami matters" in the first case are rendered as "hidden matters" in the second.

In this version of the *Nihon shoki* account, we learn further of a beautiful palace to be built for Ōanamuchi, which is called *ama no hizumi no miya* 天日隅宮 (Palace of the Heavenly Sun Corner). Eventually, however, Ōanamuchi "hides himself for ever" (*tokoshie ni kakuremashiki* 長隠), and we are informed neither of whether he actually received his palace, nor of in which way he went on to "direct the hidden matters."[16]

The term *kakuru* 隠る (to hide) is, by the way, also found in an interesting corresponding account of the retirement of the first creator god, Izanagi. After fathering various islands, plants and elements such as the wind, Izanagi finally creates the sun goddess Amaterasu, the moon god

Tsukiyomi, and the aforementioned Susanoo,[17] and thus concludes his active role in the narration. In a short note, the *Nihon shoki* mentions that upon completing these creative acts, Izanagi built a "hidden palace" (*kakure miya* 隠宮) on the island of Awaji, dwelling there forever in silence and concealment (Aston 1972, p. 34). Again we find this concealment expressed by the same characters: 長隠, "long hiding" (*Nihon shoki* 1, p. 103).

A second version in the *Nihon shoki* transfers Izanagi's place of retirement to the realm of heaven and calls it the "Small Palace of Heaven" (*ame no wakamiya* 天少宮). In the *Kojiki* version, this episode is reduced to one sentence: "Izanagi no Ōkami is enshrined in Taga of Ōmi" (*Kojiki*, p. 43; Philippi 1968, p. 73). There is indeed a famous Izanagi shrine called Taga in the province Ōmi (now Shiga prefecture). As we will see later, medieval commentators noted the parallels in the mythical accounts and tried to find all sorts of connections between the abodes of divine retirement of Izanagi and Ōkuninushi.

Before proceeding to the commentaries on the *Nihon shoki*, let me recall the three somewhat arcane elements in this episode of the myth:

1   the eighty windings
2   the opposition of "visible matters" (*arawani no koto*) to "hidden matters" (*kakuretaru koto*), also called "matters of the kami" (*kami no koto*)
3   the [Heavenly] Palace of the Sun Corner ([*ame no*] *hizumi no miya*).

While the general outline of the *kuniyuzuri* episode remained strangely uncommented upon by medieval authors, these phrases aroused particular interest. As we shall see below, however, their explanations varied quite significantly.

Urabe Kanekata's Shaku nihongi annotations

As has already been mentioned, the oldest and most important product of Urabe scholarship on the *Nihon shoki* is Urabe Kanekata's *Shaku nihongi*. It can be described as a compendium of annotations that are actually rather dry. They refer in most cases to the correct reading of terms and the identification of place names, or explain words and items no longer in use. The *Shaku nihongi* also quotes extensively from *Kojiki* and *Kuji hongi*, or from ancient regional chronicles (*Fudoki* 風土記) and other classical texts. Many explanations refer to a "teacher's comment" or to "private records" (*shiki* 私記).[18] Thus, in contrast to the often mysterious original text and the aura of exclusivity surrounding the whole subject, the *Shaku nihongi* is characterized by a distinct sense of objectivity and practicality.

The *Shaku nihongi* is divided into several chapters, each working through the entire original text and dealing with passages chosen for their specific topics. In the introduction, the relevance of the *Nihon shoki* in relation to other classics is discussed. A great deal of this chapter is also devoted to the various designations for Japan, such as Yamato, Nihon, Hi-no-moto, and so on. Another chapter lists terms according to their Sino-Japanese (*on* 音) readings, ordered by their appearance in the text. The corresponding chapter on ancient Japanese (*kun* 訓) readings is much longer, and forms one of the essential sections of the *Shaku nihongi*. Interestingly, these *kun* readings are referred to as "secret readings" (*hikun* 秘訓). Thus it appears as if the *on* readings were the normal standard whereas the *kun* readings were reserved for special, secret, or exclusive occasions, or were regarded as a kind of sacred language. The very title of the *Nihon shoki* is a case in point. Its (secret?) *kun*-pronunciation reads "*Yamato fumi*" (*Shaku nihongi*, p. 394).

The *Shaku nihongi* further includes a very detailed imperial genealogy, but the largest section (about 40 percent) is devoted to lexicon-style explanations of terms and phrases. These explanations contain much useful information on the *Nihon shoki*, even for modern students of the text. In this section, we also find references to the *kuniyuzuri* episode. However, the *Shaku nihongi* contains surprisingly little information on this topic. Most comments refer to the actual location of the Sun-Corner Palace (*ame no hizumi no miya*), the palace being ultimately identified as a designation for the Great Shrine of Izumo (*Shaku nihongi*, pp. 200–01).

To support this conclusion, there is a quite extensive discussion on two other shrines that sometimes went by the name Sun-Corner Palace and that have some ties to Ōkuninushi/Ōnamuchi: the afore mentioned Taga Shrine in Ōmi, and the Hie Shrine at the foot of Mount Hiei. Urabe Kanekata bases their identification with the Sun-Corner Palace on the following reason: the term "sun corner" (*hizumi* 日隅) refers to the direction of sunrise at summer solstice, i.e. the north-east. Seen from the ancient capitals of Nara and Kyoto, the direction of both the Hie and the Taga shrines is indeed north-east. These cities, however, did not exist in the divine age and therefore there is no reason to consider that the shrines in question were situated in any "Sun-Corner" direction. Kanekata continues by pointing out that Hie, for that matter, is inhabited not by Ōanamuchi, but by his nephew Ōyamakui 大山咋 (The Great Mountain Eater). Thus, Kanekata confirms that in the divine age, the name Sun-Corner Palace referred to Izumo, in spite of its location to the north-*west* of the present capital (*Shaku nihongi*, pp. 200–01).

In this discussion, we feel a strong concern with directions. This was probably inherited from the divinatory tradition of the Urabe at the Heian court. What seems most striking to me, however, is the strict limitation to empirical or "historical" argumentation. It is not doubted that the Sun-Corner Palace must be a real building at a precise geographical location, whereas no thought is given to a metaphysical explanation of Ōanamuchi's abode, in heaven or in the Netherworld, for instance. Thus, the deities in the text are not treated differently from physical people. The mythological accounts are taken as reports of a time on earth when the forefathers of mankind were in possession of certain superior capacities and were thus called deities, but in every other respect they acted like men.

Among the remarks on the *kuniyuzuri* episode in the *Shaku nihongi*, the location of the Sun-Corner Palace appears a matter of considerable concern. The "eighty windings," however, are mentioned only in passing in order to identify Ōkuninushi's abode with the shrine of Izumo. The third group of arcane expressions, the open, the hidden, and the kami matters, are not discussed at all.

Ichijō Kaneyoshi's Sanso

Most commentators from the first phase of Urabe history continued the tradition of Kanekata and followed more or less the same kind of reasoning. Commentaries from other angles are only found outside the Urabe tradition.[19] Much more influential and also more original in terms of argumentation is the *Nihon shoki sanso* 日本書紀纂疏 (thereafter *Sanso*)[20] by Ichijō Kaneyoshi 一条兼良 (1402–81), which deals exclusively with the divine age chapters of the *Nihon shoki*. It is a line-by-line commentary that is clearly based on Urabe philology, but extends its explanations freely into the field of metaphysical interpretation.

Ichijō Kaneyoshi is known first of all for his commentaries on *Ise-* and *Genji monogatari*, which single him out as a leading scholar of literature. In addition, he held the post of a *kanpaku* 関白 the highest position of the court hierarchy, and was closely involved in all kinds of negotiations with the shogunate. Today his interest in the *Nihon shoki* is not as well known as his other achievements,[21] but in Kaneyoshi's time it was certainly of considerable importance in *kuge* society, since Kaneyoshi, like the Urabe themselves, lectured on this topic even to the Tenno. Kaneyoshi's access to Urabe scholarship is not only explained by the above-mentioned family relations between the Ichijō and the Urabe. Also as mentioned above, the Ichijō were at that time among those exalted court families to whom the Urabe were obliged to hold lectures on the *Nihon shoki*. In Kaneyoshi's case, however, the relation of teacher and disciple changed. Like other individual members of the Ichijō, he had been initiated to the most secret family traditions of the Urabe. When his tutor, Urabe Kaneatsu 兼敦 (1368–1408), died at an early age, the continuity of the Urabe transmission was endangered, since there was no fully initiated successor. Kaneyoshi filled the gap by "returning" some of the initiations he had received from Kaneatsu to Urabe Kanetomi 兼富 in 1418.[22]

It is not entirely clear what these top-secret initiations actually consisted of but obviously they enabled Kaneyoshi to also establish himself as an authority in the field of mythological exegesis. Judging from what we know from the *Shaku nihongi*, the knowledge he received referred primarily to the correct reading of the *Nihon shoki*.[23] Kaneyoshi's *Sanso*, on the other hand, is full of comments on philosophical or metaphysical principles that he had found, for instance, in the *kuniyuzuri* episode. Here, for the first time, we find a lengthy discussion on the opposition visible–hidden:

> The visible matters, this is the way of man (*jindō* 人道), the hidden matters, this is the way of the gods (*shintō* 神道). These two ways are like day and night, Yin and Yang: They are two and yet one (*ni ni shite ichi nari* 二而為一).
>
> If people commit evil on the visible plain of Earth, they receive punishment from the emperor. If they commit evil hidden in the dark, they receive punishment from the gods (*kishin* 鬼神). In the same way, doing good leads to happiness. The matters of the kamī belong therefore to the dark realm (*meifu* 冥府), they do not refer to ceremonies and offerings (*saishi seihei* 祭祀牲幣). Ceremonies and offerings belong to the visible matters.
>
> (*Sanso*, p. 311)

The first thing to note here is that the kami are seen as different from men, as a kind of antagonistic force. They inhabit a metaphysical realm, a realm unseen and yet constantly present. They see what man cannot see, they judge on matters that happen secretly. This is the implicit explanation for the fact that in the original *Nihon shoki* text, "matters of the kami" and "hidden matters" are equated. While different in nature, kami and human beings are seen as mutually dependent. This is expressed by an eclectic mixture of Daoism and Buddhist dialectics, typical for the esoteric discourse of the time. Another typical feature of m edieval esotericism is the importance on phonetic similarities. *Shintō* (Way of the Kami, probably pronounced *jindō*)[24] and *jindō* (Way of Men) do not accidentally sound similar; this similarity is taken to be a major indication of whatever relationship the author is going to establish between the two.

Interestingly, in Kaneyoshi's view, *shintō* does not refer to any religious act ("ceremonies and offerings"). The Way of the Gods is what deities do, as opposed to the Way of Men, which includes man's reverence to the deities. This interpretation reflects a more traditional understanding of the term *shintō*, which does not aim at the establishment of any systematic religious system. Nevertheless, the above citation reveals a kind of nostalgia for the golden past, typical also for many theological-systematic discourses on Shinto: The universe is governed by the Tenno and the kami, there is no mention of any other religious or political authority. The Tenno is in charge of the visible realm, the kami govern the invisible. Humans may see only one of these realms, but the seen and the unseen are actually interdependent. Together they form one system, one body of laws. By extending this line of thought, Ōkuninushi would embody divine law, as Ninigi embodies human, or imperial law.

We may add, that such conceptions are strikingly different from Kaneyoshi's actual environment. Political authority and jurisdiction were no longer executed by the Tenno, and divine reward was generally attributed to Buddhist karma, or to kami and buddhas together. Kaneyoshi's commentary, however, evokes the mythical past as a retrospective utopia, where only two sources of authority existed, which were ultimately of the same origin and therefore "two and yet one." No doubt, Kaneyoshi preferred these circumstances to his present. The past was therefore what the present really should be. By indulging in such utopian nostalgia, Kaneyoshi shared the world view of "Loyalist" adherents of the "divine land conception" (*shinkoku shisō* 神国思想), as for instance Kitabatake Chikafusa 北畠親房 (1293–1354) or the Tendai monk Jihen 慈遍, another member of the Urabe family. Jihen, by the way, had undertaken a mythological exegesis of the *Kuji hongi* some one hundred years before Kaneyoshi's *Sanso* that may have had a direct influence on the latter work.[25]

Before concluding the discussion of Kaneyoshi's exegesis of the *kuniyuzuri* episode, I should mention his comment referring to the Sun-corner Palace. Here, Kaneyoshi repeats the *Shaku nihongi* arguments, that is the questions of orientation and the Taga Shrine, in a shortened form. There is, however, a striking remark, which brings a completely new aspect into the whole discussion: "According to another explanation, *ama no hizumi no miya* is a palace in heaven, a place where the kami live" (*Sanso*, p. 311). Again it becomes clear that the mythological kami are seen as beings from a different realm than man's, and that the discourse tends toward a theological interpretation quite different from Urabe Kanekata's scholarly prose.

Yoshida Kanetomo

The next stage in the commentary literature on the *Nihon shoki* begins with the writings of Yoshida Kanetomo and his successors, in other words, the *Nihon shoki* interpretation of Yoshida Shinto. There are quite a few extant manuscripts on this topic, all related to lecturing activities. Some are notes left by the Yoshida themselves, others are notes by disciples who had heard their lectures. These so-called *kikigaki* 聞書 (writing from hearing) are particularly interesting, as they reflect the immediate spoken language used in the sermons of Yoshida priests.

Together with the Nakatomi Purification Formula (*Nakatomi harae* 中臣祓), the *Nihon shoki* was privileged material for elucidating the basic doctrines of Yoshida Shinto in the form of lectures. Nevertheless, there is no authoritative source of Yoshida *Nihon shoki* exegesis. There only exists a range of many similar works, often with the same title, but different details. While the main arguments remain the same, each member of the

Yoshida tried to find his own words and means of explanation. Kanetomo himself left several different notes on the *Nihon shoki*. His first lectures on the topic were probably based directly on Kaneyoshi's *Sanso*, as has been argued by Okada Shōji (1981). This assumption is based on copies of the *Sanso* in Kanetomo's own hand that contain a few, but significant, changes in which Kanetomo's views obviously differed from those of his master.[26] Yet, in later lectures on the *Nihon shoki*, Kanetomo hardly ever mentioned Kaneyoshi's *Sanso*, and when he did so it was only to demonstrate where Kaneyoshi differed from "our family tradition." As with other sources of inspiration, Kanetomo methodically avoided any indication that he had relied on non-family members.

Let us now have a look at Kanetomo's interpretation of the *kuniyuzuri* episode, which he expounded in 1481 in a lecture that was written down in a *kikigaki* by the Buddhist monk and Yoshida disciple Keijo Shūrin 景徐周麟, 1440–1518). As Kaneyoshi did in the *Sanso*, Kanetomo discussed the opposition visible–hidden quite extensively, explaining it – according to Keijo's notes – in the following way:

> The visible [matters] – this is the Royal Way (*ōdō* 王道). The matters of the kami – this is the dark realm (*meifu*). What is inside the six senses and the five organs and what nurtures them – this is the divine (*shin/kami* 神), this is the secret (*mitsu* 密). The Royal Way is visible. [...] Ōanamuchi entered heaven and earth to become the divine, in man he is the heart, and thus he is preserved.
>
> (*Shinsho monjin* 神書聞塵, pp. 113–14)

In a much more hectic style (which is probably due to the colloquial nature of the *kikigaki*) this passage repeats Ichijō Kaneyoshi's point that Ōkuninushi/Ōanamuchi did not simply retire (or perhaps die), but was transformed into a state of higher being. This state, which is not visible to ordinary men, is what is meant by hidden matters. Hidden matters are, at the same time, kami matters and thus also the Way of the Kami. The equation of kami, heart, and spirit with heaven, man, and the ten-thousand phenomena (*banbutsu*), by the way, is quite frequently found in Yoshida Shinto. It points to a concept according to which kami, heart, and spirit are all manifestations of the divine in, so to speak, different states of aggregation.

An important point in comparison with the *Shaku nihongi*, regardless of the particular explanations for a given item, is the fact that it is no longer necessary – and not even desirable – to arrive at only one interpretation. Ōanamuchi is transformed into the invisible state of the divine (which is the same and yet something different from his visible existence), and is further transformed into the invisible state of the human heart, and probably also into the spirit inside "all phenomena" (although there is no mention of this transformation here). This does not imply that other kami or other beings are *not* identical with the invisible kami things and with the heart, and so on. On the contrary, they too can acquire this state of existence. Thus, Kanetomo purposefully creates a multilayered reality here, where "being A" does not imply "being not B," but "being A and B and C" on different levels of... of what? Perception? Reality? Consciousness? This question is never really discussed in Kanetomo's writings, and therefore creates an ambiguity also characteristic of other examples of medieval esoteric discourse. It is therefore not at all surprising to learn in a further statement by Kanetomo on the *kuniyuzuri* episode that *hizumi no miya* is both a palace in Heaven *and* a shrine on Earth, namely the Great Shrine of Izumo (*Shinsho monjin*, p. 114).

As we have seen already in Ichijō Kaneyoshi's *Sanso*, the new, "esoteric" exegesis of mythology laid much more importance on the opposition visible–hidden than the former "philological" approach of the Urabe. For Kaneyoshi, this opposition ultimately signified the contrast of human and divine law (*shintō*). In his *Nihon shoki* lecture, Kanetomo followed this argument, but in another context he used the opposition to establish a more systematic system of Shinto. In his *Yuiitsu shintō myōbō yōshū* 唯一神道名法要集 ("Name and Law of Yuiitsu Shinto," written around 1485; hereafter *Myōbō yōshū*), he explained that Yuiitsu Shinto consists of two parts, "open teachings" and "secret teachings":

> There are the three basic texts (*honsho* 本書); the open teachings (*kenro no kyō* 顕露教) are based on them. And there are three divine scriptures (*shinkyō* 神経); they form the secret teachings (*on'yū no kyō* 隠幽教). Yuiitsu Shinto is both open and secret teachings (*ken-mitsu no ni-kyō* 顕密二教).[27]

To readers of the present book, this distinction between open and secret teachings sounds quite familiar. It is obviously a reflection of the *ken–mitsu* 顕密 dichotomy of medieval Japanese Buddhism. Kanetomo even uses Buddhist terms – *ken* (open, visible) and *mitsu* (secret, hidden) – when he refers to the totality of both teachings (*ken–mitsu no ni-kyō*). However, he also uses more specific terms: *kenro* for "open" or exoteric, and *on'yū* for secret or esoteric. *Kenro*, lit. "clear as dew," already appears in the Chinese classics, but *on'yū* seems to be a neologism. It is a composite of "to hide" (隠) and "dark," "mysterious" (幽).

A casual reading of the *Myōbō yōshū* can easily lead to the impression that these terms are just makeshift variants, provisionally concealing the Buddhist origin of the exoteric–esoteric dichotomy in Yoshida Shinto. If we take a look at the open–secret dichotomy in the *kuniyuzuri* episode, however, we find that Kanetomo quite cleverly derived his terms from here, since already in the *Nihon shoki* "the open matters" (*arawani no koto*) are rendered with the same kanji as *kenro* 顕露, while "hidden matters" (*kakuretaru koto*) are written with the characters 隠事. Kanetomo's term for "secret" – perhaps for reasons of symmetry – happens to include the additional character *yū* ("dark"), but it becomes obvious that he alluded to the *kuniyuzuri* episode in another citation, which appears close to the end of the *Myōbō yōshū*:

> Question: Are the meanings of open and secret (*ken–mitsu*) originally derived from Buddhism or do they belong to Shinto?
>
> Answer: The distinction between open and secret has the same meaning as in Buddhism. The terms, however, come from the writings of Shinto.
> (*Myōbō yōshū*, p. 237)

What follows is a direct quote from the *Nihon shoki* version of the *kuniyuzuri* episode, where open and hidden matters are mentioned. This further leads to an explanation of esoteric ranks (*mitsui* 密位), composed of two sets of four hierarchical stages, which are strikingly similar to esoteric ranks in Shingon Buddhism.[28] Fully aware of this fact, Kanetomo goes on to explain this relationship:

> Shingon has secret [ranks] (*himitsu*), Shinto has mysterious [ranks] (*onmitsu* 隠密). These are ranks that go beyond the secret [ranks]. That is why they are called mysterious.
> (*Myōbō yōshū*, p. 237)

From this citation we can infer that Kanetomo quite consciously took Shingon Buddhism as a model when he set up his new Shinto teaching. As with other sources of inspiration, he took great pains to ensure that his teaching (which was purportedly derived from the Age of the Gods) appeared to be the original, whereas the Shingon model was presented as of a secondary, less "esoteric" grade.

In the *Myōbō yōshū* passages following the above citation, we find a systematic outline of esoteric initiations arranged in a hierarchical sequence from open to secret. The open–secret dichotomy is therefore a rationale to create an organized religious system. Since this system is allegedly derived from the divine age, it is of utmost importance to base this dichotomy on ancient myths. In Yoshida ritualism, there are indeed traces of an attempt to structure all rituals accordingly, that is to relate them to a system of progressively "secret" initiations as is found in esoteric Buddhism. The terms proposed in the *Myōbō yōshū*, however, are not used consistently in the respective ritual manuals. This leads to doubts of whether this system of esoteric initiations as sketched in the *Myōbō yōshū* was ever fully in use in Yoshida Shinto. Later texts of Yoshida Shinto suggest that the system was actually simplified a bit, but that which Kanetomo outlined in the *Myōbō yōshū* is at least as complex and detailed as the corresponding Buddhist ritual systems.

Nihon shoki *exegesis after Kanetomo*

Kanetomo's successors followed his tradition of lecturing and writing comments (*shō* 抄) on the *Nihon shoki*. Of his four known sons, Kiyohara Nobukata 清原宣賢 (1475–1550) was probably the most gifted. As an adopted heir to the Kiyohara family, which was traditionally in charge of Confucian learning (*myōgyōdō* 明経道) at the court, Nobukata stressed Yin and Yang in his commentary on the *Nihon shoki*. Thus, in regard to the *kuniyuzuri* episode, we learn that "the visible things are the way of Man, this is Yang. The way of the gods, this is Yin" (*Nihon shoki jindai no maki shō* 日本書紀神代巻抄, p. 229). This passage seems to be actually closer to the *Sanso* than to the *kikigaki* of a Kanetomo lecture. Nobukata also mentions the two possible explanations for the Sun-corner Palace, that is Izumo and "a palace in Heaven." While Kanetomo saw the two explanations as reflections of two kinds of truth, Nobukata rather takes the traditional stance of the Urabe tradition, citing both explanations and leaving it open to debate which one is true.

Similarly, a *kikigaki* of lectures of Nobukata's son Kanemigi 兼右 (1516–73), who became the head of Yoshida Shinto in 1536, exhibits a kind of return to the *Sanso*, or even to the *Shaku nihongi*, seen in its inclusion of much more philological and practical reasoning than found in Kanetomo's texts. Interestingly, the division of hidden things and visible things is not commented on. Regarding the *kuniyuzuri* episode, Kanemigi mentions the *hizumi no miya* only briefly, providing the two explanations mentioned above. There is also a note in the original *kikigaki* text, probably added on a later occasion. It refers to the palace-in-heaven explanation and says, "this is the correct meaning!"[29]

Kanetomo's heirs, therefore, exhibit a tendency to return to more "orthodox," philological arguments of *Nihon shoki* exegesis instead of developing Kanetomo's esoteric discourse further. This can be seen as an indication that the medieval culture of secrecy had already reached its climax before Kanetomo created the esoteric concepts of Yoshida Shinto. Among his successors, a new kind of historiographical scrutiny under the sway of Confucianism seems to have led to an awareness of potential points of criticism that could be used against Yoshida Shinto. Yet while later Yoshida priests did not do much to develop Kanetomo's esoteric discourse, they remained faithful to what they had inherited and continued to set his ritual system into practice.

Conclusion

By tracing the *Nihon shoki* transmission and its *textpflege* by the "house of the *Nihongi*," i.e. the Urabe family, I intended to point out the fact that secrecy in the medieval period was put to quite different uses which were not necessarily all "esoteric." In what I called the first phase of Urabe history (from the late Heian to the later medieval periods) the family employed a technology of secrecy that aimed at the conservation of "symbolic capital." They turned parts of traditional court culture (first divination and other ritual knowledge, later also philological *textpflege*) into private house canons (in the case of texts often called "oral transmissions" – *kuden* 口伝 or *kuketsu* 口決) and structured them by their degree of secrecy, the most valuable items being known only to the head of the family.[30] The aim of this technology of secrecy was primarily to keep the tradition within the possession of the family. However, as we have seen in the case of the *Nihon shoki* transmission, the canonized knowledge itself was surprisingly free from any particularly mysterious or "esoteric" interpretations. Only during the "second phase" (from the late fifteenth century onward) did the Urabe employ a secret technology that pertained to both the form and the contents of a transmission.

In this period the *Nihon shoki* was no longer conceived as a historical narrative, but as containing one or more levels of hidden meaning. It is quite telling that during this phase, the provisions against access to the text by outsiders actually loosened. The *Nihon shoki* was used to prove the existence of "secret teachings" in Shinto, but was itself regarded as part of the "open teachings." Consequently, Kanetomo and his successors lectured quite freely on the *Nihon shoki*, not only to members of court, but also to the warrior aristocracy and to Buddhist monks, mostly of Zen or Tendai provenance. What was kept secret was the body of secret rituals of Yuiitsu Shinto, to which the dichotomy open–secret allegedly referred.

These rituals – purportedly so secret that they had never been disclosed since the divine age, but in fact mostly creations by Yoshida Kanetomo – became the new core of the Urabe's symbolic capital. Taking Shingon Buddhism as a model, Kanetomo even set up a system of eight esoteric ranks that structured texts and rituals as well as the access to them. Even more importantly, these rituals and initiations were seen as a means to gain union with the kami, which substituted buddhahood in Kanetomo's Shinto. Secrecy was therefore the natural condition of the ultimate truth (or the highest state of being, in this case identical with the nature of the kami), which formed the basis of the whole esoteric system created by Kanetomo.

Structurally, the two modes of secrecy are directly opposed to each other. In the first case, something real is kept secret because it is for some reason not advisable to reveal it to everybody. In the second case, the ultimate truth is secret by definition, and can only be revealed by the employment of rituals that may or may not be protected by secrecy rules. In the first case, secrecy is a pragmatic, technical matter; in the second, it is the result of imperfect human perception. Therefore, in the first case, the *Nihon shoki* was one of the central objects of secrecy, while in the latter it became a kind of pointer to the ultimate, secret truth.

Functionally, the purpose of keeping the tradition secret seems to have been no longer motivated by the fear of competing experts alone. Rather, secrecy appears as a means of religious propaganda: The more profound the secrets, the more people will feel attracted to them. This led to an inflationary use of secrecy that already contained the roots of its crisis: While indeed more and more people became attracted to Yuiitsu Shinto, there were also more to question its secrets.

As demonstrated by many other examples of esoteric practice in this book, such characteristics can be found not only in the Urabe transmission of the *Nihon shoki*, but they occurred in all the religious and cultural traditions that were shaped and reshaped under the sway of esoteric Buddhism. What makes this transmission interesting in the discussion of medieval secrecy is the fact that the esoteric readjustments of the transmission did not occur continuously, but erupted suddenly after a long period of conservative preservation. Thus, the two technologies or modes of secrecy under discussion are surprisingly far apart in terms of their first chronological evidence. This is all the more surprising as the influence of esoteric Buddhism on the general intellectual environment had already reached its apex during the first phase of Urabe history. Other kami priests such as the Watarai of Ise already adopted esoteric Buddhism in the thirteenth century, for instance. Yoshida Shinto is hardly conceivable without these innovations, but it took another two hundred years before a priest of the Urabe applied them to his own traditions.

The reasons are probably tied to the special status of the Urabe at court, or rather to the particular conservatism of that environment. Within the court, the Urabe gained a certain degree of authority and independence through their secret traditions, but at the same time the exchange of knowledge and authority was determined by the traditional system of obligations toward their superiors. Only when this system dissolved was there a possibility and even a necessity to create something new. The employment of esotericism by the Urabe is therefore similar in many ways to examples from the long history of esoteric Buddhism in India and China:[31] it was induced by a time of crisis, i.e. the destruction of the political foundations of an earlier status, which led to a new independence. Thus an original loss was turned into an advantage.

Notes

1 The term *textpflege* (lit. taking care of a text) is borrowed from Aleida and Jan Assmann (1987). In particular, they refer to *textpflege*, "wenn es auf eine exakte wortlautgetreue, u.U. sogar intonationsgetreue Fixierung ankommt," (Assmann 1987, p. 12), a method that they regard to be typical for the process of text canonization.
2 According to our current knowledge, the composition of the *Kuji hongi* can be dated to somewhere in the tenth century. See also Kadoya Atsushi's essay in this book (Chapter 11, pp. 270–71).

3 Based on articles by Okada Shōji (1983, 1984a, 1984b), I have described the courtly career of the Urabe more thoroughly in Scheid 2001, ch. 3.

4 Kanetomo's branch of the Urabe family had changed its name to Yoshida a generation earlier. The name of Urabe was still alternatively used, however, which is why Yoshida Shinto is also known by the name of "Urabe Shinto."

5 This was specified in the bakufu's "Regulations for Shrine Priests" (*Shosha negi kannushi hatto* 諸社補宜神主法度) issued in 1665. The third of a total of five regulations demanded that "shrine priests (*shake*) without [court] rank must wear white robes. [The use of] other robes must be approved by the Yoshida house." As discussed in more detail by Hiromi Maeda (2003, pp. 83–90), this regulation entailed control over the social status of the vast majority of shrine priests by the Yoshida.

6 The *Shaku nihongi* includes reports about such events, known as *kōsho* 講書, in 812, 839, 878, 904, 936, and 965 (Onoda 1986, p. 16). There is also a reference to a lecture in 721, the year after the compilation of the text, but this is of somewhat doubtful evidence. Masuo Shinichirō (1999, p. 19) argues, however, that such a lecture is by no means unnatural since it would have made the contents of the newly compiled imperial chronicle known to the court.

7 See, for instance, Saitō 1999, p. 36. As many scholars have pointed out, "*Nihongi*" does not necessarily refer to the *Nihon shoki* text alone, in this context, but rather to the genre of Japanese ancient chronicles.

8 This statement was caused by a conversation between Masafusa and Fujiwara no Sanekane (1085–1112), who questioned the renowned scholar on the *Nihongi*, as reported by Masafusa in his *Kōdanshō* 江談抄. See Yoshihara 1999, pp. 43–44.

9 *Nihongi shō* 日本紀鈔 by Shinzei 信西 (a.k.a. Fujiwara no Michinori 藤原通憲, ?–1159). Shinzei is notorious for his political manipulations during the Hōgen and Heiji disturbances (1156–59) that eventually cost his life, but he was also a renown scholar. Interestingly, he is the son of Fujiwara no Sanekane 藤原実兼, who, in the diary by Ōe Masafusa, had demonstrated a lack of basic knowledge concerning the *Nihon shoki*, yet nevertheless some interest.

10 Before establishing closer ties with the Ichijō, the Urabe served as house-vassals (*ietsukasa* 家司) of the Shirakawa, a branch family of the Tenno house that headed the Jingi-kan from the time of Prince Akihiro (1095–1180) onward. The term *ietsukasa* refers to semi-hereditary posts that lesser court families held in addition to their official duties. In 1224, the Urabe dissolved this form of their allegiance to the Shirakawa (Okada 1984a, pp. 708–09). Okada regards this as a decisive step toward an increase in the Urabe's status as well as independence from their Jingi-kan superiors. It is probably also a sign of approval of the Urabe's philological scholarship. From this period onward, the copying activities of mytho-historical texts by the Urabe are clearly evident in the form of colophons and other scriptural sources (Onoda 1986, pp. 16–18).

11 Starting with the enthronement of Go-Uda Tenno in 1274, Nishida Nagao (1979, pp. 140–43) and Okada Shōji (1999, p. 77) have looked into several cases in which Urabe expertise in ritual matters had a decisive impact on court politics. For a summary, see Scheid 2001, pp. 91–92; see also an example mentioned by Mark Teeuwen (p. 181) in this book.

12 Klein (2002, pp. 43–44) identifies four types of early medieval commentary literature in the field of poetry: "pragmatic," "philological," "historical" (these first three being also present in the first phase of Urabe history), and "religious."

13 In this essay I generally refer to Ōkuninushi, since this is the name by which the deity is best known today. When referring specifically to the *Nihon shoki*, I

will use Ōanamuchi. It is worth noting that there is also a reference in the *Nihon shoki* explaining that Ōkuninushi is another name of Ōanamuchi, also known as Ōmononushi (the Great Leader of Things) and by several other names (*Nihon shoki* 1, p. 128; Aston 1972, vol. 1, p. 59).

14 *Nihon shoki* 1, p. 140, Aston 1972, p. 69. In the edition of NKBT 67, the respective character 隠 (*kakureru* in modern Japanese) is glossed not only as *kakuru* ("hide") but also as *makaru* ("obey," "return"; in the *Nihon shoki* often used for "to die").

15 *Nihon shoki* 1, p. 150. Translation modified from Aston 1972, p. 80.

16 Ibid., p. 151.

17 In the best-known versions, these deities were created when Izanagi washed his eyes and his nose. In contrast, the earlier acts of procreation were done in sexual union with his sibling-consort Izanami.

18 Kanekata also refers to a *Yōrō go-nen shiki* 養老五年私記, i.e. a "private record form 721," which may refer to a work related to the "lecture" on *Nihon shoki*, mentioned above (see Masuo 1999, pp. 19–20).

19 Besides the *Nihon shoki sanso* discussed here, the most prominent example is the *Jindai no maki kuketsu* 神代巻口訣 (= ST *Koten chūshaku-hen* 3, pp. 3–163), dated 1367 and attributed to Inbe no Masamichi 忌部正通, a member of another family serving at the Jingi-kan. Its date and authorship, however, are not univocally acknowledged.

Moreover, Mure Hitoshi (1996) has argued that another esoteric exegesis of ancient mythology, a text called *Shintō hiketsu* 神道秘訣, was actually written by an Urabe family member from the twelfth century, as indicated in its colophon. Mure's stress on the authenticity of the *Shintō hiketsu* would imply that the Urabe were in fact the first to advance esoteric Shinto interpretations. So far, the *Shintō hiketsu* is the only text to support such a view. It is therefore more probable to regard it as apocryphal like so many other texts of the *hiketsu* genre. See Scheid 2001, pp. 99–100, n. 50, for a further discussion.

20 The term *sanso* is an unusual compound of *san* 纂 (to compile) and *so* 疏, which may be translated as "commentary," but contains also the notion of a "report to the emperor."

21 A recent biography of Ichijō Kaneyoshi by Steven Carter (1996) does not even mention his interests in religion and mythology. On the general interests of the Ichijō in ritual matters, see Mark Teeuwen's essay in this book.

22 For the details of these circumstances, see Okada 1984b, pp. 24–26.

23 The reading of ancient texts was actually a most difficult matter. From the diary of Bonshun 梵舜 (1553–1632), a member of the Yoshida Urabe at the time of Hideyoshi and Ieyasu, we know that he, formally trained as a Buddhist monk, had an intimate knowledge of the *Nihon shoki*, but was not capable of reading it out loud.

24 As Teeuwen has pointed out in his article "From *jindō* to Shinto" (Teeuwen 2002), it is quite possible that the common pronunciation of *shintō* at that time was actually *jindō*. This would make the above sentence an even better play on words.

25 Jihen (n.d.), a brother of the famous poet Yoshida Kenkō 吉田兼好, was born in a side branch of the Urabe family that was probably no longer involved in the family's priestly duties. His esoteric Shinto writings, most prominently his *Kuji hongi gengi* 旧事本紀玄義, were based rather on Watarai Shinto than on the traditions of the Urabe.

26 Although it is not clear whether Kanetomo ever received personal instruction from Ichijō Kaneyoshi, it is at least probable. Nishida Nagao, one of the pioneers of modern research on Yoshida Shinto, reported the existence of a copy of

Kanyoshi's *Sanso* by Kanetomo in 1459, Kanetomo's twenty-fifth year. This copy seems to have been lost in Second World War (Okada 1981, p. 171).

27 *Myōbō yōshū*, p. 212. The text goes on to explain that the "open teachings" are based on *Kuji hongi, Kojiki,* and *Nihon shoki,* whereas the "secret teachings" are based on scriptures called *Tengen shinpen jinmyō kyō* 天元神変神妙経, *Jigen jinzu jinmyō kyō* 地元神通神妙経, and *Jingen shinriki jinmyō kyō* 人元神力神妙経 (p. 213). These names are derived from esoteric Buddhist terminology, yet these scriptures are mentioned at no other place in Kanetomo's writings.

28 See for instance Fabio Rambelli's article in this book for a discussion of esoteric ranks in Shingon Buddhism.

29 Yoshida Kanemigi, *Nihon shoki kikigaki* 日本書紀聞書, p. 415.

30 Only the family heads had full access to the entire body of transmissions, and they were responsible for finding a suitable successor, who had to undergo a series of initiations before he inherited it. Thus, there was always a danger that the family transmission might be interrupted if the head of a house or the prospective heir died unexpectedly.

31 See, for instance, the contributions of Ronald Davidson and Martin Lehnert in this book.

References

Primary sources

Kojiki 古事記. Aoki Kazuo 青木和夫, *et al.* (annot.), NST 1, 1982. (tr. Philippi 1968.)

Myōbō yōshū → *Yuiitsu shintō myōbō yōshū*

Nihon shoki 日本書紀 1. Ienaga Saburō 家永三郎, *et al.* (annot.), NKBT 67, 1967. (tr. Aston 1972.)

Nihon shoki jindai no maki shō 日本書紀神代巻抄, by Kiyohara Nobukata 清原宣賢. In Akiyama Kazumi (annot.), *Nihon shoki chūshaku*, vol. 3 (=ST *Koten chūshaku-hen* 4, 1988), pp. 139–247.

Nihon shoki kikigaki 日本書紀聞書, by Yoshida Kanemigi 吉田兼右. In Akiyama Kazumi 秋山一美 (annot.), *Nihon shoki chūshaku* 日本書紀註釈, vol. 3 (=ST *Koten chūshaku-hen* 4, 1988), pp. 249–434.

Nihon shoki sanso 日本書紀纂疏, by Ichijō Kaneyoshi 一条兼良. In Makabe Toshinobu 真壁俊信 (annot.), *Nihon shoki chūshaku*, vol. 2 (=ST *Koten chūshaku-hen* 3, 1986), pp. 145–351.

Sanso → *Nihon shoki sanso*

Shaku nihongi 釈日本紀, by Urabe Kanekata 卜部兼方. In Onoda Mitsuo 小野田光雄 (annot.), ST *Koten chūshaku-hen* 5, 1986.

Shinsho monjin 神書聞塵, by Keijo Shūrin 景徐周麟. In Akiyama Kazumi (annot.), *Nihon shoki chūshaku*, vol. 3 (=ST *Koten chūshaku-hen* 4, 1988), pp. 1–138.

Yuiitsu shintō myōbō yōshū 唯一神道名法要集, by Yoshida Kanetomo 吉田兼倶. In Ōsumi Kazuo 大隈和雄 (annot.), *Chūsei shintō ron* 中世神道論 (=NST 19, 1977), pp. 209–52.

Modern sources

Abe Yasurō 阿部泰郎 (1999), "*Nihongi* to iu undō" 日本紀という運動. *Kokubun-gaku kaishaku to kanshō* 64/3, pp. 6–17.

Assmann, Aleida and Jan Assmann (1987), "Kanon und Zensur," in A. Assmann and J. Assmann (eds), *Kanon und Zensur* (= Beiträge zur Archäologie der literarischen Kommunikation, vol. 2). München: W. Fink, pp. 7–27.

Aston, G.W. (1972), *Nihongi: Chronicles of Japan from the Earliest Times to A.D. 697.* Rutland, Vermont & Tokyo: Tuttle. [¹1896] (Two volumes in one book; all references refer to vol. 1.)

Carter, Steven (1996), *Regent Redux: A Life of the Statesman-Scholar Ichijō Kaneyoshi.* Ann Arbor: University of Michigan.

Klein, Susan (2002), *Allegories of Desire: Esoteric Literary Commentaries of Medieval Japan.* Cambridge, MA: Harvard University Press.

Maeda, Hiromi (2002), "Court Rank for Village Shrines: The Yoshida House's Interaction with Local Shrines during the Mid-Tokugawa Period." *Japanese Journal of Religious Studies* 29/3–4, pp. 325–58.

Maeda, Hiromi (2003), *Imperial Authority and Local Shrines: The Yoshida House and the Creation of a Countrywide Shinto Institution in Early Modern Japan.* PhD Dissertation, Cambridge, MA: Harvard University.

Masuo Shinichirō 増尾伸一郎 (1999), "Nara/Heian shoki no *Nihongi* to sono shūhen" 奈良・平安初期の〈日本紀〉とその周辺. *Kokubungaku kaishaku to kanshō* 64/3, pp. 18–25.

Mure Hitoshi 牟礼仁 (1996), "Shimabara Matsuhira bunko-zō *Shintō hisetsu* honkoku, kaidai" 島原松平文庫蔵「神道秘訣」翻刻・解題. *Kōgakkan daigaku shintō kenkyūjo kiyō* 12, pp. 95–178.

Nishida Nagao 西田長男 (1979), "Nihon shintō-shi kenkyū 日本神道史研究," vol. 5, *Chūsei-hen (ge)* 中世編（下）. Tokyo: Kōdansha.

Okada Shōji 岡田荘司 (1981), "Yoshida Kanetomo no Nihon shoki kenkyō" 吉田兼倶の日本書紀研究. *Kokugakuin zasshi* 82/11, pp. 165–77.

Okada Shōji (1983) "Yoshida Urabe-shi no seiritsu" 吉田卜部氏の成立. *Kokugakuin zasshi* 84/9, pp. 25–45.

Okada Shōji (1984a), "Yoshida Urabe-shi no hatten" 吉田卜部氏の発展, in *Shintōshi ronsō – Takikawa Masaijirō Sensei beijukinen ronbunshū* 神道史論叢：瀧川政次郎先生米寿記念論文集. Tokyo: Kokusho Kankōkai, pp. 700–720.

Okada Shōji (1984b), "Kaidai" 解題. In Okada Shōji (annot.), *Nihon shoki jindai no maki shō* 日本書紀神代巻抄 (= *Yoshida sōsho* 吉田叢書 4). Kyoto: Yoshida jinja, pp. 9–94.

Okada Shōji (1999), "Urabe-shi no Nihongi kenkyū" 卜部氏の日本紀研究. *Kokubungaku kaishaku to kanshō* 64/3, pp. 75–82.

Onoda Mitsuo 小野田光雄 (1986), "Kaidai" 解題. In Onoda Mitsuo (annot.), *Shaku Nihongi* (= ST, *Koten chūshaku-hen* 5), pp. 15–83.

Philippi, Donald L. (tr.) (1968), *Kojiki.* Tokyo: University of Tokyo Press, 1968.

Saitō Hideki 斎藤英喜 (1999), "Sekkanki no Nihongi kyōju" 摂関期の日本紀享受. *Kokubungaku kaishaku to kanshō* 64/3, pp. 34–42.

Scheid Bernhard (2001), *Der Eine und Einzige Weg der Götter: Yoshida Kanetomo und die Erfindung des Shinto.* Vienna: Austrian Academy of Sciences Press.

Teeuwen, Mark (2002), "From *Jindō* to Shinto: A Concept Takes Shape." *Japanese Journal of Religious Studies* 29/3–4, pp. 233–63.

Yoshihara Hiroto 吉原浩人, "Inseiki no Nihongi kyōju" 院政期の日本紀享受. *Kokubungaku kaishaku to kanshō* 64/3, pp. 43–50.

Part III

The demise of secrecy

13 When secrecy ends

The Tokugawa reformation of Tendai Buddhism and its implications

William M. Bodiford

The culture of secrecy so strongly associated with medieval Japanese religions largely came to an end during the Tokugawa period (1603–1868). Individual lineages of esoteric initiations continued, of course, but not the authority they once commanded. The emergence of a new culture of printed texts, public education, and the free exchange of knowledge gradually eroded the power of occult learning. Government policies and Buddhist priests accelerated this shift in values by promoting reformations that profoundly altered the ways that Japanese Buddhists (and modern scholars) would come to understand their own traditions.

Donald Keene asserts that Confucian scholars were the first ones to break free of the confines of secret lineages. Specifically, he cites 1599 – the year when Fujiwara Seika 藤原惺窩 (1561–1619) first punctuated the Chinese classics so that they could be read by any literate Japanese person – as the first step in "ending medieval traditions and opening the way to the popular" (Keene 1984, p. 120). Prior to this time, Keene notes, the punctuation of the Chinese classics had been a secret lore transmitted only within the Kiyohara 清原 and Nakahara 仲原 families of court aristocrats. Shortly thereafter, in 1603, Hayashi Razan 林羅山 (1583–1657) delivered the first public lectures on neo-Confucian texts. Japanese literature soon followed. One year later, in 1604, Matsunaga Teitoku 松永貞徳 (1571–1643) delivered the first public lectures on works of Japanese literature: *Tsurezuregusa* 徒然草 and *Hyakunin isshu* 百人一首 (Keene 1984, p. 121). By the end of that century the study of Japanese literature had passed totally out of the hands of private lineages and into the public domain, as exemplified by the massive study and translation of the *Manyōshū* 萬葉集 completed by the Buddhist monk Keichū 契沖 (1640–1701). Keichū based his interpretations of the *Manyōshū* poems on his own philological research (using Buddhist hermeneutical techniques), not on the secret traditions of the high-ranking court families (i.e. the so-called *dōjō* 堂上) that heretofore had monopolized knowledge of the text (Nosco 1986, p. 112).

The situation among Buddhists was more complicated. On the one hand, we find the same trend toward the greater public availability of previously inaccessible knowledge. The best-known example of this trend, perhaps, is the comprehensive analysis of the Buddhist scriptures by the rationalist scholar Tominaga Nakamoto 富永忠基 (1715–46), published in 1745 as his *Conversations After Emerging from Meditation* (*Shutsujō gōgo* 出定後語). Tominaga's textual analysis would have been impossible except for the explosive growth of print culture during the Tokugawa period, which included not just the importation of Buddhist texts from China, but also the publication of the entire Buddhist canon in Japan, first during the years 1637–1648 (the so-called Tenkai 天海 edition in movable type; 6,323 fascicles) and again in 1681 (the so-called Ōbaku 黄檗 woodblock edition; 6,771 fascicles). On the other hand, we also find Buddhists taking an active stance by campaigning against secret initiations, denouncing them in print, and advocating their suppression. Leaders of the True Pure Land School (Jōdo Shinshū) repeatedly published denunciations of secret teachings (*hiji bōmon* 秘事法門), of secret rituals (e.g. *fuhai hiji* 不拜秘事), and of secret initiation vaults (*dozō hiji* 土蔵秘事). While the True Pure Land School is especially renowned for their repeated campaigns against deviant faith (*ianjin* 異安心, i.e. heresy; see Dobbins 1980), they are by no means the only Buddhists to denounce secret teachings as heretical. In Sōtō Zen, for example, Menzan Zuihō 面山瑞方 (1683–1769) denounced all secret initiation documents (*danshi* 断紙, i.e. *kirikami* 切紙) that could not be reconciled with what he determined to be the authentic writings of Dōgen 道元 (1200–53).[1] Menzan's rejection of secret initiations is especially noteworthy because it forms one step in his efforts to replace the religious charisma of Dōgen as originator of the Japanese Sōtō Zen lineage with a new kind of textual charisma that emanates from Dōgen as author of authoritative texts. This new charisma was conveyed not through master–disciple initiations, but through philological analysis and textual commentaries written by scholars like Menzan (Riggs 2002).

The least noted yet most influential denunciation of secrecy within Buddhism might very well have been the so-called Anraku 安樂 reforms initiated in the Tendai school by Reikū Kōken 霊空光謙 (1652–1739). In 1689 Reikū wrote *Byakujahen* 闢邪篇 (*Repudiation of Heresies*), a polemical attack on the Tendai school's most exalted secret initiations. Reikū called these initiations *genshi kimyōdan* 玄旨帰命壇 , a name of uncertain significance (see the discussion below) which has been adopted by subsequent historians. Reikū's *Repudiations* won him the support of Kōben 公弁 (1669–1716), the royal prelate (*hōshinnō* 法親王) who ruled Tendai affairs from his position as abbot of Kan'eiji 寛永寺 temple in Edo (the seat of the military government and site of modern Tokyo). As will be explained below, Kōben's status as the son of the Heavenly Sovereign (*tennō* 天皇 , i.e. "emperor") along with Kan'eiji's prestige as chief administrative temple gave him unprecedented power with which to support Reikū's views.[2] In 1693 Kōben appointed Reikū as the first abbot of the Anrakuin 安樂院 temple on Mount Hiei, the monastic headquarters of Tendai, and granted him authority to reform discipline and education on the mountain. The following year, in 1694, Kōben wrote a preface for Reikū's *Repudiations* and published it. With the force of Kōben's endorsement, Reikū's Anraku reforms overwhelmed centuries of tradition. Thereafter all activities associated with the so-called *genshi* and the *kimyō* initiations ceased and most texts pertaining to them were burned. For all intents and purposes the year 1694 marks the beginning of the end of the medieval traditions of Tendai esoteric lore.

The rejection of secret initiations initiated by Reikū Kōken has attracted little attention, even within the Tendai school (for a standard overview, see Ishida 1986). Nonetheless, its importance cannot be over-estimated. Reikū's *Byakujahen* marks an important turning point in the history of Japanese Buddhism, one which altered the way that the monks of the Tendai tradition came to interpret their own tradition and one which has profoundly influenced and confused the way that scholars have viewed Japanese religious history as a whole. To understand why this is so, though, first we must briefly examine the larger context in which this treatise appeared. For Japanese Buddhism in general, and for the Tendai establishment in particular, the Tokugawa period presented a new intellectual milieu and new political realities. Moreover, within this new intellectual and political climate, Reikū Kōken was just one member of the larger Anraku Reform movement that struggled for control over the Tendai school.

The intellectual milieu of Tokugawa Buddhism

As I have already suggested, the intellectual climate of Tokugawa Japan witnessed a profound epistemological shift, when private initiations into secret lore could no longer satisfy the growing demands for philological and historiographic evidence. Legitimacy and authority came to derive more and more from new scholarship and philological analysis of publicly available texts. The Tokugawa government itself promoted Buddhist scholarship through the many regulations (*hatto* 法度) that it issued to Buddhist institutions from 1608 to 1618 (Bodiford 1991, p. 433). Intellectual historians, however, have examined this growing reliance on scholarship primarily in terms of Confucian developments. Thus, many studies examine important Confucian scholars, like Itō Jinsai 伊藤仁斉 (1627–1705), who advocated the study of the ancient meaning (*kogigaku* 古義学) of Confucian texts, or Ogyū Sorai 荻生祖徠 (1666–1728), whose rejection of neo-Confucian interpretations helped to start the movement called the school of Ancient Learning (*kogaku ha* 古学派). These Japanese efforts developed in parallel with similar efforts by Confucian scholars in

Qing dynasty China (1644–1912) who developed what they called evidentiary learning (*kōshōgaku* 考証学). The writings of Japanese scholars like Itō and Ogyū were reprinted in China, and there is no doubt that contemporary Qing dynasty scholarship was read in Japan. Thus, Confucian scholars on both sides of the sea navigated the same transition that Benjamin Elman (1984) has described as moving "from philosophy to philology" (cf. Riggs 2002).

The influence of developments in contemporary Chinese Buddhism on Tokugawa Japan is less well known. Previous scholarship on the influence of Chinese Buddhism of this period has focused solely on the arrival of Chinese monks like Yinyuan Longqi 隱元隆琦 (Ingen Ryūki, 1592–1673) and other supporters of the defeated Ming dynasty (1368–1644) who subsequently established the Ōbaku 黃檗 Zen lineage in Japan (Baroni 2000; Wu 2002). It is important to note, therefore, that the influence of the Chinese Buddhism extended far beyond Ōbaku or Zen circles. The arrival of Chinese monks helped to awaken new sectarian awareness among Japanese Buddhists of all backgrounds who sought to compete with Chinese rivals for patronage and who increasingly sought to justify difference between Chinese and their own Japanese traditions by citing authoritative texts. When citing texts, this new Japanese Buddhist scholarship relied greatly on Buddhist scriptures imported from China. These Chinese Buddhist texts are especially significant because they reflect Chinese doctrinal concerns, Chinese ritual practices, and Chinese monastic practices – all of which were very different from the ones that had developed in medieval Japan.

If we look at Reikū Kōken, for example, we find that he and his teacher, Myōryū Jisan 妙立慈山 (1636–90), and their disciples all insisted that Japanese Tendai monks should base their teachings and practices on Chinese standards. Henceforth the combination of Tendai (*en* 円), Tantra (*mitsu* 密), Zen 禅, and Mahāyāna precepts (*kai* 戒) introduced by Saichō 最澄 (767–822) – the unstable combination that had given birth to medieval (*chūko* 中古) Tendai's culture of secrecy – was to be judged against the standards of the Song dynasty (960–1279) Tendai orthodoxy created by Siming Zhili 四明知禮 (960–1028) and his so-called Mountain House (*sange* 山家) school. Significantly, Myōryū Jisan and Reikū Kōken based their interpretations of Zhili not on Zhili's own writings, but on the writings of later Ming dynasty Buddhist monks such as Huaize 懷則 (n.d.), Wujin Chuandeng 無盡傳燈 (fl. 1627), and Ouyi Zhixu 藕益智旭 (1599–1655).[3] Compared to Siming Zhili, all of these later Ming dynasty monks were much more polemical, sectarian, and strident in their doctrinal assertions. They insisted that only Tendai conveys the correct Buddhism and that only Siming Zhili represents correct Tendai. These Chinese writers could never have admitted that Japanese Tendai might deviate from this Chinese orthodoxy. The writings of these Ming dynasty Chinese monks would not have been available in Japan prior to the Tokugawa period. Thus, at a time when the Tokugawa government was promoting Buddhist academic scholarship and when Japanese Buddhists were re-examining the textual justifications for their own customary practices, monks like Myōryū Jisan and Reikū Kōken gained access to Ming dynasty Buddhist treatises that insisted on rigid standards of doctrinal orthodoxy.

The political setting of Tendai Buddhism

The political context of Reikū Kōken's *Repudiations* also must be considered. As mentioned earlier, this treatise was published in 1694 with a preface by the royal prelate Kōben. Without the endorsement of this royal prince, Kōken's *Repudiation of Heresies* would not have been so powerful; its effects could not have been so profound. To explain why this particular royal prelate exerted so much influence, we must examine how the Tokugawa government restructured the Tendai Buddhist institution. Prior to the Tokugawa no Tendai prelate, royal or otherwise, existed in eastern Japan. During the medieval period the most important Tendai institution, and perhaps the most important religious institution in Japan, consisted of the Enryakuji monastic compound on Mount Hiei. This was the religious site charged with responsibility for ensuring the health and long life (*honmyō* 本命) of the heavenly sovereign. For this reason, of all the religious institutions in Japan it was the one that enjoyed the closest connections to the royal family. During the medieval period Mount Hiei was governed by three royal temples (*monzeki* 門跡: Ennyūin 円融院, Myōhōin 妙法院, and Shōren'in 青蓮院.[4] Among royal temples, they were of the highest ecclesiastical status, meaning that their abbots must possess the *miya* 宮 title awarded only to legitimate princes. In other words, their abbots were high-ranking sons of the Heavenly Sovereign. Moreover, the chief abbot (*zasu* 座主) of Mount Hiei always was selected from among the abbots of these three royal temples. Thus, the upper echelons of the Tendai establishment constituted a significant branch of the royal family.

The medieval structure of Mount Hiei was destroyed in 1571 when the warlord Oda Nobunaga (1534–82) and his troops attacked and torched the mountain. Thereafter, the Tendai school, and Mount Hiei in particular, never again would be allowed to regain its former glory. The new Tokugawa government (or bakufu) allowed Mount Hiei to rebuild, but only in demilitarized form, within a much smaller scope, and a restructured format (Morioka 1967). Several Tokugawa policies limited the power of the reconstituted Hiei complex (see Somata 1985; Takano 1985). First, the bakufu issued separate regulations (*hatto*) to Buddhist denominations such as the Pure Land (Jōdoshū), Shugendō, and Rinzai Zen lineages that during the medieval period had developed in quasi-affiliation with the Tendai institutions. These separate regulations gave these groups unambiguous institutional independence from Tendai for the first time (Kashiwara 1967). Second, it ordered Buddhist schools, including Tendai, to form newly rationalized networks of head-temples and branch-temples across the country. These temple networks would take orders not from their previous monastic centers (such as Mount Hiei), but from liaison (*furegashira* 触頭) temples that were constructed in the government's new urban center, Edo. Third, the bakufu severely restricted the size and influence of royal temples within the Tendai (a total of nine *miya monzeki*), Shingon (six *miya monzeki*), and Hossō (two *miya monzeki*) schools. The government reduced the size of their land holdings and assumed supervisory positions over them. Bakufu regulations set the standard income for *miya*-class royal temples at 1,000 *koku* 石 (a unit of measurement nominally linked to rice production). Likewise, the court rank for royal abbots at the three main Tendai royal temples (Ennyūin, Myōhō'in, and Shōren'in) was set at "second class" (*nihon* 二 品). Fourth, in 1655 the bakufu created a new *miya*-class royal temple to rule over the Tendai school: Kan'eiji in Edo.[5] Tendai thereby became administratively split into an old faction linked just to the court and a new one that could be closely supervised by the military government.

Kan'eiji gave the bakufu a direct line of control over Tendai. Kan'eiji differed from the other three Tendai royal temples in that it was created by the military government. Its annual income was set at the amount of 13,000 *koku* – the highest of any royal temple and far above the other Tendai royal temples. Moreover, the royal prince who served as abbot of Kan'eiji would hold a court rank of "first class" (*ichibon* 一品). This new royal temple was given direct authority over Mount Hiei, over the other three Tendai royal temples, and over the Rinnōji 輪王寺 Tendai temple complex on Mount Nikkō. Rinnōji is the site of the mausoleum for Tokugawa Ieyasu (1542–1616) – the founder of the Tokugawa military government. It was there that Tokugawa Ieyasu was deified as the Great Avatar Shining Over the East (Tōshō Daigongen 東照大権現), a title signifying that he had become the divine Buddhist protector of Japan, a Buddhist god (*shinkun* 神君) who illuminates the East. In short, a royal prince – the heavenly sovereign's brother or son – in his role as the abbot of Kan'eiji henceforth would lead the nation in worshiping the founder of the military government. During rituals conducted in honor of Tokugawa Ieyasu, the abbot of Kan'eiji would act as chief ritualist (*dōshi* 導師) while one or more of the other royal prelates from one of the three main Tendai royal temples (Ennyūin, Myōhō'in, and Shōren'in) or from Mount Hiei would act as his assistant. As Herman Ooms (1985, p. 185) has noted, "Ritual was thus the most important means by which the Tokugawa legitimized their regime." This ritual hierarchy clearly symbolized the political hierarchy of: the military government on top, Eastern Tendai (in Edo) next, Western Tendai (i.e. Mount Hiei) below, and the royal family (who traditionally had relied on Mount Hiei for spiritual protection) at the bottom (Somata 1985). In this way the center of Japanese Tendai shifted east from Mount Hiei to Edo. This shift is symbolized by the fact that Kan'eiji was popularly known as Tō Eizan 東叡山, "the Mount Hiei of the East" (a play on "Eizan," the shortened form of Hiei-zan).

When Reikū Kōken's *Bakujahen* was published in 1694, the fact that it included a preface by Kōben, the abbot of Kan'eiji, amounted to an official bakufu endorsement of Kōken's views. The existence of this preface explains why *Bakujahen* signaled a shift in policies that would result in the elimination of Tendai traditions of oral initiation. All heretical texts were burned to avoid trouble with bakufu authorities. Kōben had become the head of Kan'eiji only one year earlier, in 1693. At that time, one of his first official acts was to order the establishment of a new temple complex on Mount Hiei to be known as the Anrakuin, which henceforth would be in charge of reforming the discipline and training of all Tendai clergy. Kōben thereupon appointed Reikū as its first physical abbot.[6] As a further indication of his particular favor, Kōben personally carved a three-sided seal, which he presented to Reikū. One side of the seal gave Reikū's formal Buddhist name (*hōki* 法諱): Shaku Kōken 釈光謙 (i.e. Kōken, the descendant of Śākyamuni Buddha). Another side of the seal gave his path name (*dōgō* 道号): Reikū. The third side read, *Tendai shōshū* 天台正宗 (the Orthodox Doctrines of Tendai). This third side indicates that the reforms to be implemented at the Anrakuin symbolized for Kōben (and for Reikū) the restoration of Tendai orthodoxy in Japan (Ishida 1986, p. 463).

The Anraku reform movement

Space does not permit a detailed overview of the Anraku reform movement in this essay. It involves many different individuals who disputed numerous complex issues of Tendai doctrine and history over a period of almost one hundred years. Here I will limit my remarks to the ways that the establishment of a new Tendai orthodoxy (initiated by the Anrakuin movement) necessitated the elimination of the competing systems of Tendai secret initiations. My interpretation of the Anraku movement is somewhat novel, since according to most accounts its reforms were concerned not with secret initiations but with vinaya ordination.

As is well known, Saichō had gained institutional independence for the Tendai school in Japan by rejecting all ordination rites based on the Buddhist codes of discipline known as vinaya (Groner 2000). Saichō labeled the vinaya as being "Hīnayāna" (*shōjō* 小乗; inferior Buddhism) and petitioned the royal court to allow him to ordain his own disciples according to unique Tendai precepts – which he called "exclusively Mahāyāna precepts" (*ikkō daijō kai* 一向大乗戒). This audacious act won independence for Japanese Tendai and changed the course of Buddhist history in Japan. Nowhere else in Asia has any orthodox, mainstream Buddhist community disavowed the vinaya. This lack of vinaya sets Japan apart. In the eyes of many Buddhists from other Asian countries, the

Japanese Buddhist samgha (religious community) without vinaya cannot be a real samgha.[7] In other words, the people commonly referred to as "monks" and "nuns" are not real monks and nuns in the sense that those terms are used in other Buddhist regions.[8] And, consequently, Japanese Buddhism is not real Buddhism. The modern Japanese perspective, of course, is very different. Since the early twentieth century, Japanese Buddhists and scholars alike have celebrated Japan's lack of vinaya as a unique achievement which renders Japanese Buddhism more Mahāyāna (i.e. superior) and Japan's samgha better suited to the demands of modern civilization.

When seen in terms of these contrasting perspectives on the importance of vinaya, it is perhaps natural that the Anraku movement's best-known reform is its revival of traditional monastic ordinations based on the *Four part vinaya* (*Shibun ritsu* 四分律). Modern scholars tend to portray the Anraku reforms simply as an anachronistic attempt by later Tendai monks to turn back eight hundred years of Tendai history and undo the one achievement for which they praise Saichō (e.g. Ishida 1986; Ueda 1976). In spite of its supposed anachronism, the Anraku revival of vinaya was largely successful. From 1693 until the Meiji Restoration of 1868 (with only a brief twenty-year interruption from 1752 to 1773) the Anrakuin temple ensured that Tendai clerics were ordained and disciplined according to the traditional forms codified by vinaya. For Reikū and Kōben, though, vinaya was only one element in a much larger agenda. Even during the brief period when vinaya ordinations were suspended, their overall agenda continued to dictate the terms of debate (Sonehara 1991).

Reikū and Kōben sought to reform Japanese Tendai so that it would never again suffer repression and destruction by the warrior government. In their eyes as long as Japanese Tendai monks clung to their own medieval systems of initiation, they would continue to reject the vinaya. As long as they rejected the vinaya, they would lack proper moral training. As long as they lacked morality, Tendai would be a threat to social order, and the Tendai establishment could never regain its former glory. In other words, Kōben and Reikū saw a direct link between maintaining social morality, promoting the vinaya (as followed by Chinese Tendai monks), and suppressing the established customs of medieval Japanese Tendai. All three of these elements were but interconnected aspects of the same reform process, just like the three sides of the seal that Kōben had presented to Reikū. This relationship between vinaya and social order is clearly expressed in the various orders issued by Kōben. In 1693 he issued a decree to establish the Anrakuin (*Anrakuin okibumi* 安樂院置文), which said in part:

> In maintaining the Buddha Dharma, nothing precedes vinaya. It is the standard for both monastics and lay people. Both the great and inferior vehicles [i.e., Mahāyāna and *hīnayāna*] flourish because of it.

Therefore when our ancestor Saichō founded this mountain he submitted the petition concerning the three types of temples [i.e., Hīnayāna, Mahāyāna, and mixed] and established the one vehicle precepts (*ichijō kai* 一乗戒) [i.e., Lotus sutra Mahāyāna precepts] of the ten grave prohibitions and the sixty-eight minor ones as the basis for becoming a fully ordained monk and the perfect, sudden ten good precepts (*jūzen kai* 十善戒) as the basis for becoming a novice (*shami* 沙弥, Skt. *śrāmaṇera*). As a result the sunlight of the Buddha has shone over Japan and the winds of the teachings have pervaded the lands of our kingdom.

Alas, our ancestors have long departed, peoples' spiritual abilities have deteriorated, and monastic decorum has declined. The winds of truth have died out. At this time we need dedicated individuals who will spurn the majority, retire to an isolated hermitage and devote themselves to the cultivation of vinaya. The Anrakuin temple in Imuro Valley was such a place. But in recent decades it lost its associate institutions and charter. How could such a fate not sadden anyone who knows of it? Therefore, based on its ancient precedents I now proclaim Anrakuin to be a center for the promotion of vinaya in the hope that vinaya will never again decline. For this point forward the abbot of the Anrakuin temple must be someone who observes the vinaya, and anyone who lacks the vinaya precepts must not be allowed to reside there. This order shall be proclaimed throughout the mountain.[9]

In 1707, Kōben issued regulations for Mount Hiei (*Enryakuji jōsei* 延暦寺條制) in which he stated that if the abuses of previous years are not corrected, then it will be impossible to win back the faith of the aristocracy or to attract able monks who want to study Tendai. Key provisions of the regulations state,

Enryakuji on Mount Hiei is the holy sanctuary that protects the monarchy and it is the ancestral home of Tendai Buddhism. Since ancient times it has trained many eminent and virtuous teachers. For this reason the kind and the aristocracy have venerated Mount Hiei beyond all others. Yet since the medieval times the religious path has lost its vibrancy to such an extant that those who have faith in the dharma can merely sigh in regret. Now our kingdom is at peace and there are no rebels within our shores. For the past thirty years the true dharma has begun to revive and its seeds are ready to bear fruit. If the evil practices are not reformed then outside the monastery it will be impossible to win the faith of the king and ministers and inside the monastery it will be impossible to attract student monks. The good will be harmed. This year as I have again been named

chief abbot (*zasu*). [...] I hereby established ten articles to encourage
study:

1   The study of Buddha Dharma must entail both understanding
    and practice. The three forms of learning [i.e., wisdom, morality,
    and mental cultivation] complete one another. [...]

2   The founder's, Saichō's, curriculum consisted of a twelve-year
    residency (*ikki* 一紀) as a bodhisattva monk (*bosatsu sō* 菩薩僧) based
    on ordination with the Brahmā-net sutra (*Bonmō-kyō* 梵網經経)
    precepts alone, after which time one would become a bodhisattva
    monk of senior standing who studies the dual discipline [i.e.,
    vinaya] of the great and inferior vehicles [i.e., Mahāyāna and
    "Hīnayāna"]. But both curriculums subsequently disappeared so
    that even their names have not been heard for quite some time.
    Recently one group of monks [i.e., Reikū and the members of
    the Anraku Movement] have started to observe the twelve-year
    residency in Tantric (*shana* 遮那) and Tendai (*shikan* 止観) study,
    and upon attaining senior standing they practice the dual disci-
    pline of the five classes of precepts [in the *Four part vinaya*]. Such
    monks are our true role models. With this standard for our student
    monks, people of religious aspiration will flourish for ages to come
    and their lineage will not perish. That is my earnest hope. [...]

3   Mahāyāna consists of various doctrines, each one of which cures
    [specific spiritual afflictions]. Therefore, a single doctrine cures,
    but many doctrines [combined together] cannot cure and cannot
    be illuminated. Therefore, students must study only their own
    [school's] doctrines. Student monks on this mountain must study
    the two vehicles of Tendai and Esoteric (*tai mitsu ryōjō* 台密両乗)
    because our founder, Saichō, propagated those two vehicles.
    Nonetheless monks of exceptional ability can also study Kegon,
    Hossō, and so forth. Once they have completed those texts, there
    is no obstacle to investigating the five Confucian classics and
    Chinese literature, just so long as they do not fall prey to ordinary
    secular teachings. Siming Zhili warned against this danger. Chinese
    Buddhist monks heed his warning. Should not people of our
    land do the same? [...][10]

The second provision is especially noteworthy. This regulation requires a
mandatory twelve-year period of residency (*ikki*) on Mount Hiei, which it
identifies as the form of practice advocated by Saichō. In fact, though,
this twelve-year residency would be devoted to study of the Chinese
Tiantai orthodoxy (i.e. Siming Zhili's Mountain House school). During
this period, the priests on Mount Hiei would be ordained with the
Mahāyāna precepts alone. At the end of their twelve years, when they

were ready to leave the mountain, they also would be ordained with the vinaya precepts (Ishida 1986, p. 468). This long period of isolation on the mountain, if enforced, would have effectively prevented Tendai monks from becoming involved in secular affairs while they were young and vigorous.

Reikū's *Repudiation*

Reikū's *Repudiation* (*Byakujahen*) developed within and reinforced the aforementioned intellectual climate, political structure, and sectarian movement that together were reshaping the landscape of Japanese Buddhism. Reikū began this work with the following assertion:

> To repudiate heresies means to repudiate the heretical teachings (*jasetsu* 邪說) of *genshi kimyōdan* 玄旨帰命壇. In our land the Tendai doctrines (*taikyō* 台教) became confused during the medieval (*chūko*) period and people with evil views (*akuken* 悪見) constructed these secret doctrines (*genshi* 玄旨). They have established [Zen-like] *kōan* 公案 [dialogues] for secret initiations during consecration (*kanjō* 潅頂; i.e., *abhiṣeka*) rituals on the altar of refuge (*kimyō dan* 帰命壇). These have been so widespread for such a long time that today people who lack Dharma vision all revere them and are under their sway. They even go so far as to say that: "[Tendai] Lotus [doctrines] and [Tendai] meditation (*shikan* 止観) [practices] are just expedient teachings that have not yet clarified the original meaning (*gen'i* 元意)!" At first I also transmitted these teachings, but later I awakened to their depravity. How could I not regret my verbal karmic transgressions and refrain from repudiating them?
>
> Now, its initiation rituals definitely cannot be found in any Buddhist scripture or treatise. The fact that the ritual procedures forcibly distort passages from commentaries and that the manuals are full of errors is perfectly obvious without one having to argue the point. Its *kōan* consist of passages taken from scriptures and treatises, but not one of them is interpreted correctly. [...][11]

In this passage Reikū specifically denounces the rituals that he calls "the secret doctrines" conveyed on "the altar of refuge" (*genshi kimyōdan*). Today we cannot know exactly what these rituals were or how they functioned in the context of Tendai monasticism. Surviving evidence suggests that instead of a single secret Tendai initiation ritual known as *genshi kimyōdan*, there might have been a series of rituals known as the "three-fold secret doctrine" (*sanjū genshi* 三重玄旨) or a pair of parallel rituals known as the "secret doctrine initiation" (*genshi kanjō* 玄旨潅頂) and the "refuge initiation" (*kimyō kanjō* 帰命潅頂). Most modern scholars, however, simply use Reikū's terminology and refer to these rituals (whatever they were) as *genshi kimyōdan*. They interpret this name (quite correctly I believe) as a generic term that – by implication at least – collectively designates all the secret initiations and oral traditions of medieval Tendai.[12] In other words, Reikū used the *genshi kimyōdan* as a target for a doctrinal attack aimed at the entire culture of Tendai secret initiations.

Of these various Tendai secret initiations, the ones known as *genshi* or as *kimyō* or by some similar designation seem to have been the most secret. Nonetheless, they were not so secret as to escape the attention of well-informed lay people. The Nativist (*kokugaku* 国学) scholar Amano Nobukage 天野信景 (1661–1733), for example, wrote that Tendai doctrines have become confused and lost. As a result, some Tendai monks have adopted Zen teaching methods in which they compose *kōan* and appended sayings (*jakugo* 著語), which are taught so as to provide seals of certification (*inka* 印可) for Tendai monks in a secret ceremony known as the "consecration ritual of secret doctrines on the altar of refuge" (*genshi kimyōdan no kanjō* 玄旨帰命壇潅頂). Amano added that the main deity (*honzon* 本尊) for this ritual is the god Matarajin 摩多羅神 (Amano Nobukage in *Shioshiri* 塩尻, fasc. 35; quoted in Sonehara 1990, p. 30). The fact that Amano links *genshi kimyōdan* to the otherwise obscure god Matarajin is significant. Although all but forgotten today, Matarajin once had been an extremely important god (see the discussion below and the essay in this book by Bernard Faure). In spite of Matarajin's importance, Reikū makes no mention of Matarajin or of any other god. It is not the links to strange gods that Reikū finds objectionable, but the Buddhist doctrines expressed by the curriculum of Zen *kōan* dialogues.

Reikū's *Repudiation* analyzes thirteen of these *kōan* dialogues (the first seven are labeled *genshi kōan* 玄旨公案 and the last six are *kimyō kōan* 帰命公案). Each analysis consists of a three-part structure, consisting of: (1) a quotation from Buddhist scriptures; (2) a series of questions and answers concerning that quotation, which represent the secret teachings conveyed in the *genshi kimyōdan* initiation ritual; and (3) Reikū's criticism of the ideas expressed by that *kōan* dialogue. The first *kōan* concerns the phrase "refraining from all evil" (*shoaku makusa* 諸悪莫作). These words occur in the well-known verse that in East Asia is titled the "Universal Precepts of the Seven Buddhas" (*Shichibutsu tsūkai ge* 七仏通戒偈). The entire verse goes,

> Not doing evils,
> Devoutly practicing every good,
> Purifying one's own mind:
> These are the teachings of all buddhas.[13]

This verse constitutes one of the earliest Buddhist teachings. It occurs in a wide variety of Buddhist scriptures which represent all historical periods and varieties of Buddhist thought. In Tendai it is especially important, since it appears in several of the commentaries traditionally attributed to Tiantai Zhiyi 天台智顗 (538–97), the de facto founder of the Tendai tradition in China.[14]

According to Reikū, in the *genshi kimyōdan* initiation ritual the *kōan* concerning this phrase goes as follows:

> *Number 1: Verse of the Universal Precepts of the Seven Buddhas*
> The teacher asks: "What is the meaning of not doing evils and devoutly practicing every good?"
>
> The student replies: "The mind not thinking of good or evil."[15]

In his analysis Reikū first acknowledges that this position has some doctrinal basis. The highest truth of Buddhism lies beyond the appearances of the mundane world. Therefore the *genshi kimyōdan* initiation emphasizes not minding. Nonetheless, Reikū points out that this approach goes totally against the actual meaning expressed in the verse on the Universal Precepts of the Seven Buddhas. The *genshi kimyōdan* initiation focuses on abstract theory (*ri* 理), while the verse actually concerns physical practice (*ji* 事). Reikū draws a clear distinction between abstract truth and its realization in practice (cf. Sonehara 1990, pp. 30–31). He writes,

> Buddha precepts may be numerous, but all of them can be reduced to either proscriptive or prescriptive injunctions. Proscriptive means stopping evil. Prescriptive means promoting good. The phrase "not doing evils" is the proscriptive precept. The phrase "devoutly practicing every good" is the prescriptive precept. For this reason these are called the universal precepts. Therefore, both of these statements concern practice, not theory. Both concern cultivation, not the [ultimate] nature of reality. How can [the *genshi kimyōdan* initiation] explicate them as if they directly concern theory or [ultimate] nature?[16]

Reikū's remarks on the third *kōan* clearly express the reasons why he so strongly wished to distinguish the need for concrete practice from the abstract truth, which should be its goal. This dialogue addresses the phrase "real mind fixed on real object" (*jisshin kei jikkyō* 実心繋実境), tradition attributed to Nanyue Huisi 南嶽慧思 (515–77), the teacher of the Tiantai patriarch Zhiyi. In a collection of Zhiyi's oral instructions on meditation practices, Zhiyi says,

> My teacher [Nanyue Huisi] would always admonish us by saying:
>
> When the real mind (*jisshin* 実心) fixes on the real object (*jikkyō* 実境),
> Then the real conditions (*jitsuen* 実縁) gradually arise.
> The real and the real successively infuse [one another],
> So that one naturally enters the real truth (*jitsuri* 実理).[17]

According to Reikū, in the *genshi kimyōdan* initiation ritual the *kōan* concerning this phrase goes as follows:

Number 3: Nanyue's verse
The teacher asks: "What is the real mind fixed on the real object?"

The student replies: "Mind and object fundamentally do not exist."

The teacher again asks: "What is real conditions gradually arise?"

The student replies: "Nothing, and suddenly they exist."

The teacher again asks: "What is the real and the real successively infusing so that one naturally enters the real truth?"

The student replies: "Wearing cloths and eating rice; ordinary life without affairs."[18]

Reikū begins his criticism of the *genshi kimyōdan* initiation by showing that it deviates from the standard Chinese commentary on this verse:

This [*genshi kimyōdan*] explanation not only disagrees with the meaning of the original passage, but also greatly violates Tendai doctrinal guidelines. Here we can see how those who created the *genshi* [initiations] wanted to confuse the hearts of men in this world. This verse concerns Master Nanyue's admonition for [the student monks in] his assembly. Master Tiantai [Zhiyi][19] commented on this verse, saying: "If the mind is fixed [i.e., concentrated] on an object, then the object certainly fixes the mind. Mind and object fixing one another is called 'real conditions.' Moreover, each successive [instant of mind] continues on this basis so that each [instant of] mind is described as 'successive mutual infusion.' In other words, mind is infusing the object and the object is infusing mind. Mind and object, in each instant of thought, are mutually infused like this so that gradually the *kṣaṇa* [moments of time] lose all duration. From following this method of contemplation, one naturally enters into a partial authentication [of the truth]. Therefore, it is called 'entering the real.'" This [passage] shows how Nanyue [Huisi] and Tiantai [Zhiyi] wanted people to establish Perfect [Tendai] cultivation (*enshu* 円修) so that they might achieve perfect results [i.e., awakening]. Therefore, they carefully admonished [their students] in this way.

The secret doctrine [initiations], however, by stating that something which is fundamentally nonexistent can suddenly exist, thereby abolishes [any need for] the cultivations of virtues (*shutoku* 修徳). It only values the ordinary mind (*byōjō shin* 平常心), which it takes to be the way of naturalness (*jinen dō* 自然道). In its opposition to the patriarchal doctrines, could anything be more extreme than this? It is as if [the devil, Māra] Pāpīyas (Hajun 波旬) entered into the hearts of men and taught them an imitation doctrine in the desire to cause living beings to slander the Buddha Dharma, to act without any restraints, and to fall forever into Avīci Hell (Abi goku 阿鼻獄) [i.e., the worst possible kind of hell]. [...][20]

In other words, instead of teaching the proper methods of mental concentration and meditation, the secret initiations assert the heresy of naturalism in which there is no karmic relationship between religious cultivation and the attainment of its fruits. By proclaiming that results can suddenly appear out of nothingness, they negate any need for the religious cultivation of virtue. This is why the secret initiations identify the attainment of ultimate truth (i.e. entering the real) with the activities of ordinary life. For Reikū nothing could be worse than this kind of antinomianism. He spells out these implications in graphic terms:

> People who transmit these secret doctrine initiations lack moral precepts or physical circumspection (*kaiki* 戒檢) and lack mental cultivation (*zenna* 禅那). They pass each day drinking alcohol and playing checkers (*go* 碁) into the night. Their sexual avarice and greed know no limits. [...][21]

Finally, Reikū concludes his remarks on this *kōan* by citing a passage from the *Śūraṅgama-sūtra* (*Shoulengyan jing* 首楞嚴經, fasc. 9; T no. 945, 19.149c–150a) where it warns against false teachers who praise violating the rules of Buddhist morality and who advocate giving in to greed and lust, or who teach that the pleasures of the senses are the true Pure Land (*gen ni bi setsu kaü jōdo* 眼耳鼻舌皆為淨土) and that men and women's sexual organs are the real source of awakening and nirvana (*danjo nikon soku bodai nehan* 男女二根即菩提涅槃). Reikū writes, "The *genshi kimyōdan* initiations truly are no different from this. How could they be anything other than the devil's teachings?" [22]

Reikū's criticisms of these two *kōan* encapsulate the crux of his argument. For Reikū, religious practice requires adherence to defined moral standards of behavior. The secret initiations, however, taught that all standards reside within one's own mind. Thus, the key issue consisted of a moral choice between objective criteria based on authoritative scriptures, commentaries, and treatises versus subjective inner experience. The secrecy of the initiations permitted their antinomian rejection of moral teachings to flourish unchecked. Therefore, Reikū concluded that these particular secret initiations – and, by extension, all other unorthodox secret initiations – must be banned.

The loss of secrecy

Reikū's arguments, backed by Kōben's political power, were remarkably successful. The medieval culture of Tendai secret initiations came to an end (Tamura 1973, p. 478). Even ritual manuals describing these initiations largely disappeared, except for a few scattered fragments.[23] Moreover, the monks of Mount Hiei were ordained according to the *Four Part Vinaya*, a practice that continued until the Meiji Restoration of 1868. These accomplishments invited opposition. Almost as soon as the Anrakuin temple was established as a center for teaching vinaya on Mount Hiei, an opposing group of Tendai monks appeared. In contrast to Reikū's seal with the slogan "Orthodox Teachings of Tendai" (Tendai shōshū), the opposing faction referred to themselves as the "Orthodox Lineage of the Mountain School" (Sange seitō 山家正統). These sobriquets might seem to suggest a dichotomy between two opposing groups, one claiming authority based on orthodox doctrines from scriptures and another relying on customary practices as authenticated by historical lineages. That was not the case. Instead, advocates of the "Orthodox Lineage of the Mountain School" adopted Reikū's style of textual scholarship. They merely disagreed to his selection of authoritative texts. Instead of the writings of the Chinese patriarch Siming Zhili (whom Reikū favored), they relied on the writings of the Japanese patriarch Saichō.[24] They were the Tendai monks who, for the first time in Japanese history, began to collect and study the writings of Saichō, which they used to argue that Saichō had firmly rejected the vinaya. Thus, Reikū and his opponents together helped create the standard explanation of Japanese Tendai that dominates modern textbooks, namely the doctrines of Siming Zhili combined with Saichō's rejection of vinaya.

This standard textbook explanation cannot clarify the medieval culture of secrecy, but can only obscure it. Secrets, once lost, cannot be revealed. Nonetheless if we are to understand medieval religion and culture, we must try to remind ourselves that these lost secrets once existed. Once upon a time they were not heretical. In fact, they animated mainstream Japanese religion and culture – and they were held dear by the high priests and institutions patronized by the most powerful social leaders. The god Matarajin is a prime example. In 1617 when the Tendai monk Tenkai 天海 (1536–1643) interred the remains of Tokugawa Ieyasu at Nikkō, he also enshrined two protective deities: Sannō Gongen 山王権現 and Matarajin. The procession of clerics who walked to Nikkō carried three sacred palanquins (*mikoshi* 神輿), one for each of these divinities (Ieyasu, Sannō, and Matarajin). In other words, prior to Reikū's reforms Matarajin had ranked as high as Sannō in the Tendai hierarchy of gods, so much so that he functioned as one of the main spiritual protectors of the Tokugawa house (Sonehara 1992, p. 286; Sugahara 1992, pp. 28–30). Scattered textual references suggest that Matarajin enjoyed this high status because he stood at the intersection of every field of cultural production, not just political power (as at Nikkō), but also meditative rites for salvation in the Pure Land of the Buddha Amitābha (Yamada 1992) and as one of the so-called "backdoor" (*ushirodo* 後戸) deities associated with the origins of Japanese professional theater (Marra 1993, pp. 56–61). He embodied the fusion of autochthonous (Shinto) and universal (Buddhism) that so characterized medieval religious life (also see the essay by Bernard Faure in this book.)

Concluding remarks

After Reikū's reforms, Matarajin sank into obscurity.[25] As Matarajin faded from view, his entire field of cultural production disappeared with him. This disappearance constitutes a rupture in Japanese Buddhist discourse. For the first time publicly available texts (published scriptures and Chinese commentaries) became more powerful than private and secret sectarian lore. The implications of this rupture for our understanding of Japanese religious history have yet to be fully explored. Since the early twentieth century when the modern academic study of Japanese religion began, scholars have constructed narratives in which they identify the development of Japanese forms of Buddhism with the classical (Heian) and early medieval (Kamakura) periods.[26] Subsequent periods supposedly witnessed institutional expansion, but no new doctrinal developments.[27] My overview of the reformation of Tendai during the Tokugawa period attempts to call into question that dominant interpretive narrative. Reikū, Kōben, and the Anraku movement illustrate how our standard academic narrative developed out of reforms and controversies during which the so-called classical and medieval doctrines were rediscovered, reconfigured, or even invented. By denouncing the past as heretical and by recovering the forgotten writings of founding figures, Reikū and other reformers succeeded in drawing attention away from their own innovations. Their elimination of the earlier cultural secret initiations – with its associated lore of political power, local gods, ritual performances, dramatic arts, and literature – created an empty space to be filled by a new kind of Buddhism that was better suited to the sensibilities of their (and subsequent) times. Pregnant with possibilities, this empty space could not be filled completely by a new form of doctrinal Buddhism alone, but provided the matrix for the emergence of new popular religious movements, Nativism, and Nativist forms of Shinto. If we are to understand accurately the religious life of medieval Japan, we must attempt not only to discover the lost culture of secrecy. Just as important, we must notice the empty space created by its loss. In short, we cannot fully understand either medieval or subsequent religious life without re-examining the Tokugawa period when secrecy ends.

Notes

1 See the "Transcripts of Private Instructions on Dharma Transmission Ceremonies," *Denbō shitsunai mitsuji monki* 伝法室内密示聞記, SoZ 15, pp. 176–77.
2 In spite of its near universal acceptance in English-language writings about Japan, I avoid translating *tennō* as "emperor" for two reasons. First, whether compared to Chinese or European contexts, the term "emperor" conveys

political connotations (e.g. supreme command over civil and military administration, rule over vast territories, lordship over foreign lands, etc.) that are completely absent from Japan. Second, the literal translation "heavenly sovereign" better captures the religious overtones (i.e. the unmoving pole star around which the heavens revolve) that were important in Japan.

3 Fukuda 1954, p. 694; Ishida 1986, p. 461; Ueda 1976, p. 111.

4 Each one of these temples was commonly known by its location, so that Ennyūin also is known as Kajii monzeki 梶井門跡, Myōhō'in also is Kōfuku goten 廣福御殿, and Shōren'in also is Awata 粟田 goten.

5 Kan'eiji also was known as "Rinnōji no Miya" 輪王寺宮, which technically was the *miya* title of its abbot.

6 *Tendai kahyō* 天台霞標, section 4, fasc. 4; reprinted in DNBZ 41, pp. 409c–410a. I use the word "physical" because when Reikū assumed this position, he posthumously enshrined his teacher Myōryū Jisan as Anrakuin's first spiritual abbot.

7 See Bodiford 2005a for a discussion of the diverse religious and social implications of vinaya in East Asian Buddhism.

8 I place the words "monks" and "nuns" inside quotation marks because recent research on the Buddhist codes of discipline (vinaya) by Gregory Schopen (2004) and others demonstrates that no members of the Buddhist samgha conform to the usual definitions of "monks" or "nuns" as those terms are used in the context of European monastic traditions.

9 *Tendai kahyō*, section 4, fasc. 4; DNBZ 41, pp. 409c–410a; cf. Ishida 1986, pp. 463–64.

10 *Tendai kahyō*, section 6, fasc. 3; DNBZ 42, p. 92c.

11 叙曰關邪者關玄旨帰壇邪説也。蓋本邦台教中古大乱悪見者私造玄旨。帰命壇潅頂以立公案密相授受。愈久愈熾廼至今時無擇法眼者往往莫不尊信而服膺焉。甚至於謂法華止観猶方便説未明斯元意。余初伝其説後悟其妄。豈可惜口業而不關之乎。蓋其壇場軌式固不見乎経論不載乎疏鈔。則実出于牽合附会之説而其為杜撰不待弁論而明矣。其案目乃雖或出于経疏然其義意全非正旨。

(Byakujahen, 1a–b; punctuation added)*

12 For an up-to-date summary of current knowledge and speculation regarding these rituals, see Yamamoto 1998, pp. 174–262.

13 諸悪莫作 衆善奉行 自淨其意 是諸佛教

14 For example *Fahua xuanyi* 法華玄義, fascs. 2 and 3; T 1716. 33.695c, 716a.

15 七佛通戒偈、第一
師問、如何是諸悪莫作衆善奉行意旨。学者答曰、無思量善悪之心。

(Byakujahen, 2a–b; punctuation added)*

16 蓋佛戒雖多要之止作二持而已矣。止持者息悪之謂也。作持者修善之謂也。諸悪莫作即止持也。衆善奉行即作持也。此其所以為通戒也。故二者皆事也、非理也。修也、非性也。何得直以理性解之乎。

(Byakujahen, 2b; punctuation added)*

17 *Tiantai Zhizhe dashi chanmen koujue* 天台智者大師禪門口訣; T 1919. 46.581c.

18 南嶽偈、第三問、如何是実心繋実境。答曰、心境本無。又問、如何是実縁次第生。答曰、無而忽有。又問、如何是実実迭相注自然入実理。答曰、着衣喫飯、平常無事。

(Byakujahen, 6b; punctuation added)*

19 This commentary actually is not by Zhiyi, but by a subsequent Tiantai patriarch named Jingxi Zhanran 荊溪湛然 (711–82). See his *Zhiguan yili* 止觀義例 (fasc. 1; T 1913. 46.453a).

20 弁曰、此説非惟不合其文意、抑又大乱於綱宗。作玄旨者欲誑惑世人之心肝斯可見矣。此一偈蓋南嶽大師所教誡大衆而天台大師精釈其文曰、「心若繋境。境必繋心。心境相繋名為実縁。復由後心後心相続。心心相繋名相注。即是心注於境注於心。心心境境念念相注如是次第刹那無間。自然從於観行相似以入分證。故云入実。」(已上天台釈文) 是則南嶽天台欲人立於円修而赴於円果。

故其叮嚀告誡如此。玄旨則示本無忽有以撥修德。但貴平常心為自然道。其反
祖宗如此甚矣何哉。意者波旬入於人心説相似法欲使衆生謗破佛法态乎三業永
堕在於阿鼻獄裏。

(Byakujahen, 6b–7b; punctuation added)

21 伝玄旨者身無戒檢心無禅那。喫酒囲碁夜以繼日。愛色貪財不知紀極。

(Byakujahen, 7b; punctuation added)

22 玄旨所伝実不異此。非魔説而何。

(Byakujahen, 8a; punctuation added)

23 The only published texts seem to be the *Genshidan hishō* 玄旨壇秘抄 (2 fasc.;
copied ca. 1614), which Mitamura Genryū 三田村玄龍 (a.k.a. Engyo 鳶魚; 1870–
1952) included in his collection of banned religious texts titled *Shinkō sōsho* 信
仰叢書 (Compilation of Superstitions; 1915), and a collection of related documents compiled by Uesugi Bunshū 上杉文秀 (1863–1936) and included as a
supplement in the second volume of his history of Japanese Tendai (1935;
reprinted 1972). Neither of these sources include any references to the kinds of
kōan dialogues attacked by Reikū.
   The only surviving description of the *kōan* initiations seems to be the *Kongōtō*
金剛幢 written in 1738 by Jōin 乗因 (1682–1739). For an analysis of this text, see
Sonehara 1992. Jōin was a former Tendai prelate who died in exile after being
banished for disseminating heretical teachings regarding the gods (*shintō* 神道).

24 Sonehara (1991, p. 60) notes that this argument over Chinese sources of
authority versus Japanese ones occurred at approximately the same time when
Confucian theories of Shinto began to be challenged by Nativist versions that
relied more heavily on Japanese ancient literature.

25 Some evidence suggests that Matarajin was not totally forgotten. The Tendai
prelate Kakushin 覚深 (1694–1776), for example, wrote a brief essay in 1738
about Matarajin (*Matarajin shikō* 摩多羅神私考; Uesugi 1972, pp. 891–92). In
this essay he notes that everyone understands why Sannō Gongen is enshrined
at Nikkō, but that the meaning of Matarajin is unclear. Then he attempts to
explain (or justify) Matarajin by identifying him with other deities mentioned
in the Buddhist scripture, such as the Tantric deity Matari jin 摩怛哩神, who
appears in a commentary by Yixing 一行 (673–727) on the **Mahāvairocana-sūtra*.
It is significant, I think, that Kakushin feels compelled to cite only scriptures
with solid Chinese pedigrees. For Yixing's reference to Matari jin, see *Dapiluzhena
chengfo jingsu* 大毘盧遮那成佛經疏, fasc. 10 (T 39.684b); cf. *Dapiluzhena chengfo
shenbian jiachi jing* 大毘盧遮那成佛神變加持經, fasc. 3 (T 18.18b).
   The priest Jōin (see note 23) provides an alternative explanation of
Matarajin. According to Jōin's *Kongōtō* (fasc. 3; Repr. pp. 308–309), Matarajin
is the dream king (*muō* 夢王) mentioned in the *Mahe zhiguan* 摩訶止観 (fasc. 1;
T 46.13a) who vouchsafes the correct attainment of samādhi. Matarajin's drum
sounds out the verse of repentance as described in the "Repentance Chapter"
(Sange bon 懺悔品) of the "Sutra of Golden Illuminating Wisdom" (*Konkōmyō
kyō* 金光明経; fasc. 2; T 16.365b). See Sonehara 1992.

26 There are three standard interpretive models of Japanese Buddhist history:
Original Enlightenment thought (*hongaku shisō* 本覚思想); Kamakura reformation; and exoteric–esoteric establishment (*kenmitsu taisei* 顕密体制). All
three of them focus exclusively on the classical and medieval periods. For a
detailed overview, see Bodiford 2005b.

27 A prime example of the dominant tendency to view Buddhism during
Tokugawa period solely in terms of institutional developments is the four-
volume series *Nihon bukkyōshi* 日本仏教史 (*History of Japanese Buddhism*) published
by Yoshikawa Kōbunkan in the late 1980s. The first two volumes, which
concern classical and medieval times, contain almost no institutional history
while the third volume on the Tokugawa period consists of nothing else.

References

Primary sources

Byakujahen 闢邪篇, by Reikū Kōken 霊空光謙 (1652–1739).
  Woodblock edition, published by Taishū Shodō 台宗書堂, 1694. Reprinted in 1698. 22 leaves. Preface (*jo* 序) by Kōben Hōshinnō 公弁法親王 (1669–1716), 3 leaves. Postscript (*batsu* 跋) by Gidō 義道, 3 leaves. Owned by Taishō University Library, Tokyo.
Denbō shitsunai mitsuji monki 伝法室内密示聞記. Compiled by disciples of Menzan Zuihō 面山瑞方 (1683–1769). SoZ 15, "Shitsunai" 室内.
Four part vinaya (a.k.a. *Dharmaguptaka vinaya*; *Sifen lü* 四分律), T. no. 1428.
Genshidan hishō 玄旨壇秘抄. 2 fasc. Copied ca. 1614.
  Reprinted in *Shinkō sōsho* 信仰叢書. Edited by Mitamura Genryū 三田村玄龍 (a.k.a. Engyo 鳶魚). Tokyo: Kokusho Kankōkai, 1915, pp. 18–122.
Kongōtō 金剛幢. 3 fasc. By Jōin 乘因 (1682–1739).
  Reprinted in *Togakushi* 戸隠 (=*Zoku Shintō Taikei*, Jinja hen 続神道大系, 社編), vol. 1. Edited by Sonehara Satoshi 曽根原理. Tokyo: Shintō Taikei Hensankai, 2001, pp. 233–327.
Matarajin shikō 摩多羅神私考, by Kakushin 覚深 (1694–1776) of Shinnyoin 眞如院 in Tō Eizan 東叡山 (i.e. Kan'eiji 寛永寺 temple), 1783. Reprinted in Uesugi 1972, pp. 891–92.
Repudiation of Heresies. See *Byakujahen*.
Tendai kahyō 天台霞標 . 7 sections of 4 fasc. each (total 28 fasc.). Section 1 (fasc. 1–3) compiled in 1771 by Konryū Keiyū 金龍敬雄 (1713–82), supplement to section 1 (1 fasc.) and section 2 (4 fasc.) compiled in 1829 and sections 3–7 (20 fasc.) compiled in 1862 by Rakei Jihon 羅溪慈本 (1794–1868). Reprinted in DNBZ 41, pp. 188–412, and 42, pp. 1–160.

Modern sources

Baroni, Helen J. (2000), *Obaku Zen: The Emergence of the Third Sect of Zen in Tokugawa Japan*. Honolulu: University of Hawai'i Press.
Bodiford, William M. (1991), "Dharma Transmission in Sōtō Zen: Manzan Dōhaku's Reform Movement." *Monumenta Nipponica* 46/4, pp. 423–51.
Bodiford, William M. (2005a), "Introduction," in William M. Bodiford (ed.), *Going Forth: Visions of Buddhist Vinaya*. Honolulu: University of Hawai'i Press, pp. 1–16.
Bodiford, William M. (2005b), "Medieval Period (11th to 16th centuries)," in Paul L. Swanson and Clark Chilson (eds), *The Nanzan Guide to Japanese Religions*. Honolulu: University of Hawai'i Press, pp. 161–81.
Dobbins, James (1980), "The Concept of Heresy in the Jōdo Shinshū." *Transactions of the International Conference of Orientalists in Japan* 25, pp. 33–46.
Elman, Benjamin A. (1984), *From Philosophy to Philology: Intellectual and Social Aspects of Change in Late Imperial China*. Cambridge, MA: Council on East Asian Studies, Harvard University.
Fukuda Gyōei 福田尭頴 (1954), *Tendaigaku gairon* 天台学概論, 2 vols. Tokyo: Bun'ichi Shuppan.
Groner, Paul (2000), *Saichō: The Establishment of the Japanese Tendai School*. Honolulu: University of Hawai'i Press. [¹1984]

Ishida Mizumaro 石田瑞麿 (1986), "Anraku ritsu no funsō" 安樂律の紛争. Reprint in *Nihon bukkyō shisō kenkyū* 日本仏教思想研究, vol. 1. Kyoto: Hōzōkan, pp. 455–82. [¹1957]

Kashiwara Yūsen 柏原祐泉 (1967), "Bukkyō shisō no tenkai" 仏教思想の展開, in Tamamuro Taijō 圭室諦成 (ed.), *Nihon Bukkyōshi* 日本仏教史 3. Kyoto: Hōzōkan, pp. 73–168.

Keene, Donald (1984), "Characteristic Responses to Confucianism in Tokugawa Literature," in Peter Nosco (ed.), *Confucianism and Tokugawa Culture*. Princeton: Princeton University Press, pp. 120–37.

Marra, Michele (1993), *Representations of Power: The Literary Politics of Medieval Japan*. Honolulu: University of Hawai'i Press.

Morioka Kiyomi 森岡清美 (1967), "Kyōdan no kōzō" 教団の構造, in Tamamuro Taijō 圭室諦成 (ed.), *Nihon Bukkyōshi* 日本佛教史 3. Kyoto: Hōzōkan, pp. 169–247.

Nosco, Peter (1986), "*Manyōshū* Studies in Tokugawa Japan." *Transactions of the Asiatic Society of Japan*, 4/1, pp. 111–146.

Ooms, Herman (1985), *Tokugawa Ideology: Early Constructs, 1570–1680*. Princeton: Princeton University Press.

Riggs, David (2002), "The Rekindling of a Tradition: Menzan Zuihō and the Reform of Japanese Sōtō Zen in the Tokugawa Era." (Ph.D. dissertation). Los Angeles: University of California.

Schopen, Gregory (2004), "What Manner of Monk is This? The Buddhist Bhikṣu's Obligation to Support his Parents in Early and Medieval India." Unpublished paper presented at the symposium, "Buddhism In (and Out of) Place," University of California, Los Angeles, 18 October 2004.

Somata Yoshio 杣田善雄 (1985), "Bakuhan-sei kokka to monzeki: Tendai zazu, Tendai monzeki o chūshin ni" 幕藩制国家と門跡、天台座主・天台門跡を中心に. *Nihonshi kenkyū* 日本史研究 277, pp. 1–34.

Sonehara Satoshi 曽根原理 (1990), "Reikū Kōken no genshi kimyōdan hihan: Bakufu no shūkyō seisaku to no kanren de" 霊空光謙の玄旨帰命壇批判、幕府の宗教政策との関連で. *Rekishi* 歴史 75, pp. 21–40.

Sonehara Satoshi 曽根原理 (1991), "Anraku ritsu o meguru ronsō: Hōreki hachi nen Anraku ritsu haishi ni itaru made" 安楽律をめぐる論争：宝暦八年安楽律廃止に到るまで, *Tōhoku daigaku fuzoku toshokan kenkyū nenpō* 東北大学附属図書館研究年報 24, pp. 37–75.

Sonehara Satoshi 曽根原理 (1992), "Kinjirareta shinkō: kinsei zen hanki no Matarajin" 禁じられた信仰：近世前半期の摩多羅神, in Minamoto Ryōen 源了円 and Tamagake Hiroyuki 玉懸博之 (eds), *Kokka to shūkyō: Nihon shisō shi ronshū* 国家と宗教：日本思想史論集. Tokyo: Shibunkaku, pp. 285–306.

Sugahara Shinkai 菅原信海 (1992), *Sannō Shintō no kenkyū* 山王神道の研究. Tokyo: Shunjūsha.

Takano Toshihiko 高埜利彦 (1985), "Edo bakufu to jisha" 江戸幕府と寺社, in Rekishigaku Kenkyūkai 歴史学研究会 and Nihonshi Kenkyūkai 日本史研究会 (eds), *Kōza Nihon rekishi* 講座日本歴史 vol. 5 (Kinsei 近世 1). Tokyo: Tōkyō Daigaku Shuppankai, pp. 79–116.

Tamura Yoshirō 田村芳朗 (1973), "Tendai hongaku shisō gaisetsu" 天台本覚思想概説, in Tada Kōryū 多田厚隆 *et al.* (eds.), *Tendai hongakuron* 天台本覚論 (=*Nihon shisō taikei* 日本思想大系9). Tokyo: Iwanami Shoten, pp. 477–548.

Ueda Tenzui 上田天瑞 (1976), *Kairitsu no shisō to rekishi* 戒律の思想と歴史. Wakayama Pref.: Mikkyō Bunka Kenkyūjo.

330 William M. Bodiford

Uesugi Bunshū 上杉文秀 (1972), "Nihon Tendai danna-ryū genshi kimyōdan hiroku shū" 日本天台壇那流玄旨帰命壇秘録集. In *Nihon Tendai shi* 日本天台史, vol. 2. Tokyo: Kokusho Kankōkai, pp. 829–96. [[1]1935]

Wu, Jiang (2002), "Orthodoxy, controversy and the transformation of Chan Buddhism in Seventeenth-century China." (Ph.D. dissertation). Cambridge: Harvard University.

Yamada Yūji 山田雄司 (1992), "Matarajin no keifu" 摩多羅神の系譜. *Geinōshi kenkyū* 芸能史研究 118, pp. 1–16.

Yamamoto Hiroko 山本ひろ子 (1998), *Ishin: chūsei Nihon no hikyōteki sekai* 異神: 中世日本の秘教的世界. Tokyo: Heibonsha.

14 Hiding the shoguns

Secrecy and the nature of political authority in Tokugawa Japan

Anne Walthall

Shogun Ienari's audience for two castaways, the ship master Daikokuya Kōdayū and sailor Isokichi, had almost nothing in common with their reception by Catherine the Great. According to Kōdayū's account, when they first saw Catherine, she was surrounded by female attendants. The chief minister took Kōdayū by the hand, led him to the empress, and told him to place his hands on top of each other. Catherine stretched out her hand and touched his palm. "I was told to suck (*name*) her fingers, and so I did." For the audience on 1793/9/18, Ienari went to the viewing stand in Fukiage park outside the main enceinte. He took his seat at the center, hidden behind bamboo blinds (*misu*). An attendant sat to his left. To his right were Matsudaira Sadanobu and other high officials. Lower-ranking officials sat at right angles to the shogun, visible to the two castaways sitting on the ground (Fig. 14.1). Ienari never addressed the castaways directly; officials mediated his questions and the castaways' replies. Portraits of Catherine circulated in Russia and Japan; portraits of Ienari did not.[1]

The Tokugawa shoguns used strategies of concealment and secrecy to enhance their authority and to maintain the status hierarchy that under-pinned the social order. Formal ceremonies performed inside castle walls put these strategies in action, but even more informal encounters such as the one described above afford glimpses of the principles that underlay them. These principles alluded to and arose from the context of conceal-ment and power developed in the Japanese political and religious tradition. Although lacking secret transmissions or anything resembling a secret enthronement ceremony, the shoguns had to strive for a different articulation. The goals of shogunal ceremony and Mikkyō initiation and ritual were not same, but both tried to manipulate power inherent in the unseen.

Shoguns flaunted their authority in massive walls and public works, but they concealed their persons. Screech has pointed to an "iconography of absence" that marked not only the shogun's relations with commoners, but also his relations with daimyo, chief retainers, and foreign emissaries.

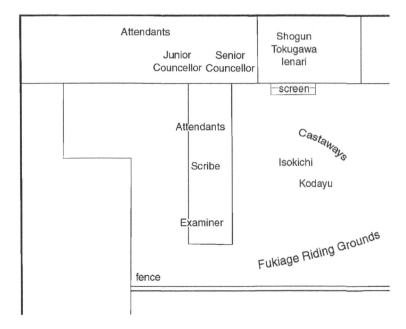

Figure 14.1 Shogun Tokugawa Ienari's interrogation of two returnees from Russia. (Adapted from Yamashita 2003, pp. 4–5.)

This iconography of absence characterized the entire ruling class from monarch and nobility in Kyoto to daimyo in the provinces (Screech 2000, pp. 112–13). I plan here to examine the politics of concealment by analyzing ceremonies at which it was contravened because the only way to see the invisible is through the visible. As Scheid has pointed out, there has to be a "dialectical give and take of concealment and disclosure" (Scheid 2002, p. 47). The question is, what was to be concealed, how was the hidden to be accessed, and what did this access mean for the parties involved?

The focus of this essay is on shogunal ceremony. Tokugawa shoguns drew on a range of practices, from the rituals crafted by their predecessors – the Ashikaga shoguns and Toyotomi Hideyoshi – to folk traditions performed to bring good luck. These they made their own by assimilating them to the regime's foundation myths, claiming, for example, that the ceremony performed on the first day of the eighth month commemorated Ieyasu's entry into the Kanto plain in 1590, rather than a long-standing belief that it was auspicious to present gifts on that day (Futaki 1986b, pp. 33–34). Regardless of the occasion, ceremonies climaxed in an audience with the shogun (Watanabe 1986, p. 142). I will first present the shogun in his most universal but also most hidden form, in death. Then I will analyze shogunal ceremonies to ascertain when and to whom the shogun disclosed or withheld his person: how he appeared to the daimyo and how he concealed himself from foreign envoys. Let us not forget the role of women in the rituals that maintained political authority, especially because this role changed from the Ashikaga to the Tokugawa period. In contrast to the shogun's interactions with men whose rank and status permitted them entry inside palace buildings, his appearances before commoners took place with them under the open sky. This spatial dimension to shogunal ceremony speaks to the hierarchy of rule, issues of secrecy and control, religion and political authority, the paraphernalia of *matsurigoto* 政, or rituals of rule in the context of the performance of power.

Shoguns and the power of the dead

The enshrinement of Ieyasu at Nikkō and his incarnation as Tōshō Daigongen 東照大権現, the eternal founder, established an ideological foundation for Tokugawa rule. Ieyasu became the spiritual protector not only of the Tokugawa lineage, but of his capital city at Edo, of the Kanto, and of Japan as a whole, as seen through the establishment of Tōshōgū dedicated to his worship in *fudai* and *tozama* domains. While only Ieyasu was given a universalizing posthumous title that proclaimed his divine protective powers, the way his descendants were buried suggests that they too had a role to play after death that corresponded to their earthly mission.[2]

Moving shogunal graves at Zōjōji in 1958 provided an unprecedented opportunity to view the remains of the shoguns and their families. Ieyasu had decided that Zōjōji was to be the family mortuary temple in 1598 because it lies south of the castle, directly opposed to Nikkō in the North, and it guards the entrance to the Tōkaidō, the Pacific Coast Highway. It is thus situated at one of the four cardinal directions at which supernatural forces needed to be brought to bear to protect the city according to Chinese geomancy. Of the six shoguns buried there, Ienobu is one of the best preserved, and he gives a good indication of how the shoguns continued to function as guardians of the state after death. The embalmed Ienobu is seated inside two wooden coffins placed in a copper coffin inside a stone chamber, all packed with ash and lime. His hair is in a topknot, and he is dressed in the formal court robes of a chief minister (*naidaijin* 内大臣) with a mace in his hands, the same clothes he would have worn in life during the ceremonies that marked the calendar year. A broadsword is at his side (Naitō 1996, p. 24). The people who buried him endeavored to preserve his body from decay in order that his corpse might embody a magical power capable of protecting the state made concrete in the city of Edo. They tried to deny the truth of what lay concealed – the fact that the shogun was dead – and to do so in such a way as to maintain his charismatic power on behalf of his city. To draw on

Taussig, we can say that the careful attention paid to the burial of the shoguns, and the memorial services performed on their behalf by their descendants, harnessed the dead for stately purposes and recharged "the circulation of power between the dead and the living" (Taussig 1997, pp. 339).

Shogun and daimyo also performed memorial services for Tokugawa ancestors in rites that emphasized the familial dimension to Tokugawa rule. As the dynasty lengthened, shoguns spent more and more days on visits to mortuary temples, to the extent that other annually scheduled observances had to be curtailed (*Shinhen Chiyodakushi tsūshi* 2, p. 519). At least ten days every month were given to these services for which the shogun purified himself by abstaining from sex. Whether he went to Zōjōji or Kan'eiji or to the mortuary hall at Momijiyama inside the castle precincts, a retinue of his closest attendants and political advisors had to accompany him (*Shinhen Chiyodakushi tsūsh* 1, pp. 363–67). Preparations for a shogun's procession included clearing his route and tidying even the side roads. Lights and fires were prohibited. Doors had to be sealed and second-storey windows closed. The procession thudded down silent streets. When it passed a daimyo compound, the daimyo had to kneel facing the street. People guarding side streets had to kneel as he passed. Watanabe has pointed out that these were the same marks of respect offered to the portable shrines (*mikoshi*) at shrine festivals (Watanabe 1986, pp. 137–38). Pilgrimages to Nikkō involved *tozama* daimyo and their retinues as well as *fudai* daimyo.[3] These processions to spiritually significant sites re-enacted the Tokugawa foundation myth and pointed to Tōshō Daigongen as the chief deity of the nation. As Naitō (1996, p. 54) has indicated, by being repeated at intervals over the years, they transformed Tokugawa military leaders into magical symbols of sacred authority.

Ceremonies for daimyo

Spatial settings

The spatial layout of Chiyoda castle reflected the principles of concealment that buttressed the shogun's authority. Closest to the main entrance was the largest reception hall, the *ōhiroma* 大広間 shaped like a squared U. The left side contained three rooms called *dan* 段, each elevated above the other. The shogun usually sat in the upper *dan*. At the bottom of the U and up its right side were the second, third, and fourth reception rooms called *ma* 間 (Fig. 14.2). Since the *ōhiroma* was the farthest from the interior, it was reserved for the most powerful *tozama* daimyo and the most formal of ceremonies. Farther in the interior was the Shiroshoin 白書院 that had two reception rooms, the upper and lower *dan* as well as two waiting rooms. It was for *fudai* daimyo and the shogun's relatives.[4]

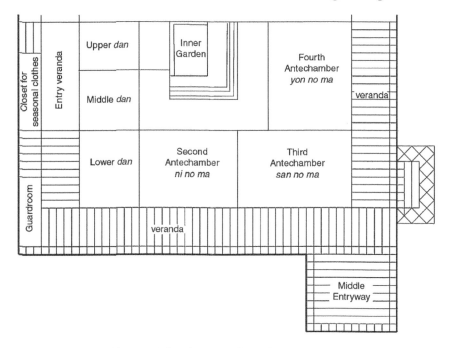

Figure 14.2 Spatial layout of the *ōhiroma*. (Adapted from Hirai 2000, p. 35.)

Deeper yet was the Kuroshoin 黒書院 for the shogun's officials, considered to be more a part of his family than his relatives (Fukai 2001–02, vol. 4, p. 4; vol. 6, pp. 3–6). It also constituted the setting for smaller, informal interactions between the chief daimyo and the shogun (Sono 2004, p. 124).[5] The shogun's private quarters lay beyond that. Deep within castle walls was the Great Interior (*ōoku* 大奥) for the shogun's women, officially off-limits to all men except the shogun. Unlike the vistas, public gardens, and plazas that distinguished Versailles, the Chinese Forbidden City, or the Ottoman sultan's Topkapi palace, the maze of rooms and corridors in Chiyoda palace was designed to confuse the unwary and conceal the shogun's whereabouts from potential enemies. Watanabe claims that the palace was an active space, meant to be viewed on the move, with fresh perspectives revealed at every corner as though unrolling a scroll (Watanabe 1986, p. 141).

Every daimyo and *hatamoto* in residence in Edo had to appear at the castle on specified days. This was their duty, the work that they performed in Edo, as demonstrated by the *kin* 勤 in *sankin kōtai* 参勤交代, usually translated as "alternate attendance" (Watanabe 1986, p. 140). Under the system established by Iemitsu in the 1630s and refined in 1648, even the daimyo's heirs had to go on duty at the castle, regardless of whether the shogun was ill, in mourning, or otherwise indisposed.[6] Also in the 1640s, the shogun started putting more distance between himself and daimyo, particularly those of lower rank while still requiring them to attend ceremonies (Futaki 2003, p. 423). His presence at Chiyoda castle summoned the daimyo just as Ieyasu's apotheosis at Nikkō and Ienobu's burial at Zōjōji summoned unseen forces on behalf of the state.

Ceremonies inside Chiyoda palace had two political functions. They forced the daimyo to acknowledge their subordination to the shogun, and they iterated the status hierarchy that divided the shogun's subordinates. One distinction reinforced with every ceremony was between those who had the right of audience with the shogun (*omemie* 御目見え) and those without. Each participant had to follow procedures that regulated where he sat in his specified room while waiting to appear before the shogun, the route he took for his audience, the greetings he exchanged en route, the precise spot where he performed his first bow at the entrance to the reception hall, the same for the second performed in front of the shogun, and what he was expected to bring with him.[7] Three days were not too long to practice the appropriate etiquette. The inspectors (*metsuke* 目付) who supervised the ritual were known to throw men out of the castle if they made a mistake (Watanabe 1986, p. 143).

The point of these formalities was to demonstrate to participant and observers his precise rank in the status hierarchy, based on familial ties, service to the shogunate, and most importantly, court rank and office bestowed by the monarch in Kyoto at the behest of the shogun.[8] Those with the highest rank approached most closely to the shogun, who sat at the center of the castle at the center of Edo at the political epicenter of the country. Like initiations into Mikkyō there was a series of levels, but unlike the initiates, a man's closeness to the center was based almost entirely on ascribed, not achieved, status. Although both the palace and the temple encompassed a hierarchy of difference, in the temple, objects and persons became progressively more concealed as the gaze moved from the periphery to the center, and this move replicated a transformation from the profane to the sacred, from the common to the pure. In the palace, the extent to which the shogun was concealed depended on the viewer's politically designated position.

Investiture ceremonies

Records of Ienobu's investiture as shogun provide evidence of how rank determined access to the shogun for the aristocratic, military, and ecclesiastical hierarchies.[9] The investiture took place on 1709/5/1 when Ienobu received his patent of authority from Kyoto. For the audience with the court nobles who had brought it, Ienobu sat in the upper *dan* of the *ōhiroma*. The two *sekke* 摂家 (houses that provided regents for the Kyoto monarch) had the privilege of a face-to-face interview (*taigan* 対顔) with him in the upper *dan*.[10] Nobles above the fifth rank presented swords and gold coins (*tachi mokuroku* 太刀目録) individually in the middle *dan*.[11] Those below the fifth court rank had to be content with a seat in the lower *dan*. Those not allowed into the ceremonial hall in Kyoto, generally below the sixth rank, had to sit on the veranda. Ten days later, the shogun held audiences for the daimyo over the course of three days, in either the Shiroshoin or the *ōhiroma* depending on their rank and status. None of them approached closer than the middle *dan*. At the end of the month, abbots, priests, and monks offered their congratulations to the new shogun. The Nikkō abbot led the way.[12] Like the two *sekke*, he had the honor of sitting with the shogun on the upper *dan* of the Shiroshoin because he was a member of the royal family. Everyone else performed obeisance in the lower *dan* in accordance with his rank (Fukai 1999, pp. 83–104).

Court rank determined whether nobles, daimyo, and priests had the privilege of individual audiences or had to be content with audiences en masse. Except for face-to-face interviews with peers, all audiences were conducted through the senior councilors, protocol chiefs (*kōka* 高家), or masters of ceremonies (*sōjaban* 奏者番), who inspected the gifts and mediated communications with the shogun. On the occasion of Yoshimune's investiture, after the privileged daimyo had individual audiences in the Shiroshoin, Yoshimune walked to the upper *dan* of the *ōhiroma*. When all was in readiness, he stood up and moved down to the entrance to the lower *dan*. On the other side of the door dividing the three *dan* from the reception rooms waited daimyo, the shogun's chief retainers, and priests. On the veranda knelt messengers from Kyoto nobles, doctors, Noh performers, and masters of the wardrobe, all with wooden swords and coins placed in front of them. When the senior councilors gave the signal, these men prostrated themselves, the senior councilors opened the sliding doors, and Yoshimune looked out over a sea of backs while the senior councilors announced that the assembled warriors offered their congratulations (Fig. 14.3).[13] Then they closed the doors. Even when Yoshimune received congratulations from high ranking daimyo, he spoke not one word (Ichioka 1989, pp. 48–65).

It is possible to draw two conclusions from the descriptions of the shogun's investiture. First, silence was equated with dignity, and dignity was equated with authority. Especially for the inauguration of his reign, the shogun needed to appear impassive, like a statue. Second, even though it might seem that the shogun displayed himself to a large number of his retainers, he did so in ways that reinforced the social hierarchy. He observed them, not the other way around. Only men of high rank glimpsed the shogun's face. The rest kept their eyes on the floor. No one had a full view of what the shogun did. The placement of screens meant that men who saw him moving down a corridor did not see him seated or standing

Figure 14.3 Standing at the door to the lower *dan*, Yoshimune surveys his
subordinates (Ichioka, pp. 62–63. Reproduction by courtesy of
Heibonsha, Tokyo.)

and vice versa. As the most solemn and portentous of the ceremonies
performed by the shogun, the investiture encapsulated the principles of
silence and the disclosure of concealment.

Seasonal festivities

The celebrations for the New Year set the tone for the shogun's interactions
with daimyo and retainers and drew on long-standing practice for infe-
riors to offer greetings of the season to their superiors.[14] All daimyo in
residence in Edo had to come to Chiyoda castle on the first, second, and
third days. On the first day the shogun would already be seated in the
upper *dan* of the Shiroshoin when the shogunal relatives, the Maeda,
and the chief *fudai* daimyo proffered their New Year's greeting and gifts –
the usual wooden swords and gold coins.[15] The senior councilors took
charge of these. After a banquet the assembled daimyo proceeded to the
ōhiroma where they sat in the lower *dan*. The senior councilors opened
the sliding doors to the reception rooms to reveal the rest of the *fudai*
and *tozama* daimyo as well as shogunal housemen, priests, and doctors,
all prostrate. The *rōjū* read a statement offering best wishes for the New
Year. Only then did the shogun seat himself in the upper *dan*. Sake was
served. The shogun then went to the Shiroshoin to receive New Year's

greetings from his personal staff – pages, painters, and Noh performers. Over the first week of the New Year, the rounds of greetings expanded to include different status hierarchies. Following the first Noh performance of the year on the third day, the shogun watched robes of the season being distributed to the performers (Fig. 14.4). The robes were clearly designated as gifts from the shogun, but they by no means came from his hand. This method of giving accentuated both the shogun's largess and the gulf between him and the performers. Elders from several *fudai* domains, the Edo city elders, and commoner officials from Kyoto, Osaka, Nara, Fushimi, and the money guilds also arrived on the third. On the sixth, shogunal retainers so low-ranking that they were normally not allowed as audience with the shogun were permitted to prostrate themselves in offering their New Year's greetings. On the first day of the second month, the Nikkō abbot arrived at the palace for a face-to-face greetings with the shogun (Ichioka 1989, pp. 132–40).[16] As at the investiture, setting the abbot apart from the daimyo served not only to confirm the shogun's control over the religious establishment, but also to assimilate him to the prestige accruing to the royal house in Kyoto.

Shogun and daimyo participated in gift exchanges designed to reiterate the hierarchy of deference that underpinned Tokugawa rule throughout the year. In addition to seasonal gifts, each daimyo had to make "morning offerings" according to a set schedule. The daimyo's representatives took these to the castle where the official who took charge of them then reported that the shogun had deigned to accept them. At a daimyo's

Figure 14.4 The shogun observes the distribution of robes to Noh actors.[17]
(Reproduction by courtesy of Anne Walthall.)

succession, he had to petition the senior councilors to confirm that he could continue the same round of gift-giving as his predecessor. These ceremonial offerings of local products proved that the lord was governing the land he had received from the shogun. They also supplemented the audiences in confirming that daimyo continued to accept the shogun's suzerainty (Ōtomo 1999, pp. 3, 22–28).

The yearly schedule for audiences included five holidays that marked the turn of the seasons, the first, fifteenth, and twenty-eighth of every month, the good luck day of 6/1, and days that celebrated events in the Tokugawa family history.[18] These occasions included the shogun's staff who lined the corridors through which he passed on his way to hold audiences for daimyo (Fukai 2001–02, vol. 3, pp. 222–25, 236–39, *passim*). They afforded the members of the ruling class an opportunity to bask in the shogun's presence. By affirming status distinctions that bound men to the shogun, they provided concrete evidence of class identity – the distinction between the in-group of rulers, the outer ring of administrators, and the outermost commoner populace. At the same time, the ceremonies leveraged the gulf between the shogun and everyone else in such a way as to make the shogun an icon of rule.

Masking the ruler

Daimyo and *hatamoto* had to perform these ritualized audiences even if the agent for the audience, the shogun, was absent. One *hatamoto* recalls his experience:

> While being guided to the Kikunoma [behind the Shiroshoin], I was really frightened. I waited just an instant before the doors to the upper *dan* slid open. At the same time, I heard a repressive whisper, *shii, shii*. I don't know where the shogun was, I was just trying to make my bow as best I could. The room is called Kikunoma because of the chrysanthemums on the sliding doors, and it is awe-inspiring (*kōgōshii* 神々しい). When I heard that *shii, shii* sound, my throat constricted. I have no idea if the shogun was really there or not.
>
> (Watanabe 1986, p. 143)

Even powerful daimyo found themselves performing ceremonies that put form over substance. When Asano Nagakoto 浅野長勲, daimyo for Hiroshima, had an audience in the Shiroshoin, he discovered that

> The shogun had taken his seat with the bamboo blind let down so that it concealed the upper half of his body. Since I was a *kunimochi* daimyo [a daimyo whose domain was as big as a province], I was seated for my audience in the middle of the antechamber (*tsugi no ma* 次の間). I could not see the shogun at all. I just had to flatten my

body and lower my head. That's why it was said that when *tozama* daimyo had their audiences in the Yanaginoma outside the *ōhiroma*, the shogun might not bother to show up.

(Watanabe 1986, p. 143)

Both of these recollections are from the last decades of shogunal rule, when ceremonies had become so routinized that regardless of whether the center was empty, the participants had to pretend it was full.

Language also served to mask the shogun. Except for the patent of investiture, the term "shogun" seldom appears in Edo period texts. This is hardly surprising, given that the higher ranked the individual, the more s/he was referred to by indirection. The populace at large called the shogun *kubō* 公方, a term meaning "the person in charge of the public" that had designated shoguns since the Muromachi period (Kinsei Shiryō Kenkyūkai 1966, p. 190). In the records describing shogunal ceremonies, he is never named, even by title.[19] Instead, his presence is implied in a verbal form that puts the verb before the honorific *go* 御. This method of referring to a superior, or a god, by not naming him or her, uses language to conceal the agent of action. In other words, the absence of language naming the shogun as subject suggests another way in which he remained hidden.

The reception of the foreign envoys

Another arena where the shoguns both concealed their persons and demonstrated their authority was in the reception of foreign envoys. The rituals surrounding these receptions took a variety of forms, depending on the importance of the envoy's country of origin, the shogun's age, and his personality. Although the shogunate kept records of these visits to serve as precedents, the rituals of diplomatic exchange were by no means fixed. Arai Hakuseki and the Hayashi family, for example, fought a notable battle over everything from the appropriate title for the shogun to the dishes to be served at a banquet for the Korean envoys in 1711. Some shoguns ended up submerged in the bureaucracy while others put their stamp on rituals. Surely such elasticity of form also characterized esoteric rituals and the leaders of lineages could decide and change the content of performances.

The most exotic foreign envoys were the Dutch. For the formal audience, they approached no closer than the outer veranda below the lower *dan* at the *ōhiroma* where they presented their credentials and received food and drink (Fukai 2001–02, vol. 1, pp. 40–41, vol. 2, p. 206, vol. 3, p. 374). According to Engelbert Kaempfer's record of his visit to Edo during Tsunayoshi's reign, for "informal audiences,"[20] the Dutch delegation was led by the senior councilors "deeper into the palace to present them for inspection and amusement to the shogunal women, as well as curious princesses of shogunal descent specially invited for the event. On this occasion his majesty and the women are hidden behind the blinds, while the councilors and high courtiers commanded to attend the audience appear in public" (Kaempfer 1999, p. 361). The Dutch delegation visited a number of daimyo residences. Each time the women of the house watched from behind blinds as the Dutch went through their tricks. On Kaempfer's second journey to Edo, he was summoned to the Yanagisawa residence where Tsunayoshi had come to watch him. Again, Tsunayoshi and the female attendants remained ostensibly hidden behind blinds. When Kaempfer stared too intently in the shogun's direction, Tsunayoshi changed his seat. In contrast to the solemnity of the official reception, the informal audience with the shogun and his women was marked by laughter (Kaempfer 1999, pp. 408–09). Kaempfer's account thus provides an unusual glimpse of the shogun's ability to manipulate the rules of concealment in the name of entertainment.

Another perspective on the dialectic between concealment and disclosure can be seen in the visits of Korean envoys to Edo to congratulate each shogun on his accession to office. Toby has pointed out that these visits served as an "important element in the political legitimation of the Tokugawa shogunate" (1986, p. 415). As with visits by Ryukyuan envoys and the Dutch delegation, daimyo from domains en route had to supply porters, sustenance, and entertainment for the envoys and their retinues. Once in Edo and lodged at Higashi Honganji in Asakusa, the delegation paraded through the streets of Edo to the audience with the shogun. At the time of the 1719 visit, print makers sold prints of the 1711 Korean delegation that showed the Korean envoys riding in an "open-sided palanquin, the better to be seen by the assembled crowds" (Toby 1986, p. 433). In the background is Mt. Fuji rising above the walls of Chiyoda castle (Fig. 14.5). Disclosed to public view are the Korean king's representatives, the actors in this enactment of the shogun's authority; concealed is the shogun, his presence marked by his castle, and his universalizing authority symbolized by the vision of the sacred mountain rising above it.

The ceremonies that dramatized the Korean envoys' subordination to the shogun also played on the dialectic of disclosure and concealment. As usual the daimyo resident in Edo and their heirs had to go to the castle and spend hours in designated rooms waiting for the signal to present themselves before the shogun. The same held true for officials from the senior councilors on down and even retainers without office. The record for 1719 shows that the shogun appeared in the afternoon in the upper *dan* of the *ōhiroma*, escorted by a retinue carrying his swords, two protocol officials, and the chief senior councilor (*tairō* 大老). Once seated, the retinue formed a backdrop of living but immobile figures. The blinds on both sides of the upper *dan* were lowered; one blind in the middle was raised. The screens dividing the other rooms were all raised. Only

Figure 14.5 The procession of Korean envoys through Edo.[21] (Reproduction by courtesy of Tokyo National Museum.)

the Kii and Mito lords sat in the middle *dan*; the senior councilors and other officials sat in the lower *dan*. "No one else was in a position to view the lord" (*Tokugawa reiten roku* 3, p. 368).

Once the stage was set, the Korean envoys preceded by their letter from the Korean king passed from their waiting room through reception rooms filled with daimyo to the wooden veranda below the lower *dan*. Once the shogun had given permission, the letter passed from one official to the next before coming to rest on a tatami mat below the upper *dan*. After the envoys had bowed and retired to the antechamber, the master of ceremony took the letter and placed it in the alcove behind the shogun. In order of rank, each of the three envoys then came back to the *ōhiroma* where they approached as far as the second tatami mat below the edge of the middle *dan* to pay their respects. While they were back in the antechamber, the gifts they had brought were displayed in the garden. They then appeared a third time to make personal greetings, again sitting in the lower *dan*. They had to go back and forth two more times, once to drink sake, the second time to eat a meal. For the drink, only the chief envoy was allowed the privilege of sitting in the middle *dan*. Having left while preparations for the banquet were being made, the shogun returned after the envoys had seated themselves in the lower *dan*. By that time the bamboo screens for the upper and middle *dan* would have been lowered, placing a double blind between the envoys and the shogun. The shogun inquired after the envoys' health by a word to the senior councilors who conveyed the query to the Tsushima lord who passed it to the interpreters and thence to the envoys. All communication between the shogun and the envoys followed this same cumbersome procedure, designed to shield the shogun from any contact with foreigners. Throughout the long hours taken by this ceremony, daimyo retired to their waiting rooms only during preparations for the banquet, but officials in the *san-no-ma* and *yon-no-ma* had to remain where they were (*Tokugawa reiten roku* 3, p. 366–79).

Notable in this account is the punctilious attention to detail. It specified not only the rooms occupied by the envoys, but also their location, and that of the daimyo, in each. Although most of the daimyo and officials were seated off to the side where they could not see the shogun, they constituted an essential audience for this ceremony by watching the Koreans parade back and forth, just as the Edo townspeople watched not the interaction between shogun and envoys, but the envoys alone. Every government uses state occasions to assert its authority through rituals of rule, but the dialectic of disclosure and concealment distinguishes shogunal ceremonies from those in modern times. In that sense, the ritual surrounding the visits of the Korean envoys marks a historical dead end.

The visit of the Ryukyuan envoys at the accession of Shogun Ietsugu in 1714 differed in detail from that for the Korean envoys five years later. Because the shogun was a child, he was completely concealed behind bamboo screens. As befitted the lower rank of the Ryukyuan king, the envoys never ventured above the lower *dan*. Rather than a letter, they brought the king's sword as a token of his submission to the shogun. Once it had been proffered, they bowed nine times. This ceremony closed with daimyo and *hatamoto* of rank four and above lining up in the reception rooms. The senior councilors opened the doors that divided the lower *dan* from the reception rooms; the shogun stood up and surveyed the assemblage, their heads lowered in a bow. Then the doors closed (*Tokugawa reiten roku* 3, pp. 307–10).

Discussion

Whether the shogun was a mature man or a boy, ceremonies for foreign envoys had many parts. In this they resembled the mandatory work of coming and going, bowing and waiting, done by the daimyo during the yearly round of scheduled audiences and the shogun's investiture. According to Alan Grapard, ceremonies are designed to be boring. Their aim is to impress the onlooker and participants with the gravitas of the occasion and demonstrate that the agent who ordered the ceremony (in this case the shogun), has the power to compel people to spend long hours doing nothing.[22] Noteworthy as well are the layers of personnel through which messages traveled back and forth between the shogun and the envoys. Like the layers of rooms furnished with screens and blinds that extended beyond the upper *dan*, they hid the shogun just as a gift is wrapped in layers of paper, boxes, paper, and more boxes. In the case of the boy shogun Ietsugu, the wrappings of language and space concealed a politically impotent center.

Even in modern industrial societies, ritual is an integral part of the political process (Kertzer 1988, p. 3). David Cannadine has argued that the more societies experience disruptive change, the more rulers need ceremonies to assert a vision of an invariant order (Cannadine 1987, p. 8). In the early seventeenth century, ceremonial formalism characterized the Tokugawa regime's determination to assert its authority across the Japanese islands. Plus, given the agricultural and commercial revolutions that contributed so much to the dynamism of the Tokugawa era, it is tempting to fit Cannadine's assertion to the contours of shogunal rule, particularly since the 1840s saw both a revival of the Nikkō pilgrimage and a special months-long series of Noh performances designed to restore magic to the state (Looser 1999, pp. 399–411). This elaboration of ceremony that involved both the living and the dead served not only to protect the state but also to support the continuance of Tokugawa family rule.

Western European monarchs showed considerably more of their persons more of the time than did the shoguns. Even when they were not parading in open carriages through the streets, their visages appeared on coins and portraits hung in public places. As Duus has pointed out, "the Tudor/Stuart courts and the Bourbon kings [staged] a 'theater of power' intended to show their audiences that power and sovereignty resided not just in the royal office, but in the royal person" (2001, p. 969). It must be said that the audience was primarily noble and ecclesiastical. This theater displayed a specifically Christian type of power, one that relied for its potency on public displays of piety even while the relationship between ruler, Christ, and people changed over time. According to Paul Monod, for most Christians in the sixteenth and early seventeenth centuries, monarchy "was a reflection of God," and the king functioned as an "intermediary between people and Christ." Kings saw themselves as representatives of God, not the nation. The rituals of consecration transformed them into "a quasi-sacred personage, a living imitator of Christ himself."[23] By the early eighteenth century, the development of absolutism forced the incorporation of greater numbers of people into the notion of the state. Much of the magic of royalty disappeared and, as a consequence, the monarch became more open to public gaze. Even the birth of the king's children took place in a crowded room in full view of the assembled courtiers.

Rituals of power for European and Japanese monarchs diverged in the seventeenth and eighteenth centuries. Can it be said that by forgoing magic while clinging to a divine right to rule that French kings put themselves in danger of disclosing the gulf between their human frailties and the pretense of innate superiority? By appearing infrequently and in immobile poses designed to conceal individual weaknesses, the shoguns tried to wrap themselves in a timeless (though in fact mutable) aura of sanctity so far removed from the mundane that it defied challenge. An essential component in the symbolic denial of the mundane was the seclusion of the shogun's women.

The shogun's women and the culture of secrecy

The public display of European royal women such as Catherine the Great stands in marked contrast to the roles assigned the shogun's women. Even more than the shogun, they were defined by the iconography of absence that conferred authority not on them, but on him. Futaki has documented the extent to which Tokugawa ceremonies replicated those of the Ashikaga shogunate, but there is one dimension he overlooks. The Ashikaga shogun's wife served as the focal point for ceremonies over the course of the year, holding audiences for Kyoto nobles and daimyo, watching Noh with the shogun and exchanging gifts.[24] Tokugawa women participated neither in the shogun's investiture nor in the yearly round of audiences. For these reasons, it would be easy to see them as inconsequential to the public display of sovereignty and to ignore them in analyzing rituals of rule. I think this would be a mistake for two reasons. First, the walls of Chiyoda castle that dominated Edo enclosed not only the shogun, but also his mother, wife, concubines, children, and scores of lady officials, attendants, and scullery maids, pressed into the service of reproducing the dynasty and building alliances with daimyo. In a system of hereditary rule, women played an essential role in securing the dynastic foundation of the state. Another reason why women should not be overlooked in discussing the public ceremonies of rule is that though they were hidden, they were implicated in crucial moments. Otherwise low-ranking *fudai* daimyo took pride in their participation in ceremonies for childbirth, betrothals, and marriage (Fukai 2001–02, vol. 6, pp. 95–134, 241, 244, 252, 422–26, *passim*). As Scheid pointed out, the *ōoku* ("Great Interior") might be seen as analogous to the treasury house at a temple, a place to hoard objects that enhanced the owner's prestige and were seldom if ever put on view (2003, p. 30).

The shogun's daughters played a conspicuous role in binding important daimyo to the shogun. Shoguns even adopted women whom they could then marry off in order to put more men under the obligation of being their in-laws. This was also an advantage to the daimyo because sons born to the shogun's daughters became members of both families. At times when daimyo had to content themselves with formal audiences in the public halls of the castle, shogunal grandsons went into the *ōoku* for informal, intimate face-to-face visits.

Participants in marriage ceremonies included shogunal officials, housemen, and daimyo. The daimyo lined the castle walkways on the bride's departure while the shogun's retainers guarded the streets through which she passed. None of them caught so much as a glimpse of her because unlike the Korean envoys, she rode in an enclosed palanquin. The groom had no control over the staff funded by the shogun that accompanied his bride, he entered her quarters only at her invitation, and she had her own gate at her new home.[25] Every year on the first day of the third month, she returned to the palace to visit the shogun and his wife. To celebrate the occasion, Noh was performed in the Great Interior. Lest actors catch unseemly sight of the shogun's women, the women watched from behind screens just as they had watched Kaempfer perform his antics (Ikenouchi 1925, p. 131).

The shogun's women sometimes participated in ritualized gift exchanges that maintained bonds between members of the ruling class and reinforced the social hierarchy. Along with the shogun, they regularly exchanged gifts with Kyoto. Whenever a retainer retired or died, he bequeathed "tokens of deference" – a sword to the shogun and a book of poetry to the shogun's wife; mother too, if she was still alive.[26] One of the ways in which Tsunayoshi had his favorite concubine treated as equal to his wife was by having her receive these tokens as well. Shelley Errington argues that the gifts offered to rulers and their women were not about loot, but about the ability to command allegiance (Errington 1989, p. 117). What is relevant here is how seldom gift exchanges took place face-to-face. After Iemitsu's last visit to Kyoto in 1634 to celebrate his niece Meishō's ascension as monarch, the shogun had no direct contact with the Kyoto court. Gifts from the shogun's retainers went to disembodied figures hidden behind castle walls. By participating in these exchanges across the divide between the visible and the invisible, the shogun's women contributed to manifesting his authority while remaining out of sight.

In many countries the ruler's women have played essential roles in bolstering the prestige of the state by performing public acts of religious piety. Tokugawa women supported priests and temples and sent processions of delegates to worship at mortuary temples.[27] For the most part, they played less prominent roles in public works projects than royal women in other countries, with the exception of Tsunayoshi's mother, Keishōin. The temple complex at Zenkōji still preserves objects commemorating her support and that of other women from the *ōoku*.[28] Another example is Gokokuji in Edo, founded in 1682 as Keishōin's private temple. In 1691, a Tōshōgu was erected in its precincts. It became a public temple in 1697 when the main hall was rebuilt. Among the deities enshrined there is Daigensui Myōō 大元帥明王, known for his prowess in defeating the enemies of the state. He had previously been enshrined at a temple in Yamashiro to protect the Kyoto-centered realm. Now he protected another sovereign – the shogun. In 1704, the year after she celebrated her seventy seventh birthday, Keishōin arranged to have the Thirty-Three Body (*sanjūsanjin* 三十三身) Buddha enshrined at Gokokuji. The bodies depict thirty-three manifestations of the Buddha's saving power as well as the guardians who protect the Buddhist teachings, represented in their most fearsome and hence magically powerful forms. Inside each of them is Keishōin's hair. One of the statues has the long hair of a layperson and may represent Keishōin herself. In this way she took her place among the protective deities assigned to guard her son (Naitō 1996, pp. 82–98).

Hidden though they were from public view, the shogun's women figured prominently as objects, both of exemplary behavior and in death rituals. It is well known that Tsunayoshi made an extravagant show of filial piety to his mother as part of his program of inculcating Confucian virtues in the military class. Every morning he sent a messenger to inquire after her health when he did not go himself. He showered her with presents. He painted pictures for her, danced for her, and did everything he could to give her pleasure (Ikenouchi 1925, p. 30). Although he performed these acts in the *ōoku*, they were meant to serve as models for the ruling class. The deaths of the shoguns' daughters, wives, and mothers required nation-wide signs of deference (Kinsei Shiryō Kenkyūkai 1966, pp. 199–200). Some were buried at Kan'eiji and Zōjōji, like the shoguns. Others were buried at smaller temples. They received posthumous names attesting to their virtue and figured in memorial services that incorporated them into the Tokugawa pantheon of guardian spirits. In this way their disembodied presence that supported temples and bound the daimyo to the dynasty continued after death to protect their descendants. Their hidden presence in the rituals of power thus provides another register in which to speak to a political authority predicated on the potency of secrecy.

Commoners and shoguns

Even though the shogun seldom showed his person to the Edo commoners, he loomed large in their lives.[29] As well as serving as guarantor of the city's continued prosperity, he contributed to its ritual life by funding festivals, inviting commoners onto palace grounds at his investiture or at New Year's, and providing for spectacular processions, both of daimyo and of his daughters. (One of the three famous sites of Edo was said to be the spot outside the castle where daimyo had to dismount their horses and clamber into palanquins.) Rituals involving commoners brought them into a more intimate relationship with the shogun, one that apparently gratified both.

The Sannō and Kanda festivals enjoyed a special relationship with the shogunate.[30] Sannō Gongen 山王権現 was the tutelary deity for the Tokugawa family and the protector of Chiyoda castle; Kanda Daimyōjin 神田大明神 was the tutelary deity for Edo.[31] Their festivals were called "festivals of the realm" (*tenka matsuri* 天下祭) because the shogunate covered some of their costs, the floats (*dashi* 山車) were allowed to enter the castle grounds, the shogunate issued orders governing the participants' appearance, and the shogun was said to take pleasure in watching the festivities (Toyoda 1999, p. 110).[32] For this purpose, he went to the viewing stand in Fukiage park where Ienari had interviewed the castaways in 1793.[33] Along with him went his wife, daughters, and their female attendants who also enjoyed watching the spectacle from behind bamboo screens.[34] By the early nineteenth century, the floats included imitations of the Korean envoys' processions, and wood block prints showed them with the same castle walls and Mt. Fuji in the background that graced the 1719 print (Toby 1986, pp. 447–53; Tōkyō-shi 1939, pp. 71, 82) (Fig. 14.6). A gold and silver signpost marked the spot where each unit in the procession stopped for the dancers to perform their best. According to Kurushima Hiroshi, "dancing where they knew the shogun would see them enhanced a sense of intimacy with him" (1986, p. 14). The more boisterous and excited the dancers, the more auspicious the occasion (*Kasshi Yawa, zokuhen* vol. 1, p. 324). The point of the festival was to celebrate peace and pray for eternal prosperity under military rule, a desire that united shogun and commoners. "It interrogated, remade, and reaffirmed their relationship" (Kurushima 1986, p. 16). During these processions, the townspeople assumed that the shogun enjoyed watching them have fun, yet they could no more see him than they could see deities carried on floats.

Figure 14.6 Festival floats recall the process of Korean envoys.[35] (Reproduction by courtesy of Tokyo National Museum.)

Another occasion that brought together commoners and shogun was *machi-iri* Noh 町入り能, first performed for the birth of Ietsuna in 1651 (*Shinhen Chiyodakushi tsūshi* 1, p. 382). At occasions auspicious for the Tokugawa house – the New Year's celebrations, the investiture of a shogun, his promotion in court rank, the birth of his heir, the heir's coming-of-age ceremony, the heir's marriage, and the shogun's trips to Nikkō – townspeople were allowed to enter Chiyoda castle for a Noh performance (Kurushima 1986, p. 18). They came for the first and most important day, an honor they shared with the most prestigious daimyo. Unlike the daimyo, they were allowed to watch only a half day's performance at a time. They had to sit to one side on the white gravel strewn between the stage and the *ōhiroma* wherein sat the shogun and daimyo. They had at best an imperfect view of action on the stage, since the actors performed for the shogun who was sitting directly across from them. While they could see the daimyo and officials who filled the rooms that stretched to the left of the shogun, they and the daimyo could see the shogun himself only when he allowed the screen that separated him from the rest of the audience to be raised (Fig. 14.7). According to an eyewitness account, when this happened, they shouted, "*yaa*" (*Kasshi yawa, zokuhen*, vol. 1, p. 324). Despite their cries, the shogun sat as rigid as a statue.

This was the sole occasion for commoners to view their ruler. For it they wore *kamishimo*, but with the whalebone stiffening in the shoulders

Figure 14.7 Crowded together the townspeople watch Noh. The shogun is hidden behind a screen directly opposite the stage (Ichioka, pp. 70–71. Reproduction by courtesy of Heibonsha, Tokyo.)

removed because they were packed in so tightly (Murai and Hirai 1988, p. 33). Each had to have an invitation.[36] As in festivals, a certain laxness in behavior was permitted, to the shogun's amusement – fights over food and drink, swiping of decorations, breaking down the fence around the stage, even smoking (Kurushima, 1986, p. 20; *Kasshi yawa, shōhen*, vol. 6, p. 293). The aim was to attain a common sense of enjoyment, a sense that commoners and shogun enjoyed the same spectacle. According to Matsudaira Nobuyoshi, seeing the shogun in this setting caused the townspeople to feel "a deepened sense of his authority." The term he used, *ikō* 威光, literally meant "the power of light" (Looser 1999, p. 348).

Conclusion

An important article by Fabio Rambelli (2002) highlights issues surrounding secret buddhas that can equally be applied to the shoguns and their women. How can buddhas convey meaning if they are hidden, and by extension, how can shoguns convey power? If a secret buddha serves as a bridge between the visible and the invisible realms, does hiding himself enable the shogun to serve as a bridge between power and authority as Herman Ooms pointed out in *Tokugawa Ideology*? In other words, if making a Buddhist icon invisible intensifies its sacredness, does making the shogun invisible intensify his authority? Insofar as that authority was predicated on the apotheosis of the founder and protected by the corpses of his descendants, in its ultimate manifestation, it could never be exposed. With some notable exceptions believed to be living buddhas, most Buddhist images subjected to a "regime of secrecy" were made visible and accessible in a ritual known as *kaichō* 開帳 when they were put on display. *Kaichō* were said to benefit the state because the object thus exposed acted to protect the people. By becoming visible, the image magnified the mystery of its secret, sacred, power. Could it not be said that when the shogun appeared unmoved and unmoving at *machi-iri* Noh, for example, that the occasion functioned as a form of *kaichō*? And this occasion showed in life how the shogun would appear in death.

Let me stretch the analogy by suggesting that if the shogun revealed himself in emulation of *kaichō*, then Chiyoda castle functioned as a temple complex. For most ceremonies, the shogun appeared immobile, often behind a screen at the highest place of honor before whom everyone bowed in the castle's main halls. Behind him and out of sight to mere men, the *ōoku* then functioned as a temple treasury. There gifts to the shogunate, both living and inanimate, were concealed and stored, their value deriving less from being used than from being hoarded, kept in reserve, the knowledge of their existence serving to guarantee their value.

Rambelli argues that "the magic of the state is always related in complex and inseparable ways to religious magic" (2002, p. 280), but perhaps my assimilation of the shogun to statues is too easy. After all, seclusion did not bestow power on the Kyoto monarch who during the Tokugawa period remained politically impotent. While it is obvious that the shogun more carefully guarded access to his person than did many European monarchs, perhaps he did so because the military campaigns of the sixteenth century as well as the traditions of secret knowledge transmitted in Noh troupes, the noble connoisseurs of poetry, other fields of cultural practices, and religious lineages had taught him the value of secrecy as a means of control. Looser has claimed that the shogun embodied all knowledge of the state (1999, p. 75), and one way to protect this knowledge was to keep it and its bearer secret. Furthermore, by appearing only at carefully selected times and remaining still, the shoguns exposed themselves as perfect beings wrapped in the dignity of silence, not as active humans who by definition are mortal and imperfect. Religion and governance were inextricably mixed, as the reading of *matsurigoto* for 政 attests. But ceremonial took on a life of its own in affairs of state, as we can see in the term for the governmental order of the shogunate, for what was the literal meaning of *kōgi* 公義 but public ceremony? (Looser 1999, p. 134) A public ceremony predicated on concealing politics.

Notes

1 See Yamashita 2003, especially pp. 4–5, 9–10, and Winkel 2004, p. 161.
2 The most prominent example is probably the third Shogun, Iemitsu. He was buried in the Taiyū-in in Nikkō in parallel fashion to Ieyasu, only lacking a Gongen 権現 title. In a bibliographical article on Iemitsu, Sugahara Shinkai (2000) has pointed out that there are actually many indications that Iemitsu wanted to become the "Second Gongen."
3 Ieharu's trip to Nikkō took nine days and required 230,000 porters, 620,000 guards, and 305,000 horses (Watanabe 1986, p. 138).
4 While waiting to appear before the shogun, the daimyo sat in assigned waiting rooms. These assignments were first made under Ietsuna in 1659 and revised by Yoshimune in 1744 (Futaki 2003, p. 381).
5 East of the ceremonial halls and the corridors that connected them were administrative offices (*Shinhen Chiyodakushi tsūshi* 1, p. 349).
6 In 1634, a toothache prevented Iemitsu from appearing at the *Kajō* 嘉祥 ceremony on 6/1, but it was held anyway. This happened in subsequent years as well (Futaki 2003, pp. 372, 416, 425).
7 Numerous records kept by shogunal officials diagram where different classes of daimyo were to sit and the procedures they were to follow for audiences before the shogun. See Fukai 2001–02, vols 1, 4, 6.
8 Futaki points out that one difference between Ashikaga and Tokugawa ceremonies was the weight placed on court rank in the latter (2003, pp. 428, 431, 439, 444).
9 According to Fukai (1999, p. 83), accounts of the ceremonies for the investitures of Ieharu, Ienari, and Iesada in *Tokugawa reiten roku* are incomplete.
10 In addition to sharing the same exalted court rank, Nijō was the natal house for Ienobu's father's wife, and Konoe was the natal house for Ienobu's wife.

11 Beginning in 1723, a wooden sword was substituted for metal (Futaki 2003, p. 391).
12 On the special relationship between the abbots of the Rinnōji in Nikkō and the Tokugawa shoguns, see William Bodiford's article in this book.
13 Hidetada began this practice for the new year's group audiences on the first, second, and third days of the new year (Futaki 2003, pp. 387, 389, 425). Iemitsu did the same, and by Yoshimune's time, it was standard practice (Fukai 2001–02, vol. 3, pp. 336–37).
14 Futaki documents how Ieyasu, Hidetada, and Iemitsu cajoled or coerced larger and larger numbers of daimyo to come to Edo for this visit (1986a, pp. 352–53, 392).
15 For greater detail, see *Shinhen Chiyodakushi tsūshi* 1, pp. 352–53.
16 On some occasions, abbot and shogun sat together in the lower *dan*, but regardless of the location, the shogun's pages made sure they were completely enclosed in screens (Fukai 2001–02, vol. 3, pp. 274–75).
17 Woodblock print by Chikanobu (1838–1912); possession of the author.
18 The ceremony of receiving cakes on 6/1 was first spelled out in 1635 under Iemitsu (Futaki 2003, pp. 352, 369).
19 Shogunal officials who kept elaborate records and made detailed drawings showing who was to go where during ceremonies almost never noted the shogun's position unless he was in motion. (Fukai 2001–02, vol. 1, pp. 38–41, 50–63, 116–17, 132–33, 142–43, 264–65).
20 These informal audiences are not mentioned in the *Tokugawa jikki* and further research is needed to find out whether they extended beyond the reign of Tsunayoshi.
21 Woodblock print by Okumura Masanobu; source: Tokyo National Museum.
22 As reported to me by William Bodiford.
23 Cf. Monod 1999, pp. 1, 3, 26, 39. Monod (p. 42) also points out that this theory of divine kingship was strongest felt in England and France; in other parts of Europe, monarchs had to be content with lesser claims.
24 At the New Year for example, the Ashikaga shogun's wife received greetings from everyone who had to pay their respects to the shogun. When the shogun paid the first visit of the year to the deputy shogun's house, his wife preceded him. Those who offered the shogun felicitations following his first bath of the year also visited the wife's quarters to greet her (Futaki 2003, pp. 45, 46, 48).
25 In 1688 Tsunayoshi issued regulations to curb the excesses of his daughter's staff in the Kii mansion (Kuroita 1931, vol. 6, p. 3). For the ceremonies for the husband's visit to such a wife see Hata 2001, pp. 156–57. Ichioka (1989) mentions the gates on p. 153.
26 See, for example, Kuroita 1931, vol. 5, pp. 378, 386, 472, 511, *passim*.
27 It was on one of these expeditions that the infamous Ejima incident occurred. An important scene in the kabuki play, *Kagamiyama kokyō no nishikie* 加賀見山旧錦絵 is also set during one of these excursions.
28 Keishōin assisted in building the main hall for Zenkōji, a project that took fifteen years (McCallum 1994, pp. 171–73).
29 Although the first three shoguns took advantage of hawking expeditions to accept petitions from commoners, this practice died out when the next four shoguns abjured the practice. When Yoshimune and his successors went hunting, they made it a practice never to go so far that they could not return to the castle by nightfall.
30 Although some records claim that the Sannō festival procession started entering the castle in 1615, the first shogun to take the opportunity to watch it was Iemitsu in 1635. The Kanda procession received the same permission

in 1688, and Tsunayoshi first watched it in 1706 (Taniguchi 1979, pp. 17–58; Tōkyō-shi 1939, pp. 84–85).

31 Iemitsu was the first to claim Sannō Gongen as his family tutelary deity (*ubusuna no kami* 産土神) (Tōkyō-shi, 1939, p. 11). Originally the protective deity of Mount Hiei, Sannō was introduced in the veneration of Ieyasu (Tōshō Daigongen) by the Tendai abbot Tenkai 天海, one of the chief religious advisors to Ieyasu and most notably Iemitsu.

32 Both the Kyōhō and the Kansei reforms had a depressing effect on the festival owing to sumptuary regulation and limitations on the size and number of floats. Without the shogun's protection, the festivals declined in Meiji (Sakumi 1996, pp. 13, 96, 137).

33 This viewing stand was also used for judicial proceedings observed by the shogun (*kōji jōchō* 公事上聴), horseback riding, archery, gunnery, and sumo. Before it was built in 1713, the shogun's position for viewing festivals varied considerably, and there is no mention of blinds (*Shinhen Chiyodakushi tsūshi* 1, pp. 373–75; Tōkyō-shi 1939, p. 129).

34 *Tokugawa jikki* states that the shogun saw the Sannō festival 71 times; the Kanda festival 3 times, suggesting that most years he did not go to the Fukiage viewing stand even though the procession always went through castle grounds up to the 1850s (Toyoda 1999, p. 110, 112). The two festivals alternated years.

35 Woodblock print by Nishimura Shigenaga; source: Tokyo National Museum.

36 According to Matsura Seizan, 5118 townspeople – 2551 in the morning and 2567 in the afternoon – saw *machi-iri* Noh (*Kasshi yawa, zokuhen*, vol. 1, pp. 3–9). On the day of the festival, they received umbrellas, cakes, and sake; afterward they received money.

References

Cannadine, David (1987), "Introduction: Divine rites of kings," in David Cannadine and Simon Price (eds), *Rituals of Royalty: Power and Ceremonial in Traditional Societies*. Cambridge: Cambridge University Press, pp. 1–19.

Duus, Peter (2001), "Presidential Address: Weapons of the Weak, Weapons of the Strong – The Development of the Japanese Political Cartoon." *Journal of Asian Studies* 60/4, pp. 965–998.

Errington, Shelly (1989), *Meaning and Power in a Southeast Asian Realm*. Princeton: Princeton University Press.

Fukai Masaumi 深井雅海 (1999), "Shōgun senge in miru kuge, daimyō, jishakata no kakushiki: rokudai shōgun 'shōgun sengeki' ni mieru 'memie' to 'furumai' ni kansuru shiryō shōkai o kanete" 将軍宣下に見る公家・大名・寺社方の格式：六代家宣「将軍宣下記」に見える「目見え」と「振舞」に関する史料紹介を兼ねて, in Hashimoto Masanobu 橋本政宣 (ed.), *Kinsei buke kan'i no kenkyū* 近世武家官位の研究. Tokyo: Zoku Gunsho Ruijū Kanseikai, pp. 83–117.

Fukai Masaumi (ed.) (2001–02), *Edo jidai buke gyōji girei zufu* 江戸時代武家行事儀礼図譜, 8 vols. Tokyo: Tōyō Shoin.

Futaki Ken'ichi 二木兼一 (1986a), "Edo bakufu shōgatsu sanga girei no seiritsu" 江戸幕府正月参賀儀礼の成立, in Hayashi Rokurō Sensei Kanreki Kinenkai (ed.), *Kinsei kokka no shihai kōzō* 近世国家の支配構造. Tokyo: Yūzankaku, pp. 389–411.

Futaki Ken'ichi (1986b), "Edo bakufu yassoku sanga girei no seiritsu" 江戸幕府八朔参賀儀礼の成立. *Nihon rekishi* 462, pp. 33–50.

Futaki Ken'ichi (2003), *Buke girei kakushiki no kenkyū* 武家儀礼格式の研究. Tokyo: Yoshikawa Kōbunkan.

Hata Hisako 畑尚子 (2001), *Edo oku jochū monogatari* 江戸奥女中物語り. Tokyo: Kōdansha.

Hirai Kiyoshi 平井聖 (2000), *Edo-jō to shōgun no kurashi* 江戸城と将軍の暮らし (=*Zusetsu Edo* 図説江戸, vol. 1). Tokyo: Gakushū Kenkyūsha.

Ichioka Masakazu 市岡正一 (1989), *Tokugawa seisei roku* 徳川盛世録. Tokyo: Heibonsha. [¹1889].

Ikenouchi Nobuyoshi 池内信嘉 (1925), *Edo no nō* 江戸の能 (=*Nōgaku seisuiki* 能楽盛衰記, vol. 1). Tokyo: Nōgakukai.

Kaempfer, Engelbert (1999), Beatrice M. Bodart-Bailey (ed. and tr.), *Kaempfer's Japan: Tokugawa Culture Observed*. Honolulu: University of Hawai'i Press.

Kasshi yawa 甲子夜話 (20 vols) by Matsura Seizan 松浦静山 (1760–1841). Nakamura Yukihito 中村幸彦 and Nakano Mitsutoshi 中野三敏 (eds). Tokyo: Heibonsha 1977–83.

Kertzer, David L. (1988), *Ritual, Politics, and Power*. New Haven: Yale University Press.

Kinsei Shiryō Kenkyūkai 近世史料研究会 (1966), *Shōhō jiroku* 正宝事録, vol. 3. Tokyo: Nihon Gakujitsu Shinkōkai.

Kuroita Katsumi 黒板勝美 (ed.) (1931), *Tokugawa jikki* 徳川実紀, vol. 6. Tokyo: Kokushi Taikei Kankōkai.

Kurushima Hiroshi 久留島浩 (1986), "Kinsei ni okeru matsuri no 'shūhen'" 近世における祭りの「周辺」. *Rekishi hyōron* 歴史評論 439, pp. 12–24.

Looser, Thomas David (1999). *The Celebration of Eternity: Space-Times of the State and Gestures of History in the Early Modern Nō Theater of Japan*. University of Chicago, Ph.D. dissertation.

McCallum, Donald F. (1994), *Zenkōji and its Icon: A Study in Medieval Japanese Religious Art*. Princeton: Princeton University Press.

Monod, Paul Kléber (1999), *The Power of Kings: Monarchy and Religion in Europe 1589–1715*. New Haven: Yale University Press.

Murai Masao 村井益男 and Hirai Kiyoshi 平井聖 (1988), *Edo-jō to ōoku* 江戸城と大奥 (=*Pikutoriaru Edo*, vol. 1). Tokyo: Gakushū Kenkyūsha.

Naitō Masatoshi 内藤政敏 (1996), *Mato Edo no toshi keikaku: Tokugawa shogunke no shirarezaru yabō* 魔都江戸の都市計画：徳川将軍家の知られざる野望. Tokyo: Yōsensha.

Ooms, Herman (1985), *Tokugawa Ideology*. Princeton: Princeton University Press.

Ōtomo Kazuo 大伴一雄 (1999), *Nihon kinsei kokka no ken'i to girei* 日本近世国家の権威と儀礼. Tokyo: Yoshikawa Kōbunkan.

Rambelli, Fabio (2002), "Secret Buddhas: The Limits of Buddhist Representation." *Monumenta Nipponica* 57/3, pp. 271–301.

Sakumi Yōichi 作美陽一 (1996), *Ōedo no tenka matsuri* 大江戸の天下祭り. Tokyo: Kawade Shobō.

Scheid, Bernhard (2003), "Conference Report: Section 8, Religion and History of Ideas." *Bulletin of the European Association of Japanese Studies* 64, pp. 29–31.

Scheid, Bernhard and Birgit Staemmler (2002), "Call for Papers: Section 8, Religion and History of Ideas" *Bulletin of the European Association of Japanese Studies* 60, pp. 46–47.

Screech, Timon (2000), *The Shogun's Painted Culture: Fear and Creativity in the Japanese State, 1760–1829*. London: Reaktion Books.

Shinhen Chiyodakushi tsūshi 新遍千代田区史通史 (1998), 2 vols. Chiyodakusei gojūnenshi hensan iinkai 千代田区政五十年史編纂委員会 (ed.). Tokyo: Chiyoda-ku.

Sono, Reiko (2004), "Imagination of Matter in Early Modern Japan." *Historical Sources and Their Usage: The Fifth International Conference of the Japan Memory Project*. Tokyo: Historiographical Institute, University of Tokyo, pp. 119–29.

Sugahara Shinkai 菅原信海 (2000), "'Nisei gongen' Iemitsu-kō" 「二世権現」家光公. *Nikkō Rinnōji* 67 (2000/4), pp. 29–44. (Special issue commemorating the 350th year after Tokugawa Iemitsu's death.)

Taniguchi Ken'ichi 谷口健一 (ed.) (1979), *Sairei* 祭礼 (=*Nihon shomin seikatsu shiryō shūsei* 日本庶民生活史料集成, vol. 22). Tokyo: San'ichi Shobō.

Taussig, Michael (1997), *The Magic of the State*. New York and London: Routledge.

Toby, Ronald P. (1986), "Carnival of the Aliens: Korean Embassies in Edo-Period Art and Popular Culture." *Monumenta Nipponica* 41/4, pp. 415–56.

Tokugawa reiten roku 徳川礼典録 (1942), 3 vols. Owari Tokugawa Reimeikai 尾張徳川黎明会 (ed.). Tokyo: Owari Tokugawa Reimeikai.

Tōkyō-shi 東京市 (ed.) (1939), *Tenka matsuri* 天下祭 (=*Tōkyō shishi gaihen* 東京市史外篇, vol. 4). Tokyo: Tōkyō Shiyakusho.

Toyoda Kazuhira 豊田和平 (1999), "Tenka matsuri to Edo no sairei bunka" 天下祭と江戸の祭礼文化, in Katō Takashi 加藤貴 (ed.), *Ōedo rekishi no fūkei* 大江戸歴史の風景. Tokyo: Yamakawa Shuppansha, pp. 109–21.

Watanabe Hiroshi 渡辺浩 (1986), "Go-ikō to shōchō: Tokugawa seiji taisei no ichi sokumen" 「御威光」と象徴—徳川政治体制の一側面. *Shisō* 740, pp. 132–154.

Winkel, Margarita (2004), *Discovering Different Dimensions: Explorations of Culture and History in Early Modern Japan*. Leiden: By the author.

Yamashita Tsuneo 山下恒夫 (ed.) (2003), *Daikokuya Kōdayū shiryōshū* 大黒屋光太夫史料集, vol. 3. Tokyo: Nihon Hyōronsha.

15 "Esoteric" and "public" in late Mito thought

Kate Wildman Nakai

As the other contributions to this book have detailed, the esotericism prevalent in medieval Japanese Buddhism had a far-reaching impact on various dimensions of religious, cultural, and intellectual life. Central among its legacies was the articulation of "Shinto," claimed by successive thinkers to be an autonomous body of doctrines and practices, but in fact owing much of its content and orientation to the matrix of esoteric Buddhism from which it emerged. What happened to this combination of elements with the rise of interest in Confucianism and the concomitant disavowal of Buddhism characteristic of early modern intellectual life? Confucian thinkers of all schools put priority on the ordering of society and the establishment of proper social relations; they also took as a given that, as categories, "public" (*kō* 公) was something positive, in contrast to "private" (*shi, watakushi* 私), which carried dubious and negative connotations. One might thus expect a commitment to Confucianism to bring with it a querying of esotericism and its attendant assumption that privileged knowledge should be guarded and transmitted only to the initiated.

In many regards this proved to be the case. A story told of Hayashi Razan 林羅山 (1583–1657) is emblematic. According to the biography compiled by his sons, Razan's career as a scholar began with a challenge to the medieval norm of privileged transmissions. Having become familiar with Zhu Xi's commentaries on the Four Books, the young Razan, so the story goes, began to offer public lectures in Kyoto on the *Analects*. The court scholar Kiyohara (Funahashi) Hidekata 清原(船橋)秀賢 (1575–1614), whose house specialized in the reading and recitation of the Confucian classics, protested that only those with an imperial sanction to do so should be allowed to conduct lectures on the classics. The newly appointed Shogun Tokugawa Ieyasu, however, the biography relates, intervened on Razan's behalf. Whether or not these events occurred precisely as described, the story is indicative of a new value assigned to the "public" over the "secret" or "private."[1]

Yet the situation was not so simple and straightforward as the story might be taken to suggest. Just as earlier generations of religious figures had drawn equations between elements of kami worship and Buddhism, many Tokugawa Confucians, Razan included, posited a unity between Confucianism and Shinto. We may assume various factors to underlie this phenomenon. There was doubtless a concern, on the one hand, to infuse Confucian practice with immediacy by linking it to an existing spiritual regimen and ritual forms. The fact that various late medieval and early modern proponents of Shinto were in the process of divesting their formulations in name, if not fully in content, from an affiliation with Buddhism facilitated reconnection with Confucianism. Confucians participating in these developments, on the other hand, also wished to reform and reorient Shinto practices by joining them more explicitly to the Confucian goal of ordering society.

Regardless of the underlying motivation, in their efforts to combine the doctrines and practices of the two traditions, early Tokugawa Confucians often fell under the sway of medieval Shinto's propensity for casting knowledge as a secret to be conveyed only to the properly initiated. They also inherited specific points of esoteric lore regarding the nature of certain kami and ritual acts and the meaning of passages from the accounts of *kamiyo* 神代 (the age of the gods) in *Nihon shoki* and other texts. Razan's *Shintō denju* 神道伝授 (Transmissions on Shinto), written in the 1640s, provides a pertinent example. To be sure, in this work Razan took steps to disassociate his version of Shinto from currently prevalent forms. The "true" form of Shinto that he propounded was, he asserted, identical with the "way of the king" (*ōdō* 王道), in other words, the Confucian Way. Drawing from Song Confucian ideas, he further identified Shinto cum *ōdō* with an inner spiritual realm linking the individual to a moral cosmic order, and he demarcated this "true" Shinto from lesser forms associated with shrine priests, whom he characterized as dealing in *shinji* 神事, technical matters of ritual and such, not Shinto.[2] But, as Bernhard Scheid has recently pointed out, Razan also composed *Shintō denju* in the form of a collection of separate secret transmissions, and he evidently conveyed, or planned to convey, individual sections of it in the *kirikami* 切紙 ("separate sheet") format traditionally used for such transmissions.[3] Many of the points to be transmitted show the direct influence of Yoshida Shinto ideas, and Razan's characterization of the metaphysical inner world of the spirit built on medieval interpretations of the initial generations of kami such as Kuni no Tokotachi 国常立 and Ame no Minakanushi 天御中主, who had been the subject of much allegorical exegesis. And, in formulating what were essentially initiations into the meaning of such matters, Razan followed the patterns for conveying esoteric knowledge by identifying one item or another as "a secret among secrets," or by stating that "this is an inner secret of Shinto; it should not be disclosed to others" (*Shintō denju*, pp. 36, 46).

The somewhat younger Confucian Yamazaki Ansai 山崎闇斎 (1618–82), known for his fervent commitment to Zhu Xi and for his emphasis on a rigorous, introspective self-cultivation, showed an equal debt to the medieval Shinto fondness for esoteric hermeneutics. His efforts to demonstrate the identity between the *kamiyo* chapters of *Nihon shoki* and Zhu Xi metaphysics, for example, depended heavily on the allegorical word play and numerical associations favored by medieval commentators. Like Razan he took Shinto to be something of universal relevance and held that it should not be treated as the privileged possession of one particular lineage. But he also continued to couch central aspects of Shinto doctrine as esoteric knowledge to be conveyed through stages of initiation.[4] Consolidated further by his followers, this aspect of Ansai's approach to Shinto became an established feature of the Suika 垂加 school of Shinto devolving from him.

But not all Tokugawa efforts to establish an identity between Confucianism and Shinto stayed within the framework of the allegorical, inward-looking perspective with its deep debt to medieval esotericism as well as Song metaphysics that we see in Razan and Ansai. The thoroughgoing critique of Song thought mounted at the end of the seventeenth century and in the first decades of the eighteenth century by the so-called Ancient Learning (*kogaku* 古学) scholars, most particularly Ogyū Sorai 荻生徂徠 (1666–1728), inevitably had an impact on such constructions as well. Sorai attacked the Song emphasis on introspective self-cultivation supported by a metaphysical apparatus that reified the "abstract and minute" as a "specious product of private speculation" (*shichi mōsaku* 私智妄作).[5] The same criticism could be readily extended to the medieval and early modern forms of Shinto, described caustically by Sorai's senior disciple Dazai Shundai 太宰春台 (1680–1747) as no more than something concocted out of "seven or eight parts Buddhism and two or three parts" Song metaphysics (*Bendō sho*, pp. 44–46).

Among the heirs to this perspective were the thinkers of the late Mito school, active from the end of the eighteenth to the mid-nineteenth century. The late Mito thinkers – Fujita Yūkoku 藤田幽谷 (1774–1826), Aizawa Seishisai 会沢正志斎 (1782–1863), and Yūkoku's son Tōko 東湖 (1806–55) – disagreed strongly with some of Sorai's propositions. Most notably, they took issue with his assertion that the Way was a human construction. To the contrary, they insisted, the Way was grounded in the natural order of things, and, in line with this position, they reiterated again and again the obligation to uphold the moral norms – the five constants of human relationships – that constituted the foundation of the Way. While they adhered to the traditional Confucian position that the Way was something natural and innate, however, the Mito thinkers had more in common with Sorai than with followers of the Song tradition. They shared Sorai's suspicion of the Zhu Xi emphasis on metaphysical analysis and reasoning and on introspection and cultivation of the self. Like Sorai they fully recognized the power of the religious impulse in human beings, and they were sensitive to the dynamics of the quest for spiritual reassurance and consolation in the face of death and the unknown. But they also saw these impulses as something potentially dangerous. To be directed to positive ends, the instinctive yearning for spiritual reassurance needed to be controlled and properly guided through effective structures of ritual.[6]

Lending urgency to the Mito thinkers' focus on these issues was their intense concern about the fractures and divisions that they saw undermining the social order of their time. These, they were convinced, might well provide an opening to foreign incursions, the way for which would be paved by insidious efforts to spread subversive forms of belief and religion. To prevent this from happening, it was essential to do away with all potential sources of divided allegiance and to develop means of fostering a spiritual unity in which "the multitudes would be of one mind" (*okuchō isshin* 億兆一心).[7]

These convictions permeated the Mito approach to Shinto. Like Razan and Ansai, the late Mito thinkers posited an "intrinsic match" (*angō* 暗合) between Shinto and the Confucian Way. The essence of both, they held, lay in the clarification and reinforcement of the moral fabric of the social and political order. Beyond that, both Shinto and the Confucian Way were founded on recognition that rituals to the spiritual forces of Heaven and Earth and ancestral rites were the most efficacious means to unify the minds of the populace and convey moral norms.[8] As evidence of this intrinsic match, the Mito scholars pointed to the passage from the *Yijing* 易経 stating that "the sage uses the divine way (*shendao*; i.e., *shintō*) to give instruction, and the entire world submits to him."[9] This, they argued, was exactly the method of rule original to Japan. Citing the phrase from the *Yijing*, Aizawa wrote of Amaterasu that "in antiquity, the Heavenly Ancestor (Tenso 天祖), using the divine way to give instruction, established the norms of human behavior by clarifying loyalty and filial piety."[10]

Shinto, according to the Mito scholars, was thus by origin an instrument for conveying moral principles and establishing order throughout society. In "using Shinto to give instruction," Amaterasu had set forth standards essential to the eternal preservation of the imperial line and to ensuring the welfare of the realm over which it ruled. The formulators of the various schools of so-called Shinto that had appeared in Japan in the wake of the introduction of Buddhism had lost sight of this purpose and had distorted Shinto's true nature. The cosmological and allegorical interpretations of the *kamiyo* texts and other works that they had elaborated were nothing more than their own "private speculations." By further framing these private speculations as stages of initiation, the medieval and early modern Shinto thinkers had, as Fujita Tōko put it, "turned the record of the accomplishments of the sagely and divine founders of the realm into something like a riddle or a secret code."[11] In these forms, Shinto could hardly provide appropriate moral guidance or serve to unify the minds of the multitudes. To meet the needs of time, it was crucial to rescue Shinto from its current state of corruption and restore its original character as a means of extending moral instruction throughout society. The Mito scholars pursued two intersecting routes to this end. One was to reclaim territory over which esoteric notions had extended a far-reaching influence; specifically this meant freeing deities such as Amaterasu of the accretion of "distorting" interpretations and resituating them within the framework of Shinto as the Mito scholars conceived it. The other was to set forth a structure of ritual appropriate to "using Shinto to give instruction."

Reclaiming esoteric territory

In place of the expansive allegorical interpretations of the *kamiyo* deities characteristic of medieval and early modern Shinto, the late Mito thinkers took a fundamentally historical approach.[12] Although a sacred entity identical with the sun, Amaterasu was also the founder of the imperial line and the polity of Japan. As such, in their view, she was analogous in many regards to the sages of ancient China.[13] Other key deities, like Ame no Koyane 天児屋根, the ancestor of the Nakatomi 中臣 lineage and its offshoot, the Fujiwara, the late Mito thinkers likewise saw as historical figures who had served Amaterasu and assisted her in establishing the foundations of the polity. To this premise the late Mito thinkers attached a sequence of interlocking propositions. The founders of the polity had provided later generations with immense benefits for which their descendants owed eternal recompense. Such recompense meant not only honoring the founders through appropriate rituals, but also continuing the tasks they had undertaken. The same charge applied to the general populace as well as the rulers of the day. Concretely, in antiquity, the ancestors of those now living had carried out diverse roles in service to Amaterasu; in the same way, the people of the present should serve the emperor, her descendant, by re-enacting the functions performed by their ancestors. They would thereby fulfill two obligations at once: loyalty to the ruler and filial piety to their ancestors. The two central moral norms, loyalty and filial piety, would be "rooted in one source" (*chūkō wa ichi ni izu* 忠孝出一), while "the present would replicate the antiquity" (*kyō wa sunawachi jōko; jōko wa sunawachi kyō* 今日即上古、上古即今日).[14] Such fusion would ensure the unification of the minds of the populace, guard against any cracks in the social fabric providing an opening to subversive forces, and secure the preservation of order and hierarchy. The late Mito thinkers summed up this sought-for dynamic with a phrase from the Chinese classics: *hōhon hanshi* 報本反始 ("recompensing the source and holding to the origin").

To inscribe (or, as they would see it, to bring to light) the mechanism of *hōhon hanshi* at the core of Japanese tradition, the late Mito thinkers concentrated attention on the "historical" deities – above all Amaterasu – whom they held to be central to its operation. Simultaneously they downplayed the significance of those *kamiyo* deities that did not fit readily within the framework of *hōhon hanshi* as they envisioned it. Among these, hardly coincidentally, were shadowy entities such as Kuni no Tokotachi and Ame no Minakanushi that were difficult to link to activities of a "historical" nature and that throughout the medieval and early modern period had been favored subjects of esoteric allegorical interpretations.

Aizawa's *Tekiihen* 迪彝編 (Exhortations about Adhering to Moral Norms), a work he wrote in 1833 for popular edification, provides a revealing example of this strategy. In this piece Aizawa did not cite directly from the original *kamiyo* texts such as *Nihon shoki*. Instead, to explain the distinctive features of the Japanese polity, he stated that he would quote from the "correct account" of the origins of the imperial line that Kitabatake Chikafusa 北畠親房 (1293–1354) had set out in his *Jinnō shōtōki* 神皇正統記 (Chronicle of the Legitimate Line of Deities and Sovereigns). Presumably Aizawa chose this method because Chikafusa's "correct account" brought out much more fully than the original texts the image of Amaterasu as a source of moral norms that the late Mito scholars wished to emphasize. In describing Amaterasu's grant to her grandson Ninigi 瓊瓊杵 of the regalia, for instance, Chikafusa had explained that she had not bestowed upon Ninigi simply tangible symbols of authority. More importantly she had provided him with teachings as to "the correct way to govern and preserve the country."[15]

But while quoting Chikafusa directly on such points, Aizawa also excised or modified elements that he found inconvenient. Among other things, he omitted almost all of Chikafusa's version of the opening section of the *kamiyo* accounts. Over the centuries this section, which described the state of primal chaos prior to the separation of Heaven and Earth and named the initial generations of deities, had been a particularly rich source for allegorical and speculative reinterpretation. Of Chikafusa's version, Aizawa kept the statement that the first deity at the beginning of Heaven and Earth was known as Kuni no Tokotachi and alternatively as Ame no Minakanushi. He added a cautionary note, however, observing that "although there are various theories about this name, it being a matter of the distant past, the details of the situation are not clear" (*Tekiihen*, pp. 251, 253–55). And through a discreet sleight-of-hand, he shifted attention away from the role that esoteric interpretations had long assigned Kuni no Tokotachi as an originary force.

Referring to Kuni no Tokotachi as Tenso (which we may translate here as Heavenly Progenitor), Chikafusa began *Jinnō shōtōki* by declaring that Japan was known as the country of the gods because "the Heavenly Progenitor set forth its foundations and the Sun Deity bequeathed its rule eternally to her descendants."[16] For Chikafusa, the involvement of Kuni no Tokotachi as an originary force was thus a crucial element in the establishment of the Japanese polity.[17] Aizawa, on the other hand, as we saw above, commonly used Tenso in the manner of the laudatory names of founders of Chinese dynasties to refer to Amaterasu. Elsewhere he specified that this term traditionally had been used in contrast to the more generic *tenjin* 天神 (heavenly deities) to distinguish Amaterasu as a sole actor.[18] In quoting the opening passage from *Jinnō shōtōki* without any reference to Chikafusa's identification of Tenso as Kuni no Tokotachi, Aizawa elided the role ascribed to the latter deity together with its various esoteric connotations. Instead he combined in Amaterasu the function of both founder and bequeather. Similarly, while reproducing in extenso the passage from *Jinnō shōtōki* concerning the regalia, through the omission of certain phrases and the modification of others, Aizawa reshaped Chikafusa's depiction of this event. Although he retained, for instance, the emphasis that Amaterasu conveyed teachings to Ninigi together with the regalia, Aizawa systematically suppressed the allegorical and inward-looking interpretations of those teachings that Chikafusa had derived from Watarai Shinto texts. Symbolic of these changes is Aizawa's substitution of the matter-of-fact phrase "[the regalia] are the divine treasure of this country" (*kono kuni no shinpō nite* この国の神宝にて) for Chikafusa's more mystical statement that Amaterasu conveyed them "as the divine spirit of this country" (*kono kuni no shinrei toshite* 此国ノ神霊トシテ). Similarly Aizawa excised the phrases in which Chikafusa characterized the regalia as the "font" (*hongen* 本源) of uprightness, compassion, and wisdom, the qualities that the emperor needed to cultivate so as to govern the realm properly.[19] In place of Chikafusa's emphasis on the process of self-cultivation incumbent upon the ruler, Aizawa stressed that Amaterasu's bequest of the regalia and command that her descendants should rule Japan eternally constituted a central pillar of the imperative to "recompense the source and hold to the origin." For the emperor, fulfillment of this imperative meant above all to uphold his filial duty to Amaterasu through preservation of the unbroken imperial line and ongoing devotion to her.

To reinforce Amaterasu's centrality within the dynamic of *hōhon hanshi*, Aizawa did not merely reorient Chikafusa's version of the events of *kamiyo* to bring out more sharply that the essence of her teachings resided in the "clarification of loyalty and filial piety." Moving outside the parameters of Chikafusa's account, he drew attention to the significance of other blessings received from Amaterasu. Apart from granting Ninigi the regalia, she had, "with her own hands," bestowed upon him sheaves of grain from her sacred field and had shown the way to cultivate silkworms as well as the use of other fibers. Through these beneficent gifts she had provided the means for the populace to sustain life and protect themselves from the cold.[20] Not only the ruler responsible for the welfare of the populace, but the people themselves had thus incurred an inexhaustible debt to Amaterasu as the source of the most fundamental necessities of human existence as well as moral teachings.

The late Mito thinkers' approach to deities like Ōkuninushi 大国主 illustrates another aspect of the challenge to esoteric understandings embedded in the resituation of the deities of *kamiyo* as "historical" actors. Described in *Nihon shoki* as having declared his readiness to yield authority over the land to the descendants of Amaterasu and to devote himself to "divine matters" or "hidden matters,"[21] Ōkuninushi could be assigned a place within the historical process of the founding of the polity. But through imaginative exegesis at the hands of medieval and early modern commentators he had also acquired a variety of other characteristics and associations. As Bernhard Scheid discusses in this book, Shinto thinkers took the passages about "divine matters" and "hidden matters" as a key sanction for esoteric interpretations and practices. In the early Tokugawa period Yamazaki Ansai had interpreted a dialogue between Ōkuninushi and his "wondrous spirit" (*sakimitama kushimitama* 幸魂奇魂) as a model for a personal spiritual regimen of introspective moral reflection.[22] Nearer in time to the late Mito thinkers, Hirata Atsutane 平田篤胤 (1776–1843) had acclaimed Ōkuninushi as the ruler of the unseen world of the spirits of the dead.[23]

For the late Mito thinkers, these interpretations of Ōkuninushi were prime examples of problematic "private speculation" that, by fostering heterodox beliefs and practices, served only to divide, not unify, the allegiance of the populace. Deflating the aura of expansive associations surrounding Ōkuninushi, the late Mito thinkers instead presented him simply as the chief of the Izumo region. As such he was one among the "many" early chiefs of this sort who had pacified local territories and done things beneficial for the populace. That the people of the regions where such chiefs had been active should revere them was only natural.[24] Ōkuninushi was further worthy of emulation as an exemplar of a local chief who, having presented his territory to the sovereign, had dispatched emissaries to the court to pay homage. And he deserved praise for his achievements in developing methods of healing.[25] But the reverence offered to him should be incorporated within an appropriate overall framework of ritual that would contribute to realization of the unifying dynamic of *hōhon hanshi*.

The efficacy of public ritual

The locus classicus of the term *hōhon hanshi* was *Liji* 礼記 (Book of Rites), and, as this suggests, the major inspiration for the late Mito thinkers' concept of a proper system of ritual likewise came from the classical Chinese canon, particularly works such as *Liji*, *Zhouli* 周礼 (Rites of Zhou), and *Shangshu* 尚書 (Book of History). In these works the Mito scholars saw a picture of society governed through ritual structures that also conveyed moral norms and that thereby guided the populace in the proper direction while simultaneously providing an outlet for its religious impulses. Put slightly differently, they found delineated in concrete form further core components of their notion of Shinto, such as the fusion of governance and doctrine (*jikyō itchi* 治教一致) and ritual and governance (*saisei itchi* 祭政一致). More than simply channeling the religious instincts of the populace into an appropriate framework, this model of government through ritual had the capacity, the Mito thinkers were convinced, to tap into the energies of the people and arouse in them the spontaneous commitment to serve the ruler summed up in the term *hōhon hanshi*. Prime examples of this ideal were the ruler's annual sacrifices to Earth and Heaven – the *she* 社 (Jap. *sha*) and *jiao* 郊 (Jap. *kō*; i.e., the Suburban Sacrifice). As described in *Liji*, the populace did not take a direct part in the rituals. Yet, the solemnity of the occasion aroused in the people an instinctive desire to contribute to their successful perform-ance. For the sacrifices to Earth, members of all levels of society went out to secure the items to be offered. For the sacrifices to Heaven, the people undertook to water and sweep the road along which the ruler would pass, "according with the wish of the ruler without being explicitly ordered to do so." The transforming effect of the ritual inspired in them a spontaneous desire to "recompense the source and hold to the origin."[26]

The late Mito thinkers' conviction that an "intrinsic match" existed between the Way of the founders of the Japanese polity and the Way of the sages carried with it the corollary that something like the types of rituals described in *Liji* must have existed in Japan. Initially, they admitted, the forms had been quite different. In antiquity, when customs had been simple and the people straightforward, the Japanese sage rulers had not found it necessary to explicate the Way through formal structures; they had merely conveyed it symbolically, as had Amaterasu in granting Ninigi the regalia and sheaves of grain. It was the natural course of things, however, for society to grow more complex over time. As a complement to simplicity (*shitsu* 質), cultured forms of expression (*bun* 文), including explicit ritual structures, became correspondingly essential. Recognizing this, the early emperors, such as the first emperor, Jinmu 神武, and the tenth emperor, Sujin 崇神, had established appropriate rituals. But the incursion of Buddhism had corrupted native practices and blinded people's perception. People no longer could grasp directly the import of what the founders had intended. To clarify the founders' intent it was thus necessary to turn to Chinese sources where the same fundamental methods and aims were set forth in more explicit written form.[27]

Armed with this proposition, the late Mito scholars identified in works such as *Nihon shoki* several key instances of the early emperors instituting forms of ritual comparable to those described in the Confucian classics. To substantiate these cases and to bring out their full implications, the Mito thinkers adopted the same interpretive strategies that we have seen them employ to establish that Amaterasu provided instruction through Shinto and to reshape Chikafusa's version of *kamiyo* to fit their own aims.

In place of the word play and numerology favored by the practitioners of medieval and early modern esoteric hermeneutics, the Mito scholars built up an argument based on analogy. Carefully selecting the relevant details of the Japanese event, they drew out its meaning (or, we might say, more accurately, infused it with the desired meaning) by enveloping those details in a web of references to the fuller Chinese accounts of the ancient Chinese "parallel." While we might see this process as entailing veiling and concealment, from their perspective it enabled the recuperation of elements of Japanese tradition that hitherto had been susceptible to esoteric distortion.

We can find an instructive example of this process in Aizawa's interpretation of the *Nihon shoki* passage that relates how Sujin moved the mirror granted by Amaterasu to Ninigi out of the emperor's residence. Prior to this, *Nihon shoki* states, the emperor had worshiped Amaterasu and the deity Yamato no Ōkunitama 倭大国魂 within his own living quarters. But following a pestilence that swept the land and popular rebellions, in response to which he begged the deities of Heaven and Earth for forgiveness, he became "fearful of the power of these deities and uneasy about living in proximity to them. He thus entrusted Amaterasu [i.e., the mirror] to Toyosukiiribime no Mikoto 豊鍬入姫命 and worshiped her at Kasanui 笠縫 in Yamato" and made arrangements as well for the separate worship of Yamato no Ōkunitama.[28] In Heian and medieval texts the transfer of the mirror to Kasanui assumed importance as the first stage in its eventual conveyance to Ise, a development that received much attention and elaboration at the hands of Watarai Shinto thinkers.

Aizawa, however, alluding to "parallel" events and practices described in Chinese classical texts, recast this episode into something quite different from both the original and the medieval versions of it. The Zhou rulers, he pointed out, had performed ancestral rites to the founder of the dynasty, King Wen 文王, in the hall where they conducted the rituals and affairs of government. By thus associating the populace of the realm with their rites to King Wen, the later Zhou rulers had manifested more fully their reverence for him. Sujin's transfer of the mirror, declared Aizawa, was motivated by similar concerns. Not only did the involvement of the populace in his rites to Amaterasu serve to enlarge Sujin's expression of filial piety to her, it also had the edifying effect of bringing the people to realize the meaning of his piety. "Conducting rites within his residence," Aizawa wrote, Sujin "might have been able to express inwardly his own sincere reverence, but he could not make clear to the realm the import of such reverence. The emperor therefore conducted rites outside his residence, revering [Amaterasu] publicly together with the people of the realm. The meaning of such reverence having been manifested to the realm, the people understood without being told."[29]

Aizawa used similar interpretive procedures to extract from the accounts of the early emperors evidence of their conducting rites comparable to the *she* and *jiao* recorded in *Liji*. As the ritual analogous to the *jiao*, the suburban sacrifices to Heaven, he singled out the *daijōsai* 大嘗祭, the ceremony of accession in which the new emperor engaged in ritual communion with Amaterasu.[30] Its transforming effect made the *daijōsai*, he held, the ultimate expression of *hōhon hanshi*. Using the language of *Liji*, Aizawa wrote evocatively, on the one hand, of the communion that occurred when the emperor, the "bequeathed body" (*itai* 遺体) of Amaterasu, offered the first fruits of the harvest to her, a devoted act of return for the grain she had granted Ninigi. It was as if "full of reverence, he could faintly see her before him, present today in her original form." But Aizawa equally stressed the impact of the occasion on others. The assembled officials felt as if they, too, "were in the presence of the Heavenly Ancestor, and looking upon the emperor, it was as if they saw the Heavenly Ancestor." And, as the descendants of those deities who had served Amaterasu and the early emperors, they contributed to the realization of *hōhon hanshi* by re-enacting the roles performed by their ancestors.[31]

Further, as with the *jiao*, the transforming effect was not limited to those immediately present. Since the "emperor takes the realm as his house and shares all his actions with the realm," originally he had involved the entire populace in the *daijōsai* through various preparatory events, such as the selection of the provinces to provide grain for the ceremonies. Lamenting that in later centuries this process had become formalistic and perfunctory, with the provinces designated to perform this function permanently fixed, Aizawa pointed out that in antiquity they had been chosen through a true divination, and thus all the realm had remained involved. "There was no province that might not be charged with providing the offering." Within the province selected, the people all gathered together to prepare the grain and send it off properly guarded. As other provinces offered tax revenues to pay for miscellaneous costs, "there was no province that did not serve the deity"; through the ceremonies of purifying the roads along which the offerings were sent, "the entire realm knew what was to be revered"; and through the emperor's distribution of celebratory offerings to the shrines of the land, "the entire realm knew that there was no deity not under the authority of the Heavenly Ancestor and her imperial descendants." In this way the people were brought to "manifest the utmost in devotion and reverence without any need for insistent explanations. [...] The emperor's devotion and reverence extended from the palace and was felt throughout the realm, and the devotion and reverence of the realm was gathered from the multitudes and focused around the seat of rule."[32]

In his presentation of Sujin's transfer of the mirror and the *daijōsai*, Aizawa emphasized the beneficial impact of making "public" ceremonies and matters usually understood as things to be carefully veiled from view. To be sure, in noting the late Mito scholars' affirmation of "public"

ritual in place of "esoteric," we need to be careful to keep our own
present-day assumptions from intruding into what they meant, as in
the passage about Sujin, by "revering [Amaterasu] publicly (*kōzen to* 公然と)
together with the people of the realm." The Mito scholars did not see
such rituals as "public" in the sense of an open display, a performance
directly before the masses. What they anticipated, rather, was that the
aura surrounding the ritual would extend beyond the immediate participants to encompass society as a whole. Nor did the late Mito thinkers
presume that rites recovered from the realm of esoteric practices would
be transparent or foster enlightened attitudes. To the contrary, in their
eyes, the power of ritual lay in its capacity to "carry" the people along
without the latter realizing what was happening, in contrast to direct
orders or didactic sermons, which often aroused resistance rather than
active cooperation. It was this ability to evoke an instinctive readiness to
assist and serve the ruler that made the "public" conduct of rites an
effective means of mobilizing the populace to carry out various crucial
social tasks.[33]

The late Mito thinkers further did not assume that public ritual meant
open or equal access to the sacred entity that was the object of the ritual.
They condemned the graded initiations to different levels of knowledge
characteristic of esoteric practices for treating as a personal possession
matters that were not "private." But they took for granted the importance
of hierarchy. Seeing their own age as rent by potential divisions, they
looked to the institution of a proper structure of ritual to restore and
reinforce the hierarchy essential to social stability. In the sacrifices to
Earth and Heaven described in *Liji*, the populace did not worship
Heaven and Earth directly; rather, each element in society contributed
to the performance of the ritual in the manner appropriate to its station.
While involving the entire populace in some way, the ritual at the same
time thus clarified and consolidated the social hierarchy. This premise
was fundamental to Aizawa's vision of the *daijōsai*. It also figured in his
identification of an analogue to the *she*.

In the rituals related to the *she*, Aizawa pointed out, the ruler honored
the land, on which the populace depended for its livelihood, and the
deities of the land, whom the people revered. The ruler further conjoined
with these sacrifices rites to those who had performed meritorious deeds
on behalf of the populace. The efficacy of these practices lay in their
capacity to unify the people and secure their allegiance. "If the emperor
takes the lead in offering rites to these deities, there is a means by which
to extend a regulating authority over the hearts of the people, and their
allegiance will be focused on one [rather than divided]." It was precisely
with this intent, Aizawa proposed, that Sujin, together with moving the
mirror from his residence and creating a public framework for his rites
to Amaterasu, had set up ritual structures for the worship of Yamato no
Ōkunitama and another deity, Ōmononushi 大物主. Aizawa categorized

both of these deities as local founders similar to Ōkuninushi. They had brought benefits to the people of the Yamato region, where the court was based, by making the land habitable. In taking measures to ensure the maintenance of appropriate sacrifices to them, Sujin had manifested his own reverence for these deities of importance to the populace of the capital region. He thereby had shown the latter that he "took the concerns of the people as his own and brought them to entrust their hopes to the court." This was just what the ancient Chinese rulers had accomplished through the *she*.[34]

As outlying regions were brought under the sway of the court, Sujin had also, Aizawa argued, paid homage to the meritorious founder deities of those areas, such as Ōkuninushi. This action, which again resembled that of the Chinese sages, had made it possible to temper uncivilized customs and had established the ground for incorporating the populace as a whole into the framework of *hōhon hanshi*.[35] Pursuing lines of interpretation of this sort, Aizawa not only played down the elements that had been used to construct esoteric approaches to deities such as Ōkuninushi, he also gave those deities a carefully defined place within a hierarchically ordered framework of public ritual centered on the court.

Efforts at implementation

Through the types of interpretive strategies touched on above, the late Mito scholars tried to show that in intent and effect the ritual forms of Japanese antiquity matched those described in the Chinese classics like the "two sides of a tally."[36] They did not undertake this demonstration simply as an abstract academic exercise. To the contrary, for them it was a preliminary step towards establishing a comparable unification of rites and governance in their own day. In the political context of the late Tokugawa period, carrying out such a project on a national scale was beyond the realm of immediate possibility. Even at the local level of the domain, efforts at implementation of more modest elements of the Mito ritual program were thwarted by factionalism and by the sharp ups and downs between 1829 and 1860 in the political situation of the scholars' patron, the strong-minded Daimyo Tokugawa Nariaki 徳川斉昭 (1800–60).[37] But even if partial and sporadic, the attempts of the Mito scholars and Nariaki to put their vision into practice throw into relief some of the implications of the Mito rejection of secrecy and concept of a system of public ritual.

The creation of a system of ritual that "would extend from the palace and be felt throughout the realm" ultimately required action by the rulers of the day. Aizawa hoped, for instance, that the court would revive the long-abandoned *ritsuryō* practice of sending offerings to important shrines throughout the land on the occasion of major court rites such as the *kinensai* (*toshigoi no matsuri*) 祈年祭, the spring rites to pray for good crops, and the *niinamesai* 新嘗祭, the autumn rites of thanksgiving. Like the open-ended divination no longer performed on the occasion of the *daijōsai*, the offerings sent out to shrines, he pointed out, were crucial means of bringing the realm as a whole within the transformative aura of court ritual. In the absence of the sought-for action from above, the efforts of the late Mito thinkers to implement their vision of the unification of rites and governance were directed primarily at devising ways to "gather the devotion and reverence of the multitudes" and "focus it around the seat of rule." To this end, in 1834, Aizawa compiled an explanation "for the ordinary people of rural districts and villages who cannot read characters" of what he regarded as the most important of the rites observed at court and by the domain rulers. One needed to take care not to be disrespectful in listing up the details of court ceremonies, he acknowledged; nevertheless, these were also precisely the things that "the populace should look up to with reverence."[38] Nariaki's forced retirement in 1844 and the eclipse of the scholars associated with him put an end to a plan to publish this work, titled *Sōen kagen* 草偃和言 (Gentle Words [to Make] the Grass Bend), and to distribute throughout the domain a simplified version of Aizawa's ritual calendar adapted to village life.[39] But from these projects we can glean a picture of the direction in which the Mito scholars hoped to move.

As with *Tekiihen*, likewise meant for popular edification, Aizawa wrote *Sōen kagen* in a straightforward Japanese rather than the ornate *kanbun*, laden with allusive references to the Chinese classics, that he favored for pieces such as the well-known *Shinron* 新論 (New Theses, 1825). The parallels with *Tekiihen* go beyond style. In *Tekiihen*, as we noted above, Aizawa based his selective account of *kamiyo* on that in Kitabatake Chikafusa's *Jinnō shōtōki*. In *Sōen kagen*, for basic information about the nature of the court rites that he described, he similarly made use of a concise fifteenth-century compendium of the yearly round of court rituals compiled by the then young court noble and scholar (and later regent) Ichijō Kaneyoshi 一条兼良 (1402–81). Aizawa pointed out that this work, titled *Kuji kongen* 公事根源 (Fundamentals of Court Ceremonial), was already "distributed widely." By making it the foundation of his own account, he thus could preserve a balance between discretion in discussing matters of the court and enlarging general awareness of the things that "the populace should look up to with reverence" (*Sōen kagen*, p. 275). But, just as with *Jinnō shōtōki*, Aizawa was also highly selective in his use of *Kuji kongen*. Through what he omitted as well as his further explanations of the significance of what he included, he modified and shifted the orientation of Kaneyoshi's work even as he built upon it.

In *Kuji kongen* Kaneyoshi listed month by month a round of more than 170 rites important to court life. These included major court ceremonies dating back to the *ritsuryō* period like the *kinensai* and *niinamesai*, festivals of various shrines, ceremonies of court appointments, various elegant activities and miscellaneous events, and a large number of Buddhist-related ceremonies. From these Aizawa selected a little fewer than thirty. As we might expect, he excluded all ceremonies of Buddhist provenance as well as those having to do with court appointments and elegant amusements. He also omitted many of the shrine festivals and various rites that had a magical import or were intended to dispel malevolent forces, such as the *Gion no goryōe* 祇園御霊会 and the *tsuina* 追儺 festivals. Where rituals of this sort were part of the original *ritsuryō* state rites, Aizawa mentioned them. He kept, for instance, the *hishizume no matsuri* 鎮火祭 (intended to prevent fires) and the *michiae no matsuri* 道饗祭 (meant to pacify and keep away malevolent entities). But he left out various details to be found in *Kuji kongen*, instead stating pointedly that these were minor rites.[40]

By contrast, Aizawa put prime emphasis on the major state rites dating from the *ritsuryō* period (in his view, of course, many could be traced to *kamiyo* or the reigns of the first emperors). Above all he elaborated on rites like the spring *kinensai*, wherein the emperor sought the assistance of the deities for the successful growing of the year's crops, and the autumn *kannamesai* 神嘗祭 and *niinamesai* in which the ruler made offerings of gratitude for the harvest. In his explanation of the import of these rites, Aizawa repeatedly stressed that the divine blessings of grain and cloth bequeathed originally by Amaterasu were what ensured the people's sustenance and that the emperor performed these rites of gratitude on their behalf as a means of fulfilling the imperative of *hōhon hanshi*.

Aizawa not only tried to enlarge his readers' awareness of these circumstances, he also urged that they engage at the local level in activities that would echo the rites performed at court. On the fourteenth day of the fourth month, for instance, the emperor sent specially woven cloth offerings to Ise. This, Aizawa noted, was in gratitude for Amaterasu's bequest of the fibers that made it possible for the populace to ward off the cold in winter. For their part, the people, "so as not to forget this sacred benefice, should put on clean clothes, whether newly made or freshly washed, and make a pilgrimage to their local shrine." Similarly they should hold rites of thanksgiving in their local shrines in the ninth month, when the emperor sent offerings of grain to Ise for the *kannamesai*, and on the occasion of the *niinamesai* in the eleventh month, when the emperor personally offered the first fruits of the harvest to the heavenly deities. Gathering together with their relatives and fellow villagers to celebrate these occasions, the people should renew their sense of the debt of obligation that they owed to Amaterasu and to the emperor for performing rites of recompense to her on their behalf (*Sōen kagen*, pp. 291, 303–04, 310). In a similar vein, the simplified version of Aizawa's ritual calendar meant to be distributed to villages in the domain stipulated that, as the *kinensai* was held on the fourth day of the second month to pray for the successful growing of the five grains, it would be appropriate for villagers to hold the Inari 稲荷 festival (likewise associated with food and grain) on this day (*Mito-han shiryō*, vol. 5 [*bekki, ge*], p. 51).

Dilemmas of practice

By bringing the entire nation within the aura of rituals emanating from the court, the Mito scholars hoped to focus the minds of the populace on one source and foster unstinting service to superiors. In an ironic paradox, however, various tensions embedded in that effort compromised precisely what the Mito thinkers hoped to accomplish. The heightened emphasis on an Amaterasu-emperor axis as the pivot of a national structure of ritual raised questions, for one thing, about the relationship of that structure to the contemporary bakufu-centered political order. Mito was one of the three main collateral Tokugawa houses, and the late Mito scholars did not question bakufu rule. They in no way intended devotion to Amaterasu to detract from the fulfillment of feudal obligations to the bakufu. To the contrary, shogunal reverence for the emperor, who offered dedicated service to Amaterasu, would, they argued, in turn encourage renewed commitment to the shogun by the daimyo and their retainers. Properly oriented reverence would have a chain effect of fostering loyalty and whole hearted service to superiors throughout the feudal hierarchy.[41] Reflecting their acknowledgment of the importance of the obligations owed the bakufu, the Mito scholars called for expressions of homage to Tokugawa Ieyasu as well as to Amaterasu. Aizawa, for instance, included the anniversary of Ieyasu's death in *Sōen kagen*. It was owing to Ieyasu's efforts that the people of the present age had enjoyed over two hundred years of peace and security, he wrote. On that day the people should gather with their relatives and neighbors to reflect with gratitude on Ieyasu's accomplishments (*Sōen kagen*, pp. 292–94). We may read in such arrangements an attempt to strike a balance between commitment to an Amaterasu-emperor axis, on the one hand, and to the bakufu, on the other. The strife between pro-court and pro-bakufu factions that left a bloody imprint on the domain's final years suggests, however, that balance was in actuality not easy to maintain.

Inherent in the emphasis on Amaterasu as the source of blessings for the entire populace and on the necessity for the realm as a whole to offer recompense was likewise the danger that it might encourage contravention of the very social hierarchy it was supposed to reinforce. The late Mito thinkers held that this should not be the case, that by specifying an appropriate role for each participant, a national structure of rites centered ultimately on reverence to Amaterasu should confirm the place of each within a class-based hierarchical order. The Mito scholars remained sensitive, nevertheless, to the potentially negative consequences of the populace expressing devotion to Amaterasu in an unmediated form. One of the grave faults of Christianity and Buddhism, Aizawa asserted, was encouraging the masses to worship Heaven or an overarching deity directly. In so doing, these doctrines inevitably sowed the seeds of disruption of the social hierarchy. Recognizing that the emperor in making offerings to Amaterasu was also acting on their behalf, the people should not presume to duplicate his role. Rather, they should feel a doubled sense of gratitude, to the emperor as well as to Amaterasu (*Tekiihen*, pp. 259–60). Referring to the ancient prohibition of private worship at Ise, Fujita Tōko emphasized that the performance of rites to Amaterasu was the prerogative of the court; ordinary people should not engage in "private" rites to her.[42] Even as the Mito scholars exalted Amaterasu as a font of blessings to the populace, they thus also called for the preservation of a respectful distance.

On the level of practice, the late Mito thinkers promoted several ways of bridging the contradiction in this situation. One was the mechanism of replication that Aizawa advocated in *Sōen kagen*. By coordinating their local village rites with the court ritual calendar, the populace should echo the rites conducted by the emperor. But they were to make their offerings to the deities of their own area, not directly to higher deities such as Amaterasu, honored by the emperor. In effect they were to engage in what we might call "honoring vicariously": that is, they were to offer rites to hierarchically appropriate deities who could in turn be linked to service to Amaterasu. As Aizawa put it, the tutelary shrines of local areas were dedicated to deities "who had all in antiquity assisted the Sun Deity (*hi no kami* 日神) in her heavenly task and had pacified and nurtured the local populace. To pay homage to these deities thus accords with the principle of thanking the Sun Deity for her blessings."[43] The choice of the deity to enshrine at the Kōdōkan 弘道館, the domain school founded under Nariaki, was based on this notion. The deity Nariaki and his advisers ultimately selected was Takemikazuchi 建雷. They saw him as particularly suitable because he was the deity of Kashima 鹿島, the leading shrine (*ichi no miya* 一宮) of Hitachi province, where Mito was located (although Kashima itself was not within Mito domain territory). As a military deity, Takemikazuchi was also an appropriate object of homage for a warrior house. Most important, his action in pacifying various unruly deities and paving the way for Ninigi's descent had provided vital assistance in the heavenly task of securing the welfare of the realm. As such it exemplified the height of service to Amaterasu. For the retainers of the Mito domain to offer rites to Takemikazuchi would inculcate in them awareness of the hierarchically correct forms of honoring Amaterasu as well.[44]

Such devices did not fully suffice, however, to contain the momentum generated by the focus on reverence for the imperial line and Amaterasu as the ultimate mechanism for ensuring that "the multitudes would be of one mind." Even among the Mito thinkers wavering can be seen on this point. In discussions in 1834 over the choice of the deity to honor at the

Kōdōkan, for instance, Nariaki initially favored enshrining Emperor Jinmu, Ōjin 応神, or Tenji 天智, or a combination of the three. A year earlier he proposed as a separate project establishing a shrine to Jinmu within the domain. Aizawa and Nariaki's other advisers demurred on the ground, in the first case, that it was not appropriate to enshrine a figure as awesome as the emperor in a school, and, in the second, that it did not accord with correct ritual for a feudal lord to offer rites to an emperor.[45] Some years later, however, Aizawa had second thoughts about this issue. Noting in 1848 the urgency of creating proper venues for meeting the spiritual needs of the populace and thus forestalling the corrupting influence of Buddhism and heterodox forms of popular worship, he called for the establishment of new shrines of orthodox antecedents. Central among those he proposed was a shrine to Jinmu at Kashihara 橿原 in Yamato, near the first emperor's putative place of burial. At the same time Aizawa also expressed regret that the plan to build a shrine to Jinmu in Mito had not come to fruition.[46]

Similarly, parallel to his emphasis on honoring Amaterasu vicariously through hierarchically differentiated modes, Aizawa also pursued ways of expressing reverence to her in a more immediate manner. As a key means of doing so while avoiding the problems of direct worship, he advocated showing "reverence from a distance" (*yōhai* 遙拝). The antecedents of this practice could be traced to the second lord of the domain, Mitsukuni 光圀 (1628–1700), who every New Year, attired in the court dress appropriate to his rank, had bowed toward the emperor in Kyoto. In 1837 Aizawa proposed to incorporate an extension of this custom in the ritual to be employed at the Kōdōkan. He recommended that a special altar (*dan* 壇) be erected to the rear of the shrine to Takemikazuchi as a site for manifesting reverence to Amaterasu and to the emperors from Jinmu down to the current occupant of the throne. On the first day of classes for the year, to be established as the day for the shrine festival, the domain lord and his retainers were to wear formal dress and from this altar bow towards Kyoto. Thereafter those present were to enter the school hall and bow in homage, first to a scroll inscribed with the genealogy of the imperial line, beginning with Amaterasu, and then to other scrolls depicting the lineage of the Tokugawa shogunal house from Ieyasu on and the lineage of the domain lord. In confirmation of the unity of Confucian and Shinto teachings supporting these expressions of devotion, the participants were then to listen to a set of ceremonial lectures on the passage from *Nihon shoki* describing Amaterasu's bestowal of the regalia on Ninigi, the liturgy (*norito* 祝詞) recited in honor of Amaterasu on occasions like the *kinensai*, and the first verse of the *Analects*.[47]

Through the creation of a structure of "public" ritual centered on Amaterasu, the Mito scholars aimed to reinforce the Tokugawa social and political order, not weaken it. In their eyes, the prevalence of "secret transmissions" purveying esoteric interpretations of Amaterasu and the events of *kamiyo* served only to encourage "private speculation" and a presumptuous manipulation of things that individuals should not treat as a personal possession. Secrecy was an invitation to social chaos. Promotion of "public" ritual centered on Amaterasu would counter the threat of chaos and inculcate throughout society the dynamic of *hōhon hanshi*. Such a public ritual would thereby also redound, they believed, to the benefit of the shogun and the Tokugawa order. In fact, however, the Mito scholars' exaltation of Amaterasu acted as an undertow, pulling their project in a direction beyond the parameters of their vision. As such it contributed, albeit inadvertently from their perspective, to the disintegration of the ideological foundations of the Tokugawa feudal system as they conceived it.

The Mito project had another unintended consequence: the move in the Meiji period and later towards the formulation of a system of public ritual that presumed mass involvement of the populace. The forms such involvement took hardly preserved the Mito scholars' ideal of a ritual structure that would embody and reinforce a class-based social hierarchy. Yet embedded in the modern imperial state was the legacy of many aspects of the late Mito deconstruction of secrecy and call for ritual embodiment of *hōhon hanshi* – from Aizawa's ritual calendar to the establishment of a shrine to Jinmu and the institution of *yōhai* of Amaterasu and the emperor as national practices.

Notes

1 For a discussion of this incident and the relevant sources, see Hori 1964, pp. 39–54.
2 Hayashi Razan, *Shintō denju*, p. 19.
3 Scheid 2002, p. 306. See also Taira 1972, p. 518.
4 See Takashima 1992, p. 3; Ooms 1985, pp. 221–86.
5 Ogyū Sorai, *Bendō*, pp. 26–28. Here and below, all citations to the *Nihon shisō taikei* (NST) edition of works written in *kanbun* are to the *kakikudashi* 書き下し version.
6 I have previously discussed some of the links between Sorai's thought and the Mito school (and have also taken up from a different perspective a number of the points addressed below) in Nakai 2002. See also Bitō 1973; Wakabayashi 1986, pp. 117–19.
7 Aizawa Seishisai, *Shinron*, p. 52. See also the translation of *Shinron* in Wakabayashi 1986, p. 152.
8 Aizawa Seishisai, *Doku Naobi no mitama*, p. 36.
9 聖人以神道設教、而天下服矣. Explanation of the *guan* 觀 (Jap. *kan*) hexagram; translation (slightly modified) from Wilhelm 1967, p. 486.
10 *Shinron*, p. 140; Wakabayashi 1986, p. 252.
11 Fujita Tōko, *Kōdōkanki jutsugi*, p. 264. In *Hitachi obi* 常陸帯, Tōko described the "so-called Shinto of the day" in terms similar to those used by Dazai Shundai: it had been fashioned by "incorporating the theories of Yin Yang and five-elements cosmology or by in effect adopting the ideas of Confucian [metaphysics] and Buddhism." Fujita Tōko, *Hitachi obi*, p. 120. The language Tōko used in *Kōdōkanki jutsugi* to describe the corruption of Shinto sums up

the Mito understanding of the phenomenon referred to in this book as "esotericism": it meant "wild private speculation" (*midari ni shichi o motte* 妄り に私智を以て), "allegorical" (*gūgen* 寓言) interpretations that turned the records of *kamiyo* into "riddles" (*sōji* 廋辞) or a "secret code" (*ingo* 隠語), and the concealing of the shallowness and dubious nature of such things by putting them in the form of "secret transmissions" (*hiketsu* 秘訣).

12 The late Mito scholars' approach to *kamiyo* was part of a broad shift from allegorical to "historical" interpretations that took place in the course of the Tokugawa period. I have discussed these developments in a contribution to a forthcoming volume based on a conference held on Maui in November 2000 that was jointly sponsored by the International Research Center for Japanese Studies, Kyoto, and the University of Hawai'i.

13 English requires gendered pronouns, and, in accordance with the assumption generally accepted today that Amaterasu was female, here I will use "she" and "her" in referring to this deity. We should keep in mind, however, that the Mito thinkers, like many other medieval and early modern figures, may not have conceived of Amaterasu in these terms. Aizawa took issue with thinkers who asserted Amaterasu was female, arguing that *Nihon shoki* and *Kojiki* were not explicit on this point. See, for instance, *Doku Kuzubana*, p. 22; *Doku Maganohire*, p. 8. As noted above and discussed further below, the Mito thinkers often alluded to Amaterasu as Tenso. Although this term could be traced back to early texts such as *Kogo shūi* 古語拾遺, the Mito scholars used it in a manner evocative of the posthumous names of the founders of Chinese dynasties. As such it also conveyed an image of Amaterasu as male rather than female. For details, see pp. 362–63 and note 19.

14 *Shinron*, p. 56; Wakabayashi 1986, p. 158; Aizawa Seishisai, *Kagaku jigen*, p. 30b.

15 Kitabatake Chikafusa, *Jinnō shōtōki*, p. 60; Varley 1980, p. 77.

16 *Jinnō shōtōki*, p. 41: 天祖ハジメテ基ヲヒラキ、日神ナガク統ヲ伝給フ. The editors of the NKBT edition gloss the characters Tenso as Amatsumioya. See also Varley 1980, p. 41.

17 Note 6 on p. 41 of the NKBT edition of *Jinnō shōtōki* indicates that Chikafusa followed Watarai Shinto ideas in substituting *tenso* for *tenjin* 天神 and specifying *tenso* to be Kuni no Tokotachi.

18 *Shinron*, p. 53; Wakabayashi 1986, p. 154.

19 *Tekiihen*, pp. 254–55. Compare *Jinnō shōtōki*, pp. 60–61; Varley 1980, pp. 76–77. Aizawa also elided phrases where Chikafusa specifically identified Amaterasu as female (compare *Tekiihen*, p. 253; *Jinnō shōtōki*, pp. 52–53; Varley, p. 66). These omissions support the supposition that Aizawa likely preferred to think of Amaterasu as male rather than female (see note 13).

20 *Tekiihen*, pp. 257–59. Chikafusa notes in passing that the rice people eat everyday is an imperial benefice originating from the seeds sown by Amaterasu (*Jinnō shōtōki*, p. 163; Varley 1980, p. 230). But the image of Amaterasu as a source of material blessings is not nearly so central to his account as it is to the Mito view.

21 *Nihon shoki*, vol. 1, pp. 150–51; Aston 1972, vol. 1, p. 80.

22 Yamazaki Ansai, *Jindaikan kōgi*, pp. 166–70; Takashima 1992, pp. 577–80.

23 See, for instance, Hirata Atsutane, *Tama no mihashira*, pp. 72–77.

24 *Shinron*, pp. 142, 148; Wakabayashi 1986, pp. 257, 264.

25 See *Kagaku jigen*, p. 43b; *Mito-han shiryō*, vol. 5 (*bekki, ge*), p. 317.

26 *Liji* 11 ("Jiaotesheng" 郊特牲), vol. 2, pp. 394–95, 398–99; Legge 1964, vol. 1, pp. 425–26, 429–31.

27 Aizawa Seishisai, *Taishoku kanwa*, pp. 237–38, 241–42. The late Mito scholars were, of course, not the only ones to find fault with existing forms of Shinto.

Their near contemporaries, the *Kokugaku* thinkers, likewise attacked Yoshida Shinto and the early Edo Confucian Shinto schools as corruptions of the true Japanese tradition. The *Kokugaku* and Mito thinkers differed sharply, however, in their conception of what constituted the true tradition. The Mito scholars criticized in particular the *Kokugaku* denial of its compatibility with Confucian norms and the methods of rule of the Chinese sages. According to the Mito scholars, a key aspect of the lack of balance in the perspective of the *Kokugaku* thinkers was their rejection of the "culture" (*bun*) that was an essential element of Confucian learning and their overexaltation of "simplicity." The "simplicity" of the supposedly "ancient" outlook that the *Kokugaku* thinkers claimed to recover was, the Mito scholars argued, in fact little more than a fictive creation of their own that drew from Taoism and even Christianity. See *Kōdōkanki jutsugi*, pp. 264–65; *Hitachi obi*, pp. 102–03.

28 *Nihon shoki*, vol. 1, pp. 238–39; Aston 1972, vol. 1, pp. 151–52.

29 *Shinron*, pp. 140–41; Wakabayashi 1986, pp. 253–54.

30 As I have noted in Nakai 2002, p. 289, Aizawa traced the first performance of the *daijōsai* to the rites that Jinmu, according to *Nihon shoki*, conducted at Tomiyama 鳥見山 following his succession. *Nihon shoki*, vol. 1, pp. 214–15; Aston 1972, vol. 1, p. 134.

31 *Shinron*, p. 55; Wakabayashi 1986, p. 157. See *Liji* 24 ("Jiyi" 祭義), vol. 2, pp. 701, 719; Legge 1964, vol. 2, pp. 211, 226.

32 *Kagaku jigen*, p. 36b. See also *Shinron*, p. 150; Wakabayashi 1986, pp. 267–68.

33 For a succinct statement of Aizawa's views on this aspect of the power of a public system of ritual, views which owe much to the ideas of Ogyū Sorai, see *Kagaku jigen*, p. 26a.

34 *Shinron*, p. 141; Wakabayashi 1986, pp. 254–55.

35 *Shinron*, pp. 142–43; Wakabayashi 1986, pp. 256–57.

36 *Shinron*, pp. 148. As he notes, Wakabayashi omits from his translation the passage containing this phrase. See Wakabayashi 1986, pp. 264, 313–14.

37 On the Mito reform program pursued by Nariaki and his advisers, see Koschmann 1987.

38 *Sōen kagen*, pp. 318, 309.

39 Aizawa revised *Sōen kagen* in 1843 in preparation for its publication; in a postscript he took note of plans to distribute the published version among the village leadership stratum. The priest of a major domain shrine ultimately sponsored its publication in 1852.

40 *Kuji kongen*, for instance, noted of both the *michiae no matsuri* and the *hishizume no matsuri* that they were managed by the Urabe 卜部 lineage and of the latter that "many secret techniques (*hijutsu* 秘術) are said to be used during this rite." Aizawa omitted these details. See Ichijō Kaneyoshi, *Kuji kongen*, p. 76; *Sōen kagen*, p. 301.

41 Fujita Yūkoku, *Seimeiron*, p. 13. See also *Shinron*, pp. 153–54; Wakabayashi 1986, pp. 271–72.

42 *Kōdōkanki jutsugi*, p. 316. Elsewhere Tōko described direct worship of Amaterasu by the populace as "tantamount to going over the head of the lord of one's domain and making a direct appeal to the court. It is an extreme abrogation of proper ritual forms." *Hitachi obi*, p. 120.

43 *Sōen kagen*, p. 304. Implicit in such a strategy, of course, was the necessity to clarify the origins of local tutelary deities and to free them of syncretic corruptions. See *Hitachi obi*, p. 120.

44 *Kōdōkanki jutsugi*, pp. 316–17; *Hitachi obi*, pp. 105–06.

45 *Mito-han shiryō*, vol. 5 (*bekki, ge*), pp. 264, 266; *Mito-han shiryō*, vol. 4 (*bekki, jō*), pp. 200–01.

46 Aizawa Seishisai, *Kōko fuken*, pp. 529–31. Aizawa urged as well creating shrines to Sujin and Tenji. There already were shrines to Ōjin (i.e., those to Hachiman 八幡), he acknowledged, and these would suffice if purged of Buddhist elements. Ibid.

47 Aizawa Seishisai, *Taimon sansaku*, p. 183. To indicate the unity of Confucianism and Shinto and the indivisibility of the civil and military arts (*bun* 文 and *bu* 武), Nariaki and his advisers also established a hall to Confucius in the Kōdōkan parallel to the shrine to Takemikazuchi. Aizawa recommended that on the day of the *sekiten* 釈奠 service performed in honor of Confucius, a ceremony similar to that conducted on the first day of classes, with lectures on the same texts, should be held before a scroll inscribed with Confucius's name. Ibid.

References

Primary sources

Bendō 弁道, by Ogyū Sorai 荻生徂徠. In *Ogyū Sorai* 荻生徂徠 (= NST 36), 1974.

Bendō sho 弁道書, by Dazai Shundai 太宰春台. In *Nihon shisō tōsō shiryō* 日本思想闘争史料, vol. 3. Tokyo: Meicho Kankōkai, 1969.

Doku Kuzubana 読葛花, by Aizawa Seishisai 会沢正志斎. In *Nihon jurin sōsho* 日本儒林叢書, vol. 4. Tokyo: Hō Shuppan, 1971.

Doku Maganohire 読末賀能比連, by Aizawa Seishisai. In *Nihon jurin sōsho* 日本儒林叢書, vol. 4. Tokyo: Hō Shuppan, 1971.

Doku Naobi no mitama 読直毘霊, by Aizawa Seishisai. In *Nihon jurin sōsho* 日本儒林叢書, vol. 4. Tokyo: Hō Shuppan, 1971.

Hitachi obi 常陸帯, by Fujita Tōko 藤田東湖. In Kikuchi Kenjirō 菊池謙二郎 (ed.), *Tōko zenshū* 東湖全集 Tokyo: Hakubunkan, 1940.

Jindaikan kōgi 神代巻講義, by Yamazaki Ansai 山崎闇斎. In *Kinsei shintō ron* 近世神道論 (= NST 39), 1972.

Jinnō shōtōki 神皇正統記, by Kitabatake Chikafusa 北畠親房. In NKBT 87, 1965.

Kagaku jigen 下学邇言, by Aizawa Seishisai. Privately published, 1892.

Kōdōkanki jutsugi 弘道館記述義, by Fujita Tōko. In *Mitogaku* 水戸学 (= NST 53), 1973.

Kōko fuken 江湖負暄, by Aizawa Seishisai. In *Mitogaku* 水戸学 (= ST, vol. *Ronsetsuhen* 論説編 15), 1986.

Kuji kongen 公事根源, by Ichijō Kaneyoshi 一条兼良. In *Jikkinshō, Kuji kongen* 十訓抄・公事根源 (=*Nihon bungaku zensho* 日本文学全書, vol. 22). Tokyo: Hakubunkan, 1892.

Liji (Raiki) 礼記. *Shinshaku kanbun taikei* 新釈漢文大系, vols 27–29. Tokyo: Meiji Shoin, 1977.

Mito-han shiryō 水戸藩史料, 5 vols. Tokyo: Yoshikawa Kōbunkan, 1970.

Nihon shoki 日本書紀. NKBT 67–68, 1965–67.

Seimeiron 正名論, by Fujita Yūkoku 藤田幽谷. In *Mitogaku* 水戸学 (= NST 53), 1973.

Shinron 新論, by Aizawa Seishisai. In *Mitogaku* 水戸学 (= NST 53), 1973.

Shintō denju 神道伝授, by Hayashi Razan 林羅山. In *Kinsei shintō ron* 近世神道論 (= NST 39), 1972.

Sōen kagen 草偃和言, by Aizawa Seishisai. In *Mitogaku* 水戸学 (= ST, vol. *Ronsetsuhen* 論説編 15), 1986.

Taimon sansaku 対問三策, by Aizawa Seishisai. In *Mitogaku* 水戸学 (=ST, vol. *Ronsetsuhen* 論説編 15), 1986.

Taishoku kanwa 退食間話, by Aizawa Seishisai. In *Mitogaku* 水戸学 (=NST 53), 1973.

Tama no mihashira 霊の真柱, by Hirata Atsutane 平田篤胤. In *Hirata Atsutane* 平田篤胤 (=NST 50), 1973.

Tekiihen 迪彝編, by Aizawa Seishisai. In *Shinron, Tekiihen* 新論・迪彝編. Tokyo: Iwanami Shoten, 1941.

Modern sources

Aston, W. G. (tr.) (1972), *Nihongi: Chronicles of Japan from the Earliest Times to A.D. 697.* Tokyo and Rutland, VT: Charles E. Tuttle (reprint; [1]1896 in 2 vols).

Bitō Masahide 尾藤正英 (1973), "Mitogaku no tokushitsu" 水戸学の特質, in *Mitogaku* 水戸学 (=NST 53), pp. 556–82.

Hori Isao 堀勇雄 (1964), *Hayashi Razan* 林羅山. Tokyo: Yoshikawa Kōbunkan.

Kaempfer, Engelbert (1999), Beatrice M. Bodart-Bailey (ed. and tr.), *Kaempfer's Japan: Tokugawa Culture Observed.* Honolulu: University of Hawai'i Press.

Koschmann, J. Victor (1987), *The Mito Ideology: Discourse, Reform, and Insurrection in Late Tokugawa Japan, 1790–1864.* University of California Press.

Legge, James (tr.) (1964), *The Li Ki* (=*The Sacred Books of the East*, vols 27–28). Delhi: Motilal Banarsidass (reprint; [1]1885).

Nakai, Kate Wildman (2002), "Chinese Ritual and Native Identity in Tokugawa Confucianism," in Benjamin A. Elman, John. B. Duncan, and Herman Ooms (eds), *Rethinking Confucianism: Past and Present in China, Japan, Korea, and Vietnam.* Los Angeles, CA: UCLA Asian Pacific Monograph Series, pp. 258–91.

Ooms, Herman (1985), *Tokugawa Ideology: Early Constructs, 1570–1680.* Princeton: Princeton University Press.

Scheid, Bernhard (2002), "Shinto as a Religion for the Warrior Class: The Case of Yoshikawa Koretaru." *Japanese Journal of Religious Studies* 29/3–4, pp. 299–324.

Taira Shigemichi 平重道 (1972), "Kinsei no shintō shisō" 近世の神道思想, in *Kinsei shintō ron* 近世神道論 (=NST 39), pp. 507–58.

Takashima Motohiro 高島元洋 (1992), *Yamazaki Ansai: Nihon Shushigaku to Suika shintō* 山崎闇斎：日本朱子学と垂加神道. Tokyo: Perikansha.

Varley, H. Paul (tr.) (1980), *A Chronicle of Gods and Sovereigns: Jinnō Shōtōki of Kitabatake Chikafusa.* New York: Columbia University Press.

Wakabayashi, Bob Tadashi (1986), *Anti-Foreignism and Western Learning in Early-Modern Japan: The New Theses of 1825.* Cambridge, MA: Council on East Asian Studies, Harvard University.

Wilhelm, Richard (tr.) (1967), *The I Ching.* Princeton, NJ: Princeton University Press.

Index

An environmentally friendly book printed and bound in England by www.printondemand-worldwide.com

PEFC Certified

This product is
from sustainably
managed forests
and controlled
sources

www.pefc.org

PEFC/16-33-415

This book is made of chain-of-custody materials; FSC materials for the cover and PEFC materials for the text pages.

#0165 - 020216 - C0 - 234/156/22 - PB - 9780415546898